Interparental Conflict and Child Development

Theory, Research, and Applications

Interparental Conflict and Child Development provides an in-depth analysis of the rapidly expanding body of research on the impact of interparental conflict on children. Emphasizing developmental and family systems perspectives, this book investigates a range of important issues including the processes by which exposure to conflict may lead to child maladjustment, the role of gender and ethnicity in understanding the effects of conflict, the influence of conflict on parent-child, sibling, and peer relations, family violence, and interparental conflict in divorced and step-families. It also addresses the implications of this research for prevention, clinical intervention, and public policy. Each chapter examines relevant conceptual and methodological questions, reviews pertinent data, and identifies pathways for future research. The book describes the "state of the art" in the field and charts the course for continued investigation into the links between marital conflict and child functioning.

John H. Grych is Assistant Professor of Psychology at Marquette University.

Frank D. Fincham is Professor and Director of Clinical Training at the University of New York at Buffalo.

Interparental Conflict and Child Development

Theory, Research, and Applications

Edited by

John H. Grych
Marquette University

Frank D. Fincham
The State University of New York–Buffalo

CAMBRIDGE
UNIVERSITY PRESS

PUBLISHED BY THE PRESS SYNDICATE OF THE UNIVERSITY OF CAMBRIDGE
The Pitt Building, Trumpington Street, Cambridge, United Kingdom

CAMBRIDGE UNIVERSITY PRESS
The Edinburgh Building, Cambridge CB2 2RU, UK
40 West 20th Street, New York, NY 10011-4211, USA
10 Stamford Road, Oakleigh, Melbourne 3 166, Australia
Ruiz de Alarcón 13, 28014 Madrid, Spain
Dock House, The Waterfront, Cape Town 8001, South Africa

http://www.cambridge.org

First published 2001

Printed in the United States of America

Typeface Palatino 10/12.5 pt   *System* QuarkXPress™   [HT]

A catalog record for this book is available from the British Library

Library of Congress Cataloging-in-Publication Data

Interparental conflict and child development : theory, research, and applications /
edited by John H. Grych, Frank D. Fincham.
     p.   cm.
  ISBN 052 165142 5
     1. Child development. 2. Family – Psychological aspects. 3. Marital conflict.
  4. Conflict management. I. Grych, John H. (John Howard), 1963 –
  II. Fincham, Frank D.
  HQ772.5 I58 2001
  305.231 – dc21

                                                        00-031275

ISBN 0 521 65142 5 hardback

To our families:

Janet, Alec, and Aaron

Susan, Alex, Camilla, and Jessica

Contents

Contributors

Christy M. Buchanan, Ph.D, Department of Psychology, Wake Forest University, Winston-Salem, NC.

Shalini Cardoza-Fernandes, M.A., Department of Psychology, Marquette University, Milwaukee, WI.

Nikeea Lynell Copeland, Ph.D, School of Public Health, Emory University, Atlanta, GA.

Martha J. Cox, Ph.D, Frank Porter Graham Child Development Center, University of North Carolina at Chapel Hill, Chapel Hill, NC.

Susan Crockenberg, Ph.D, Department of Psychology, University of Vermont, Burlington, VT.

E. Mark Cummings, Ph.D, Department of Psychology, University of Notre Dame, Notre Dame, IN.

Mark R. Dadds, Ph.D, School of Applied Psychology, Griffith University, Mt Gravatt Campus, Brisbane, Australia.

Lisa Davies, Ph.D, Social, Genetic, and Developmental Psychology, Institute of Psychiatry, London, England.

Patrick T. Davies, Ph.D, Clinical and Social Sciences in Psychology, University of Rochester, Rochester, NY.

Tammy L. Dukewich, M.A., Department of Psychology, University of Notre Dame, Notre Dame, IN.

Judy Dunn, Ph.D, Social, Genetic, and Developmental Psychology, Institute of Psychiatry, London, England.

Robert E. Emery, Ph.D, Department of Psychology, University of Virginia, Charlottesville, VA.

Frank D. Fincham, Ph.D, The State University of New York at Buffalo, Buffalo, NY.

Mark Fine, Ph.D, Department of Human Development and Family Studies, University of Missouri, Columbia, MO.

Mary Flyr, Ph.D, Department of Psychology, University of California, Riverside, Riverside, CA.

Marcie C. Goeke-Morey, Ph.D, Department of Psychology, University of Notre Dame, Notre Dame, IN.

John H. Grych, Ph.D, Department of Psychology, Marquette University, Milwaukee, WI.

Camille I. Harper, Ph.D, Department of Psychology, University of Michigan, Ann Arbor, MI.

Kristina Harter, M.A., Department of Psychology, University of North Carolina at Chapel Hill, Chapel Hill, NC.

Kelly L. Heiges, M.A., Department of Psychology, University of Miami, Coral Gables, FL.

Ernest N. Jouriles, Ph.D, Department of Psychology, University of Houston, Houston, TX.

Lynn Fainsilber Katz, Ph.D, Department of Psychology, University of Washington, Seattle, WA.

Patricia K. Kerig, Ph.D, Department of Psychology, University of North Carolina at Chapel Hill, Chapel Hill, NC.

Colleen M. Killian, M.A., Department of Psychology, University of California, Riverside, Riverside, CA.

Mina Kim, M.A., Department of Psychology, University of California, Riverside, Riverside, CA.

Adela Langrock, Ph.D, Department of Psychology, University of Vermont, Burlington, VT.

Lisa L. Lindsay, M.A., Clinical and Social Sciences in Psychology, University of Rochester, Rochester, NY.

Gayla Margolin, Ph.D, Department of Psychology, University of Southern California, Los Angeles, CA.

Renee McDonald, Ph.D, Department of Psychology, University of Houston, Houston, TX.

David J. McDowell, M.A., Department of Psychology, University of California, Riverside, Riverside, CA.

Vonnie C. McLoyd, Ph.D, Center for Human Growth and Development, University of Michigan, Ann Arbor, MI.

Anna Marie Medina, M.A., Department of Psychology, University of Southern California, Los Angeles, CA.

William D. Norwood, Ph.D, Department of Psychology, University of Houston, Houston, TX.

Pamella H. Oliver, M.A., Department of Psychology, University of Southern California, Los Angeles, CA.

Blair Paley, Ph.D, UCLA Neuropsychiatric Institute and Hospital, Child and Adolescent Psychiatry, Los Angeles, CA.

Ross D. Parke, Ph.D, Department of Psychology and Center for Family Studies, University of California, Riverside, Riverside, CA.

Beth Peters, M.A., Department of Psychology, University of Houston, Houston, TX.

Sandra D. Simpkins, Ph.D, Department of Psychology, University of California, Riverside, Riverside, CA.

Cynthia M. Turner, M.A., School of Applied Psychology, Griffith University, Brisbane, Australia.

Margaret Wild, Ph.D, University of California Extension at Riverside, Riverside, CA.

Preface

The past decade has witnessed tremendous growth in efforts to understand how interparental conflict may affect children's functioning. Nearly two-thirds of the studies included in a recent meta-analysis of this literature were published in the 1990s (Buehler et al., 1997), and significant progress has been made in describing the nature of the links between conflict and child adjustment. This is a particularly opportune time to examine the current status of the field and to contemplate its future directions. As the focus of research moves from documenting the parameters of the association between conflict and child adjustment to investigating the processes that explain how, why, and under what conditions interparental conflict may affect children, it is important to take stock of what we do and do not know about the impact of conflict on children and to identify both problems and prospects for research in the next decade.

This book is designed to facilitate exploration of the links between marital and child problems by providing an in-depth analysis of research on interparental conflict and children's development. The chapters that follow provide diverse perspectives on this literature, examine a wide range of critical issues, and discuss the conceptual and methodological questions that are most central for advancing research in this area. Two themes are given particular emphasis in the book. Although it often has been noted that children's age and the context in which conflict occurs are important for understanding its effects, our knowledge of the roles that these factors play is limited. Consequently, contributors were asked to consider how *developmental* and *systemic* processes may influence children's responses to conflict and shape its impact on them.

The book is divided into five parts. The first examines several fundamental issues for studying the potential effects of interparental conflict on children and sets the stage for more specific topics covered in the remainder of the book. It opens with chapters that critique the most prominent theoretical perspectives and research methods in the field and offer ideas for enhancing the conceptual and methodological bases of research on conflict. This part also includes examinations of how children's gender and ethnicity may influence their responses to conflict or moderate its effects. The second part of the book focuses on basic psychological processes that occur when children observe conflict. Examining children's emotional, cognitive, physiological, and coping responses may illuminate immediate and more lasting effects of witnessing angry, conflictual interactions between parents. The third part places conflict in a larger context, examining how interparental discord may affect parent–child relationships, sibling relationships, and children's interactions with peers, and discussing the impact of violent forms of interparental conflict on children. In addition, chapters examine conflict in different family forms, addressing how interparental conflict is similar and dissimilar in divorced and remarried families. The focus in the fourth part is more practical, with chapters examining implications of basic research for prevention and clinical intervention and for public policy. The final part of the book reflects on future directions for research on interparental conflict and child development.

Acknowledgments

This volume reflects the efforts of many people. We are grateful to the authors of the chapters for their willingness to offer their expertise and ideas and to share our vision for the book. We also want to thank Julia Hough and Elana Vardy of Cambridge University Press for supporting the book and guiding it along the way. Laura Klockow prepared the index, and we appreciate her diligence and hard work. Finally, we wish to thank our families – Janet, Alec, and Aaron; Susan, Alex, Camilla, and Jessica – for their love and encouragement. They are an unending source of inspiration, learning, and fulfillment, and we dedicate this book to them.

REFERENCE

Buehler, C., Anthony, C., Krishnakumar, A., Stone, G., Gerard, J., & Pemberton, S. (1997). Interparent conflict and youth problem behaviors: A meta-analysis. *Journal of Child and Family Studies, 6,* 233–247.

Interparental Conflict and Child Adjustment

An Overview

John H. Grych and Frank D. Fincham

Researchers and clinicians have long recognized that marital and child problems tend to co-occur.* Although not all would agree with Framo's assertion that "whenever you have a disturbed child you have a disturbed marriage" (Framo, 1965, p. 154), the presumption that the quality of a couple's relationship is fundamentally important for their children's development is common across a variety of theoretical perspectives (see Fincham, 1998). Empirical research supports this contention as well, showing that measures of marital dissatisfaction and discord consistently predict child adjustment problems (e.g., Buehler et al., 1997; Cummings & Davies, 1994). Marital dissatisfaction is a broad construct, however, and therefore it is critical to identify what it is about discordant marriages that may lead to child maladjustment.

In the past decade, efforts to understand the association between marital and child problems increasingly have focused on how couples express and manage conflict in their relationship. Although conflict occurs in virtually all close relationships, it tends to become more frequent and intense as marital quality erodes. Children report that observing interparental conflict is a significant stressor (Lewis, Siegal, & Lewis, 1984), and observational studies show that children typically exhibit distress when exposed to angry or aggressive interactions involving their parents (e.g., Cummings, Zahn-Waxler, & Radke-Yarrow, 1981). Moreover, interparental conflict is a better predictor of child adjustment problems than marital dissolution or global measures

---

* The terms "marital" and "interparental" are used interchangeably in this volume. Although they are not always synonymous, there tends to be considerable overlap between them, and this field traditionally has focused on married couples. However, the findings are presumed to apply to couples in committed relationships who are not legally married.

of marital dissatisfaction, and is related to child functioning even after controlling for overall level of marital quality (e.g., Jouriles, Murphy, & O'Leary, 1989). Thus, empirical evidence from different sources suggests that interparental conflict is a risk factor for the development of maladjustment.

In this introductory chapter, we provide a brief overview of this evidence to provide a backdrop for the ensuing chapters that examine varied aspects of the links between interparental conflict and child development. In general, research in this area can be viewed as addressing two issues: the association between interparental conflict and child adjustment, and children's responses to witnessing interparental conflict. As research relating to each issue tends to adopt a different level of analysis and to use different methods, we address them separately.

Research on the Association between Interparental Conflict and Child Adjustment

Most studies investigating links between conflict and child adjustment have examined the relation between global indices of the frequency with which couples argue or engage in particular conflict behaviors (e.g., verbal aggression) and global measures of child adjustment problems. Although conflict is usually assessed with parental reports, there is some evidence that children's perception of the conflict that they have witnessed more consistently predicts their adjustment (e.g., Grych, Seid, & Fincham, 1992). Several narrative reviews have concluded that there is a reliable association between these constructs (e.g., Cummings & Davies, 1994; Grych & Fincham, 1990), but in this overview we will focus on the results of a recent meta-analysis because it provides clearer indication of the strength of the relations between particular aspects of conflict and different types of child problems.

Buehler et al.'s (1997) meta-analysis of 68 studies testing the association between conflict and adjustment showed that the average effect size was .32, midway between a "small" (.20) and "medium" (.50) effect as described by Cohen (1977). This effect size is nearly twice that found for the association between divorce and child adjustment (Amato & Keith, 1991). Buehler and her colleagues' (1997) analysis also showed that effect sizes differed depending on how conflict was expressed. Studies assessing overt conflict, defined as direct expressions of hostile behavior and affect, produced a larger effect size (.35) than studies examining covert conflict (.28), in which hostility is expressed indirectly, withdrawal from conflict (.27), or studies simply measuring conflict frequency (.19). These differences indicate that the way parents manage conflict, rather than whether it occurs, is critical for understanding its impact on children.

In contrast, effect sizes were not significantly related to children's age or gender, though the magnitude of the effect size for boys (.32) was larger than that for girls (.23). Findings regarding gender differences in children's adjustment and in their immediate response to conflict have been inconsistent, and the role that gender may play in moderating the impact of conflict is a subject of current debate (see Davies & Lindsay, Chapter 3). The ethnic composition of the samples also was not related to effect sizes, but the question of whether conflict may have different effects for children from different ethnic or cultural backgrounds has not been investigated frequently enough to draw any firm conclusions (see McLoyd, Harper, & Copeland, Chapter 4).

Effect sizes also did not differ significantly for different kinds of child adjustment problems. In assessing child outcomes, researchers have tended to focus primarily on broad-band measures of problem behaviors (e.g., internalizing vs. externalizing). Although greater exposure to interparental conflict is related to elevated levels of maladjustment in general, a recent study suggests that children living in highly conflictual and aggressive homes exhibit different patterns of adjustment problems (Grych, Jouriles, McDonald, & Norwood, Swank, 2000). Grych and colleagues (2000) found that some children of battered women exhibited elevated levels of both internalizing and externalizing problems, others only internalizing or only externalizing problems, and still others demonstrated no behavior problems. Understanding how different developmental pathways may arise in children from conflictual homes is an important goal for future research (see Margolin, Oliver, & Medina, Chapter 1). In addition, even though it clearly is important to know that children exposed to high levels of conflict are at greater risk for maladjustment, it also is important to investigate whether conflict is related to other important developmental sequelae (e.g., peer or dating relationships).

Conclusions about the causal relation between interparental conflict and child adjustment are limited because the vast majority of studies conducted in this area are still cross-sectional. Nonetheless, research demonstrating the stressfulness of conflict for children suggests that exposure to conflict may well affect children's functioning, and the few longitudinal investigations examining relations between conflict and adjustment support the hypothesis that exposure to conflict predicts later adjustment problems (see Harold & Conger, 1997; Harold, Fincham, Osborne, & Conger, 1997; Katz & Gottman, 1993).

Research on Children's Immediate Responses to Witnessing Conflict

The second major issue that has been a focus of research concerns the immediate effects of witnessing conflict. Studies examining children's responses to specific conflictual interactions have sought to understand how the manner in which conflict is expressed may shape its impact on children and how other factors (e.g., gender, prior exposure to conflict) may influence children's responses as well. In this type of study, children observe one or more conflictual interactions, and their emotional, cognitive, behavioral, and/or physiological responses are assessed. These studies typically have used analog designs, using taped or staged conflicts involving actors rather than the child's parents, but several have observed children's responses to conflicts between their own parents, either at home (e.g., Cummings et al. 1981) or in a lab (e.g., Davis, Hops, Alpert, & Sheeber, 1998; Gordis, Margolin, & John, 1997). For a more detailed discussion of this methodology, see Cummings, Goeke-Morey, and Dukewich (Chapter 2).

Cummings and his colleagues have demonstrated that the level of anger and aggressiveness displayed during a conflict and the quality of its resolution are particularly important for determining how stressful conflict is for children (for a review, see Cummings & Davies, 1994). Other studies indicate that what parents are arguing about, the content of the disagreement, also can affect how it is perceived by children (Grych & Fincham, 1993; Laumakis, Margolin, & John, 1998). For example, children appear to be more threatened by conflicts involving a child-related topic and are more motivated to intervene in such conflicts (Grych & Fincham, 1993). These studies also have shown consistently that children exposed to more frequent, hostile, and poorly resolved interparental conflict become sensitized to the occurrence of conflict and feel more distressed when they witness later episodes of conflict (e.g., Cummings, Pellegrini, Notarious, & Cummings, 1989; El-Sheikh, 1994). Similarly, experiences with parent–child aggression have been linked to children's responses to interparental conflict (Grych, 1998; Hennessy, Rabideau, Cicchetti, & Cummings, 1994).

Research investigating specific conflict episodes also has been guided by an interest in determining whether children's immediate responses have implications for their broader functioning. Conceptual models proposing that witnessing conflict may have direct (i.e., unmediated by other factors, such as parenting) effects on children's development suggest that attention to children's emotional, cognitive, physiological, and/or coping responses may provide important insights into the processes that give rise to adjustment problems. The chapters in Part 2, "Basic Processes" discuss these processes in more detail.

Conclusion

We have learned a great deal about the relation between interparental conflict and child maladjustment, but many essential questions remain about the potential effects of interparental discord on children's development. The chapters that follow address some of the most critical issues in this area, and together serve both to describe the "state of the art" in the field and to chart the course for advancing understanding of this important link between interparental and child functioning.

REFERENCES

Amato, P. R., & Keith, B. (1991). Consequences of parental divorce for the well-being of children: A meta-analysis. *Psychological Bulletin, 110,* 26–46.

Buehler, C., Anthony, C., Krishnakumar, A., Stone, G., Gerard, J., & Pemberton, S. (1997). Interparent conflict and youth problem behaviors: A meta-analysis. *Journal of Child and Family Studies, 6,* 233–247.

Cohen, J. (1977). *Statistical power analysis for the behavioral sciences.* New York: Academic Press.

Cummings, E. M., & Davies, P. T. (1994). *Children and marital conflict.* New York: Guilford.

Cummings, E. M., Zahn-Waxler, C., & Radke-Yarrow, M. (1981). Young children's responses to expressions of anger and affection by others in the family. *Child Development, 52,* 1274–1282.

Cummings, J. S., Pellegrini, D. S., Notarious, C. L., & Cummings, E. M. (1989). Children's responses to angry adult behavior as a function of marital distress and history of interparent hostility. *Child Development, 60,* 1035–1043.

Davis, B. T., Hops, H., Alpert, A., & Sheeber, L. (1998). Child responses to parental conflict and their effect on adjustment. A study of triadic relations. *Journal of Family Psychology, 12,* 163–177.

El-Sheikh, M. (1994). Children's emotional and physiological responses to interadult angry behavior: The role of history of interparental hostility. *Journal of Abnormal Child Psychology, 22,* 661–678.

Fincham, F. D. (1998). Child development and marital relations. *Child Development, 69,* 543–574.

Framo, J. (1965). Rationale and techniques of intensive family therapy. In I. Boszormenyi-Nagy & J. Famo (Eds.), *Intensive family therapy* (pp. 143–212). New York: Hoeber Medical Division, Harper & Row.

Gordis, E. B., Margolin, G., & John, R. S. (1997). Marital aggression, observed parental hostility, and child behavior during triadic family interaction. *Journal of Family Psychology, 11,* 76–89.

Grych, J. H. (1998). Children's appraisals of interparental conflict: Situational and contextual influences. *Journal of Family Psychology, 12,* 437–453.

Grych, J. H., & Fincham, F. D. (1990). Marital conflict and children's adjustment: A cognitive-contextual framework. *Psychological Bulletin, 108,* 267–290.

Grych, J. H., & Fincham, F. D. (1993). Children's appraisals of marital conflict: Initial investigations of the cognitive-contextual framework. *Child Development, 64,* 215–230.

Grych, J. H., Jouriles, E. N., McDonald, R., Norwood, W., & Swank, P. (2000). Patterns of adjustment among children of battered women. *Journal of Consulting and Clinical Psychology, 68,* 84–94.

Grych, J. H., Seid, M., & Fincham, F. D. (1992). Assessing marital conflict from the child's perspective. *Child Development, 63,* 558–572.

Harold, G. T., & Conger, R. D. (1997). Marital conflict and adolescent distress: The role of adolescent awareness. *Child Development, 68,* 333–350.

Harold, G. T., Fincham, F. D., Osborne, L. N., & Conger, R. D. (1997). Mom and dad are at it again: Adolescent perceptions of marital conflict and adolescent psychological distress. *Developmental Psychology, 33,* 333–350.

Hennessy, K. D., Rabideau, G. J., Cicchetti, D., & Cummings, E. M. (1994). Responses of physically abused and nonabused children to different forms of interadult anger. *Child Development, 65,* 815–828.

Jouriles, E. N., Murphy, C. M., & O'Leary, K. D. (1989). Interspousal aggression, marital discord, and child problems. *Journal of Consulting and Clinical Psychology, 57,* 453–455.

Katz, L. F., & Gottman, J. M. (1993). Patterns of marital conflict predict children's internalizing and externalizing behaviors. *Developmental Psychology, 29,* 940–950.

Laumakis, M. A., Margolin, G., & John, R. S. (1998). The emotional, cognitive, and coping responses of preadolescent children to different dimensions of marital conflict. In G. Holden, R. Geffner, & E. Jouriles (Eds.), *Children exposed to marital violence* (pp. 257–288). Washington, DC: American Psychological Association.

Lewis, C. E., Siegal, J. M., & Lewis, M. A. (1984). Feeling bad: Exploring sources of distress among pre-adolescent children. *American Journal of Public Health, 74,* 117–122.

PART ONE. FOUNDATIONS

1 Conceptual Issues in Understanding the Relation between Interparental Conflict and Child Adjustment

Integrating Developmental Psychopathology and Risk/Resilience Perspectives

Gayla Margolin, Pamella H. Oliver, and Anna Marie Medina

Despite widespread acceptance of the belief that exposure to interparental conflict is a serious stressor for children, much remains unknown about exactly why and how this stressor translates into different outcomes across children. The assumption that marital conflict is a stressor for children stems from several explanatory frameworks – family systems theory, social learning theory, the transmission of affect, consistencies in cognitive style, genetic transmission theories, and trauma theory. These frameworks have provided both the impetus and foundation for empirical investigations of the effects of marital conflict on children. In this chapter, we review these frameworks and illustrate how a developmental psychopathology perspective can inform research in this area. Specifically, we analyze the status of marital conflict as a risk factor, consider how research on vulnerability and protective factors can delineate processes that intensify or interrupt the trajectory from marital conflict to negative child outcomes, and recommend greater attention to the resilience of many children living in highly conflictual homes. This perspective underscores the complexity of the relationship between marital conflict and child outcomes and suggests why conflict does not affect children in predictable or consistent ways.

Marital Conflict as a Risk: Empirical Evidence

Since instances and even extended periods of marital discord are quite common in marriage, children living in two-parent households generally have been exposed to some form of marital conflict. Statistics on

Preparation of this chapter has been supported by grant #99-8412 from the David and Lucile Packard Foundation.

divorce and marital violence suggest that a substantial number of children have been exposed to serious marital conflict. Approximately 40% of U.S. children age 16 or younger will live in single-parent households because of divorce (Cherlin, 1992). More than 10 million U.S. children witness physical aggression between their parents each year (Straus, 1992). The seemingly pervasive nature of marital conflict in family life results in obvious questions about whether and under what conditions marital conflict indeed is a risk factor for children.

Various sources of evidence indicate that marital conflict is a stressor for children with at least short-term, and perhaps long-term, implications for children's adjustment. First, studies designed to identify and rate the impact of many childhood events point to interparental arguments as relatively common and disruptive events in children's lives. Children rate "having parents argue in front of you" as the third worst event in a list of 20 events that make them feel bad (Lewis, Siegel, & Lewis, 1984). Adults who work with children rate increased arguments between parents, marital separation, and divorce as events that require moderate to high amounts of psychological readjustment in children of all age groups (Coddington, 1972).

Second, there is a rapidly expanding literature documenting associations between marital conflict and various indices of maladjustment in children (for reviews, see Cummings & Davies, 1994; Emery, 1999; Grych & Fincham, 1990; Margolin, 1998; Reid & Crisafulli, 1990). This literature has brought scholarly and clinical attention to the concern that children living with high levels of marital conflict may be at risk for negative developmental outcomes. The sequelae of marital conflict are multifaceted and varied, leading to the conclusion that the effects of this stressor do not follow a common pathway. Associations have been noted between marital conflict and many indices of child maladjustment, including internalizing and externalizing behavior problems, post-traumatic stress symptoms, physiological and health symptoms, and problems with mood, academics, peer relationships, and social problem-solving abilities. Since much of this literature is cross-sectional, there is substantial evidence that marital conflict and negative child behaviors co-occur but less evidence that marital conflict actually causes poor adaptation in children.

The third source of evidence comes from studies designed to assess children's immediate reactions to interparental conflict, either as they respond in real life or as they respond in analogue situations when exposed to audiotaped or videotaped samples of interadult anger. Children register their distress to adult conflict through negative emotions, physiological changes, and self-reported discomfort (e.g., El-

Sheikh & Cummings, 1995; Grych, 1998; Laumakis, Margolin, & John, 1998). These studies have also revealed the types of adult conflict that are most distressing to children, for example, those that lack resolution and include high levels of hostility, physical violence, or threats to leave.

Fourth, research on how divorce affects children informs our understanding of how marital conflict affects children. Studies on children's adaptation to divorce, although originally focused on family structure, have more recently emphasized family process (Emery, 1999; Grych & Fincham, 1997). The divorce literature points to two family process factors that influence child behavior – interparental conflict and parent–child relations. According to Amato and Keith (1991), interparental conflict accounts for more of the negative consequences of divorce than either parental absence or economic disadvantage. Moreover, prospective studies provide evidence that child adjustment problems, interparental tensions, and unsupportive parenting may be processes occurring prior to the divorce, rather than as an outcome of divorce (Block, Block, & Gjerde, 1988; Shaw, Emery, & Tuer, 1993). Hetherington, Bridges, and Insabella (1998) propose a model, also applicable to the effects of marital conflict, in which children's overall outcomes to divorce are a function of the complicated balance between risk and protective factors at specific phases of the transition through divorce, and with attention to children's developmental stage and gender.

Marital Conflict as a Risk Factor: Conceptual Foundations

The study of marital conflict as a risk factor for children's maladjustment stems from the general premise that children's behavior can best be understood in the context of important relationships. However, theories seeking to explain the link between marital conflict and child adjustment differ in the processes they propose give rise to this association. In this section, we review the most prominent theoretical perspectives guiding research on conflict and child adjustment.

Family Systems Theory

As contrasted with traditional views attributing psychopathology to individual personality factors, the *family systems* perspective understands psychopathology as a reflection of family processes. According to family systems theory, marital conflict is a risk factor for children because marital power struggles are accompanied by an intensification of either intimacy, rejection, or both in the parent–child relationship, which also are accompanied by symptomatic behaviors in the child. One proposed type of intensification is that parents distract themselves from their marital problems by uniting in their focus on a child's symptoms (Vogel & Bell, 1960). Whether the parents unite to protect or to blame a symptomatic child, they maintain an ostensibly harmonious marital relationship by magnifying the child's problems. The child, in turn, may intensify problematic behaviors that serve to reunite otherwise disengaged parents. Another proposed intensification is that marital conflict leads to inappropriate generational boundaries in which a distant marital relationship is paired with an excessively close and enmeshed cross-generational alliance between one parent and the child (Minuchin, Rosman, & Baker, 1978). Children experiencing this type of intensified parent–child relationship may feel pressed to ally with one parent against the other as well as to assume characteristics of the adult role. These children may become increasingly symptomatic over time if the enmeshed parents fail to enforce rules or to hold the child to age-appropriate standards of behavior (Nichols & Schwartz, 1995). Supporting these explanations, Lindahl and Malik (1999) report that high levels of marital conflict are found in parents who are disengaged from one another or who are united in their attacking of the child, and both of these patterns are associated with behavior problems in boys.

Social Learning Theory

A *social learning* analysis attributes problematic behavior to observational learning, reinforced performance of the behavior within a social context, and, albeit to a lesser extent, biological factors that influence what individuals learn and what they can perform (Bandura, 1977). Early models suggest that children learn aggressive behaviors from the observation of aggressive models, with parents being powerful models for aggressive behavior. Conflictual spouses may provide children with models of angry, hostile behavior and fail to provide models of warmth, caring, and productive problem solving (Margolin, 1981). Interparental hostility and aggression likely impart messages to children condoning aggression in intimate relationships. Moreover, the short-term positive outcomes often associated with aggressive behavior may teach children the functional value of such behaviors. Specific social processing deficits, for example, bias toward attributing hostile intent and inability to generate competent solutions, found in victims of child abuse (Dodge, Bates, & Pettit, 1990), may be similarly acquired by observing interparental aggression.

Patterson (1982) describes how marital conflict not only models aggressive behavior but is one of several family stressors that alter the parents' mood and disrupt parents' implementation of family management practices, such as enforcing house rules, monitoring, being contingent with consequences, and using effective problem solving. The combination of a child who exhibits high levels of aversive stimuli coupled with parents who exhibit inept child management skills results in a system characterized by coercive, attacking, and counterattacking exchanges. The system potentially spirals out of control as lack of parenting success negatively influences parental self-esteem, which feeds back to the marital relationship, leading to more mismanaged parenting, and so forth. These coercive family cycles also interact with broader social structures and contextual variables, for example, social status, neighborhood, poverty, and cultural attitudes and beliefs, in influencing children's performance of deviant behaviors (Patterson, Reid, & Dishion, 1992).

Theories Relating to the Transmission of Affect or Spillover

A common theme in explanations of how one family subsystem influences another family subsystem revolves around the transfer of mood or affect across family subsystems (Erel & Burman, 1995; Repetti, 1987). As Hinde and Stevenson-Hinde (1988) describe, the harmony or disharmony in one family relationship can affect the overall emotional climate of the family and also spill into other relationships. Although affect can be transmitted among marital, parent–child, and sibling relationships, the marital relationship plays a pivotal role (Margolin, Christensen, & John, 1996). The instrumental and emotional support that spouses provide for each other has been identified as an important influence on other family relationships, particularly parenting (Belsky, 1984). The *spillover* or contagion of affect can function in either positive or negative ways (Engfer, 1988). Whereas hostile, aversive marital relationships can be reflected in angry, power-assertive parenting styles, positive marital relationships appear to bolster parents' abilities and confidence for parenting (Easterbrooks & Emde, 1988).

A related explanation of affective transmission is the *common-factor* hypothesis, suggesting that personality characteristics of one person can influence the quality of both the parenting and marital relationships (Engfer, 1988). Hence, a parent's harsh, authoritarian interpersonal style could generalize across relationships and create tensions with both the spouse and the child. Data suggest, for example, that fathers' marital aggression is associated with fathers' authoritarian, controlling, and physically abusive behavior toward their sons (Holden & Ritchie, 1991; Jouriles & LeCompte, 1991; Margolin, John, Ghosh, & Gordis, 1996). Caspi and Elder (1988) suggest that unstable,

aversive personalities in the parents are related to aversive marital relationships and are found in the context of an overall disordered family,
thereby producing unstable, problematic children.

Theories regarding affect spillover have their roots in social psychology and sociological stress theory. Early social psychology theories
posited that aggression may be expressed toward a less powerful and
more easily available target as a substitute for the primary target
(Dollard, Doob, Miller, Mowrer, & Sears, 1939), and that anger may
lower the threshold for an aggressive response (Buss, 1961). Thus, after
a marital fight, if the child commits even a small transgression, parents
may exhibit disproportionate anger toward the child, as a safer target
than the spouse. Sociological *role strain* theory further describes how
stress is generated when expectations of one role compete with the
demands of another role (Goode, 1960). Although sometimes used to
describe how the stress of raising a difficult or chronically ill child
affects other family systems, role strain theory also can explain how the
stress of a conflictual marriage depletes energy for and competes with
the demands of parenting.

Theories Relating to Consistencies in Cognitive Style

Similar to the common-factor hypothesis of affect, family members
may apply the same types of cognitive perceptions across different
family relationships. Easterbrooks and Emde (1988) describe a *perceptual bias screen* in which a parent's negative perceptions and interpretations are applied to both the child and the marriage. Reporting on
evidence of a general attributional style, Fincham and Grych (1991)
found that distressed spouses are more likely than nondistressed
spouses to apply global attributions to both negative child behavior
and marital difficulties. Cognitive disturbances, including unrealistic
expectations and negative attributional biases, also have been reported
in abusive parents (Azar, Barnes, & Twentyman, 1988), suggesting that
cognitive styles having a negative impact in one family relationship
may also occur in another family relationship.

Genetic Transmission Theories

Although this chapter focuses on social psychological dimensions of
marital conflict as a risk for children, it is also possible that this risk
incorporates genetic similarities between parents and children as well
as genetic vulnerabilities (Rutter, 1994). Findings indicating that individual differences in parents' temperament are associated with children's adjustment have been attributed to heredity as well as to family
environment (DiLalla & Gottesman, 1991). For example, the consistent

finding that children's conduct disorders are associated with parents' antisocial behavior raises the possibility of both genetic and environmental components for the co-occurrence of negativistic, antisocial behaviors in both the parents and child. Rutter (1988) suggests that parental psychopathology and criminality, which are related to marital discord, may be proxies for genetic risk and perhaps account for some of the variance in child outcomes that is attributed to psychosocial variables.

Another possibility is that the effects of adversities in life such as marital discord are more profound in genetically vulnerable children. Since dealing with adversity requires self-regulation of attention, emotion, and behavior (Cicchetti & Toth, 1995; Masten & Coatsworth, 1998), children with genetically related cognitive or neurological limitations may be more vulnerable to the stress of marital conflict and violence. Similarly, several authors suggest that family process variables such as marital conflict and negative parenting may potentiate a genetic transmission between adult psychopathology and child psychopathology, although they conclude that, as yet, there is little evidence supporting such hypotheses (Patterson & Dishion, 1988; Rutter, 1988).

Trauma Theory and Sensitization to Marital Conflict

Chronic exposure to severe marital conflict and violence has been described as a form of child maltreatment and trauma (Hart & Brassard, 1987; Tomkins, Mohamed, Steinman, Macolini, Kenning, & Afrank, 1994). Witnessing others being severely endangered or injured can be as traumatic as being directly victimized oneself (Silvern & Kaersvang, 1989; Singer, Anglin, Song, & Lunghofer, 1995), particularly when violence is directed toward a parent upon whom the child relies for caretaking and protection. As such, interparental aggression can be a serious violation of children's dependency needs (Finkelhor & Dzuiba-Leatherman, 1994) and can create a sense of personal threat and loss (Pynoos & Eth, 1985). Moreover, as opposed to a one-time trauma that elicits intense surprise, the repeated nature of exposure to marital conflict and violence would place it in Terr's (1991) definition of Type II traumas, eliciting prolonged and anguished anticipation of this event.

Despite debate over what constitutes a traumatic stressor, there is agreement over the types of symptoms associated with traumatic experiences. Post-traumatic stress generally is recognized through symptoms of reexperiencing, avoidance, and heightened arousal. Heightened arousal, frequently reflected in emotional and physiological dysregulation, is experienced sometimes as hypervigilance and exaggerated startle and, other times, as numbing and decreased responsiveness to external stimuli (Perry, 1997). Both types of dysregulation can potentially impair concentration and attention in children.

Within the marital conflict literature, the *sensitization* hypothesis describes a process paralleling Type II trauma whereby children become increasingly reactive, or on alert to future interparental hostility. The sensitization hypothesis proposes that children's previous experience with marital conflict serves as a context for their later reactions such that children who are exposed to greater amounts of marital conflict become more vulnerable over time to its effects. According to Grych and Fincham's (1990) cognitive-contextual model, past experience with interparental discord increases children's sensitivity to conflict by creating internal representations or expectations about the course of future conflict experiences and also about their abilities to cope with conflict. According to Davies and Cummings' (1994) emotional security model, repeated exposure to destructive marital conflicts compromises children's adjustment by inducing chronic levels of arousal and emotional dysregulation, thereby fostering a variety of adjustment problems. Both of these models have undergone considerable empirical investigation with results showing that children with a history of repeated exposure to marital conflict or violence, compared to children without the exposure history, tend to be more threatened and distressed when faced with new instances of conflict.

Evidence of chronic heightened arousal also comes from physiological findings. Gottman and Katz (1989) report an inverse relationship between marital adjustment and children's urinary dopamine levels, which are an index of catecholamine concentration and an estimate of physiological arousal. Catecholamine levels, in connection with affective and behavioral reactions, were related to children playing at a developmentally lower level with their best friend, that is, parallel play rather than interactive play. These authors suggest that children exposed to marital conflict may become hypervigilant to conflict cues, experience a high level of chronic stress as indexed by their catecholamine levels, attempt to contain negative affect by playing at a low level, but still have trouble regulating emotion if anger erupts. This study, together with the previously described studies, begins to suggest theoretical connections among children's exposure to chronic marital conflict; cognitive, emotional, and physiological stress reactions; and more global negative consequences.

Developmental Psychopathology Perspective

A *developmental psychopathology* perspective assumes that a child's reactions to a stressor such as marital conflict reflect an interaction between the nature of the stressor and the child's developmental capacities to respond to that stressor (Cicchetti, 1993; Cicchetti & Toth, 1995; Finkelhor & Kendall-Tackett, 1997). Incorporating a developmental perspective into the study of marital conflict involves examining: (a) how the consequences of marital conflict vary in intensity and form at different developmental stages; (b) how outcomes are multiply determined rather than uniquely the result of marital conflict; and (c) whether and under what circumstances the risk of exposure at one age affects later development.

With a strong focus on continuities and discontinuities in development, the developmental psychopathology framework is grounded in an understanding of normal development and in the ways that one developmental task is linked to another developmental task. From this perspective, the consequences of marital conflict may not be limited to isolated effects in children but potentially may disrupt overall developmental trajectories. Stage-salient developmental tasks generally seen as vulnerable to environmental stressors include the development of attachment, the regulation of affect, the development of internalized beliefs about oneself and others, the establishment of peer relations, and adaptation to school (Cicchetti & Toth, 1995). Although existing data do not indicate that one age group is more vulnerable to marital conflict than another (Grych & Fincham, 1990), some types of caretaking risks do appear to have heightened salience for a particular developmental stage (Seifer, Sameroff, Baldwin, & Baldwin, 1992).

Comprehensive conceptualizations of the effects of marital conflict on children tend to incorporate the developmental psychopathology perspective by examining the transactional relations between the context of interparental conflict and the children's cognitive and affective processes. As one example, Grych and Fincham (1990; 1993) propose that the meaning children place on marital conflict modulates the regulation of affect arousal and coping strategies and also generalizes to broader indices of childhood functioning. Developmental stage is relevant to this model in that perceived threat and perceived ability to cope vary by child age, and the type of adjustment exhibited reflects the developmental tasks facing the child. As another example, Davies and Cummings (1994) propose that marital conflict interrupts children's attachment processes and leads to emotional insecurity. Emotional insecurity leaves children more prone to negative emotional arousal and distress, less able to regulate their emotions, and less optimistic about their abilities to cope when faced with further episodes of marital conflict (see Crockenberg and Langrock, Chapter 5).

As these two models illustrate, the marital conflict literature points to disruptions in developmental processes involving the organization, regulation, and understanding of emotional experience as well as distortions in cognitive processes regarding conflict situations. According to the developmental psychopathology literature, these types of disruptions may have significant developmental consequences (Cichetti & Toth, 1995). Although the marital conflict literature has provided considerable empirical support for the link between various dimensions of marital conflict and cognitive and affective disruptions, as well as for the link between these disruptions and child outcomes, further evaluation is needed of models that simultaneously examine all three components (see Davies & Cummings [1998] and Kerig [1998] for exceptions). Other aspects of the developmental psychopathology framework that need further attention with respect to the impact of marital conflict include: (a) whether marital conflict interacts with other stressors both within and outside the family in leading to developmental disruptions; (b) whether there is a chain of effects such that initial reactions of anxiety, fear, arousal, and distraction lead to secondary effects such as problems with peers or school, which then lead to a cascading series of more severe problems, such as antisocial behaviors, substance abuse, or illegal activities; (c) whether transitions to new developmental phases, such as adolescence, are times of heightened vulnerability due to the co-occurrence of other ongoing stressors as well as the salience of socialization processes during those times; and (d) what contributes to children's resilience such that many exhibit good adaptation despite the challenges of living in highly conflictual homes.

Application of a developmental psychopathology perspective helps to explain why marital conflict, as with other types of adversity, does not affect children in predictable or consistent ways. As described in the next section, appreciation for the wide range of outcomes related to marital conflict requires closer examination of marital conflict as a risk factor, consideration of risk and resilience models, and a description of vulnerability and protective factors that interact with marital conflict.

Difficulties in the Interpretation of Marital Conflict

Marital conflict is an enormously wide-ranging construct encompassing events viewed as common, everyday stressors (Repetti, McGrath, & Ishikawa, 1999) to events viewed as significant life traumas (Silvern & Kaersvang, 1989). The empirical literature does little to reconcile these divergent views of marital conflict. The term *marital conflict* is often used in an undifferentiated manner, encompassing a broad range of conflict behaviors. Whereas some studies conceptualize marital conflict as a continuous variable, other studies use distinct groups of high versus low conflict, suggesting that there is a meaningful cutoff point at which marital conflict is and is not detrimental to children. Some studies specifically examine the effects of exposure to interparental physical aggression, whereas other studies do not evaluate the extent to which high conflict is actually a proxy for physical aggression. As Fincham, Grych, and Osborne (1994) point out, the relatively modest associations between marital relations and child outcomes most likely reflect the wide range of phenomena being measured under the rubric of marital conflict.

The literature has begun to address the possible beneficial effects of children's exposure to low levels of marital conflict (Davies & Cummings, 1994; Grych & Fincham, 1993). It is possible that in measured dosages and with calm, productive outcomes, marital conflict serves children well by preparing them to deal constructively in conflict situations that they might encounter. On the other end of the conflict spectrum, with respect to severely hostile and violent forms of marital conflict, the literature suggests that a child's physical well-being, as well as her or his sense of order and stability in the world may be threatened (Margolin, 1998). This type of marital conflict shares many features in common with other severe stressors, such as child abuse and neighborhood violence. That is, children who are exposed to a chronically distressing situation no longer view their home as a safe haven and have no power to remove themselves from the unsafe situation.

Are there dose-response effects for children exposed to marital conflict? The trauma literature clearly points to dose-exposure gradients such that higher symptom levels are associated with the number of traumatic events experienced, physical proximity to violence, and psychological proximity to the victim (Richters & Martinez, 1993; Wright, Masten, Northwood, & Hubbard, 1997). To a certain extent, the marital conflict and violence literature suggests that there is a linear relationship between amount and severity of conflict and children's outcome, with violent conflict being associated with more severe outcomes and more severe immediate reactions than nonviolent conflict (Davies & Cummings, 1994; Fincham, Grych, & Osborne, 1994; Jouriles, Farris, & McDonald, 1991; Margolin, 1998). However, the literature does not specify whether there is a linear relationship between marital conflict and children's maladjustment or whether there is a threshold of conflict exposure, in terms of severity or amount, beyond which most children are likely to experience adverse effects.

Marital conflict frequently co-occurs with other environmental risk factors (Margolin & Gordis, in press) which together may have additive or even interactive effects on children's adjustment (Rossman, Hughes, & Hanson, 1998; Rutter, 1990). Bronfenbrenner's (1979) ecological approach indicates that development is influenced by a variety of distal and proximal environmental factors. This approach would suggest that an understanding of child outcomes to marital conflict requires examination of multiple contextual variables and, in particular, other risk factors. Exposure to marital conflict and violence tends to co-occur with child physical abuse (Appel & Holden, 1998), child sexual abuse (McCloskey, Figueredo, & Koss, 1995), and community violence (Bell & Jenkins, 1993). As suggested in the results by Cummings, Hennessy, Rabideau, and Cicchetti (1994), exposure to one type of abuse might sensitize children to another type of abuse in that physically abused children, compared to nonabused children, responded with greater fear to interadult anger. Children exposed to high levels of marital conflict or violence also may experience other types of mental-health risks, such as poverty, parental unemployment, low education level, separation from a parent, and parental substance abuse (Fantuzzo, Boruch, Beriama, Atkins, & Marcus, 1997). The co-occurrence of marital conflict with other environmental risks is potentially problematic since exposure to multiple risks is associated with worse developmental outcomes than exposure to a singular risk (Rutter, 1990; Sameroff, Seifer, Barocas, Zax, & Greenspan, 1987).

Resilience

The study of resilience (Garmezy, Masten, & Tellegen, 1984; Rutter, 1990; Werner, 1993) is relevant to understanding why, given the large number of children who experience marital conflict, only a small number appear to be affected at any one point in time. Although resilience has a number of definitions, it typically is used to describe processes that interrupt the trajectory from risk to problem behaviors, thereby explaining why some children show successful adaptation despite exposure to threatening situations. Resilience, however, is not a fixed characteristic of an individual but changes across time and circumstances. Children who show resilience in one situation may not show resilience in another situation or at another point in time (Freitas & Downey, 1998).

The study of resilience is built on the concepts of risk indicators (also called risk factors), risk mechanisms (also called vulnerabilities), and protective variables (Rutter, 1994; Werner, 1990). Risk indicators are psychosocial or biological hazards that increase the likelihood of negative developmental outcomes. Risk mechanisms or vulnerabilities explain the how and why of individual susceptibility. Whereas marital conflict is a risk indicator, dimensions of marital conflict and individual characteristics of the child are typically examined as risk mechanisms.

The resiliency literature offers three general ways that protective variables exert their beneficial effects (Freitas & Downey, 1998; Tiet et al., 1998). Distinctions are drawn among those variables that interact with the risk factor to reduce negative outcomes, those variables that have a direct or main effect on the child's adaptation regardless of risk, and those that inoculate the child through successful responses to the challenge. Variables that interact with a risk factor either intensify or ameliorate the effect of the stressor in the high-risk population but have little or no effect in the low-risk group (Rutter, 1990). These variables typically would be moderators as they affect the direction and/or strength of the association between the risk and adaptation variables. For example, data from Sandler, Tein, and West (1994) indicate that an active coping style moderates the relation between stress and child problems. The cross-sectional positive relation between stress and child conduct problems and the longitudinal relation between stress and anxiety were significant for those who used a low level of active coping but nonsignificant for those who used a high level of active coping.

The second type of protection is found when main effect variables, that is, resource factors or compensatory factors, neutralize adverse life events by their direct and independent influence on the child outcome variable (Garmezy et al., 1984). Zimmerman and Arunkumar (1994) describe how parental interest in children's education functions as a compensatory factor for family conflict in predicting children's academic competence. The third model of protection is the challenge model that suggests a moderate amount of a risk factor potentially enhances successful adaptation (Zimmerman & Arunkumar, 1994). An important dimension of this model is identifying the level of risk that, rather than immobilizing the child, actually prepares the child for the next challenge by strengthening his or her resilience. Although certain dimensions of marital conflict have been shown to have no lasting negative effects, little is known about how marital conflict actually prepares children for future conflicts they will encounter.

It is not unusual for certain protective variables to have both a main effect on child outcomes as well as an interactive effect on the risk variable. As Rutter (1988) points out, there has been much debate about whether supportive relationships constitute a main effect or serve as a buffer, exerting their influence only in the presence of stress or high-risk conditions. Some of the debate reflects different operationalization of terms. Cohen and Wills (1985) report that social support serves as a buffer if measured as the availability of interpersonal resources responsive to the needs elicited by the stressful events, but serves as a main effect if measured as the person's overall degree of integration in a large social network. Forehand and colleagues (Forehand et al., 1991) similarly report that positive parent–adolescent relationships serve as a buffer of cumulative family stressors including divorce and interparental conflict, but as a main effect on adolescent functioning.

Although this book focuses on marital conflict as a risk factor, it should be noted that some models of children's adaptation identify marital conflict as a vulnerability mechanism that explains how or why another risk factor affects children. Capaldi and Clark (1998), for example, assessed parental dyadic aggression and unskilled parenting as explanatory factors in the relationship between parents' antisocial behavior and their young adult sons' aggression toward a female partner. Their data point to unskilled parenting, more than interparental aggression, as affecting sons' later aggression, via the boys' antisocial behavior. Cowan and colleagues (Cowan, Cohn, Cowan, & Pearson, 1996) found that marital quality functioned as a mediator between fathers' insecure attachment, parenting, and child adjustment. For mothers, marital quality acted as a buffer interrupting the relationship between mothers' insecure attachment and ineffective parenting style.

Vulnerability and Protective Factors

Protective factors in children's resilience to hostile, abusive environments include both individual characteristics of the children as well as environmental characteristics (Hughes, 1997; Margolin & Gordis, in press). Individual characteristics promoting resiliency include relatively stable attributes of the child, such as intelligence, easygoing temperament, specific talents, and physical attractiveness, as well as the child's interpretation of events and ability to respond effectively when confronted with stressful situations (Masten & Coatsworth, 1998; Rutter, 1990). The key environmental characteristics identified to buffer severe risk conditions appear to be emotionally supportive and responsive caretaking either from parents or other adults in the child's life, good sibling relationships, and participation in activities that offer the child a sense of efficacy, success, and reinforcement (Egeland, Carlson, & Sroufe, 1993; Grych & Fincham, 1997; Jenkins & Smith, 1990; Masten & Coatsworth, 1998). There sometimes are important interactions between protective factors within and outside the child, for example, children with easy temperaments who actively seek relationships outside the family also are likely to get more positive feedback from the environment in support of their efforts (Hetherington, 1989; Werner, 1993).

The marital conflict literature has identified appraisals, coping responses, vagal tone, and intelligence as individual child factors that influence the relation between marital conflict and child outcomes. Parenting is the primary environmental characteristic examined as both a risk and protective variable in the marital conflict literature. A key consideration with these protective/risk variables is the iterative process between these variables and marital conflict, and between these variables and child outcomes. Even characteristics thought to be relatively stable can be modified and shaped by these feedback loops.

Appraisals. Grych and Fincham's (1990) cognitive-contextual framework posits that children's subjective cognitive evaluations of interparental conflict are integral to understanding children's responses to marital discord (see also Grych & Cardoza-Fernandes, Chapter 6). In support of this model, investigators have established links between children's appraisals of threat and self-blame and the intensity and frequency of the marital conflict (Cummings, Davies, & Simpson, 1994; Grych & Fincham, 1993). Investigators also have established links between children's appraisals and adaptational outcomes. Poorer adjustment is found in children who report higher awareness of conflict, blame themselves or their parents, and perceive higher levels of threat and less resolution (Cummings, Davies, et al., 1994; Grych & Fincham, 1993; Harold & Conger, 1997; Kerig, 1998). Appraisals of marital conflict have been put forth as both mediators and moderators of the relationship between marital conflict and children's adjustment (Grych & Fincham, 1990; Rossman & Rosenberg, 1992), with data supporting both models and also showing gender effects. Although not directly testing for mediation, Cummings, Davies, et al. (1994) present data suggesting that the link between marital conflict and child adjustment difficulties is influenced by boys' appraisals of threat and girls' appraisals of self-blame. Kerig (1998), finding more support for the moderating than the mediating hypothesis, reports that appraisals of conflict properties, threat, self-blame, and perceived control moderated links to externalizing, total problems, and anxiety in boys and to internalizing in girls.

Coping Responses. Coping is generally described as children's effortful, intentional, or purposeful physical or mental activities to alter the perceived problem or to alter their own emotional states. The literature outlines two forms of coping: (a) problem-focused coping, which serves to manage or alter the problem through strategies such as intervening directly or generating alternative solutions, and (b) emotion-focused coping, which serves to regulate stressful emotions and includes strategies such as avoidance, distancing, and selective attention (Compas, Banez, Malcarne, & Worsham, 1991; Kerig, Chapter 8; Repetti, et al., 1999). Although problem-focused coping tends to be effective for problems that children can control, e.g., failure at school, it is not particularly effective for problems that children cannot control. Since children have little or no control over their parents' marital conflicts, intervention in parents' quarrels by trying to stop the conflict, reasoning with the parents, or inserting oneself physically between the parents, has been found to be associated with poor child outcomes (Jenkins, Smith, & Graham, 1989; O'Brien, Margolin, & John, 1995). Laumakis et al. (1998) report that boys from high-conflict families, when presented with interparental conflict vignettes, report thoughts of direct intervention more frequently than boys from low-conflict families or girls from either high- or low-conflict families.

The data on children's use of outside social supports appear predictive of decreased maladjustment whereas coping through avoidance and withdrawal from marital conflict leads to mixed child outcomes. Rogers and Holmbeck (1997) observed that children's reported perceived availability of peers and use of social support moderated the link between marital conflict and child adjustment. Although avoidance of marital conflict was shown to be related to decreased maladjustment (O'Brien et al., 1995), avoidance coupled with rumination concerning loss of parental love ("worried avoidance") was associated with higher levels of child-reported depression but lower levels of teacher-reported externalizing behavior problems (O'Brien, Bahadur, Gee, Balto, & Erber, 1997). According to Rossman and Rosenberg (1992), children's beliefs in their ability to calm themselves were associated overall with adaptive child outcomes. However, endorsement of self-calming as well as intervention acted as vulnerability moderators when stress was high.

Emotion-focused coping also has been examined in several recent studies that used actual observed coping responses to conflict rather than self-reports. Children with histories of exposure to interparental physical aggression tend to use withdrawal, anxiety, and distraction during problem-oriented triadic family discussions as coded by outside observers (Gordis, Margolin, & John, 1997). Using daily home diary data from the parents, Garcia O'Hearn, Margolin, and John (1997) show that children who previously had been exposed to their parents' physical conflict, compared to children exposed to nonphysical conflict and low conflict, are more likely to leave the room, misbehave, or appear angry, and appear sad or frightened when confronted with ongoing interparental arguments in their home environments. Based on children's emotional reactivity when observing an analogue conflict between their mothers and an experimenter, Davies and Cummings (1998) report that greater marital discord predicted greater emotional distress (anxiety, freezing, sadness) and vigilance (preoccupation, verbal concern) in children, which mediated the relationship between marital functioning and children's externalizing and internalizing symptoms. Davis, Hops, Alpert, and Sheeber (1998) show that children's aggressive behavior in response to actual interparental conflicts predicted elevated aggressive child functioning one year later.

Vagal Tone. The recent literature examining exposure to environmental stressors and children's physiological functioning suggests that physiological reactivity may be a variable that potentiates or mitigates vulnerability to adverse life experiences (Pynoos, Steinberg, & Goenjian, 1996). In support of the importance of physiological reactivity to marital conflict, Katz and Gottman's work (see Katz, Chapter 7) indicates that high vagal tone serves to protect children from the deleterious effects of exposure to interparental hostility. Vagal tone, as a measure of the parasympathetic branch of the autonomic nervous system, is a physiological marker of the child's ability to focus attentional processes and to inhibit inappropriate action (Katz & Gottman, 1995). For children with low vagal tone, marital hostility at age 5 predicted antisocial behavior at age 8, whereas for children with high vagal tone, no such relationship was found. Katz and Gottman (1997) additionally report that vagal suppression buffered children from physical illness whereas high basal vagal tone buffered children from emotion dysregulation.

Intelligence. Researchers studying child and adolescent resilience in general have identified child intelligence as a significant protective factor (Garmezy et al., 1984; Tiet et al., 1998). Blechman, Prinz, and Dumas (1995) suggest that above-average intelligence fosters children's abilities to cope with adverse life experiences by facilitating language-based, prosocial coping, and cognitive restructuring. Specific to separation and divorce, intelligence is related to better coping and adaptation (Hetherington, 1989), perhaps due to children's "abilities to understand what has transpired and why" (Grych & Fincham, 1997, p. 177). Katz and Gottman (1997) show that children's intelligence partially buffered the marital risk on children's observed negative affect with peers and academic achievement.

Although intelligence appears to contribute to children's resilience, it is not yet clear whether high intelligence is a buffer, low intelligence is an independent risk factor, or intelligence is a proxy for other variables, such as coping strategies.

Parenting. Consistent evidence demonstrates that parenting effectiveness has a main effect on the healthy development of children. Although the nature of the relationship between parent and child changes across developmental stages, there is agreement concerning the parental behavioral patterns that promote optimal child development, such as responsiveness or attunement, sensitive control, warmth, and parental effectiveness in discipline, supervision, monitoring, and child management skills. Effective parenting, including emotional support and responsive caretaking, has been designated in the resiliency literature as a protective factor in the face of adverse life stress (Masten et al., 1988). As an example, Tiet et al. (1998) found parental monitoring to be a resource factor in that resilience in high-risk children was predicted by closer parental monitoring and better family functioning.

The association between marital relations and the parent–child relationship is well established (Cox, Paley, & Harter, Chapter 9; Erel & Burman, 1995). As a result of interparental conflict, parents can become emotionally unavailable or withdraw from their children (Fauber, Forehand, Thomas, & Wierson, 1990) or, alternatively, mothers may compensate for marital distress or paternal withdrawal through increased involvement and support for children (Belsky, Youngblade, Rovine, & Volling, 1991; Brody, Pillegrini, & Sigel, 1986). Empirical evidence indicates that maritally discordant parents use more power-assertive punishment, less positive reinforcement, and more inconsistent discipline (Crockenberg & Covey, 1991). In addition, the relationship between marital conflict and parenting is mediated by coparenting, the way in which parents parent together (Floyd, Gilliom, & Costigan, 1998). Distressed couples show hostile-competitive coparenting as well as discrepancies in involvement with the child (Katz & Gottman, 1996; McHale, 1995).

Theoretically, it has been suggested that marital conflict disrupts the parenting process, which then results in adverse outcomes for children (Emery, 1982; Fauber et al., 1990). This model of the effects of marital conflict on children with parenting as a mediator implies that direct associations between marital conflict and child outcomes become nonsignificant when one accounts for the effects of parenting (Holmbeck, 1997). Additionally, the implication that marital conflict disrupts parenting suggests a change in parenting over time attributable to the conflict, a conclusion requiring longitudinal data.

Studies using contemporaneous data have found both direct and indirect effects of marital conflict on child outcomes. Gottman and Katz (1989) report an indirect path from marital discord through parenting style to preschool children's social interactions and health, but a direct path from marital conflict to children's physiological arousal. Indirect effects of marital conflict through parents' rejection/withdrawal were supported for internalizing and externalizing behaviors in adolescents by Fauber et al. (1990), with direct effects of marital conflict significant for externalizing behavior problems in intact families. Miller, Cowan, Cowan, Hetherington, and Clingempeel (1993) report that positive affect and conflict in marriage have both direct and indirect effects with parental warmth serving as a pathway through which marital quality relates to lower levels of child aggression in preschoolers and early adolescents. Margolin and John (1997) also support both direct and indirect effects of marital conflict on child hostility and child depression and anxiety, with indirect effects mediated through power-assertive and positive parenting. Mann and MacKenzie (1996), finding no direct effects, indicate that marital dissatisfaction was mediated by paternal rejection, whereas overt marital conflict was mediated by lax and inconsistent maternal discipline.

Other studies with longitudinal components have examined how marital conflict and parenting at one point in time relate to subsequent child outcomes. These studies provide increased specificity in identifying the processes involved, as well as suggestive evidence for directional effects, although without repeated measurements on all variables, these studies do not address changes in parenting or child functioning. Examining specific dimensions of marital conflict, Katz and Gottman (1996) found that, when couples were hostile, fathers used intrusive and power-assertive approaches with children, which subsequently related to children's aggressive peer play. Husbands' emotional withdrawal was related contemporaneously to mother's rejecting parenting, which related to children's internalizing problems assessed three years later. According to Katz and Gottman (1997), parental warmth, scaffolding/praise, and low levels of derogatory statements completely buffered children experiencing marital conflict against the negative outcomes of academic difficulty, emotional-regulation problems, teacher ratings of negative peer relationships, and child physical illness, whereas the metaemotion variables of parent's acknowledging and helping to coach children about their emotions completely buffered against teacher ratings of negative peer relationships, negative affect with peers, and child physical illness. Behavior problems were the only negative outcomes not completely buffered by the parenting factors examined.

As noted by Fincham and colleagues (1994), marital conflict may not influence children in a simple linear manner, but rather may set into motion a causal chain of events. MacKinnon-Lewis and Lofquist (1996), for example, found evidence indicative of complexity in causal chains. An increase in marital conflict or an increase in negative mother–son interactions sets into motion distinct chains of events that included being disliked by peers with differential effects 18 months later, resulting in boys' aggressive or withdrawn behavior. Based on children's perceptions of interparental conflict as well as the parent–child relationship, Harold, Fincham, Osborne, and Conger (1997) longitudinally found both direct and indirect effects of marital conflict on adolescents' internalizing behavior problems but only indirect effects for externalizing problems. Adolescents' awareness of marital conflict was mediated by their perceptions of parent hostility towards them, which then related to externalizing behavior problems. Although the majority of studies find both direct and indirect effects of marital conflict, Neighbors, Forehand, and Bau (1997) support only a direct effects model whereby current interparental conflict and current relationships with parents were directly related to psychological adjustment of young adults. Overall, the longitudinal data presented here support models that connect interparental conflict with parent-child conflict that, through varying pathways, are linked to adjustment problems for children.

In terms of a resiliency model, there is evidence that parenting is a resource factor, a mechanism, and a protective or vulnerability factor. Although the associations between parenting and child outcomes are bidirectional and reciprocal in nature, most of these models have been tested in one direction only. With the purpose of determining how parenting protects or places children at increased risk in the face of interparental conflict, the specified direction of parent to child makes conceptual sense. Ultimately, however, fuller models would include feedback loops to examine how problematic child behavior promotes or maintains conflict in the marital and parent–child relationships.

Research Design Recommendations for Theory Development

Although already stated (Fincham et al., 1994), the necessity of longitudinal research designs cannot be overemphasized. Predominant models in understanding the effects of marital conflict on children require making causal inferences about how marital conflict directly affects children, how marital conflict indirectly affects children by disrupting other family systems, how marital conflict interacts with other risk factors to affect children, and how certain individual or environmental variables intensify or interrupt the trajectory from marital risk to maladjustment. In order to make such inferences, longitudinal designs are needed to establish the temporal ordering of risk factor and developmental outcome, and to determine whether the problem behavior emerged or changed as a result of the risk factor. To assess causal relationships among risk factors, protective/vulnerability factors, and adaptation requires that baseline measurements be made of all constructs under consideration, that the same variables be measured across time, and that assessments be made at several different points with enough time between assessments to allow for the hypothesized influences to occur (Gest, Neemann, Hubbard, Masten, & Tellegen, 1993). To integrate a developmental psychopathology perspective also requires longitudinal assessments. Longitudinal designs can determine whether the reactions are stable across time, whether there are particular periods of vulnerability, and how adaptation at one point in time affects adaptation at a later point in time (Margolin, 1998; Moffitt, 1990).

Examining children's adaptation across multiple domains of development also is essential to the study of children's reactions to marital conflict (Cicchetti & Garmezy, 1993). It is possible for a child to be functioning well in one domain, such as academic performance, but not in another domain, such as social adjustment. It is also possible that what may be adaptive in the context of a family characterized by high levels of interparental hostility may be maladaptive in other relationships (e.g., increased vigilance for cues of impending conflict may protect the child at home but may be maladaptive in other social situations). The costs of coping well also have been noted recently (Margolin & Gordis, in press). Children who exhibit problems are likely to draw attention to themselves and get help whereas children who cope successfully may not receive the same level of assistance. Apropos to the recommendation for longitudinal research, Masten and Coatsworth (1998) question whether and under what circumstances children who manifest competence at one stage exhibit negative consequences at a later stage.

Conclusions

Rich and varied conceptual underpinnings have been brought to the study of marital conflict and its impact on children. Empirical studies on this topic, however, are somewhat disconnected from the conceptual underpinnings due primarily to the lack of research designs testing whether marital conflict actually leads to problems in children's adjustment or to deterioration in the quality of parenting. It is recommended that theoretical and empirical considerations of the impact of marital conflict on children further integrate developmental psychopathology and resilience perspectives. Grounding the exploration of the effects of marital conflict within the context of normal and abnormal development will focus attention on: (a) multiple factors that interact with marital conflict to influence children's adjustment, (b) continuity and discontinuity in children's reactions across time, (c) developmental periods that may be particularly vulnerable to the effects of marital conflict, and (d) the impact of developmental problems at one age on development at a later age. A resilience perspective will focus attention on how marital conflict interacts with other risk factors and also how children's internal and external resources buffer their exposure to marital conflict. These perspectives hold considerable promise for advancing knowledge about what variables should be targeted toward the goal of promoting better adaptational outcomes in children exposed to marital conflict.

REFERENCES

Amato, P. R., & Keith, B. (1991). Parental divorce and the well-being of children: A meta-analysis. *Psychological Bulletin, 110,* 26–46.

Appel, A. E., & Holden, G. W. (1998). The co-occurrence of spouse and physical child abuse: A review and appraisal. *Journal of Family Psychology, 12,* 578–599.

Azar, S. T., Barnes, K. T., & Twentyman, C. T. (1988). Developmental outcomes in physically abused children: Consequences of parental abuse or the effects of a more general breakdown in caregiving behaviors? *The Behavior Therapist, 11,* 27–32.

Bandura, A. (1977). *Social learning theory.* New York: General Learning Press.

Belsky, J. (1984). The determinants of parenting: A process model. *Child Development, 55,* 83–96.

Belsky, J., Youngblade, L., Rovine, M., & Volling, B. (1991). Patterns of marital change and parent-child interaction. *Journal of Marriage and the Family, 53,* 487–498.

Bell, C. C., & Jenkins, E. J. (1993). Community violence and children on Chicago's southside. In D. Reiss, J. E. Richters, M. Radke-Yarrow, & D. Scharff (Eds.), *Children and violence* (pp. 46–54). New York: Guilford.

Blechman, E. A., Prinz, R. J., & Dumas, J. E. (1995). Coping, competence, and aggression prevention: 1. Developmental model. *Applied & Preventive Psychology, 4,* 211–232.

Block, J. H., Block, J., & Gjerde, P. R. (1988). Parental functioning and the home environment in families of divorce: Prospective and concurrent analyses. *Journal of the American Academy of Child and Adolescent Psychiatry, 27,* 207–213.

Brody, G. H., Pillegrini, A. D., & Siegel, I. E. (1986). Marital quality and mother-child and father-child interactions with school-aged children. *Developmental Psychology, 22,* 291–296.

Bronfenbrenner, U. (1979). *The ecology of human development.* Cambridge, MA: Harvard University Press.

Buss, A. H. (1961). *The psychology of aggression.* New York: John Wiley.

Capaldi, D. M., & Clark, S. (1998). Prospective family predictors of aggression toward female partners for at-risk young men. *Developmental Psychology, 34,* 1175–1188.

Caspi, A., & Elder, G. H. (1988). Emergent family patterns: The intergenerational construction of problem behaviour and relationships. In R. A. Hinde & J. Stevenson-Hinde (Eds.), *Relationships within families: Mutual influences* (pp. 218–240). Oxford: Clarendon Press.

Cherlin, A. J. (1992). *Marriage, divorce, remarriage* (2nd ed.). Cambridge, MA: Harvard University Press.

Cicchetti, D. (1993). Developmental psychopathology: Reactions, reflections, projections. *Developmental Review, 13,* 471–502.

Cicchetti, D., & Garmezy, N. (1993). Prospects and promises in the study of resilience. *Development and Psychopathology, 5,* 497–502.

Cicchetti, D., & Toth, S. (1995). A developmental psychopathology perspective on child abuse and neglect. *Journal of the American Academy of Child and Adolescent Psychiatry, 34,* 541–565.

Coddington, R. D. (1972). The significance of life events as etiological factors in the diseases of children: A study of a normal population. *Journal of Psychosomatic Research, 16,* 205–231.

Cohen, S., & Wills, T. A. (1985). Stress, social support, and the buffering hypothesis. *Psychological Bulletin, 98,* 310–357.

Compas, B. E., Banez, G. A., Malcarne, V., & Worsham, N. (1991). Perceived control and coping with stress: A developmental perspective. *Journal of Social Issues, 47,* 23–34.

Cowan, P. A., Cohn, D. A., Cowan, C. P., & Pearson, J. L. (1996). Parents' attachment histories and children's externalizing and internalizing behaviors: Exploring family systems models of linkage. *Journal of Consulting and Clinical Psychology, 64,* 53–63.

Crockenberg, S., & Covey, S. L. (1991). Marital conflict and externalizing behavior in children. In D. Cicchetti & S. L. Toth (Eds.), *Rochester symposium on developmental psychopathology: Vol. 3. Models and integration* (pp. 235–260). Rochester, NY: University of Rochester Press.

Cummings, E. M., & Davies, P. T. (1994). *Children and marital conflict: The impact of family dispute and resolution.* New York: Guilford Press.

Cummings, E. M., Davies, P. T., & Simpson, K. S. (1994). Marital conflict, gender, and children's appraisals and coping efficacy as mediators of child adjustment. *Journal of Family Psychology, 8,* 141–149.

Cummings, E. M., Hennessy, K. D., Rabideau, G. J., & Cicchetti, D. (1994). Responses of physically abused boys to interadult anger involving their mothers. *Development and Psychopathology, 6,* 31–41.

Davies, P. T., & Cummings, E. M. (1994). Marital conflict and child adjustment: An emotional security hypothesis. *Psychological Bulletin, 116,* 387–411.

Davies, P. T., & Cummings, E. M. (1998). Exploring children's emotional security as a mediator of the link between marital relations and child adjustment. *Child Development, 69,* 124–139.

Davis, B. T., Hops, H., Alpert, A., & Sheeber, L. (1998). Child responses to parental conflict and their effect on adjustment: A study of triadic relations. *Journal of Family Psychology, 12,* 163–177.

DiLalla, L. F., & Gottesman, I. I. (1991). Biological and genetic contributors to violence. Widom's untold tale. *Psychological Bulletin, 109,* 125–129.

Dodge, K. A., Bates, J. E., & Pettit, G. S. (1990). Mechanisms in the cycle of violence. *Science, 250,* 1678–1683.

Dollard, J., Doob, L. W., Miller, N. E., Mowrer, H. H., & Sears, R. R. (1939). *Frustration and aggression.* New Haven, CT: Yale University Press.

Easterbrooks, M. A., & Emde, R. N. (1988). Marital and parent-child relationships: The role of affect in the family system. In R. A. Hinde & J. Stevenson-Hinde (Eds.), *Relationships within families: Mutual influences* (pp. 83–103). Oxford: Clarendon Press.

Egeland, B., Carlson, E., & Sroufe, L. A. (1993) Resilience as process. *Development and Psychopathology, 5,* 517–528.

El-Sheikh, M., & Cummings, E. M. (1995). Children's responses to angry adult behavior as a function of experimentally manipulated exposure to resolved and unresolved conflict. *Social Development, 4,* 75–91.

Emery, R. E. (1982). Interparental conflict and the children of discord and divorce. *Psychological Bulletin, 92,* 310–330.

Emery, R. E. (1999). *Marriage, divorce, and children's adjustment* (2nd ed.). Thousand Oaks, CA: Sage.

Engfer, A. (1988). The interrelatedness of marriage and the mother-child relationship. In R. A. Hinde & J. Stevenson-Hinde (Eds.), *Relationships within families: Mutual influences* (pp. 104–118). Oxford: Clarendon Press.

Erel, O., & Burman, B. (1995). Interrelatedness of marital relations and parent-child relations: A meta-analytic review. *Psychological Bulletin, 118,* 108–132.

Fantuzzo, J., Boruch, R., Beriama, A., Atkins, M., & Marcus, S. (1997). Domestic violence and children: Prevalence and risk in five major U. S. cities. *Journal of the American Academy of Child and Adolescent Psychiatry, 36,* 116–122.

Fauber, R., Forehand, R., Thomas, A. M., & Wierson, M. (1990). A mediational model of the impact of marital conflict on adolescent adjustment in intact and divorced families: The role of disrupted parenting. *Child Development, 61,* 1112–1123.

Fincham, F. D., & Grych, J. H. (1991). Explanations for family events in distressed and nondistressed couples: Is one type of explanation used consistently? *Journal of Family Psychology, 4,* 341–353.

Fincham, F. D., Grych, J. H., & Osborne, L. N. (1994). Does marital conflict cause child maladjustment? Directions and challenges for longitudinal research. *Journal of Family Psychology, 8,* 128–140.

Finkelhor, D., & Dziuba-Leatherman, J. (1994). Victimization of children. *American Psychologist, 49,* 173–183.

Finkelhor, D., & Kendall-Tackett, K. (1997). A developmental perspective on the childhood impact of crime, abuse, and violent victimization. In D. Cicchetti

& S. L. Toth (Eds.), *Rochester symposium on developmental psychopathology: Vol. 8. Developmental perspectives on trauma: Theory, research, and intervention* (pp. 1–32). Rochester, NY: University of Rochester.

Floyd, F. J., Gilliom, L. A., & Costigan, C. L. (1998). Marriage and the parenting alliance: Longitudinal prediction of change in parenting perceptions and behaviors. *Child Development, 69,* 1461–1479.

Forehand, R., Wierson, M., Thomas, A. M., Armistead, L., Kempton, T., & Neighbors, B. (1991). The role of family stressors and parent relationships on adolescent functioning. *Journal of the American Academy of Child and Adolescent Psychiatry, 30,* 316–322.

Freitas, A. L., & Downey, G. (1998). Resilience: A dynamic perspective. *International Journal of Behavioral Development, 22,* 263–285.

Garcia O'Hearn, H., Margolin, G., & John, R. S. (1997). Mothers' and fathers' reports of children's reactions to naturalistic marital conflict. *Journal of the American Academy of Child and Adolescent Psychiatry, 36,* 1366–1373.

Garmezy, N., Masten, A. S., & Tellegen, A. (1984). The study of stress and competence in children: A building block of developmental psychopathology. *Child Development, 55,* 97–111.

Gest, S. D., Neemann, J., Hubbard, J. J., Masten, A. S., & Tellegen, A. (1993). Parenting quality, adversity, and conduct problem in adolescence: Testing process-oriented models of resilience. *Development and Psychopathology, 4,* 663–682.

Goode, W. J. (1960). A theory of role strain. *American Sociological Review, 25,* 488–496.

Gordis, E. B., Margolin, G., & John, R. S. (1997). Marital aggression, observed parental hostility, and child behavior during triadic family interaction. *Journal of Family Psychology, 11,* 76–89.

Gottman, J. M., & Katz, L. F. (1989). Effects of marital discord on young children's peer interaction and health. *Developmental Psychology, 25,* 373–381.

Grych, J. H. (1998). Children's appraisals of interparental conflict: Situational and contextual influences. *Journal of Family Psychology, 12,* 437–453.

Grych, J. H., & Fincham, F. D. (1990). Marital conflict and children's adjustment: A cognitive-contextual framework. *Psychological Bulletin, 108,* 267–290.

Grych, J. H., & Fincham, F. D. (1993). Children's appraisals of marital conflict: Initial investigations of the cognitive-contextual framework. *Child Development, 64,* 215–230.

Grych, J. H., & Fincham, F. D. (1997). Children's adaptation to divorce: From description to explanation. In S. A. Wolchik & I. N. Sandler (Eds.), *Handbook of children's coping: Linking theory and intervention* (pp. 159–193). New York: Plenum.

Harold, G. T., & Conger, R. D. (1997). Marital conflict and adolescent distress: The role of adolescent awareness. *Child Development, 68,* 333–350.

Harold, G. T., Fincham, F. D., Osborne, L. N., & Conger, R. D. (1997). Mom and Dad are at it again: Adolescent perceptions of marital conflict and adolescent psychological distress. *Developmental Psychology, 33,* 333–350.

Hart, S. N., & Brassard, M. R. (1987). A major threat to children's mental health: Psychological maltreatment. *American Psychologist, 42,* 160–165.

Hetherington, E. M. (1989). Coping with family transition: Winners, losers, and survivors. *Child Development, 60,* 1–14.

Hetherington, E. M., Bridges, M., & Insabella, G. M. (1998). What matters? What does not? Five perspectives on the association between marital transitions and children's adjustment. *American Psychologist, 53,* 167–184.

Hinde, R. A., & Stevenson-Hinde, J. (1988). Epilogue. In R. A. Hinde & J. Stevenson-Hinde (Eds.), *Relationships within families: Mutual influences* (pp. 365–385). Oxford: Clarendon Press.

Holden, G. W., & Ritchie, K. L. (1991). Linking extreme marital discord, child rearing, and child behavior problems: Evidence from battered women. *Child Development, 62,* 311–327.

Holmbeck, G. N. (1997). Toward terminological, conceptual, and statistical clarity in the study of mediators and moderators: Example from the child-clinical and pediatric psychology literatures. *Journal of Consulting and Clinical Psychology, 65,* 599–610.

Hughes, H. M. (1997). Research concerning children of battered women: Clinical implications. In R. Geffner, S. B. Sorenson, & P. K. Lundberg-Love (Eds.), *Violence and sexual abuse at home: Current issues in spousal battering and child maltreatment* (pp. 225–244). New York: Haworth.

Jenkins, J. M., & Smith, M. A. (1990). Factors protecting children living in disharmonious homes: Maternal reports. *Journal of the American Academy of Child and Adolescent Psychiatry, 29,* 60–69.

Jenkins, J. M., Smith, M. A., & Graham, P. J. (1989). Coping with parental quarrels. *Journal of the American Academy of Child and Adolescent Psychiatry, 28,* 182–189.

Jouriles, E. N., Farris, A. M., & McDonald, R. (1991). Marital functioning and child behavior: Measuring specific aspects of the marital relationship. *Advances in family intervention, assessment and theory* (pp. 25–46). London: Kingsley.

Jouriles, E. N., & LeCompte, S. H. (1991). Husbands' aggression toward wives and mothers' and fathers' aggression toward children: Moderating effects of child gender. *Journal of Consulting and Clinical Psychology, 59,* 190–192.

Katz, L. F., & Gottman, J. M. (1995). Vagal tone protects children from marital conflict. *Development and Psychopathology, 7,* 83–92.

Katz, L. F., & Gottman, J. M. (1996). Spillover effects of marital conflict: In search of parenting and coparenting mechanisms. *New Directions for Child Development, 74,* 57–76.

Katz, L. F., & Gottman, J. M. (1997). Buffering children from marital conflict and dissolution. *Journal of Clinical Child Psychology, 26,* 157–171.

Kerig, P. K. (1998). Moderators and mediators of the effects of interparental conflict on children's adjustment. *Journal of Abnormal Child Psychology, 26,* 199–212.

Laumakis, M. A., Margolin, G., & John, R. S. (1998). The emotional, cognitive, and coping responses of preadolescent children to different dimensions of marital conflict. In G. W. Holden, R. Geffner, & E. N. Jouriles (Eds.), *Children exposed to marital violence: Theory, research, and applied issues* (pp. 257–288). Washington, DC: American Psychological Association.

Lewis, C. E., Siegel, J. M., & Lewis, M. A. (1984). Feeling bad: Exploring sources of distress among pre-adolescent children. *American Journal of Public Health, 74,* 117–122.

Lindahl, K. M., & Malik, N. M. (1999). Marital conflict, family processes, and boys' externalizing behavior in Hispanic American and European American families. *Journal of Clinical Child Psychology, 28,* 12–24.

MacKinnon-Lewis, C., & Lofquist, A. (1996). Antecedents and consequences of boys' depression and aggression: Family and school linkages. *Journal of Family Psychology, 10,* 490–500.

Mann, B. J., & MacKenzie, E. P. (1996). Pathways among marital functioning, parental behaviors, and child behavior problems in school-age boys. *Journal of Clinical Child Psychology, 25,* 183–191.

Margolin, G. (1981). The reciprocal relationship between marital and child problems. In J. P. Vincent (Ed.), *Advances in family intervention, assessment and theory (Vol. 2)* (pp. 131–182). Greenwich, CT: JAI Press.

Margolin, G. (1998). Effects of domestic violence on children. In P. K. Trickett & C. J. Schellenbach (Eds.) *Violence against children in the family and the community* (pp. 57–102). Washington, DC: American Psychological Association.

Margolin, G., Christensen, A., & John, R. S. (1996). The continuance and spillover of everyday tensions in distressed and nondistressed families. *Journal of Family Psychology, 10,* 304–321.

Margolin, G., & Gordis, E. B. (in press). Effects of family and community violence on children. *Annual Review of Psychology, 51,* 445–479.

Margolin, G., & John, R. S. (1997). Children's exposure to marital aggression: Direct and mediated effects. In G. Kaufman-Kantor & J. L. Jasinski (Eds.), *Out of darkness: Contemporary perspectives on family violence* (pp. 90–104). Thousand Oaks, CA: Sage.

Margolin, G., John, R. S., Ghosh, C. M., & Gordis, E. B. (1996). Family interaction process: An essential tool for exploring abusive relations. In D. D. Cahn & S. A. Lloyd (Eds.), *Family violence from a communication perspective* (pp. 37–58). Thousand Oaks, CA: Sage.

Masten, A. S., & Coatsworth, J. D. (1998). The development of competence in favorable and unfavorable environments: Lessons learned from research on successful children. *American Psychologist, 53,* 205–220.

Masten, A. S., Garmezy, N., Tellegen, A., Pellegrini, D. S., Larkin, K., & Larsen, A. (1988). Competence and stress in school children: The moderating effects of individual and family qualities. *Journal of Child Psychology and Psychiatry, 29,* 745–764.

McCloskey, L. A., Figueredo, A. J., & Koss, M. P. (1995). The effects of systemic family violence on children's mental health. *Child Development, 66,* 1239–1261.

McHale, J. P. (1995). Coparenting and triadic interactions during infancy: The roles of marital distress and child gender. *Developmental Psychology, 31,* 985–996.

Miller, N. B., Cowan, P. A., Cowan, C. P., Hetherington, E. M., & Clingempeel, W. G. (1993). Externalizing in perschoolers and early adolescents: A cross-study replication of a family model. *Developmental Psychology, 29,* 3–18.

Minuchin, S., Rosman, B., & Baker, L. (1978). *Psychosomatic families: Anorexia nervosa in context.* Cambridge, MA: Harvard University Press.

Moffitt, T. E. (1990). Juvenile delinquency and attention deficit disorder: Boys' developmental trajectories from age 3 to age 15. *Child Development, 61,* 893–910.

Neighbors, B. D., Forehand, R., & Bau, J. (1997). Interparental conflict and relations with parents as predictors of young adult functioning. *Development and Psychopathology, 9,* 169–187.

Nichols, M. P., & Schwartz, R. C. (1995). *Family therapy concepts and methods* (3rd ed.). Boston: Allyn & Bacon.

O'Brien, M., Bahadur, M. A., Gee, C., Balto, K., & Erber, S. (1997). Child exposure to marital conflict and child copng responses as predictors of child adjustment. *Cognitive Therapy and Research, 21,* 39–59.

O'Brien, M., Margolin, G., & John, R. S. (1995). Relation among marital conflict, child coping, and child adjustment. *Journal of Clinical Child Psychology, 24,* 346–361.

Patterson, G. R. (1982). *Coercive family process.* Eugene, OR: Castalia.

Patterson, G. R., & Dishion, T. J. (1988). Multilevel family process models: Traits, interactions and relationships. In R. A. Hinde & J. Stevenson-Hinde (Eds.), *Relationships within families: Mutual influences* (pp. 283–310). Oxford: Clarendon Press.

Patterson, G. R., Reid, J. B., & Dishion, T. J. (1992). *Antisocial boys: A social interactional approach.* Eugene, OR: Castalia.

Perry, B. (1997). Incubated in terror: Neurodevelopmental factors in the "Cycle of Violence." In J. D. Osofsky (Ed.), *Children in a violent society* (pp. 124–149). New York: Guilford.

Pynoos, R. S., & Eth, S. (1985). Children traumatized by witnessing acts of personal violence: Homicide, rape, or suicide behavior. In S. Eth & R. S. Pynoos (Eds.), *Post-traumatic stress disorder in children* (pp. 17–44). Washington, DC: American Psychological Association.

Pynoos, R. S., Steinberg, A. M., & Goenjian, A. (1996). Traumatic stress in childhood and adolescence: Recent developments and current controversies. In B. A. van der Kolk, A. C. McFarlane, & W. Weisaeth (Eds.), *Traumatic stress* (pp. 331–358). New York: Guilford.

Reid, W. J., & Crisafulli, A. (1990). Marital discord and child behavior problems: A meta-analysis. *Journal of Abnormal Child Psychology, 18,* 105–117.

Repetti, R. L. (1987). Links between work and family role. In S. Oskamp (Ed.), *Family processes and problems: Social psychological aspects* (pp. 98–127). Newbury Park, CA: Sage.

Repetti, R. L., McGrath, E. P., & Ishikawa, S. S. (1999). Daily stress and coping in childhood and adolescence. In A. J. Goreczny & M. Hersen (Eds.), *Handbook of pediatric and adolescent health psychology* (pp. 343–360). Allyn & Bacon.

Richters, J. E., & Martinez, P. (1993). The NIMH Community Violence Project: 1. Children as victims of and witnesses to violence. In D. Reiss, J. E. Richters, M. Radke-Yarrow, & D. Scharff (Eds.), *Children and violence* (pp. 7–21). Guilford: New York.

Rogers, M. J., & Holmbeck, G. N. (1997). Effects of interparental aggression on children's adjustment: The moderating role of cognitive appraisal and coping. *Journal of Family Psychology, 11*, 125–130.

Rossman, B. B. R., Hughes, H. M., & Hanson, K. L. (1998). The victimization of school-age children. In B. B. R. Rossman & M. S. Rosenberg (Eds.), *Multiple victimization of children: Conceptual, developmental, research and treatment issues* (pp. 87–106). Binghamton, NY: Haworth.

Rossman, B. B. R., & Rosenberg, M. S. (1992). Family stress and functioning children: The moderating effects of children's beliefs about their control over parental conflict. *Journal of Child Psychology and Psychiatry, 33*, 699–715.

Rutter, M. (1988). Functions and consequences of relationships: Some psychopathological considerations. In R. A. Hinde & J. Stevenson-Hinde (Eds.), *Relationships within families: Mutual influences* (pp. 332–353). Oxford: Clarendon Press.

Rutter, M. (1990). Psychosocial resilience and protective mechanisms. In J. Rolf, A. S. Masten, D. Cicchetti, K. H. Neuchterlein, & S. Weintraub (Eds.), *Risk and protective factors in the development of psychopathology* (pp. 181–214). Cambridge: Cambridge University Press.

Rutter, M. (1994). Family discord and conduct disorder: Cause, consequence, or correlate? *Journal of Family Psychology, 8*, 170–186.

Sameroff, A., Seifer, R., Barocas, R., Zax, M., & Greenspan, S. (1987). Intelligence quotient scores of 4-year old children: Social-environmental risk factors. *Pediatrics, 79*, 343–350.

Sandler, I. N., Tein, J-Y. & West, S. G. (1994). Coping, stress, and the psychological symptoms of children of divorce: A cross-sectional and longitudinal study. *Child Development, 65*, 1744–1763.

Seifer, R., Sameroff, A. J., Baldwin, C. P., & Baldwin, A. (1992). Child and family factors that ameliorate risk between 4 and 13 years of age. *Journal of the American Academy of Child and Adolescent Psychiatry, 31*, 893–903.

Shaw, D. S., Emery, R. E., & Tuer, M. D. (1993). Parental functioning and children's adjustment in families of divorce: A prospective study. *Journal of Abnormal Child Psychology, 21*, 119–134.

Silvern, L., & Kaersvang, L. (1989). The traumatized children of violent marriages. *Child Welfare, 68*, 421–436.

Singer, M. I., Anglin, T. M., Song, L., & Lunghofer, L. (1995). Adolescents' exposure to violence associated symptoms of psychological trauma. *Journal of the American Medical Association, 273*, 477–482.

Straus, M. A. (1992). Children as witnesses to marital violence: A risk factor of lifelong problems among a nationally representative sample of American men and women. In D. F. Schwarz (Ed.), *Children and violence: Report of the twenty-third Ross roundtable on critical approaches to common pediatric problems* (pp. 98–109). Columbus, OH: Ross Laboratories.

Terr, L. C. (1991). Childhood traumas: An outline and overview. *American Journal of Psychiatry, 148*, 10–20.

Tiet, Q. Q., Bird, H. R., Davies, M., Hoven, C., Cohen, P., Jensen, P. S., & Goodman, S. (1998). Adverse life events and resilience. *Journal of the American Academy of Child and Adolescent Psychiatry, 37*, 1191–1200.

Tomkins, A. J., Mohamed, S., Steinman, M., Macolini, R. M., Kenning, M. K., & Afrank, J. (1994). The plight of children who witness woman battering: Psychological knowledge and policy implications. *Law and Psychology Review, 18,* 136–187.

Vogel, E. F., & Bell, N. W. (1960). The emotionally disturbed child as a family scapegoat. In N. W. Bell & E. F. Vogel (Eds.), *The family* (pp. 382–397). New York: The Free Press.

Werner, E., E. (1990). Protective factors and individual resilience. In S. J. Meisels & J. P. Shonkoff (Eds.), *Handbook of early childhood intervention* (pp. 97–116). Cambridge: Cambridge University Press.

Werner, D. E. (1993). Risk, resilience and recovery. Perspectives from the Kauai longitudinal study. *Development and Psychopathology, 5,* 503–516.

Wright, M. O., Masten, A. S., Northword, A., & Hubbard, J. J. (1997). Long-term effects of massive trauma: Developmental and psychobiological perspectives. In D. Cicchetti & S. L. Toth (Eds.), *Rochester symposium on developmental psychopathology: Vol. 8. Developmental perspectives on trauma: Theory, research, and intervention* (pp. 181–226). Rochester, NY: University of Rochester.

Zimmerman, M. A., & Arunkumar, R. (1994). Resiliency research: Implications for schools and policy. *Social Policy Report: Society for Research in Child Development, 8,* 1–18.

2 The Study of Relations between Marital Conflict and Child Adjustment

Challenges and New Directions for Methodology

E. Mark Cummings, Marcie C. Goeke-Morey, and Tammy L. Dukewich

While relations between marital conflict and children's adjustment are well established as a general proposition, many questions remain about the processes accounting for these relations. Various chapters in this volume are concerned with numerous substantive issues. Nonetheless, methodology is ultimately at the heart of the potential for new understanding of the psychological and systematic factors that account for children's outcomes, and the challenges are daunting. Marital conflict is a relatively rare event, especially as it occurs in front of children, may be reactive to the presence of observers in either the home or laboratory, and is not amenable for practical and ethical reasons to true experimental manipulation, particularly in the presence of children. The adequacy of current methodologies (i.e., research designs; measurement; statistical models) and the extent to which improvements and innovations can be made in the future as the envelope of knowledge expands are fundamental to the possibility of new advances.

This chapter begins with an examination of the significance of *research design* to the study of relations between marital conflict and child adjustment. Numerous child, marital, and familial factors are linked with the effects of marital conflict on child development. While all factors obviously cannot be addressed in every study, it is important to be cognizant of the breadth of possible causal influences and pathways. The cutting-edge of the field has moved beyond simple demonstrations of the correlations between marital conflict and child adjustment to a second generation of research that is concerned with

Preparation of this paper was supported in part by a grant from the National Institute of Child Health and Human Development (HD 36261) to the first author.

testing complex models of the processes accounting for these relations (Fincham, 1994). Relatedly, adequate *statistical models* are required to make sense of complex theoretical models and relations between marital conflict, family contexts, and children's functioning over time. Thus, there is an increasing need for investigators to integrate statistical and substantive issues in decisions about how and why particular methods are used. Accordingly, the discussion of research design will also include a consideration of statistical methods that are appropriate for testing complex conceptual models.

Finally, we examine the matter of the *measurement* of marital conflict and the assessment of children's responses to marital conflict, consider the pros and cons of various approaches, and present new directions being explored in our laboratory that are responsive to the challenges posed by current limitations. This issue is fundamental, because without adequate measurement, further development of conceptual and statistical models will be of limited interest. That is, the increasing emphasis being placed upon the measurement of multiple variables in complex theoretically driven research designs, and upon the use of advanced statistical procedures, should not cause researchers to lose sight of the fact that the quality of empirical research ultimately depends upon the rigor and appropriateness of the measurement of child, family, and marital variables. On the other hand, the issue is not an either/or matter, since the simultaneous use of multiple measurement approaches is likely to be superior to the reliance on any single approach to measurement for both substantive (i.e., every method has limitations) and statistical (e.g., the appropriate derivation of latent variables) reasons.

Research Design

Sufficiently Inclusive Research Designs

The complexity of relations between marital conflict and children's outcomes necessitates sufficiently inclusive research designs so that major familial influences and their pathways of influence on children's functioning are taken into account, including possible mediators and moderators of child outcomes. Figure 2.1 outlines some of the matters to consider. Notably, this figure illustrates no more than the most fundamental considerations for research design; model tests based on actual data are likely to yield far more complex patterns of relations than those portrayed in this figure (e.g., Harold, Fincham, Osborne, & Conger, 1997).

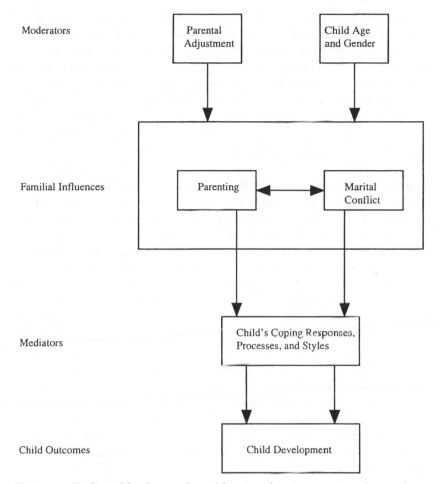

Figure 2.1. Outline of fundamental considerations for process-oriented research on marital conflict and child adjustment.

Mediators and Children's Coping Responses, Processes, and Styles

Mediators are the *generative mechanism* by which an independent variable influences outcomes. In this instance, identifying mediators means explaining precisely how and why marital conflict leads to lack of social competencies or adjustment problems in children. For example, Davies and Cummings (1994) have proposed that children's appraisals and experiences of emotional security organize and guide their responses to marital conflict and influence psychological processes related to the development of adjustment problems or social competencies over time.

An especially precise and informative level of analysis of mediating processes is obtained when investigators document reactions in terms of everyday stress and coping processes (Cummings, Zahn-Waxler, & Radke-Yarrow, 1981), tracking cumulative change over time at this level of analysis. That is, from a process-oriented perspective, it is especially interesting to show how short-term fluctuations and changes in marital relations and children's reactions translate over time into relatively stable patterns of adjustment or maladjustment in children (Cummings & Cummings, 1988). The effects of family experiences on children reflect, at the most microscopic level of analysis, the occurrence of small, frequently subtle changes in interpersonal and social behaviors emerging over time in response to the occurrence of daily stressors or positive experiences (e.g., social support, happy moments) (Cummings, 1998; Repetti, McGrath, & Ishikawa, 1995; Repetti & Wood, 1997). Thus, changes in children's responding in the short-term mediate long-term outcomes in children associated with marital conflict (see Figure 2.1) (Davis, Hops, Alpert, & Sheeber, 1998). Parental diaries of marital conflict and child reactions in the home are especially informative about children's coping processes at this level of analysis (Garcia-O'Hearn, Margolin, & John, 1997), which accounts, in part, for our particular interest in this methodology. By contrast, global self-reported assessments may (a) provide only an approximate characterization of the nature of mediating processes and (b) incorrectly imply that children's response processes are static and fixed in time, rather than dynamic and ever responsive to changes in family experience. Even pattern assessment (e.g., emotional security; see Davies & Cummings, 1994) is most robust when based upon multimethod and multiresponse assessments.

Moderators

Moderators specify the strength and/or direction of relations between an independent variable and an outcome. If moderators are identified, it means that the nature and degree of risk is not uniform across different conditions and people. Among the moderating factors that have been identified are children's age and gender (Cummings & Davies, 1994a), parental gender (Osborne & Fincham, 1996), SES (Ingoldsby, Shaw, Owens, & Winslow, 2000), and parental adjustment (Cummings & Davies, 1994b). That is, each of these factors has been shown to change the strength and/or direction of the relationship between marital conflict and child adjustment. As this literature continues to grow, it can be expected that evidence for additional moderating influences will emerge.

Marital Conflict and Parenting

Marital conflict also negatively affects parenting and parent–child attachments (Davies & Cummings, 1994; Erel & Burman, 1995), and, as indicated in Figure 2.1, assessment of effects on parenting should be included as a fundamental element of process-oriented research design. On the other hand, it is clearly the case that measuring the effects on parenting is not enough, as changes in parenting associated with marital conflict do not fully account for effects and sometimes emerge as weak predictors of child outcomes (Harold et al., 1997; Neighbors, Forehand, & Bau, 1997; Vandewater & Landsford, 1998; see discussion in Emery, Fincham, & Cummings, 1992).

New Directions in Process-Oriented Research Designs

The inclusion of mediators and moderators in research designs is only a necessary, but not sufficient, condition for adequate process-oriented investigations because of the multiplicity of factors that may possibly be influential in terms of children's development. Given that all possible variables cannot be measured in any one study, the burden upon investigators is to make informed choices guided by past research. Several frameworks have been advanced that provide additional guidelines for inclusive research designs (Cummings & Cummings, 1988; Cummings & Davies, 1996; Grych & Fincham, 1990). Informed choices may also be based upon theoretical models (Davies & Cummings, 1994), which may offer an even richer basis for research design.

However, few research designs have been tested that contain all of the elements in Figure 2.1. While some tests of mediational models have been reported recently (e.g., Davies & Cummings, 1998; Harold et al., 1997), these studies provide no more than initial steps toward articulating this direction in research. Limitations of research to date include: (a) only adequate tests of effects due to exposure to marital conflict, or effects due to parenting, but not both (e.g., an inadequate test is obtained when there is very weak assessment of one pathway and rigorous assessment of the other), (b) limited or no assessment of the response processes (i.e., children's coping processes) that might mediate either or both of these pathways, (c) limited or no assessment of possible moderating factors, or (d) tests of models in the context of cross-sectional, but not longitudinal, data sets, which limits the inferences that can be made about either causality or developmental change.

In summary, there are a variety of matters to consider for future directions in research design. A fundamental point is that research designs should be more inclusive of process-oriented variables rather than simply assessing marital conflict and child adjustment.

Statistical Models: General Considerations

Another element of moving forward with complex, multivariate tests of developmental models of relations between marital conflict and child adjustment is to consider directions toward analyzing such models. As we have argued, at this point the challenge is to do more than simply show correlations between predictor and outcome variables. For example, we know with some certainty that marital hostility is linked probabilistically with an increase in children's adjustment problems. The question now is why (i.e., what are the mediating processes?). More specifically, it is time to examine what coping responses, processes, and styles mediate relations between marital conflict and child outcomes. In addition, it is important to ask what groups are particularly affected (i.e., moderators) by exposure to marital conflict. Given that the research design is appropriate (i.e., a sufficiently broad number of variables are assessed) and measures are adequate in the assessments of variables, the next step is to use appropriate statistical procedures to test these process models.

Tests for whether particular processes mediate relations between predictors (e.g., parental depression) and outcomes (e.g., childhood disorders) have to meet several criteria, that is, demonstrations of significant relations between (a) the predictor and outcome, (b) the predictor and the process, and (c) the process and the outcome. Finally, the relation between the predictor and outcome is reduced or becomes nonsignificant when the process is factored into the analysis (Baron & Kenny, 1986). Testing simple process models at this level of analysis can be successfully accomplished with statistical methods that are well known and long-standing (e.g., regression analyses). However, given that researchers are increasingly interested in simultaneously taking into account multiple predictors, multiple mediators, and multiple outcomes in this area of research (see Figure 2.1), more advanced statistical approaches increasingly need to be considered.

Structural Equation Modeling

Structural equation modeling (SEM), that is, causal modeling, provides the researcher with a statistical methodology for testing more advanced theoretical models (Biddle & Marlin, 1987). This methodology uses the correlations among all of the measures assessed in a study to estimate the specific pathways predicted by the hypotheses of a theory. A "good fit" between a model and a theory means that the pathways predicted by the theory do not differ from the pathways derived from the observed correlations. It is also possible by this method to compare the proposed model with alternative models that add or remove relationships among the constructs. When used appropriately, this approach can provide a better estimate of true scores by statistically removing measurement error, and it can also determine how well different purported measures of a psychological variable relate to an underlying construct. SEM can be adapted to address the issues raised by mediational models (e.g., generative mechanisms), longitudinal models (i.e., developmental models), and moderational models (i.e., group differences) and can include all of these matters at the same time in a comprehensive test of theory. However, SEM does not provide a shortcut for measurement issues. One must be very careful in evaluating the measurement quality and characteristics of research before accepting conclusions based on SEM or any other analytic technique. Tests of models can only be as good as the measures, and multiple high-quality measures of each construct are needed for their optimal representation. Moreover, relatively large sample sizes are required to meet the statistical requirements of this technique. Thus, a tension inevitably results for those aiming to apply this procedure to test advanced models of theories about development for at-risk and normal groups of children. Rigorous and extensive measurement of the variables pertinent to advanced theory is expensive and time consuming, which tends to limit the sample sizes that can be included in research. For more guidance on the use of SEM, the reader is referred to several recent publications (Bollen & Long, 1993; Hoyle, 1995; Marcoulides & Schumacker, 1996).

Longitudinal Research: A Gap in the Study of Marital Conflict and Child Adjustment

Perhaps the most significant gap in research design is the relative absence of longitudinal research. Marital conflict has been shown, prospectively, to predict children's adjustment problems (e.g., Block, Block, & Morrison, 1981; Harold et al., 1997), but has often been based on limited model testing and assessments (e.g., Howes & Markman, 1989). No published longitudinal studies have employed an extensive battery of assessments, based upon multimethod and multidimensional assessments of response processes, and brought them to bear systematically on the study of the processes accounting for relations between marital conflict and children's development (see Figure 2.1). There are no prospective longitudinal tests of theoretically guided models (e.g., the emotional security hypothesis, Davies & Cummings, 1994). Also important is the need to investigate how stability and change forecast children's behavior problems, an issue that has also not yet been systematically studied. Children whose parents reduce marital conflict (or learn to manage conflicts better) should show diminished difficulties. When conflict begins or is exacerbated, there should be an escalation in children's emotional difficulties. However, these longitudinal issues have not been addressed.

We have alluded to the virtues of prospective longitudinal research for testing models of causal processes, and for charting pathways of development. Fincham, Grych, and Osborne (1994) outlined suggestions for more informative longitudinal research, including: (a) testing competing theoretical models rather than merely a theoretical vs. a null model and (b) testing whether change in conflict predicts change in adjustment, rather than adjustment in an absolute sense. However, there are also pitfalls and potential problems with this methodology, including (a) loss of the weakest marriages over time, thereby attenuating effects, (b) awareness that evidence for causality in longitudinal designs is not the same as in randomized experiments, so that causal conclusions should be stated more tentatively than is often the case, and (c) awareness that correlated variables may account for effects that are attributed to the identified independent variables (Christensen, 1998; Glenn, 1998). Moreover, analysis of longitudinal data can yield misleading results, particularly when a two-wave design is employed and the marital variable is highly stable and is highly correlated with the other variable(s) of interest (Bradbury, Cohan, & Karney, 1998). Accordingly, some modes of analysis of longitudinal data (e.g., the difference score method, the partial correlation method, and the semipartial correlation method) may sometimes yield inaccurate estimates of the association between variables, even results that are the inverse of predictions (Bradbury & Karney, 1995). Improvement in prediction results from multiwave assessments (i.e., more than two assessments) in longitudinal research designs. Another avenue toward improving statistical analysis is to assess change by means of growth-curve analysis, which we discuss next.

Growth-Curve Modeling

Growth-curve modeling (hierarchical linear modeling, or HLM) can address issues concerning change over time in longitudinal research that cannot be readily addressed by other means (Bryk & Raudenbush, 1987; Raudenbush & Chan, 1992; 1993). Given the increasing concern with pathways of development in this area, this procedure merits consideration. The advantages of growth-curve analysis include the following: (a) All waves of data are used simultaneously to create the dependent variable, (b) it provides a more precise assessment of longitudinal trajectories, and (c) more specific hypotheses about continuity and change can be tested (Bradbury et al., 1998). In particular, this approach can be used to examine interindividual differences in intraindividual change. For example, suppose one assessed relations between marital conflict and children's adjustment over a 5-year period, with assessments being conducted each year. By applying HLM to longitudinal data, one would be able to investigate interindividual differences in the developmental trajectories of children exposed to marital conflict over the 5-year period. Using this technique, one could also investigate the effects of changes in marital conflict on changes in the degree of a child's behavior problems. By contrast, multivariate approaches to repeated measures are limited to examining average intraindividual change across participants in a study (Maxwell & Delaney, 1990).

However, as with SEM, there are demanding requirements for the appropriate use of this procedure that go beyond simply statistical requirements for large sample sizes. That is, rigorous measurement of psychological variables, ideally based on multimethods as well as multiple forms of assessments, is also required for optimal testing of causal and longitudinal models. Moreover, the need to collect data for participants across multiple occasions adds to the load on the investigator's resources. On the other hand, data does not have to be gathered at all time points for all families, and intervals do not need to be the same for all families (Kenny, 1998). However, the missing data problem remains if sample attrition is nonrandom, which is likely to be the case in a longitudinal study of marriages and families (Glenn, 1998). For more guidance on the use of growth-curve modeling, the reader is referred to several recent publications (Bijleveld & van der Kamp, 1998; Bryk & Raudenbush, 1992; Kreft & De Leeuw, 1998).

Measurement

Heuristically, it must be recognized that the search in terms of measurement should not be for a procedural "silver bullet," because such a paradigm is not likely to be found. There are too many possible challenges to interpretation to be overcome by any single approach to measurement. Even with further improvements and advances, an optimal course with regard to measurement is to take advantage of the respective strengths of the various approaches, and minimize their weaknesses, by employing multiple approaches (e.g., questionnaire *and* laboratory observation) (Glenn, 1998). Like blind men feeling different parts of an elephant, each may hold an aspect of the truth, but none provides the whole picture. On the other hand, given the plethora of possibilities, informed decisions must be made with regard to measurement approaches, and particular strategies or instruments within a given measurement approach (e.g., choice of questionnaires). The following section on questionnaires explicates some of the considerations that may guide the selection of particular measurement strategies.

Questionnaires

Given supportive psychometrics, a strength of this methodology is that one can obtain the "big picture" on family functioning and child adjustment by a mode of data collection that is relatively cheap and easy to use. Moreover, the outcomes can readily be compared across studies and across the results obtained from multiple laboratories. For these reasons alone, a battery of statistically sound and conceptually relevant questionnaires should be one element of all family research on the present topic.

There are other advantages. Using questionnaires, one may assess dimensions of responding that are not readily assessed by other methods. For example, marital satisfaction cannot be directly observed. In addition, in some instances self-report is the most appropriate level of analysis of a given construct. For example, measures of an individual's attributions or perceptions of others, which may be pertinent to psychopathology in instances of distorted or biased attributions, is best assessed by carefully constructed self-reported instruments for indexing attributions. With regard to children's reports on questionnaires, their appraisals may be more significant to their own functioning and adjustment than the parents' reports. For example, children's reports of depressive symptomatology may be more sensitive to depression in children than parental reports about the children, as parents may not notice or attend to children's symptomatology. Alternatively, the children may hide or not express such feelings to the parents. Moreover, children's reports of marital conflict are more closely linked to the impact of marital conflict on the children than are the parents' reports of their own conflicts (Cummings, Davies, & Simpson, 1994).

However, there are a number of weaknesses inherent to this methodology that should be recognized, including: (a) the potential for memory or response-bias errors, (b) limitations on the specificity of dimensions of family or child responses that can be obtained, (c) limitations on the number of response dimensions that can be reliably or sensibly assessed, (d) limitations in the extent to which nonverbal behavior or other nonpublic responding can be assessed by those aside from the target individual (e.g., limitations of parental report on questionnaires about significant elements of children's functioning, such as their concealed feelings of anxiety), and (e) limitations of questionnaires for uncovering new dimensions of responding that are not already thought by investigators to be important at the time of scale construction. Another problem that is more subtle is that questionnaires are not particularly engaging and may even be tedious for some individuals to complete. Thus, children may not be particularly motivated to give their best answers, may simply fail to connect with the material, or may not truly understand what the questions are asking. Questionnaires also may require considerable aptitude for language, which limits their utility with some samples. For example, younger children may not be able to complete questionnaires about family topics reliably, particularly when the items place considerable load on representational, language, or inferential abilities. For many instruments it is not yet clear whether children younger than middle school age (i.e., 9–10 years of age) can provide psychometrically adequate responses.

While a plethora of instruments have been developed, certain measures have emerged as the standards for assessing marital functioning and children's perceptions of marital conflict. Fincham (1998) provides a detailed and incisive analysis of the pros and cons and the reader is referred to that source for more on making decisions among the various options for particular research purposes.

Laboratory Methods

Analogue Methods. Analogue methods, that is, procedures in which simulations or other constructed representations of family events (e.g., live, or recorded on videotape or audiotape) are presented to family members to obtain their reactions, are one form of laboratory method that can be used to assess children's reactions to family events. Cummings, Grych, Margolin, El-Sheikh, and their colleagues, have published numerous studies illustrating the usefulness of this methodology (see Cummings & Davies, 1994a, for a review; see Cummings, 1995, for a methodological discussion). Advantages of this approach include that various dimensions of the family event (e.g., marital conflict; parental depressive symptomatology) can be precisely specified and presented in the same way across all participants, and explicit recording of responses on multiple dimensions (e.g., cognitive, verbal, emotional, physiological) is possible. These elements make it possible to test hypotheses about causal relations under controlled conditions and to differentiate effects due to variations in histories of exposure from responses due to the particular characteristics of the present family situations. Another advantage is that such stimuli can be presented in a manner that is lively and engaging for the participants, so that even very young children can be highly motivated to participate and may be highly responsive to the questions asked of them about the family events (e.g., 4–5-year-olds, Cummings, Vogel, Cummings, & El-Sheikh, 1989). Thus, the data may provide a better reflection of how participants feel or behave than presentation formats that sometimes fail to elicit much interest or that seem somewhat vague and uninteresting to some participants.

Analogue procedures can also potentially provide a relatively inexpensive way to explore new questions (Cummings, 1995). Accordingly, this approach is most useful when the stimuli and responses are specified as precisely as possible and include scenarios to explore reactions to new dimensions of family situations. The age at which the responses of children to conflict scenarios can be obtained is further reduced when live actors simulate conflicts in the presence of children (e.g., 2-year-olds, Cummings, Iannotti, & Zahn-Waxler, 1985; J. S. Cummings, Notarius, Pellegrini, & Cummings, 1989). Using this approach, detailed observational records have been obtained on responses to conflict even for children less than 1 year of age (Shred, McDonnell, Church, & Rowan, 1991). A variation is to have the mother and an actor engage in a simulated conflict, which has the advantage of providing records of children's responses to conflicts involving a family member (J. S. Cummings et al., 1989).

A concern about this methodology is generalizability; that is, responses to these analogue procedures may not be equivalent to the responses to actual parental conflict. On the other hand, there is evidence that children's reactions to analogue presentations of marital conflict are consistent with family histories of marital conflict and children's risk for adjustment problems. That is, children from high-conflict homes report greater emotional arousal and aggression in response to analogue marital conflicts, and these reactions, in turn, are related to behavior problems (Cummings & Davies, 1994a). Thus, presumably, children's reactions are reflective of significant differences in everyday response patterns (Cummings & Davies, 1994a). Moreover, generalizability questions are a challenge for all methodologies, including behavioral observation of the family at home (e.g., does the slice of behavior observed in the home represent typical behavior?).

Notably, the goal of analogue procedures, as with any laboratory procedure, is not to recreate the exact conditions of the family environment (an impossibility), but is to induce the critical response processes and investigate the process relations that underlie responding in natural settings, such as the home. Thus, reactions to analogue stimuli are informative if they are meaningfully related to response patterns in the home, whether or not these responses are precisely the reactions that occur in the home. For example, one would not expect children to be as distressed by mild conflicts between strangers in a videotaped presentation format as by actual, and intense, marital conflicts that take place in the home. However, when assessing responses across children, one might expect that the degree and type of responding in one context would be related to the degree and type of responding in the other. Another limitation of analogue methods is that some family situations and issues may not be amenable to presentation in this way, and complex patterns of back and forth interaction in family contexts, which may be highly significant to understanding risk for psychopathology or other adjustment problems, cannot be recorded.

We are currently exploring the use of a new analogue procedure designed to provide greater experimental rigor than past procedures, testing children's responses to many more precisely defined marital conflict elements than in past work. In this procedure children are introduced to marital conflict scenarios by means of vividly described vignettes, which are followed by brief, tightly defined videotaped presentations (5–10 seconds) of target marital conflict behaviors initiated by either a female or male. In past analogue studies marital conflict simulations often included multiple modes of expression of conflict (e.g., multiple forms of expression of verbal anger) by both adults. This new research has several advantages: (a) one can elicit children's responses to very precisely defined marital conflict behaviors enacted only by one parent (i.e., female *or* male), so that one can isolate the effects of the mother's vs. father's conflict behaviors, (b) many more scenarios can be tested in a single session, which is an issue if one is concerned with mapping children's responses to multiple dimensions of constructive and destructive marital conflict behaviors, and (c) the presentation is less repetitious, and therefore more engaging, because videotaped story stems do not have to be repeatedly presented. Based on an initial test with 50 children, we have found that even very young children (e.g., 4–5-year-olds) are responsive to this methodology, and that children's reactions to 20 or more scenarios can be obtained in a single session, even among preschoolers. Moreover, children's emotional reactions to these scenarios provided empirical bases for making statistically significant and fine-grained distinctions between constructive and destructive marital conflict behaviors from their perspective (Goeke-Morey, 1999).

Observational Methods. A strength of employing observational methodologies in the laboratory is that considerable rigor in coding responses is possible. Coding of marital conflict may include detailed, microanalytic coding of live or videotaped marital interactions. Another advantage is that actual behaviors are observed, with an assumption that behavioral patterns that occur in the home are to some extent reenacted. Even if responses in the home are not recreated exactly, it is likely that there is a similarity to the process that does occur in the home. However, since interactions are allowed to vary after a context is defined for participants (e.g., a toy play task), one loses some control over the comparability of responses across participants once the task begins. That is, family members are responding to each other's behaviors and not a controlled laboratory context or situation in a traditional experimental sense, after they are allowed to interact freely. On the other hand, the interaction sequences that occur may be inherently interesting in their own right as indices of marital relations around conflict issues. There are again concerns about whether responses generalize to everyday situations in the home, and the samples of behavior obtained are brief (5–15 min), thus, only a small slice of behavior is obtained on which to base judgments of family functioning (Christensen, 1998). Nonetheless, it might be presumed that everyday interactions would be more readily elicited in response to other family members' behaviors than in response to analogue situations, which often involve actors that are strangers to the family. For an excellent analysis of the pros and cons of various procedures and coding systems for assessing marital functioning (without the child being present) the reader is referred to Fincham (1998). Finally, concerns might be raised about ethical matters pertaining to couples' participation in laboratory marital conflict resolution tasks. However, in fact, benefits are reported by the great majority of couples from research participation (Bradbury, 1994).

Our assessment is that these procedures can be made to be even more informative. That is, observational studies of responding in the laboratory are limited in assessing multidimensional responding, if only the coding of observational categories is undertaken. On the other hand, interviewing participants after social interactions may potentially obtain data on immediate cognitions, perceptions, and emotions. We are exploring procedures for obtaining parental reports following videotaping of their marital interactions, using an interview format drawn from our daily record procedures (see the section, "Parental Daily Records"), so that records of parental cognitions and emotions are obtained. Thus, we are supplementing observers' behavioral coding of marital interactions with parental reports of their own emotional, behavioral, and cognitive responding in terms of a coding system on which parents have received considerable training (see "Parental Daily Records" section).

Variation of these procedures that include the child (triadic tasks) are most directly relevant to children's responses to conflict. Several studies have been reported in which children are present during marital conflict resolution tasks (triadic interaction tasks, e.g., Davis et al., 1998; Easterbrooks, Cummings, & Emde, 1994). However, while some form of laboratory record of children's responses is desirable, showing children videotapes of parental behavior in marital conflict resolution tasks rather than having them directly participate, a method pioneered by Crockenberg and Forgays (1996), may have advantages. We are currently further exploring such a procedure. An advantage of this new direction is that multiple elements of children's covert responses to marital conflict can be obtained, and these responses can be repeatedly obtained in response to marital interactions by interviewing children on a time-sampled basis (e.g., every minute). Thus, based on the questioning of children following their viewing of the marital interaction tapes, the children's emotional reactions, their impulses with regard to intervention, and their representations of the status of interparental relations can be discovered. Although children's behavioral responses cannot be directly observed with this method, children's reactions in the laboratory are, in any case, inhibited in relation to behavior in the home, and emotional and cognitive responses that do not appear behaviorally may be more informative of the impact of marital conflict (Cummings & Davies, 1996; Grych & Fincham, 1990). Nonetheless, only a limited record (i.e., responses to one or a few situations of marital conflict resolution) can be obtained in this manner, and reactivity to the laboratory context remains an issue.

Moreover, for some investigators, ethical concerns may preclude creating a laboratory situation in which parents discuss conflictual issues in the presence of children. With regard to this matter, marital conflict resolution tasks are designed to produce reenactments of everyday family patterns, so that children are unlikely to be exposed to unfamiliar events. Nonetheless, an additional advantage of showing children videotapes of parental behavior in marital conflict resolution tasks is that records can be screened before they are shown to the children, and the experience is not so immediate and potentially threatening. An additional safeguard that we employ is that we obtain the parents' permission after they engage in the tasks, but before we show the videotapes to the children.

Disadvantages with laboratory conflict resolution tasks include considerable variability in the marital conflict scenarios that occur, which presents a limitation in terms of comparing reactions across children. Responding by parents may be reactive to both the presence of children and the laboratory context. On the other hand, although this procedure may not replicate the home responses, we expect that similar processes will be elicited by these procedures, and that variability in responding will parallel variability in responding to naturally occurring conflicts.

Parental Daily Records

Completion of daily records by spouses of marital events in the home has a long history in marital research (Margolin, 1987). The most commonly used methodology, the Spouse Observation Checklist (SOC; see Weiss, Hops, & Patterson, 1973), provides day-to-day records, including accounts of emotional and cognitive as well as behavioral responses, of marital interactions between spouses. The advantages of daily records include less demand on memory and the ability to assess specific events rather than global impressions. Moreover, the SOC has been shown to chart the effects of behavioral therapy and responses to successfully discriminate between distressed and nondistressed couples. Furthermore, spousal perceptions are a significant level of analysis in their own right and may be more predictive of the quality of marital relations, partly because of access to more information about the meaning of behaviors, than an outside rater's coding of marital behaviors (Fincham, 1998).

Thus, the notion of having spouses act as observers of their own and their partners' interactions is not a new one, but questions have been raised about whether such records can be sufficiently reliable to be considered objective records of marital exchanges. However, an alternative interpretation is that the structure and content of most procedures have severely reduced the possibility of obtaining high interrater reliabilities. For example, the SOC employs 408 items that are to be completed on a daily basis. It is questionable whether the low correlations across spouses, or between spouses and trained observers, that are reported (Christensen & Nies, 1980) reflect the potential utility of spouses as objective reporters. That is, spouses are virtually never provided with training on the use of codes or with specific behavioral definitions to support coding; the response categories are sometimes vague, ill-defined, and subjective; spouses are not tested on the reliability of the use of codes before they are employed; and the very length of the task to be completed on a daily basis is likely to place considerable loads on attention and interest that diminish performance. One must wonder how well student coders, or any other category of coder, would perform under such circumstances.

In fact, the scant evidence available suggests that interspousal reliability can be greatly increased by training. Elwood and Jacobson (1988) reported that nearly doubled kappa agreement coefficients were obtained when spouses obtained training, a result significantly higher than the interspousal agreements found in couples that did not receive training. While percent agreements were still relatively low (61–62% with training vs. 39–40% without training), the training consisted simply of spouses comparing their own checklists with each other and discussing disagreements over a 15-day period. There is certainly much room for improved training procedures. Elwood and Jacobson (1988) concluded that the results strongly challenge the view that married couples are too biased to permit reliable observation (p. 165). Moreover, spouses reported that the training procedures were enjoyable and insightful, even more so than for the parents who did not receive the training phase of the study.

The results of this study suggest the promise for obtaining reliable daily records with parent training, particularly with methodological refinement to improve the quality of the training and the use of a more user-friendly home report instrument. Diary or daily record procedures have only rarely been employed to obtain data on children's responses to marital conflicts (Cummings et al., 1981; Cummings, Zahn-Waxler, & Radke-Yarrow, 1984; Garcia-O'Hearn et al., 1997). Interestingly, parents did receive limited training in completing narrative reports about family interactions from research assistants, as well as a coding manual that described home report protocols, in the Cummings et al. studies. Moreover, a strong emphasis in training enabled parents to provide objective, narrative records that were as free as possible of any inferences about behavior. In this instance, 85% agreement was found between parents and trained research assistants in reporting about the parent's own anger expressions and their own children's responses in the home. Thus, the two instances in the literature of parents receiving training on the use of daily records strongly contradicts the conventional wisdom that parents cannot be trained to be reliable observers.

Moreover, revised diary methods are urgently needed to learn more about children's responses to actual marital conflict in the home. There does not appear to be any other procedure with the promise for obtaining a substantial record of marital conflict behaviors and children's responses within the bounds of ethical psychological science. Observation in the home by trained research assistants is impractical, and, moreover, may be insensitive to critical dimensions of conflict. Furthermore, spouses or children are potentially the best source of data on marital interactions (Fincham, 1998). There are bases for expecting that family members may well provide reliable data if they are sufficiently trained to understand the coding categories; the coding system is not too lengthy and is structured to be relatively easy to use and understand; and the temptation to infer, rather than report, is minimized. Furthermore, reports completed immediately following conflicts further reduce the load on memory and can yield quite detailed reports of specific conflict behaviors and events.

Nonetheless, the Cummings et al. procedures had significant limitations with regard to feasibility. In particular, the method required parents to dictate highly detailed narratives about family events into a tape recorder as soon as possible after the events occurred. One risk of narrative reports is that observers may, or may not, include all of the aspects of conflict behavior that are important. The completion of narratives is also time-consuming for the reporter, and narratives are very expensive and time-consuming to transcribe. The verbal and cognitive demands of composing narratives are also likely to self-select highly educated and affluent families, reducing the applicability of the procedure to the study of diverse family groupings and forms (e.g., diverse SES groupings).

Below we discuss a new daily record procedure that is based on parents' completion of checklists following everyday conflict situations and that is designed specifically to overcome the limitations of the Cummings et al. procedures. Informed by research over the past 20 years on dimensions of marital conflict that affect children, it was possible to structure the checklists to detect those specific dimensions of marital conflict behavior that have been identified as most likely to be significant. Results pertaining to the methodological matters are also described. The analyses reported are based on 23 marital dyads with children from three age groups: 9 with 5-year-olds, 12 with 8-year-olds, and 2 with 11-year-olds.

Parents and children participated in two laboratory visits, spaced two weeks apart. In the interval between visits each parent completed Daily Records. During the first visit parents were trained extensively with detailed, verbal instructions, supported by written text (to be taken home with the parents). Parents then watched a series of short videotaped segments including each of the behaviors to be scored. Parents' reactions served both as an initial reliability check and as a springboard for further discussion to clarify incorrectly coded behaviors. Parents also watched three longer and more complex, "interparental disagreements", obtaining practice using the Daily Record to code complex behavioral sequences, with further feedback provided by the experimenter.

During the training it was emphasized that all forms of disagreements or differences of opinion were to be recorded, resolved or not, positive or not, major or minor. Second, it was stressed that each parent was to respond independently. Parents were explicitly asked to not discuss their responses with each other and to decide for themselves whether a particular interaction should be scored as a conflict.

Copies of all instructions and definitions were included in separate booklets given to each of the parents. Booklets also included a supply of Daily Records. Notably, terminology notwithstanding, records were to be completed after each conflict, so that multiple Daily Records (one for each conflict) could be completed on a given day. Reliability was assessed using a videotape of the 12 categories of conflict behavior to be scored in the Daily Record (calm discussion, verbal aggression, nonverbal anger, physical aggression–person, physical aggression–object, threat, withdraw/avoid, pursue, support, humor, affection, and problem solving) and the eight categories of conflict endings that were to be scored (compromised, apologized, agree to disagree, agree to discuss it later, give in, withdraw/avoid, change topic, and cold shoulder).

In the 2-week interval between visits *each* parent separately completed Daily Records for 6 mutually agreed-upon days. Whenever conflicts occurred, parents filled out a complete report. The checklist included items concerned with the length and topic of disagreement, who initiated the disagreement, and whether the problem was an old or new one. Moreover, each parent also reported on the feelings (on separate continua of positive/support, anger, sadness, and fear) and behaviors for themselves and their spouses both during the disagreement and at the end. Spouses also separately reported the degree to which the conflict was resolved, how responsible they felt for the disagreement, the present and long-term significance of the disagreement, and whether children were present. If children were present, parents recorded children's concern during and at the end of conflicts (on a continuum from no concern to high concern), children's emotions during and at the end of conflicts (happiness, anger, sadness, and fear, each on a continuum from none to high), and children's specific behaviors during and at the end of the conflict.

During the second visit, parents were again tested on the reliability of their identification of conflict and conflict-ending categories. At the end of the visit, they were also asked to comment on their reactions to completing Daily Records. In the next section we consider some of the results of this initial study that are pertinent to the reliability and feasibility of this procedure.

Can Parents Be Trained to Be Reliable Reporters on Diaries? Parents' responses on the reliability tapes indicated that they could be trained to reliably code the categories of conflict behavior. In the first visit, percent agreements for the exact identification of conflict behaviors shown on videotapes were (wives, husbands, respectively): nonverbal anger (96%; 100%), threat (100%, 100%), physical aggression–object (100%; 86%), physical aggression–person (100%; 86%), humor (96%; 96%), withdraw/avoid (96%; 96%), affection (86%; 82%), problem-solving (96%; 77%), verbal anger (86%; 96%), support (82%; 59%), calm discussion (73%, 81%), and pursue (46%, 32%). Percent agreements for behaviors at the end of conflicts were: agree to disagree (100%; 96%), agree to discuss later (96%; 96%), compromised (100%, 82%), apologized (100%, 96%), gave-in (100%, 86%), changed topic (100%, 100%), withdraw/avoid (64%, 64%), and cold shoulder (73%, 77%). Notably, parents had to choose from among 12 and 8 alternatives, respectively, in their judgments, so chance had slight effect on percent agreements. All errors were between categories that were similar in content (e.g., verbal anger and pursue; withdrawal and cold shoulder).

Mothers' and fathers' reliabilities were similar in tests of reliability in the second visit; there was minimal observer drift, that is, degradation of understanding of coding criteria (91% vs. 84% for wives; 85% vs. 81% for husbands). (Note, collapsing across a couple of highly similar conflict categories, i.e., verbal anger and pursue; withdrawal and cold shoulder, resulted in reliabilities uniformly over 90%.)

What Is the Impact of Completing the Daily Record Procedure? Parents' comments at the end of the second visit were informative about various feasibility-related questions: *Any problems with diary procedure?* It was fun (8); no problems (15); easy to fill out (3); training was helpful (3); hard to remember to fill out forms (5). *Did the diary reporting procedure influence your interactions with your spouse?* Many said it had no influence of any type (19). Some thought it may have influenced how they behaved, but only at first (3). Many others reported that being more aware and attentive had some influence, typically about relatively subtle elements ("made me think"; "calmer"), but did not directly state that fewer disagreements resulted (19). Only one dyad said that they had fewer marital conflicts than normal in the reporting period (husband and wife independently agreed); one husband thought that he labeled responses as conflicts that he normally would not have ("the littlest things or problem we had to report it"), but no one said the rate of conflicts increased because of completing the diaries. *Did child ask any ques-*

tions or talk about the study at home? Child liked coming in and wanted to come back (17); child asked what the parents did (5). Other responses indicated that most parents were able to use the forms easily and were comfortable with, appreciated, or even enjoyed, the process, and felt their responding was not influenced, or only influenced in relatively subtle ways, by the act of completing diaries.

In summary, the analyses from this initial study strongly support the promise of training parents to provide records of marital conflicts and children's responses in the home.

Conclusion

Research design, measurement, and statistical model testing are each important methodological directions for future advances in the study of this topic. In this paper we highlighted some of the concerns that need to be examined. However, it can be expected that there will be a constant need for innovation and exploration of new methodological directions in the future. That is, as the envelope of knowledge expands, the burden will continually be on methodology to provide a foundation for the next steps in understanding. Most appropriately, methodology in this area is regarded as dynamic and always under revision, not as a static set of principles and procedures. Thus, while our discussion of methodology is intended to provide a state-of-the-art update on cutting-edge perspectives on this topic, we also hope that the concepts and ideas advanced serve to stimulate others to consider how to forge their own new directions in methodology toward the future advancement of understanding of relations between marital conflict and child adjustment. The importance of using advanced statistical procedures and more complex research designs to address complex theoretical models is evident. Finally, measurement considerations must not be neglected (Christensen, 1998; Fincham, 1998; Glenn, 1998; Parke & Buriel, 1998), and, in fact, these concerns merit special emphasis as they are perhaps the most fundamental for promoting substantial future advances in understanding.

REFERENCES

Baron, R. M., & Kenny, D. A. (1986). The moderator-mediator variable distinction in social psychological research: Conceptual, strategic, and statistical considerations. *Journal of Personality and Social Psychology, 51,* 1173–1182.

Biddle, B. J., & Marlin, M. M. (1987). Causality, confirmation, credulity, and structural equation modeling. *Child Development, 58,* 4–17.

Bijleveld, C. C., van der Kamp, L. J. (with Mooijaart, A., van der Kloot, W. A., van der Leeden, R. & van der Burg, E.) (Eds.). (1998). *Longitudinal data analysis: Designs, models, and methods.* Thousand Oaks, CA: Sage Publications.

Block, J. H., Block, J., & Morrison, A. (1981). Parental agreement-disagreement on child-rearing orientations and gender-related personality correlates in children. *Child Development, 52,* 965–974.

Bollen, K. A., & Long, J. S. (Eds.). (1993). *Testing structural equation models.* Thousand Oak, CA: Sage Publications.

Bradbury, T. N. (1994). Unintended effects of marital research on marital relationships. *Journal of Family Psychology, 8,* 187–201.

Bradbury, T. N., Cohan, C. L., & Karney, B. R. (1998). Optimizing longitudinal research for understanding and preventing marital dysfunction. In T. N. Bradbury (Ed.), *The developmental course of marital dysfunction* (pp. 279–311). Cambridge: Cambridge University Press.

Bradbury, T. N., & Karney, B. R. (1995). *Assessing longitudinal effects in marital research: A simulation study comparing three approaches.* Unpublished manuscript.

Bryk, A. S., & Raudenbush, S. W. (1987). Application of hierarchical linear models to assessing change. *Psychological Bulletin, 101,* 147–158.

Bryk, A. S., & Raudenbush, S. W. (Eds.). (1992). *Hierarchical linear models: Applications and data analysis methods.* Thousand Oaks, CA: Sage Publications.

Christensen, A. (1998). On intervention and relationship events: A marital therapist looks at longitudinal research on marriage. In T. N. Bradbury (Ed.), *The developmental course of marital dysfunction* (pp. 377–409). Cambridge: Cambridge University Press.

Christensen, A., & Nies, D. C. (1980). The spouse observation checklist: Empirical analysis and critique. *American Journal of Family Therapy, 8,* 69–79.

Crockenberg, S. B., & Forgays, D. (1996). The role of emotion in children's understanding and emotional reactions to marital conflict. *Merrill-Palmer Quarterly, 42,* 22–47.

Cummings, E. M. (1995). The usefulness of experiments for the study of the family. *Journal of Family Psychology, 9,* 175–185.

Cummings, E. M. (1998). Children exposed to marital conflict and violence: Conceptual and theoretical directions. In B. W. Holden, R. Geffner, & E. N. Jouriles (Eds.), *Children exposed to marital violence: Theory, research, and applied issues* (pp. 257–288). Washington, DC: American Psychological Association.

Cummings, E. M., & Cummings, J. S. (1988). A process-oriented approach to children's coping with adults' angry behavior. *Developmental Review, 3,* 296–321.

Cummings, E. M., & Davies, P. T. (1994a). *Children and marital conflict: The impact of family dispute and resolution.* New York: The Guilford Press.

Cummings, E. M., & Davies, P. T. (1994b). Maternal depression and child development. *Journal of Child Psychology and Psychiatry, 35,* 73–112.

Cummings, E. M., & Davies, P. T. (1996). Emotional security as a regulatory process in normal development and the development of psychopathology. *Development and Psychopathology, 8,* 123–139.

Cummings, E. M., Davies, P., & Simpson, K. (1994). Marital conflict, gender, and children's appraisal and coping efficacy as mediators of child adjustment. *Journal of Family Psychology, 8,* 141–149.

Cummings, E. M., Iannotti, R. J., & Zahn-Waxler, C. (1985). The influence of conflict between adults on the emotions and aggression of young children. *Developmental Psychology, 21,* 495–507.

Cummings, E. M., Vogel, D., Cummings, J. S., & El-Sheikh, M. (1989). Children's responses to different forms of expression of anger between adults. *Child Development, 60,* 1392–1404.

Cummings, E. M., Zahn-Waxler, C., & Radke-Yarrow, M. (1981). Young children's responses to expressions of anger and affection by others in the family. *Child Development, 52,* 1274–1282.

Cummings, E. M., Zahn-Waxler, C., & Radke-Yarrow, M. (1984). Developmental changes in children's reactions to anger in the home. *Journal of Child Psychology and Psychiatry, 25,* 63–75.

Cummings, J. S., Pellegrini, D., Notarius, C., & Cummings, E. M. (1989). Children's responses to angry adult behavior as a function of marital distress and history of interparent hostility. *Child Development, 60,* 1035–1043.

Davies, P. T., & Cummings, E. M. (1994). Marital conflict and child adjustment: An emotional security hypothesis. *Psychological Bulletin, 116,* 387–411.

Davies, P. T., & Cummings, E. M. (1998). Exploring children's emotional security as a mediator of the link between marital relations and child adjustment. *Child Development, 69,* 124–139.

Davis, B. T., Hops, H., Alpert, A., & Sheeber, L. (1998). Child responses to parental conflict and their effects on adjustment: A study of triadic relations. *Journal of Family Psychology, 12,* 163–177.

Easterbrooks, M. A., Cummings, E. M., & Emde, R. N. (1994). Young children's responses to constructive marital disputes. *Journal of Family Psychology, 8,* 160–169.

Elwood, R. W., & Jacobson, N. S. (1988). The effects of observational training on spouse agreement about events in their relationship. *Behavioural Research and Therapy, 26,* 159–167.

Emery, R. E., Fincham, F. D., & Cummings, E. M. (1992). Parenting in context: Systemic thinking about parental conflict and its influence on children. *Journal of Consulting and Clinical Psychology, 60,* 909–912.

Erel, O., & Burman, B. (1995). Interrelations of marital relations and parent-child relations: A meta-analytic review. *Psychological Bulletin, 188,* 108–132.

Fincham, F. D. (1994). Understanding the association between marital conflict and child adjustment: An overview. *Journal of Family Psychology, 8,* 123–127.

Fincham, F. D. (1998). Child development and marital relations. *Child Development, 69,* 543–574.

Fincham, F. D., Grych, J. H., & Osborne, L. N. (1994). Does marital conflict cause child maladjustment? Directions and challenges for longitudinal research. *Journal of Family Psychology, 8,* 128–140.

Garcia-O'Hearn, H., Margolin, G., & John, R. (1997). Mothers' and fathers' reports of children's reactions to naturalistic marital conflict. *Journal of the American Academy of Child and Adolescent Psychiatry, 36,* 1366–1373.

Glenn, N. D. (1998). Problems and prospects in longitudinal research on marriage: A sociologist's perspective. In T. N. Bradbury (Ed.), *The developmental course of marital dysfunction* (pp. 427–440). Cambridge: Cambridge University Press.

Goeke-Morey, M. C. (1999). *Children and marital conflict: Exploring the distinction between constructive and destructive marital conflict behaviors.* Unpublished doctoral dissertation, University of Notre Dame, Notre Dame, IN.

Grych, J. H., & Fincham, F. (1990). Marital conflict and children's adjustment: A cognitive-contextual framework. *Psychological Bulletin, 108,* 267–290.

Harold, G. T., Fincham, F. D., Osborne, L. N., & Conger, R. D. (1997). Mom and dad are at it again: Adolescent perceptions of marital conflict and adolescent psychological distress. *Developmental Psychology, 33,* 333–350.

Howes, P., & Markman, H. J. (1989). Marital quality and child functioning: A longitudinal investigation. *Child Development, 60,* 1044–1051.

Hoyle, R. H. (Ed.). (1995). *Structural equation modeling: Concepts, issues, and applications.* Thousand Oaks, CA: Sage Publications.

Ingoldsby, E. M., Shaw, D. S., Owens, E. B., & Winslow, E. B. (2000). A longitudinal study of interparental conflict, emotional and behavioral reactivity, and preschoolers' adjustment problems among low-income families. *Journal of Abnormal Child Psychology, 27,* 343–356.

Kenny, D. A. (1998). Couples, gender, and time: Comments on method. In T. N. Bradbury (Ed.), *The developmental course of marital dysfunction* (pp. 410–422). Cambridge: Cambridge University Press.

Kreft, K. & DeLeeuw, J. (Eds.). (1998). *Introducing multilevel modeling.* Thousand Oaks, CA: Sage Publications.

Marcoulides, G. A., & Schumacker, R. E. (Eds.). (1996). *Advanced structural equation modeling: Issues and techniques.* Mahwah, NJ: Lawrence Erlbaum Associates.

Margolin, G. (1987). Participant observation procedures in marital and family assessment. In T. Jacob (Ed.), *Family interaction and psychopathology: Theories, methods, and findings* (pp. 391–426). New York: Plenum Press.

Maxwell, S. E., & Delaney, H. D. (1990). *Designing experiments and analyzing data: A model comparison perspective.* Pacific Grove, CA: Brooks/Cole Publishing.

Neighbors, B. D., Forehand, R., & Bau, J. J. (1997). Interparental conflict and relations with parents as predictors of young adult functioning. *Development and Psychopathology, 9,* 169–187.

Osborne, L. A., & Fincham, F. D. (1996). Marital conflict, parent-child relationships, and child adjustment: Does gender matter? *Merrill-Palmer Quarterly, 42,* 48–75.

Parke, R. D., & Buriel, R. (1998). Socialization in the family: Ethnic and ecological perspectives. In W. Damon & N. Eisenberg (Eds.), *Handbook of child psychology, 5th ed, Vol. 3: Social, emotional and personality development* (pp. 463–552). New York: John Wiley & Sons, Inc.

Raudenbush, S. W., & Chan, W. S. (1992). Growth curve analysis in accelerated longitudinal designs. *Journal of Research in Crime and Delinquency, 29,* 387–411.

Raudenbush, S. W., & Chan, W. S. (1993). Application of a hierarchical linear model to the study of adolescent deviance in an overlapping cohort design. *Journal of Consulting and Clinical Psychology, 61*, 941–951.

Repetti, R., McGrath, E., & Ishikawa, S. (1995). Daily stress and coping in childhood and adolescence. In A. J. Goreczny & M. Hersen (Eds.), *Handbook of pediatric and adolescent health psychology.* New York: Allyn & Bacon.

Repetti, R., & Wood, J. (1997). Families accommodating to chronic stress: Unintended and unnoticed processes. In B. Gottlieb (Ed.), *Coping with chronic stress* (pp. 191–220), New York: Plenum.

Shred, R., McDonnell, P. M., Church, G., & Rowan, J. (1991, April). *Infants' cognitive and emotional responses to adults' angry behavior.* Paper presented at the biennial meeting of the Society for Research in Child Development, Seattle, WA.

Vandewater, E. A., & Landsford, J. E. (1998). Influences of family structure and parental conflict on children's well-being. *Family Relations, 47*, 323–330.

Weiss, R. L., Hops, H., & Patterson, G. R. (1973). A framework for conceptualizing marital conflict, a technology for altering it, some data for evaluating it. In L. A. Hamerlynch, L. C. Handy, & E. J. Mash (Eds.), *Behavior changes: Methodology, concepts, and practice.* Champaign, IL: Research Press.

3 Does Gender Moderate the Effects of Marital Conflict on Children?

Patrick T. Davies and Lisa L. Lindsay

Although exposure to high levels of marital conflict increases children's susceptibility to psychological maladjustment, the modest magnitude of the risk and the considerable heterogeneity in children's outcomes have precipitated the development of multivariate models designed to explicate conditions that moderate the risk of marital conflict. As part of this process, child and parent gender are assuming increasingly prominent roles as sources of the variability in child outcomes. The evolution of gender in models of interparental relations is underscored by the distinction between two generations of marital conflict research (Fincham, 1994). A first generation of research has focused on documenting an association between marital and child functioning. Within this generation of research, gender has either been commonly treated as a nuisance variable that is statistically controlled, pooled in primary analyses, or eliminated by design (e.g., exclusive focus on boys) (Davies & Windle, 1997; Johnson & O'Leary, 1987), or examined as a main effect (e.g., examining mean differences between boys and girls in the levels of exposure to interparental conflict). However, these main effects models fail to address a critical task of understanding how and why child gender may alter the association between marital conflict and child adjustment (Fincham, Grych, & Osborne, 1994; Kerig, Fedorowicz, Brown, Patenaude, & Warren, 1998).

A fundamental aim of the second generation of research is to specify the precise conditions that exacerbate or attenuate the risk posed by marital conflict (i.e., moderator models). This chapter builds on this approach by exploring child and parent gender as attributes that may protect or potentiate the risk posed by marital conflict to children's development. Yet, simply cataloging gender as a moderator is not enough. The second generation of research also calls for understanding *why* certain children are at risk under certain conditions. Gender, in particular, is only a marker variable for a complex set of more proximal processes. Therefore, another purpose of this chapter is to advance the search for the mechanisms that underlie the moderating role of child and parent gender.

Toward a Biopsychosocial Model of Gender and Marital Conflict

Two models have been commonly proposed to explain the moderating effects of child gender in the link between marital conflict and children's functioning. The first model, which we label the *male vulnerability* model, characterizes the relationship between marital conflict and child maladjustment as being stronger for boys than girls. That is, boys are posited to be more susceptible to the harmful effects of marital conflict than girls. The second model, which we label the *differential reactivity* model, hypothesizes that boys and girls may experience relatively comparable levels of distress that are manifested in different ways. Hence, in accordance with gender differences in the prevalence of internalizing and externalizing symptoms (Zahn-Waxler, 1993), boys exposed to elevated levels of marital conflict may express their distress through anger, aggression, behavioral dysregulation, and externalizing symptoms, whereas girls' distress in the face of conflict may take the form of fear, dysphoria, overinvolvement in parental problems, and ultimately internalizing symptoms.

The selective review of studies in Table 3.1 shows that research has supported the male vulnerability model with some regularity when the outcome measures include indices of general psychological adjustment (e.g., internalizing and externalizing symptoms). Our evaluation of the findings indicates that at least half of the studies provide compelling (i.e., moderate to strong) support for the male vulnerability model (Rutter, 1970) while the majority of studies fail to find a comparable level of support for the differential reactivity model (e.g., Kerig, 1996).

Although these results appear to compellingly support the male vulnerability model at first glance, a more rigorous analysis of the studies reveals that it is difficult to draw any simple conclusions regarding the role of gender. First, many of the recent studies have produced more complex and inconsistent findings (see Grych & Fincham, 1990, for a review). For example, although some recent findings continue to yield support for the male vulnerability model (Kerig, in press-b), meta-analyses and community-based studies with large samples have failed to find gender differences in the magnitude of associations between marital conflict or discord and children's psychological problems (e.g.,

Table 3.1. A Selective Review of the Moderating Role of Child Gender in the Relationship between Marital Conflict and Boys' and Girls' Global Psychological Adjustment

| | | | | Support for Models | |
				Male Vulnerability	Differential Reactivity
Study	Sample	Method	Results		
1. Buehler, Anthony, Krishnakumar, & Stone (1997)	68 studies	Meta-analysis	Although the relationship between marital conflict and problem behavior was stronger for boys (effect size = .32) than girls (effect size = .23), the difference was not significant. Marital conflict did not differentially predict internalizing and externalizing symptoms for boys and girls, respectively.	Weak	None
2. Block, Block, & Morrison (1981)	100 (3-year-old) children and their mothers and fathers (46 boys, 54 girls)	Prospective parent and teacher reports at 3, 4, and 7 years of age	The relationship between parental child-rearing disagreements at age 3 and concurrent and subsequent teacher reports of externalizing symptoms and behavioral control were significantly stronger for boys than girls. Child-rearing disagreements predicted greater inhibition among girls only, but the magnitude of relations did not significantly differ by gender.	Strong	Modest

Study	Sample	Informants	Findings		
3. Davies & Windle (1997)	443 adolescent-mother pairs (239 girls, 204 boys)	Mother and adolescent reports	The relationship between maternal reports of marital discord (conflict and dissatisfaction composite) and adolescent-reported delinquency and alcohol problems was stronger for girls than boys.	None	None
4. Emery & O'Leary (1982)	50 (8–17-year-old) children, clinic sample (25 girls, 25 boys)	Parent and child reports	Maternal reports of marital discord (disagreements, dissatisfaction) and child reports of marital conflict predicted conduct problems for boys only. Moderator analyses for gender were not conducted.	Moderate	Modest
5. Grych, Seid, & Fincham (1992)	336 (9–12-year-old) children (160 girls, 176 boys)	Parent, child, teacher, and classmate reports	The overall findings suggested that the relationship between marital conflict and children's functioning was similar for boys and girls. However, parent reported marital conflict did predict teacher/peer reports of greater internalizing symptoms for boys and lower internalizing symptoms for girls.	Weak	None

(continued)

Table 3.1 (*continued*)

Study	Sample	Method	Results	Support for Models	
				Male Vulnerability	Differential Reactivity
6. Johnston, Gonzalez, & Campbell (1987)	56 (4–14-year-old) children (28 girls, 28 boys) and their parents in divorce mediation	Observations of parent and child counseling; parent and child reports; clinician ratings	The only moderating effect of gender indicated that postdivorce interparental conflict predicted greater internalizing symptoms for girls.	None	Moderate
7. Jouriles, Bourg, & Farris (1991)	1,107 two-parent families with a 6–12-year-old child (549 girls, 558 boys)	Parent and child reports	Gender did not moderate the relationship between parent reports of marital adjustment and child and parent reports of child conduct problems.	None	None
8. Kerig (1996)	116 (7–11-year-old) children and their mothers and 79 fathers (63 boys, 51 girls)	Parent and child reports	Mother reports of destructive marital conflict more strongly predicted mother and child reports of internalizing and externalizing symptoms for boys than girls.	Strong	None

Study	Sample	Source	Findings		
9. Kerig (1999)	102 couples reporting marital aggression over the past year and their 7–11-year-old children	Mother, father, and child reports	Although it is unclear whether moderator analyses were conducted, parental reports of marital conflict were associated with a wide range of adjustment problems for boys, including child reports of anxiety and parent reports of internalizing symptoms, externalizing problems, and total problems. For girls, marital conflict only predicted parent reports of total problems and internalizing symptoms.	Moderate	Moderate
10. Wolfe, Jaffe, Wilson, & Zak (1985)	198 (4–16-year-old) children and 142 mothers from the community and abused women's shelters (98 boys, 100 girls)	Maternal reports	Although moderator analyses were not conducted, the discrepancy in clinically significant rates of behavior problems of children in maritally violent and nonviolent homes appeared to be higher for boys (47% and 16.3%, respectively) than girls (36.2% and 22.6%, respectively).	Moderate	Weak

Buehler, Anthony, Krishnakumar, & Stone, 1997; Jouriles, Bourg, & Farris, 1991).

Second, gender appears to operate in different ways across levels or domains of children's functioning. The review of studies in Table 3.2 specifically shows that the male vulnerability model cannot explain differences in boys' and girls' specific reactions to marital and adult conflict; only 2 of the 10 studies yield more than weak support for the male vulnerability hypothesis. Conversely, our interpretation of findings indicates that the majority of studies (i.e., 6 of 10) provide strong support for the differential reactivity model. For example, although findings indicate that boys are not immune to the stressful effects of conflict, the studies do indicate the girls may be especially likely to exhibit greater distress with corresponding increases in conflict hostility (Cummings, Vogel, Cummings, & El-Sheikh, 1989; Davies, Myers, Cummings, & Heindel, 1999; Grych, 1998).

Third, some of the empirical support for the male vulnerability model may be attributable to an artifact in methodological designs, especially in the older studies. Given the greater tendency for boys to exhibit externalizing symptoms and for girls to exhibit internalizing symptoms (Zahn-Waxler, 1993), biases toward the assessment of externalizing symptoms in the older studies often yielded disproportionately low samples of girls or range restrictions in the girls' maladjustment scores. The accompanying drop in statistical power may thus explain the failure to detect a consistent relationship between marital discord and child adjustment for girls. Because parents and teachers have increased difficulty in evaluating the more covert symptoms of internalizing problems, heavy reliance on adult reports (e.g., parent, teacher) of child maladjustment in some older studies may have further jeopardized the psychometric properties of internalizing symptomatology measures. In keeping with these methodological limitations, recent studies that broaden the assessment of adjustment problems and utilize child self-reports have found that boys and girls exhibit similar vulnerability to marital conflict (Grych, Seid, & Fincham, 1992). Methodological "cohort" effects, however, do not appear to fully explain the complexity of the findings. For example, the results of a multi-informant (i.e., parents, children) study assessing multiple forms of child maladjustment indicate that marital conflict was a stronger predictor of internalizing and externalizing symptoms for boys than for girls (Kerig, 1996). Therefore, conceptual explanations are integral to developing a complete account of when and why male vulnerability occurs.

In sum, even from the selective review of the gender literature, it is clear that no single explanation can fully account for the complex inter-

Table 3.2. A Selective Review of the Role of Child Gender in Children's Responses to Marital Conflict

Study	Sample	Method	Results	Support for Models	
				Male Vulnerability	Differential Reactivity
1. Buchanan, Maccoby, & Dornbusch (1991)	522 (10–18-year-old) children of divorced parents (257 girls, 265 boys)	Adolescent and parent reports	Adolescent girls were more apt to feel "caught between parents" in divorced families than boys. The moderating role of gender in the relationship between parental discord and feeling "caught" was not examined.	None	Strong
2. Cummings, Davies, & Simpson (1994)	51 (9–12-year-old) children and their mothers (25 boys, 26 girls)	Mother and child reports	The relationship between maternal reported marital discord and children's appraisals of destructive conflict, self-blame, and perceived threat were more consistent for boys than girls (67% vs. 8% significant). However, only the relationship between marital hostility and perceived threat was significantly greater for boys than girls.	Moderate	None

(continued)

Table 3.2 (continued)

Study	Sample	Method	Results	Support for Models	
				Male Vulnerability	Differential Reactivity
3. Cummings, Vogel, Cummings, & El-Sheikh (1989)	63 (4–9-year-old) children (29 girls, 34 boys)	Interview responses to videotaped adult conflicts	Gender main effects were the following: (a) Boys perceived the adults as more angry; (b) boys felt more angry in response to adult conflicts; and (c) girls proposed more specific solutions and greater involvement in the adults' problems. Moderator analyses indicated that girls were more likely to report feeling distressed than boys for very hostile adult conflicts only.	Weak	Strong
4. Davies & Cummings (1995)	64 (4–8-year-old) children (32 boys, 32 girls)	Behavioral and interview responses to simulated "live" adult conflict following a mood induction	Significant gender main effects of interactions with age or mood were below chance level.	None	None

Study	Sample	Measure	Findings		
5. Davies, Myers, Cummings, & Heindel (1999)	112 (6–19-year-old) children (56 boys, 56 girls)	Interview responses to videotaped adult conflicts	The moderating effects of gender indicated that for girls witnessing destructive conflict histories elicited greater fear and anger during a subsequent conflict than witnessing constructive conflict histories. Gender differences that varied as a function of age included the following: (a) Preadolescent boys reported greater mediation impulses than their female peers, and (b) late adolescent girls felt more sadness and expected greater interadult sadness than male peers.	Weak	Strong
6. El-Sheikh (1994)	40 (4–5-year-old) children (21 girls, 19 boys)	Mother reports; child behavioral, physiological, and interview responses to a simulated "live" adult conflict	Moderator analyses revealed an association between marital conflict histories and greater heart rate reactivity to simulated adult conflict for girls. A gender main effect indicated that boys reacted more aggressively to the conflict than girls.	Weak	Strong
7. El-Sheikh, Cummings, & Reiter (1996)	47 (4–5-year-old) children (22 girls, 25 boys)	Behavioral and interview responses to "live" simulated adult conflict histories	For girls only, witnessing unresolved conflict histories elicited greater perceived adult negativity and intervention impulses in a subsequent conflict than witnessing resolved conflict histories.	Weak	Strong

(continued)

Table 3.2 (*continued*)

Study	Sample	Method	Results	Support for Models	
				Male Vulnerability	Differential Reactivity
8. Grych (1998)	60 (7–12-year-old) children and their mothers (30 boys, 30 girls)	Interview responses to audiotaped marital conflict vignettes	Although boys' and girls' distress responses were comparable for low-intensity conflicts, girls reported experiencing more distress than boys for high-intensity conflicts. High-intensity conflicts elicited more perceived threat than low-intensity conflicts for girls.	None	Strong
9. Grych & Fincham (1993)	Study 145 (11–12-year-old) children (26 boys, 19 girls) Study 2: 112 fifth grade children (53 boys, 59 girls)	Interview responses to audiotaped marital conflict vignettes	No gender main effects or gender interactions with different conflict types or age emerged for children's affective and cognitive responses to conflict.	None	None
10. Kerig (1998a)	174 families with children between 7 and 11 years of age (86 girls, 88 boys)	Parent and child reports	Associations between marital conflict and children's perceived threat and self-calming difficulties were stronger for boys than girls.	Strong	Weak

play between gender and marital conflict. Even when coherent patterns do emerge in the data, empirical inconsistency and complexity commonly outweigh any regularity in the results. Thus, a key task facing researchers is to try to uncover the wide range of developmental and socialization pathways that lead to multifinality; that is, the multiplicity of outcomes experienced by boys and girls exposed to the same stressor of marital conflict (Cicchetti & Rogosch, 1996). As a way of organizing the complexity inherent in studying gender, the biopsychosocial model in Figure 3.1 portrays a representative, but not exhaustive, overview of the broader family and developmental systems that

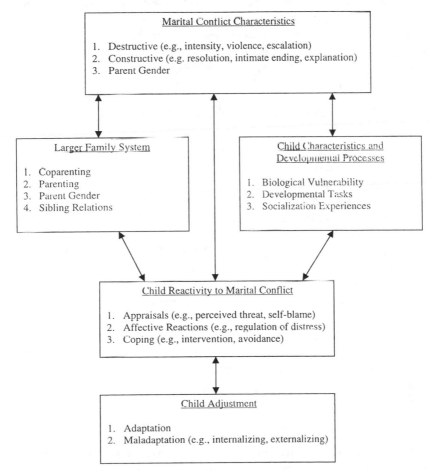

Figure 3.1. A family and developmental systems framework for understanding the role of gender in the association between interparental conflict and child development.

may account for gender-specific pathways between interparental conflict and child development. Its multifaceted nature *tentatively* addresses how boys' and girls' responses to interparental conflict are likely to vary as a function of a dynamic, transactional constellation of factors, including child characteristics (e.g., timing of developmental tasks), interparental conflict dimensions (e.g., conflict characteristics, parent gender), the larger family system (e.g., parent–child relations), and the domain of children's functioning (e.g., appraisals, coping). At the outset, however, it is important to note that variability in functioning within each gender is typically greater than the variability between the genders. Thus, even the most robust gender differences are generally modest in magnitude. Because any understanding of when and why gender differences occur requires consideration of socialization experiences, developmental processes, and intraindividual characteristics, we first turn to consider intraindividual and developmental factors relevant to children's responses to interparental conflict.

Child Characteristics and Developmental Processes

Although research largely supports models of differential reactivity and male vulnerability, the viability of these models may vary across the developmental stage of the children (Hops, 1997). For example, boys from discordant homes may be more susceptible to maladjustment than their female counterparts, especially in the development of externalizing symptoms. However, this pattern does not hold true and may even reverse during adolescence (e.g., Cummings & Davies, 1994; Davies & Windle, 1997; Hops, 1997; Petersen, 1988). For example, in a sample of middle adolescents, Davies and Windle (1997) reported that marital discord was a significantly stronger predictor of girls' delinquency and alcohol problems than it was for boys. Girls' greater susceptibility to intrafamilial stress during adolescence may also be manifested in heightened depressive symptoms and other emotional difficulties (e.g., Gore, Aseltine, & Colten, 1993). Multiple intrapersonal and developmental mechanisms may underlie these complex findings. Therefore, the following sections review some of the primary mechanisms of effect.

Biological Vulnerability

Biological vulnerability may partly explain why boys exposed to elevated levels of marital conflict are sometimes found to be at greater risk for developing problems in early childhood. Stated in the terminology of a diathesis–stress model, the weaker neuropsychological and psychobiological systems of boys may serve as a diathesis that is potentiated further by stress components, such as interparental conflict (Emery, 1982). Adequate tests of this model, however, await further empirical precision in identifying the neuropsychological mechanisms that exacerbate the stress of interparental conflict for boys. Another challenge is to trace exactly how the evolving genotype–environment coactions differ by gender. That is, the greater constitutional vulnerability for boys may give rise to behavior problems, which, in turn, may increase family stress, leading to exposure to greater interparental quarreling. Nevertheless, these biological accounts, which propose that male vulnerability is relatively stable across the life span, cannot explain why gender-specific vulnerability changes over development. It is likely then that other child and developmental processes are also responsible for this risk pattern.

Developmental Tasks

While boys and girls may face similar developmental tasks in many domains, differences in the timing and nature of some developmental challenges do vary by child gender. Puberty is perceived by girls to be a more stressful negative event (e.g., Crockett & Petersen, 1987), and girls are more likely to experience the challenge of coping with puberty in combination with the transition to the larger, more impersonal confines of secondary school systems. As girls progress through adolescence, they also report experiencing more stressful psychosocial events than boys (Windle, 1992). Thus, a plausible explanation for female vulnerability to parental conflict during adolescence is that adolescent girls' experiences with these constellations of psychosocial stressors may lower the threshold for maladaptive responding and serve as catalysts for the deleterious effects of interparental conflict.

Socialization Experiences

Age differences in gender vulnerability to marital discord may also be explained, in part, by developmental accounts of differential socialization experiences. Parents, for example, reward boys for assertiveness and independence and girls for acquiescent behavior (Kerig, Cowan, & Cowan, 1993). According to gender role theory (Helgeson, 1994), this pattern reflects a broader range of socialization pressures. Boys are hypothesized to develop greater dispositions toward agency, or interest in the self as an individual, which is specifically manifested in greater independence, self-direction, self-protection, and autonomy. Girls, on the other hand, are thought to develop a greater proclivity toward communion, or the merging of an individual within social networks; this disposition is considered to be expressed through more interpersonal connectedness and concern for the welfare of others.

These sex roles, in turn, have been posited to constrain or channel the expression of psychological problems in gender-specific ways that dovetail with the differential reactivity model. In an effort to preserve the goal of interpersonal harmony in discordant homes, girls may express their distress in a subtle, inner-directed pattern characterized by symptoms of depression and anxiety. By contrast, boys may direct their psychological distress toward external sources (e.g., delinquency, aggression) in an effort to reestablish their autonomy and assertiveness under the shadow of threat posed by marital conflict.

Although these gender differences in personality development may emerge early in childhood and have biological roots (Zahn-Waxler, 1993), the gender intensification hypothesis postulates that adolescence is a sensitive period during which the divergence in personalities between boys and girls becomes particularly pronounced (Hill & Lynch, 1983). Increasing physical differentiation between boys and girls during puberty sets in motion more pressure by socialization agents to conform to conventional social roles and greater adolescent awareness of gender differences. To relieve the resulting tension, adolescents may adhere to the imposed expectations of traditional gender roles and, as a result, further the psychological differentiation between boys and girls. Although resulting increases in communion and interpersonal concern among adolescent girls in harmonious homes may serve the adaptive functions of bolstering self-esteem and well-being (e.g., Chase-Lansdale, Wakschlag, & Brooks-Gunn, 1995), the progressively lower thresholds of interpersonal concern under conditions of marital discord may cause girls to be particularly likely to ruminate about negative family events, feel "caught" in parental problems, and become enmeshed in the family difficulties (Davies & Windle, 1997). These patterns of "caregiving burden," in turn, do not bode well for the girls' psychological health (Chase-Lansdale et al., 1995; Gore et al., 1993). In contrast, boys' greater agency, valuation of self-protection, and negotiation of independence may reduce their exposure to marital conflict and hence dilute the risk posed by family discord. In summary, any account of gender-differentiated reactions to marital conflict will not be complete without systematic attention to the effects of these developmentally based biological, personality, and socialization mechanisms.

Marital Conflict Characteristics

Increasing precision in the conceptualization of marital conflict characteristics may be another integral task in unraveling the complex role that gender plays in the effects of marital conflict. Children's interpretations of the causes of conflict and its implications for the welfare of their parents' marriage, family, and the self, hinge largely on the quality of conflict expression and the gender of the parent engaging in the conflict expression (e.g., Crockenberg & Forgays, 1996; Davies & Cummings, 1994; Grych & Fincham, 1993). Because boys and girls often place different value on the significance of the self in relation to significant others and have been found to relate differently to mothers' and fathers' conflict expressions, children's interpretations and reactions to different conflict characteristics may vary by child gender.

Constructive and Destructive Characteristics of Marital Conflict

Gender-specific patterns in children's long-term adjustment to the interparental relationship may thus depend, in part, on children's experiential histories with specific aspects of the interparental relationship. For example, Grych and Fincham (1990) tentatively concluded that global marital dissatisfaction was more closely associated with externalizing symptoms in boys and internalizing symptoms in girls (see Reid & Crisafulli, 1990), whereas the frequency of marital conflict was associated with a similar range of psychological problems in both boys and girls (see Buehler et al., 1997). However, because studies of marital conflict have focused almost exclusively on measures of global conflict frequency, they do not address the possibility that boys and girls may cope differently in experiencing interparental conflicts that vary in course (e.g., resolution, escalation), quality of expression (e.g., physical violence), and content (e.g., childrearing disagreements). Moreover, the myopic focus in research on the interparental relationship cannot account for the possibility that characteristics in the larger family system (e.g., changes in maternal and paternal parenting practices with boys and girls) accompanying marital distress may partially explain the more pronounced gender-specific patterns of child functioning that occur in the face of marital distress. Field research may thus benefit by embedding the study of marital conflict dimensions in the larger family system, broadening child assessments to include both short-term and long-term domains of functioning, and utilizing prospective research designs. Its limitations notwithstanding (e.g., low ecological validity), analogue studies, which isolate the direct effects of conflict dimensions, have provided a relatively efficient first step in exploring how the direct effects of specific marital conflict characteristics may vary by gender (Davies & Cummings, 1994).

The Course and Ending of Conflicts. If girls are socialized to exhibit greater concern for maintaining harmonious interpersonal relations, it follows that they may be particularly sensitive to conflict characteristics that are relatively accurate barometers of the quality of close adult relationships. Since ways of managing the emotional course and endings of the disagreement are among the best predictors of adult relationship quality and dissolution (e.g., Gottman, Coan, Carrere, & Swanson, 1998), girls may be specifically sensitive to the degree to which conflicts result in a mutually satisfactory resolution. Analogue designs have provided strong support for this hypothesis (Cummings et al., 1989). For girls, witnessing histories of unresolved conflicts between adults elicited greater appraisals of adult negativity and impulses to intervene in subsequent conflicts than witnessing couples who regularly resolved their conflicts (El-Sheikh & Cummings, 1995; El-Sheikh, Cummings, & Reiter, 1996). Similarly, although both boys and girls reported feeling more sadness in response to a standard interadult conflict that followed exposure to destructive adult conflict histories (i.e., proliferation of distress) than constructive conflict histories (i.e., conflict ending a mutually satisfying way), only girls reported greater negativity across all domains of affect (e.g., sad, scared, mad) in response to the cumulative experience of destructive conflicts (Davies et al., 1999).

However, evidence also suggests that boys are not completely insensitive to the emotional course and aftermath of adult conflicts. Thus, histories of exposure to unresolved adult conflicts elicited higher levels of behavioral distress (e.g., freezing, facial and gestural distress) to a standard conflict for boys and girls than did resolved conflict histories (El-Sheikh et al., 1996). Likewise, Kerig (1996) reported that parental impasses in resolving conflicts were stronger predictors of self-reported anxiety symptoms for boys than girls. Reflecting the distinctive nature of short-term response patterns and long-term functioning, interpersonal sensitivity and emotional understanding in the face of parental discord may actually serve as a protective, rather than risk, factor in girls' long-term outcomes (Grych & Fincham, 1992). By contrast, although boys seem to show a similar profile of sensitivity to the emotional course and ending of conflicts at the behavioral (i.e., unconscious or semiconscious processes) level of emotional reactivity, they may be less able to understand the interpersonal ramifications of the situation.

Form and Intensity of Conflict. In extending the finding that boys are more agentic than girls (i.e., greater concern with self-protection), one might hypothesize that boys may be particularly reactive to forms of marital conflict that hold direct and/or immediate implications for their own well-being. Interparental violence and aggression are particularly likely to spill over to compromise parent–child relations and the psychological and physical welfare of the child. Thus, boys from maritally violent homes may be particularly sensitive to intense conflicts because, in their aftermath, they are more likely to become targets of parental hostility than their counterparts from nonviolent homes. In support of this prediction, interparental violence more consistently predicts negative outcomes for boys than for girls (e.g., Kerig, 1996, 1999; Jouriles & Norwood, 1995). Thus, in contexts ridden with adult violence, boys may be especially motivated to be vigilant to any semblance of danger and may act accordingly in ways that reduce their exposure to the threat. In keeping with this notion, boys from homes with higher levels of interparental violence (a) exhibited greater anxiety and withdrawal during a family disagreement task centering on the child's behavior than their female counterparts (Gordis, Margolin, & John, 1997), and (b) reported feeling more fear in simulated interadult and mother–child conflicts than their female counterparts (El-Sheikh, 1997). Boys' tendencies to endorse fewer aggressive tactics in response to physical adult arguments versus verbal arguments have also been interpreted as reflecting their efforts to suppress misbehavior and, in the process, reduce the probability that adult aggression would involve them (El-Sheikh & Cheskes, 1995).

Parent Gender

Distinguishing between the ways in which mothers and fathers handle marital conflicts also holds considerable promise for understanding gender specificity in pathways of marital conflict. Crockenberg and Forgays (1996) have integrated social learning and family systems theories into a framework designed to describe how maternal and paternal behavior in marital conflicts may differentially affect boys and girls. The social learning component of the conceptualization presupposes that children develop similar ways of handling stressful situations by more closely identifying with and modeling the same-sex parents' ways of coping with marital conflict. Although these assumptions have yet to be fully tested, the empirical observation that mothers' hostility in marital interactions is more closely associated with girls' conduct problems than fathers' hostility does provide substantiation of the hypotheses (Johnson & O'Leary, 1987). Social learning principles may also partially explain why girls are sometimes found to be at greater risk for developing internalizing symptoms. Crockenberg and Forgays (1996) suggest that children may derive a sense of self-efficacy by observing the power and efficacy of models like their same-sex parent. Since wives still hold significantly less power on average than husbands in most areas of family decision making (e.g., Steil & Weltman, 1991), girls may identify with their mothers' powerlessness, helplessness, and dysphoria.

The family systems part of the framework postulates that greater identification with the same-sex parent also causes children to perceive the opposite-sex parent's hostility as an attack upon themselves. As a result, they may become more reactive to the opposite-sex parent's conflict behaviors. Concordant with this hypothesis, fine-grained observations of maternal and paternal belligerence in marital conflicts did prospectively predict teacher reports of internalizing problems in the opposite-sex child three years later (Katz & Gottman, 1993). Similarly, girls perceived their fathers' behavior during conflicts as more angry than boys, even though trained observers failed to note any differences in paternal anger across child gender (Crockenberg & Forgays, 1996). If identification processes play a role in shaping children's perceptions of being attacked by the opposite-sex parent, an additional assumption is that the resulting feelings of insecurity in relationships with the opposite-sex parent may have a particularly profound impact on children's development. Supporting this explanation, Osborne and Fincham (1996) found that only negative perceptions of relationships with the opposite-sex parent predicted internalizing symptoms, a form of maladjustment that most closely matches indicators of insecurity (Davies & Cummings, 1998).

Some empirical findings, however, are at odds with this two-component model. For example, Crockenberg and Forgay's (1996) own data raise questions concerning the extent to which 6-year-old children truly distinguish between maternal and paternal behavior during marital conflicts. In keeping with cognitive-developmental theories (Kohlberg, 1966), the process of identifying with same-sex models may still be in the final stages of development during the early elementary school years (Ruble, Balaban, & Cooper, 1981). Alternatively, tendencies for children to emulate a powerful competent model may override the influence of same-sex socialization agents (Bandura, 1977). For example, in drawing on the observation that fathers are commonly more powerful figures in family decisions, Crockenberg and Forgays (1996) offer an additional hypothesis that boys and girls may be more likely to imitate fathers. These conflicting notions require more fine-grained empirical scrutiny.

Larger Family System

Thus far, the chapter has addressed how characteristics of marital conflict and the child may account for variability in gender as a moderator of marital conflict. Yet, family systems theory strongly cautions that any comprehensive model of the role of gender in the link between marital conflict and child functioning must also take into account the interpersonal dynamics of the larger family system, including the coparenting, parenting, and sibling subsystems.

Co-parenting

In an effort to explain why boys are sometimes reported to exhibit greater vulnerability to marital conflict, some researchers have hypothesized that stereotypical conceptions of the psychological fragility of girls may guide parents to take greater strides to shield girls from their conflicts (e.g., Emery, 1982). However, empirical support for this hypothesis is inconsistent. On one hand, prior research has shown that girls are exposed to less interparental conflict than boys (e.g., Hetherington, Stanley-Hagen, & Anderson, 1989), and Cummings, Davies, and Simpson (1994) reported greater correspondence between child and maternal reports of marital conflict for boys than girls; given that girls have been shown to be equally or more sensitive to interadult conflict than boys, one interpretation of the latter finding is that parents better shield girls from exposure to conflict. On the other hand, the majority of studies of intact families report no gender differences in exposure to interparental conflict (e.g., Emery & O'Leary, 1982; Kerig et al., 1998). Incorporating broader family characteristics (e.g., at-risk families, families with gender stereotypical beliefs) and precisely explicating multiple dimensions of the coparenting relationship (e.g., mutual supporting in caregiving, interparental consistency in discipline) may help identify the conditions under which girls are more shielded from conflict than boys.

Parenting

The moderating role of child gender in the link between marital conflict and parenting practices may also account for why boys sometimes exhibit greater vulnerability to marital turmoil than girls. Boys are more likely to be targets of parental hostility and aggression than girls in nonclinic samples (Maccoby & Jacklin, 1974), with this gender difference becoming larger as marital conflict increases (e.g., Jouriles & LeCompte, 1991; Jouriles & Norwood, 1995). Speaking to the robust nature of these findings, a stronger pathway between marital distress and parental hostility for boys has been demonstrated to exist even in infancy (McHale, 1995). Why might this pathway differ for boys and girls? Guided by a family process model, Jouriles and Norwood (1995) hypothesized that boys' disproportionate risk for exhibiting externalizing symptoms, particularly in the context of marital discord, serves to further intensify the stress experienced by parents from high-conflict homes and, as a result, increases the probability that parents will direct their aggression toward them. Parental beliefs that boys benefit from greater discipline than girls for misbehavior may be an additional process that fuels parental use of coercion and aggression toward boys (Maccoby & Jacklin, 1974). Thus, from a family systems perspective, boys' greater concerns about their own well-being, as concretely reflected in higher levels of perceived threat and anxiety, may not simply be a by-product of their attempts to preserve their agency, but may also reflect relatively accurate appraisals about their greater probability of becoming targets of parental hostility in violent homes (El-Sheikh & Cheskes, 1995; Gordis et al., 1997). As part of an evolving, reciprocal cycle of adversity, higher levels of perceived threat engendered by parental hostility may further intensify externalizing symptoms among boys, which, in turn, evokes even greater hostility from parents.

Parent Gender

Differentiating between children's responses to maternal and paternal parenting practices may further advance an understanding of gender differences (Cummings & O'Reilly, 1997). Fathers' parenting practices have been reported to be more likely to deteriorate in the face of marital stress (Amato & Booth, 1991; Jouriles & Farris, 1992), as evidenced by disengagement, negativity, and withdrawal in their child-rearing roles (Howes & Markman, 1989; Katz & Gottman, 1996; Lindahl, Clements, & Markman, 1997). Given that children develop unique appraisals of the implications of interparental conflict for the quality of their relationships with mothers and fathers (Osborne & Fincham, 1996), these findings suggest that fathers' parenting practices may play a more robust role than mothers' parenting practices in mediating indirect linkages between marital conflict and child adjustment. One explanation for these findings is that mothers may be better able to compartmentalize their spouse and parent roles, resulting in less carry-over from marital relations to parenting (e.g., Belsky, Youngblade, Rovine, & Volling, 1991; Lindahl et al., 1997). In keeping with traditional sex roles and the disproportionate prevalence of women as primary caregivers, another potential explanation is that parenthood is regarded by women as a more fundamental role than men (Thompson & Walker, 1989). Daughters' greater assertiveness, control, and defiance in interactions with their maritally distressed fathers suggests that they may be attempting to gain the attention and involvement of emotionally disengaged fathers (Kerig et al., 1993). This transactional process, however, may actually serve to increase paternal negativity and disengagement from family life.

Further complicating the issue, researchers must consider how the match between the sex of the parents and children may moderate the relationship between interparental conflict and child adjustment. Disruptions in child-rearing practices among fathers experiencing marital discord are especially pronounced in relationships with their daughters, as evidenced by especially high rates of parental negativity and withdrawal in father–daughter interactions (Belsky, Rovine, & Fish, 1989; Kerig et al., 1993; McHale, 1995; Parke & Tinsley, 1987). This pattern may be part of a larger tendency for opposite-sex parent–child relationships to be most strained in discordant homes. For example, while Kerig et al. (1993) found evidence that higher levels of marital distress predicted the greatest parental negativity in father–daughter dyads, they also reported that reciprocation of negative affect toward children was most pronounced by maritally distressed mothers in their interactions with sons. Likewise, sons witnessing marital conflict perceived more negativity in relationships with their mothers than with fathers (Osborne & Fincham, 1996). This emerging, but not entirely consistent, pattern of greater negativity between maritally distressed parents and opposite-sex children requires further investigation. Family systems formulations postulate that parents experiencing marital problems may project greater negativity toward the opposite-sex children because they are more reminiscent of the perceived shortcomings of their partners (e.g., Osborne & Fincham, 1996). Moreover, developing and maintaining an involved role as a parent in gender-differentiated activities may be an especially challenging developmental task for the opposite-sex parent, particularly without the support, knowledge, and guidance of the same-sex parent in discordant families.

Sibling Relations

Although the sibling subsystem constitutes a fundamental component of the family system, little is known about the interplay between marital conflict and sibling relationships (see Dunn and Davies, Chapter 10). Even less is known about how the gender composition of sibling relations may alter the effects of marital conflict on children's adjustment. Thus, marital conflict has been associated with parental differential treatment of siblings (Deal, 1996), but tests of whether the results are more pronounced for certain gender compositions in sibling dyads have yet to be undertaken. Providing a possible explanation for the male vulnerability model, boys with sisters who face differential treatment by parents may be particularly vulnerable to developing adjustment problems, especially in the form of externalizing symptoms (McGuire, Dunn, & Plomin, 1995). Older opposite-sex siblings may also curtail gender-socialization processes that guide boys and girls toward different trajectories of personality styles. The resulting balance between traits of communion and agency for younger siblings or a reversal of conventional gender-specific personality patterns may attenuate gender differences in responding to marital conflict (Brody & Stoneman, 1990).

Child Reactivity to Marital Conflict: The Implications of Gender-Differentiated Patterns

Do gender differences in socialization experiences and child character-istics guide boys and girls to respond differently to the direct effects of interparental and interadult conflict? If so, what roles might they play in the development of gender-differentiated trajectories of long-term adjustment? Consistent with earlier work (Crockenberg & Forgays, 1996; Davies & Cummings, 1998; Grych & Fincham, 1990), the differen-tiation between children's reactivity to conflict and their trajectories of global adaptation or adjustment in the model highlights that (a) gen-der-specific pathways may emerge in any number of domains of func-tioning, and (b) gender differences in reactivity and coping in the face of marital conflict may develop into organized behavioral patterns that coalesce into different psychological adjustment trajectories for girls and boys.

Overall, the pattern of differences in boys' and girls' reactivity and coping patterns does not readily account for findings that support the male vulnerability model (see also Table 3.2). Observational and self-report studies fail to find any systematic evidence that the more consis-tent links between marital conflict and child adjustment among boys are due to some global liability in their affective, cognitive, or behav-ioral sensitivity to conflict. Rather, the results, though not always con-sistent, tend to favor some form of a differential reactivity model of gender and adjustment.

Girls and boys do appear to respond to conflict in ways that reflect their respective socialization experiences toward agency and commu-nion. As a possible manifestation of their greater concern with main-taining harmony in close relationships, girls appear to be more likely than boys to respond to high levels of parental discord by blaming themselves (e.g., Kerig, 1998a; Kerig et al., 1998), taking too much responsibility for repairing family relationships (Gore et al., 1993), feel-ing caught in their parents' quarrels (e.g., Buchanan, Maccoby, &

Dornbusch, 1991), and reporting greater impulses to intervene in adult conflicts (e.g., El-Sheikh et al., 1996; El-Sheikh & Reiter, 1996). Girls, at least prior to adolescence, also tend react to adult and parental conflict through more subtle, nondisruptive emotional channels of distress, worrying, and fear (e.g., Cummings, Iannotti, & Zahn-Waxler, 1985; Cummings et al., 1989; Davies, Myers, & Cummings, 1996; Hennessy, Rabideau, Cicchetti, & Cummings, 1994; Roecker, Dubow, & Donaldson, 1996). In contrast, boys have been found to be especially likely to appraise greater threat to themselves in the face of destructive interparental conflict (Kerig, 1998a; Kerig et al., 1998). An associated tendency for boys to respond with greater aggression in the context of adult and interparental conflict fits with this emphasis on protecting the self through "fight" responses (Cummings et al., 1985), particularly given that perceptions of threat to the self are theorized to correspond with hostility and egoistic (i.e., self-centered) forms of distress (Cummings et al., 1994).

Despite some evidence indicating that girls exhibit greater interpersonal concern and impulses to intervene in adult conflict, boys and girls appear to show similar levels of behavioral involvement in marital conflict. For example, observations of family interactions indicated that girls were more likely than boys to intervene in all types of family conflict *except* for interparental conflicts (Vuchinich, Emery, & Cassidy, 1988). In fact, boys endorsed more instrumental strategies toward repairing the task that caused the marital problem when conflicts ended in adult hostility (Davies et al., 1996). So, why might girls' greater motivation to repair marital relationships fail to translate into more frequent behavioral attempts to intervene in marital conflict? One possibility is that girls may be caught in a "double bind." Although they may exhibit comparatively greater sensitivity and concern for interparental relations, a diminished sense of interpersonal control instilled by socialization pressures may result in an increasing reliance on escape strategies as a way of coping with marital conflict (Crockenberg & Forgays, 1996; Kerig et al., 1998). By contrast, greater self-perceptions of agency and control over events among males may offset their lower levels of interpersonal concern (Block, 1983), guiding them to intervene by using rational strategies that address the task that caused the marital problem, rather than the uncomfortable underlying emotional issues (Davies et al., 1996).

A second, less consistent, pattern in the literature yields support for the notion that girls, on the whole, may be more sensitive to conflict than boys. Close scrutiny of children's emotional responses to experimentally manipulated histories of interadult conflict have shown that girls exhibit greater affective sensitivity to the quality of conflict histories. For example, girls are more likely to become sensitized to cumulative histories of destructive and unresolved conflict between adults, at least in the domains of subjective distress and intervention impulses (Davies et al., in press; El-Sheikh & Cummings, 1995; El-Sheikh et al., 1996; Grych, 1998). This gender-differentiated response may further reflect girls' greater concerns about repairing and maintaining interpersonal relationships in roles as emotional caretakers (Davies & Windle, 1997; Kerig, 1998a). Yet, greater interpersonal sensitivity, even under discordant conditions, does not necessarily translate into greater vulnerability and may even act as a protective factor that buffers girls from the effects of interparental adversity (Grych & Fincham, 1992). Moreover, many studies examining associations between naturalistic histories of interparental conflict and behavioral expressions of affect have failed to find gender differences that are comparable to the experimental studies (e.g., Davies & Cummings, 1998; El-Sheikh, 1994; El-Sheikh et al., 1996; Gordis et al., 1997; Grych, 1998). Thus, exposure to extensive histories of conflict between emotionally significant socialization figures may override any gender differences in brief experimental manipulations of conflict between adult strangers.

Developmental models further highlight the possibility that the applicability of any gender differences may be limited to specific developmental periods. Increases in gender-specific socialization pressures (i.e., gender intensification hypothesis) and psychosocial stressors (i.e., developmental theories of stress and coping) during adolescence may trigger changes in boys' and girls' responses to adult conflict (see "Child Characteristics" section). For example, trends for girls to respond with greater sadness than boys to unresolved interadult anger have been reported to reverse around the onset of adolescence (after age 10), so that boys actually report greater sadness in response to conflict than do girls (Cummings, Ballard, & El-Sheikh, 1991; Cummings, Ballard, El-Sheikh, & Lake, 1991). The next step toward bolstering the ecological validity of findings requires assessments of age by gender interactions in short-term responding to interparental, rather than interadult, conflict.

Child Adjustment

The integration of children's specific reactivity to conflict with their global psychological adjustment may illuminate the developmental pathways by which time- and context-specific response patterns may differentially affect boys' and girls' adjustment. Figure 3.2 selectively

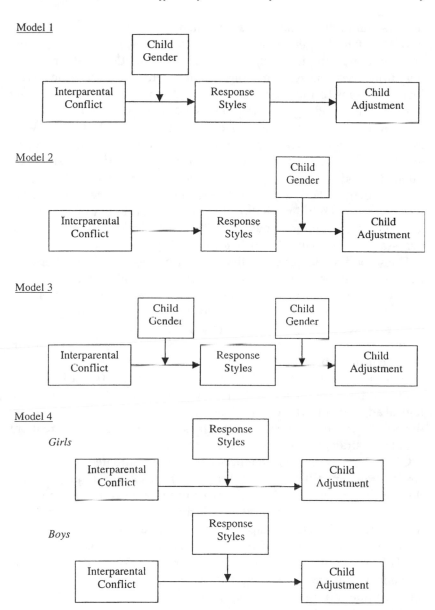

Figure 3.2. Alternative models for delineating gender differences in the links between marital conflict and children's reaction patterns, and their long-term adjustment.

depicts four of the primary ways in which children's response patterns
may elucidate the gender-specific pathways between marital conflict
and children's long-term adjustment. The first model posits that gender influences children's response patterns to marital conflict. With
increasing sensitization to parental conflict, boys' dispositions to react
with hostility and egoistic appraisals (i.e., self-centered appraisals)
may eventually crystallize into deeper, pervasive difficulties with
externalizing symptoms. Through similar sensitization processes, girls'
tendencies to respond with preoccupation, worry, and self-blame may
intensify and coalesce into subsequent internalizing symptoms
(Crockenberg & Forgays, 1996; Davies et al., 1996; Hennessy et al.,
1994). Tracing the full mediational evolution of differences in psychological problems among boys and girls from high-conflict homes is a
necessary next step in rigorously testing this model.

The second model proposes that gender moderates the link between
response patterns to interparental conflict and child adjustment (see
Figure 3.2). In other words, it is possible that the same responses may
have different implications for the adjustment of boys and girls. For
example, Kerig and colleagues (1999) found that the association
between forms of coping with conflict and children's adjustment differed considerably for boys and girls. For girls, lower levels of
approach strategies and higher levels of avoidance (i.e., distancing)
strategies for coping with conflict were associated with better psychological adjustment, whereas increases in adjustment for boys were predicted by more frequent approach strategies and less frequent
avoidance strategies in coping with conflict.

Given that individual differences are often accentuated in the face of
stress and change (Caspi & Moffitt, 1991), distancing strategies may
deter girls from the tendency toward unmitigated communion or the
progressive sacrifice of their own goals and well-being in the service of
improving family relationships. For boys, active attempts at approaching the marital problem may help them to maintain at least a minimum
level of emotional ties with family members and, as a result, offset male
tendencies toward increasing social detachment and unmitigated
agency under duress (Helgeson, 1994).

Model 3 illustrates the possibility that gender differences may occur
at both points along the mediational chain. Some empirical findings
support the notion that gender differences in appraisals of marital conflict are sequelae of marital conflict and precursors of adjustment problems. Not only has the association between marital conflict and
perceived threat been found to be stronger for boys than girls (Kerig,
1998a; Kerig et al., 1998b), but perceived threat has simultaneously been

shown to predict adjustment problems for boys only (Cummings et al., 1994; Kerig, 1998a). Conversely, self-blame was found to be a unique predictor of girls' maladjustment, particularly in the development of internalizing symptoms (Cummings et al., 1994; Kerig, 1998b; 1999).

However, important questions remain regarding the role these mediational mechanisms play in the specific adjustment trajectories of boys and girls. Can these models help explain why boys and girls from high-conflict homes are sometimes found to be at risk for different forms of psychological maladjustment (i.e., multifinality)? For example, some researchers have speculated that boys' and girls' respective tendencies to react to conflict with hostility and distress may help to explain why girls are at greater risk for internalizing symptoms and boys are at greater risk for externalizing symptoms when faced with elevated marital conflict (Davies et al., 1996; Hennessy et al., 1994). Alternatively, do gender-specific reaction patterns represent different pathways to the same form of child maladjustment (i.e., equifinality)? In support of this pathway, mediational tests have indicated that children's susceptibility to internalizing symptoms in high-conflict homes is partly accounted for by boys' tendencies to perceive threats to themselves and girls' tendencies to blame themselves (Kerig, 1999). Hence, different mechanisms explained why boys and girls in high-conflict homes were at risk for the same form of maladjustment.

Some dimensions of children's responses to marital conflict may also protect or moderate boys' and girls' risk in high conflict homes in different ways (see Figure 3.2, model 4). Kerig's (1998a) results, for example, suggested that appraisals of destructive interparental conflict accentuate the deleterious impact of interparental conflict on boys' adjustment, whereas high levels of perceived control over the conflict protected or buffered boys from the vulnerability associated with marital conflict. By contrast, girls' perceptions of having control over interparental quarreling and perceived threat actually exacerbated the risk of marital conflict, while girls' beliefs about their ability to regulate their affect during conflicts actually protected them from the effects of interparental conflict. Furthermore, consistent with differential reactivity models of gender, appraisals that were moderators of conflict were particularly useful in forecasting girls' internalizing symptoms and boys' externalizing symptoms.

Conclusion

Incorporating gender in models of interparental conflict is an integral step in identifying the precise conditions and processes by which marital conflict may affect children's developmental trajectories. Cataloging *how* gender may moderate relations between marital and child functioning will remain a central part of this task, especially in light of the complexity of previous gender research. However, the second generation of research also stipulates that progress in understanding the moderating role of gender must be supplemented with searches for *why* child and parent gender may alter the interrelationship between marital conflict and child development (Fincham, 1994). Advancing this new generation of research on gender and marital conflict will require creative integrations of theory and methods. Conceptualizing gender as a marker variable for a multivariate constellation of mechanisms multiplies the complexity of methodological designs. Without theoretical guidance and direction, efforts to capture the multivariate network will oversaturate statistical models. Thus, even though conceptual explanations for the mechanisms underlying gender as a moderator are in the early stages of development, they provide sufficient direction to advance a deeper analysis of process. Theoretical accounts of gender in the cognitive-contextual framework (Grych & Fincham, 1990), the process model of marital conflict (Crockenberg & Forgays, 1996), and the gender intensification hypothesis (Davies & Windle, 1997; Hill & Lynch, 1983) may be especially useful in narrowing the conceptual scope and developing elaborate but parsimonious empirical tests. Nevertheless, even after theoretical "tools" are used to tighten conceptualizations to a set of central constructs, this new generation of research will challenge researchers to specify more complex blends of moderator and mediator models (Kerig, 1998a; Osborne & Fincham, 1996), including models of moderated mediation, mediated moderation, and double moderation (Baron & Kenny, 1986). In presenting a heuristic model of the role gender plays in contexts of marital conflict, this chapter was designed to guide researchers in the deeper search for process that is the trademark of the second generation of research on marital conflict.

REFERENCES

Amato, P., & Booth, A. (1991). Consequences of parental divorce and marital unhappiness for adult well-being. *Social Forces, 69,* 895–914.
Bandura, A. (1977). *Social learning theory.* Englewood Cliffs, NJ: Prentice-Hall.
Baron, R. M., & Kenny, D. A. (1986). The moderator-mediator variable distinction in social psychological research: Conceptual, strategic, and statistical considerations. *Journal of Personality and Social Psychology, 51,* 1173–1182.
Belsky, J., Rovine, M., & Fish, M. (1989). The developing family system. In M. R. Gunnar & E. Thelen (Eds.), *The Minnesota Symposium on Child Psychology: Vol. 22. Systems and development* (pp. 119–166). Hillsdale, NJ: Erlbaum.

Belsky, J., Youngblade, L. M., Rovine, M., & Volling, B. L. (1991). Patterns of marital change and parent-child interaction. *Journal of Marriage and the Family, 53,* 487–498.

Block, J. H. (1983). Differential premises arising from differential socialization of the sexes: Some conjectures. *Child Development, 54,* 1335–1354.

Block, J. H., Block, J., & Morrison, A. (1981). Parental agreement-disagreement on child-rearing orientations and gender-related personality correlates in children. *Child Development, 52,* 965–974.

Brody, G. H., & Stoneman, Z. (1990). Sibling relationships. In I. E. Sigel & G. H. Brody (Eds.), *Methods of family research: Biographies of research projects. Vol 1: Normal Families* (pp. 189–212). Hillsdale, NJ: Erlbaum.

Buchanan, C. M., Maccoby, E. E., & Dornbusch, S. M. (1991). Caught between parents: Adolescents' experience in divorced homes. *Child Development, 62,* 1008–1029.

Buehler, C., Anthony, C., Krishnakumar, A., & Stone, G. (1997). Interparental conflict and youth problem behaviors: A meta-analysis. *Journal of Child & Family Studies, 6,* 223–247.

Caspi, A., & Moffitt, T. E. (1991). Individual differences are accentuated during periods of social change: The sample case of girls at puberty. *Journal of Personality & Social Psychology, 61,* 157–168.

Chase-Lansdale, P. L., Wakschlag, L. S., & Brooks-Gunn, J. (1995). A psychological perspective on the development of caring in children and youth: The role of family. *Journal of Adolescence, 18,* 515–556.

Cicchetti, D., & Rogosch, F. A. (1996). Equifinality and multifinality in developmental psychopathology. *Development and Psychopathology, 8,* 597–600.

Crockenberg, S., & Forgays, D. K. (1996). The role of emotion in children's understanding and emotional reactions to marital conflict. *Merrill-Palmer Quarterly, 42,* 22–47.

Crockett, L. J., & Petersen, A. C. (1987). Pubertal status and psychosocial development: Findings from the early adolescence study. In R. M. Lerner & T. T. Foch (Eds.), *Biological-psychosocial interactions in early adolescence: A life-span perspective.* Hillsdale, NJ: Erlbaum.

Cummings, E. M., Ballard, M., & El-Sheikh, M. (1991). Responses of children and adolescents to interadult anger as a function of gender, age, and mode of expression. *Merrill-Palmer Quarterly, 37,* 543–560.

Cummings, E. M., Ballard, M., El-Sheikh, M., & Lake, M. (1991). Resolution and children's responses to interadult anger. *Developmental Psychology, 27,* 462–470.

Cummings, E. M., & Davies, P. T. (1994). Maternal depression and child development. *Journal of Child Psychology and Psychiatry, 35,* 73–112.

Cummings, E. M., Davies, P. T., & Simpson, K. S. (1994). Marital conflict, gender, and children's appraisals and coping efficacy as mediators of child adjustment. *Journal of Family Psychology, 8,* 141–149.

Cummings, E. M., Iannotti, R. J., & Zahn-Waxler, C. (1985). The influence of conflict between adults on the emotions and aggression of young children. *Developmental Psychology, 21,* 495–507.

Cummings, E. M., & O'Reilly, A. (1997). Fathers in family context: Effects of marital quality on child adjustment. In M. E. Lamb (Ed.), *The role of the father in child development* (3rd ed., pp. 49–65). New York: Wiley.

Cummings, E. M., Vogel, D., Cummings, J. S., & El-Sheikh, M. (1989). Children's responses to different forms of expression of anger between adults. *Child Development, 60,* 1392–1404.

Davies, P. T., & Cummings, E. M. (1994). Marital conflict and child adjustment: An emotional security hypothesis. *Psychological Bulletin, 116,* 387–411.

Davies, P. T., & Cummings, E. M. (1995). Children's emotions as organizers of their reactions to interadult anger: A functionalist perspective. *Developmental Psychology, 31,* 677–684.

Davies, P. T., & Cummings, E. M. (1998). Exploring children's emotional security as a mediator of the link between marital relations and child adjustment. *Child Development, 69,* 124–139.

Davies, P. T., Myers, R. L., & Cummings, E. M. (1996). Responses of children and adolescents to marital conflict scenarios as a function of the emotionality of conflict endings. *Merrill-Palmer Quarterly, 42,* 1–21.

Davies, P. T., Myers, R. L., Cummings, E. M., & Heindel, S. (1999). Adult conflict history and children's subsequent responses to conflict. *Journal of Family Psychology, 13,* 610–628.

Davies, P. T., & Windle, M. (1997). Gender-specific pathways between maternal depressive symptoms, family discord, and adolescent adjustment. *Developmental Psychology, 33,* 657–668.

Deal, J. E. (1996). Marital conflict and differential treatment of siblings. *Family Process, 35,* 333–346.

El-Sheikh, M. (1994). Children's emotional and physiological responses to interadult angry behavior: The role of history of interparental hostility. *Journal of Abnormal Child Psychology, 22,* 661–678.

El-Sheikh, M. (1997). Children's responses to adult-adult and mother-child arguments: The role of parental marital conflict and distress. *Journal of Family Psychology, 11,* 165–175.

El-Sheikh, M., & Cheskes, J. (1995). Background verbal and physical anger: A comparison of children's responses to adult-adult and adult-child arguments. *Child Development, 66,* 446–458.

El-Sheikh, M., & Cummings, E. M. (1995). Children's responses to angry adult behavior as a function of experimentally manipulated exposure to resolved and unresolved conflict. *Social Development, 4,* 75–91.

El-Sheikh, M., Cummings, E. M., & Reiter, S. (1996). Preschoolers' responses to interadult conflict: The role of experimentally manipulated exposure to resolved and unresolved arguments. *Journal of Abnormal Child Psychology, 24,* 665–679.

El-Sheikh, M., & Reiter, S. (1996). Children's responding to live interadult conflict: The role of form of anger expression. *Journal of Abnormal Child Psychology, 24,* 401–415.

Emery, R. E. (1982). Interparental conflict and the children of discord and divorce. *Psychological Bulletin, 92,* 310–330.

Emery, R. E., & O'Leary, K. D. (1982). Children's perceptions of marital discord and behavior problems of boys and girls. *Journal of Abnormal Child Psychology, 10,* 11–24.

Fincham, F. D. (1994). Understanding the association between marital conflict and child adjustment: Overview. *Journal of Family Psychology, 2,* 123–127.

Fincham, F. D., Grych, J. H., & Osborne, L. N. (1994). Does marital conflict cause child maladjustment? Directions and challenges for longitudinal research. *Journal of Family Psychology, 8,* 128–140.

Gordis, E. B., Margolin, G., & John, R. S. (1997). Marital aggression, observed parental hostility, and child behavior during triadic family interaction. *Journal of Family Psychology, 11,* 76–89.

Gore, S., Aseltine, R. H., & Colten, M. E. (1993). Gender, social-relational involvement, and depression. *Journal of Research on Adolescence, 3,* 101–125.

Gottman, J. M., Coan, J., Carrere, S., & Swanson, C. (1998). Predicting marital happiness and stability from newlywed interactions. *Journal of Marriage and the Family, 60,* 5–22.

Grych, J. H. (1998). Children's appraisals of interparental conflict: Situational and contextual influences. *Journal of Family Psychology, 12,* 437–453.

Grych, J. H., & Fincham, F. D. (1990). Marital conflict and children's adjustment: A cognitive-contextual framework. *Psychological Bulletin, 108,* 267–290.

Grych, J. H., & Fincham, F. D. (1992). Interventions for children of divorce: Towards greater integration of research and action. *Psychological Bulletin, 111,* 434–454.

Grych, J. H., & Fincham, F. D. (1993). Children's appraisals of marital conflict: Initial investigations of the cognitive-contextual framework. *Child Development, 64,* 215–230.

Grych, J. H., Seid, M., & Fincham, F. D. (1992). Assessing marital conflict from the child's perspective. *Child Development, 63,* 558–572.

Helgeson, V. S. (1994). Relation of agency and communion to well-being: Evidence and potential explanations. *Psychological Bulletin, 116,* 412–428.

Hennessy, K. D., Rabideau, G. J., Cicchetti, D., & Cummings, E. M. (1994). Responses of physically abused and nonabused children to different forms of interadult anger. *Child Development, 65,* 815–828.

Hetherington, E. M., Stanley-Hagan, M., & Anderson, E. R. (1989). Marital transitions: A child's perspective. *American Psychologist, 44,* 303–312.

Hill, J. P., & Lynch, M. E. (1983). The intensification of gender-related role expectations during early adolescence. In J. Brooks-Gunn & A. C. Petersen (Eds.), *Girls at puberty: Biological and psychosocial perspectives* (pp. 175–201). New York: Plenum Press.

Hops, H. (1997). Intergenerational transmission of depressive symptoms: Gender and developmental considerations. In C. Mundt, M. Goldstein, K. Hahlweg, & P. Fiedler (Eds.), *Proceedings of the Symposium of Interpersonal Factors in the Origin and Course of Affective Disorders.* London: Royal College of Psychiatrists.

Howes, P., & Markman, H. J. (1989). Marital quality and child functioning: A longitudinal investigation. *Child Development, 60,* 1044–1051.

Johnson, P. L., & O'Leary, K. D. (1987). Parental behavior patterns and conduct disorders in girls. *Journal of Abnormal Child Psychology, 15,* 573–581.

Johnston, J. R., Gonzalez, R., & Campbell, L. E. (1987). Ongoing post-divorce conflict and child disturbance. *Journal of Abnormal Child Psychology, 15,* 165–173.

Jouriles, E. N., Bourg, W. J., & Farris, A. M. (1991). Marital adjustment and child conduct problems: A comparison of the correlation across subsamples. *Journal of Consulting and Clinical Psychology, 59,* 354–357.

Jouriles, E. N., & Farris, A. M. (1992). Effects of marital conflict on subsequent parent-son interactions. *Behavior Therapy, 23,* 355–374.

Jouriles, E. N., & LeCompte, S. H. (1991). Husbands' aggression toward wives and mothers' and fathers' aggression toward children: Moderating effects of child gender. *Journal of Consulting and Clinical Psychology, 59,* 190–192.

Jouriles, E. N., & Norwood, W. D. (1995). Physical aggression toward boys and girls in families characterized by the battering of women. *Journal of Family Psychology, 9,* 69–78.

Katz, L. F., & Gottman, J. M. (1993). Patterns of marital conflict predict children's internalizing and externalizing behaviors. *Developmental Psychology, 29,* 940–950.

Katz, L. F., & Gottman, J. M. (1996). Spillover effects of marital conflict: In search of parenting and coparenting mechanisms. In J. P. McHale & P. A. Cowan (Eds.), *Understanding how family-level dynamics affect children's development: Studies of two-parent families.* San Francisco, CA: Jossey-Bass.

Kerig, P. K. (1996). Assessing the links between interparental conflict and child adjustment: The conflicts and problem-solving scales. *Journal of Family Psychology, 10,* 454–473.

Kerig, P. K. (1998a). Moderators and mediators of the effects of interparental conflict on children's adjustment. *Journal of Abnormal Child Psychology, 26,* 199–212.

Kerig, P. K. (1998b). Gender and appraisals as mediators of adjustment in children exposed to interparental violence. *Journal of Family Violence, 15,* 345–363.

Kerig, P. K. (1999). Gender issues in the effects of exposure to violence on children. *Journal of Emotional Abuse, 2,* 87–105.

Kerig, P. K., Cowan, P. A., & Cowan, C. P. (1993). Marital quality and gender differences in parent-child interaction. *Developmental Psychology, 29,* 931–939.

Kerig, P. K., Fedorowicz, A. E., Brown, C. A., Patenaude, R. L., & Warren, M. (1998). When warriors are worriers: Gender and children's coping with interparental violence. *Journal of Emotional Abuse, 1,* 89–114.

Kohlberg, L. (1966). A cognitive-developmental analysis of children's sex-role concepts and attitudes. In E. E. Maccoby (Ed.), *The development of sex differences.* Stanford, CA: Stanford University Press.

Lindahl, K. M., Clements, M., & Markman, H. (1997). Predicting marital and parent functioning in dyads and triads: A longitudinal investigation of marital processes. *Journal of Family Psychology, 11,* 139–151.

Maccoby, E. E., & Jacklin, C. N. (1974). *The psychology of sex differences.* Stanford, CA: Stanford University Press.

McGuire, S., Dunn, J., & Plomin, R. (1995). Maternal differential treatment of siblings and children's behavioral problems: A longitudinal study. *Development and Psychopathology, 7,* 515–528.

McHale, J. P. (1995). Coparenting and triadic interactions during infancy: The roles of marital distress and child gender. *Developmental Psychology, 31,* 985–996.

Osborne, L. N., & Fincham, F. D. (1996). Marital conflict, parent-child relationships, and child adjustment: Does gender matter? *Merrill-Palmer Quarterly, 42,* 48–75.

Parke, R. D., & Tinsley, B. J. (1987). Family interaction in infancy: A reevaluation. *Family Coordinator, 25,* 365–371.

Petersen, A. C. (1988). Adolescent development. *Annual Review of Psychology, 39,* 583–607.

Reid, W. J., & Crisafulli, A. (1990). Marital discord and child behavior problems: A meta-analysis. *Journal of Abnormal Child Psychology, 18,* 105–117.

Roecker, C. E., Dubow, E. F., & Donaldson, D. (1996). Cross-situational patterns in children's coping with observed interpersonal conflict. *Journal of Clinical Child Psychology, 25,* 288–299.

Ruble, D. N., Balaban, T., & Cooper, J. (1981). Gender constancy and the effects of sex-typed televised toy commercials. *Child Development, 52,* 667–673.

Rutter, M. (1970). Sex differences in response to family stress. In E. J. Anthony & C. Koupernik (Eds.), *The child in his family* (pp. 165–196). New York: Wiley.

Steil, J. M., & Weltman, K. (1991). Marital inequality: The importance of resources, personal attribute, and social norms on career valuing and the allocation of domestic responsibilities. *Sex Roles, 24,* 161–179.

Thompson, E., & Walker, A. (1989). Gender in families: Women and men in marriage, work, and parenthood. *Journal of Marriage and the Family, 51,* 845–872.

Vuchinich, S., Emery, R. E., & Cassidy, J. (1988). Family members as third parties in dyadic family conflict: Strategies, alliances, and outcomes. *Child Development, 59,* 1293–1302.

Windle, M. (1992). A longitudinal study of stress buffering for adolescent problem behaviors. *Developmental Psychology, 28,* 522–530.

Wolfe, D. A., Jaffe, P., Wilson, S. K., & Zak, L. (1985). Children of battered women: The relation of child behavior to family violence and maternal stress. *Journal of Consulting and Clinical Psychology, 53,* 657–665.

Zahn-Waxler, C. (1993). Warriors and worriers: Gender and psychopathology. *Development and Psychopathology, 5,* 79–90.

4 Ethnic Minority Status, Interparental Conflict, and Child Adjustment

Vonnie C. McLoyd, Camille I. Harper, and Nikeea Lynell Copeland

Bolstered by evidence that marital conflict surrounding divorce, rather than the breakup of the family, is a major source of psychosocial problems in children from divorced households, the impact of interparental conflict on child functioning has emerged as an important focus of study. Marital conflict is associated with a number of adjustment problems, including higher levels of depression, anxiety, and aggression and lower levels of academic achievement and social competence (Emery, 1982; Grych & Fincham, 1990). In this chapter, we focus attention on the role of ethnicity in a range of issues related to interparental conflict and children's development. In particular, we consider the relation of ethnicity to the frequency, nature, and management of interparental conflict and to children's response to interparental conflict.

The chapter is divided into four major sections. First, we examine the relation between ethnicity and interparental conflict. Because research on this issue is so sparse, we also include in our discussion studies of ethnicity and marital conflict, even though the samples in these studies may include childless couples. We then turn to studies of the impact of interparental conflict, family conflict, and divorce on children from ethnic minority families. In the third section, we take up the question of whether and how ethnicity moderates children's response to interparental and family conflict. Finally, we highlight several issues whose consideration in future research may advance our understanding of the role of culture and ethnicity in the experience and impact of interparental conflict.

Several limitations of existing research mitigate against incisive analyses of and definitive conclusions about the issues discussed in

The second and third authors contributed equally to this chapter. The order of their names was determined by a coin toss.

this chapter. First, empirical studies of these issues are sparse and relevant studies of ethnic minority families other than African Americans are sparser still (Hines, 1997; Lawson & Thompson, 1994). The paucity of studies focusing expressly on ethnicity as a moderator of interparental conflict is especially glaring. Second, most of the studies we review here typify what Bronfenbrenner (1986) termed the "social address" model of analysis. That is, analyses are limited to a comparison of outcomes for spouses and children who differ in terms of ethnicity, with no empirical tests of intervening structures or processes through which ethnicity might influence these outcomes. Even when research studies include ethnically diverse samples, the absence of any theory on how ethnicity or culture might shape interparental or family conflict and its impact on children and their home environments often results in ethnicity being used as a control variable (e.g., Jekielek, 1998; Menaghan & Parcel, 1995). In such instances, ethnicity in effect is cast as a "nuisance" variable, with the amount of variance due to ethnicity partitioned as a strategy to reduce extraneous variance as much as possible to give the focal independent variables a chance to show their significance (McLoyd, 1998). In view of the limitations of the extant research literature, we draw few conclusions about the relations among ethnicity, interparental conflict, and children's adjustment. Rather, we highlight emergent themes and offer speculations about why ethnicity or culture may moderate interparental conflict and children's response to it.

Ethnic Differences in Interparental Conflict

Strong evidence exists that children's response to interparental conflict is shaped by the frequency and intensity of conflict, with more child adjustment problems being associated with more frequent exposure to interparental conflict and exposure to more intense forms of interparental conflict (e.g., physical violence). The content (e.g., parental disagreement about chores versus childrearing values) and resolution of interparental conflict also appear to moderate the latter's impact on children, but the evidence of these effects is neither plentiful nor robust (Grych & Fincham, 1990). In view of these potentially moderating influences, we first turn our attention to the question of whether ethnicity influences dimensions of marital and interparental conflict.

Frequency of Conflict

Obtaining accurate and reliable estimates of the prevalence and frequency of interparental conflict within a population is difficult. Use of divorce rates among couples with children as a proxy for the frequency and intensity of interparental conflict is highly problematic. Divorce rates are higher among African Americans than other racial or ethnic groups (in 1990, for example, the percentage of African American, European American, and Latino women aged 40–44 who were divorced after their first marriage was 45%, 35%, and 27%, respectively) (U.S. Census Bureau, 1997), and African American children are twice as likely as European American children to experience at least one parental divorce (Hetherington, Bridges, & Insabella, 1998). It is unclear, however, whether these ethnic disparities reflect differences in response to marital conflict or differences in the prevalence, frequency, or intensity of marital conflict. Because of the difficulty and expense of conducting observations, most studies of interparental conflict rely exclusively on self-report measures. One of the limitations of this measurement strategy is the difficulty of ruling out the possibility that ethnic differences in the reported frequency of conflict reflect differences in willingness to acknowledge conflict, definitions of conflict, and beliefs about disclosing family-related information. It is critical to bear this in mind when interpreting findings based on self-report measures.

Early research suggested that relations among African American couples and families were more conflictual than their European American counterparts. However, as Henggeler and Tavormina (1980) noted, such findings may have resulted from methodological flaws such as confounding of race and social class, biased sampling, and use of measures of unknown or questionable reliability and validity for African American families. Failing to control for social class when examining ethnic differences was a common error in early studies of interparental discord (O'Keefe, 1994b). Empirical study of the frequency of marital and interparental conflict across ethnic groups continues to be sparse. Acitelli, Douvan, and Veroff (1997) noted that in an exhaustive review of longitudinal research on marriages conducted by Karney and Bradbury (1995), only 8 percent of the samples in these studies included both African Americans and European Americans.

The few recent studies of ethnic differences in the frequency of marital conflict yield inconsistent findings, perhaps due partly to differences in methodology and sample characteristics. In a sample of 199 African American and 174 European American newlywed couples (5–8 months into marriage) drawn from couples filing for marriage licenses in a largely urban county in eastern Michigan, Oggins, Veroff, and Leber (1993) found no differences between the two ethnic groups in perceived frequency of marital conflict, controlling for household income, parental status, length of cohabitation before marriage, and education. In contrast, McDonald and DeMaris's (1995) analysis of data from a nationally representative sample indicated that reports of marital conflict were more common among African Americans than European Americans.

In a retrospective study of spouses in marriages that had lasted at least 20 years, Mackey and O'Brien (1998) sought to determine whether ethnic groups differed in conflict at different stages of marriage. Their findings, while intriguing, must be interpreted with considerable caution because of the real possibility of memory distortion and because the findings have not been replicated. These researchers found ethnic differences in major marital conflicts (conflicts described by respondents as highly distressing and as having significantly disruptive effects on their marital relationship) depending on the stage of the marriage. More African American couples than Mexican American and European American couples reported major conflicts during the early, prechildbearing years of marriage. However, when asked about the childrearing years, fewer African American couples reported major conflicts than did their Mexican American and European American counterparts.

Adopting a life-course perspective, Mackey and O'Brien (1998) speculated that African American couples may have had more frequent major conflicts during the early years of marriage because they were more likely to adopt nontraditional gender roles. As they explained:

Equity and sharing of role responsibilities, including the rearing of children, needed to be negotiated and may have fueled conflict among African American couples. Working out roles through negotiation was different for other respondents in which marital roles were ascribed along traditional gender lines... When roles were allocated according to accepted cultural mores ... there may have been less need to negotiate one's place in the relationship, at least in the early years of marriage. (pp. 133–138)

African American women's historically higher rate of labor force participation (as compared to their European American counterparts) has resulted in smaller gaps in power between African American spouses, a factor that may impact marital expectations and ultimately, the quality of marital relations. For example, Hatchett, Veroff, and Douvan (1995) found that among African Americans, but not among European Americans, marriages were more unstable if wives perceived role inflexibility in relation to household tasks, and if husbands reported more of a power imbalance in decision making.

Intensity and Management of Conflict

For our purposes, studies of the relation between ethnicity and intensity of marital conflict warrant special attention, as this dimension of
conflict is a substantially stronger predictor of child adjustment than is
frequency of interparental conflict (Buehler et al., 1998). Interparental
conflict marked by physical aggression and/or high levels of negative
affect, including denigration, anger, hostility, and verbal aggression, is
especially destructive to children's well-being (Buehler et al., 1998;
Hetherington et al., 1998). Children in high-conflict, nondivorced
families have more psychosocial problems than do children in
divorced families or children in low-conflict, nondivorced families
(Amato & Keith, 1991). Furthermore, children remaining in two-parent
families characterized by high marital conflict exhibit more anxiety and
depression or withdrawal than children who have experienced high
levels of parental conflict but whose parents divorce or separate
(Jekielek, 1998).

Physical Violence. Ethnicity has been linked to physical violence
among spouses. Data from almost 7,000 currently married respondents
in the National Survey of Families and Households (NSFH) indicated
that even with controls for income, education, urbanicity, age and
number of children, and duration of marriage, African Americans were
1.58 times more likely and Latinos 0.53 times less likely than European
Americans to report that marital arguments during the past year had
escalated into physical violence (i.e., hitting, shoving, throwing things
at spouse) (Sorenson, Upchurch, & Shen, 1996). Ethnicity was related to
neither the identity of the person committing the violence (wife, husband, both partners) nor the identity of the person injured. The second
National Family Violence Survey found higher rates of husband-to-
wife violence and severe violence among both African Americans and
Latinos, compared to European Americans. Rates of overall wife-to-
husband violence and severe violence for Latinos were intermediate
between those of African Americans and European Americans, with
African American females having the highest rates. Controlling for
inequalities in income and social class reduces, but typically does not
eliminate, the relation between ethnicity and spousal violence
(Hampton & Coner-Edwards, 1993). Some studies do not find these
patterns of ethnic differences, but they tend to be based on small, nonrandom community samples or samples drawn from mental health
facilities (e.g., Lockhart, 1991; Proctor, Vosler, & Sirles, 1993).

It is plausible that the effect on children of exposure to spousal violence and ethnic differences in these effects depends partly on the vic-

tim's response to and causal attributions about spousal violence. Latino women, compared to non-Hispanic white women, are reported to be more tolerant of physical aggression by their husbands and in their perception of what constitutes physical abuse (Asbury, 1993; Gondolf, Fisher, & McFerron, 1991). In addition, some research finds that Latino women in shelters have experienced longer duration of abuse, compared to African Americans and European Americans (Gondolf et al., 1991). If indeed these ethnic differences are subsequently replicated in well-controlled studies, we need to know the extent to which they are driven by disparities in economic well-being, educational credentials, and employability. Latino women in shelters tend to be poorer and less educated and have larger families than their African American and European American counterparts. In some cases, language difficulties also impede employment and economic independence and increase Latino women's vulnerability to long-term physical abuse (Gondolf et al., 1991).

Peterson-Lewis and colleagues (1988) speculate that African American women who are abused by their husbands are more likely than their European American counterparts to attribute the causes of the violence to the larger society, seeing such behavior as a reflection of the treatment that African American men receive from the dominant culture. They also are thought to be less likely to involve the police, believing that African American males are more likely to be arrested and to be the victims of police maltreatment than their European counterparts. To the extent that these reportedly ethnicity-related attitudes and attributions are communicated to children and/or temper the emotional responses to spousal violence displayed to children, the adverse psychological impact of spousal violence may be attenuated in African American and Latino children, as compared to European American children.

An important issue deserving as much attention as ethnic differences in spousal violence concerns the factors that predict couple violence within different ethnic groups. Hampton and Gelles (1994) found that lower income, younger age of couple, shorter residence in a community, unemployment of the husband, being hit as an adolescent, and witnessing parental violence were significant predictors of husband-to-wife violence within African American families. Some of these variables (i.e., income, age, witnessing parental violence) also have been found to predict couple violence in a national, ethnically diverse sample (Choice, Lamke, & Pittman, 1995). Data from the Los Angeles Epidemiologic Catchment Area (ECA) study indicate that rates of spousal violence among Mexican Americans varied according to immi-

gration status. Mexican Americans born in the United States had rates
2.4 times higher than those born in Mexico (the latter group had rates
equivalent to non-Hispanic whites) (Sorenson & Telles, 1991). We do
not know what factors mediate this difference, though several seem
worthy of exploration (e.g., perceived acceptability of violence toward
spouse, cultural conflicts, sense of relative deprivation, embeddedness
within extended family, household composition, and internalization of
mainstream values regarding autonomy and self-reliance).

Affect and Expressive Styles. Degree of negative affect or hostility
expressed by spouses and parents during conflictual encounters can
also be viewed as an indicator of the intensity of marital conflict (Grych
& Fincham, 1990). Ethnic differences have not been reported for these
types of indicators, but too little relevant work has been done to declare
the issue resolved. Controlling for lower income and education, greater
number of children, and greater experience with cohabitation for
African Americans compared with European Americans, Oggins et al.
(1993) found that African American and European American newlywed couples did not differ in the frequency with which they reportedly
responded to conflict either with destructive reactions (e.g., insulting
or calling spouse names, bringing up the past, having to have the last
word, yelling or shouting at the spouse) or constructive reactions (e.g.,
saying nice things, trying to find out how spouse was feeling, trying to
make spouse laugh).

The issue of affective responses to marital conflict is part of the
broader question of how partners cope with or handle marital conflict.
There is some evidence of ethnic differences in these outcomes, but
whether such differences translate into ethnic differences in children's
adjustment is unknown. Furthermore, the findings are conflicting.
Mackey and O'Brien's (1998) retrospective study found that reported
use of confrontational styles of conflict management for three periods
of marriage (prechildbearing years, childrearing years, empty-nest
years) was greater among African American husbands than European
American and Mexican American husbands. A confrontational style
was defined as any effort to express one's thoughts and feelings to the
spouse in a face-to-face manner. Interestingly, ethnicity was unrelated
to wives' reports of how their husbands managed marital conflict.

On the other hand, in Oggins et al.'s (1993) study of newlyweds,
African Americans were significantly more likely than European
Americans to report that they handled conflict by withdrawing (i.e.,
becoming quiet and pulling away) or leaving for a while to cool down
before talking out the disagreement. In addition, they were more likely
than European Americans to report that it is easier to talk with some-

one other than the spouse, a finding that may be linked with spouses trying to avoid the negative affect that might ensue when difficult issues are openly discussed with their partners. Ironically, African Americans also reported more disclosing communication with their spouses than did European Americans (e.g., revealing very intimate things or personal feelings, or telling spouse what you want or need from the relationship). However, the latter communicative style does not appear to extend into their styles of conflict management and resolution, given that avoidance of conflict was a more common pattern among African American couples than among European American couples. In Sistler and Moore's (1996) study of elderly couples (mean length of marriage was approximately 40 years), ethnicity was unrelated to couples' reported avoidance in response to marital conflict, but African American couples were more likely than their European American counterparts to seek social support and engage in wishful thinking to cope with marital difficulties.

The apparent disparity in the findings reported by Oggins et al. (1993) and Mackey and O'Brien (1998) may reflect differences in the retrospective period at issue and the stage of marriage that characterized the samples. Whereas Oggins et al.'s sample was comprised of newlyweds, Mackey and O'Brien studied couples who, in addition to having children who were at least age 18 or out of high school, had been married at least 20 years. In addition, as noted previously, it is highly plausible that memories elicited in Mackey and O'Brien's study, especially of the prechildbearing and childrearing years, were distorted substantially with the passage of time.

Life Course Changes in Conflict. In addition to assessing ethnic differences in marital conflict and communication at one time point in marriage, researchers have explored whether ethnic differences exist in changes in marital quality, marital conflict, and responses to marital conflict. Using a subset of the sample in Oggins et al.'s (1993) investigation, Crohan (1996) addressed these questions in a sample of couples who made the transition to parenthood within the first two years of marriage. The longitudinal study, conducted in the third year of marriage, included only those couples in this sample who did not have a child at the time of the first interview. Among both African Americans and European Americans, couples who made the transition to parenthood reported more frequent conflicts, more marital tension, and a greater decline in marital happiness than couples who remained childless. Conflict behaviors among new parents were linked to marital happiness in similar ways for African American and European American spouses. Destructive conflict (e.g., insulting spouse, calling spouse names) and active avoidance (leaving the scene of the conflict to cool down) predicted lower marital happiness for both new mothers and fathers, whereas passive avoidance predicted higher marital happiness. Scholars have cautioned that although conflict avoidance may be functional in the early years of marriage and parenthood, it may undermine marital happiness in the long run because the conflict is never adequately resolved (Crohan, 1996; Gottman & Krokoff, 1989).

Among European American couples, but not African American couples, the tendency to respond to marital conflict by becoming quiet and withdrawn (passive avoidance) increased after the birth of their child. Crohan speculated that the increase in avoidance behavior among European American couples may be due to limited time and energy that new parents have to devote to conflict resolution and/or their concern about protecting their children from the negative side of conflicts (e.g., expressions of anger). Although African American couples did not respond to parenthood with an increase in passive avoidance, it bears underscoring that levels of passive avoidance prior to the transition to parenthood were actually higher among African American couples than European American couples, whereas the two groups were roughly comparable in their reported use of this strategy following parenthood.

Qualitative data on use of confrontational styles of conflict management across the course of marriage, which presumably are negatively related to passive avoidance, are not consonant with the ethnic differences reported by Crohan (1996). Among the middle-aged and elderly couples in Mackey and O'Brien's (1998) study, husbands' use of confrontational styles of managing conflict was relatively stable from the prechildbearing years through the childrearing years, according to self-reports and reports by wives. This pattern held for African American, European American, and Mexican American couples.

Content of Conflict

The issue of ethnic differences in the content of interparental conflict has received little systematic research attention to date. It is an intriguing question in view of speculations that marital conflict concerning the child and childrearing may be more distressing to the child and more closely related to behavior problems (because it leads to inconsistent discipline) than other topics of marital conflict (Grych & Fincham, 1990; Hetherington et al., 1998). Lockhart (1991) found associations between ethnicity and sources of conflict in her study of a sample deliberately drawn to maximize social class heterogeneity. European American respondents reported more conflicts around the man's job, employment, and friends than did African American respondents. The husband's jealousy was a source of marital conflict more frequently and children a source of conflict less frequently among middle-class African Americans as compared to middle-class European Americans. Among elderly couples, ethnicity appears to be unrelated to the types of issues that evoke marital conflict (Sistler & Moore, 1996). Other research suggests that during the first year of marriage between individuals in young- to middle-adulthood, the range of topics that evoke disagreements (e.g., money, religion, children, leisure, spouse's family) is narrower among African American couples than European American couples (Oggins et al., 1993).

Summary

Ethnicity does not appear to be a reliable predictor of the frequency of marital conflict. The relation between ethnicity and intensity of marital conflict seems to depend on the marker of intensity. Whereas no relations have been reported between ethnicity and level of negative affect or verbal aggression expressed during marital conflict, links between ethnicity and physical violence among spouses have been found in national surveys, with African Americans having higher rates than Latinos and non-Hispanic whites. This apparent inconsistency may reflect the marked differences in the amount of research attention to these two types of outcomes. There is a dearth of research on all forms of spousal/partner conflict among ethnic minorities, but African Americans are more likely to be included in studies of physical violence than studies focusing primarily on nonphysical marital conflict (e.g., Julian & McKenry, 1993; Sorenson et al., 1996).

African Americans, compared to European Americans, have been found to respond more frequently to conflict by confronting their spouse (wives), withdrawing, seeking social support, and engaging in wishful thinking. Although these ethnic differences in conflict management styles do not appear altogether consistent, it is possible that ostensibly contradictory conflict management styles (e.g., withdrawal versus confrontation) may coexist. Following the transition to parenthood, both African Americans and European Americans experience more frequent conflicts, more marital tension, and a greater decline in marital happiness than couples who remain childless.

The Impact of Interparental and Family Conflict on Ethnic Minority Children

The limited amount of research bearing on the question of how interparental conflict affects adjustment in ethnic minority children suggests that family and parental conflict can adversely affect the functioning of African American and Mexican American children. African American children exposed to higher levels of family and inter-parental conflict, compared to those who experience lower levels of family and interparental conflict, report increased depression, more acute feelings of hopelessness (DuRant, Getts, Cadenhead, Emans, & Woods, 1995), more psychological distress, lower levels of satisfaction with their family climate, and less satisfaction with their social lives (Dancy & Handel, 1984). They also spend more time with their friends (Dancy & Handel, 1984), and they have lower levels of academic com-petence (grades and performance on tests of cognitive ability) and self-regulation (Brody, Stoneman, & Flor, 1995) and higher levels of externalizing behavior (Mason, Cauce, Gonzales, Hiraga, & Grove, 1994). Externalizing problems are especially likely following parental separation among African American children who blame themselves for marital conflict (Bussell, 1995). Even within the context of danger-ous or disadvantaged environments, conflictual relations within the family can have negative consequences for adolescents' mental health (DuRant et al., 1995). Furthermore, there is evidence that increased severity of family violence is associated with lower academic self-esteem among African American adolescents, and lower academic achievement among African American females (Spencer, Cole, Dupree, Glymph, & Pierre, 1984).

Child-focused studies of family conflict in Mexican American fami-lies, although rare, are distinctive from those focusing on African American children in that they explore both outcomes and mediating processes. An investigation by Dumka, Roosa, and Jackson (1997) of 121 low-income Mexican immigrant and Mexican American mothers and their fourth-grade children indicated that family conflict (par-ent–parent conflict, parent–child conflict, and parent–relative conflict) as reported by the child, but not the mother, predicted lower levels of supportive parenting among mothers and higher levels of depression and conduct disorder in children. Moreover, the researchers found evi-dence that low levels of supportive parenting among mothers medi-ated the relationship between family conflict and children's depression. In addition to its substantive contribution about process issues, this study points up the significance of the identity of the infor-mant about family conflict. It appears that children noticed and responded to events to which mothers were either oblivious or unwill-ing to disclose, lending support to the claim that children's perceptions of marital hostility and conflict are better indicators than parent reports because they represent a better estimate of what the child actually observes or experiences (Buehler et al., 1998; Emery & O'Leary, 1982).

Buehler et al. (1998) found that internalizing and externalizing behavior among Mexican American and European American youth was more strongly predicted by hostile conflict styles among parents (e.g., calling each other names, threatening each other) than frequency of disagreement among parents. Even more intriguing was their assessment of whether the associations between conflict styles and youth problem behavior are specialized. That is, they hypothesized that parents' use of an overt conflict style is uniquely associated with youth externalizing problems, whereas their use of a covert conflict style is uniquely associated with youth internalizing problems. They found support for the latter hypothesis but not the former.

In summary, studies to date suggest that ethnic minority children, like majority children, respond to family and interparental conflict with increased psychological distress and lower levels of psychosocial and academic competence. This area of research awaits progress on several fronts. More attention to parental conflict as a specific subcategory of family conflict is essential. Also needed is examination of a variety of child outcomes and identification of the conditions under which dysfunction resulting from interparental conflict is either more or less likely. The studies reviewed here examine the impact of interparental or family conflict on ethnic minority children living in a variety of physical and social environments. Whether these different environmental contexts moderate the impact of interparental conflict is unknown. Given the extreme variations in the ecologies within which these children develop, one might not expect to find a uniform pattern of findings on the impact of interparental conflict even within groups of ethnic minority children.

Ethnicity as a Moderator of Children's Response to Interparental and Family Conflict

The aforementioned studies report adverse effects of family and interparental conflict on the adjustment of African American and Mexican American children that parallel effects found among European American children. They do not tell us, however, whether or not ethnic minority status accentuates, attenuates, or has no influence on the relation between family/interparental conflict and child adjustment. Speculation has centered largely around the possibility of an attenuation effect. In particular, scholars have speculated that ethnic minority children are less vulnerable than non-Hispanic white children to the adverse effects of parental discord, separation, and divorce for two reasons. They point out, first, that ethnic minority children are more likely than non-Hispanic white children to be embedded in extended family networks and, second, that marital discord and dissolution as experienced by ethnic minority children often occurs within the context of an overabundance of ethnic- and race-related stressful events and ongoing conditions, muting the unique effects of marital discord and dissolution. Because non-Hispanic white children generally live in more favorable environmental and social contexts and enjoy greater opportunities for positive growth than ethnic minority children, it is thought that parental discord, separation, and divorce may have more pronounced effects on the former than the latter (Amato & Keith, 1991; Smith, 1997). Although the attenuation hypothesis lacks strong, direct empirical support, three kinds of evidence converge to bolster its plausibility.

First, Amato and Keith's (1991) meta-analysis comparing effect sizes across studies of parental divorce and adult well-being indicated that the negative consequences of parental divorce were significantly greater for European American adults than for African American adults. In particular, European American adults from divorced families of origin showed greater increases in separation, divorce, and one-parent family status and larger decreases in educational attainment than did their African American counterparts.

Two prospective studies focusing on child behavior following marital transitions, one race comparative and the other not, offer evidence somewhat along the same lines. Mason et al. (1994) found that African American adolescents in one-parent households had higher rates of externalizing behavior than those in two-parent households, but adolescents living in two-parent households where the second parent was a stepparent did not differ in rates of misbehavior from those living with both biological parents. In Shaw, Winslow, and Flanagan's (1999) prospective study of low-income boys living in always-two-parent, to-be-divorced, already-divorced, and always-single-parent families, to-be-divorced Black mothers were observed to be more rejecting than their White counterparts, and more rejecting than Black or White mothers in always-two-parent families. Nonetheless, it was White boys, not Black boys, whose externalizing behavior was significantly affected by marital group differences. Two-year-old White boys from to-be-divorced families had higher externalizing scores than White boys from always-two-parent families. In contrast, Black boys in to-be-divorced versus always-two-parent families did not differ in their level of externalizing behavior. But race neither moderated the effects of marital group differences on internalizing behavior, nor distinguished how children responded to living in an already-divorced versus always-two-parent family.

Second, a few scattered findings in the literature intimate differential responses to interparental conflict as a function of ethnicity. For example, in Buehler et al.'s (1998) study of youth in grades 5 to 8, the association between overt hostile conflict styles among parents (e.g., calling each other names, threatening each other) and youth externalizing problems was much weaker among Mexican American youth than among European American – the slope for the latter group (which included some ethnically mixed youth) was twice that of the slope for Mexican American youth. Likewise, Smith (1997) reported that the impact of parental separation on the school grades of seventh and ninth graders was smaller among African Americans than European Americans. However, in Lindahl and Malik's (1999) recent study, marital discord was found to affect externalizing behavior similarly in Latino and White boys.

O'Keefe (1994a) found that 7–13-year-old Latino and African American children residing in temporary shelters with their battered mothers (the majority of mothers were married or cohabitating) had elevated scores (relative to normative samples) for internalizing and externalizing problems equivalent to those for their European American counterparts. However, African American mothers rated their children significantly higher in social competence than did either European American or Latino mothers. Although this finding may reflect biases in mothers' perceptions of their children, it also may be indicative that African American children from violent homes are forced to assume greater responsibility at an earlier age compared to children from other ethnic backgrounds. Evidence exists that African American parents in the general population expect children to overcome dependency needs and assume responsibility at an earlier age than do European American parents (Bartz & Levine, 1978). Echoes of this theme emerged in McKenry and Fine's (1993) study of reported maternal behavior following divorce. Although African American mothers did not differ from European American mothers in parenting behavior, involvement, or satisfaction following a divorce, they had higher expectations for child competence (e.g., being independent, controlling temper, complying with parents' requests) than European American mothers. In addition, African American mothers rated the quality of their child's life more positively than did European American mothers. It is possible that these differences in perceptions and expectations will differentially influence children's adjustment to divorce. Given that these reports likely reflect mothers' actual views about their child's life as well as their feelings about their current situation, the ethnic differences may indicate a higher level of optimism in

African American mothers in the face of relationship difficulties. Indeed, a number of studies report more positive psychological functioning among African American women than European American women following separation and divorce (see Lawson & Thompson, 1994, for a review of these studies).

Finally, indirect support for the attenuation hypothesis comes from a large international survey study of college students from 39 countries on six continents. Gohm, Oishi, Darlington, and Diener (1998) found that the negative association of parental marital status and conflict (constructed as a single variable with 7 levels) to life satisfaction and affect balance (negative affect minus positive affect) was weaker in students from collectivist countries (e.g., Ghana, Zimbabwe, China, Colombia) than students from individualistic countries (e.g., United States, Germany, Japan, Italy). Collectivism lessened both the impact of divorce following a high-conflict marriage and the impact of marital conflict when a parent remarried. The authors interpreted these findings as evidence that increased levels of social support offered by members of the extended family in countries that are more collectivistic than individualistic ameliorates the negative impact of parental divorce and parental marital conflict on child adjustment. They argue forcefully that "the availability of social support is an important aspect of the broad cultural dimension of individualism-collectivism" (p. 321), noting that individualistic cultures emphasize the importance and desirability of personal independence and autonomy, while collectivist cultures encourage interdependence, stress the importance of obligations to others rather than self-interest, and encourage harmony with others rather than autonomy.

Partly as a strategy to ease economic hardship, extended family coresidential arrangements and sharing of resources among extended family members have traditionally been more prevalent among African American and Latino families. Research on social support networks among African Americans consistently reports a pattern of frequent socializing among family members, a high degree of residential propensity among related households, and an emphasis on participation in family occasions. Embeddedness in extended family networks has been found to improve the quality of care children receive and to temper the negative effects on achievement and social adjustment of growing up in a mother-headed household. The bulk of evidence suggests that these networks have more indirect than direct effects on the child through their effects on the mother (e.g., improved psychological functioning, higher educational achievement) (for a review of relevant studies, see Wilson, 1986; Wilson & Tolson, 1990). In Isaacs and Leon's (1987) study of disrupted families, African American fathers reportedly visited their children far less frequently following marital separation than did European American fathers. Among the factors that accounted for this disparity was the increased tendency of African American mothers, compared to European American mothers, to move in with their own parents following marital separation. Extended family support, while a deterrent to paternal visitation, may have enhanced children's adjustment by increasing economic resources, increasing the number of adults offering nurturance and support, and reducing children's exposure to interparental conflict following separation. A tenable hypothesis evoked by these findings about ethnic minority families, juxtaposed to those reported by Gohm et al. (1998), is that even within the American context, embeddedness in extended family networks protects children against the negative psychosocial effects of interparental conflict and that variation in extended family embeddedness may account partially for ethnic differences in children's response to interparental conflict.

Explicating the Role of Culture and Ethnicity in the Experience and Impact of Interparental Conflict: Recommendations for Future Research

Although previous findings have been scarce and inconsistent, they can be used to formulate testable hypotheses about ethnic group differences. While studies of between-group differences in interparental conflict are important in that they provide information about a family-level factor that has consistently been found to negatively impact child development, our goal should be developing a more complex understanding of the role of ethnic minority status in interparental conflict and marital transitions. Among other things, this means understanding what factors determine intragroup variation and mediate ethnic group differences in interparental conflict and children's responses to it. Researchers will need to make a more concerted effort to identify the experiences, conditions, and adaptations to conditions unique to members of these groups, whether inside or outside of families, that may attenuate or exacerbate the impact of interparental conflict. We have already mentioned some of these factors. In the following sections, we present a fuller discussion of some of these issues with the hope that an appreciation of them will strengthen and enrich future research in this area.

Economic Factors

Several studies provide support for the important role of family financial concerns in shaping marital conflict. Money and financial matters often are cited as a major source of disagreement for married couples (Berry & Williams, 1987; Hobart, 1991; Price, 1992). Brody, Stoneman, and Flon (1995) found that per capita income is negatively associated with interparental conflict among African American families living in the rural South. Systematic differences in family income across ethnic groups might account for ethnic differences in the frequency of interparental conflict. Given the disproportionate representation of African American and Latino families among those living in poverty or extreme hardship, it might be expected that interparental conflict among these groups would be more frequent or extreme relative to other ethnic groups.

In most existing studies of the relation of ethnicity to the frequency and intensity of conflict, current family income is controlled in order to identify the independent impact of ethnicity. However, in controlling only for current family income, the study authors have not completely eliminated the potential influence of family finances on interparental conflict. Ethnic differences are found not only in current family income, but also in longer term accrual of family income, stability of family income, and wealth accumulation. African Americans are more likely to experience work interruption and African American children are more likely to experience poverty following events that reduce a family's financial resources (McLoyd, 1990). Given that African American families have far fewer financial assets and less net worth than European American families, even among those of similar income levels (McLoyd & Ceballo, 1998), there is little doubt that many African American families are in a precarious economic situation. African American families are less able to manage their more frequent financial emergencies. Faced with this level of financial insecurity and uncertainty, conflict between African American partners may be more likely. Oggins et al.'s (1993) finding of significantly less marital happiness among African American couples compared to European American couples might be explained by the greater economic insecurity within African American families. As this effect was independent of the marital interaction and demographic variables assessed in the study (e.g., current household income, education), the authors speculate that the racial disparity is due to the greater social pressures that African Americans face (e.g., discrimination, reduced economic and employment opportunities).

Family Structure and Household Composition

The prevalence of single parent families in the African American community also should be considered when thinking about racial or cultural differences in the experience of interparental conflict. In 1996, only 33% of African American children under 18 lived in two-parent households, whereas 53% lived in mother-only households. For Latino and non-Hispanic white children, the numbers were 62% and 29%, and 75% and 18%, respectively (Population Reference Bureau, 1999). Differences in family arrangements, themselves, will be expected to shape the frequency and nature of interparental conflict to which children are exposed. When parents live in separate households, it is possible that interparental conflict may be experienced less frequently, but (depending on the history of the relationship) may be more intense when it does occur.

A longer history or greater acceptance of single-parent households in a particular community may have allowed for the development of a wider variety of support networks, whether comprised of friends and neighbors, or extended family members. The role of the extended family itself should be explored more closely. The receipt of social support from a source outside the nuclear family consistently has been identified as an important protective factor for children and adolescents (Werner, 1992). As Smith (1997) suggests, support from extended family members may lessen the negative impact of parental separation on African American children's psychosocial functioning. Direct tests of whether embeddedness in an extended family network accounts for within-group variation in ethnic minority children's response to interparental conflict and/or for ethnic group differences in children's adaptation to interparental conflict are long overdue. Such studies should take a broad view of the nature of such networks, however, because for both parents and children alike, extended family support may have its downside (Stack, 1974; Wilson, 1986). Depending on the degree to which extended family members participate in childrearing and share childrearing ideologies and practices, it may contribute to the total amount of conflict experienced by children within the family.

Experiences of Racial or Ethnic Discrimination

Occupational stress is a risk factor for divorce (Lawson & Thompson, 1994), and for ethnic minority adults, significant sources of this stress may be race-related attitudes and behavior (e.g., greater scrutiny of African American employees) as well as outright racial oppression in the workplace. These issues have received remarkably little empirical attention. One of the few investigations focused on a sample of African American police officers. Johnson (1989) assessed the direct and indirect effects on marital relations (e.g., satisfying communication with spouse, receipt and expression of emotional support, enjoyable sex life) of three types of perceived racism in the workplace – being judged by the actions of other officers because of race, being penalized more than other officers because of race, and being barred from certain assignments because of race. The latter two stressors had significantly negative, direct effects on the quality of marital relations, that, in turn, increased the degree to which couples had considered divorce. With respect to indirect effects, being judged by the actions of other African Americans officers had an especially potent and negative impact on marital interaction, mediated through an increased tendency to behave callously and impersonally. In addition, being barred from assignments because of race adversely influenced marital relations by increasing feelings of fatigue and emotional depletion and increasing officers' desire to quit their jobs. In subsequent analyses of data from a comparable sample of European American police officers, desire to quit the job was more predictive of marital discord among African Americans than European Americans, apparently because it constituted a more serious economic threat as a result of the reduced job opportunities available to African Americans.

Spousal work-related attitudes and race-linked occupational stresses also appear to promote marital conflict among African Americans. For example, there is evidence that feelings of competition and resentment between spouses engendered by the husband's perception that African American women face fewer barriers to career advancement than do African American men undermine marital happiness among dual-career African American couples, as does lack of racial or ethnic diversity and social isolation in the workplace (Cazenave, 1983; Thomas, 1990).

Future research examining the ways in which culture and ethnicity shape the experience of interparental conflict must consider the potential influence of multiple contexts. It is possible that the negative consequences of marital disruption for African American children may result as much from conditions outside the family as those within the family. As an example, racial bias in classroom settings may be important in understanding the effects of interparental conflict on ethnic minority children's development. Smith (1997) found significant ethnic differences in the impact of the timing of parental separation on children's school grades. Among European American children, grades were negatively affected only when parental separation occurred after the second grade, whereas among African American children, grades declined only when separation occurred before kindergarten. Smith's finding is especially intriguing when juxtaposed with evidence that poverty during early childhood has more detrimental effects on children's years of completed school than poverty during middle child-hood and adolescence, especially among African Americans (Duncan, Yeung, Brooks-Gunn, & Smith, 1998). One explanation offered for the latter effect might help to account for Smith's (1997) finding that African American children are especially vulnerable to parental separation that occurs during the preschool years. The timing effect of poverty may reflect the influence of school readiness, and in turn, teachers' affective responses and expectancies, both of which predict later school achievement (Alexander, Entwisle, & Thompson, 1987; Brooks-Gunn, Guo, & Furstenberg, 1993; Rist, 1970). The timing effect may be stronger among African American children because they experience greater difficulty than European American children overcoming weak academic skills upon entry to public school due to negative racial stereotypes about their cognitive ability (Steele, 1992). In short, because of racial prejudice, early school difficulties, whether due to poverty or the experience of family discord, may be more likely to set African American children than European American children on a trajectory toward underachievement.

Religiosity

Religiosity occupies a more central role in the lives of African Americans than European Americans. In a study of newlywed's narratives, the theme of religion was significantly more prominent in the narratives of African American couples than European American couples (Chadiha, Veroff, & Leber; 1998). A number of studies have identified religious factors as important predictors of marital adjustment and marital quality (Ellison, 1994; Heaton & Pratt, 1990; Wilson & Filsinger, 1986). For example, Filsinger and Wilson (1984) found that religiosity was not only a strong predictor of marital adjustment, but explained roughly twice as much of the variance in marital adjustment as did socioeconomic rewards or family development characteristics. Given the link between religiosity and marital quality and adjustment, it is reasonable to speculate that the frequency of interparental conflict may be influenced by religiosity.

In theory, religiosity, especially religious homogamy between spouses, is associated with value accordance (Albrecht, Bahr, & Goodman, 1983) in a number of content areas that are potential sources of conflict for couples (i.e., childrearing, gender roles, choice of friends). Further, it is reasonable to assume that the social networks derived from religious affiliations may promote marital stability and "provide some consensus regarding appropriate resolution of marital problems" (Heaton & Pratt, 1990, p. 192). Consonant with these propositions, Brody et al. (1996) found that greater maternal formal religiosity predicted less interparental conflict among African Americans. Booth, Johnson, Branaman, and Sica's (1995) longitudinal study of a national sample of over 2,000 married persons under age 55 indicated that increases in religiosity predicted a decline in couples' inclination to consider divorce or discuss it with others, but was unrelated to marital disagreement, abusive behavior, joint engagement in activities, and marital happiness. No analyses were undertaken to determine if ethnicity moderated the strength of these relations. Unfortunately, African Americans and Latinos were underrepresented in the waves of data that contained detailed measures of religiosity.

Just as religion can serve as a marital stabilizer, it also may be a source of marital tension for some couples (i.e., amount of time spent at church, choice of a church, financial contributions, rituals). In an exploratory study of African American men and marital distress, differences in religious behavior and the centrality of church attendance as a manifestation of spiritual commitment were reported as factors that contributed to disagreements and ultimately, marital disruption (Lawson & Thompson, 1996). African American wives often pressured husbands to attend church services and serve on deacon boards, while African American husbands often wanted to pursue leisurely activities on the weekends rather than to attend church (Lawson & Thompson, 1994). Data from an investigation by Hatchett and colleagues (1995) revealed that "religiosity is not sufficient to weather the problematic situations faced by black couples" (p. 203).

The intensity of interparental conflict may be affected by religious attitudes and beliefs as well, though there is a paucity of empirical work that addresses this issue. The principles of most religions espouse nonviolent means of conflict resolution, but the extent to which these principles shape beliefs as well as behavior in conflict situations is unclear. In Sorenson et al.'s (1996) study of violence and injury in marital arguments, Protestants were significantly less likely to report that their arguments escalated into violence. However, Catholics and those of other faiths did not differ from respondents who reported no religion. More research is needed to address this issue as well as the interplay of ethnicity and religiosity on the intensity of conflict.

Religious coping, a more salient resource among African American than European Americans, may influence parents' as well as children's responses to interparental conflict. This form of coping may include religious avoidance (i.e., reading the Bible or becoming involved in religious activities), seeking religious support (Pargament et al., 1990), and making causal attributions of a religious nature (Gorsuch & Smith,

1983). In the context of interparental conflict, religious coping strategies may involve turning to clergy for marital counseling, praying to God for intervention, and looking for answers to marital problems in the Bible. Lawson and Thompson (1996) found that African American men reported that increased involvement in church activities and a religious community helped them cope with divorce. Religious attributions may cause spouses to resist finding fault in the perpetrators of conflict and to view the conflict as having a divine purpose or as a test from God. This predilection may cause feuding spouses to turn to God rather than to each other to handle conflict. Children's responses to interparental conflict may be similarly shaped by religiosity. In a study of university students who had experienced the divorce of their parents during adolescence, Shortz and Worthington (1994) found that those who viewed the divorce as part of God's plan used religion to cope actively. Given the salience of religiosity in the lives of many African Americans, future studies of interparental conflict should include an examination of religiosity and its effects on the frequency, intensity, and content of interparental conflict and on children's and parents' responses to conflict.

Conclusion

Studies of the relation between ethnicity and frequency of marital conflict report inconsistent findings, but there is growing evidence of ethnic differences in partners' responses to marital conflict. However, because little effort has been devoted to examining how parents' perceptions of and response to marital conflict impacts children, it remains unclear how these potential ethnic variations might differentially shape ethnic minority children's experience of interparental conflict. What is clear from within-group studies, though, is that ethnic minority children, like majority children, respond to interparental conflict with increased psychological distress and lower levels of psychosocial and academic competence. Several types of research lend indirect support for the notion that these adverse effects may be attenuated in ethnic minority children, compared to majority children. Given its tenability and popularity, direct tests of this hypothesis and the potentially moderating processes clearly are warranted.

Our understanding of issues raised in this chapter would benefit from a greater number of studies developed and conducted with attention to the need for methodological consistency. Advances also might be more likely if researchers developed a more theoretical approach to the question of how ethnic background might shape the impact of interparental conflict on children. Central to such an approach would be consideration of the unique histories, environments, and cultural orientations of minority and majority families. High priority should be given to economic factors, access to social services, language barriers, and the nature of relations with extended family members. These, as well as more subjective factors such as perceptions of mainstream institutions (e.g., justice system), spousal and gender expectations, the meaning of gender differentials in educational attainment, role strain, perceptions of racism, and religiosity all might be expected to influence how minority versus majority couples manage conflict and how their children respond to marital conflict and particular conflict management strategies.

REFERENCES

Acitelli, L., Douvan, E., & Veroff, J. (1997). The changing influence of interpersonal perceptions of marital well-being among black and white couples. *Journal of Social and Personal Relationships, 14,* 291–304.

Albrecht, S. L., Bahr, H. M., & Goodman, K. L. (1983). *Divorce and remarriage.* Westport, CT: Greenwood.

Alexander, K., Entwisle, D., & Thompson, M. (1987). School performance, status relations, and the structure of sentiment: Bringing the teacher back in. *American Sociological Review, 52,* 665–682.

Amato, P. R., & Keith, B. (1991). Parental divorce and adult well-being: A meta-analysis. *Journal of Marriage and the Family, 53,* 43–58.

Asbury, J. (1993). Violence in the families of color in the United States. In R. Hampton, T. Gullotta, G. Adams, E. Potter, & R. Weissberg (Eds.), *Family violence: Prevention and treatment* (pp. 159–178). Newbury Park, CA: Sage.

Bartz, K., & Levine, E. (1978). Child rearing by black parents: A description and comparison to Anglo and Chicano parents. *Journal of Marriage and the Family, 40,* 709–719.

Berry, R. E., & Williams, F. L. (1987). Assessing the relationship between quality of life and marital and income satisfaction: A path analytic approach. *Journal of Marriage and the Family, 49,* 107–116.

Booth, A., Johnson, D. R., Branaman, A., & Sica, A. (1995). Belief and behavior: Does religion matter in marriage? *Journal of Marriage and the Family, 57,* 661–671.

Brody, G. H., Stoneman, Z., & Flor, D. (1995). Linking family processes and academic competence among rural African American youths. *Journal of Marriage and the Family, 57,* 567–579.

Brody, G. H., Stoneman, Z., & Flor, D. (1996). Parental religiosity, family processes, and youth competence in rural, two-parent African American families. *Developmental Psychology, 32,* 696–706.

Bronfenbrenner, U. (1986). Ecology of the family as a context for human development: Research perspectives. *Developmental Psychology, 22,* 723–742.

Brooks-Gunn, J., Guo, G., & Furstenberg, F. (1993). Who drops out and who continues beyond high school? A 20-year follow-up of black urban youth. *Journal of Research on Adolescence, 3,* 271–294.

Buehler, C., Krishnakumar, A., Stone, G., Anthony, C., Pemberton, S., Gerard, J., & Barber, B. (1998). Interparental conflict styles and youth problem behavior: A two-sample replication study. *Journal of Marriage and the Family, 60,* 119–132.

Bussell, D. (1995). A pilot study of African American children's cognitive and emotional reactions to parental separation. *Journal of Divorce and Remarriage, 24 (3/4),* 1–22.

Cazenave, N. A. (1983). Black male-black female relationships: The perceptions of 155 middle-class black men. *Family Relations, 32,* 341–350.

Chadiha, L. A., Veroff, J., & Leber, D. (1998). Newlywed's narrative themes: Meaning in the first year of marriage for African American and white couples. *Journal of Comparative Family Studies, 29,* 115–130.

Choice, P., Lamke, L., & Pittman, J. (1995). Conflict resolution strategies and marital distress as mediating factors in the link between witnessing interparental violence and wife battering. *Violence and Victims, 10,* 107–119.

Crohan, S. E. (1996). Marital quality and conflict across the transition to parenthood in African American and white couples. *Journal of Marriage and the Family, 58,* 933–944.

Dancy, B., & Handal, P. (1984). Perceived family climate, psychological adjustment, and peer relationship of black adolescents: A function of parental marital status or perceived family conflict. *Journal of Community Psychology, 12,* 222–229.

Dumka, L. E., Roosa, M. W., & Jackson, K. M. (1997). Risk, conflict, mothers' parenting, and children's adjustment in low-income, Mexican immigrant, and Mexican American families. *Journal of Marriage and the Family, 59,* 309–323.

Duncan, G., Yeung, W., Brooks-Gunn, J., & Smith, J. (1998). How much does childhood poverty affect the life chances of children? *American Sociological Review, 63,* 406–423.

DuRant, R., Getts, A., Cadenhead, C., Emans, S., & Woods, E. (1995). Exposure to violence and victimization and depression, hopelessness, and purpose in life among adolescents living in and around public housing. *Developmental and Behavioral Pediatrics, 16,* 233–237.

Ellison, C. G. (1994). Religion, the life stress paradigm, and the study of depression. In J. S. Levin (Ed.), *Religion in aging and health: Theoretical foundations and methodological frontiers* (pp. 78–121). Thousand Oaks, CA: Sage.

Emery, R. E. (1982). Interparental conflict and the child of discord and divorce. *Psychological Bulletin, 92,* 310–330.

Emery, R. E., & O'Leary, K. D. (1982). Children's perceptions of marital discord and behavior problems of boys and girls. *Journal of Abnormal Child Psychology, 10,* 11–24.

Filsinger, E. E., & Wilson, M. R. (1984). Religiosity, socioeconomic rewards, and family development: Predictors of marital adjustment. *Journal of Marriage and the Family, 46,* 663–670.

Gohm, C. L., Oishi, S., Darlington, J., & Diener, E. (1998). Culture, parental conflict, parental marital status, and the subjective well-being of young adults. *Journal of Marriage and the Family, 60,* 319–334.

Gondolf, E., Fisher, E., & McFerron, R. (1991). Racial differences among shelter residents: A comparison of Anglo, Black, and Hispanic battered women. In R. Hampton (Ed.), *Black family violence: Current research and theory* (pp. 103–113). Lexington, MA: Heath.

Gorsuch, R. L., & Smith, C. S. (1983). Attributions of responsibility to God: An interaction of religious beliefs and outcomes. *Journal for the Scientific Study of Religion, 22,* 340–352.

Gottman, J. M., & Krokoff, L. J. (1989). Marital interaction and satisfaction: A longitudinal view. *Journal of Consulting and Clinical Psychology, 57,* 47–53.

Grych, J. H., & Fincham, F. D. (1990). Marital conflict and children's adjustment: A cognitive-contextual framework. *Psychological Bulletin, 108,* 267–290.

Hampton, R. L., & Coner-Edwards, A. (1993). Physical and sexual violence in marriage. In R. Hampton, T. Gullotta, G. Adams, E. Potter, & R. Weissberg (Eds.), *Family violence: Prevention and treatment* (pp. 113–141). Newbury Park, CA: Sage.

Hampton, R. L., & Gelles, R. (1994). Violence toward Black women in a nationally representative sample of Black families. *Journal of Comparative Family Studies, 25,* 105–119.

Hatchett, S., Veroff, J., & Douvan, E. (1995). Marital instability among Black and White couples in early marriage. In M. B. Tucker & C. Mitchell-Kernan (Eds.), *The decline in marriage among African Americans: Causes, consequences, and policy implications* (pp. 177–218). New York: Russell Sage.

Heaton, T. B., & Pratt, E. L. (1990). The effects of religious homogamy on marital satisfaction and stability. *Journal of Family Issues, 11,* 191–207.

Henggeler, S., & Tavormina, J. (1980). Social class and race differences in family interaction: Pathological, normative, or confounding methodological factors. *Journal of Genetic Psychology, 137,* 211–222.

Hetherington, M., Bridges, M., & Insabella, G. (1998). What matters? What does not? Five perspectives on the association between marital transitions and children's adjustment. *American Psychologist, 53,* 167–184.

Hines, A. (1997). Divorce-related transitions, adolescent development, and the role of the parent-child relationship: A review of the literature. *Journal of Marriage and the Family, 59,* 375–388.

Hobart, C. (1991). Conflict in remarriages. *Journal of Divorce and Remarriage, 15,* 69–86.

Isaacs, M. B., & Leon, G. (1987). Race, marital dissolution and visitation: An examination of adaptive family strategies. *Journal of Divorce, 11,* 17–31.

Jekielek, S. M. (1998). Parental conflict, marital disruption and children's emotional well-being. *Social Forces, 76,* 905–935.

Johnson, L. B. (1989). The employed black: The dynamics of work-family tension. Ethnicity and interparental conflict *Review of Black Political Economy, 17,* 69–85.

Julian, T., & McKenry, P. (1993). Mediators of male violence toward female intimates. *Journal of Family Violence, 8,* 39–56.

Karney, B. R., & Bradbury, T. N. (1995). The longitudinal course of marital quality and stability: A review of method, theory, and research. *Psychological Bulletin, 118,* 3–34.

Lawson, E. J., & Thompson, A. (1995) Black men make sense of marital distress and divorce. *Family Relations, 44,* 211–218.

Lawson, E. J., & Thompson, A. (1996). Black men's perceptions of divorce-related stressors and strategies for coping with divorce: An exploratory study. *Journal of Family Issues, 17,* 249–277.

Lawson, E., & Thompson, A. (1994). Historical and social correlates of African American divorce: Review of the literature and implications of research. *Western Journal of Black Studies, 18,* 91–103.

Lindahl, K. M., & Malik, N. M. (1999). Marital conflict, family processes, and boys' externalizing behavior in Hispanic American and European American families. *Journal of Clinical Child Psychology, 28,* 12–24.

Lockhart, L. (1991). Spousal violence: A cross-racial perspective. In R. Hampton (Ed.), *Black family violence: Current research and theory* (pp. 85–101). Lexington, MA: Heath.

MacDonald, W., & DeMaris, A. (1995). Remarriage, stepchildren, and marital conflict: Challenges to the incomplete institutionalization hypothesis. *Journal of Marriage and the Family, 57,* 387–398.

Mackey, R. A. & O'Brien, B. A. (1998). Marital conflict management: Gender and ethnic differences. *Social Work, 43,* 128–141.

Mason, C. A., Cauce, A. M., Gonzales, N., Hiraga, Y., & Grove, K. (1994). An ecological model of externalizing behaviors in African American adolescents: No family is an island. *Journal of Research on Adolescence, 4,* 639–655.

McKenry, P., & Fine, M. (1993). Parenting following divorce: A comparison of Black and White single mothers. *Journal of Comparative Family Studies, 24,* 99–111.

McLoyd, V. C. (1990). The impact of economic hardship on black families and children: Psychological distress, parenting, and socioemotional development. *Child Development, 61,* 311–346.

McLoyd, V. C. (1998). Changing demographics in the American population: Implications for research on minority children and adolescents. In V. C. McLoyd & L. Steinberg (Eds.), *Studying minority adolescents: Conceptual, methodological, and theoretical issues* (pp. 3–28). Mahwah, NJ: Erlbaum.

McLoyd, V. C., & Ceballo, R. (1998). Conceptualizing and assessing economic context: Issues in the study of race and child development. In V. C. McLoyd & L. Steinberg (Eds.), *Studying minority adolescents: Conceptual, methodological, and theoretical issues* (pp. 251–278). Mahwah, NJ: Erlbaum.

Menaghan, E., & Parcel, T. (1995). Social sources of change in children's home environments: The effects of parental occupational experiences and family conditions. *Journal of Marriage and the Family, 57,* 69–84.

O'Keefe, M. (1994a). Linking marital violence, mother–child/father–child aggression, and child behavior problems. *Journal of Family Violence, 9,* 63–78.

O'Keefe, M. (1994b). Racial/ethnic differences among battered women and their children. *Journal of Child and Family Studies, 3,* 283–305.

Oggins, J., Veroff, J., & Leber, D. (1993). Perceptions of marital interaction among black and white newlyweds. *Journal of Personality and Social Psychology, 65,* 494–511.

Pargament, K. I., Ensing, D. S., Falgout, K., Olsen, H., Reilly, B., Haitsma, K. V., & Warren, R. (1990). God help me: Religious coping efforts as predictors of the outcomes to significant negative life events. *American Journal of Community Psychology, 18,* 793–824.

Peterson-Lewis, S., Turner, C. W., & Adams, A. M. (1988). Attributional processes in repeatedly abused women. In G. W. Russell (Ed.), *Violence in intimate relationships* (pp. 107–130). New York: PMA Publication Corporation.

Population Reference Bureau (1999). The challenge of change: What the 1990 Census tells us about children, Table 14 with data from the Bureau of the Census, 1980 Census of Population, "General Social and Economic Characteristics", PC80-1-C1, United States Summary, tables 100, 121, and 131; and Census of Population and Housing 1990, Summary Tape File 3, tables P-19, P-20, and P-21. Center for the Study of Social Policy. Available: http://aspe.os.dhhs.gov/hsp/97trends/PF2-1.htm]

Price, R. H. (1992). Psychosocial impact of job loss on individuals and families. *Current Directions in Psychological Science, 1,* 9–11.

Proctor, E. K., Vosler, N. R., & Sirles, E. A. (1993). The social-environmental context of child clients: An empirical exploration. *Social Work* (May), *38,* 256–262.

Rist, R. (1970). Student social class and teacher expectations: The self-fulfilling prophecy in ghetto education. *Harvard Educational Review, 40,* 411–451.

Shortz, J. L., & Worthington, E. L. (1994). Young adults' recall of religiosity attributions, and coping in parental divorce. *Journal for the Scientific Study of Religion, 33,* 172–199.

Shaw, D. S., Winslow, E. B., & Flanagan, C. (1999). A prospective study of the effects of marital status and family relations on young children's adjustment among African American and European American families. *Child Development, 70,* 742–755.

Sistler, A. B., & Moore, G. M. (1996). Cultural diversity in coping with marital stress. *Journal of Clinical Geropsychology, 2,* 77–82.

Smith, T. E. (1997). Differences between Black and White students in the effect of parental separation on school grades. *Journal of Divorce & Remarriage, 27,* 25–42.

Sorenson, S. B., & Telles, C. A. (1991) Self-reports of spousal violence in a Mexican American and non-Hispanic white population. *Violence and Victims, 6,* 3–16.

Sorenson, S. B., Upchurch, D. M., & Shen, H. (1996). Violence and injury in marital arguments: Risk patterns and gender differences. *American Journal of Public Health, 86,* 34–40.

Spencer, M. B., Cole, S., DuPree, D., Glymph, A., & Pierre, P. (1993). Self-efficacy among urban African American adolescents: Exploring issues of risk, vulnerability, and resilience. *Development and Psychopathology, 5,* 719–739.

Stack, C. B. (1974). *All our kin: Strategies for survival in a Black community.* New York: Harper & Row.

Steele, C. (1992, April). Race and the schooling of Black Americans. *Atlantic Monthly,* 68–78.

Thomas, V. G. (1990). Problems of dual-career black couples: Identification and implications for family interventions. *Journal of Multicultural Counseling and Development, 14,* 177–185.

U. S. Census Bureau (1997). *Statistical abstract of the United States: 1997.* Washington, DC: U.S. Government Printing Office.

Werner, E. E. (1992). The children of Kauai: Resiliency and recovery in adolescence and adulthood. *Journal of Adolescent Health, 13,* 262–268.

Wilson, M. N. (1986). The black extended family: An analytical consideration. *Developmental Psychology, 22,* 246–258.

Wilson, M. N., & Tolson, T. (1990). Familial support in the black community. *Journal of Clinical Child Psychology, 19,* 347–355.

Wilson, M. R., & Filsinger, E. E. (1986). Religiosity and marital adjustment: Multidimensional interrelationships. *Journal of Marriage and the Family, 48,* 147–151.

PART TWO. BASIC PROCESSES

5 The Role of Emotion and Emotional Regulation in Children's Responses to Interparental Conflict

Susan Crockenberg and Adela Langrock

The 1990s has witnessed an explosion of theories and research directed toward understanding the processes by which specific external events and experiences impact children in ways that impede development and increase the likelihood of behavioral problems. Scholars have moved beyond establishing associations between the events to which children are exposed and their current and subsequent behavioral adjustment, to identifying and investigating internal cognitive and emotional processes that could explain these associations. This focus on process is nowhere more apparent than with respect to the well-established connection between marital conflict and children's externalizing and internalizing behaviors (Emery, 1988).

In a seminal paper, Grych and Fincham (1990) proposed a model in which children's perceptions of marital conflict mediate its impact on their behavior. These perceptions are influenced in turn by characteristics of the marital conflict context, interpreted through the lens of children's past experience with conflict and their age-related cognitive abilities to make causal inferences, engage in causal reasoning, and take the perspective of others. In their model, affect is the result of cognitive processing, but also influences attributions, memory, contemplation of coping strategies in relation to the marital conflict, and hence behavior. Nevertheless, in discussing the implications of their framework, Grych and Fincham emphasized cognitive mediating processes, noting only that "children's ability to regulate emotional arousal (*and other variables*) ... are also likely to be important factors" (p. 286).

In two subsequent conceptualizations of the processes linking marital conflict and children's behavioral adjustment, Crockenberg and Forgays (1994; 1996), in their specific emotions model, and Davies and Cummings (1994; 1995), in their emotional security model, elaborated Grych and Fincham's (1990) framework, giving emotion a more pivotal explanatory role. In these models, knowledge of children's emotional reactions to interparental conflict and of the way they regulate emotions is essential for understanding how such exposure impacts children's overt behavioral responses to the conflict and ultimately their adjustment. In this chapter we present an elaborated version of the specific emotions model, document similarities and differences between it and the emotional security model, and show how it helps to both organize empirical findings and identify directions for empirical inquiry.

Emotion-Focused Models of Marital Conflict Effects

A Specific Emotions Model of Marital Conflict and Child Adjustment

In the specific emotions model (see Figure 5.1) marital conflict is a multifaceted, recurrent event with two adult characters exhibiting an array of discrete behaviors and emotions (Christensen, 1988; Gottman, 1979; Margolin, 1988). When children witness marital conflict, these interparental behaviors constitute one aspect of their knowledge of the event. They serve as data children use in constructing the meaning of the conflict for themselves, the basis of their emotional reactions.

Marital conflict is expected to affect children's behavior, and with repetition their behavioral adjustment, through their assessment of the relevance of the conflict for themselves and their associated emotional reactions. The solid line connecting the boxes in the center of Figure 5.1 identifies this pathway. The ability to assess interparental conflict for relevance varies with children's age-related cognitive abilities, and relevance is a function of goals that may vary by age and gender, as shown by the solid line connecting these characteristics with children's evaluations. Children's constitutionally based temperamental characteristics (i.e., the speed and intensity of their initial physiological responses and physiologically based regulatory capacities) also impact children's emotional reactions, as indicated by the solid line connecting these features of the model.

Behaviors parents engage in during interparental conflict serve also as models for children's behavior, with children attending to and displaying disproportionately the behavior of same-gender parents, for reasons we explain below. The solid line connecting interparental behavior directly with children's behavioral adjustment identifies this pathway. The broken line from child gender, which represents its moderating effect on this process, intersects it. A second intersecting line from parental behavior identifies the potential moderating impact of

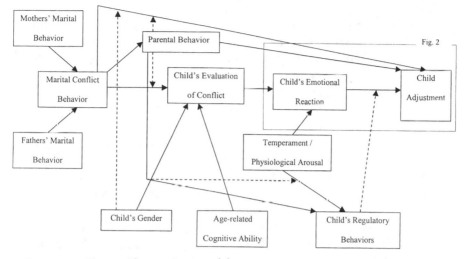

Figure 5.1　The specific emotions model.

parental behavior on children's display of observed interparental behaviors. If parent-imposed consequences for engaging in a behavior outweigh goal-related benefits, children are less likely to engage in behavior they observe between parents.

Additionally, marital conflict is expected to affect children's behavior indirectly through the parent-child relationship, in what is commonly referred to as spillover, illustrated in Figure 5.1 by the solid lines linking marital and parental behavior, and the latter with children's behavioral adjustment. Parental behavior can also moderate the emotion-linked effects of marital conflict on children's adjustment through its impact on children's goals, as indicated by the broken line between parental behavior and children's evaluations, and by fostering the development of socially competent ways of regulating emotions. The solid line connecting parental behavior to children's regulatory behaviors and the broken line connecting those behaviors with children's behavioral adjustment show the latter effect.

Children's temperamental characteristics (i.e., the intensity of their physiological arousal and their ability to self-soothe) impact the regulation process directly and also as moderated by parental behavior (see Katz, Chapter 7). This effect is represented by the solid line connecting temperament with regulatory behavior and by the broken line from parental behavior that intersects it, indicating the moderating effect.

In the sections that follow, we elaborate on each of the direct pathways, emphasizing the core pathway from marital conflict to children's behavioral adjustment through meaning and emotion. We explain also how children's initial behavioral responses to interparental conflict develop into patterns of behavioral adjustment as experiences with conflict are repeated and children develop internalized schemas that link cognitions, emotions, and behaviors.

Meaning and Emotion. In the model, it is the meaning of the marital conflict to children that influences their emotional reactions, and their specific emotions that relate to the patterns of behavior they develop. Meaning is established in the course of children's experiences with conflicts that occur between their parents and that impinge on their age-related goals. Children have a number of goals that might be put at risk (i.e., threatened) by marital conflict. Marital conflict can impact security goals (i.e., to be loved and protected), concrete relationship goals (i.e., to participate with parents in planned activities or anticipated family routines), and other concrete goals (i.e., to be able to have or do things over which parents exercise control).

Certain goals may be more salient to children at different ages, or more easily threatened by virtue of their age-related ability or inability to understand the nuances of the conflict and its possible implications. Thus, younger children may be more upset than older children by threats to their emotional security (e.g., a parent leaving the house and driving away during an interparental conflict) because of their greater dependence on parents and their more limited understanding of time, which affects their assessment of when the parent is likely to return.

Congruent with Mandler's (1975) interruption hypothesis of emotion, failure to attain or maintain goals is assumed to be unpleasant, and accordingly, when children perceive that their goals are jeopardized, their emotional reactions are expected to be negative. Initially, when children are exposed to marital conflicts, they may not know how their goals will be affected. As a consequence, their negative emotional reactions may be determined to a considerable degree by the intensity and negativity of the observed interparental behavior, as these features of the conflict carry greater cross-contextual meaning for children (e.g., physical aggression means that someone will get hurt; yelling means that someone will get in trouble). With repeated exposure, children learn the consequences that accompany overt expressions of anger in their own families and begin to recognize other types of interparental conflicts that jeopardize their goals (i.e., increase the likelihood that something bad will happen). When such conflicts occur, children feel mad, sad, or anxious/afraid.

As marital conflicts are repeated, children perceive similarities across them, and integrate them into a single interpretation (Tompkins, 1979).

These interpretations include everything children know about the conflict, whether or not they are aware of or can articulate it, and most important, how it impinges on their goals. Initially, we believe that the usual pattern is for children's goal-related interpretations of marital conflicts to trigger their emotional reactions, as shown in Figure 5.1. With repetition, however, cognitive and affective responses become linked together in memory in what Jenkins and Oatley (1998) refer to as "emotion schemas" that serve as organizing structures for future experiences. As schemas coalesce, linear connections between cognitions and emotions blur, and children's emotional responses to specific marital conflicts become increasingly automatic. Thus, a child who witnesses marital conflicts in which one or both parents are verbally aggressive and finds repeatedly that family plans are disrupted as a consequence, comes to interpret the verbal aggression to mean, "I'm not going to get to do what I had expected to do," and feels bad. Whether the feeling is anger, sadness, fear/anxiety, *or some combination thereof* depends on other features of the conflict and on the child's experiences with threats to goal attainment or maintenance, as we explain next.

Children's emotional responses are central in this model in part because they represent the meaning of marital conflict to individual children. If children interpret the conflict benignly, it should have no negative emotional impact, although associations between marital and child behavior may occur through modeling.

Emotion and Behavior. The link between emotion and behavior, included on the right side of Figure 5.1, locates emotion at the heart of the process connecting parents' behavior during marital conflict with children's behavioral maladjustment. A central tenet of all functionalist theories of emotion is that emotions serve specific functions, one of which is to organize and direct behavior (Campos, Mumme, Kermoian, & Campos, 1994; Frijda, Kuipers, & ter Shure, 1989; Saarni, Mumme, & Campos, in press). A related assumption is that people prefer to be in pleasurable states and avoid unpleasant ones, and that much human behavior is carried out in the service of achieving and maintaining pleasure and avoiding pain. It follows that negative emotions prompt efforts to reduce aversive states, and further, that the nature of the negative emotion (i.e., anger, sadness, or fear) influences the type of behavior the child adopts.

Both innate predispositions and experience may explain why specific emotions are associated with specific types of behaviors. Oatley (1992) and others argue that certain emotion-behavior patterns have been selected for in the course of evolution because they have increased the likelihood of survival. As a consequence, specific emotions prime the brain for certain types of response. Thus, anger occurs when goals are threatened and elicits attempts to dominate others (aggression); sadness occurs in response to loss or defeat and elicits assistance or caregiving; fear occurs when there is threat or danger and elicits attempts to protect oneself.

Experience is important also in individuals' evaluations of the nature of the threat and their own ability to meet it effectively. According to Stein and Levine (1987), certain types of experience defined in relation to success or failure of goal attainment are linked in predictable ways to specific emotions. They propose that whether an event elicits anger, sadness, or fear is related in part to children's estimates of how likely it is that the goal can be reinstated, or maintained if threatened. If reinstatement is perceived as probable, children feel angry and act to reinstate goals. If reinstatement is perceived as improbable, they feel sad and will abandon their original goal and possibly pursue an alternative goal. If the outcome is potentially negative but uncertain, and if, in addition, children think they cannot influence whether the negative outcome occurs, they feel anxious or afraid and will act to protect themselves against the source of the feelings or the feelings themselves. If several goals are impacted by the marital conflict, children may experience multiple emotions, which influence behavior in more complex ways.

Marital conflict may elicit more than one emotion because the child is responding to two adults, each of whom may elicit a different emotional reaction, or because the same adult elicits more than one emotion. A child may feel angry with the parent who is the aggressor and sad or afraid for the parent who is the victim of the aggression, or for themselves if they think a parent's aggressive behavior might spill over into the parent–child relationship. Under any of these circumstances, a child might display both internalizing and externalizing problems, a pattern of comorbidity that is fairly common in children (McConaughy & Achenbach, 1994). Alternatively, a child may be angry when a parent behaves aggressively during marital conflict, but also afraid to express anger overtly if the cost of doing so is high (e.g., could result in physical or verbal attack). Under these circumstances, fear could inhibit the expression of anger and elicit social withdrawal. In Figure 5.2, the broken line from fear that intersects the broken line between anger and internalizing identifies this moderating effect.

As articulated in Crockenberg and Forgays (1996), the fearful inhibition of anger is expected to occur more frequently in girls than boys

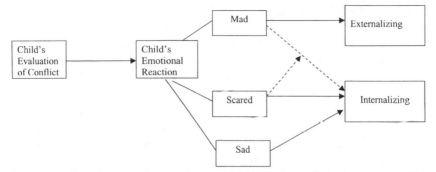

Figure 5.2. Detailed specific emotions model highlighting links between specific emotions and specific behaviors.

given the strong disapproval of female aggression that characterizes American culture. This disapproval makes the overt expression of anger risky for girls, who must weigh anxiety about the consequences of behaving aggressively against any gains to be achieved through its use. It is well documented that girls experience more pressure than boys to inhibit aggressive or assertive behavior during the early school years, that both fathers and mothers are implicated in applying that pressure (Kerig, Cowan, & Cowan, 1993), and that school-age children understand that aggressive behavior is less accepted and more likely to be punished in girls than boys (Perry, Perry, & Weiss, 1989). Suppression of anger is not unique to girls, but it is more characteristic of girls than boys (Crick, Casas, & Mosher, 1997).

Although emotions occur in response to assessments of the impact of events on goals, they may also alter goals. If children believe they cannot attain or reinstate the original goal (e.g., to prevent physical harm), they can only hope to reduce the aversive emotional state. This goal transformation is helpful in understanding why children who experience a threat to or loss of a goal sometimes engage in behaviors such as revenge or withdrawal. Although neither behavior is likely to facilitate attainment of the original goal, each may temporarily reduce the child's aversive emotional state and thus be negatively reinforced. Revenge is sweet; it replaces pain with pleasure by assuring that the perpetrator pays for the transgression. Avoidance may reduce sadness or fear by removing the child from the context that elicits the negative emotion. Emotions generated in these ways are unlikely to have long-term benefits for children's development, however, because they fail to advance, and they may in fact reduce the possibility of attaining important goals, the most reliable source of positive emotion.

Children's beliefs about their ability to protect and reinstate important goals are based on their reservoirs of experience with their parents in the context of marital and other family conflicts, and the inferences they have drawn from those experiences. The anticipated links between specific emotions and specific behaviors are illustrated in Figure 5.2. Initially, children's responses to marital conflict may be quite variable as they experiment with different types of responses to different conflicts. Over time, if a child believes that she, or people like her, typically get what they want when they attempt to dominate others in their efforts to reinstate goals, anger will become a pervasive response to marital conflict, and aggression or coercion (externalizing) will be the behavior of choice when personal goals are threatened. On the other hand, if a child believes that she or others like her are unable to reverse losses or prevent harm through active intervention, sadness or fear will become characteristic responses to marital conflict, and submission or withdrawal (internalizing) the likely behavioral response. These characteristic behavioral responses are the ways children behave in an attempt to maintain their goals and reduce negative feelings that persist when they are unable to do so, and they define children's behavioral adjustment.

Emotional Regulation. In the model, children who have repeated, specific negative emotional reactions to marital conflict are more likely than other children to develop specific types of behavior problems (i.e., anger with externalizing, fear with internalizing), but negative emotions are not invariably associated with dysfunctional behavior. Children develop adaptive ways to express emotions and attain goals that lead to divergent pathways between negative emotions and behavioral adjustment, strategies that Eisenberg (1997) refers to as "emotion-related behavioral regulation" and Compas, Connor, Thomsen, Saltzman and Wadsworth (1999) label "primary control coping."

In the regulatory process, specific negative emotions direct and to some extent constrain the child's behavioral adaptation by stimulating behaviors consistent with the particular emotion and the appraisal it represents. To illustrate, when a child is angry, behavior is directed toward attaining or protecting a threatened goal. Thus, efforts to reduce the likelihood of an aggressive response require substitution of an alternative behavior (e.g., negotiation) that will be as effective as aggression in achieving that end, all things considered, *or* reduction of the angry emotion (i.e., decreasing intensity or substituting sadness or happiness for anger). The dual dimensions of primary control coping represent these alternatives, including both active efforts to modulate arousal and to solve problems, with the preferred approach depending on the controllability of the emotion-arousing event.

Differences in the capacity to modulate felt emotions moderate associations between specific emotions and behavior, with different regulatory strategies predicting different behavioral outcomes. To the extent that these regulatory behaviors allow children to advance certain goals without unduly compromising other goals, they are adaptive. To the extent that they allow them to do so without intruding on the ability of other people to pursue their goals, they are socially competent (Crockenberg, Jackson, & Langrock, 1996).

Specific regulatory behaviors develop initially in the course of family interactions during which parents comfort children, engage them in collaborative conflict resolution, talk about specific emotions and the events that elicit them, and coach adaptive coping strategies (Kliewer, Fearnow, & Miller, 1996; Nathan-Ailor, 1999). As shown in Figure 5.1, such parental behaviors help to buffer children from the potentially negative impact of marital conflict by enhancing certain regulatory behaviors and discouraging others. Children may also learn to regulate negative emotions vicariously by observing how parents deal with their own negative emotions in the course of marital conflict, as we discuss next.

Modeling Effects of Marital Conflict. The direct link between marital conflict and children's behavior reflects the expectation that children will imitate marital behavior if they think it will be or discover that it is effective in attaining desired goals. That there are two parents of different genders engaged in the marital conflict introduces additional complexity. If mothers and fathers differ in conflict behaviors (e.g., fathers aggressive, mothers avoidant), children will use gender to select which behavior to imitate. By the time children are 5 to 6 years old, they have incorporated gender-relevant scripts into their personal identities. These scripts or schemas are packets of gender-related information, understanding, knowledge, and beliefs that direct cognition and thereby contribute to the development of gender-specific behavior. Gender or gender schemas influence what information young children attend to, process, and remember, with boys focusing more on male-relevant information, and girls focusing on female-relevant information (Bauer, 1993; Levy & Boston, 1992). Although children gain information about the other gender as well, according to Levy and Fivush (1993), their in-depth knowledge of gender-typed content is biased toward accrual of same-sex information, which they use to guide their own gender-appropriate behavior. Even if children learn behaviors displayed by both parents, they may not perform the behavior of the opposite-gender parent because they anticipate negative consequences for doing so (Bandura, 1965; Bandura, Ross, & Ross, 1963).

The Emotional Security Hypothesis of Marital Conflict Effects

According to Davies and Cummings (1994), the implications of marital conflict for children's emotional security determine the meaning of the marital conflict, and through its impact on emotional regulation and coping, their behavioral adjustment. From this perspective, *emotional security* is the goal most likely to be threatened by marital conflict. When children feel emotionally secure, they are confidant that marital conflicts will eventually ameliorate and that their parents will continue to be psychologically and physically available. When they perceive that this goal is threatened by marital conflict, children feel emotionally insecure, which undermines their ability to cope and promotes emotional and behavioral dysregulation in response to everyday stresses.

Davies and Cummings (1994) postulate three interrelated processes to explain how emotional security or insecurity affect children's functioning. The first is through its impact on emotional arousal and regulation, which may occur in several ways: (1) Chronic exposure to destructive marital conflict may induce chronic arousal, resulting in dysregulation as psychological energy is depleted and children have fewer resources to deploy in modulating emotions. (2) Repeated emotional arousal may result in sensitization, the intensification of responses with more frequent exposure. (3) Negative emotions may predispose children to attend to and remember negative characteristics of marital conflict (i.e., to make negative appraisals of marital conflicts), increasing the likelihood of negative emotional reactions.

Second, children may attempt to increase their feelings of emotional security by attempting to reduce or end the interparental conflict. Paradoxically, this technique may have the opposite effect if intervention involves misbehavior that targets children as recipients for their parents' anger or if the behavioral intervention is effective in halting the conflict, resulting in reinforcement of problematic behavior.

Third, children's past experiences with marital conflict may influence their appraisals of the marital conflict, such that a child who is emotionally insecure as a result of past exposure to intense marital conflicts may more readily perceive threat, eliciting emotional arousal and initiating a process by which behavioral maladjustment becomes more likely. Moreover, children may learn about regulating their own emotions by observing parents' marital behaviors.

Comparing the Specific Emotions and Emotional Security Hypotheses

These models are similar in many ways. In each, emotion reflects the meaning of the marital conflict to a specific child, with meaning derived from that child's past experiences with marital conflict in relation to his or her own goals, stored in memory as internal representations. In each, emotion serves as an impetus for external behavior in pursuit or defense of those goals. In each, children's ability to regulate/cope with negative emotion alters the impact of marital conflict on their behavioral adjustment. In each, parents influence the way children regulate/cope with marital conflict-linked negative emotions.

There are notable differences between the two emotion-focused models as well. They differ formally in the degree to which goals are distinguished from the cognitive and emotional processes activated when significant goals are threatened by interparental conflict. In the Davies and Cummings model, emotional security, the belief that one is loved and will be cared for, is both a goal that may be threatened by marital conflict and a set of cognitive and affective processes that define and reflect the construct. In contrast, in the specific emotions model, emotional security is one of several goals, which, when threatened, elicit a range of emotions that both reflect the consequences of previous behavior and motivate child behavior in the present. Goals are distinct from emotions and emotions from behavior, although all are linked in clearly specified ways. These propositions provide the basis for testable hypotheses about the conditions under which and the processes through which marital conflict results in different types of behavioral problems.

The specific emotions and emotional security models differ more specifically in several other ways, each of which is addressed in turn.

Emotional Security or Multiple Goals. A key difference between the specific emotions and emotional security models is their respective focus on an idiosyncratic set of goals, any of which might be impacted by marital conflict and give rise to negative emotions, versus an exclusive focus on emotional security as the goal threatened when parents engage in marital conflicts. From the emotional security perspective, children appraise the conflict for its impact on their security, and differences in appraisals reflect the seriousness of the threat and the child's ability to deflect the threat (efficacy). From the specific emotions perspective, children appraise the conflict in relation to several goals, threats to which might elicit one or more emotions, which may be linked singly or in combination to behavior. This differential emphasis is reconciled easily enough by stipulating that emotional security, although only one of the goals threatened by marital conflict, is both a significant goal and one that is often impacted when parents engage in angry and aggressive marital conflicts.

Specific Emotions and General Distress. In the emotional security model, general emotional distress mediates between children's appraisal of the marital conflict and their behavioral responses. Differences in the way children cope with distress moderate its expression and explain behavioral differences. The nature of the negative emotion is of no significance in the model.

In the specific emotions model, children's feelings of anger, sadness, and fear *and* their capacity and strategies for regulating these emotions are linked. Specific emotions reflect, in part, children's experience-based assessments of their effectiveness in maintaining or reinstating goals impacted by the conflict (i.e., their appraisal of what might work), and function to elicit or stimulate behaviors consistent with those assessments. From this perspective, a child's behavioral response to an emotionally arousing event is constrained by the specific emotion experienced. If a child is angry, we expect behavior directed toward attaining or protecting a threatened goal. When that behavior is consistent with cultural or contextual expectations for the appropriate expression of anger, it is viewed as normative and adaptive. When it deviates from the norm, it is viewed as dysfunctional and maladaptive. In either case, the behavior serves the same function.

Additionally, the specific emotions model introduces the possibility that children will experience multiple emotions in response to marital conflict (e.g., anger and fear), resulting in several possible behavioral patterns. They may display the behavior associated with each emotion sequentially, first aggressing then withdrawing before the aggressive conflict escalates further. They may display different behaviors in different contexts, expressing anger overtly when they think it will be effective (e.g., with the less powerful parent or with peers), withdrawing when the costs of aggressing are too high (e.g., with the more powerful parent). Alternatively, one emotion may mask another without reducing it (e.g., fear of negative social consequences may inhibit the overt expression of anger as aggression, but the child may remain angry). In contrast, the emotional security model provides no guidance regarding the type of behavior a child is likely to display when distressed, and it is unable to explain the moderating effects of dual emotions on behavior.

Gender-Linked Processes. In the emotional security model, gender has no specified role, although in some studies investigators have examined gender differences in children's responses to marital conflicts. In contrast, gender is a central feature of the specific emotions model through its impact on children's appraisals of conflicts, on the consequences children experience for expressing specific emotions in certain ways, and on children's selection of which parent's behavior to model. Nevertheless, gender differences are conditional; they are expected to vary across studies as a function of sample characteristics. If mothers are as overtly aggressive as fathers during marital conflicts and girls are not disproportionately punished for aggression, there may be no significant gender differences in maritally linked externalizing behavior. Alternatively, if boys and girls are equally fearful in response to marital conflict, there may be no maritally linked gender differences in internalizing behavior.

Even in the absence of mean gender differences in emotions or behaviors, gender may be important in understanding the processes by which marital conflict impacts children's behavioral adjustment. Certain pathways of influence may be more common for girls and boys, or vice versa, as we have suggested with respect to the fearful inhibition of anger, and contribute to different developmental trajectories. Thus, the somewhat higher incidence of internalizing behavior in girls than boys at adolescence may reflect girls' increasing awareness and anxiety that expressing anger will diminish their attractiveness to the opposite sex, a concern that is considerably less important for adolescent boys.

Research on the Emotional Processes Linking Marital Conflict with Behavioral Adjustment

We now consider four primary questions about the role of emotion processes in understanding the impact of marital conflict on children's behavioral adjustment. First, do certain types of marital conflicts elicit negative emotional reactions in children, and do children vary in their emotional reactions to the same or similar marital behaviors? Second, are children's appraisals of the marital conflict related to the variation in their emotional reactions, with more negative appraisals in relation to children's own goals associated with more negative emotional reactions? Third, do children's emotional reactions to marital conflicts predict their behavioral adjustment, serving as either mediating or moderating variables? Fourth, do other characteristics of children (e.g., their social competence or ability to cope effectively in relationships) moderate the association between maritally linked negative emotions and behavior?

Children's Emotional Reactions to Marital Conflict

There is considerable convergent evidence that, as a group, children experience and express negative emotions in response to physically or verbally aggressive interadult conflict between strangers (see Davies & Cummings, 1994 for a review), and that children's distress to such conflicts varies in relation to their histories of physically and verbally aggressive interparental conflict (Cummings, Pellegrini, Notarius, & Cummings, 1989; Davies & Cummings, 1998; El-Sheikh, 1994).

Notably, in relation to specific emotions theory, El-Sheikh and colleagues reported that children's specific emotional reactions varied in relation to specific characteristics of simulated, videotaped interadult conflicts. Physical anger elicited higher levels of behavioral distress than verbal or covert forms of anger, whereas covert anger elicited greater emotional distress (i.e., sad or scared feelings) than verbal forms of angry conflict (El-Sheikh & Reiter, 1996). Additionally, children raised in homes characterized by either any physical or frequent verbal interparental aggression reported more fear in response to both interparental and adult–child angry interactions than children from low-conflict homes (El-Sheikh, 1997).

Children demonstrate intense and diverse emotional reactions to conflicts between their own parents as well. Crockenberg and Forgays (1996) videotaped parents working to resolve significant conflicts and then showed segments of those interactions, which included negative parental emotion and behavior, to their 6-year-old children. Using a narrative interview, children were questioned about the nature and intensity of their emotional reactions to the interparental conflict, after ascertaining that they understood emotion terms and could use them to describe their own reactions. Children reported a range of negative emotions (mad, sad, scared, and various combinations thereof), with sadness more frequent than anger, and frequent happy or okay responses in this nonclinical sample. Additionally, they were more likely to report negative emotions when *fathers* exhibited invalidating, critical, belligerent, and domineering behaviors during the course of the marital interaction.

Crockenberg and Langrock (1998a) interviewed children about specific interparental conflicts that parents reported they had witnessed recently. Children were asked to remember everything they could about each conflict and how they felt as it was happening. If a child reported an emotion, the interviewer queried her about the intensity, and then asked if she had any other feelings during the disagreement. Consistent with earlier findings, when fathers reported using aggressive strategies during marital conflicts, daughters reported more negative emotions of all types (mad, sad, and scared). When fathers who used physical aggression were excluded, only correlations with girls' sadness and fear remained significant.

Grych (1998) and Grych and Fincham (1993) reported comparable associations between interparental conflict and children's negative emotions using an analogue procedure. Children listened to audiotapes of conflicts between a male and female adult, which varied in intensity (i.e., hostility, interruptions, and use of disparaging remarks), while imagining the disagreement occurring between their own parents. Then they rated how mad, sad, worried, and ashamed they would feel. Children's reports of specific negative emotions (Grych & Fincham, 1993) and a composite measure of negative affect (Grych, 1998) were greater in response to high-intensity than to low-intensity vignettes, although in the 1998 study this difference was significant only for girls. Also, younger children (7–9 years) reported more negative affect than older children (10–12 years). Additionally, children's negative emotional reactions to the audiotaped conflicts intensified only in relation to mother-reported *mother-to-father* physical aggression. O'Hearn, Margolin, and John (1997) confirmed the negative emotional impact of physical marital conflict on 8–11-year-old children using parents' diary reports of marital conflicts. Parents described children as angry, sad, or frightened, or as displaying no emotional reaction to marital conflicts. When conflicts were physically aggressive, fathers reported that children were more angry, sad, or frightened, whereas mothers reported that boys expressed greater sadness or fear than boys in either nonphysically aggressive or low-conflict families. O'Brien, Balto, Erber, and Gee (1995) reported similar results with college students using an analogue procedure.

Analysis. These data confirm the anticipated links between agonistic marital conflict and both generalized negative emotion and children's specific emotions of anger, sadness, and fear. Children's emotional reactions are most strongly and consistently negative in response to physical interparental aggression, as would be expected. Nevertheless, children report intense negative emotional reactions to hostile, nonphysical conflicts as well, often sadness or fear, in response to their own parents as well as to simulated interadult conflict. Differences among studies in the emotional impact of nonphysical interparental conflict may be due to differences in the way children's emotions were assessed and to whether specific emotional reactions were distinguished. If verbal aggression is less likely than physical aggression to elicit anger, combining emotional reactions may obscure the emotional impact of that form of interparental behavior. Between-sample differences in the nature and intensity of the nonphysical aggression engaged in by parents and in child age may also explain differences in findings. Older children may be less distressed because they understand when yelling and other types of aggressive, nonphysical interparental behavior carry no threat.

Consistent with a meaning-filtered theory of marital conflict effects, in which benign assessment of an event portends the absence of a negative emotional response, a significant number of children reported no negative emotional reactions to interparental conflict (Crockenberg & Forgays, 1996; Crockenberg & Langrock, 1998a; O'Hearn, Margolin, & John, 1997). Although in some instances the lack of an emotional reaction can be attributed to the nonaggressive character of the interaction, in others children fail to react negatively to demonstrably aggressive interparental behavior.

Typically, researchers have not attempted to distinguish between effects of maternal and paternal behavior on children's emotional reactions to marital conflict, and hence conclusions about their relative impact must be tentative. In community samples, however, fathers' aggressive behavior is more strongly associated with children's negative emotional reactions than mothers', perhaps because their apparently comparable behavior differs qualitatively in ways that alter children's appraisals of threat to personal goals. Fathers may be louder than mothers, display more extreme facial expressions of anger, and engage in more "in your face" behavior by moving their typically larger bodies closer to their partners in concert with other negative verbal or nonverbal emotional cues. In contrast, in families selected for their prior history of interpartner violence, mothers may engage in more high-intensity behavior with partners, increasing the likelihood of children responding emotionally to mothers' marital behavior.

Nor is there consistent evidence that girls experience more negative emotion than boys in response to more intensely negative marital conflict. Whereas both Crockenberg and Langrock (1998b) and Grych (1998) found that only girls' self-reports of negative emotions increased with the intensity of interparental conflict, O'Hearn et al. (1997) found increases for boys' parent-reported emotional reactions to physical aggression. Again, these differences may be attributable to variations in samples and methodology. Parents may underestimate the emotional impact of physically aggressive marital conflict on girls because girls are more covert in their expressions of emotion and less likely to intervene in marital conflicts than boys, an act that may signal emotional distress (Vuchinich, Emery, & Cassidy, 1988). Alternatively, girls may react more negatively primarily to fathers, whereas boys may react more negatively to mothers when they identify more closely with the parent of the same gender and perceive the opposite-gender parent as responsible for the conflict, as we discuss next.

Children's Appraisals of Marital Conflict in Relation to Their Emotional Reactions

Evidence that children's histories of interparental conflict are associated with their emotional responses to interadult conflict provides indirect evidence that experience-based memories influence appraisals of current conflicts (J.S. Cummings, et al., 1989; El-Sheikh, 1994; 1997). More direct evidence comes from studies in which children's perceptions of the marital conflict were associated with their emotional reactions to it. In Crockenberg and Forgays' (1996) research, children's perceptions of interparental conflicts were their responses to the question of whether their parents were talking or arguing and their perceptions of parents' negative emotions during the videotaped "disagreement." Consistent with the expectation that children's appraisals are linked to their emotional reactions, children who viewed parents as arguing were more likely to report negative emotional reactions *to fathers,* and children who perceived mothers and fathers as feeling bad during the conflict were more likely to report negative emotional reactions themselves.

In Grych's (1998) study, children's appraisals were their responses to questions about whether the conflict would escalate and they would be drawn into it (threat), and the extent to which the child, mother, and father were responsible (blame) for the analogue argument they imagined happening in their own families. Their appraisals of efficacy were their ability to do something about the conflict and its likely effectiveness. Appraisals of threat, efficacy expectations, and efficacy outcomes all correlated significantly and substantially with each reported negative emotion (mad, sad, worried, ashamed), whereas perceptions that *fathers* were at fault for the argument were associated only with children's anger. These results confirmed Grych and Fincham's (1993) finding that children's perceptions of threat were associated with their self-reported negative emotions. Additionally, the 11–12-year-old children in the 1993 study reported greater distress and shame when they blamed themselves for the conflict.

Davies and Cummings (1998) reported similar associations between analogue-based measures of children's internal representations of marital conflict and a composite measure of children's emotional reactivity to conflict observed between their mothers and a stranger. The more hostile the internal representations of the marital conflicts, the more negative emotions children reported to a mother–stranger conflict.

Langrock and Crockenberg (1999) reported significant associations between children's narrative-based evaluations of their parents con-flictual interactions and their own emotional responses. When children evaluated conflicts as threatening, either to themselves (parents direct-ing anger toward the child) or for the marital relationship (thoughts of separation and divorce, escalation of negative behaviors), they were more likely to report feeling scared than angry. Additionally, children's evaluations of anger eliciting marital conflicts varied as a function of child gender. Consistent with previous findings (Crockenberg & Forgays, 1996), girls focused their anger toward fathers for blocking or threatening mothers' goals, whereas boys reported anger when marital conflicts jeopardized their own concrete goals (e.g., wanting to have or do something specific).

Analysis. Data linking children's perceptions and appraisals of interparental conflicts with their negative emotional reactions to mari-tal or other conflicts support the theory-based proposition that the meaning conflicts have for children influences their emotional reac-tions. That children's perceptions and appraisals of interparental con-flict show stronger relations with children's emotions than behaviors parents engaged in during marital conflicts (Crockenberg & Forgays, 1996; Grych, 1998) lends further support to this thesis, although method variance may contribute to these associations. Moreover, it appears that meaning is defined in part by the threat conflict poses to children's goals and further, that different types of goal threat are asso-ciated with different emotional reactions in children.

That appraisals of fathers' marital behavior are more strongly linked to children's negative emotions than appraisals of mothers' behavior demonstrate again the unique impact of fathers on children's emo-tional development. Either fathers are more likely to threaten chil-dren's goals than mothers or appear more likely to do so by virtue of the intensity of their behavior. Children may respond more negatively to fathers also because they blame them for the conflict, as Grych (1998) and Langrock and Crockenberg (1999) reported.

The hypothesized mediating effect of children's appraisals between the marital conflict and children's negative emotional reactions has not yet been tested. Regardless, evidence that cognitions mediate between events and emotions would not support the inference that cognitions necessarily precede emotional reactions as negative mood states may also lead to biased information processing (Gotlib & MacLeod, 1997).

Linking Children's Emotional Reactions to Behavior

If children's emotional reactions to marital conflict reflect their appraisals of its impact on goals and their efficacy in protecting those goals, we would expect associations between children's negative emotions and behavior. Additionally, we would expect negative emotions to mediate or moderate the associations between hostile/aggressive interparental conflict behavior and children's behavioral adjustment.

Several investigators have reported associations between children's specific emotional reactions to marital conflict and their behavioral adjustment. Crockenberg and Forgays (1996) reported that children's negative emotional reactions to fathers were associated with their internalizing behavior, and, consistent with specific emotions theory, that children who reported sad reactions to angry fathers tended to be more highly internalizing than children who did not. Similarly, Crockenberg and Langrock (1998) reported that girls' fearful reactions to fathers' interparental aggression correlated with their internalizing behavior and remained so when physically aggressive fathers were excluded (Crockenberg & Langrock, 1999). Boys' emotional reactions to interparental conflict interacted with fathers' interparental aggression to predict their behavioral adjustment. Consistent with specific emotions theory, when boys reported fear in reaction to marital conflicts, fathers' self-reported marital aggression predicted sons' internalizing behavior, whereas when boys expressed anger, fathers' marital aggression predicted sons' externalizing behavior. When fathers who were physically aggressive were excluded, only the interactive impact of fathers' hostile, nonphysical aggression and fear on boys' internalizing behavior remained significant (Crockenberg & Langrock, 1999).

Davies and Cummings (1998) reported a link between children's emotional reactions to a mother–stranger conflict and their behavioral adjustment. A composite measure of children's negative emotional reactivity correlated significantly with their internalizing and externalizing symptoms and partially mediated associations between mother-reported marital discord and both types of child behavior.

Analysis. Associations between children's specific emotional reactions to interparental conflict and both internalizing and externalizing behavior have been confirmed empirically. In the only study to test for interactive effects, anger increased the likelihood of externalizing behavior, whereas fear increased the likelihood of internalizing behavior in boys exposed to high levels of paternal marital aggression. Congruent with El-Sheikh and Reiter's (1996) findings using simulated interadult conflict, anger interacted with fathers' physical aggression and fear with fathers' hostile, nonphysical aggression to predict externalizing and internalizing behavior, respectively. Taken together, these findings support the usefulness of children's specific emotional reactions to interparental conflict in understanding the development of specific patterns of behavioral adjustment.

Moderating Effects of Emotional Regulation on Children's Behavioral Adjustment

In both emotion-focused models of marital conflict effects, as well as in Grych and Fincham's (1990) initial conceptualization, children are expected to vary in their behavioral expressions of felt emotions by virtue of differences in their regulatory capacities. Although there are convincing data that children's coping strategies moderate the association between stress and behavior (Compas et al., 1999), few investigators have assessed coping in relation to marital conflict, and even fewer have considered how children regulate specific emotions (i.e., anger or fear) (see Kerig, Chapter 8).

Two studies provide indirect support for the moderating effect of emotional regulation by demonstrating interactions between hostile marital conflict and children's regulatory capacities. Katz and Gottman (1995) reported that the impact of marital hostility assessed when children were 5, in conjunction with measures of vagal tone, predicted their externalizing behavior 3 years later. Marital hostility strongly predicted externalizing behavior for children with low vagal tone, but not for children with high vagal tone, a physiological measure of the child's capacity to regulate arousal. Similarly, Kerig (1998) found that parent-reported marital conflict was associated with girls' self-reported anxiety in the absence of self-calming strategies. When girls said they were able to modulate their distress during marital conflicts, there was no association between marital conflict and anxiety. Regulation was not assessed in relation to emotion, but it is reasonable to infer that hostile marital conflict is a marker for maritally linked distress in these studies. If there were no emotional arousal, presumably no calming would be necessary.

Additionally, Crockenberg and Langrock (1999) demonstrated that the specific emotion of anger has different behavioral correlates in girls, depending on their regulatory capacities. Six-year-old girls who were angry about interparental conflicts had inflated levels of externalizing behaviors only when they lacked social competence. Girls who were angry but socially competent were no more externalizing than girls who were not angry. In contrast, girls who were both angry and fearful in reaction to marital conflict were more internalizing than other girls.

There is evidence also that parents foster children's ability to regulate their emotional reactions to interparental conflict. Katz and Gottman (1997) reported that certain behaviors exhibited during parent–child interactions (e.g., parental warmth and praise) and parents' metaemotion philosophy (i.e., parents' attitudes and response to children's emotions) buffered children from the negative outcomes characteristically associated with marital conflict. Another aspect of the parent–child relationship that serves as a buffer for children is the presence of conversations about marital conflicts. Children were less likely to engage in externalizing behavior when parents talked with them about their interparental conflicts, reassuring children of their love for each other or for them, explaining that they were no longer upset with each other and that conflict between parents is normal (Crockenberg & Langrock, 1998).

Analysis. Although data are scant, they demonstrate that emotional regulation alters the association between children's maritally linked negative emotions and their behavior and, further, that parents facilitate children's ability to regulate negative emotions associated with marital conflicts. They indicate also that the nature of the regulatory behavior is related to the type of behavior the child manifests. Both engagement and withdrawal may reduce the overt expression of anger associated with interparental conflict, if they decrease the threat to the child's goals, either those threatened by the conflict or those generated by the child's negative emotional reaction to it. Nevertheless, the latter strategy may be less adaptive if children develop emotional schemas that generalize to situations in which avoidance interferes with their attainment of other goals.

Directions for Future Research

Development of valid methods for assessing specific emotional reactions to interparental conflict is essential to future research efforts. To ensure the validity of self-reports of emotions, children must be able to consider and report both the experience and intensity of multiple, specific emotions. They must be invited to consider a range of emotions, be able to distinguish between different emotions and intensities based on their personal experience, and, if a narrative method is employed, to feel comfortable talking about emotions. When parents inform about children's emotional reactions to interparental conflict, differences in their ability to recognize emotions and a related tendency to report their own, rather than their child's reaction, are potential sources of error. Levine, Stein, and Liwag (1999) reported discordance between parents' and children's appraisals of children's emotional responses to the same event, most notably for fear and anger, when parents' and children's goals in the emotion-eliciting context differed.

Method-based variance in measures of specific emotions can be minimized by questioning children sequentially first about the experience and then about the intensity of each specific emotion or by using global questions to reduce suggestibility in conjunction with a pictorial array of specific emotions to remind children of the possibilities. Failure to take these precautions contributes to an artificially high degree of intercorrelation between measures of emotions that may obscure associations between specific emotions and specific behaviors.

Additionally, children's emotions should be assessed in relation to interparental conflict, actual or analogue. If the eliciting stimulus is some other kind of conflict (e.g., between a parent and child or parent and stranger), it is uncertain whether children react similarly to interparental conflict and claims to this effect are unwarranted.

Interparental Behavior in Relation to Appraisals, Emotions, and Behaviors

Although the emotional impact of any specific, repeated pattern of interparental conflict depends on children's schema-based appraisals, certain behaviors, such as physical aggression, are more likely than others to adversely impact children's goals, and hence to elicit negative appraisals. The reviewed research is consistent with this model-based prediction, but mixed in demonstrating a comparable link between hostile, nonphysical interparental behavior and children's appraisals and emotions. Discrepancies may be attributable to variation in the way nonphysical interparental hostility or aggression is defined, to sample differences in the amount or degree of nonphysical aggression and its co-occurrence with physical aggression, or to the type of exposure, analogue or actual, in different studies. Analogue procedures may underestimate the impact of nonphysical interparental conflict by attenuating the goal-linked meaning of the event. Whereas physical aggression may have a generalized negative meaning for children because of its potential for physical harm, nonphysical hostility may have more idiosyncratic meanings as a function of the way it impacts children's goals in specific families. Comparisons are needed of children's emotions using both methods, as well as in audio and video-based analogue procedures.

A related issue has to do with the impact of other types of interparental conflict behavior on children. In appraisal studies, the focus has been on the influence of hostile physical and nonphysical interparental behavior for obvious reasons. Other types of interparental behavior may influence children's appraisals as well. When parents avoid conflict, they may undermine their children's sense of efficacy in relation to goal attainment, prompting feelings of sadness, and expose them to an avoidant regulation strategy that interferes with their competence to pursue and protect goals.

During interparental conflicts, children are exposed to the behavior of both parents, with the behavior of each potentially influencing their appraisals of the conflict. As a couple, they may approach conflict similarly or differently. Research is needed comparing children's appraisals, emotions, and behavior when mothers and fathers approach their conflicts similarly or differently. Moreover, as children's goal-linked appraisals are expected to vary as a function of their own and parents' gender (e.g., girls may be more frightened than boys when fathers are aggressive toward mothers), data must be analyzed separately for same and opposite-gender parent–child dyads.

Appraisals and Emotions

Research on children's appraisals of interparental conflict has focused primarily on children's perceptions of threat and blame, with threat defined in relation to escalation of the conflict and their involvement in it (Grych, 1998; Grych & Fincham, 1990), or in relation to emotional security (Davies & Cummings, 1994). There is preliminary evidence, however, that children appraise interparental conflicts in relation to multiple goals (security, relationship, and tangible concrete goals), and that different types of goal threat are linked to specific emotions, sometimes in gender-specific ways (Langrock & Crockenberg, 1999).

Additional research on appraisals is needed to understand what children find threatening about interparental conflict and to identify more precisely the circumstances under which children's emotional reactions to interparental conflicts differ. As suggested previously, children may perceive different types of threat as more or less controllable, with controllability determining emotion and the type of behavior that will ensue, although not its particular form. Comparisons of appraisals by gender are needed to test the model-based prediction that children evaluate interparental conflicts through a gendered filter that contributes to differences in emotional reactions. Comparisons of appraisals in relation to both analogue and actual interparental conflicts could help to explain the varying results regarding the emotional impact of hostile, non-physical interparental conflict on children.

Emotions and Behavior

Specific emotions are expected to increase the likelihood of certain behaviors occurring and decrease the likelihood of others (e.g., anger is expected to be associated with overt attacks on others, whereas fear is expected to be associated with withdrawal). Additionally, however, the links between specific emotions and specific behaviors are expected to vary as a function of individuals' regulatory capacities and strategies. The data are consistent with this prediction, but scant. More research is needed to test model-based hypotheses about the factors influencing children's emotional regulation in the context of interparental conflict and the processes through which that regulation occurs. One hypothesis is that specific emotions constrain behavior by influencing which regulatory strategies will be effective (e.g., to regulate anger, actions must be directed toward goal attainment and protection or toward anger reduction). Another is that the intensity of emotion impacts regulatory behavior by focusing on the threat and limiting access to alternative, goal-directed strategies in the child's behavioral repertoire (e.g., intense anger impedes problem solving and increases the likelihood of overt aggression, whereas mild anger may facilitate it). A third hypothesis is that parents influence children's emotional regulation through behaviors they model during conflicts and through behaviors they engage in with children which moderate the association between temperamental reactivity and emotional regulation (e.g., talking about interparental conflicts and what they mean, teaching children to self-soothe).

Conclusion

The data reviewed establish the usefulness of emotion and emotion regulation as explanatory constructs linking hostile interparental conflict to both externalizing and internalizing behavior in children. We believe that they demonstrate also the utility of specific emotions in explaining how and why children develop different patterns of behavioral adjustment in response to marital conflict, although the empirical basis for this conclusion is relatively thin. More research is needed on the hypothesized links between specific emotions and specific patterns of behavioral adjustment. We need valid measures of specific emotions to investigate further (1) the differential impact of different patterns of marital conflict behavior on children's appraisals, emotions, and behavior; (2) the features of appraisals associated with different emotional reactions in children; (3) the mediating and moderating effects of specific emotions on associations between interparental conflict and children's adjustment; (4) the ways different regulation strategies moderate associations between emotion and behavior; and (5) the impact of parent and child gender and child age on each aspect of the transmission process.

REFERENCES

Bandura, A. (1965). Influence of models' reinforcement contingencies on the acquisition of imitative responses. *Journal of Personality and Social Psychology, 1,* 589–595.

Bandura, A., Ross, D., & Ross, S. A., (1963). Imitation of film-mediated aggressive models. *Journal of Abnormal and Social Psychology, 66,* 3–11.

Bauer, P. (1993). Memory for gender-consistent and gender-inconsistent event sequences by twenty-five-month-old children. *Child Development, 64,* 285–297.

Campos, J. J., Mumme, D. L., Kermoian, R., & Campos, R. G. (1994). A functionalist perspective on the nature of emotion. In N. A. Fox (Ed.), The development of emotion regulation: Biological and behavioral considerations. *Monographs of the Society for Research in Child Development, 59* (Serial No. 240, pp. 284–303.)

Christensen, A. (1988). Dysfunctional interaction patterns in couples. In P. Noller & M. A. Fitzpatrick (Eds.), *Perspectives on marital interaction* (pp. 31–52). Avon, England: Multilingual Matters.

Compas, B., Connor, J., Thomsen, A., Saltzman, H., & Wadsworth, W. (1999). *Coping with stress during childhood and adolescence: Progress, problems, and potential in theory and research.* Manuscript submitted for publication.

Crick, N., Casas, J. F., & Mosher, M. (1997). Relational and overt aggression in preschool. *Developmental Psychology, 33,* 579–588.

Crockenberg, S., & Forgays, D. (1994, April). *The role of emotion in children's understanding of and reactions to conflict.* Paper presented at the Biennial Conference on Human Development, Pittsburgh, PA.

Crockenberg, S., & Forgays, D. (1996). The role of emotion in children's understanding and emotional reactions to marital conflict. *Merrill-Palmer Quarterly, 42,* 22–47.

Crockenberg, S., Jackson, S., & Langrock, A. (1996). Effects of parenting and gender on children's social competence. In M. Killen (Ed.), *Children's autonomy, social competence, and interactions with adults and other children: New directions in child development research, 73* (pp. 41–56). San Francisco, CA: Jossey-Bass.

Crockenberg, S., & Langrock, A. M. (1998a). *Marital conflict as a gendered experience: How patterns of inter-adult behavior and children's specific negative emotions influence behavioral adjustment.* Paper presented at the biennial meeting of the International Society for Behavioral Development, Berne, Switzerland.

Crockenberg, S., & Langrock, A. M. (1998b). *Buffering children from the potentially negative impact of verbally aggressive marital conflict.* Poster presented at the biennial meeting of the International Society for Behavioral Development, Berne, Switzerland.

Crockenberg, S., & Langrock, A. M. (1999). *Marital conflict, parenting, and children's behavioral adjustment: Understanding modeling and emotion processes and gender-linked trajectories.* Unpublished manuscript, University of Vermont.

Cummings, J. S., Pellegrini, D. S., Notarius, C. I., & Cummings, E. M. (1989). Children's responses to angry adult behavior as a function of marital distress and history of interparent hostility. *Child Development, 60,* 1035–1043.

Davies, P., & Cummings, E. M. (1994). Marital conflict and child adjustment: An emotional security hypothesis. *Psychological Bulletin, 116,* 387–411.

Davies, P., & Cummings, E. M. (1995). Children's emotions as organizers of their reactions to interadult anger: A functionalist perspective. *Developmental Psychology, 31,* 677–684.

Davies, P., & Cummings, E. M. (1998). Exploring children's emotional security as a mediator of the link between marital relations and child adjustment. *Child Development, 69,* 124–139.

El-Sheikh, M. (1994). Children's emotional and physiological responses to interadult angry behavior: The role of history of interparental hostility. *Journal of Abnormal Child Psychology, 22,* 661–678.

El-Sheikh, M. (1997). Children's responses to adult-adult and mother-child arguments: The role of parental marital conflict and distress. *Journal of Family Psychology, 11,* 165–175.

El-Sheikh, M., & Reiter, S. L. (1996). Children's responding to live interadult conflict: The role of form of anger expression. *Journal of Abnormal Child Psychology, 24,* 401–415.

Emery, R. E. (1988). *Marriage, divorce, and children's adjustment.* Newbury Park, CA: Sage.

Eisenberg, N. (1997, April). *Emotion-related regulation.* Master lecture presented at the Biennial meetings of the Society for Research in Child Development, Washington, DC.

Frijda, N. H., Kuipers, P., & ter Schure, E. (1989). Relations among emotion, appraisal, and emotional action readiness. *Journal of Personality and Social Psychology, 57,* 212–228.

Gotlib, I. H., & MacLeod, C. (1997). Information processing in anxiety and depression: A cognitive-developmental perspective. In J. A. Burack et al. (Eds.), *Attention, development, and psychopathology* (pp. 350–378). New York: Guilford Press.

Gottman, J. M. (1979). *Marital interaction: Experimental investigations.* New York: Academic Press.

Grych, J. H. (1998). Children's appraisals of interparental conflict: Situational and contextual influences. *Journal of Family Psychology, 12,* 437–453.

Grych J. H., & Fincham, F. (1990). Marital conflict and children's adjustment: A cognitive-contextual framework. *Psychological Bulletin, 108,* 267–290.

Grych, J. H., & Fincham, F. (1993). Children's appraisals of marital conflict: Initial investigations of the cognitive-contextual framework. *Child Development, 64,* 215–230.

Jenkins, J. M., & Oatley, K. (1998). The development of emotion schemas in children: Processes of emotion elicitation that underlie psychopathology. In W. Flack & J. D. Laird (Eds.), *Emotions in psychopathology: Theory and research.* Oxford: Oxford University Press.

Katz, L., & Gottman, J. M. (1995). Marital interaction and child outcomes: A longitudinal study of mediating and moderating processes. In D. Cicchetti & S. Toth (Eds.), Emotion, cognition, & representation *Rochester Symposium on Developmental Psychopathology*, Vol. 6, Rochester, NY: University of Rochester Press.

Katz, L., & Gottman, J. M. (1997). Buffering children from marital conflict and dissolution. *Journal of Clinical Child Psychology, 26*, 157–171.

Kerig, P. D., Cowan, P. A., & Cowan, C. P. (1993). Marital quality and gender differences in parent-child interaction. *Developmental Psychology, 29*, 931–939.

Kerig, P. K. (1998). Moderators and mediators of the effects of interparental conflict on children's adjustment. *Journal of Abnormal Child Psychology, 26*, 199–212.

Kliewer, W., Fearnow, M. D., & Miller, P. A. (1996). Coping socialization in middle childhood: Tests of maternal and paternal influences. *Child Development, 67*, 2339–2357.

Langrock, A. M., & Crockenberg, S. (1999, April). *The impact of interparental conflict on children: Direct, indirect, and interactive effects*. Paper presented at the biennial meeting of the Society for Research in Child Development, Albuquerque, New Mexico.

Levine, L., Stein, N., & Liwag, M. (1999). Remembering children's emotions: Sources of concordant and discordant accounts between parents and children. *Developmental Psychology, 35*, 790–801.

Levy, G. D., & Boston, M. B. (1992, May). *Recall of gender scripts by preschool children*. Paper presented at the meetings of the Midwestern Psychological Association, Chicago, IL.

Levy, G. D., & Fivush, R. (1993). Scripts and gender: A new approach for examining gender-role development. *Developmental Review, 13*, 126–146.

Mandler, G. (1975). *Mind and emotion*. New York: Wiley.

Margolin, G. (1988). Marital conflict is not marital conflict is not marital conflict. In R. DeV. Peters & R. J. McMahon (Eds.), *Social learning and systems approaches to marriage and the family* (pp. 193–216). New York: Brunner/Mazel.

McConaughy, S. H., & Achenbach, T. M. (1994). Comorbidity of empirically based syndromes in matched general population and clinical samples. *Journal of Child Psychology and Psychiatry, 35*, 1141–1157.

Nathan-Ailor, J. (1999). *Coping and optimism in children: Parental influences*. Unpublished doctoral dissertation, University of Vermont.

Oatley, K. (1992). *Best laid schemes: the psychology of emotions*. New York: Cambridge University Press.

O'Brien, M., Balton, K., Erber, S., & Gee, C. (1995). College students' cognitive and emotional reactions to simulated marital and family conflict. *Cognitive Therapy & Research, 19*, 707–724.

O'Hearn, H. G., Margolin, G., & John, R. S. (1997). Mothers' and fathers' reports of children's reactions to naturalistic marital conflict. *Journal of the American Academy of Child & Adolescent Psychiatry, 36*, 1366–1373.

Perry, D. G., Perry, L. C., & Weiss, R. J. (1989). Sex differences in the consequences that children anticipate for aggression. *Developmental Psychology, 25*, 312–319.

Saarni, C., Mumme, D., & Campos, J. J. (in press). Emotional development: Action, communication, and understanding. In W. Damon (Series Ed.) and N. Eisenberg (Vol. Ed.), *Social, emotional and personality development: Vol. 3: Handbook of child psychology*. New York: Wiley.

Stein, N. L., & Levine, L. (1987). Thinking about feelings: The development and organization of emotional knowledge. In R. Snow & M. Farr (Eds.), *Aptitude, learning and instruction* (Vol. 3, pp. 165–197). Hillsdale, NJ: Erlbaum.

Tomkins, S. S. (1979). Script theory: Differential magnification of affects. In H. E. Howe & R. A. Dienstbier (Eds.), *Nebraska Symposium on Motivation, 1978* (pp. 201–236). Lincoln, NE: University of Nebraska Press.

Vuchinich, S., Emery, R. E., & Cassidy, J. (1988). Family members as third parties in dyadic family conflict: Strategies, alliances, and outcomes. *Child Development, 59*, 1293–1302.

6 Understanding the Impact of Interparental Conflict on Children

The Role of Social Cognitive Processes

John H. Grych and Shalini Cardoza-Fernandes

Research on interparental conflict has shown clearly that witnessing angry, conflictual interactions between parents can be a stressful experience for children (see Cummings & Davies, 1994). However, this work shows equally clearly that children differ in how they respond to interparental conflict. Even when children observe standardized conflict stimuli in laboratory settings, consistent individual differences in their responses are found (for a review, see Cummings & Davies, 1994). Similarly, children exposed to high levels of interparental conflict and violence exhibit a variety of adjustment outcomes, with some experiencing internalizing problems, others externalizing problems, and still others exhibiting no adjustment problems at all (Grych, Jouriles, Swank, McDonald, & Norwood, 2000). Investigating why children respond differently to conflict and whether their responses are linked to broader patterns of functioning are important goals for understanding how exposure to conflict affects children's development.

Conceptual models seeking to explain how children respond to conflict emphasize different intervening processes, but a common theme in these models is that the meaning of the interaction for children is critical for determining its effects (Crockenberg & Forgays, 1996; Davies & Cummings, 1994; Grych & Fincham, 1990). This perspective is consistent with the position of stress and coping theorists who have argued that how individuals evaluate events shapes their impact (Rutter, 1983; Garmezy, 1983; Compas, 1987), and with research implicating children's perceptions and interpretation of events in the development of internalizing and externalizing problems (see Dodge, 1993).

The emphasis on children's subjective evaluation of conflict suggests that attention to social cognition, which concerns "the social construction and development of meanings about the self and social world" (Noam, Chandler, & LaLonde, 1995, p. 424), is likely to enhance understanding of the short-and long-term effects of exposure to interparental conflict. Social cognitive theories traditionally have focused either on information processing or information transformation (Dodge, 1993; Estes, 1991). Information-processing theories attempt to describe the mental events that occur "online" in response to particular situations or stimuli (e.g., peer conflict), whereas information-transformation theories describe how experiences are stored in memory and guide later processing and behavior. Though they are conceptually distinct, these cognitive activities are intimately related: mental representations of prior experiences influence children's perceptions and interpretations in new situations, and their situational processing in turn affects what is stored in memory. For example, a child who is inadvertently bumped by a peer on the playground may interpret the behavior as intentional because he holds the general belief that other children are hostile toward him, and his interpretation of this experience will provide more "evidence" to support the belief (see Crick & Dodge, 1994).

In this chapter, we examine how studying children's immediate processing of interparental conflict and the transformation of those experiences into more long-lasting mental structures may illuminate the impact of interparental conflict on child adjustment. First, we describe theory and research on social cognitive processes proposed to occur when children observe interparental conflict, and then consider how witnessing interparental conflict may affect the development of children's beliefs and expectations regarding interpersonal relationships. We then discuss some of the challenges involved in assessing social cognitive processes and close by identifying directions for future research in this area.

Children's Immediate Responses to Interparental Conflict

Information-processing theories generally propose a sequence of steps or stages that describe how stimuli are perceived, interpreted, and acted upon (Dodge, 1993; Massaro & Cowan, 1993). Progression through the stages is considered to be linear for a given stimulus, but processing can occur simultaneously at multiple steps as individuals evaluate the ongoing circumstances in a particular situation. Cognitive processing is not necessarily conscious; in fact, often it is highly automatized and occurs outside of awareness (see Bargh & Chartrand, 1999). Automatization makes very rapid processing possible because multiple cognitive activities can occur in parallel and without use of limited attentional resources, whereas controlled (or conscious) processing occurs serially and requires effort and attention (e.g., Shiffrin & Schneider, 1977).[1]

Information-processing models typically focus on cognitive activities such as encoding and response evaluation, but also may include emotional and motivational constructs such as goals and regulation of arousal (Dodge, 1993). Although there is a long history of debating the primacy of cognition versus emotion in human experience, more recent theorizing recognizes that emotion and cognition are closely intertwined and in some cases inseparable (Bretherton, Fritz, Zahn-Waxler, & Ridgeway, 1986; Campos, Campos, & Barrett, 1989; Stein & Liwag, 1997). Goodnow (1996) commented on this shift, noting that rather than viewing either emotions or cognitions as necessarily giving rise to the other, "ideas themselves are seen as suffused with affect" (p. 424). For example, fear involves both a subjective emotional experience and the perception of threat in the environment (Campos et al., 1989). The challenge is to understand more fully how cognition and emotion together influence the impact of conflict on children, including how thoughts may give rise to particular emotions and how emotions may influence cognitive processing.

Grych and Fincham (1990) proposed a conceptual framework for understanding children's responses to interparental conflict that reflects an information-processing perspective. Because this framework presents the most detailed analysis of social cognitive processes involved in children's responses to interparental conflict, we will use it to guide our examination of cognition in this part of the chapter.

The cognitive-contextual framework (see Figure 6.1) describes psychological processes hypothesized to occur when children witness a parental disagreement. It proposes that children's *appraisals* mediate the impact of conflict and guide their coping efforts. The appraisal process represents children's attempt to understand the interaction and its implications for them and their family. Cognition and affect are proposed to have a dynamic, reciprocal relationship in this process: children's perceptions and interpretations of interparental conflict modulate their initial affective response, and emotions, in turn, can color their interpretations of the interaction. The appraisals that children make in a given situation are proposed to be a function of the way the conflict is expressed (e.g., emotional intensity, resolution) and contextual factors, such as children's prior exposure to conflict and the

---

[1] The distinction between parallel and serial processing is not clear cut, however. They represent ends of a continuum, rather than discrete categories, and may occur simultaneously in many situations.

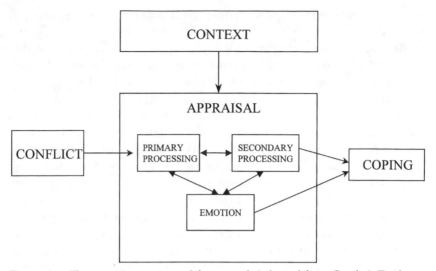

Figure 6.1. The cognitive-contextual framework (adapted from Grych & Fincham, 1990).

quality of parent–child relations. The appraisal process may continue throughout the course of the conflict and does not necessarily stop when the conflict ends; children may ruminate about an interaction later and elaborate or change their understanding of the conflict based on their ruminations or new information (e.g., a parent explaining the reason for the conflict to the child) (see Baker-Ward, Ornstein, & Principe, 1997). In the following sections, we describe the role of appraisals in more detail and review the small but growing body of research examining children's appraisals of conflict.

The Appraisal Process

Following Lazarus' work on adults' response to stressful events, appraisal is described as a two stage process in which children first evaluate whether the conflict is relevant or threatening to them ("primary processing"). If so, they engage in further processing ("secondary processing") in an attempt to understand why the conflict is occurring, how they can respond to it, and what is likely to happen next. Because children's perception and understanding of the social world changes with age, their appraisals also are likely to change developmentally.

Primary Processing. Interparental conflict may be relevant to children for two reasons. Conflict typically involves the expression of negative affect, and emotional communications, especially between family members, are salient and emotionally arousing to children (Campos et al., 1989). Emotions also provide cues about how an individual is likely to act (e.g., Banerjee, 1997). Anger, the emotion most closely associated with conflict, may predict aggressive behavior, and so attending to such signals is essential for children's safety and well-being. Children recognize facial and vocal expressions of anger in infancy (Terwogt & Harris, 1993), but the cues that they use to infer others' emotions and their capacity to recognize and distinguish between subtle expressions of anger change developmentally (for a review see Banerjee, 1997). Preschoolers tend to focus primarily on facial expressions to judge others' affect whereas older children learn to integrate facial cues, situational information, and knowledge of others' internal states (e.g., motivation) to infer another person's emotion (Gnepp, 1983; Reichenbach & Masters, 1983). Consequently, whether an interaction is perceived as conflictual or angry may differ for children of different ages. Davies, Myers, and Cummings (1996) found evidence of developmental shifts in children's perceptions of conflict, reporting that early adolescents more accurately used affective cues to determine whether a couple had resolved the problem that led to a disagreement than did 7–9 year olds.

Although parents' negative affect alone is likely to elicit an emotional response from children, the meaning of interparental conflict goes beyond the recognition that parents are angry with each other. Considering how conflict may affect children's goals – what is "at stake" for them (Lazarus & Folkman, 1984) – also is important for understanding why conflict can be upsetting to children (also see Crockenberg & Langrock, Chapter 5; Lazarus, 1991; Stein & Liwag, 1997). Interparental conflict may be perceived as posing a direct threat to children's physical or emotional well-being or to their desire to have harmonious, stable family relationships (Davies & Cummings, 1994), as well as a host of more transient, situation-specific goals, such as a family taking a trip to the zoo. Stein and Liwag (1997) argue that children as young as 4 months of age are capable of appraising events in relation to basic goals, but the breadth and type of goals affected by conflict is likely to change with age. Younger children may tend to focus primarily on immediate, concrete concerns (e.g., will Dad yell at me?) whereas older children are more aware of longer-term and more abstract consequences (e.g., will Dad be angry for the rest of the weekend?). As children get older and learn that some parents separate and divorce, they also are more likely to fear that expressions of discord may affect the future of the marriage.

Secondary Processing. If children perceive that a parental interaction is relevant to them, they then try to determine why the interaction is occurring and how they should respond. Understanding the causes and consequences of significant events, particularly those that are threatening or aversive, is adaptive because it enhances individuals' ability to respond effectively, anticipate others' behavior, and predict subsequent events (e.g., Fabes, Eisenberg, Nyman, & Michealieu, 1992; van den Broek, 1997) and may play an important role in determining the focus of individuals' coping efforts (Doherty, 1981a). However, certain attributions may exacerbate the stressfulness of conflict. In particular, perceiving that they are at fault for their parents' disagreements is upsetting for children and motivates them to seek a way to help resolve the conflict and alleviate their emotional distress (Grych & Fincham, 1993). Even if they do not blame themselves for starting a parental disagreement, children may see themselves as responsible for stopping or preventing conflicts (O'Brien, Margolin, & John, 1995). Becoming involved in the conflict, however, makes the child more vulnerable to becoming a target of parental anger or aggression or being triangulated in marital problems. Even though children's efforts may be successful in ending the conflict at the time, child involvement in marital issues is likely to have adverse long-term effects on the functioning of the family system (Emery, 1989).

Attributing responsibility for interparental conflict to the parents is likely to be more adaptive and accurate, but also may have important implications for family relationships. Research on attributions in marriage indicates that blaming a partner for marital problems leads to greater anger toward that partner and diminishing relationship quality over time (see Fincham, 1998). Children who repeatedly perceive one parent as responsible for causing discord in the marriage may become angry and resentful toward that parent and side with the parent they perceive as less blameworthy, contributing to the formation of cross-generational coalitions.

Children's understanding of the causes of interparental conflict is dependent on their capacity for causal reasoning, which exhibits a developmental trend from focusing primarily on observable factors temporally proximal to the event to internal states or characteristics of individuals (for reviews see Miller & Aloise, 1989; van den Broek, 1997). Because their own behavior is highly salient to them, young children may tend to focus on things that they have done or failed to do prior to the conflict as possible causes, particularly if the content of the disagreement is related to the child or parenting issues. Recognizing that conflict is caused by a disagreement in the marital relationship also requires that children understand that parents have a relationship that is separate from their role as parents. Several studies have shown that children's understanding of family roles and relationships becomes more differentiated over time (e.g., Bretherton, Prentiss, & Ridgeway, 1990; Fu, Goodwin, Sporakowki, & Hinkle, 1988) and it may be difficult for young children to recognize that a conflict in the marriage may be unrelated to their parents' relationship with them.

We know very little about how children make attributions for naturally occurring family events. Early studies indicated that young children tend to view their own behavior as a primary cause of parental anger (e.g., Covell & Abramovitch, 1987), but in these studies children were simply asked to report what they thought could make their parents angry, and their perceptions may be different when the anger arises from a parental disagreement. A study specifically assessing children's attributions for interparental conflicts found that 7–12-year-old children ascribed the least blame to the child in the vignettes, but that younger children tended to make more child-blaming attributions (Grych, 1998). Grych (1998) also found that attributions were related to other appraisals: perceiving either children or fathers to be responsible for causing a conflict was associated with greater threat and more pessimistic expectations for children's coping efforts, whereas attributing greater blame to mothers was associated with lower threat and more positive coping expectations.

The final type of appraisal highlighted in the cognitive contextual framework is coping efficacy. Bandura (1986) distinguished between two types of beliefs related to coping, efficacy expectations and outcome expectations. Efficacy expectations refer to individuals' belief that they have the capacity to engage in a coping behavior in a particular situation, and outcome expectations refer to whether that behavior is expected to be effective. High efficacy and outcome expectations are likely to lead to sustained coping efforts, whereas low expectations may lead to helplessness and avoidance (Doherty, 1981b). Children who feel able to respond effectively when conflict occurs also are expected to experience less threat than children who feel helpless, and Grych (1998) found that children's appraisals of threat correlated with both types of coping efficacy, but were particularly strongly linked to outcome expectancies.

The limited existing research suggests that children have relatively high efficacy expectations, but less certain outcome expectations, when conflict occurs. Covell and Miles (1992) found that 4–9-year-old children were very confident that they could change their parents' mood when they were angry, primarily by intervening directly or providing comfort to the parent. The 4–9-year-olds also viewed direct intervention in the conflict (telling the parents not to fight) as more likely to be effective than did 10–12-year-olds, a perception that was shared by their parents (Covell & Miles, 1992); whereas most parents of 4–9 year olds reported that their children's efforts to directly intervene would be successful in decreasing their anger, very few parents of 10–12-year-olds thought such tactics would be effective. Thus, age differences in coping expectations may reflect actual differences in parents' responses to children's behavior at different ages, rather than cognitive limitations on the part of younger children.

Although young children may tend to see anger as a highly changeable state and have considerable confidence in their ability to change a parents' mood (e.g., Covell & Abramovitch, 1987), their outcome expectations may be somewhat different when anger arises during marital conflict. After children listened to the conflict vignettes in Grych's (1998) study, they were asked what they would do if they observed a similar conflict between their own parents and what they thought would happen following their response. Virtually all of the children were able to generate a strategy for coping with the conflict, but their beliefs about whether their response would lead to resolving the conflict or decreasing their own distress were more pessimistic. Younger children reported lower levels of both types of efficacy (Grych, 1998), which may reflect limitations in their coping resources and ability to regulate the distress that can arise from parental conflict. Children's coping efficacy is likely to increase as they develop a broader repertoire of coping responses and a more accurate sense of how their behavior can (and cannot) affect parental interactions.

Influences on Children's Appraisals

The cognitive-contextual framework holds that children's appraisals are shaped by both the specific properties of the conflict (e.g., intensity, content) and contextual factors, which consist of psychological characteristics that the child brings into the interaction (e.g., prior experiences with conflict, gender). In some situations, the properties of the conflict are likely to have a more powerful effect on children's appraisals than contextual factors. For example, conflict that escalates into violence is likely to be perceived as highly threatening by all children regardless of their conflict history. In other instances, such as when information about the interaction is ambiguous, unclear, or incomplete, contextual factors may be more influential.

Studies examining children's appraisals of standardized conflict vignettes support the hypothesis that children's appraisals are systematically related to both conflict properties and contextual factors. As the level of anger and hostility expressed in a conflict increases, children tend to perceive greater threat, experience more negative affect, and have lower efficacy expectations (e.g., Cummings, Vogel, Cummings, & El-Sheikh, 1989; Grych 1998; Grych & Fincham, 1993). One study also found that children made more child-blaming attributions when conflicts were more hostile (Grych & Fincham, 1993), perhaps because they felt more responsible for trying to stop interactions that create more distress. The content of the conflict, specifically whether it concerns a child-related (e.g., discipline) or marital issue (e.g., finances), also has been linked to appraisals. When conflict topics are child-related, child-blaming attributions increase and children report greater coping efficacy (Grych, 1998; Grych & Fincham, 1993). Finally, successful resolution of conflict tends to significantly reduce children's negative affect (Cummings & Davies 1994).

The contextual factors that have received the most attention are children's prior exposure to conflict and aggression in the family, age, and gender. Children who have witnessed more frequent, aggressive, and poorly resolved conflict report more negative affect, greater fear that the conflict will escalate or involve them, and lower confidence in the efficacy of their coping efforts (e.g., El-Sheikh, 1994, Grych, 1998). Grych (1998) found that both father-to-mother and mother-to-father conflict behavior independently predicted perceptions of threat and outcome expectations, and that physical aggression was a more powerful predictor of these appraisals than verbal aggression. Aggression occurring between parents and their children also was correlated with perceived threat and outcome expectations, and children exposed to higher levels of both parent–child and interparental aggression tended to show the highest levels of threat and most negative outcome expectations. Taken together, these studies suggest that children's belief that they can do something to cope (efficacy expectation) may be affected more by the parameters of the situation, and how effective they believe that their coping strategy will be (outcome expectation) dependent more on their prior experiences with interparental conflict.

Empirical research also indicates that children's appraisals change developmentally. Younger children in Grych's (1998) sample of 7–12-year-olds generally reported more threat, more child blame, lower coping efficacy, and more negative outcome expectations, and there was some indication that older children's affective responses were more sensitive to the content of the conflicts than were younger children's. Boys and girls differed in some appraisals as well. Girls' perceptions of threat were linked more closely to the affect expressed during the conflict than were boys', and they blamed the fathers less for causing the conflicts than did boys.

Appraisals and Adjustment

The cognitive-contextual framework also proposes that children's appraisals have implications for children's longer-term functioning. Studies examining associations between conflict appraisals and child adjustment problems consistently document significant correlations between these constructs (e.g., Cummings, Davies, & Simpson, 1994; Grych, Seid, & Fincham, 1992; Harold, Fincham, Osborne, & Conger, 1997; Kerig, 1998a,b). However, these findings do not indicate *how* appraisals may be related to children's adjustment. As research in this area evolves from describing to explaining the links between conflict and adjustment, it is essential to develop and test hypotheses that describe specific processes by which conflict may give rise to broader problems in functioning. One of the key issues that arises in relation to cognitive processes is whether appraisals are best understood as mediators or moderators (see Holmbeck, 1997).

Mediators "explain how external physical events take on internal psychological significance" (Baron & Kenny, 1986, p. 1176) and thus are accorded a causal role in linking conflict and adjustment. To serve as mediators, the appraisals children make must be influenced by the characteristics of the conflict they observe, and in turn, their appraisals must increase the likelihood that maladjustment will occur (Baron & Kenny, 1986; Holmbeck, 1997). In contrast, a moderator influences the strength or direction of the association between the constructs, but is not the cause of the association. Conceptualized as moderators, appraisals are better understood as reflecting individual differences in how children perceive events than as a response to the conflict they witness. The analogue studies described earlier indicate that appraisals are influenced both by conflict characteristics and contextual factors (Grych, 1998; Grych & Fincham, 1993), and thus can support either mediational or moderational pathways.

A handful of studies have tested mediational or moderational hypotheses empirically, and though the data have not been entirely consistent, they provide relatively more support for a mediational pathway. For example, Grych, Fincham, Jouriles, and MacDonald (in press) hypothesized that perceived threat and self-blame mediate the relation between children's exposure to conflict and their internalizing, but not externalizing, problems and tested this hypothesis with two large samples of children, one drawn from the community (ages 10–14) and another from battered women's shelters (ages 10–12). Both perceived threat and self-blame were found to independently mediate the association between children's exposure to conflict and internalizing problems for boys in both samples and girls in the shelter sample. For girls in the community sample, only threat was a significant mediator. No significant mediational results were found for externalizing problems. Other recent studies similarly have found support for a mediational pathway linking appraisals and internalizing problems (Dadds, Atkinson, Turner, Blums, & Lendich, 1999; Davies & Cummings, 1998; Kerig, 1998b), though not all studies have replicated these findings (Kerig, 1998a).

Moderating hypotheses have received less consistent support. Kerig (1998a) found that perceptions of self-blame and threat moderated relations between interparental conflict and externalizing problems for boys and internalizing problems for girls in a community sample. Studying beliefs about their ability to control conflict, Rossman and Rosenberg (1992) reported that, for children reporting high levels of family stress, higher control beliefs were related to lower perceived competence, but there was no association between these constructs for children reporting lower levels of stress. In contrast, Grych and colleagues (1999) found no support for a moderational role for threat and blame appraisals, and Rogers and Holmbeck (1997) failed to find moderational effects for a measure of appraisal that assessed children's fear of abandonment, paternal and maternal blame, and peer avoidance.

Conclusions about the causal effects of attributions on children's adjustment are limited by the cross-sectional designs of the studies, but existing research suggests that appraisals may be a mechanism by which exposure to interparental conflict gives rise to internalizing problems. More limited evidence indicates that appraisals may moderate the association between conflict and adjustment, particularly externalizing problems. Longitudinal research is needed to adequately test the nature of the relations among conflict, appraisals, and adjustment. In addition, because much of this work has focused on children between the ages of 10 and 14, we know little about how developmental changes may influence how children perceive and respond to conflict from early childhood through adolescence.

Summary

Conceptual and empirical work on children's appraisals of interparental conflict indicates that social cognitive processes may be important for understanding the short- and long-term effects of conflict on children. In the next section, we consider how exposure to conflict in turn may influence children's social cognitive development. Specifically, we examine how children's experiences with conflict may affect how they perceive and respond to conflict, both within the family and in other relationships.

The Development of Schemas for Interparental Conflict

The idea that mental representations of experiences affect children's later functioning is prominent in developmental psychology. One of the most well-known theories of this kind was offered by Bowlby (1973), who proposed that early caregiver interactions have lasting effects on children's development because they give rise to the development of "internal working models" comprised of beliefs and expectations about close relationships. There have been several recent attempts to describe how children may mentally represent experiences with interparental conflict and aggression and the implications of those representations for their development (Davies & Cummings, 1994; Graham-Bermann, 1998; O'Brien & Chin, 1998; Rossman, 1998). For example, Davies and Cummings (1994) proposed that children's observations of parental conflict lead to a set of representations that include beliefs about the typical course and resolution of interparental conflicts, the stability and predictability of the marital relationship, and the threat posed by conflict to their own well-being. These representations form one of the foundations of children's emotional security.

Reference to mental representations, working models, and related constructs such as schemas and scripts is fairly common in the psychological literature, but these terms often are neither defined nor measured with precision. In order for such constructs to be useful for understanding the impact of interparental conflict on children's development, it is essential to operationalize them in clear, testable terms. This process will be facilitated by anchoring the investigation of children's representations of conflict in preexisting theory, methodology, and empirical findings. In this section we examine how research on schemas can guide investigation of children's representations of their experiences with interparental conflict. Although this term has been used loosely in many investigations (see Abelson & Black, 1986), there is a sufficient body of research on schemas in cognitive and social psychology to provide a firm foundation for conceptualizing and measuring children's representations of parental conflict.

Schemas

Schemas typically are defined as organized clusters of knowledge, beliefs, and expectations about a particular subject or situation. They serve to guide attention, memory, and behavior when new instances of the subject are encountered, and are used to "fill in the gaps" when social stimuli are missing, unclear, or ambiguous (for a review see Wyer & Carlston, 1994). Schemas also may include affective "tags," or emotional responses associated with the situation (Fiske & Havelchak,

1986; Wyer & Carlston, 1994), and scripts that describe particular behavioral sequences likely to occur in the situation (Baldwin, 1999). Although schemas have been studied most often in relation to the self, other people, or particular situations, several theorists have proposed that individuals also develop schemas for interpersonal relationships (for a review, see Baldwin, 1992). Children's experiences with interparental conflict are prime candidates for representation as schemas because events that are salient, emotionally arousing, and personally relevant are highly likely to be remembered, and even very young children rapidly form abstracted, generalized representations of such events (Farrar & Goodman, 1990; Fivush, Kuebli, & Clubb, 1992; Hudson, 1990).

To be adaptive, cognitive representations must be "tolerably accurate" reflections of the actual interactions that occurred (Bowlby, 1973, p. 202; also see Bretherton, Ridgeway, & Cassidy, 1990), and so there should be considerable correspondence between children's experiences with interparental conflict and the content of their schemas. However, what is represented also depends on how children perceive, interpret, and understand the events they observe (Baker-Ward et al., 1997; Wyer & Carlston, 1994; Stein & Liwag, 1997). Baker-Ward and colleagues (1997) write that "an event representation is based on an individual's *understanding* of that event as it is being experienced [emphasis added]. As such, expectation and prior knowledge guide interpretation of the experience and enable the generation of a representation that typically includes more information than that explicitly available in the event itself" (p. 89). Thus, children's appraisals should play a significant role in shaping what children encode and remember about interparental conflict, as well as being influenced by preexisting representations.

Research indicates that the process of forming an event representation is quite similar across a wide age range (see Baker-Ward et al., 1997) but that the content of schemas changes developmentally. Children from the age of 3 years on are able to remember the central details of personally relevant events and to recall them in the proper temporal order (Bauer & Mandler, 1990; Hamond & Fivush, 1991; Peterson & Bell, 1996), but as children get older their schemas become more elaborate and are more likely to include reports of affect, explanations for events (rather than simply descriptions), and inferences that go beyond the events that occurred (Baker-Ward et al., 1997; van den Broek, 1997). Children also may utilize their schemas to a greater extent as they get older. For example, O'Brien and Chin (1998) found that 10–12-year-old children showed stronger schema-consistent processing of aggressive and nonaggressive words than did 7–9-year-olds.

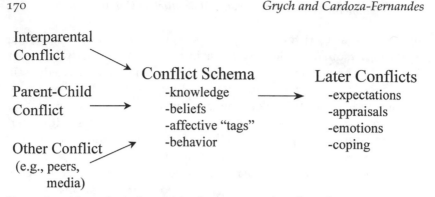

Figure 6.2. A hypothetical model for the operation of conflict schema.

Investigating how children mentally represent their experiences with conflict is a promising direction for research because it provides a mechanism for linking children's experiences with interparental conflict with their later functioning. More specifically, interparental conflict schema are likely to (a) shape children's appraisals, affect, and behavior when they witness parental conflict and (b) guide their processing and behavior when conflict arises in other close relationships. These functions, illustrated in Figure 6.2, are described in more detail below.

Conflict Schema and Children's Responses to Parental Disagreements

First, interparental conflict schemas are proposed to guide children's responses when they encounter new instances of parental conflict. Perceiving parental anger or discord is expected to activate children's conflict schema, eliciting the emotions, expectations, and appraisals associated with their prior experiences with conflict. These schematic processes are likely to combine with situational cues to determine children's initial perception of the threat posed by the conflict. Similarly, children's appraisals and coping efforts are proposed to be influenced by situational information and their beliefs about the causes of interparental conflict, recall of prior coping attempts (with overlearned and previously effective behaviors most accessible to memory), and expectations for the effectiveness of particular coping behaviors.

This process provides an explanation for the "sensitization" effect documented in prior empirical research: Children who have frequently witnessed aggressive interparental conflict are more adversely affected by and reactive to later occurrences of conflict (see Cummings & Davies, 1994). These children likely have developed the expectation that parental conflicts will escalate, be poorly resolved, and be emotionally upsetting, and, if they have coped unsuccessfully with previous conflicts, that they will not be able to respond effectively. At the first sign of interparental conflict, these expectations and emotional experiences will lead to greater perceived threat, negative affect, and increased physiological arousal. In contrast, children who have witnessed predominantly constructive conflict are likely to perceive lower levels of threat and negative affect because they expect that it will be effectively resolved and have no implications for their well-being or that of the family. The findings reported earlier that children's exposure to interparental aggression predicted their appraisals of specific conflict episodes (Grych, 1998) support this hypothesis.

In addition to differences in *what* they expect, children may differ in the extent to which their appraisals are driven by their schema versus the specific characteristics of the conflict. Children whose parents have been consistent in how they express and resolve conflict should develop strong expectations for the course and outcome of conflict and consequently may rely more on these generalized beliefs than situational factors in appraising a conflict. In contrast, children who have witnessed very little conflict or conflicts in which their parents' behavior varied widely are likely to have weaker expectations when a new disagreement occurs and consequently may attend more closely to the features of the conflict in appraising it.

Finally, there also may be differences in the process of schematic functioning (Baldwin, 1999). Schemas vary in their accessibilty, or the ease with which they are activated. For children who have witnessed frequent conflict or for whom conflict is especially threatening (e.g., those living in violent families), only minimal cues may be needed to activate their schema. In fact, for some children, their conflict schema may be chronically accessible, leading them to be highly sensitive to the occurrence of anger or discord and quick to respond when it is perceived.

Conflict Schemas and Functioning in Interpersonal Relationships

Experiences with interparental conflict also may shape children's general beliefs about what happens when disagreements arise in other relationships and consequently affect how children manage conflicts outside of the family. The generalization of interparental conflict schemas thus provides a process by which these family experiences may have pervasive effects on children's social development.

Crittendon and Ainsworth (1989) similarly argued that experiences of physical abuse may lead children to develop working models in which relationships in general are seen as threatening, and Dodge, Bates, and Pettit (1990) linked children's experiences with conflict and aggression in the family to their tendency to attribute hostility to their peers. Because romantic relationships are more similar to marriage than are peer or sibling relations, schemas developed from observing inter-parental conflict are likely to be most salient when children face conflict in intimate relationships. Children whose exposure to interparental conflict leads them to expect conflict to be destructive may become fearful and avoidant when disagreements arise with peers or dating partners, or may become angry when others disagree with them or obstruct their goals (also see Rossman, 1998). They also may engage in coercive and aggressive behavior in order to get "the upper hand" first. This latter pattern may be especially likely if children perceive parental behaviors as normative or effective in attaining their goals.

Likewise, experiences in other relationships may influence children's schema for interparental conflict. In particular, children's experiences with their parents and observations of interactions between their parents and siblings may shape their expectations of what occurs when parents become angry or manage conflictual situations. In Figure 6.2, the arrow from parent–child conflict to children's conflict schema represents this influence.

Little is known about the architecture of children's representations of interpersonal experiences, but Collins and Read (1994) proposed a hierarchical model for attachment representations that may apply in this context as well. At the top of their hierarchy are very general ideas about close relationships which branch into beliefs and expectations specific to certain kinds of relationships (e.g., parent–child, peer), and then into relationships with particular people (e.g., mother, younger sibling). Similarly, children may have fairly global ideas about how conflict is managed in relationships that is subdivided into more specific categories pertaining to particular types of relationships and people. To the extent that children have had similar experiences in different relationships, these schemas will be consistent and perhaps more poorly differentiated. Activation of one may spread quickly to others, making them more accessible as well. On the other hand, if children's experiences have been quite different in different kinds of relationships, the schema for one may have little influence on others.

Indirect evidence for linkages between children's experiences in different relationships comes from studies that examined associations between children's responses to interparental conflict and their previous exposure to both interparental and parent–child conflict. Grych (1998) found that measures of parent–child relations predicted children's thoughts and feelings about the interparental disagreement, but less strongly than their history of interparental conflict. Moreover, exposure to aggressive behavior in the two types of relationships had an interactive effect on children's perceptions of threat and coping expectations: children exposed to higher levels of both interparental aggression and father–child aggression reported the highest levels of threat and lowest coping efficacy. Hennessy, Rabideau, Cicchetti, and Cummings (1994) found that for maltreated children, parent–child aggression was a better predictor of their responses to interadult conflict than interparental conflict. The severity of the abuse the children suffered may have made parent–child experiences more salient than their observations of interparental conflict and consequently more influential in shaping their emotional responses to later conflict.

Summary

Investigating how children mentally represent experiences with interparental conflict may shed light on the long-term effects of conflict on children's responses to discord both inside and outside of the family. Conceptual work on this issue is just beginning, and there have been few empirical tests of the existence or operation of conflict schema. The study of social cognitive processes, including both appraisals and schema, depends on reliable and accurate measurement of covert mental events, and in the next section we discuss some of the critical issues and questions that arise in assessing these constructs.

Methodological Issues in the Study of Social Cognitive Processes

Assessing Conflict Appraisals

Because they are private mental events, the most straightforward way to assess children's appraisals is to ask children to report them. In analog designs, children watch or listen to a conflict involving two strangers involved in a disagreement, or in some cases, their parent and a stranger, and are asked a series of questions designed to tap their cognitions and/or emotions. An important methodological issue that arises with this approach is how to elicit children's appraisals. The kinds of questions asked have important implications for what children report and therefore what conclusions can be drawn about the appraisal process. On one end of the continuum, questions can ask directly about specific thoughts and feelings. For example, attributions could be tapped with a question such as "who do you think is to blame for the conflict?" On the other end of the continuum are very general items that do not address specific constructs. For example, instructions could be given to children to report whatever they were thinking while listening to a taped conflict (e.g., O'Brien, Margolin, John, & Krueger, 1991). Such general questions tend to use an open-ended response format, but more specific questions could be either open-ended or closed-ended.

The advantage of using questions that tap particular thoughts and feelings is that they provide information on constructs of theoretical interest to the investigator, whereas children may not refer to these constructs if they are asked more general questions. In contrast, the advantage of general, open-ended questions is that they provide greater confidence that the children's report occurred spontaneously and is not an artifact of the research context; even though a child may provide an attribution if asked to do so, there is no assurance that he or she would have made the attribution had the question not been asked.

However, it is important to note that children's responses to general, open-ended questions cannot be assumed to be a veridical report of the mental activity that occurred while observing the conflict. There are two primary reasons for this. First, the mere act of soliciting children's thoughts and feelings may produce different cognitive processes than would have occurred naturally. Even instructions to report what comes to mind may shift the focus of children's attention and change the way they approach the task. Second, children's self-reports can only include thoughts and feelings of which children are consciously aware *and* choose to share with the researcher. As previously noted, many cognitive processes are automatized and therefore operate nonconsciously (e.g., Bargh & Chartrand, 1999; Fletcher & Kininmonth, 1991; Shiffrin & Schneider, 1977). In addition, what children report in response to general, open-ended questions is influenced by their beliefs about the kind of material that is pertinent in the situation, and they are likely to omit information that seems obvious, redundant, or irrelevant (see Schwartz, 1999). Consequently, the failure to report particular thoughts or feelings does not mean that they did not occur. For example, individuals have been found to make attributions about social events without being aware of them or consciously intending to do so (Uleman, 1987).

More specific questions about children's thoughts may make some (though not necessarily all) of their automatic processing available to conscious awareness by focusing children's attention on particular aspects. In addition, asking such questions or providing response options can enhance the quality of children's responses by clarifying the task, making more explicit what kinds of responses are relevant to report, and directing their attention toward material that they were aware of but had not considered reporting (Schwartz, 1999). Although the issue of whether these responses would occur naturally remains salient, their validity is supported to the extent that children's answers are meaningfully related to other relevant constructs. Thus, although neither general nor specific questions can be assumed to reflect children's naturally occurring mental activity, they both can provide useful information, and one may be more appropriate for a particular purpose. Used in conjunction, they are likely to give a more complete description of how children process interparental conflict.

Because analogue designs typically have been used to assess children's thoughts and feelings about conflict, it is not clear if the same appraisals would be made in the affectively laden context of the family. Attempting to assess cognitions during the course of an actual interaction is fraught with difficulties (see Fletcher & Kininmonth, 1991), but several investigators have effectively assessed individuals' cognitions following an interaction. One approach that has been used in marital and family research involves videotaping an interaction and then replaying it in order to elicit participants' reactions during the conflict. For example, Sanders, Dadds, Johnston, and Cash (1992) videotaped family problem-solving interactions and later played the tape to children and asked them to report their thoughts and feelings during the interaction. Of course, these retrospective accounts may differ from the processing that actually occurred in the situation, but there are ways to reduce – though not eliminate – participants' reconstruction of their thought processes (see Fletcher & Kininmonth, 1991).

Assessment of appraisals need not be constrained to verbal self-reports; continuous measurement of nonverbal dimensions of children's responses to conflict also may provide useful information. For example, Gottman and Levenson (1985) videotaped couples engaged in a problem-solving discussion and then played the tape to them, asking each partner to turn a dial to indicate the positivity–negativity of their affect throughout the interaction. Similarly, continuous measurement of children's physiological responses has been used in prior studies (e.g., El-Sheikh, 1994), though interpretation of such responses in isolation is problematic because they are multiply determined. For example, electrodermal activity (EDA) is traditionally considered a measure of emotional responding, but also has been used as a measure of information processing (Dawson, 1990). Combining these continuously recorded nonverbal measures with verbal reports of cognition may provide an effective means for assessing children's perceptions of threat, and perhaps other appraisals as well.

Children's perceptions of conflict they have witnessed between their parents also have been assessed with questionnaires (e.g., Emery & O'Leary, 1982; Grych et al., 1992). For example, the Children's Perception of Interparental Conflict Scale (CPIC, in Grych et al., 1992) assesses child reports of specific conflict properties (intensity, frequency, resolution) and their appraisals of threat and blame. These measures tap more generalized beliefs and memories than do the situation-specific measures used in analogue studies, and so will be addressed in the next section.

Assessing Conflict Schemas

For schemas to be something more than a useful heuristic, it is essential to develop rigorous methods for measuring them. Questionnaires that focus on children's recall of conflictual interactions tap one aspect of conflict schema: Their responses reflect what they have attended to and how they have perceived and stored these experiences in memory. However, methods that simply assess children's memories for events confound representation with remembering because they measure only what children recall and can or will report (Baker-Ward et al., 1997). To assess mental representations, it is necessary to use indicators of representation that are not also simply indicators of memory (Baker-Ward et al., 1997). The choice of appropriate measures can be guided by considering two defining features of schemas: They are an *organized* set of beliefs, emotions, and expectations, and they are *constructive*, in that they actively guide information processing.

Schemas Are Organized. One of the strongest organizational principles for children's mental representations is the temporal order in which events occur (e.g., Bauer & Mandler, 1990; Nelson, 1986). Children's schemas for interparental conflict are proposed to include a description of what typically happens when parents disagree (script), and so methods that tap children's thoughts about how interparental conflicts typically unfold may be quite useful for assessing conflict schemas. Nelson and Gruendel (1981) pioneered investigation of children's event representations using semistructured interviews, sometimes supplemented with props to facilitate their responses. They interviewed children as young as 3 years of age about common events that occurred in their lives, asking questions such as "what happens when you go to the store?" The language children use in these interviews suggests that their responses reflect generalized representations rather than recall of specific events. When talking about a situation that has been stored as a generalized representation, children tend to use impersonal pronouns and the timeless present tense to describe what happens (Bauer & Fivush, 1992; Hudson, 1990). For example, a child describing a birthday party might say, "you bring a present, play games, and eat cake." In contrast, recollection of specific past events is generally reported in the past tense: "Last year I went to Disneyworld on my birthday."

Variations of this basic procedure have been used to assess children's schemas or scripts for a range of events and topics. For example, Baldwin (1999) proposes that interpersonal scripts include links between particular behaviors and outcomes, or "if … then…" contingencies, and that activation of one behavior automatically increases the accessibility of its consequent (also see Abelson, 1981). These contingencies are assessed by prompting individuals with an "if" statement intended to elicit a schema-relevant construct ("if I depend on my partner…") and asking them to rate the likelihood of various outcomes (e.g., my partner will leave, my partner will support me) (see Baldwin, 1999).

More elaborate procedures also have been developed to elicit children's representations. For example, the MacArthur Story Stem Battery (Bretherton, Oppenheim, Buchsbaum, Emde, & The MacArthur Narrative Group, 1990) is a narrative procedure designed to assess working models of attachment in 3–5-year-old children. Using dolls, toy furniture, and other props to stimulate interest and involvement, the researcher presents the child with a series of story-stems designed to elicit attachment themes. The child is asked to complete the stories and his or her narratives are coded to identify beliefs, expectations, and emotions relevant to parental and family relationships. Narrative approaches (often adaptations of the MacArthur) are being used with increasing frequency to assess other kinds of representations, including children's beliefs about interparental conflict (Bastion, Schudlich, & Shamir, 1999; Grych & Wachsmuth-Schlaefer, 1999). Their story-telling format is particularly well-suited for young children who may have difficulty responding to abstract questions.

These procedures suggest that the content of children's interparental conflict schema can be revealed by asking them open-ended questions about what happens when parents disagree or by presenting particular behaviors (e.g., "if my dad gets mad at my mom") and assessing their perception of various outcomes. Spontaneous reports and narratives are subject to the same limitations discussed in relation to open-ended questions about appraisals, and, in addition, procedures based on temporal relations assume that there is some regularity in the manner in which interparental disagreements unfold, an assumption that will be more or less true in different families. Although the sequence of events that occurs during interparental conflict may not be as predictable as some prototypical script situations (e.g., going to a restaurant), there is likely to be sufficient consistency in most parents' strategies for expressing and resolving disagreements for children to develop expectations about the general nature of these interactions. Moreover, even though variability in the elements of a script tends to slow the process of forming generalized event representations, children as young as 4-years-old are still able to construct coherent, ordered representations after only a few experiences (Bauer & Fivush, 1992).

Schema assessments do not necessarily have to focus on scriptlike sequences. The content of mental representations can be described in a number of ways. For example, Burks and her colleagues (Burks, Dodge, Price, & Laird, 1999) attempted to assess children's "knowledge base" related to aggression in peer relations. They asked children a series of open-ended questions (e.g., what kind of kids do you like, what kind of kids do you dislike) and coded the appropriateness (whether children listed positive qualities as reasons for liking and negative qualities as reasons for disliking), density (the number of responses to the questions), and accessibility (proportion of responses that reflected prosocial or antisocial constructs) of their representations.

Schemas Are Constructive. A basic function of schemas is to guide the processing of new information: material that is schema-consistent is more likely to be encoded, stored, and retrieved than information that does not fit or is not relevant to a particular schema. Tasks that provide an opportunity to systematically examine how children recall schema-relevant and -irrelevant information thus can provide insight into the content of their schemas (e.g., O'Brien & Chin, 1998; Rudolf, Hammen, & Burge, 1995). For example, O'Brien and Chin (1998) attempted to activate children's schema for interparental conflict by having them complete questionnaires about interparental conflict and listen to audiotapes of two adults arguing. The children then were given an incidental recall task in which they were presented with a list of words and asked to remember which they had heard on the questionnaires or the tape. The words referred either to aggressive (e.g., "hit", "yell") or constructive behaviors (e.g., "discuss, explain"), and either had been presented previously or were new. Children's recall was consistent with expected differences in the content of their schemas: Children who had been exposed to higher levels of interparental conflict accurately recalled more aggressive words and were more likely to falsely recall aggressive words that had not been previously heard than children exposed to lower levels of conflict.

Establishing that children exhibit schematic functioning in regard to interparental conflict is the first step in examining whether these mental constructs predict their responses to specific episodes of conflict or their behavior in peer or dating situations. The methods discussed in this section provide a variety of ways to assess interparental conflict schema that go beyond children's reports of the behaviors they have witnessed in the home. Some adjustment in these procedures will be needed for younger and older children, but the basic format is likely to prove useful across ages.

Future Directions in the Study of Social Cognition and Interparental Conflict

Work is just beginning on social cognitive processes important for understanding the impact of interparental conflict on children, and there are many important questions yet to answer. In addition to the need for longitudinal tests of the proposed relations between cognition, affect, and behavior that we noted earlier, we identify three issues that deserve attention in future research

Expanding the Conceptualization of Cognition

First, it may be productive to consider other cognitive constructs that may play a role in children's response to conflict. For example, children's goals (see Crockenberg & Langrock, Chapter 5), perception of control (e.g., Rossman & Rosenberg, 1992) and evaluation of coping options (e.g., Crick & Dodge, 1994) may be important for understanding how they respond to conflict. Because the appraisals described in the cognitive-contextual framework are proposed to be linked specifically to internalizing problems (Grych et al., in press), it is particularly important to consider whether there are cognitions related to the development of externalizing behavior. Children's perceptions of the efficacy and moral acceptability of parents' behavior may be relevant here. Children who view aggressive behavior as effective for "winning" an argument or exerting control may be more likely to remember those behaviors and use aggressive or coercive strategies in their own conflicts. On the other hand, viewing aggressive or coercive behavior as morally wrong may make children less likely to engage in these behaviors themselves. This kind of evaluation also may affect children's immediate response to conflict. Stein and Liwag (1997) propose that

anger arises from the judgment that a person violated a moral obliga-
tion, and so a child who perceives a parent as behaving in morally
unacceptable ways during conflict may become angry toward that parent and perhaps intervene on the side of the other parent (also see
Averill, 1978).

Second, our discussion of conflict schema focused primarily on the
content of children's representations, but investigating process or functional aspects of these schema (e.g., accessibility) also may prove valuable. Development of methods to assess schematic processing will
provide a valuable complement to the methods used to assess the content of conflict schema. For example, reaction time measures may be
more sensitive to individual differences in the accessibility of conflict
schema than measures based on recall of particular kinds of content.

Putting Cognition in Context

Social cognitive processes are not expected to account fully for the
association between interparental conflict and child adjustment.
Examining how children's perceptions of conflict are related to other
aspects of family functioning is important for integrating these
processes with other constructs hypothesized to mediate or moderate
the effects of conflict. The meaning children ascribe to a parental conflict is likely to be influenced by broader family factors, including children's interactions with each parent and how anger and conflict is
managed in other family relationships. For example, if a father frequently expresses hostility towards his son, the father may be perceived as more threatening or blameworthy when interparental
conflicts occur. Even though children's direct observation of interparental conflict is expected to have the most powerful influence on
children's schemas, conflict schemas are likely to be influenced by
other kinds of experiences as well. Anderson (1993) noted that cultural
norms, mass media, information provided by third parties (e.g.,
friends), and observation of others' relationships also influence the formation of relational schemas, and these factors similarly may shape
children's beliefs about conflict. Children's appraisals also may affect
how they relate to other family members, and it will be important to
consider how interpretations of interparental conflict may affect children's feelings and behavior toward each parent.

Linking Representations of Conflict with Other
Cognitive Constructs

Children's schemas for interparental conflict exist in a complex network of representations about their family and social world.

Investigating how children's understanding of this aspect of marital interaction relates to their beliefs about other relationships may provide insight into the way children organize information about the world and integrate different kinds of experiences. A first step in this direction could involve examining links between conflict schema and children's representations of potentially related interactions. For example, it is possible that children's experiences with interparental conflict contribute to the development of hostile attributional biases in aggressive children (Crick & Dodge, 1994; Dodge, 1993). In addition, examining links between how children represent aggressive behavior occurring in parent–child interaction and between their parents may provide a more comprehensive account of the influence of family interactions on the development of children's beliefs about themselves and others. It would be possible to test such linkages by using a priming procedure to activate one schema and assessing the speed with which other types of representations are accessed.

Finally, it will be useful to consider a broader question of how perceiving, appraising, and remembering interparental conflict relates to the development of more pervasive cognitive styles. Lazarus (1991) proposed that people develop generalized appraisal styles based on appraisals made in specific situations, and it may be that children who develop consistent ways of interpreting interparental conflict may apply these ways of thinking to other situations (also see Doherty, 1981b). The relation between situational and general appraisal styles is likely to be transactional. As children make appraisals in a variety of contexts, they may develop characteristic ways of perceiving and thinking about the world, and general ways of thinking in turn are likely to influence how children appraise specific events. For example, children who blame themselves for conflict may develop more general tendencies to blame themselves for other kinds of negative or distressing events. In turn, this attributional style makes it more likely that they will blame themselves when conflict occurs in the future.

Conclusion

In this chapter, we have discussed how investigating social cognitive processes may enhance our understanding of individual differences in children's short- and long-term responses to interparental conflict. More specifically, we reviewed research on links between children's appraisals, emotions, and coping behavior and suggested that applying research on schemas to children's experiences with conflict may shed light on how exposure to conflict guides children's responses to conflict in other contexts. This area of study is in an early stage of development, and a number of important conceptual and methodological issues need to be addressed. Moreover, work on social cognition ultimately must be integrated with research on emotion, physiology, parent–child relationships, and family functioning if we are to develop a comprehensive understanding of the effects of conflict on children's development.

REFERENCES

Abelson, R. P. (1981). Psychological status of the script concept. *American Psychologist, 36*, 715–729.

Abelson, R. P., & Black, J. P. (1986). Introduction. In J. A. Galambos, R. P. Abelson, & J. P. Black (Eds.), *Knowledge structures* (pp. 1–18). Hillsdale, NJ: Erlbaum.

Anderson, P. A. (1993). Cognitive schemata in personal relationships. In S. Duck (Ed.), *Individuals in relationships* (pp. 1–29). Newbury Park, CA: Sage.

Averill, J. R. (1978). Anger. In H. Howe & R. Dienstbier (Eds.), *Nebraska Symposium on Motivation* (pp. 1–80). Lincoln, NE: University of Nebraska Press.

Baker-Ward, L., Ornstein, P. A., & Principe, G. F. A. (1997). Revealing the representation: Evidence from children's reports of events. In P. van den Broek, P. J. Bauer, & T. Bourg (Eds.), *Developmental spans in event comprehension and representation* (pp. 79–107). Mahwah, NJ: Lawrence Erlbaum Associates.

Baldwin, M. W. (1992). Relational schemas and the processing of social information. *Psychological Bulletin, 112*, 461–484.

Baldwin, M. W. (1999). Relational schemas: Research into social-cognitive aspects of interpersonal experience. In D. Cervone & Y. Shoda (Eds.), *The coherence of personality: Social-cognitive bases of consistency, variability, and organization* (pp. 126–154) New York: Guilford.

Bandura, A. (1986). *Social foundations of thought and action: A social-cognitive theory*. Englewood Cliffs, NJ: Prentice-Hall.

Banerjee, M. (1997). Peeling the onion: A multilayered view of children's emotional development. In S. Hala (Ed.), *The development of social cognition* (pp. 241–272). Philalphia, PA: Psychology Press.

Bargh, J. A., & Chartrand, T. L. (1999). The unbearable automaticity of being. *American Psychologist, 54*, 462–479.

Baron, R. M., & Kenny, D. A. (1986). The moderator-mediator variable distinction in social psychological research: Conceptual, strategic, and statistical considerations. *Journal of Personality and Social Psychology, 51*, 1173–1182.

Bastion, Q., Schudlich, T. D., & Shamir, H. (1999). *Assessing children's representations of family relationships as a function of marital conflict and other family relations*. Poster presented at the biennial meeting of the Society for Research on Child Development, Albuquerque, NM.

Bauer, P. J., & Fivush, R. (1992). Constructing event representations: Building on a foundation of variation and enabling relations. *Cognitive Development, 7*, 381–401.

Bauer, P. J., & Mandler, J. M. (1990). Remembering what happened next: Very young children's recall of event sequences. In R. Fivush & J. A. Hudson (Eds.), *Knowing and remembering in young children* (pp. 9–29). Cambridge: Cambridge University Press.

Bowlby, J. (1973). *Attachment and loss: Vol. 2. Separation.* New York: Basic Books.

Bretherton, I., Fritz, J., Zahn-Waxler, C., & Ridgeway, D. (1986). Learning to talk about emotions: A functionalist perspective. *Child Development, 57,* 529–548.

Bretherton, I., Oppenheim, D., Buchsbaum, H., Emde, R., & The MacArthur Narrative Group (1990). *MacArthur Story Stem Battery coding manual.* Unpublished manuscript.

Bretherton, I., Prentiss, C., & Ridgeway, D. (1990). Family relationships as represented in a story-completion task at thirty-seven and fifty-four months of age. In I. Bretherton & M. W. Watson (Eds.), *New directions for child development: Children's perspectives on the family, 48,* 85–105.

Bretherton, I., Ridgeway, D., & Cassidy, J. (1990). Assessing internal working models of the attachment relationship. In M. T. Greenberg, D. Cicchetti, & E. M. Cummings (Eds.), *Attachment in the preschool years* (pp. 273–308).

Burks, V. S., Dodge, K. A., Price, J. M., and Laird, R. D. (1999). Internal representational models of peers implications for the development of problematic behavior. *Developmental Psychology, 35,* 802–810.

Campos, J. J., Campos, R. G., & Barrett, K. C. (1989). Emergent themes in the study of emotional development and emotion regulation. *Developmental Psychology, 25,* 394–402.

Collins, N. L., & Read, S. J. (1994). Cognitive representations of attachment: The content and function of working models. In K. Bartholomew & D. Perlman (Eds.), *Advances in personal relationships* (Vol. 5, pp. 53–90). London: Jessica Kingsley.

Compas, B. E. (1987). Coping with stress during childhood and adolescence. *Psychological Bulletin, 101,* 393–403.

Covell, K., & Abramovitch, R. (1987). Understanding emotion in the family: Children's and parents' attributions of happiness, sadness, and anger. *Child Development, 58,* 985–991.

Covell, K., & Miles, B. (1992). Children's beliefs about strategies to reduce parental anger. *Child Development, 63,* 381–390.

Crick, N. R., & Dodge, K. A. (1994). A review and reformulation of social information-processing mechanisms in children's social adjustment. *Psychological Bulletin, 115,* 74–101.

Crittenden, P. M., & Ainsworth, M. D. S. (1989). Child maltreatment and attachment theory. In D. Cicchetti & V. Carlson (Eds.), *Child maltreatment: Theory and research on the causes and consequences of child abuse and neglect* (pp. 432–463). Cambridge: Cambridge University Press.

Crockenberg, S., & Forgays, D. K. (1996). The role of emotion in children's understanding and emotional reactions to marital conflict. *Merrill-Palmer Quarterly, 42,* 22–48.

Cummings, E. M., & Davies, P. T. (1994). *Children and marital conflict.* New York: Guilford.

Cummings, E. M., Davies, P. T., & Simpson, K. S. (1994). Marital conflict, gender, and children's appraisals and coping efficacy as mediators of child adjustment. *Journal of Family Psychology, 8,* 141–149.

Cummings, E. M., Vogel, D., Cummings, J. S., & El-Sheikh, M. (1989). Children's responses to different forms of expression of anger between adults. *Child Development, 60,* 1392–1404.

Dadds, M. R., Atkinson, E., Turner, C., Blums, G. J., & Lendich, B. (1999). Family conflict and child adjustment: Evidence for a cognitive-contextual model of intergenerational transmission. *Journal of Family Psychology, 13,* 194–208.

Davies, P. T., & Cummings, E. M. (1994). Marital conflict and child adjustment: An emotional security hypothesis. *Psychological Bulletin, 116,* 387–411.

Davies, P. T., & Cummings, E. M. (1998). Exploring children's emotional security as a mediator of the link between marital relations and child adjustment. *Child Development, 69,* 124–139.

Davies, P. T., Myers, R. L., & Cummings, E. M. (1996). Responses of children and adolescents to marital conflict scenarios as a function of the emotionality of conflict endings. *Merrill-Palmer Quarterly, 42,* 1–21.

Dawson, M. E. (1990). Psychophysiology at the interface of clinical science, cognitive science, and neuroscience. *Psychophysiology, 27,* 243–255.

Dodge, K. A. (1993). Social-cognitive mechanisms in the development of conduct disorder and depression. *Annual Review of Psychology, 44,* 559–584.

Dodge, K. A., Bates, J. E., & Pettit, G. S. (1990). Mechanisms in the cycle of violence. *Science, 250,* 1678–1683.

Doherty, W. J. (1981a). Cognitive processes in intimate conflict: 1. Extending attribution theory. *American Journal of Family Therapy, 9,* 3–13.

Doherty, W. J. (1981b). Cognitive processes in intimate conflict: 2. Efficacy and learned helplessness. *American Journal of Family Therapy, 9,* 35–44.

El-Sheikh, M. (1994). Children's emotional and physiological responses to interadult angry behavior: The role of history of interparental hostility. *Journal of Abnormal Child Psychology, 22,* 661–678.

Emery, R. E. (1989). Family violence. *American Psychologist, 44,* 321–328.

Emery, R. E., & O'Leary, K. D. (1982). Children's perceptions of marital discord and behavior problems in boys and girls. *Journal of Abnormal Child Psychology, 12,* 411–420.

Estes, W. K. (1991). Cognitive architectures from the standpoint of an experimental psychologist. *Annual Review of Psychology, 42,* 1–28.

Fabes, R. A., Eisenberg, N., Nyman, M., & Michealieu, Q. (1991). Young children's appraisals of others' spontaneous emotional reactions. *Developmental Psychology, 27,* 858–866.

Farrar, M. J., & Goodman, G. S. (1990). Developmental differences in the relation between scripts and episodic memory: Do they exist? In R. Fivush & J. A. Hudson (Eds.), *Knowing and remembering in young children* (pp. 30–64). Cambridge: Cambridge University Press.

Fincham, F. D. (1998). Child development and marital relations. *Child Development, 69,* 543–574.

Fiske, S. T., & Havelchak, M. A. (1986). Category-based vs. piecemeal-based affective responses: Developments in schema-triggered affect. In R. M.

Sorrentino & E. T. Higgins (Eds.), *Handbook of motivation and cognition* (pp. 167–203). New York: Guilford Press.

Fivush, R., Kuebli, J., & Clubb, P. A. (1992). The structure of events and event representations: A developmental analysis. *Child Development, 63,* 188–201.

Fletcher, G. J. O., & Kininmonth, L. (1991). Interaction in close relationships and social cognition. In G. Fletcher & F. Fincham (Eds.), *Cognition in close relationships* (pp. 235–256). Hillsdale, NJ: Lawrence Erlbaum.

Fu, V. R., Goodwin, M. P., Sporakowski, M. J., & Hinkle, D. E. (1988). Children's thinking about family characteristics and parent attributes. *Journal of Genetic Psychology, 148,* 153–166.

Garmezy, N. (1983). Stressors of childhood. In N. Garmezy & M. Rutter (Eds.), *Stress, coping, and development in children* (pp. 43–84). New York: McGraw-Hill.

Gnepp, J. (1983). Children's social sensitivity: Inferring emotions from conflicting cues. *Developmental Psychology, 19,* 805–814.

Goodnow, J. J. (1996). Social cognition and family relationships: A comment. *Journal of Family Psychology, 10,* 422–430.

Gottman, J. M., & Levenson, R. W. (1985). A valid procedure for obtaining self-report of affect in marital interaction. *Journal of Consulting and Clinical Psychology, 57,* 47–52.

Graham-Bermann, S. A. (1998). The impact of woman abuse on children's social development: Research and theoretical perspectives. In G. W. Holden, R. Geffner, & E. N. Jouriles, (Eds.), *Children exposed to marital violence* (pp. 21–54). Washington, DC. American Psychological Association.

Grych, J. H. (1998). Children's appraisals of interparental conflict: Situational and contextual influences. *Journal of Family Psychology, 12,* 437–453.

Grych, J. H., & Fincham, F. D. (1990). Marital conflict and children's adjustment: A cognitive-contextual framework. *Psychological Bulletin, 108,* 267–290.

Grych, J. H., & Fincham, F. D. (1993). Children's appraisals of marital conflict: Initial investigations of the cognitive-contextual framework. *Child Development, 64,* 215–230.

Grych, J. H., Fincham, F. D., Jouriles, E. N., & McDonald, R. (in press). Interparental conflict and child adjustment: Testing the mediational role of appraisals in the cognitive-contextual framework. *Child Development.*

Grych, J. H., Jouriles, E. N., Swank, P. R., McDonald R., & Norwood, W. D. (2000). Patterns of adjustment among children of battered women. *Journal of Consulting and Clinical Psychology, 68,* 84–94.

Grych, J. H., Seid, M., & Fincham, F. D. (1992). Assessing marital conflict from the child's perspective. *Child Development, 63,* 558–572.

Grych, J. H., & Wachsmuth-Schlaefer, T. (1999). *The impact of family violence on children's working models of relationships.* Paper presented at the International Conference on Children Exposed to Domestic Violence, Vancouver, B. C.

Hamond, N. R., & Fivush, R. (1991). Memories of Mickey Mouse: Young children recount their trip to Disneyworld. *Cognitive Development, 6,* 433–448.

Harold, G. T., Fincham, F. D., Osborne, L. N., & Conger, R. D. (1997). Mom and dad are at it again: Adolescent perceptions of marital conflict and adolescent psychological distress. *Developmental Psychology, 33,* 333–350.

Hennessy, K. D., Rabideau, G. J., Cicchetti, D., & Cummings, E. M. (1994). Responses of physically abused and nonabused children to different forms of interadult anger. *Child Development, 65,* 815–828.

Holmbeck, G. N. (1997). Toward terminological, conceptual, and statistical clarity in the study of mediators and moderators: Examples from the child-clinical and pediatric psychology literatures. *Journal of Consulting and Clinical Psychology, 65,* 599–610.

Hudson, J. A. (1990). Constructive processes in children's event memory. *Developmental Psychology, 26,* 180–187.

Kerig, P. K. (1998a). Moderators and mediators of the effects of interparental conflict on children's adjustment. *Journal of Abnormal Child Psychology, 26,* 199–212.

Kerig, P. K. (1998b). Gender and appraisals as mediators of adjustment in children exposed to interparental violence. *Journal of Family Violence, 15,* 345–363.

Lazarus, R. S. (1991). Cognition and motivation in emotion. *American Psychologist, 46,* 352–367.

Lazarus, R. S., & Folkman, S. (1984). *Stress, appraisal, and coping.* New York: Springer.

Massaro, D. W., & Cowan, N. (1993). Information processing models: Microscopes of the mind. *Annual Review of Psychology, 44,* 383–425.

Miller, P. H., & Aloise, P. A. (1989). Young children's understanding of the psychological causes of behavior: A review. *Child Development, 60,* 257–285.

Nelson, K. (1986). *Event knowledge: Structure and function in development.* Hillsdale, NJ: Erlbaum.

Nelson, K., & Gruendel, J. M. (1981). Generalized event representations: Basic building blocks of cognitive development. In M. E. Lamb and A. L. Brown (Eds.), *Advances in developmental psychology: Vol. 1* (pp. 131–158). Hillsdale, NJ: Erlbaum.

Noam, G. G., Chandler, M., & LaLonde, C. (1995). Clinical-developmental psychology: Constructivism and social cognition in the study of psychological dysfunctions. In D. Cicchetti & D. J. Cohen (Eds.), *Developmental psychopathology: Vol. 1. Theory and methods* (pp. 424–466). New York: Wiley & Sons.

O'Brien, M., & Chin, C. (1998). The relationship between children's reported exposure to interparental conflict and memory biases in the recognition of aggressive and constructive conflict words. *Personality and Social Psychology Bulletin, 6,* 647–656.

O'Brien, M., Margolin, G., & John, R. S. (1995). Relations among marital conflict. Child coping, and child adjustment. *Journal of Clinical Child Psychology, 24,* 346–361.

O'Brien, M., Margolin, G., John, R. S., & Krueger, L. (1991). Mothers' and sons' cognitive and emotional reactions to simulated marital and family conflict. *Journal of Consulting and Clinical Psychology, 59,* 692–703.

Peterson & Bell (1996). Children's memory for traumatic injury. *Child Development, 67,* 3045–3070.

Reichenbach, L., & Masters, J. C. (1983). Children's use of expressive and contextual cues in judgements of emotion. *Child Development, 54,* 993–1004.

Rogers, M. J., & Holmbeck, G. N. (1997). Effects of interparental aggression on children's adjustment: The moderating role of cognitive appraisal and coping. *Journal of Family Psychology, 11*, 125–130.

Rossman, B. B. R. (1998). Descartes' error and post-traumatic stress disorder: Cognition and emotion in children who are exposed to parental violence. In G. W. Holden, R. Geffner, & E. N. Jouriles, (Eds.), *Children exposed to marital violence* (pp. 223–256). American Psychological Association. Washington, D.C.

Rossman, B. B. R., & Rosenberg, M. (1992). Family stress and functioning in children: The moderating effects of children's beliefs about their control over parental conflict. *Journal of Child Psychology and Psychiatry, 33*, 699–715.

Rudolf, K. D., Hammen, C., & Burge, D. (1995). Cognitive representations of self-family, and peers in school-aged children: Links with social competence and sociometric status. *Child Development, 66*, 1385–1402.

Rutter, M. (1983). Stress, coping, and development: Some issues and some questions. In N. Garmezy & M. Rutter (Eds.), *Stress, coping, and development in children* (pp. 1–41). New York: McGraw-Hill.

Sanders, M. R., Dadds, M. R., Johnston, B. M., & Cash, R. (1992). Childhood depression and conduct disorder: 1. Behavioral, affective, and cognitive aspects of family problem-solving interactions. *Journal of Abnormal Psychology, 101*, 495–504.

Schwartz, N. (1999). Self-reports: How the questions shape the answers. *American Psychologist, 54*, 93–105.

Shiffrin, R. M., & Schneider, W. (1977). Controlled and automatic human information processing: 2. Perceptual learning, automatic attending, and a general theory. *Psychological Review, 84*, 127–190.

Stein, N. L., & Liwag, M. D. (1997). Children's understanding, evaluation, and memory for emotional events. In P. van den Broek, P. J. Bauer, & T. Bourg (Eds.), *Developmental spans in event comprehension and representation* (pp. 199–235). Mahwah, NJ: Erlbaum.

Terwogt, M. M., & Harris, P. L. (1993). Understanding of emotion. In M. Bennett (Ed.), *The development of social cognition* (pp. 62–86). New York: Guilford.

Uleman, J. S. (1987). Consciousness and control: The case of spontaneous trait inferences. *Personality and Social Psychology Bulletin, 13*, 337–354.

van den Broek, P. (1997). Discovering the cement of the universe: The development of event comprehension from childhood to adulthood. In P. van den Broek, P. J. Bauer, & T. Bourg (Eds.), *Developmental spans in event comprehension and representation* (pp. 321–342). Mahwah, NJ: Erlbaum

Wyer, R. S., & Carlston, D. (1994). The cognitive representation of persons and events. In R. S. Wyer & T. K. Srull (Eds.), *Handbook of social cognition* (pp. 41–98). Hillsdale, NJ: Lawrence Erlbaum Associates.

7   Physiological Processes as Mediators of the Impact of Marital Conflict on Children

Lynn Fainsilber Katz

Investigations have consistently demonstrated a relationship between marital distress and conflict and problem behaviors in children. Marital distress and conflict have been associated with depression, withdrawal, poor social competence, health problems, poor academic performance, and conduct-related difficulties in children (e.g., Cummings & Davies, 1994; Gottman & Katz, 1989; Grych & Fincham, 1990; Hetherington, Cox, & Cox, 1982; Rutter, 1971). Physical marital violence also has profound effects on children's socioemotional adjustment. Children living in maritally violent homes exhibit higher levels of conduct problems (Hershorn & Rosenbaum, 1985; Jouriles, Murphy, & O'Leary, 1989), more internalizing and externalizing behavior problems (Sternberg et al., 1993; Jaffe, Wolfe, Wilson & Zak, 1986; Wolfe, Jaffe, Wilson & Zak, 1985), and more depressive symptoms (Sternberg et al., 1993) than children from nonmaritally violent homes.

While it is clearly understood that interparental conflict relates to a host of behavioral problems, there is less known about the mechanisms underlying the relationship between marital conflict and child maladjustment. In this chapter, the notion that physiological processes may serve as mediators of the impact of marital conflict on children is explored. A discussion of the limitations and advantages of physiological measures is presented, followed by a basic description of physiological methods and measures. Empirical evidence supporting the idea that physiological processes act as mediators of the impact of marital conflict on children is then reviewed, followed by a discussion of remaining issues that have yet to be explored in understanding the role of physiological arousal and regulation in children's reactions to marital conflict.

Misconceptions and Advantages of Psychophysiological Approaches

There is a common misconception about the benefits of understanding children's psychophysiological reactions to marital conflict. This misconception is rooted in the belief that the measurement of physiological processes provides a "true" or more objective index of children's reactions to marital conflict. The extreme form of this popular misconception is that psychophysiological data can provide a more accurate index of children's reactions to marital conflict than can be obtained from observations or children's own report. This belief largely rests on the assumption that biological processes are outside of conscious awareness and therefore cannot be controlled or modified. Another form this misconception can take is the belief that physiological indices are not subject to the same limitations as other measurement approaches. There has been long-standing concern that children's reports of their own reactions to interparental conflict or parental reports of children's reactions to marital conflict are subject to denial, minimization, or other self-presentation issues. Similar concerns related to self-presentation have been raised about observational methods, along with questions about reactivity or ecological validity of laboratory-based observations. The implication, therefore, is that assessment of psychophysiological responding is not subject to the same limitations as self-report and observational data.

However, there is substantial evidence that biological processes can be perceived and placed under conscious control. Brener (1977) highlighted the relationship between visceral perception and visceral self-control and asserted that people who can discriminate a visceral response should display improvement in their ability to control that response. Visceral control has also been the central process tapped by clinicians using biofeedback as a method of monitoring and reducing physiological arousal. Large individual differences in cardiac perception have also been found (Katkin, 1985), suggesting that physiological processes are subject to some of the same limitations as other methodologies and do not hold any special status as being more "accurate" or "truer" indices of psychological events.

Instead, the application of psychophysiological concepts to the study of social behavior has an important role in the development of theoretical models to explain social and interpersonal processes. This integration of physiological and social processes is not in the service of a reductionistic model which views biological processes as more primary or fundamental than social processes. The addition of a psychophysiological approach, with its unique theoretical perspective and concepts, may provide a small increment of understanding that will ultimately help in the final goal of building theory. As such, it may provide another "avenue of knowing." Biological mechanisms can be considered critical process measures that link psychosocial factors (e.g., marital distress) with behavioral outcomes (e.g., child externalizing behavior).

The integration of psychophysiological principles into understanding family processes is consistent with Cicchetti's (1993) call for an interdisciplinary approach to developmental psychopathology. The incorporation of psychophysiological principles into developmental thinking can foster a fruitful cross-fertilization between the two disciplines. Understanding how an individual's stereotypical form of biological responding is affected by negative environmental events can help clarify why particular maladaptive behavioral responses are chosen. For example, if a husband reacts to his wife's continued conflict engagement with high cardiovascular reactivity, his subsequent withdrawal from interaction may be an attempt to reduce physiological arousal. The husband's withdrawal, while serving the husband's immediate individual goal of reducing cardiovascular activation, has negative consequences for the long-term stability of the marriage (Gottman, 1994).

An integrated model of the interactive effects of biological and socioemotional functioning can also open up more avenues for prevention and intervention. If children from maritally distressed homes manifest behavioral difficulties that are related to difficulties regulating arousal, interventions can be focused not only on behavioral difficulties but also on reducing the physiological arousal itself. Interventions at the physiological level might include relaxation techniques or breathing exercises that activate the respiratory–vagal connection.

Physiological Constructs and Measures

Having argued against the reductionist view that physiological processes simply "explain" behavior, cognitive processes or emotional states, it is perhaps not surprising that a one-to-one relationship does not exist between a specific psychological construct and a single physiological state. In the area of emotion, there has been a lively and long-standing historical debate about specificity in function of physiological systems, with some arguing that the body functions on an all-or-none basis and that emotion is best indexed by the level of physiological arousal or activation (Duffy, 1957; Malmo, 1957), and others suggesting that there are specific physiological patterns associated with unique emotional states (Arnold, 1970; Ax, 1953; Ekman, Levenson & Friesen, 1983).

Physiological response patterning associated with the orienting and defensive responses to novel or strong stimuli have also been found. The orienting response (OR), first described by Pavlov (1927), occurs in the presence of novel stimuli. With repeated presentations of the same stimulus, the OR habituates, but any change in the intensity and magnitude of the stimulus will elict the OR again. One of the hallmark physiological signs of orienting is heart rate deceleration, which Lacey and Lacey (1967) found occurs with environmental intake (Graham & Clifton, 1966). Consistent with this finding, the OR functions to enable the organism to attend to a novel stimulus and facilitates an adaptive response to it. Once the stimulus is no longer novel, the OR habituates. The orienting response is comprised of several psychophysiological patterns that include the constriction of peripheral vessels, decreased heart rate, increase skin conductance, increased somatic or muscular tone, and a turning of the eyes toward the stimulus (Cacioppo & Petty, 1983; Sokolov, 1963).

The defensive response (DR) is elicited by a strong stimulus that may be painful or dangerous. In contrast to the OR, the defensive response habituates very slowly. Its function is to protect the organism from intense stimulation. The DR is associated with the constriction of peripheral blood vessels, muscular changes that facilitate moving or turning away from the stimulus, and increases in heart rate (Cacioppo & Petty, 1983; Sokolov, 1963; Stern et al., 1980).

The most common physiological measures used in studies of marital conflict are indices of cardiovascular and electrodermal functioning. Interest in psychophysiological measures is partly rooted in an attempt to apply theoretical concepts such as orienting and defensive response to understand children's reaction to marital conflict, and partly by a rapidly growing literature on cardiovascular reactivity to stress and its links with the development of coronary heart disease and hypertension (Boyce & Jemerin, 1990; Matthews, Rakaczky, & Stoney, 1987; Manuck, Kaplan, & Matthews, 1986).

Cardiovascular Measures

Several specific measures are used to assess cardiovascular functioning. The most common ones are reviewed below.

Heart Rate/Cardiac Interbeat Interval. Heart rate and cardiac interbeat interval are two measures of what we commonly think of as the rate at which the heart is beating. Heart rate measures the number of heart beats per minute. Cardiac interbeat interval (IBI) is measured by calculating the time interval between successive spikes, or R-waves, in the electrocardiogram (EKG). The EKG is detected using two electrodes, usually attached to the sides of the subject's chest. Assessment of cardiac functioning can yield information about heart rate as well as heart rate variability.

Heart rate is generally under reciprocal influence from both the sympathetic and parasympathetic branches of the autonomic nervous system (ANS). The sympathetic nervous system (SNS) is the "fight or flight" system that is responsible for the body's mobilization of resources; it functions to increase heart rate. The parasympathetic nervous system (PNS) is the branch of the autonomic nervous system most related to soothing and the restoration of calm in the body; it functions to decrease heart rate. In most conditions, the IBI is controlled by the parasympathetic branch (PNS) of the autonomic nervous system, but in conditions of acute stress its regulation may come under control of the sympathetic nervous system (SNS). Given the reciprocal influences of the SNS and PNS, it is difficult to tease them apart, but for purposes of theory building and our understanding of mechanism, it is important to do so.

Vagal Tone. Recent advances in statistical methodology and understanding of basic biological processes can now enable us to separate out effects of PNS activation on cardiovascular functioning (Porges, 1995) using a measure called vagal tone. *Vagal tone* is an index of the tonus of the vagus nerve, the main nerve of the parasympathetic branch of the autonomic nervous system. Vagal tone is measured by the rhythmic fluctuations in heart rate that accompany respiration.

Porges (1984) has suggested that vagal tone provides a theoretical basis for the child's ability to focus attention and inhibit inappropriate action. The vagal contribution to attentional processes has been established in both adult and child populations (Porges, 1995). In children, high vagal tone has been associated with longer periods of looking at a novel stimuli during test trials of a recognition memory task, better recognition memory, and better sustained attention (Linnemeyer & Porges, 1986; Porges & Humphreys, 1997). Vagal tone has also been related to emotional expressivity (Stifter, Fox, & Porges, 1989), appropriate emotional reactivity (Stifter & Fox, 1990) and the ability to regulate emotion in infants (Fox, 1989), and with children's negative interaction with peers and poor prosocial behavior during the preschool and school-age years (Eisenberg, Fabes, Karbon, et al., 1996; Eisenberg, Fabes, Murphy, et al., 1995; Gottman, Katz, & Hooven, 1997).

The *suppression* of vagal tone also serves an important physiological regulatory function. In general, vagal tone is suppressed during states that require focused or sustained attention, mental effort, focusing on relevant information, and organized responses to stress. Vagal suppression during challenging situations is related to better state regulation, greater self-soothing and more attentional control in infancy (DeGangi, DiPietro, Greenspan, & Porges, 1991; Huffman et al., 1998), and the ability to sustain attention in school-age children (Suess, Porges, & Plude, 1994). Poor vagal suppression has been associated with behavior problems and poor sustained attention in children. In comparing hyperactive to retarded children, Porges, Walter, Korb, and Sprague (1975) found that the retarded children do not suppress vagal tone and had a lower baseline heart rate variability, whereas hyperactive children were more likely to have normal levels of baseline heart rate variability but a deficit in suppression during task demands. Porges, Doussard-Roosevelt, Portales, and Greenspan (1996) found that 9-month-old infants who had lower baseline vagal tone and less vagal suppression during the Bayley examination had the greatest behavioral problems at age 3. Calkins (1997) also reported fewer behavior problems and more appropriate emotion regulation in preschool aged children with better vagal suppression.

Finger Pulse Volume. This is an estimate of the relative volume of blood reaching the finger on each heartbeat. FPV is a useful measure because it provides some indication of changes in peripheral blood flow. The SNS is capable of changing the distribution of central versus peripheral blood flow by constricting or dilating the peripheral blood vessels. FPV is commonly detected from a finger photoplethysmograph, and a computer measures the valley-to-peak amplitude on the signal after each heartbeat.

Blood Pressure. Blood pressure (BP) refers to the force exerted by the blood against the walls of the blood vessels, and its primary function is to drive the output of the heart through the circulatory system. When a person becomes active either due to increased physical activity or response to psychologically significant events, increased sympathetic activation leads to increases in heart rate and contractility and to greater constriction of the major arteries. Together, these factors serve to increase arterial BP. However it would be erroneous to consider sympathetic activation as the only factor contributing to changes in BP. Many different cardiodynamic and hemodynamic events can affect BP; as a result, BP can provide only a general index of cardiovascular activity rather than reflect specific physiological mechanisms.

Blood pressure is commonly measured using an automated monitor and a cuff on the child's arm circumference. This instrument has been shown to be highly reliable and to yield readings that agree closely with directly obtained radial artery readings in children (Park & Menard, 1987). The maximum pressure exerted in the artery following each heartbeat is called the systolic blood pressure (SBP), and the minimum pressure is called the diastolic blood pressure (DBP). Measures of systolic and diastolic blood pressure have been obtained both under resting conditions and in reaction to stress. There has been considerable interest in the BP response to stress since an exaggerated BP response has been associated with increased incidence of hypertension and cardiovascular disease (Fredrikson & Matthews, 1990; Manuck & Krantz, 1986; Wood, Sheps, Elveback, & Shirger, 1984). Several methods of stimulating blood pressure reactivity have been developed, including the cold-pressor test (Menkes et al., 1989), orthostasis (Parker et al., 1987), dynamic exercise (Dlin, Hanne, Silverberg, & Bar-Or, 1983) and mental challenges (Matthews et al., 1987).

Electrodermal Functioning

Skin Conductance Level. This measure is sensitive to changes in the levels of sweat in the eccrine sweat glands located in the palms of the hand. These sweat levels are thought to change in response to emotional stimuli as opposed to temperature. Measures of sweat gland activity are unique and are useful insofar as the sweat glands are one of the few organs that are innervated almost entirely by the sympathetic nervous system and only slightly by the parasympathetic nervous system. In addition, they are the only organs served by the SNS that are not strongly affected by circulating adrenaline, as they do not have an adrenaline- or noradrenaline-based chemistry. At a practical level, this simply means that the measures based on sweat gland activity have the potential for relatively independent action. The SCL is commonly obtained by passing a small voltage between electrodes attached to the middle segment of the first and third fingers of the nondominant hand.

What We Know about Children's Physiological Responses to Conflict

Two main approaches have been used to assess children's physiological functioning in relation to marital conflict. One approach has been to examine children's physiological reactions while listening to or observing simulated conflict between two unfamiliar adults. In these studies, unfamiliar adults have either been female pairs (e.g., El-Sheikh,

Cummings, & Goetsch, 1989) or male–female pairs (El-Sheikh, 1994). This approach has the advantage of having strong experimental control over the type of interadult conflict that children are exposed to. The main disadvantage has to do with ecological validity – that is, the concern over whether children would exhibit the same physiological reactions to their parents' marital conflict as they do to conflict between unfamiliar adults.

A second approach has been to examine physiological reactions of children living in maritally distressed and nondistressed homes to emotion-arousing stimuli and events and to link those physiological reactions to children's social, emotional, and cognitive development. The major advantage of this approach is that reactions of children who are actually living in highly maritally distressed homes can be assessed and tied to their psychological adjustment. The major disadvantage to these studies is that they typically have not directly assessed children's physiological reactions *to marital conflict itself*. Instead, they either index children's reactions to neutral events or look more generally at baseline functioning to obtain a more "traitlike" index of physiological functioning, or children's reactions to emotional events that do not involve interpersonal conflict are examined, with the assumption that children living in maritally conflictual homes develop physiological reactions to stressful interpersonal interactions that generalize to other stressful situations.

Children's Physiological Reactions to Nonparental Interadult Conflict

In a series of investigations, El-Sheikh and Cummings examined children's physiological reactions to interadult conflict. El-Sheikh, Cummings, and Goetsch (1989) hypothesized that children's behavioral reactions to interadult anger would predict individual differences in cardiovascular responding. Four- and five-year-old children were divided into three groups based on their behavioral and verbal responses to two female experimenters engaged in a friendly interaction, verbally angry interaction, and an interaction in which they apologized and reconciled their differences. Angry or ambivalent children exhibited both negative and positive emotional responses (ambivalent behavior) or anger expression towards the actors (anger), or both. Concerned or distressed children only displayed distress towards the actors, while unresponsive children did not exhibit any emotional response. Heart rate, systolic and diastolic blood pressure, and finger pulse volume were measured before, during, and after each interaction between experimenters (i.e., friendly, angry, apology and reconciliation), and comparisons were made between heart rate changes from the end of one interactive episode (e.g., the angry interaction) to the beginning of another interactive episode (e.g., the apology and reconciliation interaction).

Differences in heart rate were found between the end of the friendly interaction, and the beginning of the angry interaction. With the onset of the angry interaction, heart rate decreased for the angry or ambivalent group but increased for the concerned or distressed group. Unresponsive children showed no significant change in heart rate in response to any of the interactive episodes. No other differences were found between children's physiological reactions. The authors suggest that the heart rate decrease of angry or ambivalent children may reflect their attentiveness and/or interest in the fight (Graham & Clifton, 1966), or that they may have experienced empathic sadness since heart rate deceleration is characteristic of an empathic reaction of sadness (Eisenberg et al., 1988).

El-Sheikh and Cummings (1992) examined the effects of perceived control on children's physiological responses to interadult anger. Efforts to examine the role of perceived control in children's coping with marital conflict is consistent with Grych and Fincham's (1990) suggestion that children's attributions for the causes of marital conflict and judgments of blame and responsibility are likely to influence coping behavior during instances of marital conflict. Preschoolers were exposed to interadult anger and were given the option of terminating exposure by pushing an escape button or proposing an intervention for an experimenter to carry out. Although no physiological differences were found between those children who pushed the button versus those who did not exercise that option, children who had the chance to escape the argument by pushing the button exhibited higher heart rate and skin conductance level than those who did not have this option. Thus, the availability of control was associated with greater autonomic reactivity to anger in comparison to the lack of availability of control. The authors suggest that the availability of control may have drawn the children's attention to the aversive aspects of the situation, or that control may have stress-inducing properties that leave children more aroused and activated, but repeated exposure to arousing interactions between adults in which children do not have control may cause them to feel less involved and less empowered.

El-Sheikh (1994) examined children's physiological reactions as a function of history of interparental conflict. Four- and five-year-old children were divided into high- and low-conflict groups based on parental report of the history of verbal and physical aggression in the marriage.

Exposure to interadult conflict occurred in two phases. An adult walked into the laboratory, briefly expressed anger toward an unseen adult, and then left the laboratory. Children then heard an audiotaped argument through loudspeakers, ostensibly conveying that the previous argument was continuing. Children described their own emotional reactions to the argument and their perceptions of the arguing adults' emotions, and physiological recordings were obtained as children listened to the interadult conflict. Distinct gender differences in the physiology–behavior link were found. Girls from high-conflict homes exhibited more heart rate reactivity in response to interadult conflict than those from low-conflict homes. No differences in physiological functioning were found for boys from high- and low-conflict homes; however, there was some evidence that higher levels of marital violence were associated with lower heart rate reactivity in boys.

El-Sheikh, Ballard, and Cummings (1994) examined whether children's physiological state governed their choice of the intensity of the angry interactions they wished to view. Children watched two videotaped angry interactions between adults while their heart rates and skin conductance responses and levels were monitored. Before the second argument, children were given the perceived choice of watching an intense or mildly angry interchange. They found that children who chose to watch intense anger exhibited a lower decline in heart rate upon the presentation of the argument than those who chose to watch mild anger. In comparison to boys who chose mild anger, boys who chose intense anger had lower baseline heart rates, higher nonspecific skin conductance responses during one of the baseline periods, and exhibited a higher skin conductance response decline upon the presentation of the argument. Boys who had higher levels of externalizing problems also tended to choose intense versus mild anger, and were more likely to have lower baseline heart rates, higher skin conductance responses, and higher skin conductance response decline upon the presentation of the argument. The authors suggest that these findings are consistent with theorizing that individuals who engage in activities that are highly stimulating (i.e., sensation seekers) tend to have lower baseline heart rates than individuals who are low sensation seekers (Zuckerman, 1990). Boys in this study who had lower baseline heart rates may have sought a higher level of stimulation to increase arousal to an optimal level, while those with higher baseline heart rates might have chosen a lower level of stimulation (mild anger) to avoid further arousal.

In a clinical extension of this work, Ballard, Cummings, and Larkin (1993) examined cardiovascular, behavioral, and self-reported emotional responses to interadult emotional expressions (including anger) and to challenging tasks in 10–14-year-old children of hypertensive and normotensive parents. They found that sons of hypertensive parents showed greater systolic blood pressure reactivity to interadult anger and to a digit span task than sons of normotensive parents, but a consistent pattern was not found for girls. Marital distress and overt maternal anger expressions predicted children's verbal and behavioral responses to interadult anger, but there was no analysis of whether marital distress and overt maternal anger expressions related to children's physiological reactions.

Physiological Reactions in Children in Maritally Distressed and Nondistressed Families

A different approach has been to examine physiological reactions of children living in maritally distressed and nondistressed homes to emotion-arousing stimuli and events and to link those physiological reactions to children's social, emotional, and cognitive development. Gottman and Katz (1989) developed a theoretical model to explain the mechanism by which marital conflict impacts children's interactions with peers and their physical health. In one pathway through the model, they found that marital distress was associated with higher levels of urinary catecholamines (i.e., stress-related hormones), which in turn related to low levels of children's play with a best friend. Children from maritally distressed homes with high levels of stress-related hormones were not as skillful at coordinating play or engaging in fantasy play with their friend. Since the establishment of common-ground activities and fantasy play requires the ability to negotiate roles and resolve conflict when differences arise, these children may be too physiologically aroused to successfully manage interpersonal conflict and are therefore more likely to engage in a level of play that requires less interpersonal engagement and negotiation (e.g., parallel play).

In another pathway through the model, they found that negative parenting produced anger and noncompliance, negative peer interaction, and poor health in children. Negative parenting was related to a cluster of three variables: the amount of blood in the child's finger, the child's refusal to make a fear face during a modified Directed Facial Action (DFA) task (Ekman, Levenson, & Friesen, 1983), and the child's willingness to make the anger and disgust faces. Ekman, Levenson, and Friesen (1983) found higher hand temperature to be characteristic of anger and lower hand temperature to be characteristic of fear, and so more blood in the hand might be related to the child's anger. This interpretation has received some support, as both blood amplitude in the finger and the child's willingness and ability to make the anger and disgust faces were related to the child's negative interaction with a best friend. However, because the data are derived from the DFA task, there are problems in interpreting a measure of the ability to pose anger and disgust as an index of how angry and disgusted a child is in general or is made by the parent–child interaction. Nonetheless, it is also not known what relative roles voluntary versus spontaneous facial expressions play in actual social interaction.

Voluntary expressive behavior might play a large role in children's social-emotional communication. Given our prediction of negative peer interaction, it may be reasonable to interpret the child's posing of anger and disgust in the DFA task as being related to the expression of negative affect in actual social interaction. The child's refusal to pose the fear facial expression was at first puzzling to us as an individual differences variable. Several interpretations are possible: The child may be defending against feeling afraid; the refusal could be part of a "tough" stance with respect to fear; or the refusal could be part of a construct of anger, stubbornness, and noncompliance. At this time, it is unclear what the correct interpretation of this cluster of variables is. The cluster is related to the child's illness and was interpreted as the combined psychological states of anger and helplessness.

Children's physiological processes have not only been linked to behavioral maladjustment, but also to resilience in the face of marital conflict. Katz and Gottman (1995) examined several different protective mechanisms that may reduce deleterious correlates of marital conflict and marital dissolution in young children. One set of potential buffers focused on parent–child interaction: parental warmth, parental scaffolding or praise, and inhibition of parental rejection. As a second set of potential buffers, each parent was interviewed about their "metaemotion philosophy," that is, their feelings about their own emotions, attitudes, and responses to their children's anger and sadness. The third set of potential buffers concerned intraindividual characteristics of the child, including the child's intelligence and regulatory physiology (basal vagal tone and vagal suppression). Fifty-six families with a preschool child were studied at two time points: at Time-1 when the children were 5-years-old and again at Time-2 when the children were 8-years-old. At Time-1, naturalistic observations of parent–child interaction were conducted and assessment of child regulatory physiology was obtained through measures of basal vagal tone and suppression of vagal tone. Parents were also interviewed individually about their feelings about their own and their children's emotions, and children's intelligence was assessed. At Time-2, assessment of child outcomes

were obtained, including observations of peer interaction, mother ratings of behavior problems, mother and teacher ratings of peer aggression, mother ratings of child physical illness, and measures of
achievement.

With respect to physiological measures, results indicated that in the
face of marital conflict, basal vagal tone and vagal suppression
buffered children against negative outcomes on the child's negative
affect with peers, academic achievement, and child behavior problems.
Vagal suppression also buffered children from physical illness while
basal vagal tone buffered children from negative outcomes in terms of
emotion dysregulation. In addressing whether these physiological
variables were complete or partial buffers against negative outcomes, it
was found that the vagal tone variables provide complete buffers
against negative outcomes in emotional regulation and child physical
illness. These findings suggest that children's physiological functioning may index an underlying process that reduces children's vulnerability to the negative outcomes associated with marital conflict.
Huffman et al. (in press) argue that vagal tone represents a physiological substrate of a temperamental characteristic. Evidence of considerable stability in vagal tone from 9 to 36 months of age (Porges,
Doussard-Roosevelt, Portales, & Suess, 1994) suggests that vagal tone
may be measuring a lasting child characteristic. However, the degree to
which this physiological substrate represents genetic influences or an
interaction between genetic and environmental factors remains
unclear. Environmental influences might include prenatal intrauterine
conditions (e.g., Denenberg & Rosenberg, 1967) as well as social interactions with significant others.

Katz and Gottman (1995) also found that the child's vagal tone may
be related to qualities of the parent–child relationship. Children's basal
vagal tone was associated with parental coaching of emotion and low
levels of parental derogation, and vagal suppression was marginally
related to scaffolding or praising. Children with high vagal tone may
be more flexible and responsive to parental input, and may therefore
elicit more positive and less negative behavior from their parents.
These children may also be better able to make use of parental coaching
attempts, which in turn may reinforce parental coaching and create a
dynamic interaction between parent and child that increases the likelihood of resilience in the face of marital conflict. Alternatively, the quality of parent–child interactions may shape the child's physiological
reactivity to environmental events. Through parental coaching and a
climate of positive interaction, parents may teach children how to regulate their emotions by helping them gain control over their physiolog-

ical reactivity to emotional events. Thus, it is important not only to examine the child's individual physiological characteristics but also the environmental factors that may be impacting their physiological reactions to stressful family events.

Of significant import is the question of whether children's physiological reactions to marital conflict are related only to variation in adaptive functioning within the normal range or are also linked with clinically significant levels of child disturbance. Katz (in press) has been examining physiological and marital processes related to the development of conduct problems in preschool-aged children. Children were divided into three groups: (1) conduct-problem children who met criteria for Oppositional Defiant Disorder, (2) conduct-problem children who did not meet criteria for Oppositional Defiant Disorder (i.e., high-risk group), and (3) controls. Group differences in physiological reactions were assessed and current efforts are underway to link these to the degree of marital violence in the home. We reason that the high level of threat and sense of unpredictability characteristic of maritally violent homes may over long periods of time lead a child to exhibit hypervigilance towards threat. This hypervigilance includes a cognitive monitoring of the environment for cues of threat and may also be expressed in a pattern of physiological functioning that supports the attentional demands needed for continuous scanning of the environment. In adult PTSD victims, prolonged stress response has been linked to changes in the functioning of the hypothalamic-pituitary-adrenocortical axis and increased autonomic nervous system arousal (Griffin, Nishith, Resick, & Yehuda, 1997; Shalev, 1997; van der Kolk, 1996). In our model, we proposed that children from maritally hostile homes may exhibit increased vagal reactivity during threat (i.e., failure to suppress vagal tone). Heightened vagal tone in response to threat may help with attention deployment and threat detection so the child is readily prepared for action.

Assessments were made of baseline vagal tone and suppression of vagal tone under baseline conditions and under conditions of interpersonal threat. Interpersonal threat consisted of Dodge and Somberg's (1987) simulated peer provocation which involved the target child expecting to interact with a peer with whom he might get into a conflict. Through a speaker system, the target child heard a prerecorded audiotape consisting of a staged "conversation" between the experimenter and "another child" in which the "other child" stated his dislike for the experimenter and for any child with whom he would have to work. Vignettes of peer provocation were presented before and after the threat manipulation (i.e., under relaxed and threat conditions).

Physiological recordings were made while children viewed peer provocation vignettes under relaxed and threat conditions and while the target child listened to the interpersonal peer threat.

Preliminary results indicate that ODD children had lower basal vagal tone than controls and also showed increases in vagal tone from baseline to the interpersonal peer threat. We hope to examine whether baseline vagal tone or vagal reactivity to interpersonal threat is related to marital violence. Increased vagal reactivity would be consistent with findings that adult male batterers who as children experienced a high level of bidirectional violence between their parents show high vagal reactivity during interpersonal threat (Gottman et al., 1995).

Summary of Findings

Some consistencies emerge across these studies. Children from maritally conflicted homes who are showing signs of externalizing problems appear to respond to interadult conflict with reduced heart rate or heart rate reactivity. This decreased cardiovascular response is consistent with the idea of increased attentiveness or hypervigilance to the display of negative emotion between adults. This decreased cardiovascular response is a somatic quieting that allows resources to be allocated to the attentional system and prepares the body to mobilize in the service of action. Children from maritally conflictual homes may be in a constant state of preparedness because their home environments are unpredictable and increases in parental conflict may signal impending danger. We do not know whether this state of readiness is limited to their parent's marriage or is a general state that gets activated during other forms of interpersonal conflict. Dodge's notions that aggressive children have a hostile attributional bias and are hypervigilant to cues of threat in the peer context may suggest that this process can be generalized to other social contexts (Crick & Dodge, 1994; Dodge & Frame, 1982).

Within more normative samples, there is some evidence that marital conflict is associated with increased physiological arousal. Moreover, physiological activation is also linked with negative behavioral outcomes. Children from maritally distressed homes show increased urinary catecholamines and increased urinary catecholamines were associated with lower levels of imaginative play with a best friend.

Physiological abilities also appear to be associated with greater resilience in the face of marital conflict. Children with higher baseline vagal tone and greater ability to suppress vagal tone during challenge were less affected by difficulties in their parents' marriage. This may be a temperamental marker or may reflect the child's greater ability to benefit from parental efforts at shielding them from a bad marriage. In either case, these data suggest that interventions focused on reducing physiological arousal and improving physiological self-regulatory abilities may provide relief to those children experiencing significant distress living in maritally distressed homes.

Unexplored Issues and Future Directions

As can be seen from these reviews, only a handful of studies have directly examined children's physiological reactions to marital conflict. There are many unexplored issues to address and many directions to take before a fuller understanding of how physiological processes mediate the impact of marital conflict on children will emerge.

Developmental Issues

Effects of Development in the Child. We know little about how development affects children's physiological reactions to marital conflict. At the very simplest level, it is important to understand whether there are critical periods in a child's development in which marital conflict has its strongest effect on physiological functioning. Nor do we understand whether children's physiological reactions have a more detrimental effect on socioemotional functioning at different developmental periods.

We also know little about whether children from maritally distressed homes continue to show strong physiological reactions with development, or whether they habituate physiologically. Evidence that children are behaviorally sensitized to marital conflict suggests that they are likely to continue to show the same physiological reactions with development, but there is no longitudinal data that directly addresses this issue. As a result, it is difficult to determine whether the physiological reactions observed are due to the child's developmental status or the length of time that marital conflict has been going on. By far the majority of existing data has examined physiological reactivity in preschool-aged children. In discussing physiology–behavior links in aggressive children, Venables (1988) suggests that there may be a developmental shift in the physiological correlates of antisocial behavior. Citing evidence that at age 3 aggressive children are highly physiologically aroused to emotional events but that the underarousal pattern normally seen in aggressive adults appears to be present by age 11, he suggests that there may be a transitional point between these two ages at which a developmental shift in the physiological correlates of antisocial behavior may occur. The developmental course of children's physiological reactions to marital conflict is as yet unchartered territory.

Effects of Development and Change in the Marriage. We also know little about whether changes in the marriage affect children's physiological reactions to marital conflict. For example, do children's physiological reactions change when their parent's marriage improves, or when parents divorce and children are (hopefully) no longer exposed to marital conflict? This is part of the larger question of whether children's physiological reactions are transient and context specific, or are longer-lasting and become part of the child's reaction to stressful interpersonal or emotion-arousing situations.

A related question is whether children's physiological reactions show increases in physiological arousal as the marital relationship inches closer towards dissolution. Katz and Woodin (1999) found that the worst behavioral functioning was found in children from hostile-detached marriages, where the marriages are closer to dissolution. The same pattern may hold for children's physiological functioning, in that children from families in which the marriage is on the road to dissolution may be more physiologically sensitized to marital conflict.

There is also little understanding of how children's physiological reactions are related to normative developmental changes in the marital relationship. We know, for example, that in 70% of couples marital satisfaction decreases with the birth of the first child and stays down until the children leave home (Cowan & Cowan, 1992). There is also some evidence that marital satisfaction decreases with the birth of successive children (Cowan & Cowan, 1992). If so, there may be temporal effects related to birth order, since marital satisfaction has been lower for a longer period of time for later children than for first children. To the extent that this is true, later born children may show stronger or more stable physiological reactions to marital conflict than first-born children.

Children's Physiological Reactions as a Function of Severity or Type of Marital Conflict

Greater understanding of the effects of different forms of marital conflict is also needed. One particular distinction in need of greater clarification is the boundary between marital distress and marital violence. Are there differences in children's physiological reactions to parents who are extremely verbally contentious versus those who are physically violent?

Understanding the effects of different types of marriages on children is also needed. There is also increasing evidence that couples have unique styles of resolving conflict within their marriage. Attempts at characterizing these styles have yielded several new typologies of marriage. For example, Fitzpatrick (1984) characterized marriages based on each spouse's perception of their degree of interdependence within the relationship. Based on their self-reported relational style, couples were categorized as either traditional, separate, independent, or mixed (e.g., one spouse was traditional and one independent). Gottman and Levenson (1992) identified couples as regulated and nonregulated based on the ratio of positive to negative speaker behaviors over the course of a high conflict discussion. They found that nonregulated couples had lower marital satisfaction, more negative and less positive emotional expression, more stubbornness and withdrawal, more defensiveness, and a greater likelihood of divorce compared to regulated couples. We need to better understand the implications for children of living in homes characterized by these different marital communication styles. For example, Gottman (1994) identified a subgroup of couples who are unhappily married but their relationship is stable; these couples have a low likelihood of dissolution despite their high level of distress. Whether these varied styles of managing conflict have implications for children's physiological or behavioral functioning have yet to be determined.

Expanding Physiological Measurement Domains and Approaches

Assessing different physiological measurement domains can help expand our understanding of how children process and react to marital conflict. One interesting application is the use of electroencephalographic (EEG) recordings made from a variety of scalp sites, including frontal, parietal, and temporal regions. The work of Davidson and Fox (Davidson, 1994; Davidson & Fox, 1989; Davidson & Tomarken, 1989; Fox, 1991; Fox & Davidson, 1986) suggests that the patterning of frontal brain activation is linked to approach and withdrawal emotions, with the left frontal regions serving as a major approach system in the brain and the right frontal region serving as a withdrawal system. Davidson (1994) suggests that anger, joy, and interest are approach affects (lateralized on the left) because they engage people with one another and the world, whereas disgust, sadness, and fear disengage people from the world and one another and are therefore withdrawal emotions.

Frontal brain asymmetries appear very early in life. Relative right frontal activation is present in young infants during expression of disgust and crying and relative left frontal activation is present during expression of happiness (Bell & Fox, 1994; Davidson & Fox, 1989; Fox &

Davidson, 1988). Measures of resting frontal EEG activity have also been found to predict how an infant will respond emotionally to stressful situations. For example, Davidson and Fox (1989) found that infants with greater right than left frontal EEG activation during a baseline condition were much more likely to cry when later separated from their mothers.

Examining EEG activation to marital conflict can provide additional insight into individual differences in children's reaction to marital conflict. It may be that some children respond to marital conflict through withdrawal while others respond by approaching. This is consistent with evidence that some children report wanting to intervene in the marital conflict (e.g., Cummings & Davies, 1994). Such approach-withdrawal tendencies detected by EEG activation may not necessarily be observed at the behavioral level. For example, studies of offspring of depressed mothers indicate that while infants of nondepressed mothers show greater left than right frontal activation during interactive play with their mothers, infants of depressed mothers failed to show differential hemispheric activation (Dawson, Grofer Klinger, Panagiotides, Hill, & Spieker, 1992). Interestingly, behavioral coding of mothers, and infants' affective behavior during interaction did not reveal significant differences between the two groups, suggesting that the physiological measures may have been more sensitive than the behavioral measures.

It would also be conceptually useful to examine whether children in maritally distressed homes exhibit increased activation of the frontal cortex during the expression of negative emotions. Theoretically, such increased brain activation could be related to a decreased threshold for the expression of negative emotions. This in turn might help explain why exposure to dysfunctional marital conflict is associated with increased risk for behavior problems.

Measurement of EEG activation can also help separate out questions of whether children's reactions to marital conflict are individual differences related to the tendency to express specific emotions or are markers of the intensity of emotional expression.

Measures of *asymmetric* frontal EEG activity are better predictors of individual differences in the tendency to express specific emotions, such as distress and sadness, whereas measures of *generalized* frontal EEG activity are better predictors of individual differences in the intensity of emotional expression (Dawson, 1996). Dawson, Panagiotides, Grofer Klinger, and Spieker (1994) found increased activation in both the right and left frontal regions in infants of depressed mothers relative to infants of nondepressed mothers, but differences in the pattern of asymmetry were not found. This suggested that infants of depressed mothers are experiencing negative emotions more frequently and intensely. From a physiological perspective, this may result in selective amplification of those neural circuits involved in these negative emotions and lead to a lower threshold for the activation of negative emotions and a possible resulting deficit in emotion regulation.

Conclusion

In the latter part of the twentieth century, the link between marital conflict and children's socioemotional difficulties was well-established. Our task for the early stages of the next century are to fully explicate those processes that mediate and moderate the relationship between marital conflict and negative child outcomes. There is now clear evidence that children's physiological reactivity can serve such a mediational role. However, children's physiological reactions cannot be viewed in isolation from their emotional and social behavior. Nor can we consider children's physiological (or behavioral) reactions without understanding the destructive interactional processes that characterize their parent's marriage. It is only through integrating our understanding of both biological and behavioral processes that we can get a complete picture of the effects of marital conflict on the whole child.

REFERENCES

Arnold, M. B. (1970). Perennial problems in the field of emotions. In M. B. Arnold (Ed.), *Feelings and emotions.* New York: Academic Press.

Ax, A. F. (1953). The physiological differentiation between fear and anger in humans. *Psychosomatic Medicine, 15(5),* 433–442.

Ballard, M. E., Cummings, E. M., & Larkin, K. (1993). Emotional and cardiovascular responses to adults' angry behavior and to challenging tasks in children of hypertensive and normotensive parents. *Child Development, 64,* 500–515.

Bell, M. A. & Fox, N. A. (1994). Brain development over the first year of life: Relations between EEG frequency and coherence and cognitive and affective behaviors. In G. Dawson & K. Fischer (Eds.), *Human behavior and the developing brain* (pp. 314–345). New York: Guilford Press.

Boyce, W. T., & Jemerin, J. M. (1990). Psychobiological differences in childhood stress response: I. Patterns of illness and susceptibility. *Journal of Developmental and Behavioral Pediatrics, 11(2),* 86–94.

Brener, J. (1977). Sensory and perceptual determinants of voluntary visceral control. In G. E. Schwartz & J. Beatty (Eds.), *Biofeedback: Theory and research* (pp.29–66). New York: Academic Press.

Cacioppo, J. T., & Petty, R. E. (1983). Foundations of social psychophysiology. In J. T. Cacioppo & R. E. Petty (Eds.), *Social psychophysiology.* New York: Guilford Press.

Calkins, S. D. (1997). Cardiac vagal tone indices of temperamental reactivity and behavioral regulation in young children. *Developmental Psychobiology, 31,* 125–135.

Cowan, C. P., & Cowan, P. A. (1992). *When parents become partners.* New York: Basic Books.

Cicchetti, D. (1993). Developmental psychopathology: Reactions, reflections and projections. *Developmental Review, 13*(4), 471–502.

Crick, N. R., & Dodge, K. A. (1994). A review and reformulation of social information processing mechanisms in children's social adjustment. *Psychological Bulletin, 115*(1), 74–101.

Cummings, E. M., & Davies, P. T. (1994). Maternal depression and child development. *Journal of Child Psychology & Psychiatry & Allied Disciplines, 35,* 73–112.

Davidson, R. J. (1994). Development of emotion expression and emotion regulation in infancy: Contributions of the frontal lobe. In G. Dawson & K. Fischer, (Eds.), *Human behavior and the developing brain* (pp. 346–379). New York: Guilford Press.

Davidson, R. J., & Fox, N. A. (1989). Asymmetrical brain activity discriminates between positive versus negative affective stimuli in human infants. *Science, 218,* 1235–1237.

Davidson, R. J., & Tomarken, A. J. (1989). Laterality and emotion: An electrophysiological approach. In F. Boller & J. Grafman (Eds.). *Handbook of neuropsychology* (Vol. 3, pp. 419–441). Amsterdam: Elsevier.

Dawson, G., (1996). Frontal electroencephalographic correlates of individual differences in emotional expression in infants: A brain system perspective on emotion. In N. A. Fox (Ed.), *Emotion regulation: Behavioral and biological considerations. Monographs for the Society for Research in Child Development.* Chicago: University of Chicago Press.

Dawson, G., Grofer Klinger, L., Panagiotides, H., Hill, D., & Spieker, S. (1992). Frontal lobe activity and affective behavior of infants of mothers with depressive symptoms. *Child Development, 63,* 725–737.

Dawson, G., Hessel, D., & Frey, K. (1994). Social influences of early developing biological and behavioral systems related to risk for affective disorders. *Development and Psychopathology, 6,* 759–779.

DeGangi, G. A., DiPietro, J. A., Greenspan, S. I., & Porges, S. W. (1991). Psychophysiological characteristics of the regulatory disordered infant. *Infant Behavior and Development, 14,* 37–50.

Dennenberg, V. H., & Rosenberg, K. M. (1967). Nongenetic transmission of information. *Nature, 216,* 549–550.

Dlin, R. A., Hanne, N., Silverberg, D. S., & Bar-Or, O. (1983). Follow-up of normotensive men with exaggerated blood pressure response to exercise. *American Heart Journal, 106,* 316–320.

Dodge, K. A., & Frame, C. L., (1982). Social cognitive biases and deficits in aggressive boys, *Child Development, 53*(3), 620–635.

Dodge, K. A., & Somberg, D. R. (1987). Hostile attributional biases among aggressive boys are exacerbated under conditions of threats to the self. *Child Development, 58,* 213–224.

Duffy, E. (1957). The psychological significance of the concept of "arousal" or "activation". *Psychological Review, 64(5),* 265–275.

Eisenberg, N., Fabes, R. A., Karbon, M., Murphy, B. C., Smith, S., & Maszk, P. (1996). The relations of children's dispositional prosocial behavior to emotionality, regulation, and social functioning. *Child Development, 67,* 974–992.

Eisenberg, N., Fabes, R. A., Murphy, B. C., Maszk, P., Smith, S., & Karbon, M. (1995). The role of emotionality and regulation in children's social functioning: A longitudinal study. *Child Development, 66,* 1360–1384.

Ekman, P., Levenson, R. W., & Friesen, W. V. (1983). Autonomic nervous system activity distinguishes among emotions. *Science, 221,* 1208–1210.

El-Sheikh, M. (1994). Children's emotional and physiological responses to interadult angry behavior: The role of history of interparental hostility. *Journal of Abnormal Child Psychology, 22,* 661–678.

El-Sheikh, M., Ballard, M., & Cummings, E. M. (1994). Individual difference in preschoolers' physiological and verbal responses to videotaped angry reactions. *Journal of Abnormal Child Psychology, 22,* 303–320.

El-Sheikh, M., & Cummings, E. M. (1992). Availability of control and preschoolers' responses to interadult anger. *International Journal of Behavioral Development, 15,* 207–226.

El-Sheikh, M., Cummings, E. M., & Goetsch, V. L. (1989). Coping with adults' angry behavior: Behavioral, physiological, and verbal responses in preschoolers. *Developmental Psychology, 25,* 490–498.

Fitzpatrick, M. (1984). A typological approach to marital interaction: Recent theory and research. *Advances in Experimental Social Psychology, 18,* 1–47.

Fox, N. (1989). The psychophysiological correlates of emotional reactivity during the first year of life. *Developmental Psychology, 25,* 364–372.

Fox, N. (1991). If it's not left, it's right: Electroencephalography asymmetry and the development of emotion. *American Psychologist, 46,* 863–872.

Fox, N. A. & Davidson, R. J. (1986). Taste-elicited changes in facial signs of emotion and the asymmetry of brain electrical activity in human newborns. *Neuropsychologia, 24,* 417–422.

Fox, N. A., & Davidson, R. J. (1988). Patterns of brain electrical activity during facial signs of emotion in 10-month-old infants. *Developmental Psychology, 24,* 230–236.

Fredrikson, M., & Matthews, K. A. (1990). Cardiovascular responses to behavioral stress and hypertension: A meta-analytic review. *Behavioral Medicine, 12,* 30–39.

Gottman, J. M. (1994). *What predicts divorce?* Hillsdale, NJ: Lawrence Erlbaum Press.

Gottman, J. M., Jacobson, N. S., Rushe, R. H., Short, J. W., Babcock, J., LaTaillade J. J., & Waltz, J. (1995). The relationship between heart rate reactivity, emotionally aggressive behavior, and general violence in batterers. *Journal of Family Psychology, 9,* 227–248.

Gottman, J. M., & Katz, L. F. (1989). The effects of marital discord on young children's peer interaction and health. *Developmental Psychology, 25,* 373–381.

Gottman, J. M., Katz, L. F., & Hooven, C. (1997). *Meta-emotion: How families communicate emotionally.* Mahwah, NJ: Lawrence Erlbaum.

Gottman, J. M., & Levenson, R. W. (1992). Marital processes predictive of later dissolution: Behavior, physiology and health. *Journal of Personality and Social Psychology, 63,* 221–233.

Graham, R. K., & Clifton, R. K. (1966). Heart rate change as a component of the orienting response. *Psychological Bulletin, 65,* 305–320.

Griffin, M. G., Nishith, P., Resick, P. A., & Yehuda, R. (1997). Integrating objective indicators of treatment outcome in post-traumatic stress disorder. In R. Yehuda & A. C. Alexander (Eds.), *Psychobiology of post-traumatic stress disorder. Annals of the New York Academy of Sciences* (Vol. 821, pp. 388–409). New York: New York Academy of Sciences.

Grych, J. H., & Fincham, F. D. (1990). Marital conflict and children's adjustment: A cognitive contextual framework. *Psychological Bulletin, 108,* 267–290.

Hershorn, M., & Rosenbaum, A. (1985). Children of marital violence: A closer look at the unintended victims. *American Journal of Orthopsychiatry, 55,* 260–265.

Hetherington, E. M., Cox, M., & Cox, R. (1982). Effects of divorce on parents and children. In M. Lamb (Ed.), *Nontraditional families* (pp. 233–288). Hillsdale, NJ: Lawrence Erlbaum Associates.

Huffman, L. C., Bryan, Y., del Carmen, R., Pederson, F., Doussard-Roosevelt, J., & Porges, S. W. (1998). Infant temperament and cardiac vagal tone: Assessments at twelve weeks of age. *Child Development, 69,* 624–635.

Jaffe, P. G., Wolfe, D. A., Wilson, S. K., & Zak, L. (1986). Family violence and child adjustment: A comparative analysis of girls' and boys' behavioral symptoms. *American Journal of Psychiatry, 143,* 74–77.

Jouriles, E. N., Murphy, C. M., & O'Leary, K. D. (1989). Interspousal aggression, marital discord, and child problems. *Journal of Consulting and Clinical Psychology, 57,* 453–455.

Katkin, E. S. (1985). Blood, sweat and tears: Individual differences in autonomic self-perception. *Psychophysiology, 22,* 125–137.

Katz, L. F. (in press). Living in a hostile world: Toward an integrated model of family, peer and physiological processes in childhood aggression. In K. A. Kerns, J. Contreras, & A. M. Neal-Barnett (Eds.), *Linking two social worlds: Family and peers.* Thousand Oaks, CA: Sage Publications Inc.

Katz, L. F., & Gottman, J. M. (1995). Vagal tone protects children from marital conflict. *Development and Psychopathology, 7,* 83–92.

Katz, L. F., & Woodin, E. (1999). Hostility, hostile-detachment and conflict engagement in marriages. Effects on child and family functioning. Manuscript submitted for publication.

Lacey, J., & Lacey, B. (1967). Somatic response patterning and stress: Some revisions of activation theory. In M. H. Appley and R. Trumbull (Eds.). *Psychological Stress: Issues in Research* (pp. 14–37). New York: Appleton-Century-Crofts.

Linnemeyer, S. A., & Porges, S. W. (1986). Recognition memory and cardiac vagal tone in 6-month-old infants. *Infant Behavior and Development, 9,* 43–56.

Malmo, R. B. (1957). Anxiety and behavioral arousal. *Psychological Review, 64(5),* 276–287.

Manuck, S. B., & Krantz, C. S. (1986). Psychophysiologic reactivity in coronary heart disease and essential hypertension. In K. A. Matthews et al. (Eds.), *Handbook of stress, reactivity and cardiovascular disease*. New York: Wiley-Interscience.

Matthews, K. A., Rakaczky, C. J., & Stoney, C. M. (1987). Are cardiovascular responses to behavioral stressors a stable individual difference variable in childhood? *Psychophysiology, 24,* 464–473.

Menkes, M. S., Matthews, K. A., Krantz, D. S., Lundberg, V., Mead, L. A., Qaqish, B., Liang, K. Y., Thomas, C. B., & Pearson, T. A. (1989). Cardiovascular reactivity to the cold pressor test as a predictor of hypertension. *Hypertension, 14,* 524–530.

Park, M. K., & Menard, S. M. (1987). Accuracy of blood pressure measurement by the Dinamap monitor in infants and children. *Pediatrics, 79(6),* 907–914.

Parker, F. C., Croft, J. B., Cresenta, J. L., Freedman, D. S., Burke, G. L., Weber, L. S., & Berenson, G. S. (1987). The association between cardiovascular response tasks and future blood pressure levels in children: Bogalusa heart study. *American Heart Journal, 113,* 1174.

Pavlov, I. P. (1927). *Conditioned reflexes.* Oxford: Oxford University Press.

Porges, S. W. (1984). Heart rate oscillation: An index of neural mediation. In M. G. H. Coles, J. R. Jennings, & J. A. Stern (Eds.), *Psychophysiological perspectives: Festschrift for Beatrice and John Lacey.* New York: Van Nostrand Reinhold.

Porges, S. W. (1995) Orienting in a defensive world: Mammalian modifications of our evolutionary heritage: A Polyvagal Theory. *Psychophysiology, 32(4),* 301–318.

Porges, S. W., Doussard-Roosevelt, J. A., Portales, A. L., & Greenspan, S. I. (1996). Infant regulation of the vagal "brake" predicts child behavior problems: A psychobiological model of social behavior. *Developmental Psychobiology, 29,* 697–712.

Porges, S. W., Doussard-Roosevent, J. A., Portales, A. L., & Suess, A. (1994). Cardiac vagal tone: Stability and relation to difficultness in infants and 3-year-olds. *Developmental Psychobiology, 27,* 289–300.

Porges, S. W., & Humphreys, M. M. (1997). Cardiac and respiratory responses during visual search in non-retarded children and retarded adolescents. *American Journal of Mental Deficiency, 82,* 162–169.

Porges, S. W., Walter, G. F., Korb, R. J., & Sprague, R. L. (1975). The influences of methylphenidate on heart rate and behavioral measures of attention in hyperactive children. *Child Development, 46,* 727–733.

Rutter, M. (1971). Parent-child separation: Psychological effects on the children. *Journal of Child Psychology and Psychiatry, 12,* 233–260.

Shalev, A. Y. (1997). Acute to chronic: Etiology and pathophysiology of PTSD: A biopsychosocial approach. In C. S. Fullerton & Robert J. Ursano (Eds.), *Post-traumatic stress disorder: Acute and long-term responses to trauma and disaster. Progress in psychiatry series* (No. 51, pp. 209–240). Washington, DC: American Psychiatric Press.

Sokolov, E. N. (1963). *Perception and the conditioned reflex.* New York: Pergamon Press.

Stern, R. M., Ray, W. J., & Davis, C. M. (1980). *Psychophysiological recording.* New York: Oxford University Press.

Sternberg, K. J., Lamb, M. E., Greenbaum, C., Cicchetti, D., Dawud, S., Cortes, R. M., Krispin, O., & Lorey, F. (1993). Effects of domestic violence on children's behavior problems and depression. *Developmental Psychology, 29,* 44–52.

Stifter, C. A., & Fox, N. A. (1990). Infant reactivity: Physiological correlates of newborn and 5-month temperament. *Developmental Psychology, 26,* 582–588.

Stifter, C. A., Fox, N. A., & Porges, S. W. (1989). Facial expressivity and vagal tone in 5- and 10-month old infants. *Infant Behavior and Development, 12,* 127–137.

Suess, P. E., Porges, S. W., & Plude, D. J. (1994). Cardiac vagal tone and sustained attention in school-age children. *Psychophysiology, 31,* 17–22.

van der Kolk, B. A. (1996). The body keeps score: Approaches to the psychobiology of posttraumatic stress disorder. In B. A. van der Kolk and A. C. McFarlane (Eds.), *Traumatic stress: The effects of overwhelming experience on mind, body, and society* (pp. 214–241). New York: Guilford Press.

Venables, P. H. (1988). Psychophysiology and crime: Theory and data. In T. E. Moffitt & S. A. Mednick (Eds.), *Biological contributions to crime causation* (pp. 3–13). Dordrecht: Martinus Nijhoff Publishers.

Wolfe, D. A., Jaffe, P., Wilson, S. K., & Zak, L. (1985). Children of battered women: The relation of child behavior to family violence and maternal stress. *Journal of Consulting and Clinical Psychology, 53,* 657–665.

Wood, D. L., Sheps, S. B., Elveback, L. R., & Schirger, A. (1984). Cold pressor test as a predictor of hypertension. *Hypertension, 6,* 301–306.

Zuckerman, M. (1990). The psychophysiology of sensation seeking. *Journal of Personality, 58,* 313–345.

8   Children's Coping with Interparental Conflict

Patricia K. Kerig

As evidence for the negative effects of exposure to interparental conflict has accumulated, investigators in the field have turned their attention to the task of uncovering the factors that might help children to be resilient in the face of family stress (Depner, Leino, & Chun, 1992). Central to the concept of resiliency are children's coping efforts (Compas, 1998; Rutter, 1990). Successful coping with stress allows children to overcome adversity and to face future life challenges with optimism. However, depending on the match between the stressor and the strategy used to respond to it, coping can either be a help or a hindrance. For example, in the case of children exposed to interparental conflict, active problem solving may exacerbate the problem by placing children in the middle of their parents' quarrels. Consequently, coping has been given a place in the leading models of the risks and protective factors associated with exposure to interparental conflict (Cummings & Cummings, 1988; Davies & Cummings, 1994; Grych & Fincham, 1990). This chapter reviews the literature concerning the conceptualization and measurement of children's coping, summarizes the empirical evidence on children's responses to interparental conflict and violence, and explores directions for future research.

What is Coping?

The past decade has seen an explosion in the research on children's coping (for reviews, see Boekarets, 1996; Repetti, McGrath, & Ishikawa, 1996; and Wolchik & Sandler, 1997). However, no theories specific to the understanding of children's coping have yet been developed, and work on this topic continues to rely on models devised for adults. The most influential of these models is that of Lazarus and Folkman (1987), who define coping as "cognitive and behavioral efforts to manage specific external and/or internal demands that are appraised as taxing or exceeding the resources of the person" (p. 141). This definition guides our thinking in a number of important ways. First, the term *coping* refers to the *attempts* to manage stress, rather than to the outcomes of such attempts. Thus, rather than using the term coping to refer to good adaptation (e.g., Hetherington, 1992), this definition is specific to coping as the *process* by which children respond to stress. Second, this definition defines coping as *effortful* behavior, rather than reactive or unconscious processes, thus differentiating coping from defense mechanisms and symptoms of distress. A third feature of Lazarus and Folkman's model is that it gives *appraisals* a primary place in the coping process, just as Grych and Fincham's (1990) cognitive-contextual model posits that children's appraisals of interparental conflict – such as whether they are to blame for starting the quarrel or are responsible for controlling it – guide their choice of coping strategy. However, there are divergent models of coping (see Compas, 1998), each of which has been applied to the study of children exposed to interparental conflict with benefits and limitations.

How is Coping Conceptualized?

Problem Focus versus Emotion Focus. The most widely cited typology of coping is that proposed by Lazarus and Folkman (1987), who distinguish between coping strategies oriented toward solving the problem (problem-focused coping; e.g., taking action) and strategies designed to decrease distress and arousal (emotion-focused coping; e.g., self-calming). Each form of coping is assumed to be suited to a particular kind of stressor. For stressors that are controllable, and thus can be resolved through direct action, problem-focused coping should be associated with better adjustment. In contrast, when children are coping with an uncontrollable stressor, such as interparental conflict, emotion-focused coping is more adaptive. The distinction between problem-focused vs. emotion-focused strategies has been applied to a number of studies involving children (e.g., Band & Weisz, 1988; Compas, Banez, Malcarne, & Worsham, 1991) and provides an important conceptual underlay to much of the hypothesizing about the effectiveness of specific various coping strategies for children exposed to interparental conflict (Kerig, 1997). However, in the study of children and interparental conflict, global categories such as problem-focused coping fail to distinguish among such conceptually different subcategories as direct problem solving (e.g., stepping between parents in order to stop the argument) and indirect problem solving (e.g., being "extra good" in order to relieve tension in the family; Kerig, 1999a).

Clearly, these coping strategies have different implications for the child and for child–family relationships, and conceptualizations sensitive to these distinctions are needed to advance the study of children and marital discord.

Approach versus Avoidance. A second widely utilized typology is Billings and Moos's (1981) distinction between approach and avoidance. Approach coping involves focusing attention on a stressor, whether behaviorally or cognitively (e.g., thinking about or acting upon it), while avoidance refers to attempts to focus attention away from a stressor (e.g., denial or minimization). Although often used interchangeably with the terms problem-focused and emotion-focused coping, the approach–avoidance distinction is nonetheless distinct. For example, cognitive restructuring (e.g., construing the problem in a more positive way) is considered to be emotion-focused coping in Lazarus and Folkman's system, but would be typed as approach coping in Billings and Moos'. The approach–avoidance typology has been used successfully in a number of studies of children and adolescents (e.g., Herman-Stahl, Stemmler, & Peterson, 1995; Kliewer, 1991). In fact, even among measures designed to capture the problem-focused versus emotion-focused distinction, the approach–avoidance construct is the one most frequently validated in the study of children's responses to stress in general (Altshuler & Ruble, 1989; Ayers, Sandler, West, & Roosa, 1996) and to interparental conflict in particular (Fedorowicz & Kerig, 1999; Sandler, Tein, & West, 1994). However, like the problem-vs. emotion-focused categorization scheme, the approach–avoidance scheme may collapse distinctions that it would be helpful to maintain. For example, Sandler et al. (1994) make a conceptually important and empirically validated distinction between simple avoidance and distraction. While avoidance may be helpful by allowing children to muster their resources, its habitual use may prevent children from responding to the stressor in a more constructive way. Engaging in distracting actions, on the other hand, may be a more effective method of keeping a child's mind off of a stressor, and such activities (e.g., listening to music, doing artwork, playing with a friend) may be rewarding and healthful in and of themselves. Therefore, because categories such as approach and avoidance enfold such disparate coping strategies, this system, like the problem- vs. emotion-focused distinction, lacks the specificity that helps us to understand what children do, or should do, in order to cope with their parents' quarrels.

Nonconstructive Coping. A third type of coping has been variously labeled nonconstructive (Fedorowicz & Kerig, 1999), maladaptive (Aldwin, 1994), antisocial–asocial (Blechman, Prinz, & Dumas, 1995), or internalizing–externalizing (Causey & Dubow, 1992). These terms refer to misguided strategies to change the situation or to modify one's emotions that are destructive to the self or others. For example, substance abuse may be utilized in an attempt to self-calm; obsessional worrying may be an attempt to ferret out the "ideal" solution; self-blame may be a form of penitence; physical aggression may comprise an attempt to deflect the stressor. As Skinner & Edge (1998) state: "It seems relatively straightforward to identify the socially repellent properties of maladaptive coping: Opposition and self-blame beget defense and coercion, dependency and whining use up others' resources and patience" (p. 362). The construct of nonconstructive coping has been called into question because of the difficulty in distinguishing such coping strategies from negative *outcomes* of the coping process (Stanton, Danoff-Burg, Cameron, & Ellis, 1994). However, there are some reasons to retain the nonconstructive category for the study of children's coping with interparental conflict. Empirically, a separate factor comprised of such nonconstructive strategies has emerged in measures of adults' and children's coping (e.g., Causey & Dubow, 1992; Fedorowicz & Kerig, 1999; Spirito, Stark, & Williams, 1988). Conceptually, Lazarus and Folkman's model posits that coping comprises all effortful responses, not only those that are effective. In addition, the family systemic perspective takes a *functional* view of children's behavior as comprising an attempt to cope with interparental conflict. For example, Jouriles and Norwood (1995) propose that boys may act out in an attempt to deflect parents from their argument, whereas girls may become overcontrolled in an attempt to ease the tension in the family. Last, as is discussed in the following section, a developmental perspective suggests that nonconstructive coping may be particularly relevant to the study of children's coping.

Coping Categories Specific to Interparental Conflict. As noted previously, coping typologies derived from the study of general stress lack the specificity needed in order to further our understanding of children's responses to interparental conflict. Of particular concern are the ways in which children's attempts to cope might lead to inappropriate involvement in their parents' quarrels (Grych & Fincham, 1993). Children's cognitive egocentrism leads them to believe that external events are within their control, and this is particularly true in the family context. Thus, despite the fact that interparental conflict is objectively not children's responsibility, children often report that they are to blame for their parents' marital problems (Kurdek & Berg, 1987) and have control over them (Rossman & Rosenberg, 1992). Consequently, children frequently place themselves in the middle of their parents' conflicts. For example, Jenkins, Smith, & Graham (1989) found that 71% of 9–12-year-olds reported intervening directly in interparental quarrels: "Children may feel that by intervening in a quarrel they gain some direct control over an event that otherwise would make them feel helpless" (p. 187).

Far from being helpful, however, intervening in the conflict may have negative consequences, such as burdening children with developmentally inappropriate responsibilities (Johnston, Gonzales, & Campbell, 1987) or causing the marital aggression to spill over into parent–child relationships (Engfer, 1988). The dangers to the child are particularly salient when interparental conflicts are violent, as is attested to by the co-occurrence of spousal battery and child abuse (Edleson, 1999). Yet, children's inclination to intervene increases as interparental conflicts become more intense (Grych & Fincham, 1993), physically aggressive (O'Brien, Margolin, John, & Krueger, 1991), child-related (Grych & Fincham, 1993), and unresolved (e.g., El-Sheikh, Cummings, & Reiter, 1996). Thus, as children become distressed, they increasingly utilize coping strategies that put them at risk for becoming involved in the conflict and thus potentially generate even more distress.

Is Coping Dispositional or Situational?

Another major debate in the literature concerns whether coping is dispositional or situational in nature. The idea that children have dispositional coping styles that are stable across situations has been supported in work on children undergoing divorce. For example, Ayers et al. (1996) compared children's responses to a dispositional coping measure and a situational measure (the charmingly named "How I Coped Under Pressure Scale," or HICUPS), and found moderate to high consistency between them. In fact, the associations between the dispositional and situational measures was higher than is seen typically in adults, suggesting that children's dispositional styles may be more important in guiding their responses to stress than the contextual factors and appraisals that guide adult coping.

In contrast, others have argued that children's coping is inherently situational in nature, given that different coping strategies are appropriate for different situations (Forsythe & Compas, 1987). Consistent with this idea, studies generally show only moderate correspondence between children's reports of coping with disparate stressors such as interparental conflict, peer conflicts, and academic problems (e.g., Causey & Dubow, 1992; Fedorowicz, 1998; Roecker, Dubow, & Donaldson, 1996). Further, as Sandler et al. (1994) note, a limitation of dispositional measures is that they do not take into account the

"match" between coping efforts and the demands of the specific situation. For example, while problem-focused coping generally is associated with better adaptation (e.g., Ayers et al., 1996; Causey & Dubow,
1992), emotion-focused coping is more efficacious in situations in
which the child cannot control the stressor (Compas, Worsham, & Ey,
1992), such as is the case with interparental conflict and violence. In a
seeming contradiction, studies using dispositional measures have
found that the adjustment of children of divorce is positively related to
the use of active coping (Sandler et al., 1994), while avoidance is associated with maladjustment (Armistead et al., 1990; Kliewer & Sandler,
1993). However, because the measures used were dispositional, these
results cannot be interpreted as showing that active coping *with interparental conflict* is helpful for children of divorce. Children of divorce
must cope with such disparate stressors as parental distress, financial
constraints, loss of the noncustodial parent, and ongoing interparental
conflict (Grych & Fincham, 1997). Therefore, it is necessary to ask,
"Coping with what?"

Coping Efficacy. Another construct that may comprise a dispositional difference in children's responses to interparental conflict is that
of *coping efficacy* (Cummings, Davies, & Simpson, 1994), sometimes
referred to as *efficacy expectations* (Grych & Fincham, 1990), or *outcome
expectations* (Grych, 1998). Children's belief that they will be able to successfully cope with interparental conflict may affect how they respond
to it (Forsythe & Compas, 1987). For example, low coping efficacy has
been linked with negative appraisals and emotional dysregulation in
the face of interparental conflict (Grych & Fincham, 1990, 1993; Davies
& Cummings, 1994), while high coping efficacy is linked to good
adjustment (El-Sheikh & Cummings, 1992). Coping efficacy may also
arise out of experience rather than disposition. Parents who respond
positively to children's efforts to cope with interparental conflicts may
enhance children's sense of efficacy and perceived control.

Does Coping Change Over Development?

As noted earlier, much of the theorizing on children's coping has
relied on downward extensions of the study of adults; however, adult
models may not be adequate for the study of children. For example,
Band and Weisz (1988) found that 40% of children's responses on a coping interview could not be coded using categories derived from the
adult literature. How is children's coping likely to differ from that of
adults? First, the stressors children face in life are less likely to be under
their control than those encountered by adults (Ryan-Wenger, 1992).
For example, while parents may choose to divorce, children are help-

less victims of marital dissolution. Secondly, children are still in the process of developing adaptive skills and have a more restrictive repertoire of coping strategies to draw on than adults (Fedorowicz, 1998). Therefore, given that these are the only weapons in their armamentarium at times, children may resort to nonconstructive coping strategies such as aggression (Tangney et al., 1996) or ruminative worrying (Brown, O'Keefe, Sanders, & Baker, 1986).

Coping also may change as children move through development (Losoya, Eisenberg, & Fabes, 1998; Skinner & Edge, 1998). In general, development is associated with increasing cognitive sophistication (see Grych and Cadoza-Fernandes, Chapter 6) and an expanded range of coping skills. For example, while problem-focused coping strategies are seen in children as young as 6 years of age, the use of more cognitively demanding emotion-focused strategies (e.g., wishful thinking, fantasizing, and seeking understanding) increases through late childhood and adolescence (e.g., Altshuler & Ruble, 1989; Band & Weisz, 1988; Compas et al., 1992). In short, with age, children are able to manage stress through cognition rather than behavior (Kliewer, 1991). Development increases children's repertoire of coping strategies in other ways as well. Older children are more mobile and have more extensive peer networks, and thus are better able to cope through distancing themselves from the family and engaging in thoroughly engrossing distracting activities outside the home (Hetherington, 1992). Further, as cognitive development proceeds, children's appraisals may become more accurate and may guide their coping efforts in more systematic ways. For example, older children are able to reason in complex ways about the causes of marital conflict and to recognize that they are not responsible for the problem (Kurdek & Berg, 1987; Mazur, 1993). Thus, with age, children come to feel less helpless in the face of interparental quarreling (Davies, Myers, & Cummings, 1996) and perceive themselves to be more efficacious (Grych, 1998).

While some studies find no age differences in children's coping with interparental conflict (e.g., Johnston et al., 1987; Roecker et al., 1996), a well-replicated paradoxical finding is that, despite the greater availability of emotion-focused coping strategies across development, with age children are increasingly likely to attempt to use problem-focused or approach coping to respond to their parents' quarrels. For example, Cummings, Vogel, Cummings, and El-Sheikh (1989) found that children's willingness to intervene in the conflict increased from ages 4 to 9, and Davies, Myers, and Cummings (1996) found that adolescents were more likely than school-aged children to involve themselves in the argument. Creasey, Lustig, Catanzaro, Reese, and Herman (1995) found not only that first graders were more likely than kindergarteners to use approach coping (e.g., "get mom and dad to stop arguing"), but that the efficacy of children's coping efforts changed with age: Approach coping was related to better adjustment in first graders, while avoidance was related to better adjustment in kindergarteners. Further, Cummings, Ballard, El-Sheikh, and Lake (1991) found that 14-year-olds were more likely to endorse intervening in the argument than either older (19-year-old) or younger (5-year-old) children. Kerig (1999a), in turn, found that the age-related increase in intervening was specific to boys.

The explanation for this age effect, Cummings et al. (1991) argue, is that older children are both able to conceptualize potential solutions and are highly motivated to implement them. For example, Davies et al. (1996) found that adolescents were more likely to propose intervening in interparental conflicts in more sophisticated ways. In this way, cognitive development may actually *increase* children's disposition to intervene given that they are able to do so effectively, whether by devising a clever distracting maneuver, mediating a workable compromise, or, in cases of domestic violence, making a 911 call that elicits a speedy response. Yet, despite the advantages to possessing more sophisticated interpersonal problem-solving strategies, the attempt to apply them to interparental arguments is likely to compound children's stress. Playing the role of arbiter of parental disputes places a strain on children, particularly when it leads to triangulation in the marital relationship (Jenkins et al., 1989; Kerig, 1999a).

Are There Gender Differences in Children's Coping?

In addition to developmental differences, there may be gender differences in children's responses to stress. Zahn-Waxler (1993) captured these in a pithy way, characterizing boys as "warriors" who take action against what threatens them, while girls are "worriers" who internalize their distress (see Davies & Lindsay, Chapter 3). Some support for the warrior–worrier distinction has been found in studies of children's responses to interparental conflict (Kerig, 1999b). For example, boys are more likely than girls to respond to interparental quarreling with aggression (Cummings et al., 1989) and active, problem-focused coping (Davies et al., 1996), whereas girls respond with support-seeking and worrying (Roecker et al., 1996). Further, Laumakis, Margolin, and John (1998) found that boys from high-conflict marriages were more likely to endorse physically intervening in the conflict, whereas girls were more likely to suggest trying to smooth over the problem (e.g., "help clean the mess"). Again, however, evidence is mixed. Some studies have failed to find gender differences in children's coping with interparental conflict (e.g., Grych & Fincham, 1993), violence (e.g., Kerig, Fedorowicz, Brown, Patenaude, & Warren, 1998), and divorce (Sandler et al., 1994). Other findings belie gender stereotypes; for example, El-Sheikh et al. (1996) found that girls were almost four times more likely than boys to endorse intervening in interadult arguments. In sum, the literature is inconsistent regarding gender differences. The explanation for this may be, at least in part, because of the inconsistent topologies and measures used in the studies cited; therefore it is important to consider the implications of these disparate methodologies.

How Do We Know How Children Cope with Interparental Conflict?

Methodological Issues in the Studies of Children's Coping

Although it is beyond the scope of this chapter to thoroughly review all of the methodological issues in the study of children's coping, a number of these must be noted. (For recent critiques, see Fedorowicz, 1998; Fields & Prinz, 1996; Knapp, Stark, Kurkjian, & Spirito, 1991; and Ryan-Wenger, 1992). As the studies summarized in Table 8.1 show, one significant complication is that almost every study to date has utilized a different model of coping and a different way of assessing children's coping strategies. Many of these measures utilized are "homespun" and have not undergone rigorous psychometric evaluation; evidence for validity, in particular, is sparse. Scale validation has usually been limited to the use of exploratory factor analysis rather than more stringent confirmatory analytic procedures. In brief, both methodologically and conceptually, the study of children's coping is still in its infancy.

Analogue versus Actual Interparental Scenarios. One dilemma in the coping literature concerns whether children should respond to hypothetical dilemmas or to describe their own actual experiences with interparental conflict. Benefits of the analogue methodology include that all children are responding to the same scenario, and that the investigator can control and even manipulate dimensions of conflict, such as intensity, violence, and resolution. This approach has spawned a rich program of research by Cummings and his colleagues (1989, 1991; El-Sheikh et al., 1996) in which children's responses are elicited to taped or live simulated conflicts (see also Laumakis et al., 1998; Grych & Fincham, 1993; O'Brien, Bahadur, Gee, Balto, & Erber, 1997).

There are a number of potential limitations of analogue studies. For example, is the question "what would you do" the same as "what did

Table 8.1. Measures and Major Findings of Studies of Children's Coping with Interparental Conflict and Violence

Sample	Measure (Psychometrics)	Method	Dimensions	Major Findings
		Dispositional coping strategies		
Divorce: N = 258; ages = 7–13 (Sandler et al., 1994)	Children's Coping Strategies Checklist (Program for Prevention Research, 1992) (Reliability: α = .76 to .90; Validity: confirmatory factor analysis, replicated across samples)	45-item questionnaire	Active Avoidance Distraction Support	Longitudinally, active coping and distraction associated with lower internalizing. Support seeking associated with depression.
Conflict: N = 80; ages = 11–15 (Rogers & Holmbeck, 1997)	Children's Coping Strategies Scale (Jose et al., 1994) (Reliability: α = .60 to .84; Validity: confirmatory factor analysis, replicated across samples)	32-item questionnaire	Problem solving Rejuvenation Social support Aggression Drug use	Maladaptive coping associated with externalizing, internalizing, depression, and low self-worth. Support seeking associated with lower externalizing and depression.
		Situational coping strategies		
Conflict: N = 417, grades = 4–8, (Roecker et al., 1996); N = 99, grades = K–1 (Creasey et al., 1995)	Self-Report Coping Scale (Causey & Dubow, 1992); Coding system based on Causey & Dubow (1992) (Reliability: α = .58 to .84; Validity: exploratory factor analysis, replicated across situations; r with peer reports)	34-item questionnaire; Open-ended interview, categorical coding	Problem solving Distancing Social support Internalizing Externalizing	Girls used more support seeking and internalizing than boys; exposure to interparental conflict related to maladaptive coping.

Sample	Measure	Method	Variables	Findings
Conflict: N = 174, ages = 7–11 (Kerig, 1997) Violence: N = 72, ages = 7–11 (Kerig et al., 1998)	Children's Coping Questionnaire (Fedorowicz & Kerig, 1999) (Reliability: α = .67 to .83; Validity: confirmatory factor analysis, replicated across gender and situation; r with parent and other child self report)	81-item questionnaire	Approach Avoidance Venting Coping efficacy	Avoidance moderated girls' internalizing; approach and venting exacerbated girls' maladjustment Coping efficacy moderated boys' internalizing.

Coping strategies specific to interparental conflict

Sample	Measure	Method	Variables	Findings
Conflict (postdivorce): N = 56, ages = 4–12 (Johnston et al., 1987)	Role of Child in Dispute Scale; Role-Reversal Scale (Reliability: rho = .75 to .85)	Clinician rating	Involvement Role reversal	Role reversal with father related to depression and withdrawal. Role reversal with mother related to reduced withdrawal.
Conflict: N = 98, ages = 5–19 (Cummings et al., 1991)	Author-created coding system (Reliability: κ = .84)	Open-ended interview; continuous ratings	No involvement Background intervention Brief intervention Involved intervention	14-year-olds more likely to become involved than older or younger children.
Conflict: N = 45, ages = 11–12 (Grych & Fincham, 1993)	Author-created coding scheme (Reliability: κ = .95)	Open-ended interview; categorical coding	Do nothing Withdrawal Indirect intervention Direct intervention	Intervening related to conflicts concerning child; explanations that absolve child of blame related to decreased intervening.

(continued)

Table 8.1 (continued)

Sample	Measure (psychometrics)	Method	Dimensions	Major Findings
		Coping strategies specific to interparental conflict		
Conflict: N = 83, ages = 8–11 (O'Brien et al., 1995); N = 43, ages = 8–12 (O'Brien et al., 1997)	Children's Marital Conflict Coping Strategies Interview (Reliability: κ = .85; test-retest over 3 weeks)	Semistructured interview; categorical codes	Avoid/Self-rely Seek social support Self-blame Self-involve	Involvement associated with child reports of low self-esteem, anxiety, and hostility; avoidant coping associated with lower anxiety.
Conflict: N = 48, ages = 7–15 (Davies et al., 1996)	Author-created coding scheme (Reliability: κ = .94 to 1.00)	Open-ended interview; categorical coding	Superficial involvement Task-oriented involvement Triangulation involvement	Involvement more intense when conflict endings hostile and children older. Boys more likely than girls to endorse task-oriented involvement.
Conflict: N = 47, ages = 4–5 (El-Sheikh, Cummings, & Reiter, 1996)	Author-created scheme	Multiple choice format; categorical	Nothing Ignore the people Leave the room Yell at the people Hit the people Stop the fight	Girls more likely than boys to endorse intervening, especially when arguments unresolved.
Conflict: N = 43, ages = 8–12 (O'Brien et al., 1997)	Postconflict questionnaire (Reliability: α = .62 to .78)	16-item questionnaire	Avoidance Self-involvement Appraisals	Involvement related to depression and low self-esteem; Worried avoidance related to depression.

Sample	Measure	Method	Categories	Findings
Conflict: N = 90, ages = 9–13 (Gordis et al., 1997)	Author-created coding scheme (Reliability: r = .70 to .72)	Observational coding	Withdrawal Distraction	For boys, marital hostility related to distraction in violent homes and to withdrawal in non-violent homes.
Conflict/violence: N = 74, ages = 8–11 (Laumakis et al., 1998)	Follow-up questionnaire (Reliability: r = .66 to .81)	Open-ended interview, categorical coding	Seek others Self-protect Express emotions Child-directed Solution Intervention	Boys from high-conflict families most likely to endorse directly intervening, especially during violent conflicts.
Conflict: N = 56, ages = 6–9 (Davies & Cummings, 1998)	Author-created coding system (Reliability: κ = .83 to .93)	Observational coding system, rating scale	Avoidance Intervention	Coping strategies not related to marital discord or to child adjustment.
Conflict/violence N = 206, ages = 7–11 (Kerig, 1999)	Child Intervening in Interparental Conflict (Kerig, 1994) (Reliability: κ = .85 to .98; Validity: rs with parent report and other child report measure)	Open-ended interview, categorical coding; 9-item questionnaire, continuous ratings	Detriangulation No involvement Cognitive Involvement Caregiving Indirect prosocial behavior Indirect misbehavior Direct interrupting Direct mediation Direct triangulation	Older boys intervened most vigorously, especially through misbehavior, girls used more cognitive involvement and caregiving. Intervening exacerbated effects of conflict on internalizing

you do?" It is difficult to know whether children's hypothetical responses reflect their actual behavior during interparental conflicts or whether the simulated conflicts reflect what the child actually sees in the home; thus, their external validity is open to question. These methods also require of the child some degree of abstraction, whether to construe a hypothetical response to the observed scenario (e.g., "what are all the things you would have done," Laumakis et al., 1998) or to imagine that their own parents are enacting the scenario (Cummings, Hennessy, Rabideau, & Cicchetti, 1994). In addition, conflicts between actors may not be as engaging or arousing as actual marital conflicts. For example, Grych & Fincham (1993) found that children expressed unrealistically high confidence in their ability to cope with an enacted conflict. As Cummings et al. (1991) note, "Considerable care should also be taken in generalizing these results to a family context. Watching 1-minute videotapes of interacting strangers is far removed from observing actual interparental conflict" (p. 469).

On the other hand, the validity of self-reports regarding witnessed interparental conflicts is also limited by children's ability to accurately recall and report on past experiences. In addition, as noted above, the data are complicated by the fact that children are not reporting on episodes that are uniform on conflict dimensions. In sum, neither method is immune from threats to validity and reliability.

Level of Analysis: General versus Specific. Methods used to elicit children's strategies for coping with interparental conflict also differ in terms of the level of analysis used; i.e., whether children are asked to describe a *specific* episode or to *generalize* across episodes of parental quarreling. For example, at one end of the continuum, O'Brien, Margolin, and John (1995) ask children to recall a single episode of observed interparental conflict, while other investigators ask children what they generally do when their parents argue (Kerig, Fedorowicz, Brown, Patenaude, & Warren, 1998). There are potential benefits and shortcomings to inquiring about specific situations versus general tendencies. Just as it may be beyond the cognitive capacities of young children to reason abstractly about hypothetical stressors (Knapp et al., 1991), it may be difficult for them to generalize across situations. Consequently, young children may need to be grounded in concrete references to the behaviors they engaged in during a specific episode. However, a limitation of the situation-specific approach is that children may choose to report on an unusual episode, and thus not describe what is representative of their actual family life.

Methods Used to Assess Children's Coping with Interparental Conflict

A number of different methods have been used to assess children's coping with interparental conflict, including interviews, self-report questionnaires, parent reports, and observations. Each of these methods has its strengths and limitations, described next. Table 8.1 provides a summary of the coping categories, psychometric properties, samples and studies in which each measure has been used, as well as the major findings.

Interviews. Content coding of children's responses to interview questions has been used to good effect in a number of studies of children's coping with interparental conflict. Davies et al. (1996) recommend the use of open-ended questions with children rather than directed questioning, given that the demand characteristics of specific questions may lead children to endorse thoughts and emotions they did not actually experience. In addition, interviews are less cognitively taxing to young children than lengthy multiple-choice questionnaires, are better able to maintain the child's interest level, and reduce the likelihood of socially desirable responding (Creasey et al., 1997). For example, a methodologically strong series of studies have been completed using the Children's Marital Conflict Coping Strategies Interview (CMC-CSI; see O'Brien et al., 1995). Interviews have also been coded regarding children's responses to analogue conflict scenarios (e.g., Creasey et al., 1997; Cummings et al., 1991; Cummings, Hennessy et al., 1994; Grych & Fincham, 1993; Laumakis et al., 1998).

Shortcomings of content coding systems include that the coping scales are derived rationally rather than empirically, internal consistencies are not always reported, and scales are seldom validated. Further, as is often the case for categorical coding, the number of responses within each category varies greatly; in some cases, as few as 9% of children utilize a given category (O'Brien et al., 1995), and low means and high standard deviations result from rating the presence or absence of scale items (Davies et al., 1996). In general, continuous rating systems pose a number of methodological advantages over categorical content-coding systems.

Questionnaires to Assess Dispositional Coping. A number of measures of dispositional coping style have been applied to the study of children's responses to interparental conflict. For example, Rogers & Holmbeck (1997) studied children's coping with interparental conflict using Jose, Cafasso, and D'Anna's (1994) well-validated questionnaire. An alternative dispositional measure is the Children's Coping

Strategies Checklist (CCSC; Program for Prevention Research, 1992). This measure has strong psychometric properties, and its factor structure has replicated in several other samples, including school-aged children of divorce (Sandler et al., 1994). As noted above, a strength of this measure is its differentiation of avoidance and distraction. However, to date this measure has been used only to assess children's coping with general postdivorce life stress rather than the specific stressor of interparental conflict.

Questionnaires to Assess Situational Coping. Other measures ask children to rate their use of coping strategies in regard to a specific situation, such as interparental conflict. For example, the Self-Report Coping Survey (SRCS; Causey & Dubow, 1992) assesses the extent to which children use various coping strategies in regard to a specific stressor, such as interparental conflict (e.g., "When the adults in my home argue, fight, or disagree, I...") This is one of the few measures that have been validated by comparison with others' reports; in this case, those of peers. The Children's Coping Questionnaire (CCQ; Fedorowicz & Kerig, 1999) also has been used in studies of school-aged children's coping with interparental conflict, violence, and divorce and has been subjected to external validation with parent reports and other child-report measures (Kerig & Fedorowicz, 1998).

Questionnaires Specific to Interparental Conflict. A limitation of general coping measures is that the categories do not always capture distinctions of interest regarding a particular stressor. In this regard, Lazarus (1993) recommends that investigators adapt general coping measures in order to capture dimensions specific to the situation at hand. For example, in the context of children and interparental conflict, the global category of approach coping may involve many different kinds of behaviors, ranging from thinking about the problem in a more positive way to physically intervening in the quarrel. To fill this gap, O'Brien, Bahadur, Gee, Balto, and Erber (1997) developed a Post-Conflict Scale (PCS) to supplement their interview measure, assessing avoidance and involvement in the conflict. To meet a similar end, the Child Intervening in Interparental Conflict scale (CIIC; see Kerig, 1994) supplements the CCQ by typologizing children's strategies for intervening in their parents' quarrels.

Observational Approaches. One of the benefits to observational methods is that they allow the investigator to view the child's reactions in the laboratory rather than relying on self-report. Children may cope in ways that are discrepant from their self-perceptions, and only direct observation can reveal their actions independently of their appraisals (Kerig, in press). Among observational studies, Davies and Cummings

(1998) rated children's avoidance or involvement in a simulated conflict between the mother and a research confederate. Other investigators have observed children's responses to actual disagreements between parents (e.g., Easterbrooks, Cummings, & Emde, 1994; Gordis, Margolin, & John, 1997). While ecological validity is a concern, given that parents may engage in less destructive forms of conflict under the gaze of the videocamera than they do in unguarded moments at home (Margolin, 1990), observational data are invaluable in allowing for an objective assessment of children's coping not influenced by cognitive limitations or socially desirable responding.

Parent Reports. A few investigators have elicited parents' reports of children's strategies for coping with interparental conflict (e.g., Jenkins et al., 1989; Johnston, Campbell, & Mayes, 1985; Miller, Kliewer, Hepworth, & Sandler, 1994). Kerig and Fedorowicz (1998) compared child and parent reports of children's coping with interparental conflict on the CCQ, and found that, while children's reports were modestly correlated with parents' reports, agreement was low regarding strategies such as avoidance. This may be because avoidant strategies are less observable to others and less readily identifiable as coping efforts. For example, "tuning out" the conflict by putting on a set of headphones may be interpreted by parents as an indicator that a child is unconcerned, rather than as an effortful attempt to cope with the problem. In the same vein, it would be difficult for an observer to know whether a quiet child were engaging in worrying, decision making, or positive cognitive restructuring. Therefore, given that many emotion-coping strategies cannot be seen by parents or observers, there is a strong case to be made eliciting children's self-reports of coping.

What Do We Know about Children's Coping with Marital Discord?: Empirical Findings

Children Coping with Nonviolent Interparental Conflict

Johnston et al. (1985) provide a descriptive picture of children's coping with postdivorce interparental conflict, based on parents' reports. Younger school-aged children were more likely than older children to attempt to control their parents' quarrels through distraction, sometimes even through self-destructive behavior (e.g., one boy put his fist through a window). Younger children were also more likely to attempt to control the fight through mediating the dispute, telling parents to stop, or preventing them from meeting. In contrast, older children were likely to take sides and to become active participants in the quarrel.

Children who avoided the conflict (e.g., ignoring the fight, closing their ears, or leaving the scene) were judged to be the most well-adjusted overall.

Jenkins et al. (1989), in contrast, obtained school-aged children's descriptions of their methods for coping with interparental conflict, using a semistructured interview. The most frequently reported coping strategy was direct intervention, followed by attempting to comfort parents and seeking support from siblings. Among intervention attempts, the most frequently reported were telling the parents to stop fighting and attempting to get them to make up afterwards. Children also were sensitive to different types of parental quarrels and gauged their interventions strategies appropriately – one strategy for a "mild row" and another for a "severe row." In addition, Jenkins et al. investigated the outcomes of children's intervention efforts. Surprisingly, over half of the children and their mothers reported that parents stopped quarreling in response to children's interventions. However, despite the apparent success of their intervention efforts, children who made the most vigorous interventions were also the most symptomatic. Kerig (1999a) also found that, while children who intervened in their parents' conflicts were often successful in an immediate sense, for example, by causing their parents to quiet down, children's increasing involvement in the argument was associated with higher levels of maladjustment, particularly in the form of internalizing symptoms.

Subsequent research has refined our understanding of the contextual factors that lead children to intervene in interadult arguments. A history of exposure to unresolved arguments is associated with increased likelihood that children will intervene in the quarrel (El-Sheikh et al., 1996). Children are also more inclined to intervene when they blame themselves for the dispute (Grych & Fincham, 1993), while harmonious conflict resolutions dampen children's motivation to intervene in the conflict (Davies et al., 1996).

Do children adapt their coping strategies to the specific situation of interparental conflict? Roecker et al. (1996) used Causey and Dubow's (1992) measure to compare how children cope with interparental versus peer conflicts. Children were more likely to utilize direct problem-solving and internalizing coping (e.g., worrying, crying, feeling sorry for themselves) to cope with interparental conflict than with peer conflict. As levels of interparental conflict in the home increased, children reported using more nonconstructive strategies, suggesting that children find it difficult to muster an adaptive response to this uncontrollable stressor.

A few studies have examined the efficacy of children's coping efforts in response to interparental conflict. Using the CCSC, Rogers and Holmbeck (1997) found that nonconstructive coping was associated with externalizing and internalizing symptoms. In addition, tests for moderation showed that as interparental conflict increased, social support seeking was associated with lower levels of externalizing and depression. O'Brien et al. (1995) found that coping through involvement in interparental conflict was positively correlated with children's depression, anxiety, hostility, and low self-esteem, while avoidant coping and support-seeking were associated with fewer internalizing symptoms. Involvement in the conflict was a strong predictor of low self-esteem, anxiety, and hostility even when amount of conflict, demographic variables, and life stress were taken into account. Sometimes gender differences complicate the results. For example, Kerig (1997) found that avoidant coping buffered girls from the effects of interparental conflict, while approach and maladaptive coping exacerbated girls' adjustment problems. In contrast, for boys, perceived coping efficacy moderated the relationship between interparental conflict and internalizing.

O'Brien et al. (1997) took an intriguing approach to typologizing children's responses, using factor analysis to combine coping and appraisal items from the CMC-CSI and PCS. Four factors emerged: Self-Involvement, Threatened/Critical, Confident Avoidance, and Worried Avoidance. There were strong correlations between the Self-Involved factor and children's internalizing symptoms, while Threatened/Critical and Worried Avoidance were also related to children's reports of depression. Self-Involved, Threatened/Critical, and Worried Avoidance predicted child aggression. In addition, Threatened/Critical and Worried Avoidance contributed to the prediction of teacher's reports of children's externalizing, but the direction of effects was such that children who engaged in these negative cognitions demonstrated *fewer* behavior problems. Although the results of this study are challenging to interpret, they do illustrate the importance of distinguishing qualitatively amongst children's coping responses. Simply avoiding interparental conflict is not associated with relief from stress unless it is accompanied by self-calming and a sense of gaining self-control (Lengua & Sandler, 1996); children whose avoidance is accompanied by ruminative worrying or self-blame do not reap these benefits.

On the other hand, it should be noted that not all investigators find children's coping to be a strong predictor of adjustment. Davies and Cummings (1998) rated children's avoidance and intervention in response to a simulated interadult conflict, and found that children's coping strategies were not related to their adjustment, while noting that the simulation might not elicit the intense loyalty conflicts and threats to emotional security that motivate children to intervene in conflicts between their own parents. A number of studies (Jenkins et al., 1989; O'Brien et al., 1995, 1997) find coping to be related to children's own reports of symptoms but not to parents' reports. The explanation for this may lie in the fact that coping is more likely to be predictive of internalizing symptoms, about which children may be the best reporters. However, these findings are also vulnerable to monoinformant bias, and further research is needed utilizing multiple reports of children's coping.

Children Coping with Interparental Violence

Some investigations have differentiated the coping responses of children in nonviolent homes from those who are exposed to interparental violence. Gordis et al. (1997) utilized an observational coding system to analyze school-aged children's attempts to withdraw or distract parents during an interparental disagreement. Marital violence was related to boys' use of distraction during interparental conflict, whereas, for boys from nonviolent homes, family hostility was associated with withdrawal. Puzzlingly, none of the variables were significantly predictive of girls' coping responses. The authors suggest that, for boys exposed to nonviolent parental arguments, withdrawal may be an adaptive coping strategy in that it allows the child to escape from the situation or detriangulate him from the argument. In contrast, in violent households, children's high anxiety and distress preclude withdrawal from acting as sufficient coping strategy. Instead, boys in violent homes may resort to misbehavior in order to distract their parents from the argument.

Subsequent work from this laboratory showed that school-aged boys from high-conflict families were more likely than other children to endorse directly intervening in simulated interparental conflict, especially when interparental violence was involved (Laumakis et al., 1998). In fact, boys from high-conflict homes were almost twice as likely to endorse intervening in a physically aggressive scenario as were girls or children exposed to nonviolent conflicts. Gender roles may compel boys to take on responsibility for ending situations of domestic violence, even to the point of placing themselves in harm's way (Kerig, 1999b).

Studies of the efficacy of children's coping with interparental violence similarly have been complicated by gender differences. Kerig et al. (1998)

found that, for girls exposed to interparental violence, approach coping was associated with higher depression and anxiety, whereas, for boys, approach coping tended to be associated with lower adjustment problems. In turn, avoidant coping was negatively associated with maternal reports of externalizing and internalizing problems for girls, but was positively associated with self-reported depression for boys. It appears that girls are particularly affected by being entangled in their parents' conflicts, whereas boys are distressed when they feel they can do nothing more than merely passively avoid the problem.

How Do Children Develop Their Coping Strategies?

Appraisals

How do children determine the coping strategies available to them, and by what mechanisms do they learn them? As noted in the previous sections, Grych and Fincham's (1990) cognitive-contextual model posits that children's appraisals of interparental conflict guide their choice of coping responses. For example, children who feel more threatened by the conflict or who blame themselves for causing it may be more likely to intervene, whereas low coping efficacy may lead children to take a passive, helpless approach. Consistent with this model, children's appraisals of interparental conflict have been linked to the strategies they use to cope. Grych & Fincham (1993) found that children were more likely to endorse directly intervening in the conflict when they perceived the child to be at fault for causing it. Similarly, Roecker et al. (1996) found that perceived control was related to approach coping; however, appraisals were not predictive of children's use of avoidant coping.

Kerig (1997) also investigated the relationship between coping and appraisals in children exposed to interparental conflict. Approach coping was related to perceived control for both boys and girls, while nonconstructive coping was related to perceived threat and self-blame. Coping efficacy was negatively related to conflict properties and threat, and positively related to perceived control. In a subsequent study of children coping with interparental violence, Kerig et al. (1998) found that, for girls, the tendency to use approach coping increased as perceived control increased. Further, perceived self-control was positively related to both approach and avoidant coping for girls, suggesting coping flexibility. Girls also were more likely to cope through avoidance as conflict properties became more negative, and they endorsed more nonconstructive coping as perceived threat increased. For boys, in contrast, perceived direct control and self-blame were related to the use of nonconstructive coping, while perceived threat was related to avoidance.

In general, while some support has been found for the idea that children's coping strategies are predicted by their appraisals, the pattern of findings is complex and the strength of relationships modest. In particular, emotion-focused or avoidant strategies have proven difficult to predict. As Compas et al. (1991) note, problem-focused coping may be cued by appraisals of control, whole emotion-focused coping may be related to cues of emotional distress. It may be that, under the conditions of intense distress and emotional insecurity triggered by interparental conflict (Davies & Cummings, 1994) children resort to primitive and automatic responses rather than engaging in logical cognitive processing (Fedorowicz, 1998). Further, as Grych (1998) notes, young children's thinking is egocentric and concrete, and thus they are less likely than adolescents to make attributions concerning the psychological causes of interpersonal behavior. Thus, the links between coping and appraisals may be forged only over the course of development, and the sufficiency of adult models to explain children's coping is again called into question.

Parental Influences

A small body of work has been dedicated to determining whether parents play an active role in influencing children's coping. Two potential mechanisms have been explored: parents as models or parents as active socialization agents. The *parent modeling* hypothesis proposes that children imitate the ways that their parents cope with stress (Kliewer, Fearnow, & Miller, 1996). However, in a test of the modeling hypothesis in the context of interparental conflict, Brown and Kerig (1995) found that children's self-reported strategies were only modestly correlated with parents' reports of their own strategies for coping with marital problems, and showed complicated patterns related to gender. A second potential mechanism is *parent socialization* of children's coping (Brown, Kerig, Fedorowicz, & Warren, 1996; Kliewer et al., 1996). Parents may socialize children by providing advice as to how to handle upsetting feelings (e.g., "try not to think about it"; "talk to someone if you're feeling bad"). Miller et al. (1994) found that divorced mothers' encouragement of dispositional coping strategies of distraction, positive cognitive restructuring, and support seeking were related to mother's reports of children's use of those coping strategies. There also was a relationship between parental socialization and modeling: divorced mothers tended to encourage children to adopt the same coping strategies they themselves used. Thus, support for the socialization hypothesis was found; however the findings were limited solely to mothers' reports.

Family Systemic Processes

The leading models in the field are relatively child-centered in their explanation of how children elect to cope with interparental conflict, focusing on internal processes such as appraisals and emotional security. However, we might ask *why* would children hold themselves responsible for starting or stopping interparental quarrels? A family systemic perspective might help to uncover the origins of the appraisals and emotional insecurities that guide children's coping efforts. Family processes – triangulation, scapegoating, and boundary dissolution – may entangle children in interparental quarrels (Johnston et al., 1987; Kerig, 1995; Minuchin, 1974). For example, children may feel "caught in the middle" when they are asked to side with one parent, carry messages back and forth, or listen to one parent disparage the other (Buchanan, Maccoby, & Dornbusch, 1991; Johnston et al., 1987). Generational boundaries may be violated when children are encouraged to act as substitute spouses or caregivers to their parents (Brown & Kerig, 1999; Johnston et al., 1987). Each of these dynamics may pull children in the direction of intervening in interparental conflicts.

O'Brien et al. (1995) note the link between children's involvement in interparental conflict and the family systems concepts of boundary dissolution and "scapegoating." Parents may involve children in their conflicts due to lack of demarcation between the marital and parent–child subsystems. Alternatively, children may be triangulated in interparental conflicts through the process Minuchin (1974) refers to as detouring: Through deflecting marital conflict onto the child, the family system may reorganize so as to protect a vulnerable marriage. While parents may initiate this process, systemic accounts also depict children as actively volunteering for the role of scapegoat in order to keep the family intact (Kerig, 1995; Jouriles & Norwood, 1995). For example, Johnston et al. (1987) asked clinicians to make ratings of parents' attempts to draw children into postdivorce interparental conflicts (involvement), and child-initiated behaviors such as comforting or protecting a parent or acting as a coparent (role reversal). Results showed that paternal involvement of the child was related to poor adjustment, and that child-initiated role reversal, again in relation to the father, was related to depression and withdrawal. Thus, the effects of interparental conflict may be mediated by systemic family dynamics such as parent–child boundary dissolution.

Also consistent with the family systems perspective, Grych and Fincham (1993) found that parents' messages to children about who is to blame for interparental conflict predict children's coping. In particular, children were most likely to endorse intervening in the conflict when the scenario involved the parents blaming the child, or when no causal explanation was given. In contrast, when parents took clear responsibility for their marital problems, children were less likely to feel compelled to intervene. As Grych and Fincham (1993) note, more needs to be known about maladaptive family processes such as triangulation. In particular, little has been done in regard to Minuchin's detouring family form, in which children intervene in ways that deflect attention onto themselves, for better or worse.

Future Directions

How Can We Improve Methodology in the Study of Children's Coping?

The literature on children's coping with interparental coping is a pastiche of idiosyncratic measures, each of which reflects a limited number of dimensions. Sometimes coping strategies with the same label are construed differently across studies; for example, distraction has negative connotations in some measures (e.g., Gordis et al., 1997) and positive connotations in others (e.g., Sandler et al., 1994). Thus, it is challenging to synthesize the research or to compare the results of different studies. Moreover, the validity of various methods remains mostly unproved. For example, when studies use analogue measures that require children to respond to hypothetical scenarios, it is difficult to know whether children's responses reflect their real-life behaviors. Inquiries regarding children's actual experiences are not inured to this concern, either, given the general absence of external validation. Clearly, continued measurement development is needed in the study of children's coping with interparental conflict. To date, the most well-validated measures are those that assess general coping strategies or dispositions, rather than those that would be more informative by assessing coping strategies specific to interparental conflict. In addition, despite the availability of multiple measures of children's coping, including questionnaires, interviews, observations, and parent reports, almost every study has used only a single measure; thus, monomethod and monoinformant biases abound. What is needed to advance the field is programmatic research that uses multiple measures to assess conceptually related constructs.

Are There Gender and Developmental Differences in Children's Coping?

Evidence is mixed regarding the existence of age or gender differences in children's coping with interparental conflict. An interesting question that has been broached, however, concerns not whether there are mean differences between groups, but rather whether the pattern of relationships among variables differs (Cummings, Davies, et al., 1994). For example, even if there are no overall differences in how children cope with interparental conflict, there may be age or gender differences in the efficacy of children's coping efforts (e.g., Armistead et al., 1990; Creasey, Mitts, et al., 1995; Kerig, 1997; Roecker et al., 1996). Systematic attention to these issues is needed, comparing samples across gender and developmental periods.

Does Coping Help?

Empirical evidence supports the hypothesis that children's coping efforts can buffer them from the negative effects of family stress. Specifically, coping strategies in which children distance themselves from the conflict are associated with better adjustment than are coping strategies that involve the child in the argument. Further, simply avoiding interparental conflict is not associated with relief from stress unless it is accompanied by self-calming and a sense of gaining self control (Lengua & Sandler, 1996; O'Brien et al., 1997). It is interesting that social support seeking does not consistently act as a buffer; in fact some studies show that support seeking exacerbates children's response to divorce-related stress (Sandler et al., 1994; Radovanovic, 1993). Perhaps children are rebuffed when they attempt to seek support from distressed parents; similarly, their siblings may be sources of stress rather than succor (Hetherington, 1992). Thus, social support may not be readily available to children in conflictual families, even if the children actively seek it.

On the other hand, overall effect sizes in studies of coping efficacy are generally small. Another limitation is that children's coping appears to be a more powerful moderator of internalizing than externalizing symptoms (e.g., Kerig; 1997, 1999; O'Brien et al., 1995), despite the fact that exposure to interparental conflict is associated with both forms of behavior problems. Common-method variance may explain this result when children's reports of both coping and internalizing are elicited, but this pattern has emerged for maternal reports of internalizing as well (Kerig, 1997; O'Brien et al., 1995). The primacy of internalizing problems is consistent with other research on the moderators and mediators of the effects of interparental conflict on children's' adjustment (see Davies & Cummings, 1998). More attention needs to be paid to discovering the predictors of externalizing, and perhaps the nonconstructive coping category can be helpful in this regard.

How Can We Better Understand the Coping Process?

Most of the studies to date are not longitudinal, and therefore the direction of effects has not been established. For example, Sandler et al.'s (1994) longitudinal analysis showed that anxiety predicted avoidant coping, rather than the reverse; thus, the findings are consistent with the hypothesis that distress leads to the use of particular coping strategies rather than that those coping strategies cause or relieve distress. Aldwin and Revenson's (1987) question "does coping help?" cannot be answered by correlational designs that take a still photograph of a child at one point in time. Lazarus and Folkman's model of coping is a transactional one, in which children's appraisals, responses, and reappraisals shape the coping process over time. Thus, the study of coping requires the use of process models that investigate the factors predictive of children's selection of particular coping strategies, as well as the outcomes associated with their coping efforts (Cummings & Cummings, 1988). However, too few studies have taken such a multidimensional perspective, nor followed children over time as the coping process unfolds.

How Can We Help Children to Cope?

Another avenue for future research concerns the development of effective interventions that teach children adaptive ways to cope with interparental conflict (see Wolchik & Sandler, 1997). For example, interventions for children of divorce have helped children to distinguish between solvable problems and those that are unsolvable, such as interparental conflict, thereby enhancing their coping efficacy (Alpert-Gillis, Pedro-Carroll, & Cowen, 1989). Interventions with parents might focus on enhancing their ability to model adaptive coping strategies during spousal conflicts. As Cummings et al. (1991) state, "Within certain ill-defined bounds, exposure to anger between parents and others … may even be a necessary experience in the development of adequate coping skills" (p. 469).

Conclusion

The interest in understanding children's coping with interparental conflict has stimulated a rich body of literature, though much work remains to be done in order to explicate the processes underlying children's responses to their parents' quarreling. The existing research is limited particularly by the use of single measures, most of which are homespun and have undergone little validation. Consequently, because the methods used vary markedly from study to study, the literature offers a pastiche of inconsistent findings. However, much of the existing research has arisen in the past decade. The field is young and lively, and much new progress can be anticipated as needed advancements are made in devising methodologies that are sensitive to the specific context of interparental conflict. In addition, much of the literature is lacking in sensitivity to developmental issues on both methodological and conceptual levels. Developmental considerations are especially relevant, given that exposure to interparental conflict is a stressor particularly associated with childhood, which, along with other childhood stressors such as bullying, peer pressure, and differential teacher treatment, have unique characteristics and implications that merit attention. While adult-derived theories provided a secure base for early theorization on children's coping, perhaps the time has arrived for the field to take first steps toward individuation. Further, although much of the impetus for studying children's coping arose from the desire to uncover sources of resiliency in children exposed to family stress, the research has also shown that children's coping can also exacerbate the effects of exposure to their parents' conflicts. In particular, children's direct involvement in their parents' disputes, even if effective in ending the immediate conflict, is associated with increasing anxiety and depression. While these findings are illuminating regarding the negative side of the coping equation, more attention needs to be paid to understanding how it is that resilient children avoid triangulation in the marital relationship, as well as to uncovering the interpersonal, cognitive, and emotional processes that allow children to cope effectively with family stress.

REFERENCES

Aldwin, C. M. (1994). *Stress, coping, and development: An integrative perspective.* New York: Guilford.

Aldwin, C. M., & Revenson, T. A. (1987). Does coping help? A reexamination of the relation between coping and mental health. *Journal of Personality and Social Psychology, 53,* 337–348.

Alpert-Gillis, L. J., Pedro-Carroll, J. L., & Cowen, E. L. (1989). The children of divorce intervention program: Development, implementation, and evaluation of a program for young urban children. *Journal of Consulting and Clinical Psychology, 57,* 583–589.

Altshuler, J. L., & Ruble, D. N. (1989). Developmental changes in children's awareness of strategies for coping with uncontrollable stress. *Child Development, 60,* 1337–1349.

Armistead, L., McCombs, A., Forehand, R., Wierson, M., Long, N., & Fauber, R. (1990). Coping with divorce: A study of young adolescents. *Journal of Consulting and Clinical Psychology, 19,* 79–84.

Ayers, T. S., Sandler, I. N., West, S. G., & Roosa, M. W. (1996). A dispositional and situational assessment of children's coping: Testing alternative models of coping. *Journal of Personality, 64*, 923–958.

Band, E. B., & Weisz, J. R. (1988). How to feel better when it feels bad: Children's perspectives on coping with everyday stress. *Child Development, 24*, 247–253.

Billings, A. G., & Moos, R. H. (1981). The role of coping responses and social resources in attenuating the stress of life events. *Journal of Behavioral Medicine, 4*, 139–157.

Blechman, E. A., Prinz, R. J., & Dumas, J. E. (1995). Coping, competence, and aggression prevention: Part 1. Developmental model. *Applied and Preventive Psychology, 4*, 211–232.

Boekarerts, M. (1996). Coping with stress in childhood and adolescence. In M. Zeidner & N. S. Endler (Eds.), *Handbook of coping: Theory, research, and applications* (pp. 452–484). New York: Wiley.

Brown, C. A., & Kerig, P. K. (1995). *Parents' and children's coping with interparental conflict.* American Psychological Association, Toronto.

Brown, C. A., & Kerig, P. K. (1999). *Boundary dissolution in single-parent families: The effects of role-reversal and gender on the relationship between maternal and child adjustment.* Poster presented at the Society for Research in Child Development, Albuquerque, NM.

Brown, C. A., Kerig, P. K., Fedorowicz, A. E., & Warren, M. (1996). *Parent socialization of child coping strategies.* Poster presented at the Meetings of the American Psychological Association, Toronto.

Brown, J. M., O'Keefe, J., Sanders, S. H., & Baker, B. (1986). Developmental changes in children's cognition to stressful and painful situations. *Journal of Pediatric Psychology, 11*, 343–357.

Buchanan, C. M., Maccoby, E. E., & Dornbusch, S. M. (1991). Caught between parents: Adolescents' experience in divorced homes. *Child Development, 62*, 1008–1029.

Causey, D. L., & Dubow, E. F. (1992). Development of a self-report coping measure for elementary school children. *Journal of Clinical Child Psychology, 21*, 47–59.

Compas, B. E. (1998). An agenda for coping research and theory: Basic and applied developmental issues. *International Journal of Behavioral Development, 22*, 231–237.

Compas, B. E., Banez, G. A., Malcarne, V. L., & Worsham, N. (1991). Perceived control and coping with stress: A developmental perspective. *Journal of Social Issues, 47*, 23–34.

Compas, B. E., Worsham, N. L., & Ey, S. (1992). Conceptual and developmental issues in children's coping with stress. In A. M. La Greca, L. J. Siegel, J. L. Wallander, & C. E. Walker (Eds.), *Stress and coping in child health* (pp. 7–24). New York: Guilford.

Creasey, G., Lustig, K., Catanzaro, S., Reese, M., & Herman, K. (1995, March). *Coping with adult-generated interpersonal conflict: Developmental differences between kindergartners and first graders.* Society for Research in Child Development, Indianapolis, IN.

Creasey, G., Mitts, N., & Catanzaro, S. (1995). Associations among daily hassles, coping, and behavior problems in nonreferred kindergartners. *Journal of Clinical Child Psychology, 24*, 311–319.

Creasey, G., Ottlinger, K., DeVico, K., Murray, T., Harvey, A., & Hesson-McInnis, M. (1997). Children's affective responses, cognitive appraisals, and coping strategies in response to the negative affect of parents and peers. *Journal of Experimental Child Psychology, 67,* 39–56.

Cummings, E. M., Ballard, M., El-Sheikh, M., & Lake, M. (1991). Resolution and child's responses to interadult anger. *Developmental Psychology, 27,* 462–470.

Cummings, E. M., & Cummings, J. S. (1988). A process-oriented approach to children's coping with adults' angry behavior. *Developmental Review, 8,* 266–321.

Cummings, E. M., Davies, P. T., & Simpson, K. S. (1994). Marital conflict, gender, and children's appraisals and coping efficacy as mediators of child adjustment. *Journal of Family Psychology, 8,* 141–149.

Cummings, E. M., Hennessy, K. D., Rabideau, G. J., & Cicchetti, D. (1994). Responses of physically abused boys to interadult anger involving their mothers. *Development and Psychopathology, 6,* 31–41.

Cummings, E. M., Vogel, D., Cummings, J. S., & El-Sheikh, M. (1989). Children's responses to different forms of expression of anger between adults. *Child Development, 60,* 1392–1404.

Davies, P. T., & Cummings, E. M. (1994). Marital conflict and child adjustment: An emotional security hypothesis. *Psychological Bulletin, 116,* 387–411.

Davies, P. T., & Cummings, E. M. (1998). Exploring children's emotional security as a mediator of the link between marital relations and child adjustment. *Child Development, 69,* 124–139.

Davies, P. T., Myers, R. L., & Cummings, E. M. (1996). Responses of children and adolescents to marital conflict scenarios as a function of the emotionality of conflict endings. *Merrill-Palmer Quarterly, 42,* 1–21.

Depner, C. E., Leino, E. V., & Chun, A. (1992). Interparental conflict and child adjustment: A decade review and meta-analysis. *Family and Conciliation Courts Review, 30,* 323–341.

Easterbrooks, M. A., Cummings, E M., & Emde, R. N. (1994). Young children's responses to constructive marital disputes. *Journal of Family Psychology, 8,* 160–169.

Edleson, J. L. (Ed.). (1999). Interventions and issues in the co-occurrence of child abuse and domestic violence [Special issue]. *Child Maltreatment, 4* (2).

El-Sheikh, M., & Cummings, E. M. (1992). Availability of control and preschoolers' responses to interadult anger. *International Journal of Behavioral Development, 15,* 207–226.

El-Sheikh, M., Cummings, E. M., & Reiter, S. (1996). Preschoolers' response to ongoing interadult conflict: Role of prior exposure to resolved versus unresolved arguments. *Journal of Abnormal Child Psychology, 24,* 665–679.

Engfer, A. (1988). The interrelatedness of marriage and the mother–child relationship. In R. A. Hinde & J. Stevenson-Hinde (Eds.), *Relationships within families: Mutual influences* (pp. 104–118). Oxford: Clarendon Press.

Fedorowicz, A. E. (1998). *Children's coping and cognitive appraisals: An investigation of stressor and gender specificity.* Unpublished doctoral dissertation, Simon Fraser University, Burnaby, British Columbia, Canada.

Fedorowicz, A. E., & Kerig, P. K. (1999). *Children's coping questionnaire: Development and validation.* Manuscript submitted for publication.

Fields, L., & Prinz, R. J. (1997). Coping and adjustment during childhood and adolescence. *Clinical Psychology Review, 17*, 937–976.

Forsythe, C. J., & Compas, B. E. (1987). Interaction of cognitive appraisal of stressful events and coping: Testing the goodness of fit hypothesis. *Cognitive Therapy and Research, 11*, 473–485.

Gordis, E. B., Margolin, G., & John, R. S. (1997). Marital aggression, observed parental hostility, and child behavior during triadic family interaction. *Journal of Family Psychology, 11*, 76–89.

Grych, J. H. (1998). Children's appraisals of interparental conflict: Situational and contextual influences. *Journal of Family Psychology, 12*, 437–453.

Grych, J. H., & Fincham, F. D. (1990). Marital conflict and children's adjustment: A cognitive-contextual framework. *Psychological Bulletin, 108*, 267–290.

Grych, J. H., & Fincham, F. D. (1993). Children's appraisals of interparental conflict: Initial investigations of the cognitive-contextual framework. *Child Development, 64*, 215–230.

Grych, J. H., & Fincham, F. D. (1997). Children's adaptation to divorce: From description to explanation. In S. A. Wolchik & I. N. Sandler (Eds.), *Handbook of children's coping* (pp. 159–193). New York: Plenum.

Herman-Stahl, M. A., Stemmler, M., & Petersen, A. C. (1995). Approach and avoidant coping: Implications for adolescent mental health. *Journal of Youth and Adolescence, 24*, 649–665.

Hetherington, E. M. (1992). Coping with marital transitions: A family systems perspective. In Hetherington, E. M. and Clingempeel, W. G. (Eds.), Coping with marital transitions. *Monographs of the Society for Research in Child Development, 57*, 1–14.

Jenkins, J. M., Smith, M. A., & Graham, P. J. (1989). Coping with parental quarrels. *Journal of the American Academy of Child and Adolescent Psychiatry, 28*, 182–189.

Johnston, J. R., Campbell, L. E., & Mayes, S. S. (1985). Latency children in post-separation and divorce disputes. *Journal of the American Academy of Child Psychiatry, 24*, 563–574.

Johnston, J. R., Gonzales, R., & Campbell, L. E. (1987). Ongoing postdivorce conflict and child disturbance. *Journal of Abnormal Child Psychology, 15*, 493–509.

Jose, P. E., Cafasso, L. L., & D'Anna, C. A. (1994). Ethnic group differences in children's coping strategies. *Sociological Studies of Children, 6*, 25–53.

Jouriles, E. N., & Norwood, W. D. (1995). Physical aggression toward boys and girls in families characterized by the battering of women. *Journal of Family Psychology, 9*, 69–78.

Kerig, P. K. (1994). *Child intervening in interparental conflict scale.* Unpublished measure, Simon Fraser University, Burnaby, British Columbia, Canada.

Kerig, P. K. (1995). Triangles in the family circle: Effects of family structure on marriage, parenting, and child adjustment. *Journal of Family Psychology, 9*, 28–43.

Kerig, P. K. (1997). Gender and children's coping as moderators of the effects of interparental conflict on adjustment. In K. M. Lindahl & L. F. Katz

(Chairs), *Marital conflict and children's adjustment: Risk and protective mechanisms in family subsystems.* Society for Research in Child Development, Washington, DC.

Kerig, P. K. (1999a). "Put a sock in it!" Predictors and consequences of children's attempts to intervene in interparental conflict. Paper presented in G. Harold (Chair), *Gender and children's coping with interparental conflict.* Society for Research in Child Development, Albuquerque, NM.

Kerig, P. K. (1999b). Gender issues in the effects of exposure to violence on children. *Journal of Emotional Abuse, 2,* 87–105.

Kerig, P. K. (in press). Conceptual issues in family observational research. In Kerig, P. K. & Lindahl, K. M. (Eds.), *Family observational coding systems: Resources for systemic research.* Hillsdale, NJ: Erlbaum.

Kerig, P. K., & Fedorowicz, A. E. (1998). *Multiple perspectives on children's coping with interparental conflict.* Poster presented at the American Psychological Association, San Francisco.

Kerig, P. K., Fedorowicz, A. E., Brown, C. A., Patenaude, R. L., and Warren, M. (1998). When warriors are worriers: Gender, appraisals, and children's strategies for coping with interparental violence. *Journal of Emotional Abuse, 1,* 89–114.

Kliewer, W. (1991). Coping in middle childhood: Relations to competence, Type A behavior, monitoring, blunting, and locus of control. *Developmental Psychology, 27,* 689–697.

Kliewer W., Fearnow M. D., and Miller P. A. (1996). Coping socialization in middle childhood: Tests of maternal and paternal influence. *Child Development, 67,* 2339–2357.

Kliewer, W., & Sandler, I. N. (1993). Social competence and coping among children of divorce. *American Journal of Orthopsychiatry, 63,* 432–440.

Knapp, L. G., Stark, L. J., Kurkjian, J. A., & Spirito, A. (1991). Assessing coping in children and adolescents: Research and practice. *Educational Psychology Review, 3,* 309–334.

Kurdek, L. A., & Berg, B. (1987). Children's beliefs about parental divorce scale: Psychometric characteristics and concurrent validity. *Journal of Consulting and Clinical Psychology, 55,* 712–724.

Laumakis, M. A., Margolin, G., & John, R. S. (1998). The emotional, cognitive, and coping responses of preadolescent children to different dimensions of marital conflict. In G. W. Holden, R. Geffner, & E. N. Jouriles (Eds.), *Children exposed to marital conflict: Theory, research, and applied issues.* Washington, DC: American Psychological Association.

Lazarus, R. S. (1993). Coping theory and research: Past, present, and future. *Psychosomatic Medicine, 38,* 245–254.

Lazarus, R. S., & Folkman, S. (1987). Transactional theory and research on emotions and coping. *European Journal of Personality, 1,* 141–169.

Lengua, L. J., & Sandler, I. N. (1996). Self-regulation as a moderator of the relation between coping and symptomatology in children of divorce. *Journal of Abnormal Child Psychology, 24,* 681–701.

Losoya, S., Eisenberg, N., & Fabes, R. A. (1998). Developmental issues in the study of coping. *International Journal of Behavioral Development, 22,* 287–313.

Margolin, G. (1990). Marital conflict. In G. H. Brody & I. E. Sigel (Eds.), *Methods of family research: Biographies of research projects. Vol. 2: Clinical populations* (pp. 191–225). Hillsdale, NJ: Lawrence Erlbaum Associates.

Mazur, E. (1993). Developmental differences in children's understanding of marriage, divorce, and remarriage. *Journal of Applied Developmental Psychology, 14,* 191–212.

Miller, P., Kliewer, W., Hepworth, J., & Sandler, I. (1994). Maternal socialization of children's post-divorce coping: Development of a measurement model. *Journal of Applied Developmental Psychology, 15,* 457–487.

Minuchin, S. (1974). *Families and family therapy.* Cambridge, MA: Harvard University Press.

O'Brien, M., Bahadur, M. A., Gee, C., Balto, K., & Erber, S. (1997). Child exposure to marital conflict and child coping responses as predictors of child adjustment. *Cognitive Therapy and Research, 21,* 39–59.

O'Brien, M., Margolin, G., John, R. S., & Krueger, L. (1991). Mothers' and sons' cognitive and emotional reactions to simulated marital and family conflict. *Journal of Consulting and Clinical Psychology, 59,* 692–703.

O'Brien, M., Margolin, G., & John, R. S. (1995). Relation among marital conflict, child coping, and child adjustment. *Journal of Clinical Child Psychology, 24,* 346–361.

Program for Prevention Research. (1992). *Divorce adjustment program documentation.* Unpublished manuscript, Arizona State University, Tempe, AZ.

Radovanovic, H. (1993). Parental conflict and children's coping styles in litigating separated families: Relationships with children's adjustment. *Journal of Abnormal Child Psychology, 21,* 697–713.

Repetti, R. L., McGrath, E. P., & Ishikawa, S. S. (1999). Daily stress and coping in childhood and adolescence. In A. J. Goreczny & M. Hersen (Eds.), *Handbook of pediatric and adolescent health psychology* (pp. 247–362). Boston: Allyn & Bacon.

Roecker, C. E., Dubow, E. F., & Donaldson, D. (1996). Cross-situational patterns in children's coping with observed interpersonal conflict. *Journal of Clinical Child Psychology, 25,* 288–299.

Rogers, M. J., & Holmbeck, G. N. (1997). Effects of interparental aggression on children's adjustment: The moderating role of cognitive appraisal and coping. *Journal of Family Psychology, 11,* 125–130.

Rossman, B. B. R., & Rosenberg, M. S. (1992). The moderating effects of children's beliefs about their control over parental conflict. *Journal of Child Psychology and Psychiatry, 33,* 699–715.

Rutter, M. (1990). Psychosocial resilience and protective mechanisms. In J. Rolf, A. S. Masten, D. Cicchetti, K. H. Nuechterlein, & S. Weintraub (Eds.), *Risk and protective factors in the development of psychopathology* (pp. 181–214). Cambridge: Cambridge University Press.

Ryan-Wenger, N. M. (1992). A taxonomy of children's coping strategies: A step toward theory development. *American Journal of Orthopsychiatry, 62,* 256–263.

Sandler, I. N., Tein, J., & West, S. G. (1994). Coping, stress, and the psychological symptoms of children of divorce: A cross-sectional and longitudinal study. *Child Development, 65,* 1744–1763.

Skinner, E., & Edge, K. (1998). Reflections on coping and development across the lifespan. *International Journal of Behavioral Development, 22,* 357–366.

Spirito, A., Stark, L. J., & Williams, C. (1988). Development of a brief coping checklist for use with pediatric populations. *Journal of Pediatric Psychology, 13,* 555–574.

Stanton, A. L., Danoff-Burg, S., Cameron, C. L., & Ellis, A. P. (1994). Coping through emotional approach: Problems of conceptualization and confounding. *Journal of Personality and Social Psychology, 66,* 350–362.

Tangney, J. P., Hill-Barlow, D., Wagner, P. E., Marschall, D. E., Borenstein, J. K., Sanftner, J., Mohr, T., & Gramzow, R. (1996). Assessing individual differences in constructive versus destructive responses to anger across the lifespan. *Journal of Personality and Social Psychology, 70,* 780–796.

Wertlieb, D., Weigel, C., & Feldstein, M. (1987). Measuring children's coping. *American Journal of Orthopsychiatry, 57,* 548–560.

Wolchik, S., & Sandler, I. N. (Eds.). (1997). *Handbook of children's coping.* New York: Plenum.

Zahn-Waxler, C. (1993). Warriors and worriers: Gender and psychopathology. *Development and Psychopathology, 5,* 79–89.

PART THREE. FAMILY AND PEER CONTEXTS

9 Interparental Conflict and Parent–Child Relationships

Martha J. Cox, Blair Paley, and Kristina Harter

A considerable body of literature documents the relation between marital conflict and emotional and behavioral problems in children (e.g., Cummings & Davies, 1994; Emery, 1982; Grych & Fincham, 1990). The field has now moved on to consider the mechanisms and processes through which marital conflict undermines the emotional and behavioral competence of children (Fincham, 1994). Much of the theorizing about such processes has centered on the parent–child relationship, and numerous studies have examined whether marital conflict influences child development because of its impact on the parent–child relationship. Although this is a seemingly straightforward question, it is more complex than it first appears to be. Our understanding of human development is as much dependent upon asking the appropriate questions as it is on finding the answers. We propose that systems theory will be helpful in generating the appropriate questions.

Systems theories as applied to family or individual development (Cox & Paley, 1997; Sameroff, 1994) lead to a consideration of the mutual influence between family relationships. Systems perspectives suggest the importance of the constant interplay over time between levels and elements of a system. Thus, we should be asking not only how marital conflict affects parent–child relationships, but also how the development of parent–child relationships feeds back into the course of the marital relationship. Does conflict in the parent–child relationship lead to marital conflict? Does the nature of the parent–child relationship affect children's responses to marital conflict? Also, how do the responses of individual children to marital conflict feed back into the family system? Additionally, it is important to consider how the relation between these elements may change over time at different developmental stages for the family and the child. Thus, to understand how marital conflict affects the way parent–child relationships develop, it is important to conceptualize the family as a system with multiple, mutually influential levels and relationships existing across time. Unfortunately, very little research addresses the link between marital conflict and parent–child relationships in this way. These and other issues are considered in this chapter. We begin the chapter with a discussion of the different pathways that may link marital and parent–child relationships. We then turn to consider whether these relations differ by gender of child and parent. Finally, we conclude with a discussion of future directions.

Models Linking Marital Conflict and Parent–Child Relationships

In investigating the pathways between marital conflict and parent–child difficulties, Coiro and Emery (1998) note that it may be important to distinguish between the *quality* of parenting and the *quantity* of parenting. Marital conflict may influence the quality of parent–child relationships, as parents may be less sensitive and responsive to the needs of their children. Effects also may be seen in the harshness with which parents treat children, particularly in discipline encounters. Unresolved marital conflict may result in parents spending less time in family activities, which serves to reduce the amount of time that parents spend with their children. Parents may be less focused on their children, providing less supervision and monitoring. Current investigations have suggested a variety of pathways or mechanisms through which marital processes and parent–child relationships may be linked.

The Spillover Hypothesis

There is a fair amount of empirical support for the *spillover hypothesis,* or the notion that the affect experienced and expressed in one relationship system can be transferred or carried over to other relationship systems (Coiro & Emery, 1998; Engfer, 1988; Erel & Burman, 1995). That is, negative affect arising in marital conflict is thought to spread to and contaminate or disrupt interactions between parent and child.

Parents who are angry, exhausted, or demoralized from marital conflict may simply be less emotionally available or attuned to their children (e.g., Katz & Gottman, 1996; Volling & Belsky, 1991). At the most basic level, they may be unable to perceive or detect their children's emotional needs. Even if such needs are detected, parents may be unable to respond in a supportive fashion if they are preoccupied with their own marital problems. Parent–child relationships may be even more seriously threatened when the anger or withdrawal engendered by marital conflict leads parents to be actively rejecting, hostile, or physically aggressive with their children (Easterbrooks & Emde, 1988; Fauber, Forehand, Thomas, & Wierson, 1990; Gottman & Katz, 1989; Jouriles, Barling, & O'Leary, 1987). Evidence for a link between marital discord and less sensitive and responsive parenting also can be found in the documented association between marital conflict and children's insecure attachments to their parents (e.g., Belsky, 1984; Cox & Owen, 1993; Goldberg & Easterbrooks, 1984), where presumably less sensitive parenting has mediated the relation between marital conflict and attachment (Owen & Cox, 1997).

Emotional Security Hypothesis

Cummings and Davies (Cummings, 1998; Davies & Cummings, 1994) have proposed an "emotional security hypothesis" as a way of conceptualizing how marital conflict may threaten the emotional aspects of parent–child relationships. These authors note that children do not just react to the occurrence of marital conflict, but also to the meaning of such conflict, especially the extent to which it threatens the safety of their emotional life and the integrity of their family system. They further propose that children's emotional security is a function of three "component regulatory systems," including emotional regulation, internal representations of family relations, and regulation of exposure to family affect.

It is not difficult to conceive how marital conflict may compromise all three of these systems via, in part, disturbances in the parent–child relationship. Maritally conflicted parents' insensitivity or "misattunement" to their child's emotional states may impede their child's development of emotional regulation skills, as it is through the empathic and supportive responses of a parent that children learn to regulate their own affective states (Katz & Gottman, 1995; Thompson, 1994). Secondly, if maritally conflicted parents displace harsh or angry feelings onto their children, then parents may come to represent a source of fear rather than a source of comfort (Cummings & Davies, 1995). Finally, children may attempt to reduce threats to emotional security by mediating or distracting from marital conflict (Jenkins, Smith, & Graham, 1989). This may inadvertently increase their exposure to marital conflict, since children's efforts to terminate marital conflict may be largely unsuccessful (Cummings, 1994; O'Brien, Margolin, & John, 1995). Clearly, there are multiple avenues by which marital conflict may jeopardize children's felt sense of security in their family environment through disruptions in parent–child relationships.

Parental Withdrawal

Researchers have also highlighted other aspects of caregiving that may suffer in the wake of marital conflict. For example, Katz and Gottman (1996) have speculated that parents who are preoccupied with their own marital problems may withdraw from their children, and this withdrawal may be evident in "a lack of 'cognitive room' allocated to their children" (p. 74). For example, parents who are focused on conflicts with their spouse may be less likely to know the names of their children's friends and teachers, or less likely to remember upcoming events in their children's lives, such as the school play. Similarly, parental withdrawal may be evident in parents' failure to perform instrumental caregiving tasks for their children, such as preparing their children's dinner or driving them to soccer practice. Although a lack of cognitive room and lapses in instrumental caregiving may be distinct from emotional unavailability, children may experience these other forms of withdrawal from the parent–child relationship as signs of parental rejection, or at least disinterest. Consequently, they also may pose a threat to children's sense of emotional security in their relationships with their parents.

Scapegoating, Detouring, Triangulation, and Boundary Dissolution

Concepts from the family therapy literature also have been useful in understanding the processes by which marital conflict may spread to and disrupt the parent–child relationship. Family systems theorists have long noted the dynamics of *scapegoating* (Vogel & Bell, 1960) or *detouring* (Minuchin, Rosman, & Baker, 1978), wherein the child takes on symptoms of the family pathology and becomes identified as the problematic member of the family system. Rather than directing anger or criticism toward one another, parents focus the negativity on the child, and the parent–child conflict serves to distract from the tension in the marital subsystem (Fauber et al., 1990).

Triangulation refers to the pattern of family interaction in which one or both parents attempt to recruit the child into a coalition against the other parent (Minuchin, 1974). A number of studies have found such patterns in maritally conflicted families (e.g., Kerig, 1995; Lindahl, Clements, & Markman, 1997). Lindahl and colleagues (1997), for example, found that couples' prenatal negative escalation during marital interactions was predictive of husbands' triangulation of the child into the couples' marital conflict. Patterns of weak marital alliances relative to other alliances in the family have also been found to characterize distressed families (e.g., Christensen & Margolin, 1988). Cross-generational coalitions or alliances would likely threaten the child's relationship with the parent *against* whom they are expected to align, but also their relationship with the parent *with* whom they are expected to align. The child may feel anger or resentment towards the parent with whom he or she is expected to align for asking the child to, in essence, betray the other parent.

Triangulation and cross-generational coalitions may jeopardize parent–child relationships in less direct ways as well. Researchers (Brody, Stoneman, & McCoy, 1994; Deal, 1996; Reiss et al., 1994) have examined the association between marital conflict and differential treatment of siblings, and hypothesized that a particular child in the family may be co-opted into an alliance with one parent, and consequently receive preferential treatment from that parent. The nonpreferred sibling(s) of the co-opted child may be, at best, simply ignored by that parent, and at worst, actively rejected by that parent. A number of studies have in fact documented a significant association between marital conflict and differential treatment of siblings (e.g., Brody et al., 1994; Deal, 1996).

There may be other pathways between marital, sibling, and parent–child conflict. For example, marital conflict may lead to sibling conflict more directly, perhaps by siblings modeling their parents' conflict behavior. In turn, as Reiss et al. (1994) have suggested, such sibling conflict may result in the establishment of differential relationships with the parents. This may occur if siblings seek out one parent or the other as their protector, or if one or both parents feel it necessary to protect one sibling from the other (i.e., perhaps a younger sibling from an older sibling).

Marital conflict also may lead to weakened boundaries between marital and parent–child subsystems and disturbances in parent–child relationships when children attempt to intervene in their parents' disputes. There is some evidence that children who respond to interparental conflict by involving themselves in the conflict exhibit higher levels of maladjustment than children who respond by distancing themselves from the conflict (Jenkins et al., 1989; O'Brien et al., 1995). Children who attempt to intervene may be more vulnerable because they are more apt to become targets for parents' displaced anger (Rosenberg, 1987). Nonetheless, some children in maritally discordant families have articulated a conscious strategy of acting out in order to redirect their parents' anger away from one another and onto themselves (O'Brien et al., 1995). These children may see a conflicted parent–child relationship rather than a conflicted marital relationship as the lesser of two evils, although it appears that ultimately this option is to the child's detriment. Children who intervene in interparental disputes may also be at increased risk for parentification or role reversal and be seen as potential confidantes by parents in a weakened marital subsystem. Johnston (1993) has noted that "when the parental alliance breaks down and parents are less able to distinguish their own needs from those of their children, the children are often induced to assume inappropriate roles or attempt to fulfill spousal/parent functions" (p. 205). Moreover, if children fall short of their parents' demands for nurturance or support, they may be rejected and abandoned (Johnston, 1993; Johnston & Campbell, 1988). While there is not a great deal of empirical work on the dynamic of parentification in intact maritally conflicted families, researchers have documented what Wallerstein (1985) termed the phenomenon of the "overburdened child" in divorced families, especially those with high levels of conflict (Johnston & Campbell, 1988; Wallerstein, 1985). Moreover, a number of clinical accounts of such a pattern have been provided by family therapists (Hoffman, 1981).

Learning Perspectives

Researchers have proposed that modeling may represent another mechanism by which marital conflict and parent–child difficulties are linked (Easterbrooks & Emde, 1988; Erel & Burman, 1995). In the context of marital conflict, children may reject their parents as models, causing them to be less likely to imitate any positive parental behavior, and instead to seek out more inappropriate models (Emery, 1982). Alternatively, children exposed to conflict between their parents may be inclined to imitate their parents' negative behavior in their own interactions with their parents. Christensen and Margolin (1988), for example, found that in distressed families, marital conflict sequences increased the probability of parent–child conflict sequences. Similarly, Davis, Hops, Alpert, and Sheeber (1998) recently demonstrated that when parents exhibited marital conflict, adolescents behaved aggressively toward their parents, especially toward their mothers. In observing triadic interactions between fathers, mothers, and infants, Fivaz-Depeursinge, Frascarolo, and Corboz-Warnery (1996) noted that many infants were quite content merely observing their parents interact and further proposed that "successful interparental discourse helps infants to regulate their own state" (p. 33). In contrast, children whose parents model poor affect regulation during marital interactions may be more vulnerable to dysregulation themselves, which in turn may heighten the risk for negative parent–child interactions.

Another pathway by which interparental conflict compromises parent–child relationships may be through a coercive family process

(Patterson, 1982), whereby marital conflict spurs children to act out towards their parents, who consequently stop fighting in order to deal with their aggressive children. The disruption of marital conflict (even if it is only temporary) negatively reinforces the child-to-parent aggression, thus increasing its likelihood in the future (Emery, 1989; Patterson, 1982).

Parental Discipline

One aspect of the link between marital and parent–child relationships that has received a great deal of attention is the way in which marital conflict may compromise parental discipline (Fauber et al., 1990; Stoneman, Brody, & Burke, 1989). A parent who is experiencing discord with a partner may exhibit harsh, permissive, or inconsistent discipline (Fauber et al., 1990; Stoneman et al., 1989). Harsh parenting may be a function of the parent's displaced anger onto the child, or alternatively, a sense that the parent must compensate for the chaos or disruption created by the marital conflict by "buckling down" on the child. Permissive parenting may reflect parents' absorption in their own marital difficulties, leaving them little energy to devote to more careful monitoring of their children. Inconsistent parenting may be exhibited by parents who are sufficiently disorganized by their problems with their spouses that they have difficulty sustaining a consistent approach to discipline. Alternatively, a parent's inconsistencies may be due to a parent behaving one way toward their children when the spouse is present, and another way when the spouse is absent (Holden & Ritchie, 1991).

Additionally, parents who are experiencing a great deal of marital conflict and are having difficulty communicating in general may also have difficulties communicating about discipline and childrearing, thus leading to disagreements between parents about how the children should be raised (Erel & Burman, 1995). There is some evidence that parents' disputes about childrearing are especially distressing for children (Cummings, 1998). While there is some speculation that this distress may reflect children's feelings of guilt for being the source of interparental conflict, it may also reflect children's confusion about what the rules are in the family, whose directives they should be following, and in essence, with which parent they should align.

Effects on Co-Parenting

Researchers interested in the manner in which marital conflict may lead to inconsistencies between parents have highlighted the importance of co-parenting as a distinct family construct (Belsky, Crnic, &

Gable, 1995; Katz & Gottman, 1996; McHale & Cowan, 1996). McHale and colleagues (McHale, Kuersten, & Lauretti, 1996) propose that there are both overt and covert co-parenting dynamics that may be adversely affected by marital discord. Overt co-parenting processes, or those involving direct interactions between the parents regarding the child, may become hostile and competitive in the context of marital discord. One parent may actively interfere with or undermine the other parent's interactions with the child, perhaps trying to engage the child in a more appealing task or making disparaging comments about the other parent's behavior or character. Such hostility and competitiveness would likely leave children "caught in the middle," having to choose with which parent to interact, or whether to defend or align against a parent being verbally attacked by the other parent. Alternatively, difficulties in overt co-parenting may be reflected in discrepancies in levels of mothers' and fathers' involvement in family interactions (McHale et al., 1996; Katz & Gottman, 1996).

Covert co-parenting activities are those occurring when either parent is alone with the child rather than those directly observable in the context of family interactions (McHale & Rasmussen, 1998). For example, dyadic parent–child interactions may provide the opportunity for one parent to support ("Your dad really loves you") or undermine ("Your dad should really spend more time with you") the child's relationship with the other parent. Covert co-parenting processes may also serve to either reinforce the child's sense that his/her parents are united as a team in their parenting ("I really agree with Mom that you shouldn't have broken your curfew"), or instead align with the child against the other parent ("I'm sorry Mom's being so tough on you").

Not surprisingly, McHale and Rasmussen (1998) found that conflict between parents when their child was an infant was predictive of more negative covert co-parenting during the child's preschool years. Moreover, studies support co-parenting processes as phenomena distinct from processes involved in dyadic parent–child interactions in that dyadic parenting behavior and co-parenting behavior have been found to make unique contributions to the prediction of children's adjustment (Belsky, Putnam, & Crnic, 1996; Brody & Flor, 1996; McHale et al., 1996).

The Compensatory Hypothesis

Although there is a wealth of both empirical and theoretical work examining the ways in which marital conflict may adversely affect the parent–child relationship, there has been speculation that, in some families, parents may compensate for marital discord by focusing their efforts on their relationships with their children. The compensatory hypothesis suggests that parents may seek fulfillment in the parent–child relationship to make up for dissatisfactions they experience in their marriage (Erel & Burman, 1995). Some empirical evidence suggests a negative association between marital and parent–child relationships (e.g., Amato, 1986; Belsky, Youngblade, Rovine, & Volling, 1991; Brody, Pellegrini, & Sigel, 1986).

The challenge in testing the compensatory hypothesis, however, is to distinguish genuinely positive parent–child relationships from seemingly positive relationships that actually meet the needs of the adult, rather than the child. There may be positive parent–child relationships that truly withstand and rise above the strain of marital conflict. In contrast, there may be parent–child dynamics in which a parent appears to be very involved with and devoted to their child, but where such involvement or devotion has become intrusive or burdensome to the child, or is largely motivated by efforts to win the child as an ally against the other parent. Parents' attempts to compensate for marital difficulties may more likely result in parentification, triangulation, and cross-generational coalitions than in genuinely healthy parent–child relationships.

Indeed, Erel and Burman (1995) have proposed that "it is questionable whether a close relationship fueled by a parent's negative relationship with his or her spouse is truly positive" (p. 110). Moreover, these authors have noted that even if the processes of triangulation and cross-generational coalitions allow for the formation of a positive relationship with one parent, such processes would necessarily occur at the expense of the relationship with the other parent. Thus, to date, there is not a great deal of empirical support for the compensatory hypothesis (Coiro & Emery, 1998; Erel & Burman, 1995). However, it will be important to explore whether there are families in which parents can truly overcome the strain of marital conflict and provide sensitive, responsive parenting that remains focused on the child's needs.

Further Considerations in Investigating Causal Pathways

It is likely that different pathways linking marital and parent–child relationships may become more influential at different points in children's development. For example, researchers have noted that children's emulation of parents increases during the early years of childhood (Easterbrooks & Emde, 1988), but perhaps begins to wane as children enter school and are exposed to a wider variety of adult and peer models. Alternatively, although toddlers may rarely intervene in their parents' conflicts (although they may attempt to comfort parents), by preschool age, children may play an active role in mediating parental disputes, and this pattern appears to increase through adolescence (Cummings, 1994). Recently, researchers have suggested that it is important to also consider the child's appraisal of marital conflict in order to understand the impact of the marital conflict on parenting relationships (Osborne & Fincham, 1996). Children at different developmental points may understand marital conflict in different ways because of differences in cognitive development (see Chapter 6 by Grych & Cardoza-Fernandes), and such differences may affect their view of their parents.

In general, we know little about the way in which different processes may operate at different developmental periods as many studies have either focused on children in a single developmental period, or combined children at different development stages into one group. Longitudinal studies have given us a great deal of information about the long-term consequences of marital conflict for children's adjustment, but generally have not tracked how the linkages between marital difficulties and parent–child difficulties may evolve over time.

A systems framework may be especially helpful in advancing our understanding of the multiple pathways between marital conflict and parent–child difficulties, as it suggests that marital conflict, rather than producing one effect (for example, less sensitive parenting), produces a network of effects on the family system that then feed back into the system. For example, marital conflict may result simultaneously in less sensitive parenting, less time spent in parenting, and a less well-regulated child who is highly sensitized to parental conflict. A number of different, disadvantageous pathways of effects for the child will have been created. The less involved parenting of one spouse may further undermine the marriage; a more difficult child may make parenting more difficult.

A systems perspective also highlights the importance of examining how parent–child relationships affect marital relationships. Research on the transition to parenthood demonstrates that becoming a parent constitutes a challenge for the marital relationship (e.g., Cox, Paley, Burchinal, & Payne, 1999; Cowan, Cowan, Heming, & Miller, 1991), but we know little about the interplay between parenting and marital processes over time. Future investigations that are guided by a systems perspective will ideally entail more comprehensive and longitudinal designs that allow for the examination of multiple and reciprocal pathways between marital conflict and disturbances in parent–child relationships over time.

The Role of Gender

Another important issue to be examined is how individual characteristics of family members may moderate the relation between marital conflict and parent–child difficulties. We know from work by clinicians that it is not uncommon for one child in a family to be more negatively influenced by parents' conflict than other children in the family either through scapegoating, triangulation, boundary dissolution, or other processes (Minuchin, 1974). It appears that most of the research on individual characteristics involves gender of either the parent or the child. For example, several researchers have suggested that father–child relationships are more influenced by marital relationships than mother child relationships (e.g., Brody et al., 1986; Cowan & Cowan, 1987; Goldberg & Easterbrooks, 1984; O'Keefe, 1994). However, studies differ in their approaches to defining and assessing both marital conflict and parent–child relationship quality, making it hard to conclude how and why mothers and fathers may be differentially influenced.

Given these inconsistencies in the literature, it is not surprising that reviews examining the effects of the marital relationship on mothering versus fathering have come to different conclusions. Parke and Tinsley (1987) and Crockenberg and Covey (1991) both conclude in their reviews that quality of the marriage is more strongly associated with fathers' than mothers' interactions with children. However, in their meta-analysis, Erel and Burman (1995) did not find evidence that gender moderates the association between marital quality and parenting. None of these reviews were specific to marital conflict. In contrast, Coiro and Emery (1998) specifically examined the differential effects of marital conflict on mothers' and fathers' parenting. They conclude that the parenting of both mothers and fathers is adversely affected by marital conflict, although fathering appears slightly more related to marital conflict than mothering.

There are several reasons why fathering might be more affected or affected differently by marital conflict when compared to mothering (Coiro & Emery, 1998). The father role may be more tenuous and less defined by social conventions and thus more vulnerable to the disruption and disorganization associated with marital conflict (Erel & Burman, 1995). Fathers are less socialized into the caregiving role than mothers and thus may require greater support from their spouse to adapt to their parenting role (Dickie, 1987; Park & Tinsley, 1987). Moreover, mothers who are dissatisfied with their spouse might not facilitate situations that would enhance fathering, and dissatisfied fathers might not seek out such situations. Additionally, women may differentiate roles of mother and wife more than men differentiate roles of father and husband. Thus fathers who experience conflict in their marital relationship may be more likely than mothers to perceive or elicit such patterns in their interaction with their child. In support of this hypothesis, Brody, Arias, and Fincham (1996) found that wives' attributions for their husbands' behavior were specific to their husbands and distinct from attributions for other family members. In contrast, husband's attributions for their wives' behavior were similar to their attributions for other family members.

However, these arguments may apply best to marital satisfaction or general marital quality, rather than to overt marital conflict. Destructive marital conflict may overwhelm both mothers' and fathers' ability to parent well. Most of the studies that find stronger links between marital relationships and father's parenting have considered constructs other than marital conflict, such as marital satisfaction, marital quality, or marital involvement (e.g., Belsky & Volling, 1987; Easterbrooks & Emde, 1988; Volling & Belsky, 1991). What research we have may suggest that the effects of marital conflict on father's parenting as compared to mother's parenting may simply be different.

Crockenberg and Covey (1991) suggest that "there are two patterns of dysfunctional paternal behavior associated with marital conflict – one that is engaged, but intrusive, the other in which the father withdraws from the child" (p. 244). These authors further speculate that when fathers in distressed marriages engage in rejecting or intrusive parenting, mothers may attempt to compensate for their spouses' behavior by being especially nurturing of their children. However, when fathers withdraw from their children and mothers carry the full burden of parenting, mothers may be more likely to carry over the effect of marital conflict to their interactions with their children, adopting a power-assertive style of interaction. Mothers' withdrawal from marital conflict also seems to affect their parenting. Cox and her colleagues (Cox et al., 1999) found that mothers who withdrew from marital conflict prenatally showed more flat affect, less responsiveness and warmth, and more detachment in later interactions with their infant. Thus, there is evidence for marital conflict affecting both mothers' and fathers' parenting.

It is also possible that effects of marital conflict on the parent–child relationship vary with the child's gender. Some studies suggest a greater impact on sons (e.g., Cummings, Ballard, El-Sheikh, & Lake, 1991; Gordis, Margolin, & John, 1997), whereas other research suggests a greater impact on daughters (e.g., Davies & Windle, 1997; Jaycox & Repetti, 1993). This lack of agreement may mean that parent–son and parent–daughter relationships are adversely affected in different ways. Indeed, research indicates that during triadic family interactions between maritally distressed parents and their infants, couples vary their behavior depending upon the gender of the child. For example, McHale (1995) found that maritally distressed parents of boys more commonly displayed hostile-competitive coparenting behavior, whereas distressed parents of girls were more likely to show greater discrepancy in amount of maternal versus paternal involvement. Other research suggests that daughters are more likely to be inappropriately involved in marital conflicts. Jacobvitz and Bush (1996) found that fathers in emotionally distant marriages sought intimacy and affection from their daughters instead of their wives, whereas mothers in conflictual marriages sought intimacy from their daughters instead of their husbands. Additional findings suggest that sons are more likely to be scapegoated because of marital distress, particularly when marital conflict is characterized by intense hostility and aggression (e.g., Jouriles & Norwood, 1995).

Of interest also is the possible interaction between parent and child gender so that marital conflict may be more likely to affect opposite-sex parent–child relationships than same-sex parent–child relationships. Several studies suggest that the quality of the mother–son relationship suffers more than the mother–daughter relationship when children are exposed to marital conflict. Osborne and Fincham (1996) found that child-perceived marital conflict was more strongly associated with negativity in mother–son than father–son relationships. This result may be explained in part by research indicating that mothers' perceptions of their son's behavior are more closely tied to the quality of the marital subsystem (Burman, John, & Margolin, 1987). Mothers experiencing marital conflict also may be more negatively attentive to boys than to girls if the sons remind them of their husbands (O'Leary, 1984) and thus, may be more likely to make disapproval statements to boys than to girls. Furthermore, Cummings and Davies (1994) found that boys appear more attuned and less shielded from marital conflict, as evidenced by higher correlations between mothers' and sons' reports of marital conflict than mothers' and daughters' reports.

There is also some evidence that father–daughter relationships are more susceptible to effects of marital conflict than other parent–child dyads. However, the findings are inconsistent, and many studies consider general marital satisfaction or quality, rather than marital conflict. Marital satisfaction has been linked with secure father–daughter attachments, whereas the security of mother–child attachments was unrelated to marital adjustment (Goldberg & Easterbrooks, 1984).

Similarly, Kerig, Cowan, and Cowan (1993) found that fathers with lower marital satisfaction were more negative and less assertive with first-born daughters, compared to first-born sons, and their daughters were less compliant to their commands. In contrast, Simons and his colleagues (Simons, Lorenz, Conger, & Wu, 1993) conclude that marital–parental relations are more closely linked for same-sex dyads. Cummings and O'Reilly (1997) suggest that boys and girls may be equally likely to help either parent in satisfied marriages, but boys take sides with their fathers and girls take sides with their mothers in distressed marriages. In sum, given these inconsistent findings, more research is needed on the effects of marital conflict on same-sex versus opposite-sex parent–child dyads.

Future Research Directions

The current literature relating marital conflict and parent–child relationships is rich in terms of suggesting mechanisms through which the marital and the parent–child subsystems in the family are associated. However, more research needs to follow families over time to understand the transactions between the two systems and how they mutually influence each other. For example, most of the research cited investigates models that assume that marital conflict will cause problematic parent–child relationships without exploring the ways in which problematic parent–child relationships may engender conflict in the marital relationship.

Attention needs to be paid in this research to the measurement of marital conflict and to distinguishing between constructive and destructive conflict. Work by Cummings and his colleagues (e.g., Cummings, Ballard, El-Sheikh, & Lake, 1991; Cummings & Wilson, 1999) suggests that conflict is not necessarily a negative event for children, particularly when conflicts are resolved or dealt with constructively. This work suggests that constructive conflict can help children learn appropriate ways to handle interpersonal difficulties. Because conflict can be a way to work out differences that may cause resentment, anger, or negative emotions and withdrawal (Gottman, 1994), parents who engage in constructive conflict may actually be better able to parent than those who withdraw from conflict. The potentially positive aspects of constructive conflict for family relationships have not been sufficiently explored.

In addition, a number of more specific issues regarding marital–parenting linkages merit further investigation. Such issues include a greater consideration of the unit of analysis used in marriage–parenting studies, greater focus on these linkages during adolescence, increased consideration of how positive parent–child relationships might develop in a climate of destructive marital conflict, and greater recognition of the need for studies of diverse samples.

Unit of Analysis

One issue highlighted by recent studies of co-parenting is that much of the research on marital–parenting linkages is limited to a focus on dyadic parent–child relationships. Most studies involve observations of separate mother–child and father–child interactions (if fathers are included at all), thus ignoring the experience that children have with both parents. However, a number of studies have documented differences in parent–child interactions depending on whether such interactions occur in the absence or presence of the other parent (e.g., Clarke-Stewart, 1978; Gjerde, 1986). This differential pattern of parenting may be particularly pronounced among conflicted couples (Coiro & Emery, 1998). Recent work by Lauretti and McHale (1997) found that mothers who exhibited less sensitive parenting in triadic interactions (with fathers present) than in dyadic interactions were more likely to be in distressed marriages than those mothers whose sensitivity did not vary across dyadic and triadic interactions. Studying triads and whole family interactions can provide important information not only about co-parenting and the contextual effects of dyads versus triads on parenting, but also about important processes such as children's attempts to mediate conflicts and the formation of coalitions in the family.

Marital Conflict and Parent–Adolescent Relationships

The majority of studies examining marital–parenting links have focused on the early or middle childhood years, whereas relatively few studies have focused on adolescents (for some exceptions, see Conger et al., 1992, 1993; Fauber et al., 1990), and even fewer have compared children and adolescents. Thus, we know little about the dynamic linkages between marital conflict and parent–adolescent relationships, and moreover, whether such linkages are unique to adolescence.

There is some evidence that adolescents as opposed to younger children may be more likely to intervene in parents' marital disputes (Cummings, 1994). Thus, adolescents may be more likely to become targets of displaced or redirected anger, particularly in violent marriages. Parents also may be more prone to attempt to enlist them into coalitions against the other parent. As adolescents presumably have a greater capacity to provide emotional support than younger children, they may be more often targets for parentification, as their parents look to them to provide what they perceive to be missing from their marriage. Amato (1986) found, for example, that marital conflict was related to greater closeness between mothers and adolescent sons, but decreased closeness between mothers and younger sons, suggesting mothers of adolescent boys may turn to their sons for intimacy they aren't experiencing with their husbands.

On the other hand, adolescents may also be more resistant to parents' attempts to triangulate or parentify them, and such resistance may result in greater conflict between parents and adolescents. Adolescents in general may also be more likely to react to interparental aggression with their own aggression, perhaps because of longer histories of observing dysregulated affect in their families. Davis et al. (1998) found that adolescents reacted to interparental conflict with their own aggressive behavior toward their parents, especially toward their mothers, but it remains unknown whether sequential analyses of parents and younger children's interactions would reveal similar patterns. Parent–adolescent relationships may also be affected differently by the inconsistent, lax, or overly harsh discipline that can often characterize maritally conflicted families. Adolescents may be even more resentful than younger children of parents who either fail to set appropriate limits, or attempt to set overly strict limits, when they perceive their parents as incapable of managing their own lives. Thus, there are multiple ways in which marital conflicts may impact parent–adolescent relationships differently than parent–child relationships, but such possibilities have yet to be investigated.

Development of Positive Parent–Child Relationships in Maritally Conflicted Families

Another understudied area concerns the processes that allow positive parent–child relationships to develop and maintain despite the presence of marital conflict. As noted earlier, some studies have found evidence for the compensatory hypothesis – some parents in conflicted marriages nonetheless appear to have positive relationships with their children (Amato, 1986; Belsky et al., 1991). Such findings are seen as providing support for the notion that some parents may compensate for what is lacking in their marriage by focusing their energy on developing a positive relationship with their child. However, some parents might develop or maintain a positive relationship with their child in spite of a conflicted marriage, rather than because of a conflicted marriage. There may be parents who are nurturing, sensitive, and involved with their children, not in an effort to make up for deficits in their marriage, but rather because they have been able to adequately separate their marital disputes from their parenting responsibilities.

Although such parents may be unusual, they would seem to be an important group to study, as there is evidence that a positive parent–child relationship can buffer children from many of the negative consequences of marital conflict (Emery, 1989; Katz & Gottman, 1995). In particular, the question remains as to the processes or factors that allow such parents to successfully disentangle parenting from marital disputes. Perhaps such parents have certain ground rules, such as always supporting one another's parenting, even if they disagree about other issues – that is, cooperative co-parenting is a paramount goal. Perhaps such parents are characterized by different forms of marital conflict than those parents who are unable to separate marital disputes from parenting–that is, the former may engage in heated arguments, but they avoid the contempt, criticism, and withdrawal that Gottman (1994) has proposed is so destructive to marriages. Cowan and McHale (1996) have proposed that couples with better emotional regulation skills may be more able to prevent marital conflict from spilling over into parenting. These authors have suggested that "there may be families in which the parents fight (or ignore each other) a great deal when the child is not present but manage to maintain an effective working partnership that keeps their marital distress under control when they function as coparents" (p. 103). Clearly, such families will be an important focus for future study.

Diversity in Family Systems

Finally, there is a need to study linkages between marital conflict and parent–child relationships in more diverse samples. The majority of studies reviewed for this chapter utilized samples comprised mostly or entirely of European-American families (for exceptions, see Brody & Flor, 1996; Lindahl & Malik, 1999), whereas other studies contained no information regarding the ethnicity of the sample. Thus, it remains unknown whether there are different linkages between marriage and parenting across different ethnic groups, and equally importantly, whether there are differences *within* various ethnic groups. We also know relatively little about marriage–parenting linkages among families of varying socioeconomic statuses. Few of the extant studies in this area focus on lower class or poverty samples, yet there is strong evidence that economic stress has an impact on marital and parenting processes (Conger et al., 1992, 1993). Moreover, if studies are to be undertaken examining differences between various ethnic groups, then it will be important to account for economic factors, as socioeconomic status and ethnicity are often confounded. Finally, there is very little information on links between interparental relationships and parent–child relationships in nontraditional families, including adoptive families, families headed by gay and lesbian parents, and families in which parents are cohabitating, but not legally married. And while there may be similarities between traditional and nontraditional families in terms of interparental and parent–child relationships, there may also be unique issues faced by nontraditional families that impact the connections between interparental relationships and parenting. For example, most, if not all, gay and lesbian couples are likely to experience unique pressures from living in societies in which large segments of the population do not sanction their relationship. For some couples, such pressures may have the effect of dividing them as a couple, and thus compromise their parenting. For other couples, such pressures may lead them to pull together in the face of adversity, and form an even more cohesive and supportive co-parenting relationship, enhancing their parenting both as a couple and as individuals. As with any group, these nontraditional families are likely to make various adaptations in terms of interparental and parent–child relationships, yet the processes that characterize such adaptations remain largely unexplored.

Conclusion

Clearly, significant advances have been made in identifying important mechanisms and processes through which interparental conflict affects parent–child relationships, as well as factors that may moderate marriage–parenting linkages. However, we suggest that a broader family systems perspective would greatly enrich our understanding of the multiple and reciprocal pathways that may exist between marital conflict and parent–child difficulties, as well as how the associations between marital and parent–child relationships may evolve over time and in accordance with the developmental capacities of children and their families.

REFERENCES

Amato, P. R. (1986). Marital conflict, the parent-child relationship, and child self-esteem. *Family Relations, 35,* 403–410.
Belsky, J. (1984). The determinants of parenting: A process model. *Child Development, 55,* 83–96.
Belsky, J., Crnic, K., & Gable, S. (1995). The determinants of coparenting in families with toddler boys: Spousal differences and daily hassles. *Child Development, 66,* 629–642.

Belsky, J., Putnam, S., & Crnic, K. (1996). Coparenting, parenting, and early emotional development. In J. P. McHale & P. A. Cowan (Eds.), *New directions for child development: No. 74. Understanding how family level dynamics affect children's development: Studies of two-parent families* (pp. 45–55). San Francisco: Jossey-Bass.

Belsky, J., & Volling, B. L. (1987). Mothering, fathering and marital interaction in the family triad: Exploring family systems processes. In P. Berman & F. Pedersen (Eds.), *Men's transitions to parenthood: Longitudinal studies of early family experience* (pp. 37–63). Hillsdale, NJ: Lawrence Erlbaum Associates.

Belsky, J., Youngblade, L., Rovine, M., & Volling, B. (1991). Patterns of marital change and parent-child interaction. *Journal of Marriage and the Family, 53,* 487–498.

Brody, G. H., & Arias, I., & Fincham, F. D. (1996). Linking marital and child attributions to family processes and parent-child relationships. *Journal of Family Psychology, 10*(4), 408–421.

Brody, G. H., & Flor, D. L. (1996). Coparenting, family interactions, and competence among African-American youths. In J. P. McHale & P. A. Cowan (Eds.), *New directions for child development: No. 74. Understanding how family level dynamics affect children's development: Studies of two-parent families* (pp. 77–91). San Francisco: Jossey-Bass.

Brody, G. H., Pellegrini, A. D., & Sigel, I. E. (1986). Marital quality and mother-child and father-child interactions with school-aged children. *Developmental Psychology, 22,* 291–296.

Brody, G., Stoneman, Z., & McCoy, K. (1994). Forecasting sibling relationships in early adolescence from child temperaments and family processes in middle childhood. *Child Development, 65,* 771–784.

Burman, B., John, R. S., & Margolin, G. (1987). Effects of parent-child relations on children's adjustment. *Journal of Family Psychology, 1*(1), 91–108.

Christensen, A., & Margolin, G. (1988). Conflict and alliance in distressed and nondistressed families. In R. A. Hinde & J. Stevenson-Hinde (Eds.), *Relationships within families: Mutual influences* (pp. 263–282). New York: Oxford University Press.

Clarke-Stewart, K. A. (1978). And daddy makes three: The father's impact on mother and young child. *Child Development, 49,* 466–478.

Coiro, M. J., & Emery, R. E. (1998). Do marriage problems affect fathering more than mothering? A quantitative and qualitative review. *Clinical Child and Family Psychology Review, 1,* 23–40.

Conger, R. D., Conger, K. J., Elder, G. H., Jr., Lorenz, F. O., Simons, R. L., & Whitbeck, L. B. (1992). A family process model of economic hardship and adjustment of early adolescent boys. *Child Development, 63,* 526–541.

Conger, R. D., Conger, K. J., Elder, G. H., Jr., Lorenz, F. O., Simons, R. L., & Whitbeck, L. B. (1993). Family economic stress and adjustment of early adolescent girls. *Developmental Psychology, 29,* 206–219.

Cowan, C. P., & Cowan, P. A. (1987). Men's involvement in parenthood: Identifying the antecedents and understanding the barriers. In P. W. Berman and F. A. Pedersen (Eds.), *Men's transitions to parenthood: Longitudinal studies of early family experience.* Hillsdale, NJ: Lawrence Erlbaum Associates.

Cowan, C. P., Cowan, P. A., Heming, G., & Miller, N. B. (1991). Becoming a family: Marriage, parenting, and child development. In P. A. Cowan & M. Hetherington (Eds.), *Family transitions* (pp. 79–109). Hillsdale, NJ: Erlbaum.

Cowan, P. A., & McHale, J. P. (1996). Coparenting in a family context: Emerging achievements, current dilemmas, and future directions. In J. P. McHale & P. A. Cowan (Eds.), *New directions for child development: No. 74. Understanding how family level dynamics affect children's development: Studies of two-parent families* (pp. 93–106). San Francisco: Jossey-Bass.

Cox, M. J., & Owen, M. T. (1993, March). *Marital conflict and conflict negotiation: Effects on infant-mother and infant-father relationships.* Paper presented at the biennial meeting of the Society for Research in Child Development, New Orleans, LA.

Cox, M. J., & Paley, B. (1997). Families as systems. *Annual Review of Psychology, 48,* 243–267.

Cox, M. J., Paley, B., Burchinal, M., & Payne, C. C. (1999). Marital perceptions and interactions across the transition to parenthood. *Journal of Marriage and the Family, 61,* 611–625.

Crockenberg, S. L., & Covey, S. (1991). Marital conflict and externalizing behavior in children. In D. Cicchetti & S. Toth (Eds.), *Rochester symposium on developmental psychopathology: Vol. 3. Models and integrations.* Rochester, NY: University of Rochester Press.

Cummings, E. M. (1994). Marital conflict and children's functioning. *Social Development, 3,* 16–36.

Cummings, E. M. (1998). Children exposed to marital conflict and violence: Conceptual and theoretical directions. In G. W. Holden, R. Geffner, & E. N. Jouriles (Eds.), *Children exposed to marital violence: Theory, research, and applied issues* (pp. 55–93). Washington, DC: American Psychological Association.

Cummings, E. M., Ballard, M., El-Sheikh, M., & Lake, M. (1991). Resolution and children's responses to interadult anger. *Developmental Psychology, 27* (3), 462–470.

Cummings, E. M., & Davies, P. (1994). *Children and marital conflict: The impact of family dispute and resolution.* New York: Guilford Press.

Cummings, E. M., & Davies, P. T. (1995). The impact of parents on their children: An emotional security perspective. *Annals of Child Development, 10,* 167–208.

Cummings, E. M., & O'Reilly, A. W. (1997). Fathers in family context: Effects of marital quality on child adjustment. In M. E. (Ed.), *The role of the father in child development.* (Third Edition) (pp. 49–65). New York: John Wiley & Sons.

Cummings, E. M., & Wilson, A. (1999). Contexts of marital conflict and children's emotional security: Exploring the distinction between constructive and destructive conflict from the children's perspective. In M. Cox & J. Brooks-Gunn (Eds.), *Conflict and closeness in families: Causes and consequences* (pp. 105–129). Mahwah, NJ: Erlbaum.

Davies, P. T., & Cummings. E. M. (1994). Marital conflict and child adjustment: An emotional security hypothesis. *Psychological Bulletin, 116,* 387–411.

Davies, P. T. & Windle, M. (1997). Gender-specific pathways between maternal depressive symptoms, family discord, and adolescent adjustment. *Developmental Psychology, 33* (4), 657–668.

Davies, B. T., Hops, H., Alpert, A., & Sheeber, L. (1998). Child responses to parental conflict and their effect on adjustment: A study of triadic relations. *Journal of Family Psychology, 12,* 163–177.

Deal, J. E. (1996). Marital conflict and differential treatment of siblings. *Family Process, 35,* 333–346.

Dickie, J. R. (1987). Interrelationships within the mother-father-infant triad. In P. W. Berman & F. A. Pederson (Eds.), *Men's transitions to parenthood: Longitudinal studies of early family experience* (pp. 113–143). Hillsdale, NJ: Lawrence Erlbaum.

Easterbrooks, M. A., & Emde, R. N. (1988). Marital and parent-child relationships: The role of affect in the family system. In R. A. Hinde & J. Stevenson-Hinde (Eds.), *Relationships within families: Mutual influences* (pp. 83–103). Oxford: Clarendon Press.

Emery, R. E. (1982). Interparental conflict and the children of discord and divorce. *Psychological Bulletin, 92,* 310–330.

Emery, R. E. (1989). Family violence. *American Psychologist, 44,* 321–328.

Engfer, A. (1988). The interrelatedness of marriage and the mother-child relationships. In R. A. Hinde & J. Stevenson-Hinde (Eds.), *Relationships within families: Mutual influences* (pp. 104–118). Oxford, U.K.: Clarendon.

Erel, O., & Burman, B. (1995). Interrelatedness of marital relations and parent-child relations: A meta-analytic review. *Psychological Bulletin, 118,* 108–132.

Fauber, R., Forehand, R., Thomas, A. M., & Wierson, M. (1990). A mediational model of the impact of marital conflict on adolescent adjustment in intact and divorced families: The role of disrupted parenting. *Child Development, 61,* 1112–1123.

Fincham, F. D. (1994). Understanding the association between marital conflict and child adjustment: Overview. *Journal of Family Psychology, 2,* 123–127.

Fivaz-Depeursinge, E., Frascarolo, F., & Corboz-Warnery, A. (1996). Assessing the triadic alliance between fathers, mothers, and infants at play. In J. P. McHale & P. A. Cowan (Eds.), *New directions for child development: No. 74. Understanding how family level dynamics affect children's development: Studies of two-parent families* (pp. 27–44). San Francisco: Jossey-Bass.

Gjerde, P. (1986). The interpersonal structure of family interactional settings: Parent-adolescent relations in dyads and triads. *Developmental Psychology, 48,* 711–717.

Goldberg, W. A., & Easterbrooks, M. A. (1984). Role of marital quality in toddler development. *Developmental Psychology, 20,* 504–514.

Gordis, E. B., Margolin, G., & John, R. S. (1997). Marital aggression, observed parental hostility, and child behavior during triadic family interaction. *Journal of Family Psychology, 11* (1), 76–89.

Gottman, J. M. (1994). *What predicts divorce.* Hillsdale, NJ: Erlbaum.

Gottman, J. M., & Katz, L. F. (1989). Effects of marital discord on young children's peer interaction and health. *Developmental Psychology, 25,* 373–381.

Grych, J. H., & Fincham, F. D. (1990). Marital conflict and children's adjustment: A cognitive-contextual framework. *Psychological Bulletin, 108,* 267–290.

Hoffman, L. (1981). *Foundations of family therapy: A conceptual framework for systems change.* New York: Basic Books.

Holden, G. W., & Ritchie, K. L. (1991). Linking extreme marital discord, child rearing, and behavior problems: Evidence from battered women. *Child Development, 62,* 311–327.

Jacobvitz, D. B., & Bush, N. F. (1996). Reconstruction of family relationships: parent-child alliances, personal distress, and self-esteem. *Developmental Psychology, 29,* 931–939.

Jaycox, L. H., & Repetti, R. L. (1993). Conflict in families and the psychological adjustment of preadolescent children. *Journal of Family Psychology, 7*(3), 344–355.

Jenkins, J. M., Smith, M. A., & Graham, P. J. (1989). Coping with parental quarrels. *Journal of the American Academy of Child and Adolescent Psychiatry, 28,* 182–189.

Johnston, J. R. (1993). Family transitions and children's functioning: The case of parental conflict and divorce. In P. A. Cowan et al. (Eds.), *Family, self, and society: Toward a new agenda for family research* (pp. 197–234). Hillsdale, NJ: Erlbaum.

Johnston, J. R., & Campbell, L. E. G. (1988). *Impasses of divorce: The dynamics and resolution of family conflict.* New York: The Free Press.

Jouriles, E. N., Barling, J., & O'Leary, K. D. (1987). Predicting child behavior problems in maritally violent families. *Journal of Abnormal Child Psychology, 15,* 165–173.

Jouriles, E. N., & Norwood, W. D. (1995). Physical aggression toward boys and girls in families characterized by the battering of women. *Journal of Family Psychology, 9* (1), 69–78.

Katz, L. F., & Gottman, J. M. (1995). Marital interaction and child outcomes: A longitudinal study of mediating and moderating processes. In D. Cicchetti & S. L. Toth (Eds.), *Rochester symposium on developmental psychopathology: Vol. 6. Emotion, cognition, and representation* (pp. 301–342). Rochester, NY: University of Rochester Press.

Katz, L. F., & Gottman, J. M. (1996). Spillover effects of marital conflict: In search of parenting and coparenting mechanisms. In J. P. McHale & P. A. Cowan (Eds.), *New directions for child development: No. 74. Understanding how family level dynamics affect children's development: Studies of two-parent families* (pp. 57–76). San Francisco: Jossey-Bass.

Kerig, P. K. (1995). Triangles in the family circle: Effects of family structure on marriage, parenting, and child adjustment. *Journal of Family Psychology, 9,* 28–43.

Kerig, P. K., Cowan, P. A., & Cowan, C. P. (1993). Marital quality and gender differences in parent-child interaction. *Developmental Psychology, 29,* 931–939.

Lauretti, A., & McHale, J. (1997, April). *Shifting patterns of parenting styles between dyadic and family settings: The role of marital quality.* Paper presented at the biennial meeting of the Society for Research in Child Development, Washington, D.C.

Lindahl, K. M., Clements, M., & Markman, H. (1997). Predicting marital and parent functioning dyads and triads: A longitudinal investigation of marital processes. *Journal of Family Psychology, 11,* 139–151.

Lindahl, K. M., & Malik, N. M. (1999). Marital conflict, family processes, and boys' externalizing behavior in Hispanic American and European American families. *Journal of Clinical Child Psychology, 28,* 12–24.

McHale, J. P. (1995). Coparenting and triadic interactions during infancy: The roles of marital distress and child gender. *Developmental Psychology, 31,* 985–996.

McHale, J. P., & Cowan, P. A. (1996). *New directions for child development: No. 74. Understanding how family level dynamics affect children's development: Studies of two-parent families* (pp. 57–76). San Francisco: Jossey-Bass.

McHale, J. P., Kuersten, R., & Lauretti, A. (1996). New directions in the study of family-level dynamics during infancy and early childhood. In J. P. McHale & P. A. Cowan (Eds.), *New directions for child development: No. 74. Understanding how family level dynamics affect children's development: Studies of two-parent families* (pp. 5–26). San Francisco: Jossey-Bass.

McHale, J. P., & Rasmussen, J. (1998). Coparental and family group-level dynamics during infancy: Early family precursors of child and family functioning during preschool. *Development and Psychopathology, 10,* 39–59.

Minuchin, S. (1974). *Families and family therapy.* Cambridge, MA: Harvard University Press.

Minuchin, S., Rosman, B., & Baker, L. (1978). *Psychosomatic families: Anorexia nervosa in context.* Cambridge, MA: Harvard University Press.

O'Brien, M., Margolin, G., & John, R. S. (1995). Relation among marital conflict, child coping, and child adjustment. *Journal of Clinical Child Psychology, 24,* 346–361.

O'Keefe, M. (1994). Linking marital violence, mother-child/father-child aggression, and child behavior problems. *Journal of Family Violence, 9*(1), 63–78.

O'Leary, K. D. (1984). Marital discord and children: Problems, strategies, methodologies and results. *New Directions for Child Development, 24,* 35–46.

Osborne, L. N., & Fincham, F. D. (1996). Marital conflict, parent-child relationships, and child adjustment: Does gender matter? *Merrill-Palmer Quarterly, 42,* 48–75.

Owen, M. T., & Cox, M. J. (1997). Marital conflict and the development of infant-parent attachment relationships. *Journal of Family Psychology, 11,* 152–164.

Parke, R. D., & Tinsley, B. J. (1987). Family interaction in infancy. In J. Osofsky (Ed.), *Handbook of infant development* (pp. 579–641). New York: Wiley.

Patterson, G. (1982). *Coercive family process.* Eugene, OR: Castalia.

Reiss, D., Plomin, R., Hetherington, M., Howe, G., Rovine, M., Tryon, A., & Hagan, M. (1994). The separate worlds of teenage siblings: An introduction to the study of the nonshared environment and adolescent development. In M. Hetherington, D. Reiss, & R. Plomin (Eds.), *Separate social worlds of siblings: The impact of nonshared environment on development* (pp. 63–109). Hillsdale, NJ: Lawrence Erlbaum Associates.

Rosenberg, M. S. (1987). Children of battered women: The effects of witnessing violence on their social-problem solving abilities. *The Behavior Therapist, 4,* 85–89.

Sameroff, A. (1994). Developmental systems and family functioning. In R. D. Parke & S. G. Kellam (Eds.), *Exploring family relationships with other social contexts. Family research consortium: Advances in family research* (pp. 199–214). Hillsdale, NJ: Erlbaum

Simons, R. L., Lorenz, F. O., Conger, R. D., & Wu, C. (1993). Support from spouse as mediator and moderator of the disruptive influence of economic strain on parenting. *Child Development, 64,* 1282–1301.

Stoneman, Z., Brody, G. H., & Burke, M. (1989). Marital quality, depression, and inconsistent parenting: Relationship with observed mother-child conflict. *American Journal of Orthopsychiatry, 59,* 105–117.

Thompson, R. A. (1994). Emotional regulation: A theme in search of a definition. In N. A. Fox (Ed.), The development of emotional regulation: Biological and behavioral considerations. *Monographs of the Society for Research in Child Development, 59* (Serial No. 240), 25–52.

Vogel, E. F., & Bell, N. W. (1960). The emotionally disturbed child as a family scapegoat. In N. W. Bell & E. F. Vogel (Eds.), *A modern introduction to the family* (pp. 382–397). New York: Free Press.

Volling, B. L., & Belsky, J. (1991). Multiple determinants of father involvement during infancy in dual-earner and single-earner families. *Journal of Marriage and the Family, 53,* 461–474.

Wallerstein, J. S. (1985). The overburdened child: Some long-term consequences of divorce. *Social Work, 30,* 116–123.

10 Sibling Relationships and Interparental Conflict

Judy Dunn and Lisa Davies

In this chapter, we consider the links between interparental conflict and sibling relationships. Why a focus on siblings? Differences in the quality of sibling relationships are marked both across families and within families. Some siblings quarrel fiercely and frequently; among others, hostility, irritability, and fighting are rare, and affection, intimacy, and cooperation are the key features of their relationship. Yet other siblings show both affection and conflict in their relationships: They argue frequently but are also good companions and friends. These differences are evident in siblings in very early childhood, in middle childhood and adolescence, and can show considerable continuity over time (Dunn, Slomkowski, Beardsall, & Rende, 1994b). Importantly, such individual differences in siblings' relations are related to two key aspects of children's development.

The first is children's adjustment. The shaping role of siblings on children's aggressive behavior, for instance, has been documented by Patterson and his colleagues (Bank, Patterson, & Reid, 1996; Patterson, 1986). Aggressive experiences with siblings were linked with children's aggressive behavior with their peers, and with rejection by peers in MacKinnon-Lewis et al.'s study (1997). And both internalizing and externalizing behavior problems in middle childhood and early adolescence have been found to be associated with individual differences in sibling relationships years earlier – in the preschool period (Dunn et al., 1994b). Negative relations between siblings have been linked to adjustment problems in a recent large-scale community study (Dunn et al., 1998), whereas within stepfamilies, sibling negativity has also been linked with later increases in externalizing behavior (Hetherington & Clingempeel, 1992).

The second aspect of development that has been linked to the quality of early sibling relationships is the domain of social understanding –

specifically individual differences in children's ability to "read" other people's minds and emotions and to understand the connections between what someone thinks or feels and their behavior. This central aspect of social and cognitive development, which is importantly associated with the quality of children's later relationships, has been found in a number of independent studies to be linked to children's positive experiences with their siblings. Preschool children who have experienced cooperative relations with an older sibling (especially the sharing of pretend play), for instance, show particularly mature understanding of mind and emotion (Dunn, Brown, Slomkowski, Tesla, & Youngblade, 1991; see also Howe & Ross, 1990; Lewis, Freeman, Kyriakidou, Maridaki-Kassotaki, & Berridge, 1996). In research on adolescents, differences in sibling relations have been linked to developments in social understanding, sensitivity, conflict management, and caregiving (Anderson, Hetherington, Reiss, & Plomin, 1994).

So, individual differences in the relative hostility or friendliness children express and feel about their siblings are developmentally important, and the question of what factors contribute to these differences deserves attention. A range of different aspects of children's characteristics and experiences is likely to contribute to the marked differences in sibling relations including, for example, the temperamental characteristics of children (Brody, Stoneman, & McCoy, 1994; Stocker, Dunn, & Plomin, 1989); family relationships are thought to be of particular importance. Most research attention has been paid to the links between parent–child and sibling relationships (see the next section); however, we focus in particular on the possibility that the quality of relations between children's parents – and especially conflict between parents – is linked to the positivity and negativity of children's sibling relationships.

To address this issue, we need to consider a series of questions about links between family relationships. If there are connections between interparental relationships and sibling relationships, are these mediated through each child's relations with the individual parents? That is, are the links between spousal relations and sibling relationships *indirect*, connected through the quality of parent–child relationships? Or is there also evidence for *direct* connections between interparental relations and sibling relationships – patterns of association that are not mediated by the parent–child relationship, but reflect the direct impact on children of witnessing conflict or affection between their parents? And what do we know about the underlying processes that might be implicated in explaining the connections between relationships within the family or the direction of causal influences in the network of relationships? Is there evidence that sibling relationships can affect interparental relations?

We first consider each of these questions, then we focus in particular on the issue of whether patterns of connections between interparental and sibling relationships differ for the increasing numbers of families that do not fit traditional patterns in which all members are biologically related, that is, stepfamilies. In the final section, some of the methodological issues raised by the research on these issues and the implications for future research are discussed.

Interparental, Parent–Child, and Sibling Relations

Associations between interparental and sibling relationships have been much less extensively researched than links between interparental conflict and affection and children's adjustment. As described in other chapters in this volume, associations between marital conflict and children's adjustment have been widely reported – for instance, with children's depressive symptomatology, antisocial behavior, conduct disorder and aggression (Emery & O'Leary, 1982; Emery, 1988; Fincham & Osborne, 1993; Jenkins & Smith, 1990; Johnston, Gonzales, & Campbell, 1987). Both direct and indirect pathways have been suggested to explain such associations (e.g., Erel & Burman, 1995).

In terms of indirect pathways, there is considerable evidence that conflict between parents is linked with difficulties in parent–child relations and thus indirectly to children's adjustment (see Cox et al., Chapter 9). Interparental conflict has, for example, been associated with unresponsive parenting (Gottman & Katz, 1989), inconsistent parental discipline (Emery, 1982), harsh parenting and aggressive parent–child relations, and insecure parent–child relations (Howes & Markman, 1989). The mediating role of parent–child relations in contributing to the link between marital conflict and child adjustment is illustrated in the research of Conger and his colleagues (Conger et al., 1992; Conger et al., 1993; Conger, Ge, Elder, Lorenz, & Simons, 1994).

There is also evidence that interparental conflict can have a more direct impact on children. Evidence has accumulated that the experience of witnessing conflict between parents causes distress and disturbance in young children; this is powerfully shown, for instance, in experimental studies (Cummings & Davies, 1994; Grych & Fincham, 1993). It is important to place the findings of this research within the framework of recent developmental research that has documented the extent to which children monitor and respond to the interactions between other family members. We know that children are vigilant observers of the relations between their parents and siblings, for instance, even when they are very young (Dunn, 1988; Dunn & Kendrick, 1982), and of the relations between their parents (Zahn-Waxler & Radke-Yarrow, 1982). The emotions expressed by other family members during their interactions are of particular salience to young children (Dunn & Munn, 1985). The evidence from the experimental studies by Cummings and his colleagues and by Grych and Fincham fits well with the results from such naturalistic studies of family interaction. Among older children, the significance of children's perceptions and appraisals of conflict in predicting their adjustment has received increasing support (Harold, Fincham, Osborne, & Conger, 1997). It appears very plausible that the effects of marital conflict on children's adjustment include the direct impact of observing and reflecting on conflict between parents, as well as the indirect pathways in which the effects of interparental conflict are mediated by difficulties in the parent–child relationship. The developmental work on young children as family members indicates that these processes begin as early as the second year.

While this evidence has established that there are both direct and indirect links between interparental conflict and children's adjustment, relatively few studies have considered associations between such interparental conflict and sibling relationships. Yet the evidence for links between poor sibling relationships and children's externalizing and internalizing problems suggests that parental conflict may well be associated with hostility and problems in the relations between siblings. Indeed, the studies conducted so far report that in families in which there are relatively high levels of conflict or dissatisfaction between the parents and less affection, there is more conflict between siblings. This has been reported for siblings in early and middle childhood (Dunn, Deater-Deckard, Pickering, Beveridge, & the ALSPAC Study Team, 1999; Erel, Margolin, & John, 1998; Jenkins, 1992; MacKinnon, 1989; Stocker, Ahmed, & Stall, 1997) and in adolescence (Brody, Stoneman, McCoy, & Forehand, 1992; Hetherington et al., in press). A key question that follows such evidence concerns the processes that link interparental and sibling relationships– is the connection mediated by the quality of the parent–child relationship? Is there also evidence for more direct associations between interparental and sibling relationships in which the parent–child relationship is not directly implicated?

Indirect Pathways

Links between mother–child and sibling relationship quality have been documented in several studies over the last decade – though it should be emphasized at the outset that much of this work is cross-sectional in design and does not permit inferences about the direction of effects. Mothers' negative behavior toward their children has been reported to be related to the conflict and rivalry between the siblings, and maternal affection associated with warmth and supportiveness between siblings (Brody, Stoneman, & Burke, 1987; Stocker et al., 1989). It is not surprising, then, to find that in those studies of siblings that have included both assessments of the relationships between adult partners, and between parents and children, the findings support the view that indirect pathways are important in linking mother–partner and sibling relationships.

Two studies of different scale and methods can serve as illustration. In a study of same-sex adolescent siblings by Brody and his colleagues (Brody et al., 1994), 71 white middle-class families were studied at time points 4 years apart (a notable exception to the cross-sectional research on family relationships). Self-report measures of marital and sibling relationships were employed, and observations of parent–child interaction conducted. Three important points regarding the links between family relationships stand out from their findings.

First, parental conflict was linked to the quality of both mothers' and fathers' relationships with their children – with less negativity and more positivity in the parent–child relationships of those families with less interparental conflict. However, the second point is that higher levels of overt parental conflict were linked to more *differential* parent–child negativity, and it was this differential negativity that was associated with greater sibling negativity 4 years later. Parents who were in conflict with their partners were more likely to behave with more negativity and rejection to one of their children than the other, and this differential negativity is, we now know, of particular significance for children's relations with their siblings (Dunn & Plomin, 1990). More hostile, rivalrous sibling relationships have been found in families in which parents showed differential affection or discipline to their different children. Third, some links were found between lack of conflict between parents, the positivity of the mother–younger child relationship, and lower negativity of the younger siblings towards the older.

The second study that illustrates the importance of indirect links between mother–partner and sibling relationships was conducted within the framework of an epidemiological study – a longitudinal study of 3,681 pairs of young siblings participating in the Avon Longitudinal Study of Pregnancy and Childhood (ALSPAC; Dunn et al., 1998). ALSPAC is an ongoing community study of women, their children, and their partners in the geographical area of Avon in England, which includes both urban and rural areas and is demographically similar to Great Britain as a whole. Participants in ALSPAC completed questionnaires at repeated intervals during their pregnancy and the infancy and childhood years of their children; information was obtained at various time points from mothers and their partners on their psychosocial adjustment and the quality of their relations with each other, and from the mothers on their relationship history, financial situation, the mothers' and partners' relationships with child and sibling, the siblings' relationships with one another, the marital and stepfamily status of the family, age and sex of the children, and other variables (see, for instance, Deater-Deckard, Pickering, Dunn, Golding, & the ALSPAC Study Team, 1998; Dunn et al., 1998; O'Connor, Hawkins, Dunn, Thorpe, & Golding, 1998). In this sample, which included both boys and girls and families from a very diverse range of social backgrounds, we found that the quality of marital relations, as reported by both mother and partner, was associated with the individual differences in children's behavior toward their siblings assessed 4 years later.

For example, the level of hostility between mother and partner was positively related to the negative behavior shown by older siblings (on average 7-years-old) toward their 4-year-old siblings, and this link was mediated in part by the negativity within the parent–older sibling relationship. These paths are illustrated in Figure 10.1 (paths a and b). There was also a significant indirect link between lack of mother–partner affection and higher parent–child negativity (Figure 10.1, path c) and more negativity shown by older siblings toward younger siblings.

The positive aspects of the sibling relationships in the large ALSPAC sample were also related to the quality of the interparental relationship assessed 4 years earlier. High levels of affection between mother and partner were associated with lower parent–child negativity (path c in Figure 10.2) and thus indirectly to the friendliness the older siblings showed to their younger siblings (paths a and b in Figure 10.2). Interparental hostility was related to negativity in the parent–child relationship and thus indirectly to less friendliness from older to younger sibling (path a in Figure 10.2). For the 4-year-old younger siblings in this study, there was also evidence for indirect links between the level of hostility in the relationship between mother and partner and the children's hostility to their older siblings.

Direct Pathways

The large-scale ALSPAC study also showed that direct paths between the hostility and affection of the relationship between mother

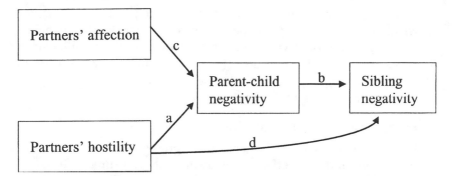

Figure 10.1. Prediction of sibling negativity in nonstepfamilies 4 years after assessment of mother–partner relationship. Significant direct links (d) and indirect links (a and c) via parent–child relationships (b).

and partner contributed significantly to the hostility and friendliness of the siblings' relationships. That is, the association between the hostility and affection of their parents and the quality of siblings' relationships 4 years later was not completely explained by the quality of the parent–child relationship as mediator. Rather, there were significant direct links between the hostility reported between parents and the children's negativity toward their siblings (path d in Figure 10.1), and between the affection of the adult partners for one another, and the siblings' friendliness to each other (path e in Figure 10.2).

This pattern is not surprising, given the evidence of increased levels of aggression in children who have witnessed conflict between their parents (Cummings & Cummings, 1988), and given the research

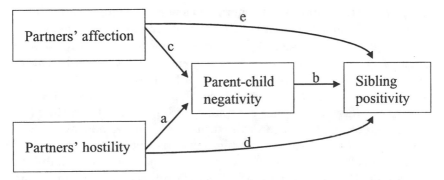

Figure 10.2. Prediction of sibling positivity in nonstepfamilies 4 years after assessment of mother–partner relationship. Significant direct links (d and e) and indirect (a and c) via parent–child relationships (b).

demonstrating the interest and attention children pay to interactions – particularly emotional interactions – between other family members. The sibling relationship is one that is characteristically uninhibited; if children feel aggressive or angry (for instance, following exposure to parental conflict), they are likely to show this aggression toward siblings, who themselves are likely to react aggressively.

Processes and Direction of Effects

While such an account is plausible, the processes involved in these "direct" and "indirect" effects remain unclear. The direct effects we found in the associations between interparental and sibling relations in both the domains of negativity and affection are compatible with accounts that emphasize social learning or genetic continuities. Children who grow up with quarrelling parents may have learned ways of responding to frustration or conflict that are then expressed in their sibling relationships. Genetics too may have played a part in the continuities in the expression of conflict or affection across different family members (Reiss, Neiderheiser, Hetherington, & Plomin, in press). In relation to indirect effects, the evidence was compatible with the hypothesis, developed in the study of adolescents' family relationships, that appraisals of marital conflict by adolescents influence their perceptions of parent–child relationships (Harold et al., 1997). Specifically, Harold and colleagues' argument is that children who have witnessed conflict between their parents interpret parent–child conflict as more threatening than children who have been less exposed to hostility between their parents.

The findings in the ALSPAC study raise a further question about processes over time. The assessment of marital conflict was made *before* the birth of the younger child. How then can the link between interparental hostility and the younger child's negativity toward his or her sibling be explained? It could be that stability in mother–partner hostility over the 4 years between the antenatal assessment and the assessment of sibling relations is important. In addition, it is possible that the negativity of the older sibling from early in the younger sibling's infancy plays a key contributory role. Such negativity toward a new sibling is likely to be higher in families with high marital conflict (see Dunn, Slomkowski, & Beardsall, 1994a). With these data we cannot compare the relative support for these various possibilities, and indeed it seems likely that many different processes may be involved. But the longitudinal evidence for patterns linking conflict and affection in marital relations with later sibling relations over this 4-year period is at least consistent with causal interpretations for the impact of interparental conflict on sibling relationships. Of course, this does not rule out the possibility that highly conflicted sibling relations also contribute to difficulties in the parents' own relationship, too.

The possibility of bidirectional effects in the associations between the parent–child and sibling relationships in the ALSPAC study is clear. The data on both were collected at the same time point, and we know that conflict between siblings is a powerful precipitant of conflict between children and their parents, as well as vice versa. In parallel, friendly and affectionate relations between siblings could, in principle, lead to parents being less irritable and negative in their interactions with each of their children as individuals.

A note of caution should be sounded about the possibility of "compensatory" effects in the pattern of family relationships. The path models for both older and younger siblings indicate that there were significant links between mother–partner hostility and positivity between siblings (path d in Figure 10.2). These echo the findings of Engfer (1988) that warm sibling relationships may develop in families with disharmonious mother–partner relationships; Jenkins's (1992) study indicated that such warm sibling relationships can provide significant sources for support in families with high conflict between mothers and their partners.

Patterns of Relationships in Stepfamilies

Increasing numbers of families in Europe and the United States do not fit the traditional family structure of two married parents and their biological children (see also Fine, Chapter 14). Stepfamilies, for instance, are increasingly common, and can include stepfathers, stepmothers, siblings who share one parent (half siblings) or who have no parent in common (stepsiblings), as well as full siblings. Do the patterns of relationships among partners, parents, and siblings we have described so far hold for these families – who have frequently experienced major disruption and social and financial stresses as well as changes in structure?

First, it should be noted that siblings are reported in some studies of stepfamilies to be more negative toward each other than in nondivorced families. Thus in Hetherington's series of studies more rivalry and less positive sibling relationships were found in stepfamilies (Hetherington, 1988; Hetherington, 1989; Hetherington, 1993; Hetherington & Clingempeel, 1992; Hetherington & Jodl, 1994), while in the ALSPAC study, older siblings in stepfamilies were more negative to their younger siblings than those in nonstepfamilies, and younger siblings in nonstepfamilies were less negative than those in complex or blended stepfamilies (those in which both adult partners brought children from previous relationships to the family) (Dunn et al., 1998). We know that the range of social and economic stresses that are faced by divorced and remarried families can contribute to the impact of family transitions on children's adjustment outcome (e.g., McLanahan & Booth, 1989), and these may also play a contributory role in the poor sibling relations – a point to which we will return.

In addition, there is the possibility that the links among partners' relationships, parent–child relationships, and sibling relations differ in these different family settings. In 1988, Hetherington reported a striking finding: In the families with stepfathers that she studied, positive qualities in the mother–stepfather relationships were associated with *high levels of negativity in parent–child relationships* (both mother–child and stepfather–child relations). This is, as we have seen, in direct contrast with the patterns found in nonstepfamilies. In a very different study of stepfamilies, in which 50 adults who had grown up in stepfamilies described and reflected on their childhood family experiences, Gorrell Barnes and her colleagues make a similar point concerning the significance of mother–partner relations for parent–child relationships (Gorell Barnes, Thompson, Daniel, & Burchardt, 1998). In contrast, Fine and Kurdek (1995) report findings from the National Survey of Families and Households (Sweet, Bumpass, & Call, 1988) suggesting that the relation of perceived marital quality and the perceived quality of stepparent–stepchild relationships was similar in direction to that in nonstepfamilies, but stronger than the relation between perceived marital quality and quality of the biological parent–child relationships. Bray and Berger (1993) noted in their longitudinal study of stepfamilies that while marital relationships were significant predictors of parent–child interactions, these associations were moderated by family group, and some relations varied with the length of the remarriage. Given these interesting and varied findings, we investigated the possibility that the patterns of relations shown in Figures 10.1 and 10.2 would differ in nonstep and stepfather families within the large-scale ALSPAC data set, and two general points stand out from the analyses (which are reported in detail in Dunn et al., 1999).

First, in general, the models for the prediction of sibling relations were similar in the nonstep and stepfamilies in terms of the patterns of associations and variance explained. So, for instance, parent-child negativity (path b in Figures 10.1 and 10.2) was importantly related to sibling outcome measures in both types of family. However, the second point is that there was an interesting difference between the paths linking mother–partner relations and parent–child relations in the two types of family. Specifically, in stepfather families, the path from interparental hostility to parent–child negativity (path a in Figures 10.1 and 10.2) was not significant in models predicting either older sibling positivity or negativity, in contrast to the paths found in nonstepfamilies. This difference in the links between interparental and parent–child relations was significant for the two family types. We did not find that there was a difference in the links with *positive* interpartner relations – that is, the results did not parallel those of Hetherington and her colleagues; however, the findings of both studies remind us that we should not assume that the associations between family relationships established in research on families with two biological parents will be found in families which do not conform to this structure, a point also stressed by Gorrell Barnes and her colleagues (Gorell Barnes et al., 1998).

To investigate the possible contributory role of socioeconomic adversities in the prediction of sibling relations in stepfamilies, we included a measure of income in the models we tested, and found that financial resources were more important in relation to children's behaviour toward their siblings in stepfather families than in nonstepfamilies. It remains likely that among other family settings, too, such as single-parent families, the socioeconomic stresses faced by the families contribute to the hostility and conflict within family relationships (Dunn et al., 1998).

Developmental Issues

To what extent do the patterns of family relationships change as children grow up? We should be cautious about generalizing from studies of families with young siblings to those with children in middle childhood or early adolescence, for several reasons. First, the sibling relationship may change over time in quality and intensity and in the balance of friendliness and hostility (it is often a relationship characterized by very mixed emotions). Studies of sibling relationships indicate that with increasing age, siblings tend to show not only less hostility but also less friendly behavior toward their siblings (see Buhrmester & Furman, 1990; Dunn et al., 1999). And developmental changes in the expression of intense negative emotions toward siblings are marked during early childhood (Dunn, Creps, & Brown, 1996). While there is evidence for considerable continuity in individual differences in sibling relations, there is also evidence for change, and transitions in family circumstances – such as negative life events – are implicated in such changes (Dunn et al., 1994b). Second, parent–child relationships are also likely to change as children grow up, especially as they reach adolescence. And third, it is possible that the links between these relationships also show changes with age. We would certainly expect that processes of appraisal of family relationships, which are linked to later adjustment (Harold et al., 1997) increase in significance after the early childhood period (see Grych, Seid, & Fincham, 1992). It seems quite plausible that such processes would be linked to changes in the quality of sibling relationships, and assessing this possibility would be a useful direction for future research.

Implications for Future Research and Methodological Issues

The research to date has highlighted just how important it is for the prediction of sibling relationships to include a focus on the relationship between the adult partners in the family. It has also raised a host of questions about what processes maybe implicated. Studies of stepfamilies and divorced parents have shown us that these family patterns may differ for different family settings and have raised the issue of how social and economic adversities contribute to different family patterns. But the gaps in what we know about the links between interparental conflict and sibling relationships are clear. The following stand out:

- We lack key information on the developmental questions – how the patterns of associations linking parents' and siblings' relationships change or show stability as children grow up, and whether the processes implicated in the connections change.
- The issue of whether the links between family relationships differ in different cultural and community groups remains relatively unexplored (see Chase-Lansdale, Gordon, Coley, Wakschlag, & Brooks-Gunn, 1999, for an exception, and McLoyd et al., Chapter 4.)
- We know very little about how father–child relationships may differ from mother–child relationships in the pattern of associations within family networks and what their implications are for sibling relationships (see Volling & Belsky, 1992). Many studies either focus on mothers or combine mother and father information into parent composites, which are useful and appropriate for answering some questions, but leave us uncertain of how we should generalize across parents. The question of whether fathers view and report interparental conflict and parent–child and sibling relationships in ways that differ from mothers needs to be considered, as

does the issue of whether fathers' reports of family relationships explain differences in children's sibling relationships independently of mothers' reports. In our longitudinal study of a subsample of families from ALSPAC we found that both father–child and mother–child negativity independently explained variance in children's internalizing and externalizing problems (Davies et al., submitted).

- We have some information for families with adolescents on the significance of the genetic relatedness between parent and child (Hetherington et al., in press) for parent–child relationships, but as yet know little about the contribution of genetics to differences in the quality of sibling relationships, especially in early and middle childhood. Yet this may well be a key factor in accounting for the marked variation in how siblings get along within stepfamilies.

In addition to these gaps in information from research, it is notable that there are inconsistencies in the results of those relatively few studies that have investigated the marital, parent–child, and sibling relationships. How far are these related to different research strategies – and what are the lessons we can learn from a consideration of the inconsistent findings? The methods of the studies vary, as do the samples on which they are based, and such differences may account for some of the lack of agreement in the details of the findings. For example, as we have seen, several studies report that positive aspects of the sibling relationship are linked to positive aspects of the relationship between parents and negatively to the conflict between parents (e.g., Brody et al., 1994; Dunn et al., 1999; Hetherington et al., in press; Stocker et al., 1997). Yet in Erel and colleagues' study (1998), which employed brief observations of young siblings together, no links were found between positive aspects of the marital, parent–child, and sibling relationships. One possibility is that 10-minute observations are not likely to reveal representative differences in the affectionate, positive aspects of young children's sibling relationships. (After 20 years of studying siblings with a variety of observational and interview techniques, this appears to us to be very likely.) Another possibility is that *father–child* relationships are of particular importance, and that studies that do not include fathers are at a disadvantage for understanding the influences on siblings' positive relations (see Davies et al., submitted; Volling & Belsky, 1992, for support for this position).

Erel, Margolin, and John (1998) raise an interesting issue concerning inconsistencies in the research findings on direct and indirect links between marital and sibling relationships. They suggest that studies reporting evidence for direct effects tend to examine children's short-term or immediate response to exposure to conflict (e.g., Cummings, Ballard, El-Sheikh, & Lake, 1991; O'Brien, Margolin, John, & Krueger, 1991), whereas those reporting indirect linkages examine the long-term effects of exposure to conflicted parental relations (e.g., Brody et al., 1994). Further, they propose that studies which investigate both direct and indirect links within a single-study design support the indirect model, whereas studies that support the direct effects model do not also investigate the possibility that indirect effects are operating. But as we have seen here, the study based on ALSPAC (Dunn et al., 1999) does in fact investigate both direct and indirect effects, and finds evidence for both, over a 4-year period. The general lesson is that if we are to make progress toward answering these difficult questions about the links between family relationships, we need research strategies that ideally combine experimental and interview methods, are longitudinal, and are designed to test for both direct and indirect processes of influence. If these studies are focused on young children, then the inclusion of naturalistic observation is an important added advantage, which gives us a window on siblings' emotional relations with one another. For sibling relationships – in which emotions play such a substantial part – this has particular significance.

REFERENCES

Anderson, E. R., Hetherington, E. M., Reiss, D., & Plomin, R. (1994). Parents' nonshared treatment of siblings and the development of social competence during adolescence. *Journal of Family Psychology, 8,* 303–320.

Bank, L., Patterson, G. R., & Reid, J. B. (1996). Negative sibling interaction as predictors of later adjustment problems in adolescent and young adult males. In G. H. Brody (Ed.), *Sibling relationships: Their causes and consequences* (pp. 197–229). Norwood, NJ: Ablex Publishing Corporation.

Bray, J. H., & Berger, S. H. (1993). Developmental issues in stepfamilies research project: Family relationships and parent-child interactions. *Journal of Family Psychology, 7,* 76–90.

Brody, G., Stoneman, Z., & Burke, M. (1987). Child temperaments, maternal differential behavior, and sibling relationships. *Developmental Psychology, 23,* 354–362.

Brody, G. H., Stoneman, Z., & McCoy, J. K. (1994). Forecasting sibling relationships in early adolescence from child temperaments and family processes in middle childhood. *Child Development, 65,* 771–784.

Brody, G., Stoneman, Z., McCoy, J. K., & Forehand, R. (1992). Contemporaneous and longitudinal associations of sibling conflict with family relationship assessments and family discussions about sibling problems. *Child Development, 63,* 391–400.

Buhrmester, D., & Furman, W. (1990). Perceptions of sibling relationships during middle childhood and adolescence. *Child Development, 61,* 1387–1398.

Chase-Lansdale, P. L., Gordon, R. A., Coley, R. L., Wakschlag, L. S., & Brooks-Gunn, J. (1999). Young African-American multigenerational families in poverty: The contexts, exchanges, and processes of their lives. In E. M. Hetherington (Ed.), *Coping with divorce, single parenting and remarriage: A risk and resiliency perspective.* Mahwah, NJ: Lawrence Erlbaum Associates.

Conger, R. D., Conger, K. J., Elder, G. H., Lorenz, F. O., Simons, R. L., & Whitbeck, L. B. (1992). Linking economic hardship to marital quality and instability. *Journal of Marriage and the Family, 52,* 643–656.

Conger, R. D., Conger, K. J., Elder, G. H., Lorenz, F. O., Simons, R. L., & Whitbeck, L. B. (1993). Family economic stress and adjustment of early adolescent girls. *Developmental Psychology, 29,* 206–219.

Conger, R. D., Ge, X., Elder, G. H., Lorenz, F. O., & Simons, R. L. (1994). Economic stress, coercive family process, and developmental problems of adolescence. *Child Development, 65,* 541–561.

Cummings, E. M., Ballard, M., El-Sheikh, M., & Lake, M. (1991). Resolution and children's responses to interadult anger. *Developmental Psychology, 27,* 462–470.

Cummings, E. M., & Cummings, J. S. (1988). A process-oriented approach to children's coping with adults' angry behavior. *Developmental Review, 8,* 296–321.

Cummings, E. M., & Davies, P. (1994). *Children and marital conflict: The impact of family dispute and resolution.* New York: Guilford.

Davies, L., Dunn, J., Pickering, K., O'Connor, T., Deater-Deckard, K., Golding, J., & the ALSPAC Study Team. (1999). *Fathers, mothers and children's adjustment: A comparison of step and non-step families.* Manuscript submitted for publication.

Deater-Deckard, K., Pickering, K., Dunn, J., Golding, J., & the ALSPAC Study Team. (1998). Family structure and depressive symptoms in men preceding and following the birth of a child. *The American Journal of Psychiatry, 155*(6), 818–823.

Dunn, J. (1988). *The beginnings of social understanding* (1st ed.). Cambridge, MA: Harvard University Press.

Dunn, J., Brown, J., Slomkowski, C., Tesla, C., & Youngblade, L. (1991). Young children's understanding of other people's feelings and beliefs: Individual differences and their antecedents. *Child Development, 62*(6), 1352–1366.

Dunn, J., Creps, C., & Brown, J. (1996). Children's family relationships between two and five: Developmental changes and individual differences. *Social Development, 5*(3), 230–250.

Dunn, J., Deater-Deckard, K., Pickering, K., Beveridge, M., & the ALSPAC Study Team. (1999). Siblings, parents and partners: Family relationships within a longitudinal community study. *Journal of Child Psychology and Psychiatry, 40,* 1025–1037.

Dunn, J., Deater-Deckard, K., Pickering, K., O'Connor, T., Golding, J., & the ALSPAC Study Team. (1998). Children's adjustment and pro-social behaviour in step-single and non-step family settings: Findings from a community study. *Journal of Child Psychology and Psychiatry, 39*(8), 1083–1095.

Dunn, J., & Kendrick, C. (1982). *Siblings: Love, envy and understanding*. London: Grant McIntyre, Ltd.

Dunn, J., & Munn, P. (1985). Becoming a family member: Family conflict and the development of social understanding in the second year. *Child Development, 56*, 764–774.

Dunn, J., & Plomin, R. (1990). *Separate lives: Why siblings are so different* (1st ed.). New York: Basic Books.

Dunn, J., Slomkowski, C., & Beardsall, L. (1994a). Sibling relationships from the preschool period through middle childhood and early adolescence. *Developmental Psychology, 30*(3), 315–324.

Dunn, J., Slomkowski, C., Beardsall, L., & Rende, R. (1994b). Adjustment in middle childhood and early adolescence: Links with earlier and contemporary sibling relationships. *Journal of Child Psychology and Psychiatry and Allied Disciplines, 35*(3), 491–504.

Emery, R. E. (1982). Interparental conflict and the children of discord and divorce. *Psychological Bulletin, 92*, 310–330.

Emery, R. E. (1988). *Marriage, adjustment and children's adjustment*. Newbury Park, CA: Sage.

Emery, R., & O'Leary, K. (1982). Children's perception of marital discord and behavior problems of boys and girls. *Journal of Abnormal Child Psychology, 10*, 11–24.

Engfer, A. (1988). The interrelatedness of marriage and the mother-child relationship. In R. A. Hinde & J. Stevenson-Hinde (Eds.), *Relationships within families: Mutual influences* (pp. 104–118). Oxford: Oxford University Press.

Erel, O., & Burman, B. (1995). Inter-relatedness of marital relations and parent-child relations: A meta-analytic review. *Psychological Bulletin, 118*, 108–132.

Erel, O., Margolin, G., & John, R. S. (1998). Observed sibling interaction: Links with the marital and the mother-child relationship. *Developmental Psychology, 34*(2), 288–298.

Fincham, F. D., & Osborne, L. (1993). Marital conflict and children: Retrospect and prospect. *Clinical Psychology Review, 13*, 75–88.

Fine, M. A., & Kurdek, L. A. (1995). Relation between marital quality and (step)parent-child relationship quality for parents and stepparents in stepfamilies. *Journal of Family Psychology, 9*, 216–223.

Gorell Barnes, G., Thompson, P., Daniel, G., & Burchardt, N. (1998). *Growing up in stepfamilies*. Oxford: Clarendon Press.

Gottman, J. M., & Katz, L. F. (1989). Effects of marital discord on young children's peer interaction and health. *Developmental Psychology, 25*, 373–381.

Grych, J. H., & Fincham, F. D. (1993). Children's appraisal of marital conflict: Initial investigations of the cognitive-contextual framework. *Child Development, 64*, 215–230.

Grych, J. H., Seid, M., & Fincham, F. D. (1992). Assessing marital conflict from the child's perspective: The Children's Perception of Interparental Conflict Scale. *Child Development, 63*, 558–572.

Harold, G. T., Fincham, F. D., Osborne, L. N., & Conger, R. D. (1997). Mom and Dad are at it again: Adolescents' perceptions of marital conflict and adolescent psychological distress. *Developmental Psychology, 33,* 333–350.

Hetherington, E. M. (1988). Parents, children and siblings: Six years after divorce. In R. A. Hinde & J. Stevenson-Hinde (Eds.), *Relationships within families: Mutual influences.* Oxford: Oxford University Press.

Hetherington, E. M. (1989). Coping with family transitions: Winners, losers, and survivors. *Child Development, 60,* 1–14.

Hetherington, E. M. (1993). An overview of the Virginia Longitudinal Study of Divorce and Remarriage: A focus on early adolescence. *Journal of Family Psychology, 7,* 39–56.

Hetherington, E. M., & Clingempeel, W. G. (1992). Coping with marital transitions: A family systems approach. *Monographs of the Society for Research in Child Development, 57*(2–3, Serial No. 227).

Hetherington, E. M., Henderson, S. H., Reiss, D., Anderson, E. R., O'Connor, T., Jodl, K. M., & Skaggs, M. J. (in press). Family functioning and adolescent adjustment of siblings in nondivorced families and diverse types of stepfamilies. *Monographs of the Society for Research in Child Development.*

Hetherington, E. M., & Jodl, K. M. (1994). Stepfamilies as settings for child development. In A. Booth & J. Dunn (Eds.), *Stepfamilies: Who benefits? Who does not* (pp. 55–79). Hillsdale, NJ: Lawrence Erlbaum Associates.

Howes, P., & Markman, H. (1989). Marital quality and child functioning: A longitudinal investigation. *Child Development, 60,* 1044–1051.

Howe, N., & Ross, H. (1990). Socialization, perspective-taking, and the sibling relationship. *Developmental Psychology, 26,* 160–165.

Jenkins, J. M. (1992). Sibling relationships in disharmonious homes: Potential difficulties and protective effects. In F. Boer & J. Dunn (Eds.), *Children's sibling relationships: Developmental and clinical issues.* Hillsdale, NJ: Lawrence Erlbaum Associates.

Jenkins, J., & Smith, M. A. (1990). Factors protecting children in disharmonious homes: Maternal reports. *Journal of the American Academy of Child and Adolescent Psychiatry, 29,* 60–69.

Johnston, J. R., Gonzales, R., & Campbell, L. E. (1987). Ongoing post-divorce conflict and child disturbance. *Journal of Abnormal Child Psychology, 15,* 497–509.

Lewis, C., Freeman, N. H., Kyriakidou, C., Maridaki-Kassotaki, K., & Berridge, D. M. (1996). Social influences on false belief access: Specific sibling influences or general apprenticeship? *Child Development, 67,* 2930–2947.

MacKinnon, C. (1989). An observational investigation of sibling interactions in married and divorced families. *Developmental Psychology, 25,* 36–44.

MacKinnon-Lewis, C., Starnes, R., Volling, B., & Johnson, S. (1997). Perceptions of parenting as predictors of boys' sibling and peer relations. *Developmental Psychology, 33,* 1024–1031.

McLanahan, S., & Booth, K. (1989). Mother-only families: Problems, prospects, and politics. *Journal of Marriage and the Family, 51,* 557–580.

O'Brien, M., Margolin, G., John, R. S., & Krueger, L. (1991). Mothers' and sons' cognitive and emotional reactions to simulated marital and family conflict. *Journal of Consulting and Clinical Psychology, 59,* 692–703.

O'Connor, T. G., Hawkins, N., Dunn, J., Thorpe, K., & Golding, J. (1998). Family type and maternal depression in pregnancy: Factors mediating risk in a community sample. *Journal of Marriage and the Family, 60*(3), 757–770.

Patterson, G. R. (1986). The contribution of siblings to training for fighting: A microsocial analysis. In D. Olweus, J. Block, & M. Radke-Yarrow (Eds.), *Development of antisocial and prosocial behavior* (pp. 235–261). New York: Academic Press.

Reiss, D., Neiderheiser, J. M., Hetherington, E. M., & Plomin, R. (in press). *The relationship code.* Cambridge, MA: Harvard University Press.

Stocker, C., Ahmed, K., & Stall, M. (1997). Marital satisfaction and maternal emotional expressiveness: Links with children's sibling relationships. *Social Development, 6,* 373–385.

Stocker, C., Dunn, J., & Plomin, R. (1989). Sibling relationships: Links with child temperament, maternal behavior, and family structure. *Child Development, 60*(3), 715–727.

Sweet, J. A., Bumpass, L. L., & Call, V. R. A. (1988). *The design and content of the National Survey of Families and Households.* Madison, WI: University of Wisconsin, Center for Demography and Ecology.

Volling, B. L., & Belsky, J. (1992). The contribution of mother-child and father-child relationships to the quality of sibling interaction: A longitudinal study. *Child Development, 63,* 1209–1222.

Zahn-Waxler, C., & Radke-Yarrow, M. (1982). The development of altruism: Alternative research strategies. In N. Eisenberg (Ed.), *The development of prosocial behavior.* New York: Academic Press.

11 Managing Marital Conflict: Links with Children's Peer Relationships

Ross D. Parke, Mina Kim, Mary Flyr,
David J. McDowell, Sandra D. Simpkins,
Colleen M. Killian, and Margaret Wild

In recent years there has been an increasing recognition of the association between marital conflict and children's adjustment (Fincham, 1998; Grych & Fincham, 1990). In spite of the increase of attention to the effects of familial conflict on children's functioning, there has been little attention devoted to children's competence with peers. The goal of this chapter is to address this relatively unexplored issue of the links between marital conflict and children's peer relationships.

Importance of Examining Links between Marital Conflict and Peer Relationships

Understanding children's social competence with peers as an outcome of marital conflict is critical for several reasons. First, the correlates and predictive associations of social incompetence (including truancy, school dropout, and criminality) have been well documented (Parker & Asher, 1987). Second, as Wasserstein and La Greca (1996) found in their investigation of marital discord and peer support among children in middle childhood, children's close friendships moderate the negative effects of marital discord. This finding highlights the importance of understanding the links between marital discord and children's peer relationships. Third, although most past research in this area has used unitary measures of child adjustment (e.g., internalizing or externalizing problems), these global evaluations need to be complemented by more specific indices in order to identify particular outcomes that may be more proximal or distal to particular aspects of marital conflict (Grych & Fincham, 1990). These global problems may, in fact, be associated with peer relationships, but there is little research that has investigated how children from families high in marital conflict are perceived socially by their peers and teachers and their level of acceptance in peer contexts. Specifically, children exhibiting internalizing and externalizing problems either act out in the classroom or withdraw from social interaction, which impact their level of social acceptance and competence. Social maladjustment, in turn, may instigate further internalizing and externalizing symptoms that result in a cyclic pattern of behavior and interactions that have implications not only for further interactions with peers but family interactions as well.

Theoretical Assumptions

Interparental conflict is only one source of family influence and to fully appreciate how family conflict may impact children's peer relationships, a family systems perspective is valuable. According to this viewpoint, the various relationships within the family including parent–child, sib–sib, and parent–sibling need to be considered as well as interparental conflict, and the interdependence among these family subsystems needs to be recognized (Parke, 1988; Dunn, 1993). Consistent with this perspective is the commonly made distinction between direct or witnessed and indirect effects of interparental conflict on children's functioning (Fincham, 1998). These two perspectives – direct effects model and indirect effects model – serve as a theoretical guide for this chapter. According to the direct effects model (Figure 11.1), children's exposure to marital conflict will have an impact on their peer relationships; we propose that these direct effects of marital conflict on peer competence are, in part, mediated by two sets of intervening processes: (1) children's perspectives of conflict and (2) emotional regulation. According to the indirect effects model (Figure 11.2), marital conflict alters children's peer outcomes by modifying the nature of parent–child interaction. In addition, the link between the parent–child relationship and peer outcomes is mediated by children's emotion regulatory abilities.

Direct Effects of Marital Conflict on Children's Peer Relationships

Theoretical Perspectives

This section is devoted to discussing the mechanisms that have been proposed by which children are directly impacted by overt marital conflict. In the following section we will explore the indirect paths by which children are at risk for maladjustment, such as through parenting practices and the parent–child relationship. The processes that have

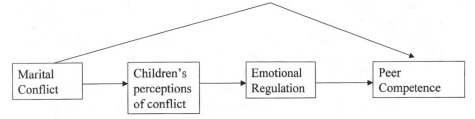

Figure 11.1. Direct effects model of the relation of marital conflict to peer competence (modified from Grych & Fincham, 1990).

been proposed to link marital conflict and child adjustment include
modeling (Cummings, Iannotti, & Zahn-Waxler, 1985; Emery &
O'Leary, 1982), emotional stress (Cummings & Davies, 1994), children's
understanding and appraisal of conflict (Grych & Fincham, 1990), and
children's sense of emotional security (Davies & Cummings, 1994).

According to the modeling hypothesis (Emery & O'Leary, 1982),
marital conflict may impact children's peer relationships by exposure
to frequent bouts of conflict exhibited by parents in the presence of the
child. Furthermore, parents in discordant and unsatisfying marriages
may demonstrate greater and more maladaptive levels of anger that
the child may imitate in negotiating conflicts with peers. Through
observations of interparental conflict, children learn about interpersonal relationships and perhaps become less inhibited in using particular strategies such as aggression in dealing with distressing situations.
Overt marital conflict also serves as a stressor for children. Exposure to
conflict may cause children to regress to earlier, immature strategies
such as aggression in order to cope with distressing situations
(Cummings & Davies, 1994).

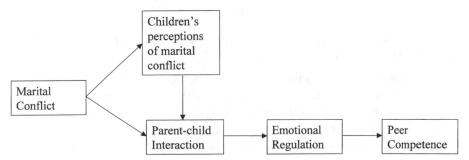

Figure 11.2. Indirect effects model of the relation between marital conflict and peer
competence.

The cognitive-contextual framework (Grych and Fincham, 1990) emphasizes the need to understand the properties of conflict (frequency, intensity, duration, resolution), the child's processing of conflict (both a general evaluation of threat level as well as specific attributions of cause and blame), and the overall context of conflict, including the child's experiential history with marital disputes, the child's perception of family relationships, and the child's temperament, gender, and mood. Dimensions at all three levels (characteristics associated with conflict, context, and child) will dictate children's coping responses (see Figure 11.1).

The emotional security hypothesis proposed by Davies and Cummings (1994) states that children actively work toward maintaining a sense of emotional well-being that guides their reactions to parental conflict. This sense of security derives from and may be either enhanced or undermined by both the parent–child relationship (specifically, the parent–child attachment relationship) and the marital relationship. Both types of relationships either contribute to or threaten family cohesion and harmony. Emotional security or insecurity directly affects children's coping efficacy and their abilities in emotional regulation via a number of processes, such as persistent and intense arousal that may impair emotional regulatory abilities. Another process linking emotional security to effective coping and regulation is the child's attempts to regulate parental conflict either directly by intervening during marital disputes or indirectly through detracting parental attention from marital conflict by engaging in problem behaviors. Furthermore, children's internal working models of self and social relationships stemming from attachment relationships as well as the child's experiences with past conflict alter future reactions to parental discord. In a recent test of the emotional security hypothesis, Davies and Cummings (1998) found that the specific component processes of emotional reactivity and internal representations did indeed mediate the relationship between marital discord and child adjustment.

Review of Research on Direct Links between Marital Conflict and Peer Relationships

As noted in the introduction, most work has focused on global measures of child adjustment, and little information is available concerning the impact of marital conflict on children's peer relationships. To fill this gap, Long, Forehand, Fauber, and Brody (1987) examined the relationship between marital conflict and recent divorce with self-perceived and independently observed social and cognitive competence among adolescents. Both independently observed and teacher-evaluated cognitive and social competence were related to high levels of marital conflict. Specifically, children from high-conflict homes were rated by their teachers as less socially competent and as having more conduct problems. Data taken from the observational measures indicated high conflict to be significantly related to poor problem-solving skills.

Similarly, Snyder, Klein, Gdowski, Faulstich, and LaCombe (1988) found that marital distress was associated with social skills deficits among children and adolescents. Parents' reports of their dissatisaction with the parent–child relationship as well as marital conflict over child-rearing practices emerged as the most powerful correlates of children's social skills deficits. Neither a global assessment of marital conflict nor conflict in areas other than childrearing emerged as significant correlates of children's emotional and behavioral problems.

As reviewed in this volume and elsewhere (Cummings & Davies, 1994), a major modifier of the effects of marital conflict on children's adjustment is the manner in which the conflict is resolved. Other support for the direct links between parental marital conflict resolution style and children's peer relationships comes from a recent study by Lindahl, Clements, and Markman (1998). Mothers' use of negative conflict resolution strategies in their marital relationship before the child's birth predicted children's poorer peer relations at 5 years of age. The fact that these relations were across both time and context is particularly impressive.

Recent Findings from the UCR Social Development Project

With the exception of the study conducted by Long et al. (1987), few researchers in this area have utilized multiagent reports of children's competence. To accurately assess children's social competence in a variety of contexts, multiple raters must be incorporated in future studies. As those individuals who are in daily contact with children from discordant marriages are likely to be classmates, there must be an incorporation of sociometric ratings and/or nominations in order to assess children's functioning in the school setting. Recent efforts in our lab have incorporated both peer and teacher ratings of children's social competence in order to illuminate the marital-conflict–child-social-outcome relationship. Two recent sets of analyses shed new light on the relations between marital conflict and children's peer relationships.

The Relationship between Marital Conflict and Children's Peer Relationships. As a first step, the issue of whether marital conflict is related to poorer peer relationships was addressed. A study by O'Neil, Parke, Flyr, and Wild (1999) examined links between marital conflict and interparental communication styles on emotional regulatory abilities and cognitive representations of parent–child relations that then influence peer group social relationships of children in early adolescence. Fifty families and their sixth-grade children (34 boys; 26 girls) participated. Marital communication and conflict management style was observed during a problem-solving procedure developed by Hooven, Rushe, and Gottman (1988). Measures of peer and teacher rated behavioral characteristics were used to index children's social competence.

Results revealed that more negative paternal problem-solving strategies were associated with greater peer-rated avoidance and lower teacher-rated acceptance. Similarly, when mothers exhibited better problem-solving skills, adolescents were rated as less avoidant by peers. Poorer maternal problem-solving and communication strategies were linked to teacher ratings of less social engagement. These findings confirm our anticipated link between marital conflict and children's peer relationships. Although the links between conflict and peer relationships are clear, this represents only the first step. Although it is plausible that modeling of parental conflictful tactics for solving disagreements may, in part, account for the findings, this is unlikely to be the only process. As Grych and Fincham (1990) argue, children's perceptions of marital conflict may serve as a mediator; in addition, emotional regulatory abilities may be a further mediating process that could, in part, account for the marital-conflict–social-outcome relation. In the next section, we explore these possibilities (see Figure 11.1).

Potential Mediators between Marital Conflict and Children's Peer Competence. To assess factors that may be possible mediators between parental conflict and peer competence, two assessments were made, namely children's perceptions of marital conflict and children's emotional regulatory abilities. First, we examined the relation between indices of marital conflict and children's perception of interparental conflict. Kim, Parke, and O'Neil (1999) obtained parental reports of marital conflict using the O'Leary-Porter Scale, while children's reports of marital conflict were obtained using an adapted version of Grych, Seid, and Fincham's (1992) "Children's Perceptions of Interparental Conflict Scale." Children's reports on this measure correlated with parents' reports of marital conflict in both grades 5 and 6, which is consistent with previous work (Grych & Fincham, 1990). Moreover, mothers and fathers agree on the amount of conflict at both assessment points. In a second set of analyses, O'Neil et al. (1999) examined the relations between observations of marital communication and conflict management and children's perceptions of interparental conflict. Using the grade 6 sample, results showed that when fathers expressed more negative affect during discussion of a marital disagreement, adolescents reported more frequent and intense interparental conflict. When fathers used more negative problem-solving strategies (e.g., hostility, denial, disruptive process), adolescents reported more intense interparental conflict. In contrast, when fathers used better problem-solving strategies (e.g., negotiation, listener responsiveness), adolescents reported less frequent and less intense conflict. Less perceived personal threat and greater resolution also was associated with interparental conflict. Mothers' observed communication and conflict management strategies were virtually unrelated to adolescents' perceptions of interparental conflict. Together, these two sets of analyses suggest a reliable relation between both self-report and observed indices of parental marital conflict and children's perceptions of marital conflict.

As a next step in the evaluation of the model, we examined the relation between children's perceptions of marital conflict and children's competence with peers. Kim et al. (1999) examined this issue across a 2-year period (grades 5 and 6). Both concurrent and predictive analyses revealed that the frequency of parental conflict and the content of marital conflict, specifically, children's perception that they were the source of the conflict, yielded the most robust relations with children's social competence. Teacher ratings of disruptive behavior in grade 5 were associated with frequent parental conflict and children's self-blame for parental conflict. In addition, the frequency of conflict and children's self-blame were associated with teacher ratings of verbal and physical aggression. In grade 6, frequent parental conflict was associated with teacher ratings of shy behavior and sadness, while children's self-blame was related to a host of negative outcomes, including peer ratings of dislike, verbal and physical aggression, and peer and teacher ratings of excluding behavior. Children's self-blame was negatively associated with peer ratings of friendliness and peer and teacher ratings of prosocial behavior. Furthermore, children's perception of the frequency of parental conflict in fifth grade was associated with sixth-grade peer ratings of excluding behavior. In addition, the content of conflict or children's self-blame in grade 5 was associated with both peer and teacher ratings of sadness, peer ratings of physical aggression, and teacher ratings of excluding behaviors in grade 6. In sum, there are clear relations among parental reports of marital conflict, children's perception of marital conflicts, and children's peer competence.

According to our model, children who perceive high levels of marital conflict may, in turn, have more difficulty in their self-regulation of emotion. According to prior research, this ability is an important correlate of children's peer competence (Parke & O'Neil, 1997; Eisenberg &

Fabes, 1994). Moreover, Cummings and Davies (1994) suggest that emotional reactivity in response to conflict may, in fact, mediate the links between marital conflict and child outcomes. In a direct test of the model, Davies and Cummings (1998) assessed the links among children's emotional security, the level of destructive and constructive marital functioning, and children's internalizing and externalizing behaviors. As predicted by the emotional security model, the links between marital discord and children's internalizing symptoms were mediated by measures of emotional security.

In our lab, we (O'Neil et al., 1999) have provided a further evaluation of the relation between marital conflict and children's emotional regulatory abilities. Children's emotion regulatory ability was measured by a self-report index of emotional reactivity and strategies for coping with emotional upset (Eisenberg & Fabes, 1994). We found several linkages between marital communication and conflict management style with children's regulation of emotion. The rate and tone of the mother's verbal and listening behaviors with her spouse were inversely related to children's reports of displayed anger. In addition, mom's willingness to negotiate with her husband to settle differences were positively related to a child's feelings of security and decreases in feelings of anxiety. Finally, a child's calm response to situations related to a less intrusive maternal communication style in her marriage. These analyses also revealed relations between the rate and tone of the father's listener responsiveness, positive mood, and involvement in problem solving with his spouse and to a child's report of displayed anger. In addition, a child's calm response to situations was positively related to the rate of a father's verbal engagement in the marriage.

These data are consistent with earlier work that suggests a link between marital conflict and children's emotional regulatory abilities. As in prior studies, fathers' as well as mothers' style of dealing with marital conflict was related to children's emotional regulatory abilities (Katz & Gottman, 1993).

The Relation between Emotional Regulatory Ability and Children's Peer Competence. Several recent theorists have suggested that these emotional competence skills are, in turn, linked to social competence with peers (Denham, 1998; Eisenberg & Fabes, 1994; Parke, 1994). Research from our lab supports the relation between emotional regulation and social competence. In our study, 105 fourth-grade children (53 boys, 52 girls) responded to a series of vignettes representing situations that might generate anger, frustration, or excitement. Measures of children's level of emotional reactivity and their modes of response and regulation (e.g., be angry, be sad, distract themselves, be nervous or fidgety, or understand why) were obtained. Children who reported greater emotional reactivity are described by peers and teachers as less prosocial and more aggressive or disruptive, while children who report using temper tantrums and displays of anger to cope with emotional upset are less socially accepted by peers and viewed as less prosocial by both peers and teachers. Clearly, children's ability to manage emotions in a constructive fashion may be an important correlate of their social acceptance and social competence (see Denham, 1998; Eisenberg & Fabes, 1994). Children who are less emotionally reactive and who respond with less anger and more positive coping strategies are more socially competent. The role of child gender remains unclear and warrants further attention.

Summary

In this section we have outlined a direct effects model of the relations between marital conflict and children's peer relationships. Two mediating mechanisms were proposed – children's perceptions of marital conflict and children's emotional regulatory abilities – that may, in part, account for the links between marital conflict and children's peer relationships. Several issues remain to be examined. First, the work reported here represents a partial and incomplete test of the model. Path analytic or LISREL approaches would provide the opportunity to test the overall model. This step is critical since it is unclear whether children's perceptions of marital conflict and emotional regulation are independent mediators or are themselves part of the causal chain outlined in the model. Specifically, it may be that children's perceptions, in turn, modify children's emotional regulatory strategies, which subsequently modify children's social relationships with peers.

In addition, a variety of other "affect management skills" (Parke, Burks, Carson, & Cassidy, 1992) beyond emotional regulation are probably serving as mediators between marital conflict and children's peer competence. Prior work in our lab (Parke, et al., 1992; Parke, Burks, Carson, Neville, & Boyum, 1994; Parke & O'Neil, 1999) and elsewhere (see Denham, 1998) have suggested that encoding and decoding of emotion, as well as cognitive understanding of the causes and consequences of emotion are linked to peer competence. In addition, evidence suggests that these affect management skills are probably learned in the context of family interaction. To date, little attention has been devoted to an examination of the direct relations between marital conflict and these aspects of children's emotional management and emotional understanding.

Indirect Effects Model of Marital Conflict and Children's Peer Competence

As outlined in Figure 11.2, the impact of marital conflict on children's adjustment is not only direct, but indirect as well. According to this model, marital conflict is an indirect influence on children's adjustment which operates through its effect on family functioning and the quality of parenting (Fauber & Long, 1991). Factors such as affective changes in the quality of the parent–child relationship, lack of emotional availability, and adoption of less optimal parenting styles each have been implicated as potential mechanisms through which marital discord disrupts parenting processes. However, as argued elsewhere, conceptualizing indirect effects as involving only parent–child interaction patterns may be too narrow a framing of the possible ways in which parents influence their children's social-emotional development, including their peer relationships. Briefly we (Parke et al., 1994) have categorized these pathways into three components, namely, parent–child interaction, parents as direct advisors or social coaches, and parents as gatekeepers who regulate opportunities for social interaction with others outside the family. Each of these components is described briefly in the next section, followed by examples from our own research that illuminate these indirect pathways that affect children's social competence.

Review of Research

Parent Modes of Influence and Children's Peer Relationships. Parental influence is exerted through parental childrearing practices and styles of interaction, and, in turn, these practices are related to peer competence. First, we will examine the links between the parent–child relationship and peer competence and then research that suggests that the nature of the quality of the parent–child relationship is, in part, determined by the quality of the marital relationship.

Research on the links between parent–child interaction and peer relationships is based on the assumption that face-to-face interaction may provide the opportunity to learn, rehearse, and refine social skills that are common to successful social interaction with peers. This work has yielded several conclusions (for fuller discussion of this work, see Parke & O'Neil, 1997). First, the nature of the style of the interaction between parent and child is linked to peer outcomes. Consistent with Baumrind's (1973) early classic studies which found that authoritative parenting was related to positive peer outcomes, more recent studies have confirmed that parents who are responsive, warm, engaging, and synchronous are more likely to have children who are more accepted by their peers (Harrist, Pettit, Dodge, & Bates, 1994). In contrast, parents who are hostile, overcontrolling, and express negative affect have children who experience more difficulty with agemates (MacDonald & Parke, 1984; Boyum & Parke, 1995; Carson & Parke, 1996). Family interaction patterns not only relate to concurrent peer relationships, but cross-time relationships as well (Barth & Parke, 1993; Isley, O'Neil, & Parke, 1996).

Learning about relationships through interaction with parents can be viewed as an indirect pathway since the goal is often not explicitly to influence children's social relationships with extrafamilial partners such as peers. In contrast, parents may influence children's relationships directly in their role as a direct instructor, educator, or advisor. In this role, parents may explicitly set out to educate their children concerning appropriate ways of initiating and maintaining social relationships (see Parke & O'Neil, 1997). Direct parental influence in the form of supervision and advice giving can significantly increase the interactive competence of young children and illustrate the utility of examining direct parental strategies as a way of teaching children about social relationships. Parents influence their children's social relationships as well by providing opportunities for children to form social ties and practice social contact with extrafamilial social partners. This management can assume several forms, including parental monitoring, parental initiation of contact between their own children and play partners, and parental facilitation of children's participation in unstructured or organized peer activities (see Parke & O'Neil, 1997).

To date, there has been only limited attention paid to the impact of marital conflict on either parents as advisors or parents as providers of opportunities. Our own research has failed to detect a relation between marital conflict, parental monitoring, or parental supervision. This null set of findings may be due to the fact that our sample was not selected to represent extremes in marital conflict. Moreover, in light of the links between stress, single parenthood, divorce, and monitoring (e.g., Forgatch, Patterson, & Ray, 1996), it would be worthwhile to examine directly the relations between marital conflict and the subsequent impairment of parental management of children's social lives. It is anticipated that marital conflict would result in deterioration of social networks, less involvement of children in extrafamilial social activities, and less active and effective monitoring.

The Relation between Marital Interaction or Conflict and Parenting Behavior. In this section, we examine the links between marital conflict and parent–child interaction. Katz and Kahen (1993) found that when parents used a mutually hostile pattern of conflict resolution, fathers were more likely to be intrusive and children were more likely to express anger during a parent–child interaction task. In addition, fathers' intrusiveness predicted more negative peer play and more aggressive play with a best friend. Interestingly, this study also suggests that an individual parent's style of handling conflict may be related to the quality of the *partner's* relationships with children in the family. When fathers were angry and withdrawn in a conflict resolution task, mothers were more critical and intrusive during interactions with their child. Maternal criticism and intrusiveness, in turn, was associated with unresponsiveness or "tuning out" by the child during mother–child interactions and also with higher levels of teacher-rated internalizing symptoms. Similarly, Cowan, Cowan, Schulz, and Hemming (1994) examined the influence of marital quality on children's social adaptation to kindergarten with results suggesting evidence of both direct and indirect links to children's social adjustment. Interestingly, internalizing difficulties (e.g., shy or withdrawn qualities) were predicted by the influences of marital functioning on parenting quality, whereas externalizing difficulties (e.g., aggressive or antisocial qualities) were predicted directly by qualities of marital interaction.

Family systems theory suggests that not only does marital discord interfere with dimensions of the mother–child or father–child relationship, it also may impair qualities of the mother–father–child triadic relationship by interfering with the effectiveness of how the mother and father work together with the child. In a study that examined the contribution of marital adjustment to the effectiveness of joint mother–father supportiveness, Westerman and Schonholtz (1993) found that fathers', but not mothers', reports of marital disharmony and disaffection were significantly related to the effectiveness of joint parental support toward their children's problem-solving efforts. Joint parental support was, in turn, related to fathers' and teachers' reports of children's behavior problems. Men's lack of involvement in the triadic family process could account for these findings, since women tend to engage and confront, while men tend to withdraw, in the face of marital disharmony (Gottman, 1994).

Evidence from the UCR Social Development Project

To shed further light on the links between marital relationships, parent–child interaction, and peer outcomes was the goal of a recent set of analyses by McDowell, Parke, and Wang (1999). As described earlier, third-grade children and their mothers and fathers participated in a family discussion task involving common family problems (e.g., privacy, homework, money). Parental controlling behavior and disruptive and facilitative parental behaviors were coded as well as the misbehavior and coerciveness of the child. Children of parents who use a controlling or directive interactive style are rated as less competent by their peers. In turn, the level of marital satisfaction (assessed by the Locke-Wallace Scale) was related to the child's behavior during the family interaction task. Mothers who had higher marital satisfaction were found to have lower levels of disruptiveness in the task and higher levels of effectiveness. In turn, maternal disruptiveness in the family interaction was related to the children's social competence. Mothers who were more disruptive had children who were rated as more negative and less positive by peers. Furthermore, fathers who reported less marital satisfaction were more likely to have a child who was coercive or misbehaving during the family interaction.

While it is critical to recognize that this global measure of marital satisfaction is not a substitute for more specific measures of marital conflict (Fincham, 1998), the pattern of our findings suggests that triadic interaction patterns are related to both levels of marital satisfaction and to children's peer competence. As suggested by a family systems perspective, parents in dissatisfied marital relationships may, in turn, express some of their negativity toward their children, which, in turn, interferes with the development of their peer competence. The value of examining the role of parental marital conflict in family interaction contexts is underscored by these preliminary findings.

Potential Mediators

Recent research suggests that parental support and acceptance of children's emotions is related to children's ability to manage emotions in a constructive fashion. It is assumed that the same emotional regulatory processes will be operative in the indirect as well as the direct model. For example, parental comforting of children when they experience negative emotion has been linked with constructive anger reactions (Eisenberg & Fabes, 1994). Similarly, parental willingness to discuss emotions with their children is related to children's awareness and understanding of others' emotions (Dunn & Brown, 1994; Denham, 1998).

This pattern of findings is consistent with recent work by Gottman, Katz, and Hooven (1996) on parents' emotion philosophy, or metaemotion. By *metaemotion* these researchers refer to parents' emotions about their own and their children's emotions; metaemotion structure refers to an organized set of thoughts, a philosophy, and an approach to one's own emotions and to one's children's emotions. In a longitudinal analysis, Gottman et al. (1996) found that fathers' acceptance and assistance with their children's sadness and anger at 5 years of age was related to higher social competence with peers at 8 years of age.

Other evidence supports the role that chronic, intense marital conflict plays in undermining children's emotion regulatory abilities. Gottman and Katz (1989) found that maritally distressed couples employed a parenting style that was cold, unresponsive, angry, and low in limit setting and structuring. Children who were exposed to this style of parenting exhibited high levels of stress hormones and displayed more anger and noncompliance; these children tended to play at low levels with peers and displayed more negative peer interactions.

Findings from our lab suggest that the strategies parents employ to manage children's negative emotion are associated with children's emotional reactivity, coping, and social competence (O'Neil, Parke, Isley, & Sosa, 1997). When mothers reported that they encouraged the expression of negative affect when their child was upset, children indicated that they would be less likely to use social withdrawal as a strategy to deal with emotional upset. Similarly, mothers who reported that they would help the child find solutions to deal with emotional distress had children who reported that they would be more likely to use reasoning to cope with emotional upset. Mothers who expressed more awareness and sensitivity to their child's emotional state in a family problem-solving task had children who expressed less positive affect and more negative affect in the problem-solving task. When mothers modeled problem-solving approaches to handling disagreement and upset, children were less likely to report becoming angry when faced with an upsetting event, less likely to express negative affect during the parent-child discussion task, were clearer in their emotional expressions, and were more likely to adopt problem-solving strategies in the discussion task.

Fathers' regulation of children's emotions was also related to social competence. Fathers who reported being more distressed by their child's expressions of negative affect had children who were more likely to report using anger and other negative emotions to cope with distressing events. When fathers reported using strategies to minimize distressing circumstances, children were more likely to report using reasoning to cope with a distressing situation. Fathers who reported emotion- and problem-focused reactions to the expression of negative emotions had children who were described by teachers as less aggressive or disruptive. This work highlights the role of fathers in learning about relationships, especially in learning the emotion regulatory aspects of relationships. Fathers provide a unique opportunity to teach children about emotion in the context of relationships due to the wide range of intensity of affect that fathers display and the unpredictable character of their playful exchanges with their children (Parke, 1995, 1996).

Summary

Together, these studies suggest that various aspects of emotional development – encoding, decoding, cognitive understanding, and emotional regulation – play an important role in accounting for variations in peer competence. Our argument is that these aspects of emotion may be learned in the context of family interaction and serve as mediators between the parents and peers. The extent to which parental practices, which, in turn, influence their children's affect management processes, are modified by marital conflict remains unclear. As noted in our discussion of the direct effects model, the work of Davies and Cummings (1998) and Gottman and Katz (1989) suggests that these hypothesized pathways between marital conflict and emotional regulation are feasible. Similarly, more attention needs to be devoted to exploration of how marital conflict modifies parent–child relationships and the potential mediating role of children's perception of the marital conflict in the hypothesized model. Finally, the relative importance of direct exposure to marital conflict (e.g., Cummings & Cummings, 1988) or the indirect effect of marital conflict through the modification of parent–child interaction is unclear. Both pathways are likely to be important in accounting for shifts in children's emotional regulatory abilities.

Marital Conflict, Sibling Relationships, and Peer Competence

Among the possible pathways between marital conflict and peer relationships, it is important to recognize sib–sib relationships as well as parent–child relationships. Although there is a large, if somewhat inconclusive, literature concerning the links between sibling and peer relationships, there has been less attention devoted to the possible marital antecedents of variations in the quality of sibling relationships (see Dunn & Davies, Chapter 10). However, it is plausible that the level and type of marital conflict may alter sibling relations, which, in turn, are related to children's peer relationships. Two issues need to be considered. First, is there a relation between the marital relationship and children's sibling relationships? Second, are there links between sibling conflict and children's peer relationships?

Prior evidence supports the link between these two family subsystems. In families characterized by high marital conflict there is a higher level of conflict in sibling relationships (Hetherington, 1991; Reid & Patterson, 1989; Straus, 1979). Because conflictful and coercive parent–child relationships are also associated with more conflictual sibling ties, it is unclear whether there is a direct or indirect pathway between marital conflict and sibling conflict.

Children's experiences with siblings provide a context in which interaction patterns and social understanding skills may generalize to relationships with other children (McCoy, Brody, & Stoneman, 1994). According to Stocker and Dunn (1990), interactions with siblings provide a setting in which children "develop social understanding skills which may enable them to form particularly close relationships with a child of their choice, a close friend" (p. 227). Sibling relationships may provide the background in which children learn conflict resolution skills that carry over to relationships with peers. Within the safety of one of the most long-lasting relationships children can have, they learn to disagree, oppose, compromise, and conciliate. These constructive conflicts enhance children's social understanding and problem-solving skills (Vandell & Bailey, 1992). In general, there appears to be a mixed body of evidence in support of links between sib–sib patterns of interaction and interaction styles that develop in the context of friendships and more general peer relationships. The pattern of findings from the small but growing number of studies provide a modest and somewhat inconsistent picture of the connections between children's sibling relationships and peer relationships. Some studies report modest evidence of straightforward carryover of interaction styles between children's relationships with siblings and peers. Others report little evidence of a carryover effect between siblings and peers (e.g., Abramovitch, Corter, Pepler, & Stanhope, 1986). Moreover, little attention has been given to the specific aspects of sibling conflict that are linked to specific aspects of peer conflict.

In sum, the links between sibling conflict and children's peer relationships are evident, but not always consistent. As Dunn (1993) has wisely noted, the goal is to specify "for *which* children, at *which* stages of development, *which* dimensions of particular relationships are likely to show associations with other relationships."

Toward a More Complete Understanding of the Links between Marital Conflict and Peer Relationships

A variety of issues remain to be examined in this area.

Beyond Peer Acceptance

Perhaps the most important issue that merits increased attention is the need for more specific measures of peer–peer conflict. Prior research has found clear links between marital conflict and peer relationships, but has failed to provide links between particular aspects of marital conflict and a similar level of analysis in the peer domain. For example, are the levels of peer conflict and types of peer resolution strategies linked to marital conflict and marital conflict resolution strategies? At the same time, it is important to remember that peer and family relationships have unique characteristics, including differences in the equality of power across partners. In a typical parent–child interaction, a vertical relationship, the parent controls the situation; whereas, with two children of similar age, a horizontal relationship, the power is proportionately distributed between the two participants (Laursen, Hartup, & Koplas, 1996). Conflicts occurring in horizontal and vertical relationships are likely to have different processes, strategies, and outcomes due to the distribution of power. One may assume that the strategies and patterns of conflict in any horizontal relationship should be similar to another horizontal relationship; yet, even within the range of children's horizontal peer relationships, there is considerable variation to the distribution of power.

Although we have focused largely on measures of sociometric status and peer acceptance, other types of peer relationships need to be distinguished, namely friendships and peer victimization. Although friendships, social acceptance, and peer victimization are all considered horizontal relationships, the distribution of power in each relationship differs. A reciprocal friendship probably has the most equal distribution of power, whereas peer victimization is the most disproportionate. Conflict in all these peer relationships could differ because of the distribution of power and also children's goals for the relationship's future. For instance, friends behave in a way that ensures the continuation of the relationship. It would be worthwhile to examine the relations between children's exposure to couples' conflict resolution strategies and children's typical conflict resolution tactics with friends. Similarly, examination of bully–victim relationships and their links to marital conflict would be useful. Although there is no information available concerning the impact of marital conflict on these types of peer relationships, it could be expected that victims may be shielded more from marital conflict, while bullies are more likely to be witnesses to more intense and likely unresolved marital conflict.

A more complete understanding of this issue would include links between specific aspects of marital conflict and specific characteristics of peer–peer conflict. This attention to the extent to which marital conflict relates to peer conflict would result in a more differentiated picture of the links between these two contexts. As argued, marital conflict is a multidimensional issue; similarly peer conflict is a multi-faceted construct.

Mediating Processes

More attention needs to be given to the mediating processes that account for the links between these domains. Although we have focused on emotional regulation, other processes may be involved, especially cognitive models of social relationships. In our prior work (Cassidy, Kirsh, Scolton, & Parke, 1996; Parke & O'Neil, 1999), we have shown links among parental cognitive models, children's cognitive models and children's social competence. A recent study (Goodman, Barfoot, Frye, & Belli, 1999) provided support for this potential mediator. Mothers who reported higher frequency and higher negativity of marital conflict had children who exhibited less effective social problem-solving solutions. In light of related work in the marital arena, which stresses the important role of cognitive processes (especially attributions about spousal behavior), it is likely that there will be interesting ties between marital cognitions and other cognitive representations about other social relationships among family members (Fincham, 1998).

Mothers, Fathers, and Families are Not Interchangeable

The differential role that mothers and fathers play needs closer scrutiny. Do children perceive that mothers and fathers play different roles in initiating marital conflict and in its resolution? These perceptions may influence children's reactions to the conflict and, in turn, alter their potential impact on peers. Finally, a family systems perspective suggests the value of examining the family as a unit of analysis, whereby some families have different levels of conflict, different ways of expressing conflict, and distinctive strategies for resolving conflict. Earlier work by Moos and Moos (1981) on distinctive family climates and styles of responding to events (Reiss, 1989) represents this family level approach.

Conflict May Sometimes Help

It is important to distinguish among various forms of family conflict and to underscore that some forms and levels of conflict may, in fact, have beneficial effects on children's functioning by teaching them how to cope effectively with conflict. Conflict may not always be bad for children. As Katz, Kramer, and Gottman (1992) note, exposure to some form of conflict – especially if it is not too intense and is resolved – can actually benefit children, by teaching them how to resolve conflict and alerting them to the normality of some level of conflict in interpersonal relationships.

Beyond White, Middle-Class Samples

Little is known about how variations in ethnicity, race, and class influence the links between marital conflict and children's peer relationships (see McLoyd et al., Chapter 4; Parke & Buriel, 1998). Variations across ethnic lines represent important opportunities not only to explore the universality of processes and mechanisms, but they also provide naturally occurring variations in the relative salience of certain key determinants such as interactive style or emotional expressiveness. As we become aware of our own cultural diversity, it becomes important that we begin to make a serious commitment to an exploration of this diversity – both theoretically and through systematic empirical inquiry. The search for a balance between processes that are universal and processes that are unique to particular cultural, racial, or ethnic groups represents an important challenge for the future.

Transmission of Similar versus Complementary Influence

Another issue that needs attention is the specification of the conditions under which children learn similar rather than complementary lessons about relationships from significant others. The bulk of the evidence suggests that most children learn to adopt similar styles and models of relationships. However, there is other evidence from adults that suggests that they compensate for their earlier, often poor, relationships by developing a very different approach to relationships. Involved fathers, for example, often report that their own fathers were uninvolved and their current views of father–child relationships are in response to their own relationship history (Parke, 1996). The factors that promote similarity versus compensatory relationships are not well understood. Perhaps children who are exposed to marital conflict seek to avoid conflict and confrontational situations or are motivated to seek out other strategies for dealing with conflict.

Peer Relationships as a Buffer against Marital Conflict

Although we have treated peer relationships as an outcome variable, a more complete appreciation of the relations between marital and peer systems requires that the bidirectional nature of the links be recognized. For example, Wasserstein and LaGreca (1996) found that children's close friendships moderate the negative effects of marital discord. Similarly, Hetherington and Stanley-Hagan (1999) have found that adolescents whose parents are undergoing separation and divorce spend more time with friends as a way of coping with the conflictful family situation. More work is needed to specify the conditions under which children seek out friends in time of marital conflict or crisis and to articulate the characteristics of friendships and/or peer relationships that are more or less effective in buffering children from family conflict.

Beyond Unidirectional Models: Transactional Models of Family-Conflict and Peer Relationships

Although, it is assumed in this literature that marital conflict alters children's social outcomes, the reverse direction of causality merits recognition as well. Children who have difficulty with peers may, in turn, lead to increased marital conflict and/or altered parent–child relationships. Parents may blame each other for the child's problematic behavior or disagree about the best correctives for the problem. Across time, these increases in marital conflict may, in turn, exacerbate children's social adaptation with peers, as suggested by transactional models of development (Sameroff, 1994). Longitudinal work could usefully examine this cycle or transactional model of the relation between marital conflict and children's peer competence.

Conclusion

Direct and indirect models of the links between marital conflict and children's peer relationships were examined. Support for both models was evident, and more attention to the independent and cumulative impact of these influence pathways is needed. Mediating mechanisms of children's cognitive processing of marital conflict and their emotional regulatory abilities are both viewed as important in accounting for the links between marital conflict and children's relationships with peers. By achieving a better understanding of the links and these processes, we will be able to mount more effective, theory-based intervention and prevention programs aimed at the reduction of marital conflict and limiting its negative effects on children's peer relationships.

REFERENCES

Abramovitch, R., Corter, C., Pepler, D. J., & Stanhope, L. (1986). Sibling and peer interaction: A final follow-up and a comparison. *Child Development, 57,* 217–229.

Barth, J. M., & Parke, R. D. (1993). Parent-child relationship influences on children's transition to school. *Merrill-Palmer Quarterly, 39,* 173–195.

Baumrind, D. (1973). The development of instrumental competence through socialization. In A. D. Pick (Ed.), *Minnesota Symposium on Child Psychology* (Vol. 7, pp. 3–46). Minneapolis: University of Minnesota Press.

Boyum, L., & Parke, R. D. (1995). Family emotional expressiveness and children's social competence. *Journal of Marriage and Family, 57,* 593–608.

Carson, J., & Parke, R. D. (1996). Reciprocal negative affect in parent-child interactions and children's peer competency. *Child Development, 67,* 2217–2226.

Cassidy, J., Kirsh, S., Scolton, K., & Parke, R. D. (1996). Attachment and representations of peer relationships. *Developmental Psychology, 32,* 892–904.

Cowan, P. A., Cowan, C. P., Shulz, M. S., & Hemming, G. (1994). Prebirth to preschool family factors in children's adaptation to kindergarten. In R. D. Parke & S. G. Kellam (Eds.), *Exploring family relationships with other social contexts* (pp. 75–114). Hillsdale, NJ: Lawrence Erlbaum Associates.

Cummings, E. M., & Cummings J. L. (1988). A process-oriented approach to children's coping with adults' angry behavior. *Developmental Review, 8,* 296–321.

Cummings, E. M., & Davies, P. T. (1994). *Children and marital conflict: The impact of family dispute and resolution.* New York: Guilford.

Cummings, E. M., Iannotti, R. J., & Zahn-Waxler, C. (1985). The influence of conflict between adults on the emotions and aggression of young children. *Developmental Psychology, 21,* 495–507.

Davies, P. T., & Cummings, E. M. (1994). Marital conflict and child adjustment: An emotional security hypothesis. *Psychological Bulletin, 116 (3),* 387–411.

Davies, P. T., & Cummings, E. M. (1998). Exploring children's emotional security as a mediator of the link between marital relations and child adjustment. *Child Development, 69 (1),* 124–139.

Denham, S. A. (1998). *Emotional development in young children.* New York: Guilford.

Dunn, J. (1993). *Young children's close relationships.* Newbury Park, CA: Sage Publications.

Dunn, J. (1995). Children as psychologists: The later correlates of individual differences in understanding emotions and other minds. *Cognition and Emotion, 9,* 187–201.

Dunn, J., & Brown, J. (1994). Affect expression in the family, children's understanding of emotions and their interactions with others. *Merrill-Palmer Quarterly, 40,* 120–137.

Eisenberg, N., & Fabes, R. A. (1994). Emotion, regulation and the development of social competence. In M. Clark (Ed.), *Review of personality and social psychology.* Newbury Park, CA: Sage.

Emery, R. E., & O'Leary, K. D. (1982). Children's perceptions of marital discord and behavior problems of boys and girls. *Journal of Abnormal Child Psychology, 10 (1),* 11–24.

Fauber, R. L., & Long, N. (1991). Children in context: The role of the family in child psychotherapy. *Journal of Consulting and Clinical Psychology, 59,* 813–820.

Fincham, F. D. (1998). Child development and marital relations. *Child Development, 69,* 543–574.

Forgatch, M. S., Patterson, G. R., & Ray, J. A. (1996). Divorce and boys' adjustment problems: Two paths with a single model. In E. M. Hetherington & E. Blackman (Eds.), *Stress, coping, and resiliency in children and families* (pp. 67–105). Mahwah, NJ: Erlbaum.

Goodman, S. H., Barfoot, B., Frye, A. A., & Belli, A. M. (1999). Dimensions of marital conflict and children's social problem-solving skills. *Journal of Family Psychology, 13*, 33–45.

Gottman, J. M. (1994). *What predicts divorce?* Hillsdale, NJ: Erlbaum.

Gottman, J. M., & Katz, L. F. (1989). Effects of marital discord on young children's peer interaction and health. *Developmental Psychology, 25*, 373–381.

Gottman, J. M., Katz, L. F., & Hooven, C. (1996). *Meta-emotion: How families communicate emotionally.* Mahwah, NJ: Erlbaum.

Grych, J. H., & Fincham, F. D. (1990). Marital conflict and children's adjustment: A cognitive-contextual framework. *Psychological Bulletin, 108 (2),* 267–290.

Grych, J. H., Seid, M., & Fincham, F. D. (1992). Assessing marital conflict from the child's perspective: The Children's Perception of Interparental Conflict scale. *Child Development, 63*, 558–572.

Harrist, A. W., Pettit, G. S., Dodge, K. A., & Bates, J. E. (1994). Dyadic synchrony in mother-child interaction–relation with children's subsequent kindergarten adjustment. *Family Relations, 43*, 417–424.

Hetherington, E. M. (1991). The role of individual differences and family relationships in children's coping with divorce and remarriage. In P. A. Cowan & E. M. Hetherington (Eds.), *Family transitions* (pp. 165–194). Hillsdale, NJ: Erlbaum.

Hetherington, E. M., & Stanley-Hagan, M. (1999). The adjustment of children with divorced parents: A risk and resiliency perspective. *Journal of Child Psychology and Psychiatry and Allied Disciplines, 40*, 12–140.

Hooven, C., Rushe, R., & Gottman, J. (1988). *The Play-by-Play Interview Manual.* Unpublished manuscript.

Isley, S., O'Neil, R., & Parke, R. D. (1996). The relation of parental affect and control behavior to children's classroom acceptance: A concurrent and predictive analysis. *Early Education and Development, 7*, 7–23.

Katz, L. F., & Gottman, J. M. (1993). Patterns of marital conflict predict children's internalizing and externalizing behaviors. *Developmental Psychology, 29*, 940–950.

Katz, L. F., & Kahen, V. (1993). *Marital interaction patterns and children's externalizing and internalizing behaviors: The search for mechanisms.* Paper presented at the biennial meeting of Society for Research in Child Development, New Orleans, LA.

Katz, L. F., Kramer, L., & Gottman, J. M. (1992). Conflict and emotions in marital, sibling, and peer relationships. In C. U. Shantz & W. W. Hartup (Eds.), *Conflict in child and adolescent development* (pp. 122–149). Cambridge: Cambridge University Press.

Kim, M., Parke, R. D., & O'Neil, R. (1999, April). *Marital conflict and children's social competence: Concurrent and predictive analyses.* Poster presented at the annual meeting of the Western Psychological Association, Irvine, CA.

Laursen, B., Hartup, W. W., & Koplas, A. L. (1996). Towards understanding peer conflict. *Merrill-Palmer Quarterly, 42*, 76–102.

Lindahl, K., Clements, M., & Markman, H. (1998). The development of marriage: A 9-year perspective. In T. Bradbury (Ed.), *The developmental course of marital dysfunction* (pp. 205–236). New York: Cambridge University Press.

Long, N., Forehand, R., Fauber, R., & Brody, G. H. (1987). Self-perceived and independently observed competence of young adolescents as a function of parental marital conflict and recent divorce. *Journal of Abnormal Child Psychology, 15* (1), 15–27.

MacDonald, K., & Parke, R. D. (1984). Bridging the gap: Parent-child play interaction and peer interactive competence. *Child Development, 55,* 1265–1277.

Margolin, G. (1988). Marital conflict is not marital conflict, is not marital conflict. In R. De V. Peters & R. S. McMahon (Eds.), *Social Learning and systems approaches to marriage and the family* (pp. 193–216). New York: Brunner/Mazel, Inc.

McCoy, J. K., Brody, G. H., & Stoneman, Z. (1994). A longitudinal analysis of sibling relationships as mediators of the link between family processes and youths' best friendships. *Family Relations, 43,* 400–408.

McDowell, D. J., Parke, R. D., & Wang, S. J. (1999). *Differences between mothers' and fathers' advice-giving style and structure: Relations with social competence and psychosocial functioning in middle childhood.* Unpublished manuscript, University of California, Riverside.

Moos, R., & Moos, B. S. (1981). *The family environment scale.* Palo Alto, CA: Consulting Psychology Press.

O'Neil, R., Parke, R. D., Flyr, M., & Wild, M. (1999). Marital interaction and children's peer competence. Unpublished manuscript. University of California, Riverside.

O'Neil, R., Parke, R. D., Isley, S., & Sosa, R. (1997, April). *Parental influences on children's emotion regulation in middle childhood.* Paper presented at the biennial meeting of the Society for Research in Child Development, Washington, DC.

Parke, R. D. (1988). Families in life-span perspective: A multi-level developmental approach. In E. M. Hetherington, R. M. Lerner, & M. Perlmutter (Eds.), *Child development in life span perspective* (pp. 159–190). Hillsdale, NJ: Erlbaum.

Parke, R. D. (1994). Progress, paradigms and unresolved problems: A commentary on recent advances in our understanding of children's emotions. *Merrill Palmer Quarterly, 40,* 157–169.

Parke, R. D. (1995). Fathers and families. In M. H. Bornstein (Ed.), *Handbook of Parenting* (Vol. 3, pp. 27–63). Hillsdale, NJ: Erlbaum.

Parke, R. D. (1996). *Fatherhood.* Cambridge: Harvard University Press.

Parke, R. D., & Buriel, R. (1998). Socialization in the family: Ethnic and ecological perspectives. In W. Damon (Gen. Ed.), *Handbook of child psychology* (Vol. 3). New York: Wiley.

Parke, R. D., Burks, V. M., Carson, J. L., & Cassidy, J. (1992). Family contributions to peer relationships among young children. In R. D. Parke & G. Ladd (Eds.), *Family-peer relationships: Modes of linkage* (pp. 107–134). Hillsdale, NJ: Erlbaum.

Parke, R. D., Burks, V., Carson, J., Neville, B., & Boyum, L. (1994). Family-peer relationships: A tripartite model. In R. D. Parke & S. Kellam (Eds.), *Advances in family research: Vol. 4. Family relationships with other social systems* (pp. 115–145). Hillsdale, NJ: Erlbaum.

Parke, R. D., & O'Neil, R. (1997). The influence of significant others on learning about relationships. In S. Duck (Ed.), *The handbook of personal relationships* (2nd ed., pp. 29–60) New York: Wiley.

Parke, R. D., & O'Neil, R. (1999). Social relationships across contexts: Family-peer linkages. In W. A. Collins & B. Laursen (Eds.), *Relationships as developmental contexts: The Minnesota symposium on child psychology* (Vol. 30, pp. 211–239). Mahwah, NJ: Erlbaum.

Parke, R. D., O'Neil, R., Flyr, M., & Wild, M. (1999, April). *Early adolescents' exposure to marital conflict: Links to relationships with parents and peers.* Poster presented at the biennial meeting for the Society for Research in Child Development.

Parker, J. G., & Asher, S. R. (1987). Peer relations and later personal adjustment: Are low-accepted children at risk? *Psychological Bulletin, 102 (3),* 357–389.

Reid, J. B., & Patterson, G. R. (1989). The development of antisocial behavior patterns in childhood and adolescence. *European Journal of Personality, 3,* 107–119.

Reiss, D. (1989). The represented and practicing family: Contrasting visions of family continuity. In A. J. Sameroff & R. N. Ende (Eds.), *Relationship disturbances in early childhood* (pp. 186–214). New York: Basic Books.

Sameroff, A. (1994). Developmental systems and family functioning. In R. D. Parke & S. G. Kellam (Eds.), *Exploring family relationships with other social contexts* (pp. 199–214). Hillsdale, NJ: Erlbaum.

Snyder, D. K., Klein, M. A., Gdowski, C. L., Faulstich, C. & LaCombe, J. (1988). Generalized dysfunction in clinic and nonclinic families: A comparative analysis. *Journal of Abnormal Child Psychology, 16 (1),* 97–109.

Stocker, C., & Dunn, J. (1990). Sibling relationships in childhood: Links with friendship and peer relationships. *British Journal of Developmental Psychology, 8,* 227–244.

Straus, M. A. (1979). Measuring intrafamily conflicts and violence: The conflict tactics (Ct) scales. *Journal of Marriage and Family, 41,* 75–88.

Vandell, D. L., & Bailey, M. D. (1992). Conflicts between siblings. In C. Uhlinger Shantz & W. W. Hartup (Eds.), *Conflict in child and adolescent development* (pp. 242–269). New York: Cambridge University Press.

Wasserstein, S. B., & La Greca, A. M. (1996). Can peer support buffer against behavioral consequences of parental discord? *Journal of Clinical Child Psychology, 25,* 177–182.

Westerman, M. A., & Schonholtz, J. (1993). Marital adjustment, joint parental support in a triadic problem-solving task, and child behavior problems. *Journal of Clinical Child Psychology, 22,* 97–106.

12 Domestic Violence and Child Adjustment

Ernest N. Jouriles, William D. Norwood, Renee McDonald, and Beth Peters

Wife abuse is now recognized as an important health and social problem that can have devastating short- and long-term consequences. Although women are the most obvious victims of wife abuse, it has become increasingly clear that their children are affected as well. This chapter reviews the empirical literature on the link between wife abuse (and marital violence, see the following paragraph) with child adjustment. We explore some of the parameters of this association and note conceptual, methodological, and practical issues confronting researchers in the area. We also highlight several controversial issues in the conceptualization of violence and note gaps in our knowledge that limit what can be concluded about this association. We conclude by offering several suggestions for future research.

It should be noted at the outset that in most of this literature the terms *wife abuse* and *violence toward women* are used interchangeably with the terms *marital violence* and *interparent violence* (Jouriles, McDonald, Norwood, & Ezell, in press). Similarly, the phrase *children of battered women* is often used interchangeably with phrases such as *children of maritally violent parents*. These terms, however, should refer to different constructs, depending on whether the intended focus is on violence against women, specifically, or interspousal violence in general. We discuss this conceptual distinction in more detail later in this chapter, and we attempt to maintain this distinction when referring to violence throughout this review. Specifically, we use the terms *wife abuse* and *violence toward women* to refer to acts of physical aggression directed toward women by a male intimate partner, and *children of battered women* is reserved for the children in families characterized by such violence. We use *marital violence* to refer to physical aggression between intimate partners without respect to the perpetrator's gender, and we use *violence* and *domestic violence* to be inclusive of both wife abuse and marital violence. Unfortunately, given the current state of the literature any attempt to strictly maintain this distinction in a review of the research in this area is almost impossible.

We should also point out that our review focuses primarily upon children's exposure to *physical* violence, as opposed to other forms of wife abuse or interparent aggression. Most researchers classify families as "violent" or "nonviolent" on the basis of reports of physical aggression (e.g., pushed, grabbed, kicked, bit, hit with a fist). Violence and abuse certainly are not limited to acts of physical aggression; indeed, victims of wife abuse often report that nonphysical forms of abuse (e.g., verbal degradation) are as damaging to them, and some times much more so, than the physical aggression (Schwartz, 1998). However, virtually all of the published research in this area has focused on physical violence, and thus we must do so as well.

Some discussion is also warranted on the distinction between marital violence and marital conflict. In some published work, marital violence is conceptualized as an "intense" form of marital conflict (e.g., Grych & Fincham, 1990), whereas in other work violence and conflict appear to be conceptualized as related but separate constructs (e.g., Rossman & Rosenberg, 1992). Although this distinction has received little empirical attention, we believe important conceptual distinctions can be made between marital violence and marital conflict. For example, conflict can be thought of as a manifestation of disagreement, whereas violence does not always occur in the context of a disagreement (even though the most commonly used measures situate violence in the context of resolving disagreements). In fact, feminist theorists maintain that much violence toward women is spurred by the motive to control or intimidate one's partner, and sometimes comes from "out of the blue" with no apparent precipitating event (Yllö, 1993). It could also be argued that conflict as disagreement is ubiquitous in marriage; marital violence and wife abuse certainly are not, particularly when these constructs are defined by acts of physical aggression. Distinctions between violence and conflict will be revisited in the section of the chapter that addresses the conceptualization of violence.

The Link between Domestic Violence and Child Adjustment Problems

Concurrent Child Problems

Early studies of domestic violence and child adjustment did not include nonviolent samples for comparison; they do, however, provide descriptive information about a range of problems experienced by children of battered women. These studies typically sampled children from shelters for battered women or other agencies serving victims of domestic violence. As a group, these studies suggest that the children of battered women experience a wide range of adjustment difficulties including symptoms of trauma, fear and anxiety, sleep difficulties and somatic complaints, aggressive and defiant behavior, delinquent behavior, and difficulties at school (e.g., Carlson, 1984; Layzer, Goodson, & Delange, 1986). Although most of these initial studies had serious methodological limitations, they document the range of adjustment problems among children in violent families and have called attention to these invisible or unintended victims of wife abuse.

These initial investigations were followed by a series of case-controlled studies in which the children of battered women, usually living with their mothers at women's shelters, were compared to children living at home with nonviolent parents. Most of these studies examined child adjustment on the two broadband indices of externalizing and internalizing problems. This early research clearly shows that children of battered women exhibit higher levels of problems than children in community comparison families (Margolin, 1998). It is noteworthy that in several of these studies the violent families were recruited from the community (and not from women's shelters or other service agencies where the violence tends to be very frequent and severe; Johnson, 1995; Jouriles et al., in press), and violence was still associated with increased risk for child adjustment problems (e.g., Fantuzzo et al., 1991; Doumas, Margolin, & John, 1994; Kempton, Thomas, & Forehand, 1989; Spaccarelli, Sandler, & Roosa, 1994). It is also noteworthy that several of these studies indicate that wife abuse and interparent violence are more potent risk factors for child problems than is verbal conflict or general marital discord (Fantuzzo et al., 1991; Jouriles, Murphy, & O'Leary, 1989; Rossman & Rosenberg, 1992), although at least two studies have failed to support this conclusion (Hershorn & Rosenbaum, 1985; Rosenbaum & O'Leary, 1981). Another important and consistent finding is that a substantial proportion of children in violent families score above clinical levels on standard measures of child problems. For example, McDonald and Jouriles (1991) reported that between 25% and 70% of children from families characterized by violence exhibited clinical levels of behavior problems compared to 10% to 20% of children in community comparison groups. These results are consistent with a later review in which estimates were aggregated across studies: About 40% of children from families characterized by violence were exhibiting problems at clinical levels versus

10% of comparison group children (Holden, 1998). Although the specific type of problems exhibited by children of domestically violent parents compared to children of nonviolent parents varies across studies, this case-controlled research leaves little doubt that the children of battered women are at risk for behavior problems.

Other areas of child functioning that have been studied include cognitive functioning and social behavior. There is evidence, for example, that children of battered women exhibit deficits in cognitive leveling or sharpening. A child who *sharpens* uses new information more quickly and more accurately, whereas a child who *levels* uses new information more slowly and less accurately. Rossman (1998) found that children of sheltered battered women showed greater leveling of aggressive cues relative to children in comparison families. Much of the research on cognitive functioning, however, suggests that children exposed to violence do not differ from children from nonviolent homes. For example, general intellectual functioning does not appear to be related to exposure to wife abuse (Christopoulos et al., 1987; Rossman, 1998; Rossman & Rosenberg, 1992).

On measures of social competence and social skills, children of battered women fare worse than children of nonviolent parents. For example, Graham-Bermann and Levendosky (1998) found preschool-aged children of battered women to differ from children of nonviolent parents during play interactions on a number of social variables. Children of battered women were more likely to express negative affect; were more likely to bite, hit, or slap others without provocation; and were more likely to insult or call other children names. Hinchey and Gavelek (1982) found preschool-aged children of battered women to be less empathic than preschool-aged children of nonviolent parents.

Descriptive studies of children of battered women and anecdotal clinical reports suggest a number of additional areas of concern. For example, there are reports that children of battered women are often in poor physical health (Campbell & Lewandowski, 1997). Many of these children come to believe that violence is an appropriate and effective means of obtaining power and control, and male children of battered women tend to be aggressive toward female targets in particular (Jaffe, Wolfe, & Wilson, 1990). Some of these children have also been reported to "tattle" to their fathers about their mothers' "misdeeds" in order to elicit violent responses (Wolfe & Korsch, 1994). Although this is not an exhaustive list of problems derived from clinical data, these examples illustrate the breadth of problems that may be experienced and the subtlety of some of the presumed effects of violence.

A handful of laboratory studies also have investigated children's immediate reactions to physically aggressive interchanges between adults (who are not the children's parents) and how exposure to physical aggression may alter children's reactions to conflict in general. Laboratory exposure to physical aggression, relative to verbal conflict, elicits more distress from children, prompts children to report more negative emotions, and causes children to perceive the interactions and the actors in a more negative light (Cummings, Vogel, Cummings, & El-Sheikh, 1989; Cummings, Zahn-Waxler, & Radke-Yarrow, 1981; Laumakis, Margolin, & John, 1998). Furthermore, children's exposure to interparent violence appears to sensitize them to further episodes of conflict. For example, community children with a history of exposure to interparent violence are more likely than children without such a history to be distressed by subsequent nonviolent conflict (Cummings et al., 1989; Garcia, O'Hearn, Margolin, & John, 1997), to appraise marital conflict as more negative (Grych, 1998), to interfere or become actively involved in parents' conflict (Cummings et al., 1981; O'Brien, Margolin, John, & Kruger, 1991), and to engage in a variety of distracting, support-seeking behaviors (Cummings, Pellegrini, Notarius, & Cummings, 1989; O'Brien, Margolin, John, & Kruger, 1991).

Longer-Term Problems

Most of the case-controlled studies on children of battered women focus on children living at women's shelters with their mothers. Although these studies indicate that children of battered women exhibit higher levels of adjustment problems than children of nonviolent parents, it is unclear whether these problems persist over time (i.e., as families move out of shelter and establish nonviolent residences). Only three studies have addressed this question, albeit indirectly. In a cross-sectional study, Wolfe, Zak, Wilson, and Jaffe (1986) assessed current women's shelter residents' reports of their children's behavior problems and social competence and compared them to those of former shelter residents (out of shelter at least six months). Children of current shelter residents were reported to be less socially competent (fewer interests, fewer social activities, lower school performance) than children of former shelter residents, but no differences were found on reports of externalizing or internalizing problems. In a short-term longitudinal study, Holden, Stein, Ritchie, Harris, and Jouriles (1998) assessed mothers' perceptions of their children's externalizing and internalizing problems during shelter residence and again six months after shelter exit. Mean levels of mothers' reports of children's externalizing and internalizing problems were higher during shelter residence than after shelter departure. Another short-term longitudinal study focused on children who were exhibiting clinical levels of externalizing problems at the time of shelter residence (Ware et al., in press). In this study, mothers' reports of child externalizing problems remained stable between shelter residence and two months following shelter departure, whereas mothers' reports of child internalizing problems decreased during this period. Thus, there is evidence suggesting that although internalizing problems and possibly difficulties in social functioning may diminish after shelter departure, externalizing problems appear to be more stable.

Finally, the relation between exposure to violence during childhood and long-term outcomes has been investigated in several studies. One long-term follow-up study indicates that boys' exposure to marital violence is one of the few childhood factors that predict adult criminal activity (McCord, 1979). Retrospective data consistently indicate that boys' exposure to violence toward women relates to wife abuse in their own adult intimate relationships (Hotaling & Sugarman, 1986). Retrospective data also indicate that children's exposure to interparent violence relates to internalizing symptoms such as depression, low self-esteem, and trauma in adulthood (Forsstrom-Cohen & Rosenbaum, 1985; Henning, Leitenberg, Coffey, Turner, & Bennett, 1996; Silvern et al., 1995). There is also evidence from retrospective studies that childhood exposure to interparent violence relates to dating violence among college students, particularly for males (Bernard & Bernard, 1983; Foo & Margolin, 1995; O'Keefe, Brockopp, & Chew, 1986; Riggs, O'Leary, & Breslin, 1990). Taken together, these studies suggest that children who are exposed to marital violence are at increased risk for long-term negative consequences. However, methodological limitations of these studies – in particular their reliance on retrospective, self-report data – preclude firm conclusions and point to a serious need for well-designed, prospective studies over long periods.

Factors Associated with Detrimental Impact

Although children of battered women are at increased risk for an array of adjustment problems, there is substantial variability in behavioral and emotional adjustment among these children. Using children's reports of internalizing problems and self-esteem and mothers' reports of externalizing problems, Grych, Jouriles, Swank, McDonald, and Norwood (2000) identified five distinct patterns of adjustment among 8–14-year-old children residing in battered women's shelters. One group of children (31%) was functioning well within the normal range on all of the adjustment measures. A second group (19%) demonstrated elevated levels of both externalizing and internalizing problems, with externalizing problems predominating. Children in a third group (21%) displayed high levels of externalizing problems and high self-esteem, but few internalizing problems. A fourth group (18%) had slightly elevated scores on measures of internalizing problems and very low levels of externalizing problems. A final group (11%) displayed high levels of both internalizing and externalizing problems, with internalizing problems predominating. Hughes and Luke (1998) identified almost identical patterns of adjustment among children at battered women's shelters in an earlier study. Studies such as these clearly illustrate that children's exposure to wife abuse is associated with heterogeneous child outcomes.

The theoretical and empirical literatures on children's responses to stressful events suggest several factors that may amplify or deflect the negative effects of wife abuse and marital violence on children. These include child variables (e.g., gender, age), parameters of the violence itself (e.g., frequency, severity), and family and community variables (e.g., child abuse, quality of the parent-child relationship, family income), among others. Although few of these variables have been investigated systematically among children of battered women or maritally violent parents, a number of interesting findings have emerged.

Child Variables

Child gender is often discussed as an important factor in the relation between violence and child adjustment, but little systematic attention has been given to this issue. In fact, only a couple of studies have directly (i.e., statistically) tested whether the association between domestic violence and child adjustment differs for girls and boys, and the results of these studies are conflicting. Jouriles and Norwood (1995) found boys to be more adversely affected by wife abuse than girls, whereas Moore and Pepler (1998) found girls to be more adversely affected than boys. Many investigators have presented their findings separately for boys and girls, and report differences for one sex or the other (and often both). However, the specific pattern of results is not consistent across studies. For example, some studies have found that male children of violent parents exhibit more externalizing problems than male children of nonviolent parents (Jaffe, Wolfe, Wilson, & Zak, 1986), but others have not (Christopoulos et al., 1987; Moore & Pepler, 1998; Rosenbaum & O'Leary, 1981). Similarly, some studies indicate that male children of violent parents exhibit greater levels of internalizing problems than male children of nonviolent parents (Graham-

Berman, 1996; Jaffe et al., 1986), but others do not (Christopoulos et al., 1987; Moore & Pepler, 1998). Inconsistent findings have emerged for girls as well. In sum, firm conclusions cannot yet be drawn regarding gender differences in the relation between domestic violence and child adjustment.

Child age has also received some attention, but, again, not as much as one might hope. Differences between violent and nonviolent comparison groups on child problems have been found in fairly homogeneous samples of preschoolers (e.g., Fantuzzo et al., 1991), young school-aged children (e.g., Sternberg et al., 1993) and adolescents (e.g., Carlson, 1990). However, many studies have included children of widely varying age (e.g., 4–16 years), and have not considered child age in the data analysis. In a notable exception to this approach, Hughes (1988) found that differences between children of battered women and children of nonviolent parents are larger for younger (preschool-aged) as opposed to older children, but this finding needs to be viewed very cautiously given the small number of younger children in this study.

Aside from child gender and age, very few other child variables have been investigated. There are some data on child ethnicity that have been interpreted to suggest that Caucasian boys exhibit higher levels of externalizing problems in response to domestic violence than African-American boys (O'Keefe, 1994; Stagg, Wills, & Howell, 1989). However, this interpretation needs to be viewed as tentative given the absence of nonviolent comparison groups in this research. There is also evidence that children's appraisals of their parents' marital conflict relate to adjustment difficulties within samples of children of battered women. Specifically, one study found that children (particularly those between the ages of 10 and 12, rather than younger children) who blame themselves for their parents' conflict or who feel more threatened by their parents' conflict are more likely to experience adjustment problems (Jouriles, Spiller, Stephens, McDonald, & Swank, in press). Children's ability to distract and comfort themselves also appears to mitigate the negative impact of exposure to violence (Rossman & Rosenberg, 1992).

Parameters of Violence

Research on marital conflict (as distinguished from marital violence) and child adjustment has uncovered several dimensions of conflict that appear to be useful in the prediction of child behavior problems. These include the frequency, intensity, resolution, and content of the conflict. In general, the more frequent and intense the marital conflict, the greater the likelihood of child difficulties; witnessing poorly resolved or unresolved marital conflict is more detrimental to children than witnessing resolved conflict; and overt marital conflict about children or childrearing appears more detrimental than overt marital conflict about other issues (Grych & Fincham, 1990; Davies & Cummings, 1994).

The empirical literature on parameters of violence related to child adjustment has focused primarily upon the frequency of the violence. Not surprisingly, the frequency of violence relates positively to children's externalizing and internalizing problems (Jouriles, Norwood, McDonald, Vincent, & Mahoney, 1996; O'Keefe, 1994; Spaccarelli, Coatsworth, & Bowden, 1995). Recent investigations also indicate that children's exposure to particular types of violence, such as interparent violence involving knives or guns, may be more detrimental to children than exposure to other forms of violence (Jouriles et al., 1998; Spaccarelli et al., 1995). Other parameters of violence have received little empirical attention. However, it is interesting to note that a number of investigators have reported that children, childrearing, and responsibilities in childcare are often the topics of arguments that culminate in episodes of wife abuse (Edleson, Eisikovits, Guttmann, & Sela-Amit, 1991; Straus, Gelles, & Steinmetz, 1980). In fact, there is some evidence that arguments about children and childrearing precede marital violence more often than arguments about other topics (Straus et al., 1980) and that children are sometimes blamed by the parents for their fathers' assaults (Holden et al., 1998).

Family and Community Variables

Domestic violence typically occurs in the context of other risk factors for child problems such as marital conflict, child abuse, poor parent–child relationships, and community violence. Some of these variables may play key roles in the development of violence, others may be a consequence of the violence, while still others may simply occur with violence but are neither cause nor consequence. Researchers are just beginning to explore how violence interacts with other family and community variables in the development of child problems.

Several studies have examined the relations among domestic violence, nonviolent marital conflict, and child adjustment problems. This research suggests that violent and conflictual interactions may have independent effects on child adjustment. For example, wife abuse and marital violence contribute in the prediction of child adjustment problems after accounting for nonviolent marital conflict (Fantuzzo et al., 1991; Jouriles et al., 1989; Rossman & Rosenberg, 1992). Similarly, verbal aggression toward a partner (e.g., insults, threats) has been found to be associated with variance in child adjustment problems that is unrelated to marital violence (Jouriles et al., 1996).

A potentially important variable for understanding the effects of violence on child adjustment is parental physical aggression toward children. Domestic violence and child abuse often co-occur (Appel & Holden, 1998), and as one might expect, children who are both victims of parental physical abuse and witnesses to domestic violence appear to be at greater risk for problems than those who only witness violence (Davis & Carlson, 1987; Hughes, Parkinson, & Vargo, 1989; O'Keefe, 1994). Some research suggests that the effects of these two forms of family violence each contribute uniquely in the prediction of child adjustment problems (O'Keefe, 1994). Other studies, however, emphasize the greater risk associated with parent–child aggression (Jouriles, Barling, & O'Leary, 1987). Physical child abuse also appears to affect children's reactions to interparent conflict and violence. For example, physically abused boys have reported greater fear than nonabused boys when presented with an episode of interadult conflict (Hennessy, Rabideau, Cicchetti, & Cummings, 1994).

Domestic violence is also associated with poor parent–child relationships. For example, Holden and Ritchie (1991) found that mothers reported that violent men were less involved than nonviolent men in childrearing, less physically affectionate with their children, less likely to use inductive reasoning with their children, and more likely to physically punish their children. Few differences were found in the parenting of battered women versus women in nonviolent relationships in this study. In contrast, O'Keefe (1995) reported that within families characterized by wife abuse, the mother–child relationship is more problematic than the father–child relationship, and McCloskey, Figueredo, and Koss (1995) reported that violence is related to child reports of lower levels of parental warmth and nurturance. Reviews of the literature on protective factors (e.g., Rutter, 1987) suggest that a good parent–child relationship can buffer children from the negative consequences of stressful events. Although it is unclear if such a buffering effect occurs in families characterized by violence (McCloskey et al., 1995), this is one mechanism by which children from violent homes may continue to function well despite their exposure to this stressor.

Several investigators have examined the relation of child problems to violence in the context of other family and community variables. For example, in a sample of inner city families, children's witnessing of marital violence correlated with parental divorce and single-parent status, lower family income, lower maternal education, frequent family moves, parental drinking, and father's incarceration (Spaccarelli et al.,

1994). After controlling statistically for these correlates, witnessing marital violence still contributed unique variance in the prediction of girls' conduct problems as well as boys' and girls' depressive symptomatology. Wolfe, Jaffe, Wilson, and Zak (1985) found wife abuse to be correlated with maternal distress and the frequency of family moves; however, wife abuse did not contribute uniquely in the prediction of child problems after controlling for these other variables.

Summary of the Literature on Child Outcomes

The research literature supports the conclusion that children in homes characterized by marital violence or wife abuse are at risk for immediate, and perhaps longer-term, adjustment problems. Furthermore, a number of factors have been identified that influence the association between exposure to violence and child outcomes. These include child variables, parameters of violence, and family and community variables. Empirical efforts to flesh out our understanding of these variables and the mechanisms by which they influence children's responses to violence are just beginning.

Issues in the Conceptualization of Violence

Wife Abuse versus Marital Violence

Issues related to the conceptualization and operationalization of wife abuse and marital violence are complex and controversial. As we indicated at the beginning of this chapter, the terms *wife abuse* and *violence toward women* and the terms *marital violence* or *interparental violence* should be reserved for different constructs. Specifically, the former terms focus on violence directed toward a female target, whereas the latter terms denote violence between spouses or parents, regardless of the gender of the perpetrator. Researchers and advocates have argued quite compellingly that male-to-female violence differs greatly from female-to-male violence and that the two should not be equated or used interchangeably, and a number of studies now document that the consequences of male-to-female violence are much more devastating to the targets of such violence (with respect to physical injury and psychological sequelae) than female-to-male violence (Holtzworth-Munroe, Smutzler, & Bates, 1997).

A related conceptual distinction is the one between ordinary or common couple violence versus wife abuse or patriarchal terrorism. The terms *ordinary* or *common couple* violence, coined by Straus (1990) and

Johnson (1995), respectively, refer to infrequent low-level acts of physical aggression engaged in by both partners. This is the type of violence documented in much of the national survey research (e.g., Straus & Gelles, 1990) and it is thought to emerge when marital conflict occasionally gets "out of hand" (Johnson, 1995). In contrast, the terms *wife abuse* or *patriarchal terrorism* refer to frequent and severe violence that is primarily unidirectional (man-to-woman) and intended to subjugate or harm the woman. This is the type of violence typically documented among residents at battered women's shelters, and it is theorized to be a "form of terroristic control of wives by their husbands that involves the systematic use of not only violence, but economic subordination, threats, isolation, and other control tactics" (Johnson, 1995, p. 284).

At this point, it is important to highlight again that the majority of studies on children of battered women recruit their violent samples (or at least portions of their violent samples) from women's shelters or other agencies that serve victims of violence. In fact, over 70% of the studies in this area have recruited at least a portion of their "violent" sample from a battered woman's shelter (Margolin, 1998; Ware et al., in press). Three studies have included a direct comparison of violent samples, in which children recruited from women's shelters were compared to children recruited from the community; two of these studies indicated that the children at shelters exhibited higher levels of adjustment problems (Fantuzzo et al., 1991; Rossman & Rosenberg, 1992) and one did not (McCloskey et al., 1995). Our point here is not to minimize the potential importance of ordinary or common couple violence. Rather, we wish to draw attention to the issue that most of our knowledge on domestic violence and children is based on women's shelter samples, and findings from shelter samples may not necessarily generalize to children in the broader community who are exposed to domestic violence.

Narrow versus Broad Definitions of Violence

As indicated at the outset of this chapter, much of the research in this area has focused on children's exposure to *physical* violence. Some scholars argue that the construct of violence should be considered much broader, and that its measurement should not be limited to acts of physical aggression alone. The working definition used by the American Psychological Association Task Force on Male Violence against Women provides examples of the domains of behavior encompassed by a broader view of violence. The Task Force defines violence as "physical, visual, verbal, or sexual acts that are experienced by a woman or girl as a threat, invasion, or assault and that have the effect of hurting her or degrading her and/or taking away her ability to control contact (intimate and otherwise) with another individual" (Koss et al., 1994, p. xvi). Those taking this broader view of violence believe that researchers should broaden their measurement approaches accordingly.

On the other hand, some researchers have argued for a narrow definition of violence because it maintains a clear distinction between marital violence and marital conflict (e.g., Gelles, 1998) and that it is more useful for practical purposes (e.g. differential allocation of public resources; Emery & Laumann-Billings, 1997). It is probably the case that different definitions are appropriate for different purposes. For example, Emery and Laumann-Billings' (1997) recommendation for a definition centering on the potential for injury may prove a useful and prudent guide to policy makers concerned with efficient allocation of scarce resources. However, a broader definition of violence that includes acts other than physical aggression alone may contribute more to our understanding of the effects of violence (Jouriles et al., 1996).

From a research perspective, other considerations should also be kept in mind. If definitions of violence are too broad, the greater variability among persons identified as violent may impede the detection and interpretation of group differences. Specifically, a broad definition would equate men who verbally denigrate their spouses with men who choke and stab their wives; although their motives may be the same (to coerce or control), differences in their observable behavior may impact children in substantially different ways. Alternatively, if violence is defined too narrowly (e.g., physical aggression only), men who verbally denigrate their spouses and control their access to resources are equated with men who do not mistreat their wives in any way, thus introducing greater variability into nonviolent control groups.

Conceptualization of Children's Exposure to Violence

The meaning of a child's exposure to violence is often not well articulated. *Exposure* can be defined a number of ways. It may include seeing and hearing (e.g., from another room), observing the immediate consequences (injuries, broken furniture), or otherwise becoming aware of the violence (mom talks about it, siblings talk about it, mom explains how she was injured or why the family is moving to a shelter). Alternatively, it might simply include living in a home characterized by violence. Clearly, further refinement of what is meant by exposure needs to be incorporated into future studies, with more careful attention to the distinctions among the occurrence of violence, children's observation of violent acts, and/or children's awareness of the frequency and types of violence which occur in the home.

Additional Issues and Future Directions

The conceptual issues that we have presented bear directly on our ability to interpret the research on children's exposure to violence. Given the potential importance to public policy of research on children exposed to domestic violence, the assumptions underlying theory and constructs in this area ought to be given full consideration. Of equal importance, however, are the nuts and bolts of all research: issues of measurement. Measurement of violence and its correlates, including child outcomes, present thorny problems that require creativity on the part of researchers.

Improving the Measurement of Wife Abuse and Marital Violence

The methods and procedures used to assess violence – however it is defined and conceptualized – require greater attention than they have been given by researchers thus far. As in the assessment of any behavior associated with social desirability, disclosure is likely to be influenced by factors such as embarrassment and fears of reprisal or negative social evaluation, in addition to the typical biases (e.g., memory errors) that are associated with self-report data. Several researchers argue that a degree of trust has to be established between the researcher and study participants before many are willing to disclose an episode of violence (Koss, 1993). Thus, interviews may yield better estimates of violence than paper-and-pencil surveys. There is also evidence that even very basic variations in procedures – such as how often during the course of an assessment specific inquiries are made about the occurrence of violent acts – influence self-report (Smith, 1987).

Who provides information regarding violence also appears to be very important. Intimate partners often do not agree with each other on reports of the occurrence of violence (e.g., Jouriles & O'Leary, 1985), or whether children in the family have seen or heard acts of violence (O'Brien, John, Margolin, & Erel, 1994). This lack of concordance suggests that one family member's report of violence (whether presence/absence or frequency) cannot be used as a proxy for the report of other family members (see Moffitt et al., 1997, for an alternative point of view). Also, there is some indication that results may differ according to who is reporting the violence. For example, Kempton et al. (1989)

found fathers' but not mothers' reports of physical and verbal aggression to relate to teacher reports of adolescents' social and behavioral problems.

Although concerns about accuracy and convergence provide the impetus for gathering information from multiple informants, there are other reasons for doing so as well. Differences across reporters may be meaningful in their own right. For example, differences in reports across family members may reflect differences in the perceived salience of various violent events across family members. Children and mothers may endorse the occurrence of different events because those events are perceived as more important to them, and such differences may be important to our understanding of the effects of violence on children. Mothers may recall violent events that are psychologically as well as physically painful or humiliating, whereas children may recall events that are particularly frightening or threatening to themselves (regardless of the emotional pain inflicted on their mother). Alternatively, children may recall and report events that make their mothers cry, but fail to report violent events that simply leave their mothers angry and upset, but not in tears. The choice of who is the most appropriate informant about the violence is, of course, dependent upon the research question of interest, and researchers should give careful thought to how and who to ask about violence. For example, if the focus of inquiry is on children's appraisals of violent events, it would be important to ask children what they recall having seen or heard occur between their parents as opposed to relying solely on parental reports of child exposure. On the other hand, if one were interested in the impact of violence on child adjustment, regardless of whether the child witnessed it or not, then sole reliance on children's reports of violence would be inadequate.

Considering Violence in Combination with Other Factors

Wife abuse and marital violence do not occur in isolation; they are part of a package of factors that are known to adversely affect child development. Interpreting the data linking domestic violence with problematic child outcomes should be done with great caution because it may well be the case that a *combination* of factors, rather than wife abuse or marital violence alone, is responsible for an observed increase in risk. In fact, one can make a compelling argument on the basis of the empirical literature that child physical abuse plays a large role in the problems experienced by children in families characterized by wife abuse or marital violence (Jouriles, Barling, & O'Leary, 1987; O'Keefe, 1994). To understand the specific role of violence, we need to make a

special effort to measure and document the most relevant related phenomena. We also need much more work on the relations and influences
among wife abuse or marital violence and other family and community
variables in the development of child problems.

Expanding Assessment of Child Outcomes

Much of our knowledge about the functioning of children in families
characterized by wife abuse is limited to the two broadband indices of
children's adjustment, internalizing and externalizing problems. As we
noted earlier, there have been several efforts to explore other important
child outcomes such as cognitive functioning, social skills and competence, and physical health. However, other variables that have been
identified as precursors to problematic adjustment also need to be
studied. Such areas include academic adjustment and school failure,
peer relations, parental supervision, and coercive family interaction
patterns. It might also be argued that more attention should be given to
problematic behavior patterns that are not severe enough to warrant or
capture clinical attention, but that nonetheless contribute to problems
in living. Such problems might include gender prejudice and beliefs
about gender roles, the ability to function under hierarchical systems of
authority, the ability to manage emotions adaptively (anger and others), attitudes about social and communal responsibility, the capacity
for compassion and empathy, prosocial coping with adversity, and general problem-solving abilities.

Developing and Integrating Theory

A number of theory-based arguments have been put forth to explain
why or how exposure to marital violence or wife abuse should affect
children, but very few empirical investigations have been explicitly
guided by theory (Margolin, 1998). A few researchers have formally
tested theory-based hypotheses (e.g., Grych, Fincham, Jouriles, &
McDonald in press; Holden & Ritchie, 1991; Jouriles et al., 1989), but
there has been little attempt to integrate findings across studies into a
broader theory. In general, the existing research has not focused as
much as it could on testing and advancing theory, or in situating children's responses to violence within the broader scientific literature on
child development. Research on children's adaptation to other adverse
family environments would likely inform our understanding of children's adjustment in the context of domestic violence, and the study of
domestic violence has the potential to inform theory and research in
other areas (such as resiliency). More theory-guided research and theoretical "cross-fertilization" is clearly warranted.

Concluding Remarks

We know a good deal about the association between domestic violence and child adjustment, and we now have a number of leads with which to further advance our knowledge. We have devoted a good portion of this chapter to describing some of the limitations of our current knowledge. This has not been intended to be an exercise in methodological criticism; rather, we have attempted to think about where existing research fits into the broader picture and to consider how best to proceed from here. Understanding children's responses to their parents' violence requires consideration of the complex mix of resources, stressors, and supports available to the child and family. Such seemingly mundane considerations as the conceptualization and measurement of constructs are in reality central to the extent and quality of knowledge we gain from studying domestic violence and children's exposure to it. This research area, arguably, is still in its infancy stage; hopefully, this chapter will provide a base from which researchers can further the development of coherent models of child development in the context of domestic violence.

REFERENCES

Appel, A. E., & Holden, G. W. (1998). The co-occurrence of spouse and physical child abuse: A review and appraisal. *Journal of Family Psychology, 12,* 578–599.

Bernard, M. L., & Bernard, J. L. (1983). Violent intimacy: The family as model for love relationships. *Family Relations, 32,* 283–286.

Campbell, J. C., & Lewandowski, L. A. (1997). Mental and physical health effects of intimate partner violence on women and children. *Psychiatric Clinics of North America, 20,* 353–374.

Carlson, B. E. (1984). Children's observations of interpersonal violence. In A. Roberts (Ed.), *Battered Women and Their Families* (pp. 147–167). New York: Springer.

Carlson, B. E. (1990). Adolescent observers of marital violence. *Journal of Family Violence, 5,* 285–299.

Christopolous, C., Cohn, D. A., Shaw, D. S., Joyce, S., Sullivan-Hanson, J., Draft, S. P., & Emery, R. E. (1987). Children of abused women: 1. Adjustment at time of shelter residence. *Journal of Marriage and the Family, 49,* 611–619.

Cummings, J. S., Pelligrini, D. S., Notarius, C. I., & Cummings, E. M. (1989). Children's responses to angry adult behavior as a function of marital distress and history of interparent hostility. *Child Development, 60,* 1035–1043.

Cummings, E. M., Vogel, D., Cummings, J. S., & El-Sheikh, M. (1989). Children's responses to different forms of expression of anger between adults. *Child Development, 60,* 1392–1404.

Cummings, E. M., Zahn-Waxler, C., & Radke-Yarrow, M. (1981). Developmental changes in children's reactions to anger in the home. *Journal of Child Psychology and Psychiatry, 25,* 63–74.

Davies, P. T., & Cummings, E. M. (1994). Marital conflict and child adjustment: An emotional security hypothesis. *Psychological Bulletin, 116,* 387–411.

Davis, L., & Carlson, B. (1987). Observation of spouse abuse: What happens to the children? *Journal of Interpersonal Violence, 2,* 278–291.

Doumas, D., Margolin, G., & John, R. S. (1994). The intergenerational transmission of aggression across three generations. *Journal of Family Violence, 9,* 157–175.

Edleson, J. L., Eisikovits, Z. C., Guttman, E., & Sela-Amit, M. (1991). Cognitive and interpersonal factors in women abuse. *Journal of Family Violence, 6,* 167–182.

Emery, R. E., & Laumann-Billings, L. (1997). An overview of the nature, causes, and consequences of abusive family relationships: Toward differentiating maltreatment and violence. *American Psychologist, 53,* 121–135.

Fantuzzo, J. W., DePaola, L. M., Lambert, L., Martino, T., Anderson, G., & Sutton, S. (1991). Effects of interparental violence on the psychological adjustment and competencies of young children. *Journal of Consulting and Clinical Psychology, 59,* 258–266.

Foo, L., & Margolin, G. (1995). A multivariate investigation of dating aggression. *Journal of Family Violence, 10,* 351–378.

Forsstrom-Cohen, B., & Rosenbaum, A. (1985). The effects of parental marital violence on young adults: An exploratory investigation. *Journal of Marriage and the Family, 47,* 467–472.

Garcia, H., O'Hearn, H., Margolin, G., & John, R. S. (1997). Mothers' and fathers' reports of children's reactions to naturalistic marital conflict. *Journal of the American Academy of Child and Adolescent Psychiatry, 36,* 1366–1373.

Gelles, R. J. (1998). *Estimating the incidence and prevalence of violence against women: National data system and sources.* Background papers for a workshop on building data systems for monitoring and responding to violence against women. Arlington, VA.

Graham-Bermann, S. A. (1996). Family worries: The assessment of interpersonal anxiety in children from violent and nonviolent families. *Journal of Clinical Child Psychology, 25,* 280–287.

Graham-Bermann, S. A., & Levendosky, A. A. (1998). The social functioning of preschool-age children whose mothers are emotionally and physically abused. *Journal of Emotional Abuse, 1,* 59–84.

Grych, J. H. (1998). Children's appraisals of interparental conflict: Situational and contextual influences. *Journal of Family Psychology, 12,* 437–453.

Grych, J. H., & Fincham, F. D. (1990). Marital conflict and children's adjustment: A cognitive-contextual framework. *Psychological Bulletin, 108,* 297–290.

Grych, J. H., Fincham, F. D., Jouriles, E. N., & McDonald, R. (in press). Interparental conflict and child adjustment: Testing the mediational role of appraisals in the cognitive-contextual framework. *Child Development.*

Grych, J. H., & Jouriles, E. N., Swank, P. R., McDonald, R., & Norwood, W. D. (2000). Patterns of adjustment among children of battered women. *Journal of Consulting and Clinical Psychology, 68,* 84–94.

Henning, K., Leitenberg, H., Coffey, P., Turner, T., & Bennett, R. T. (1996). Long term psychological and social impact of witnessing physical conflict between parents. *Journal of Interpersonal Violence, 11,* 35–51.

Hennessy, K. D., Rabideau, G. J., Cicchetti, D., & Cummings, E. M. (1994). Responses of physically abused and nonabused children to different forms of interadult anger. *Child Development, 65,* 815–828.

Hershorn, M., & Rosenbaum, A. (1985). Children of marital violence: A closer look at the unintended victims. *American Journal of Orthopsychiatry, 55,* 260–266.

Hinchey, F. S., & Gavelek, J. R. (1982). Empathic responding in children of battered mothers. *Child Abuse and Neglect, 6,* 395–401.

Holden, G. W. (1998). Introduction: The development of research into another consequence of family violence. In G. W. Holden, R. Geffner, & E. N. Jouriles (Eds.), *Children exposed to marital violence: Theory, research, and applied issues* (pp. 1–20). Washington, DC: American Psychological Association.

Holden, G. W., & Ritchie, K. L. (1991). Linking extreme marital discord, child rearing, and child behavior problems: Evidence from battered women. *Child Development, 62,* 311–327.

Holden, G. W., Stein, J. D., Ritchie, K. L., Harris, S. D., & Jouriles, E. N. (1998). The parenting behaviors of battered women. In G. W. Holden, R. Geffner, & E. N. Jouriles (Eds.), *Children exposed to marital violence: Theory, research, and applied issues* (pp. 289–334). Washington, DC: American Psychological Association.

Holtzworth-Munroe, A., Smutzler, N., & Bates, L. (1997). A brief review of the research on husband violence. Part 3: Sociodemographic factors, relationship factors, and differing consequences of husband and wife violence. *Aggression and Violent Behavior, 2,* 285–307.

Hotaling, G. T., & Sugarman, D. B. (1986). Analysis of risk markers in husband to wife violence. The current state of knowledge. *Violence and Victims, 1,* 101–122.

Hughes, H. M. (1988). Psychological and behavioral correlates of family violence in child witnesses and victims. *American Journal of Orthopsychiatry, 58,* 77–90.

Hughes, H. M., & Luke, D. A., (1998). Heterogeneity in adjustment among children of battered women. In G. W. Holden, R. Geffner, & E. N. Jouriles (Eds.), *Children exposed to marital violence: Theory, research, and applied issues* (pp. 185–221). Washington, DC: American Psychological Association.

Jaffe, P., Wolfe, D., & Wilson, S. K. (1990). *Children of battered women.* Newbury Park, CA: Sage.

Jaffe, P., Wolfe, D., Wilson, S. K., & Zak, L. (1986). Family violence and child adjustment: A comparative analysis of girls' and boys' behavioral symptoms. *American Journal of Orthopsychiatry, 143,* 74–77.

Johnson, M. P. (1995). Patriarchal terrorism and common couple violence: Two forms of violence against women. *Journal of Marriage and the Family, 57,* 283–294.

Jouriles, E. N., Barling, J., & O'Leary, K. D. (1987). Predicting child behavior problems in maritally violent families. *Journal of Abnormal Child Psychology, 15,* 165–173.

Jouriles, E. N., McDonald, R., Norwood, W. D., & Ezell, E. (in press). Documenting the prevalence of children's exposure to domestic violence: Issues and controversies. In S. Graham-Berman & J. Edleson (Eds.), *Children and domestic violence.* Washington, DC: American Psychological Association.

Jouriles, E. N., McDonald, R., Norwood, W. D., Ware, H. S., Spiller, L. C., & Swank, P. R. (1998). Knives, guns, and interparent violence: Relations with child behavior problems. *Journal of Family Psychology, 12*, 178–194.

Jouriles, E. N., Murphy, C. M., & O'Leary, K. D. (1989). Interspousal aggression, marital discord, and child problems. *Journal of Consulting and Clinical Psychology, 57*, 453–455.

Jouriles, E. N., & Norwood, W. D. (1995). Physical aggression toward boys and girls in families characterized by the battering of women. *Journal of Family Psychology, 9*, 69–78.

Jouriles, E. N., Norwood, W. D., McDonald, R., Vincent, J. P., & Mahoney, A. (1996). Physical violence and other forms of marital aggression: Links with children's behavior problems. *Journal of Family Psychology, 10*, 223–234.

Jouriles, E. N., & O'Leary, K. D. (1985). Interspousal reliability of reports of marital violence. *Journal of Consulting and Clinical Psychology, 53*, 419–421.

Jouriles, E. N., Spiller, L. C., Stephens, N., McDonald, R., & Swank, P. (in press). Variability in adjustment of children of battered women: The role of child appraisals of interparent conflict. *Cognitive Therapy and Research.*

Kempton, T., Thomas, A. M., & Forehand, R. (1989). Dimensions of interparental conflict and adolescent functioning. *Journal of Family Violence, 4*, 297–307.

Koss, M. P., (1993). Detecting the scope of rape: A review of prevalence research methods. *Journal of Interpersonal Violence, 8*, 198–222.

Koss, M. P., Goodman, L., Browne, A., Fitzgerald, L., Keita, G. P., & Russon, N. F. (1994). *No safe haven.* Washington, DC: American Psychological Association.

Laumakis, M. A., Margolin, G., & John, R. S., (1998). The emotional, cognitive and coping responses of preadolescent children to different dimensions of marital conflict. In G. W. Holden, R. Geffner, & E. N. Jouriles (Eds.), *Children exposed to marital violence: Theory, research, and applied issues* (pp. 257–288). Washington, DC: American Psychological Association.

Layzer, J. I., Goodson, B. D., & Delange, C. (1986). Children in shelters. *Response to the victimization of women and children, 9*, 2–5.

Margolin, G. (1998). Effects of domestic violence on children. In Trickett, P. K. & Schellenbach, C. J. (Eds.), *Violence against children in the family and in the community.* Washington, DC: American Psychological Association.

McCloskey, L. A., Figueredo, A. J., & Koss, M. P. (1995). The effects of systemic family violence on children's mental health. *Child Development, 66*, 1239–1261.

McCord, J. (1979). Some child rearing antecedents to criminal behavior in adult men. *Journal of Personality and Social Psychology, 37*, 1477–1486.

McDonald, R., & Jouriles, E. N. (1991). Marital aggression and child behavior problems: Research findings, mechanisms, and intervention strategies. *The Behavior Therapist, 14*, 189–192.

Moffitt, T. E., Caspi, A., Kruger, R., Magdol, L., Margolin, G., Silva, P., & Sydney, R. (1997). Do partners agree about abuse in the relationship? A psychometric evaluation of interpartner agreement. *Psychological Assessment, 9*, 47–56.

Moore, T. E., & Pepler, D. J. (1998). Correlates of adjustment in children at risk. In G. W. Holden, R. Geffner, & E. N. Jouriles (Eds.), *Children exposed to marital violence: Theory, research, and applied issues* (pp. 157–184). Washington, DC: American Psychological Association.

O'Brien, M., John, R. S., Margolin, G., & Erel, O. (1994). Reliability and diagnostic efficacy of parents' reports regarding children's exposure to marital aggression. *Violence and Victims, 9,* 45–62.

O'Brien, M., Margolin, G., John, R. S., & Kruger, L. (1991). Mothers' and sons' cognitive and emotional reactions to simulated marital and family conflict. *Journal of Consulting and Clinical Psychology, 59,* 692–703.

O'Keefe, M. (1994). Linking marital violence, mother-child/father-child aggression, and child behavior problems. *Journal of Family Violence, 9,* 63–78.

O'Keefe, M. (1995). Predictors of child abuse in maritally violent families. *Journal of Interpersonal Violence, 10,* 3–25.

O'Keefe, M., Brockopp, K., & Chew, E. (1986). Teen dating violence. *Social Work, 31,* 465–468.

Riggs, D., O'Leary, K. D., & Breslin, F. C. (1990). Theoretical model of courtship aggression. In M. A. Pirog-Good & J. E. Stets (Eds.), *Violence in Dating Relationships: Emerging Social Issues* (pp. 53–71). New York: Praeger.

Rosenbaum, A., & O'Leary, K. D. (1981). Children: The unintended victims of marital violence. *American Journal of Orthopsychiatry, 51,* 692, 699.

Rossman, B. (1998). Descartes's error and posttraumatic stress disorder: Cognition and emotion for children who are exposed to parental violence. In G. W. Holden, R. Geffner, & E. N. Jouriles (Eds.), *Children exposed to marital violence: Theory, research, and applied issues* (pp. 223–256). Washington, DC: American Psychological Association.

Rossman, B., & Rosenberg, M. (1992). Family stress and functioning in children: The moderating effects of children's beliefs about their control over parental conflict. *Journal of Child Psychology and Psychiatry, 33,* 699–715.

Rutter, M. (1987). Psychosocial resilience and protective mechanisms. *American Journal of Orthopsychiatry, 57,* 317–331.

Schwartz, M. D. (1998). *Methodological issues in the use of survey data for measuring and characterizing violence against women.* Background papers for a workshop on building data systems for monitoring and responding to violence against women. Arlington, VA.

Silvern, L., Karyl, J., Waelde, L., Hodges, W. F., Starek, J., Heidt, E., & Min, K. (1995). Retrospective reports of parental partner abuse: Relationships to depression, trauma symptoms and self-esteem among college students. *Journal of Family Violence, 10,* 177–201.

Smith, M. D. (1987). The incidence and prevalence of woman abuse in Toronto. *Violence and Victims, 2,* 33–47.

Spaccarelli, S., Coatsworth, J. D., & Bowden, B. S. (1995). Exposure to serious family violence among incarcerated boys: Its association with violent offending and potential mediating variables. *Violence and Victims, 10,* 163–182.

Spaccarelli, S., Sandler, I., & Roosa, M. (1994). History of spouse violence against mother: Correlated risks and unique effects in child mental health. *Journal of Family Violence, 9,* 79–98.

Stagg, V., Wills, G. D., & Howell, M. (1989). Psychopathology in early childhood witnesses of family violence. *Topics in Early Childhood Special Education, 9,* 73–87.

Sternberg, K. J., Lamb, M. E., Greenbaum, C., Cicchetti, D., Dawud, S., Cortes, R. M., Krispin, O., & Lorey, F. (1993). Effects of domestic violence on children's behavior problems and depression. *Developmental Psychology, 29,* 44–52.

Straus, M. A. (1990). Injury and frequency of assault and the "Representative Sample Fallacy" in measuring wife beating and child abuse. In M. A. Straus & R. J. Gelles (Eds.), *Physical violence in American families: Risk factors and adaptations to violence in 8,145 families* (pp. 75–91). New Brunswick, NJ: Transaction Publishers.

Straus, M. A., & Gelles, R. J. (1990). *Physical violence in American families: Risk factors and adaptations to violence in 8,145 families.* New Brunswick, NJ: Transaction Publishers.

Straus, M. A., Gelles, R. J., & Steinmetz, S. K. (1980). *Behind closed doors: Violence in the American family.* Garden City: Doubleday Press.

Ware, H. S., Jouriles, E. N., Spiller, L. C., McDonald, R., Swank, P. R., & Norwood, W. D. (in press). Conduct problems among children at battered women's shelters: Prevalence and stability of maternal reports. *Journal of Family Violence.*

Wolfe, D. A., Jaffe, P., Wilson, S. K., & Zak, L. (1985). Children of battered women: The relation of child behavior to family violence and maternal stress. *Journal of Consulting and Clinical Psychology, 53,* 657–665.

Wolfe, D. A., & Korsch, B., (1994). Witnessing domestic violence during childhood and adolescence. *Pediatrics, 94,* 594–599.

Wolfe, D. A., Zak, L., Wilson, S. K., & Jaffe, P. (1986). Child witnesses to violence between parents: Critical issues in behavioral and social adjustment. *Journal of Abnormal Child Psychology, 14,* 95–104.

Yllö, K. A. (1993). Through a feminist lens: Gender, power, and violence. In R. J. Gelles & D. R. Loseke (Eds.), *Current controversies on family violence* (pp. 47–62). Newbury Park, CA: Sage Publications.

13 When Conflict Continues after the Marriage Ends

Effects of Postdivorce Conflict on Children

Christy M. Buchanan and Kelly L. Heiges

Divorce is one option exercised by parents who experience conflict with one another. Yet when both parents retain some involvement with their children after a divorce, they are required to continue a relationship as parents. Co-parenting may be active (e.g., parents interacting directly with one another to establish rules and expectations for the child or make decisions about the child's life) or passive (e.g., parents avoiding contact with one another but being available to parent when it is their "turn"). In either case, co-parenting necessitates continuing ties between the once-conflicting parties; thus, the opportunity for continued conflict remains. Furthermore, even (or perhaps especially) in instances where one parent has no contact with the rest of the family, angry or hostile feelings on the part of the remaining parent may create a residue of conflict that affects children.

In this chapter we explore several questions concerning postdivorce interparental conflict. To what extent does divorce reduce the conflict to which children are exposed? And to what extent is conflict after divorce an important factor in how children adjust? Is interparental conflict after divorce different from conflict that occurs within nondivorced families? And does its impact on children differ by family structure? After addressing these questions, we examine the role of parenting in understanding the link between postdivorce conflict and children's adjustment. Finally, we look at the impact of conflict in different postdivorce living arrangements to see whether conflict's impact depends on the type of custody or visitation a child experiences. In sum, we examine what conflict after divorce is like, its relative importance to children's adjustment, the reasons for its importance, and the conditions that influence its importance.

Interparental Conflict following Divorce

To what extent is divorce effective in reducing conflict among couples who must continue to co-parent? Initially, conflict in divorcing couples is typically quite high, reflecting in many cases a history of high conflict, but also a peak that is related to resolving issues of the divorce itself (Cummings & Davies, 1994; Johnston, Campbell, & Tall, 1985). Furstenberg and Cherlin (1991) reported that over two-thirds of couples who separate experience high conflict during the process and need intermediaries to help them in resolving disputes. Hetherington, Cox, and Cox (1976) found that two-thirds of the exchanges between ex-spouses in the two months after their divorce involved conflicts.

After the first year or two following separation and divorce, however, there are decreases in conflict and increases in disengagement between ex-spouses (Forehand et al., 1991; Furstenberg & Cherlin, 1991; Maccoby & Mnookin, 1992). A minority (approximately 10–25%) of couples continues to experience moderate to high levels of hostility and conflict after the initial postseparation period (Ambert, 1989; Maccoby & Mnookin, 1992; Spanier & Thompson, 1984), and these are often couples who experienced the highest levels of conflict during marriage (Kelly, 1993; Nelson, 1989).

For some couples, conflict decreases because one parent no longer has contact with the family. Up to 10% of children have no contact with a noncustodial parent (typically the father) after parental divorce; 40–50% have irregular and infrequent contact (Ambert, 1989; Buchanan, Maccoby, & Dornbusch, 1996; Furstenberg & Harris, 1992; Seltzer, 1991). When one parent has little to no contact with the family, children are unlikely to be exposed to much active conflict between parents. But even in families where contact between children and noncustodial parents is maintained at frequent and regular intervals, increasing disengagement between parents and a lowering of negative feelings and hostility over time are typical (Ahrons, 1981; Forehand et al., 1991; Furstenberg & Cherlin, 1991; Maccoby & Mnookin, 1992). In fact, disengaged parenting between divorced parents may function to limit conflict between them (Furstenberg & Cherlin, 1991).

In sum, frequent conflict following the initial aftermath of divorce is the exception, although for 10–20% of families conflict remains an important matter with respect to children's adjustment.

The Importance of Interparental Conflict to Children after Divorce

Early research on divorce, conducted in the 1960s and 1970s, typically characterized divorce as a static situation – as a "social address"

(Bronfenbrenner, 1979) or a single *event*. This research compared the adjustment of children in divorced and nondivorced homes and frequently found children of divorce to be more poorly adjusted (e.g., Gibson, 1969; Hetherington, 1972; Parish & Taylor, 1979). By the 1980s, however, investigators began to recognize the variability in family circumstances and child adjustment in divorced homes, and thus the need to understand divorce as a *process* that goes on over some time and differs for different families. Investigators also recognized problems inherent in implicating divorce as a cause of children's problems from correlational research. Research identifying a variety of individual and family factors that mediate or moderate the impact of divorce on children has emerged since that time (see Buchanan, in press, for a summary of many such factors); postdivorce interparental conflict has emerged as one of the most important of these factors.

In 1982, Emery published a landmark paper presenting persuasive evidence that interparental conflict is a more important predictor of children's adjustment than is divorce, per se. An important implication of this evidence was that if a divorce reduced conflict between parents, this would be less damaging to children than the choice to stay in a high-conflict marriage. Nearly two decades later, there is much converging evidence that conflict between parents predicts children's adjustment better than does family structure, and that in many instances divorce "effects" actually reflect effects of conflict associated with divorce (e.g., Borrine, Handal, Brown, & Searight, 1991; Cherlin et al., 1991; Dixon, Charles, & Craddock, 1998; Forehand, McCombs, Long, Brody, & Fauber, 1988; Hayashi & Strickland, 1998; Kozuch & Cooney, 1995; Kurdek, 1991; Long, Forehand, Fauber, & Brody, 1987; Mechanic & Hansell, 1989; Vandewater & Lansford, 1998).

Research is also consistent in showing that continuing interparental conflict is one of the most important predictors of variability in children's postdivorce adjustment (Amato, 1993). As early as the first year after divorce or litigation, children fare better when conflict is reduced than when conflict remains high (Kitzmann & Emery, 1994; Long, Slater, Forehand, & Fauber, 1988). Continuing conflict is a significant predictor of variability in several aspects of adjustment, including externalizing problems, internalizing problems, self-esteem, social competence, cognitive competence, academic achievement, and young adult attitudes toward marriage and quality of romantic relationships. Internalizing problems seem most likely to emerge when conflict is extremely high or in situations where the child is unduly exposed to or used in the conflict (Johnston, Gonzalez, & Campbell, 1987; Shaw & Emery, 1988).

Thus, research unequivocally points to an important role for inter-parental conflict in understanding children's adjustment after parental divorce. The relations between postdivorce conflict and adjustment may be greater for some children than others, however, depending on characteristics of the child such as age or sex.

Age Differences

Survey research suggests that the longer-term impact of divorce is, on average, worst for children who are youngest (i.e., under six years of age) at the time of marital disruption (Allison & Furstenberg, 1989; Zill, Morrison, & Coiro, 1993). Data examining the role of age in shorter-term adjustment is more difficult to assess because of the diffi-culty in disentangling age at time of measurement from age at time of divorce as well as other methodological problems (Emery, 1999; Grych & Fincham, 1998). However, there is some evidence that differences between children of divorced and nondivorced homes are somewhat greater during the elementary and secondary school years than before or after (Amato & Keith, 1991). In contrast, more qualitative or clini-cally oriented accounts have emphasized that children of different ages have different types of reactions to divorce, and therefore there is no age at which children are immune to effects of marital disruption (Hetherington, 1989; Kalter & Rembar, 1981; Wallerstein & Kelly, 1980).

Very little research has explored the impact of postdivorce conflict by age, but the research that does is in agreement with the conclusion that children of all ages show some type of negative reaction to conflict. In one longitudinal study that compared the association between marital conflict and antisocial behavior at different ages using a nationally rep-resentative sample *combining* divorced and nondivorced families, the authors found that the association between marital conflict and antiso-cial behavior was of a similar magnitude for adolescents and elemen-tary-aged children, and the association did not decline until individuals were young adults (Sim & Vuchinich, 1996).

Further evidence that children of all ages react negatively to postdi-vorce parental discord emerges from studies of the most highly con-flicted divorced families (Garrity & Baris, 1997; Johnston et al., 1987); these studies also describe some typical reactions for different age groups. Preschool children tend to become irritable or clingy. Beginning with school age, loyalty conflicts become more common. Early adolescent children are more likely to align with one parent and less likely to experience loyalty conflicts than younger (Garrity & Barris, 1997; Johnston & Campbell, 1988) or older (Buchanan et al., 1996) children. As will be discussed later, both loyalty conflicts and alignments are likely to be linked with less-than-optimal adjustment of children, although specific manifestations of problems might vary.

Although it seems that children of all ages are affected by marital conflict after divorce, there is also some evidence suggesting that the link between marital conflict and children's problems may be *somewhat* stronger during a child's early adolescence than at other times (Johnston et al., 1987; Wierson & Forehand, 1992). A greater impact of conflict at early adolescence may be the result of a tendency for a greater number of stressors to occur at this stage (Simmons, Burgeson, Carlton-Ford, & Blyth, 1987); other simultaneous stressors may decrease the child's ability to deal with marital conflict as a stressor.

In sum, the research on children's age as a moderator of children's reactions to marital conflict is extremely limited but suggests differences in ways of reacting more so than in degree of impact. Early adolescence may be a period in which children have somewhat less ability to handle the stress that accompanies marital conflict due to co-occurring stressors.

Sex Differences

Behavioral difficulties are more often seen in school-aged boys than in school-aged girls after divorce; this difference is often attributed to higher exposure to discord accompanying the divorce for boys (Hetherington, 1990; Hetherington, Cox, & Cox, 1982; Pagani-Kurtz & Deverensky, 1997). There is some corresponding evidence that interparental conflict is more likely to predict behavior problems prior to adolescence in boys than in girls (Amato & Rezac, 1994; Fidler & Saunders, 1988; Hetherington et al., 1982). Conflict may, however, be more likely to predict internalizing problems among preadolescent girls than preadolescent boys (Johnston et al., 1987).

There is some evidence for an increased impact of stressors, including divorce, on girls during adolescence as compared to before adolescence (Hetherington, 1990; Simmons et al., 1987; Zahn-Waxler, Cole, & Barrett, 1991), leading to an elimination or even reversal of the sex differences in response to stress found among preadolescents. Little research has looked at whether this pattern of sex-differentiated change applies to interparental conflict as a stressor. In line with the possibility that adolescent girls are more sensitive to such conflict than are adolescent boys, Buchanan et al. (1996) found adolescent girls to experience more loyalty conflicts than adolescent boys after divorce. These investigators also found the relation between interparental hostility and lower closeness to the noncustodial parent to be especially strong for father-custody girls.

In general, information on sex differences in reaction to postdivorce conflict is consistent with the literatures on divorce and on marital conflict more generally. Both boys and girls are affected by conflict, but the effect may show up on different indices of adjustment (externalizing for boys, internalizing for girls) and at different time periods (with stronger effects for girls during adolescence) (Buchanan, in press; Camara & Resnick, 1988; Emery, 1982; 1988; Purcell & Kaslow, 1994).

Summary

Postdivorce conflict is clearly an important factor in understanding the adjustment of children after divorce. This is true for children of all ages and both sexes, although the specific manifestation of problems associated with conflict may vary by developmental status or between boys and girls. There are very likely other important factors that moderate the association between interparental conflict and children's adjustment after divorce. One of these may be the quality of relationships between parents and children, and we discuss evidence for this later in the section on parenting. Another may be the existence of other simultaneous life stressors, which is indicated by the findings reported here concerning early adolescence, as well as findings from research showing that children adjust better to divorce when there are fewer co-occurring life stressors (Amato, 1993; Buchanan et al., 1996; Buehler, Hogan, Robinson & Levy, 1985–1986; Tschann, Johnston, Kline, & Wallerstein, 1990). Virtually no research has directly examined the moderating influence of other factors such as life stressors, however, on the way that children of divorce respond to ongoing conflict between their parents.

Characteristics of Conflict in Divorced versus Married Parents

Dimensions of conflict such as frequency, intensity, topic, mode of expression, and resolution may be important in how children react to interparental conflict (Gano-Phillips & Fincham, 1995; Fincham & Osborne, 1993). To understand how the impact of conflict in situations of divorce compares to its impact in maritally intact families, it would be useful to have comparisons of these dimensions by family type. In this section we summarize what is known about specific dimensions of conflict in divorced families, and how these characteristics of conflict compare between parents who have divorced and parents within a marital relationship.

Frequency of Conflict

Earlier, we summarized trends in the frequency of conflict in divorced couples over time. How does frequency of postdivorce interparental conflict compare with frequency of conflict in nondivorced homes? The little research available suggests that the answer depends on how long it has been since the divorce. Mothers of adolescents who had been divorced less than 2 years reported frequencies of adolescent-observed interparental conflict (Forehand, Thomas, Wierson, Brody, & Fauber, 1990) and interparental conflict related to marital and child issues (Forehand & McCombs, 1989) that were no different than those reported by married mothers of adolescents. Mothers who had been divorced for 2 to 3 years, however, reported *less* interparental conflict in front of their adolescent children than did mothers from nondivorced homes (Forehand & Thomas, 1992). The opportunity to argue with an (ex)spouse in front of one's children inevitably lessens after divorce, and the research cited here suggests that divorce may in fact decrease young adolescents' exposure to active disagreements between their parents. Research addressing this question is limited, however, and research on children of different ages is especially needed.

Topic of Conflict

The topics that lead to conflict among both intact and divorced couples are heterogeneous. However, there are necessarily different topics of conflict that emerge in each family type. Economic stress, and subsequent conflict over finances, is one of the biggest difficulties after divorce (Hetherington et al., 1976). Besides finances, issues of visitation, childrearing, children's adjustment to divorce, and ex-spouses' intimate relations with others are topics most likely to lead to conflict among divorced couples (Ahrons, 1981; Hetherington et al., 1976). Disputes over custody and visitation constitute a specific, highly emotional form of child-related conflict that can occur between divorced parents but not between married parents. Although only 10–20% of families need legal help in resolving custody and visitation issues, the initial expressed preferences of parents concerning custody often conflict, indicating that many parents take part in bargaining about custody and visitation outside the legal arena (Maccoby & Mnookin, 1992). And given that most of their continuing interactions are due to shared children, divorced parents' conversations and conflicts are more likely to be about parenting than nonparenting issues (Ahrons, 1981; Cummings & Davies, 1994; Maccoby & Mnookin, 1992).

Married parents, like divorced parents, experience conflict over financial issues. But in contrast to divorced parents, married parents tend to discuss more spousal issues – or issues that are not directly about the children – such as division of labor, leisure time, religion, and friends. Conflict over child-related issues among married parents is more likely to revolve around daily routines and concerns than is child-related conflict among divorced parents (Forehand & McCombs, 1989; Maccoby & Mnookin, 1992).

Intensity of Conflict

Little is known about the intensity of conflict in different family forms, but there is some evidence that the arguments of married parents are less heated than those of divorced parents, at least in families of adolescents. Thus, although children of divorce may be exposed to less frequent conflict, children in divorced families may be exposed to a higher percentage of angry, intense arguments (Forehand & McCombs, 1989).

Mode of Expression and Resolution of Conflict

As noted earlier, divorced parents often avoid conflict-provoking topics (Ahrons, 1981); they are more likely than married parents to use avoidance as a response to conflict (Camara & Resnick, 1989; Forehand & Thomas, 1992). Although active disagreements may be uncommon, conflict in divorced families may more often take the form of hostility or an ongoing negative attitude toward one's ex-spouse (Forehand & McCombs, 1989). When overt conflict does occur, it may be more likely to involve verbal attacks and less likely to involve compromise in divorced as compared to married couples (Camara & Resnick, 1989).

Summary

Immediately following divorce, children may be exposed to especially high levels of conflict between their parents. After this initial period and up to about 2 years after divorce, children of divorce probably experience levels of interparental conflict very similar to levels in nondivorced families. As time since divorce lengthens beyond the first 2 years, children may in fact experience less frequent conflict between their parents in divorced than nondivorced homes. The conflict to which children of divorce are exposed may be more subtle than that in nondivorced families. It may take the form of hostility and avoidance more than active conflict, and it is less likely to involve compromise. The active conflicts that do take place are likely to be more intense, with more verbal attacks. The topic of conflict is more likely to involve child-related matters in divorced than in nondivorced families.

Interparental Conflict and Children's Adjustment in Divorced versus Nondivorced Homes

Earlier we documented a link between interparental conflict and children's adjustment after divorce. Is this link similar among children of divorced and married parents? There are several reasons why conflict might be expected to have a bigger impact in divorced than nondivorced family situations. Conflict after divorce tends to be more intense when it happens, and on average, it has probably taken place over a longer time period. The conflict is more likely to be over child-related issues. Divorced parents are also more likely to use destructive, ineffective techniques for resolving the conflict. All of these are factors linked to worse outcomes for children in the face of conflict (Camara & Resnick, 1988; Emery, 1982; Grych & Fincham, 1993; Grych, Seid, & Fincham, 1992). Furthermore, conflict after divorce is more likely to be accompanied by other life stressors such as parental depression and unhappiness (Cummings & Davies, 1994; Demo & Acock, 1996; Forehand, Thomas, et al., 1990) and financial difficulties (Duncan & Hoffman, 1985; Furstenberg & Cherlin, 1991). Because marital conflict is a stronger predictor of problems in situations of higher family stress (Cummings & Davies, 1994), one might expect conflict to have a more negative impact on children of divorce than on children of intact marriages. This may be especially true when considering internalizing problems, which are more likely than externalizing problems to emerge when there is a confluence of psychological distress and conflict (Cummings & Davies, 1994).

Also, children of divorce, having experienced more conflict – and more poorly resolved conflict – in their past, may be more highly sensitized to any conflict that does occur (Cummings, Pelligrini, Notarius, & Cummings, 1989; Cummings & Davies, 1994). And marital conflict in nondivorced families, more so than in divorced families, may be cushioned by positive features of the marital relationship (Gabardi & Rosen, 1992).

Thus, for several reasons it seems that children of divorce ought to be more adversely affected by continuing interparental conflict. Yet, a stronger negative impact of conflict within nondivorced homes might be expected for different reasons. First, children in nondivorced families with conflict are likely to be exposed to active disagreements and conflicts more frequently than children of divorce, particularly if the divorce is not recent. It is also possible that conflict itself has a less negative impact on parenting in divorced than nondivorced homes, at least among families that are not in extreme states of distress. We speculate that divorced parents who argue only occasionally with their ex-spouses may be better able to isolate the conflict from their parenting than are married parents who argue occasionally, other life stressors being equal. Divorced parents in this example are otherwise not in the presence of the person who elicits the negative emotions that presumably make it difficult to engage fully and positively with one's children. If, as we will argue in the next section, parenting is an important mediator of the conflict-adjustment link, the less negatively that conflict affects parenting, the less negative the impact of that conflict on the child should be.

Few studies have explicitly compared the conflict-adjustment link by family structure. Of those that have, most show the link to be similar in magnitude in nondivorced and divorced homes (Borrine et al., 1991; Cummings & Davies, 1994; Hayashi & Strickland, 1998; Kinnaird & Gerrard, 1986; Kozuch & Cooney, 1995; Long et al., 1987; Shaw & Emery, 1988; Vandewater & Lansford, 1998). Yet some exceptions exist, most of which show a stronger link between interparental conflict and adjustment problems among children of divorce. For example, Forehand et al. (1988) found that interparental conflict predicted lower cognitive competence among adolescents more in recently divorced than nondivorced homes. The authors suggest that marital problems among recently divorced parents may be especially likely to interfere with parental attention and supervision.

In support of the possibility that conflict is more likely to predict negative parent–child interactions in recently divorced than in nondivorced homes, there is a stronger association of interparental conflict with parent–adolescent disagreement (Forehand et al., 1991) and with maternal rejection/withdrawal (Fauber, Forehand, Thomas, & Wierson, 1990) in families who have divorced within the previous year or two than in maritally intact families. Forehand et al. (1991) speculate that interparental conflict is "more detrimental to the family environment … in divorced families because the positive aspects of the parental relationship are not present to offset the parental conflict" (p. 108). It is important to note, however, that this research supporting a more detrimental role for conflict in divorced homes was conducted with adolescents from recently divorced families. The null results from studies with more variance in children's age and time since divorce (e.g., Borrine et al., 1991; Vandewater & Lansford, 1998) call into question whether differences in the impact of conflict by family structure exist more broadly.

In contrast to findings showing a greater impact of conflict in divorced homes, one study of young adults' attitudes toward marriage and family indicated that parental conflict was a stronger predictor of disenchantment toward marriage as a lifetime commitment among children of intact marriages as compared to children of divorce (Kozuch & Cooney, 1995). The authors hypothesize that children of divorce are more likely to realize that divorce does not always end marital conflict; they thus are less likely than children of high-conflict intact marriages to endorse divorce as a good alternative to such conflict. It is important to note that in this sample, the link between interparental conflict and many other family and marital attitudes did not differ by family structure.

The studies cited here suggest that, overall, conflict probably has a similar overall impact on children's well-being regardless of family structure (see also Emery, 1982), but they also raise the possibility that the impact of conflict differs by family structure at certain times or on certain types of outcomes. For example, it is possible that interparental conflict has a stronger impact on parenting and child adjustment in divorced as compared to nondivorced families, but only in the immediate aftermath of a divorce. Perhaps after more time has passed and the frequency and intensity of conflict diminish, the differential impact disappears. Also, under some circumstances, the impact of conflict may be greater for children whose parents remain married, due to factors such as decreased (or less continual) impact of a noncustodial parent on the custodial parent's daily moods in a divorced situation (as explained previously).

It is also possible that interparental conflict affects children equally in both divorced and nondivorced family structures, but that the effect may occur for different reasons in divorced compared to nondivorced families. Importantly, most studies linking conflict with adjustment use measures of conflict that emphasize frequency and intensity of conflict. Yet, children of intact marriages may be affected more by the frequency of conflict, whereas children of divorce may be affected more by the intensity or the negative modes of resolution employed. The typical study that uses general, composite measures of conflict may not elucidate these different influences. Similarly, research that neglects to examine specific mediators (e.g., different aspects of parenting or the parent–child relationship) may fail to turn up different mechanisms of impact by family structure. For example, it seems plausible that alignment by the child with one parent as a result of interparental conflict would be more common among children of divorce simply because it is easier to stay angry at or distant from a parent the less you see him or her. This hypothesis has not received support at present, but the one study testing it (Buchanan & Louca, 1999) was limited to relatively low-conflict families; differences may emerge only or mainly among families experiencing higher levels of conflict. The point to be emphasized here is that conflict may lead to different patterns of parent–child relationships (e.g., alignments, loyalty conflicts) in different family structures, producing problems in each case but for different reasons.

Some support for different mechanisms of effect in different family structures comes from research examining young adolescents' perceptions of their parents' conflict as a mediator of conflict and adjustment. Forehand, Wierson, McCombs, Brody, & Fauber (1989) found that interparental conflict was more likely to have a direct link to adjustment problems when parents were divorced; in nondivorced families, there was an indirect path from interparental conflict to externalizing behavior via adolescents' perceptions of the conflict. The authors suggest that the meaning of conflict is clear for adolescents of divorce; these children know their parents no longer care for each other and cannot get along. For adolescents in nondivorced families, the meaning of conflict is more ambiguous, and the impact of conflict may thus depend more on an adolescent's interpretation.

In summary, as currently assessed, the magnitude of the relation between conflict and adjustment is similar in divorced and nondivorced families. When there are differences by family structure, conflict seems to have a greater impact in divorced homes. But it is premature to draw conclusions concerning differential impact by family structure, as studies have addressed this question in only a superficial and limited way. It may be that the association between conflict and adjustment differs by family structure at certain times after the divorce, at different levels of conflict, at different ages of the child, or under different contexts of other life stressors. Furthermore, global measures of conflict frequency and intensity may not fully capture the reasons for a relation between conflict and adjustment in different family structures. And the ways in which parenting and other mediators operate in the two family structures may differ. In the next section, we examine in more detail evidence for the role of parenting in mediating and moderating the link between interparental conflict and child adjustment after divorce.

The Role of Parenting in Understanding the Conflict-Adjustment Link

Interparental conflict may have a negative impact on parenting and parent–child relationships, which may in turn lead to poorer adjustment for children. Thus, parenting may mediate the conflict-adjustment link. In addition, some parents in conflict may be better at isolating interparental conflict from the parent–child relationship than others and at maintaining effective parenting and positive relationships with their children despite conflict with their partner. Thus, parenting may also function as a moderator of the conflict-adjustment link in that children may show negative effects of interparental conflict when there is – in addition – poor parenting, but not when parenting remains effective. What is the evidence that parenting plays each of these roles – both mediator and moderator – in the conflict-adjustment link?

Parenting as a Mediator

On average, divorced homes are characterized by less effective parenting and less positive parent–child relationships than nondivorced homes, and variability in adjustment after divorce has also been linked to variability in such factors (Amato, 1993; Buchanan, in press; Cummings & Davies, 1994). Given evidence for both interparental conflict *and* parenting as mediators of divorce and adjustment, and given that marital conflict and parenting are linked in nondivorced families (Fincham & Osborne, 1993), it seems plausible that interparental conflict may be linked with poor outcomes in children of divorce at least partly because of the impact of conflict on parenting and parent–child relationships. Surprisingly little research has directly examined this hypothesis in divorced families, perhaps because the focus of research is typically on whether *either* interparental conflict *or* parenting mediates the impact of divorce on adjustment.

One important study provides evidence that parenting by the custodial parent mediates the impact of conflict in divorced as well as nondivorced families (Fauber et al., 1990). In recently divorced families with adolescents, higher conflict predicted more psychological control and more rejection/withdrawal among mothers. Maternal rejection/withdrawal, in turn, predicted internalizing and externalizing problems. There was no direct relation between conflict and adjustment when rejection/withdrawal was accounted for. Thus, the impact of conflict on both internalizing and externalizing problems within the first year following divorce was mediated by maternal rejection of or withdrawal from adolescent children. In another study of recently divorced mothers of young adolescent children, similar results were found, with the impact of interparental conflict being mediated in this case by conflict in the parent–adolescent relationship (Forehand et al., 1991).

Do similar results emerge in other age groups, or when more time has elapsed since the divorce? Because conflict and levels of distress decrease for most divorced couples over time, one might expect relations such as those documented by Fauber et al. (1990) to decline as time since the divorce passes. Among families varying greatly in time since divorce and age of child but in very high conflict, empathic mother–child relationships mediated interparental conflict and children's adjustment (Tschann et al., 1990). Possible differences in the strength of mediation by time since divorce or age of child were not reported. Among adolescents from families representing a wider range of conflict, interparental conflict was not related to adolescents' perceived closeness to the custodial parent, although it did predict less closeness to the noncustodial parent and perceptions of more discrepant parenting between homes (Buchanan et al., 1996). Lack of closeness to the noncustodial parent and perceptions of discrepant parenting were both linked to poorer adjustment, but explicit tests of mediation were not conducted. Other research shows parental mediation of the conflict-adjustment relationship in samples combining adolescents from divorced and nondivorced families (e.g., Vandewater & Lansford, 1998; Wierson & Forehand, 1992), but tests of whether the mediation pathways vary by family structure are not reported.

A related line of research examines the impact of conflict on parent–child relationships in divorced homes from a family systems theory and focuses on how interparental conflict influences the pattern of relationships a child has with *both* parents. A systems perspective predicts that children will have difficulty being close to two parents who are in conflict with one another (Emery, 1988; Johnston & Campbell, 1987; Heider, 1958). Heider's (1958) balance theory emphasizes the probability of alignments between a child and one parent in response to interparental conflict and accompanying pressure on the child to take sides. However, children may also respond to such pressure by trying to maintain loyalties with both parents and becoming caught between them or by withdrawing from both parents (Emery, 1999; Emery, Joyce, & Fincham, 1987; Minuchin, 1974), both responses that alter the triadic relationships among mother, father, and child.

The results reported earlier showing that parental conflict and hostility are related to less perceived closeness on the part of adolescents toward their noncustodial parents primarily may suggest an alignment of sorts (Buchanan et al., 1996). Although adolescents were not especially close to their custodial parent in situations of high conflict, they were more likely to feel distant from their noncustodial parent. Accounting for level of visitation did not eliminate the relation between conflict and closeness to the noncustodial parent. Thus, negativity in the interparental relationship may have an emotional and psychological cost in terms of souring adolescents on the relationship with the least-seen parent, as predicted by balance theory (Heider, 1958). Alternatively, characteristics of the noncustodial parent in high conflict families may contribute to more distant parent–child relationships. At present, we know only that high conflict between parents is likely to be accompanied by adolescents' emotional distancing from the noncustodial parent in particular. Because closeness to the noncustodial parent was linked in some small but significant ways to adolescents' adjustment, it may be that alignment mediates a conflict-adjustment relation.

Data on alignment in the stronger sense – where children develop a strong preference for one parent and reject or experience extreme anger toward the other parent (as opposed to simply reporting a lack of closeness to one parent) – suggest that such alignment is relatively common in situations of high conflict (Johnston & Campbell, 1987; 1988; Lampel, 1996). How strong alignments are related to adjustment is unclear; alignment may relieve some of the anxiety associated with parental conflict but also may allow children to harbor anger and resentment that interfere with the development of mature social relationships (Lampel, 1996).

Somewhat more data are available on loyalty conflicts as a possible mediator of conflict and adjustment. A link between levels of postdivorce conflict and the experience of being caught between parents has been documented among both school-aged and adolescent children (Buchanan, Maccoby, & Dornbusch, 1991; 1996; Healy, Stewart, & Copeland, 1993; Johnston et al., 1987; Johnston, Kline, & Tschann, 1989; Tschann et al., 1990). Both objective measures of being used in parents' conflicts and subjective feelings of loyalty conflicts mediate a relationship between interparental conflict or aggression and children's adjustment on indices such as self-blame, behavior problems, and depression or anxiety (Buchanan et al., 1991, 1996; Healy et al., 1993; Johnston et al., 1989; Tschann et al., 1990). Thus, the strain of participating in the conflict and trying to remain loyal to and impartial toward *two* parents who are in conflict with one another may help explain conflict's impact.

Finally, there is some evidence that in high-conflict homes after divorce, children are at risk of role reversal with one or both parents (Johnston et al., 1987). Role reversal, in the sense of having to care for a parent (particularly if that parent is a father) or the family in very adult ways, is linked to negative adjustment among both children and adolescents (Buchanan et al., 1996; Johnston et al., 1987). Further research is needed to clarify the conditions under which conflict is related to role reversal, as well as the particular conditions under which role reversal is a negative factor in adjustment.

In sum, interparental conflict after divorce may interfere with effective parenting and healthy parent–child relationships. And both parenting and parent–child relationships are important predictors of postdivorce adjustment. Thus, among children of divorce as well as children of intact marriages, the impact of conflict appears to be mediated in some important ways through conflict's impact on parenting. Research needs to address these links more systematically, to see whether the evidence for mediation varies based on factors such as age of child, time since divorce, or characteristics of the conflict itself.

Parenting as a Moderator

A good relationship with one, and preferably both, parents can buffer the impact of divorce for children (Buchanan et al., 1996; Hess & Camara, 1979; Hetherington, Cox, & Cox, 1979; Wolchik et al., 1993). It may be that the impact of postdivorce conflict is influenced by the nature of the child's relationship with one or both parents as well. Two studies addressing this question among early adolescents report conflicting results. Brody and Forehand (1990) found that adolescents who had poor relationships with their noncustodial father in the first year after divorce were more likely to have internalizing problems linked to interparental conflict than those with good relationships. In contrast, Lutzke, Wolchik, and Braver (1996) found that the custodial mother–child relationship did not cushion adolescents from negative effects of conflict. Although the Lutzke et al. (1996) sample was large, it may have been biased toward more effective and involved parents because they were participants in a divorce intervention program. Perhaps this restricted the range of parent–child relationships represented. Further research, particularly using children spanning a wider range of ages, is needed to examine whether the impact of conflict is moderated by parent–child relationships.

Visitation, Custody, and the Impact of Conflict

Is conflict more damaging when children continue to see both parents a great deal after divorce? Common sense, and some data (Nelson, 1989; Pagani-Kurtz & Deverensky, 1997), suggest that when children see both parents frequently, there are increased opportunities for parents to engage in conflict, thereby increasing the amount of conflict to which children are exposed. Yet in some families, visitation is reduced or curtailed because of one parent's (usually the mother's) hostility toward the other (Buchanan et al., 1996), suggesting that some low-contact children are exposed to high maternal hostility. And several studies show that after the first year or two following divorce, conflict, cooperation, and hostility between parents vary little by custody or visitation arrangement (Buchanan et al., 1996; Furstenberg & Nord, 1985; Maccoby & Mnookin, 1992; Steinman, 1981).

A direct link between contact and conflict may be weak or inconsistent because many high-conflict parents avoid contact with one another despite having their children spend time in both homes. Even when parents avoid contact, however, conflict might have more potential for damage when children have more contact with both parents, because there are more opportunities for parents to use children in ongoing conflict (e.g., having them carry messages). Research on children in mother custody generally shows that high conflict between parents at minimum prevents benefits of visitation and may increase the likelihood of adjustment problems (Amato & Rezac, 1994; Felner & Terre, 1987; Johnston & Campbell, 1988). Research on joint custody has a similar message. Joint custody that is voluntarily chosen by low-conflict parents has been associated with positive adjustment in children (Luepnitz, 1986; Shiller, 1986); joint custody that is court-imposed on high-conflict parents has been associated with problems in adjustment (Johnston, 1995; Johnston et al., 1989; Steinman, Zemmelman, & Knoblauch, 1985). Conflict is also especially likely to predict loyalty conflicts among adolescents in joint custody (Buchanan et al., 1996). Overall adjustment among these joint custody adolescents was not especially poor, apparently because other benefits of joint custody offset the negative impact of loyalty conflicts. However, the potential for heightened harm due to being used in parental conflict was present, and has in fact been documented among extremely conflictual families (Johnston et al., 1989).

In contrast, a smaller number of studies suggest that visitation can sometimes help reduce the negative impact of conflict, presumably via the buffering impact of maintaining a good relationship with both parents. Forehand, Wierson, et al., (1990) found that early adolescents whose divorced parents were in high conflict and visited their noncustodial parents scored no differently on measures of social and academic competence from adolescents whose parents were low in conflict (regardless of visitation frequency). Adolescents of high-conflict parents who did not visit their noncustodial fathers scored significantly lower than all other groups. Similarly, the link between interparental conflict and less closeness to the noncustodial parent (Buchanan et al., 1996) was more common for adolescents who rarely saw their noncustodial parent. Thus, continued visitation with noncustodial parents may help adolescent children maintain a good relationship with that parent even in the face of continued conflict, and that relationship itself may have benefits to the child under some circumstances.

The mixed findings concerning how conflict and visitation interact indicate that there are yet other factors that influence the ultimate impact of conflict on children. Although high conflict, on average, probably makes high visitation more risky, the level of risk also depends on how conflict is handled and to what extent the visitation allows or reflects a good relationship with the visited parent (Buchanan, 1997). Thus, it would be helpful to know more about how specific forms of conflict or different ways of handling conflict affect children in different custody or visitation arrangements.

Fewer data are available on whether conflict and its impact differ between mother and father custody. Buchanan, Maccoby, and Dornbusch (1992) found that hostility between parents was higher in father-custody homes than in both mother- and joint-custody homes. Conflict also had a stronger link to adjustment in father custody than in mother or joint custody. Exposure to a father's anger may be experienced as more threatening or stressful by children than a mother's anger. Or because, on average, fathers are less practiced at parenting tasks, hostility may interfere more with their parenting than it does with a mother's (Belsky & Rovine, 1990; Belsky, Youngblade, Rovine, & Volling, 1991).

In summary, although visitation and custody arrangements are not strong or consistent predictors of the amount of conflict to which a child will be exposed, the way conflict is expressed or handled may differ by arrangement. Research probing more specific characteristics of conflict such as intensity and mode of expression, as well as the impact of conflict on parenting in different arrangements, might illuminate more clearly the impact of conflict in different postdivorce situations.

Directions for Future Research

Interparental conflict after divorce has important associations with children's adjustment after divorce. Yet there is much we do not know about why and when conflict is important in children's adjustment. Our suggestions for future research on postdivorce conflict revolve around elucidating: (1) the specific characteristics of conflict in divorced situations, including which of these characteristics are most important to children; (2) the circumstances under which conflict is most likely to influence parenting and parent–child relationships negatively; (3) the specific ways in which conflict after divorce differs from conflict in intact marriages and the mechanisms by which conflict influences children in different family structures; and (4) moderators of the impact of such conflict.

Almost all research on the impact of conflict after divorce conceptualizes conflict in terms of overall frequency and intensity. This research is consistent in showing that conflict is one of the more important predictors of postdivorce functioning in children, and that reductions in conflict as a result of divorce can benefit children. Yet, the interparental conflict to which children are exposed after their parents' divorce varies in degree and expression, and we know little about the relative importance of different facets of conflict. For example, how damaging is it for children to be exposed to infrequent but poorly handled conflict after divorce? What if there is infrequent active conflict but an ongoing hostile attitude toward one parent by the other? One way in which knowledge in this field can be pushed forward is for investigators to look more closely at dimensions of conflict other than frequency and intensity.

Interparental conflict after divorce appears to affect parenting and parent–child relationships, although the research is correlational and further research is needed to rule out confounding variables and increase confidence that interparental conflict is in fact a cause of problems in parenting. Existing research suggests that any impact of conflict on parenting and parent–child relationships may be strongest in the early stages following divorce and for the noncustodial parent. Thus, future research needs to clarify at what times (e.g., when divorce is recent?), under what circumstances (e.g., when there exist many additional stressors in the parent's life?), and for what manifestations of conflict (e.g., when conflict is intense?) a negative impact on parenting is most likely.

Although the link between conflict and adjustment appears similar in divorced and nondivorced families, we have argued that certain aspects of postdivorce conflict (e.g., its tendency to be child-related; its coincidence with other life stressors) ought to make conflict more damaging, while other aspects (e.g., its more infrequent or sporadic occurrence) ought to make conflict less damaging. Research addressing more specific aspects of conflict might illuminate what characteristics of conflict are most common and most important to child adjustment in each family type. In addition, a closer look at conflict in each family structure would illuminate whether conflict affects parenting and parent–child relationships differently depending on whether both parents are present in the child's life on a daily basis. And although this chapter has focused on parenting as a mediator of interparental conflict and child adjustment, this argument may apply for other potential mediators (e.g., child's interpretation of conflict) as well.

Finally, the impact of conflict depends on many other factors including a child's age and sex. Factors not reviewed in this chapter, such as a child's temperament or IQ, are also likely to be important. The number of other stressors in the life of a parent or a child might also affect the degree to which either one can cope with the stress of interparental conflict. The ability of a good parent–child relationship to moderate conflict's impact seems intuitive, but is not well documented by research. And although high visitation with both parents may magnify the negative impact of conflict, the relations among conflict, contact, and adjustment are complex and depend on other factors such as how the conflict is handled and the quality of relationships engendered by contact. Thus, an important role for future research is to test possible moderating factors, recognizing that moderated relationships are very likely complex and will involve more than two variables.

REFERENCES

Ahrons, C. R. (1981). The continuing coparental relationship between divorced spouses. *American Journal of Orthopsychiatry, 51,* 416–428.

Allison, P. D., & Furstenberg, F. F., Jr. (1989). Marital dissolution affects children: Variations by age and sex. *Developmental Psychology, 25,* 540–549.

Amato, P. R. (1993). Children's adjustment to divorce: Theories, hypotheses, and empirical support. *Journal of Marriage and the Family, 55,* 23–38.

Amato, P. R., & Keith, B. (1991). Parental divorce and the well-being of children: A meta-analysis. *Psychological Bulletin, 100,* 26–46.

Amato, P. R., & Rezac, S. J. (1994). Contact with nonresidential parents, interparental conflict, and children's behavior. *Journal of Family Issues, 15,* 191–207.

Ambert, A. (1989). *Ex-spouses and new spouses: A study of relationships.* Greenwich, CT: JAI Press.

Belsky, J., & Rovine, M. (1990). Patterns of marital change across the transition to parenthood: Pregnancy to three years postpartum. *Journal of Marriage and the Family, 52,* 5–19.

Belsky, J., Youngblade, L., Rovine, M., & Volling, B. (1991). Patterns of marital change and parent-child interaction. *Journal of Marriage and the Family, 53,* 487–498.

Borrine, M. L., Handal, P. J., Brown, N. Y., & Searight, H. R. (1991). Family conflict and adolescent adjustment in intact, divorced, and blended families. *Journal of Consulting and Clinical Psychology, 59,* 753–755.

Brody, G., & Forehand, R. (1990). Interparental conflict, relationship with the noncustodial father, and adolescent post-divorce adjustment. *Journal of Applied Developmental Psychology, 11(2),* 139–147.

Bronfenbrenner, U. (1979). *The ecology of human development: Experiments by nature and design.* Cambridge, MA: Harvard University Press.

Buchanan, C. M. (1997). Issues of visitation and custody. In G. Bear, K. Minke, & A. Thomas (Eds.), *Children's needs 2: Development, problems, and alternatives* (pp. 605–613). Bethesda, MD: National Association of School Psychologists.

Buchanan, C. M. (in press). The impact of divorce on adjustment during adolescence. In R. D. Taylor & M. Weng (Eds.), *Resilience across contexts: Family, work, culture, and community.* Mahwah, NJ: Lawrence Erlbaum Associates.

Buchanan, C. M., & Louca, M. (April, 1999). The association between marital conflict and parent-child relationships: Differences by age and family structure. Paper presented in C. M. Buchanan & S. Walper (Chairs), *Marital conflict and communication and children's adjustment: Family systems and developmental perspectives.* Symposium presented at the biennial meeting of Society for Research in Child Development, Albuquerque, NM.

Buchanan, C. M., Maccoby, E. E., & Dornbusch, S. M. (1991). Caught between parents: Adolescents' experience in divorced homes. *Child Development, 62,* 1008–1029.

Buchanan, C. M., Maccoby, E. E., & Dornbusch, S. (1992). Adolescents and their families after divorce: Three residential arrangements compared. *Journal of Research on Adolescence, 2,* 261–291.

Buchanan, C. M., Maccoby, E. E., & Dornbusch, S. M. (1996). *Adolescents after divorce.* Cambridge, MA: Harvard University Press.

Buehler, C. A., Hogan, M. J., Robinson, B. E., & Levy, R. J. (1985–1986). The parental divorce transition: Divorce-related stressors and well-being. *Journal of Divorce, 9,* 61–81.

Camara, K. A., & Resnick, G. (1988). Interparental conflict and cooperation: Factors moderating children's post-divorce adjustment. In E. M. Hetherington & J. D. Arasteh (Eds.), *Impact of divorce, single parenting, and stepparenting on children* (pp. 169–195). Hillsdale, NJ: Lawrence Erlbaum Associates.

Camara, K. A., & Resnick, G. (1989). Styles of conflict resolution and cooperation between divorced parents: Effects on child behavior and adjustment. *American Journal of Orthopsychiatry, 59,* 560–575.

Cherlin, A. J., Furstenberg, F. F., Jr., Chase-Lansdale, P. L., Kiernan, K. E., Robins, P. K., Morrison, D. R., & Teitler, J. O. (1991). Longitudinal studies of effects of divorce on children in Great Britain and the United States. *Science, 252,* 1386–1388.

Cummings, E. M., & Davies, P. (1994). *Children and marital conflict: The impact of family dispute and resolution.* New York: The Guilford Press.

Cummings, J. S., Pelligrini, D., Notarius, C., & Cummings, E. M. (1989). Children's responses to angry adult behavior as a function of marital distress and history of interparent hostility. *Child Development, 60,* 1035–1043.

Demo, D. H., & Acock, A. C. (1996). Singlehood, marriage, and remarriage: The effects of family structure and family relationships on mothers' well-being. *Journal of Family Issues, 17,* 388–407.

Dixon, C., Charles, M. A., & Craddock, A. A. (1998). The impact of experiences of parental divorce and parental conflict on young Australian adult men and women. *Journal of Family Studies, 4,* 21–34.

Duncan, G. J., & Hoffman, S. D. (1985). Economic consequences of marital instability. In M. David & T. Smeeding (Eds.), *Horizontal equity, uncertainty, and economic well-being.* Chicago: University of Chicago Press.

Emery, R. E. (1982). Interparental conflict and the children of discord and divorce. *Psychological Bulletin, 92,* 310–330.

Emery, R. E. (1988). *Marriage, divorce, and children's adjustment*. Newbury Park, CA: Sage Publications.

Emery, R. E. (1999). *Marriage, divorce, and children's adjustment (2nd ed.)*. Newbury Park, CA: Sage Publications.

Emery, R. E., Joyce, S. A., & Fincham, F. D. (1987). Assessment of child and marital problems. In K. E. O'Leary (Ed.), *Assessment of marital discord: An integration for research and clinical practice* (pp. 223–262). Hillsdale, NJ: Lawrence Erlbaum.

Fauber, R., Forehand, R., Thomas, A. M., & Wierson, M. (1990). A mediational model of the impact of marital conflict on adolescent adjustment in intact and divorced families: The role of disrupted parenting. *Child Development, 61*, 1112–1123.

Felner, R. D., & Terre, L. (1987). Child custody dispositions and children's adaptation following divorce. In L. A. Weithorn (Ed.), *Psychology and custody determinations: Knowledge, roles, and expertise* (pp. 106–153). Lincoln, NE: University of Nebraska Press.

Fidler, B. J., & Saunders, E. B. (1988). Children's adjustment during custody/access disputes: Relation to custody arrangement, gender, and age of child. *Canadian Journal of Psychiatry, 33(6)*, 517–523.

Fincham, F. D., & Osborne, L. N. (1993). Marital conflict and children: Retrospect and prospect. [Special Issue: Marital conflict.] *Clinical Psychology Review, 13*, 75–88.

Forehand, R., & McCombs, A. (1989). The nature of interparental conflict of married and divorced parents: Implications for young adolescents. *Journal of Abnormal Child Psychology, 17*, 235–249.

Forehand, R., McCombs, A., Long, N., Brody, G. H., & Fauber, R. (1988). Early adolescent adjustment to recent parental divorce: The role of interparental conflict and adolescent sex as mediating variables. *Journal of Consulting and Clinical Psychology, 56*, 624–627.

Forehand, R., & Thomas, A. M. (1992). Conflict in the home environment of adolescents from divorced families: A longitudinal analysis. *Journal of Family Violence, 7*, 73–84.

Forehand, R., Thomas, A. M., Wierson, M., Brody, G., & Fauber, R. (1990). Role of maternal functioning and parenting skills in adolescent functioning following parental divorce. *Journal of Abnormal Psychology, 99*, 278–283.

Forehand, R., Wierson, M., McCombs, A., Brody, G., & Fauber, R. (1989). Interparental conflict and adolescent problem behavior: An examination of mechanisms. *Behaviour Research and Therapy, 27*, 365–371.

Forehand, R., Wierson, M., Thomas, A. M., Armistead, L., Kempton, T., & Fauber, R. (1990). Interparental conflict and paternal visitation following divorce: The interactive effect on adolescent competence. *Child Study Journal, 20*, 193–202.

Forehand, R., Wierson, M., Thomas, A. M., Fauber, R., Armistead, L., Kemptom, T., & Long, N. (1991). A short-term longitudinal examination of young adolescent functioning following divorce: The role of family factors. *Journal of Abnormal Child Psychology, 19*, 97–111.

Furstenberg, F. F., Jr., & Cherlin, A. J. (1991). *Divided families: What happens to children when parents part*. Cambridge, MA: Harvard University Press.

Furstenberg, F. F., Jr., & Harris, K. M. (1992). The disappearing American father?: Divorce and the waning significance of biological parenthood. In S. J. South & S. E. Tolnay (Eds.), *The changing American family* (pp. 197–223). Boulder, CO: Westview Press.

Furstenberg, F. F., Jr., & Nord, C. W. (1985). Parenting apart: Patterns of child-rearing after marital disruption. *Journal of Marriage and the Family, 47,* 893–904.

Gabardi, L., & Rosen, L. A. (1992). Intimate relationships: College students from divorced and intact families. *Journal of Divorce and Remarriage, 18,* 25–56.

Gano-Phillips, S., & Fincham, F. D. (1995). Family conflict, divorce, and children's adjustment. In M. A. Fitzpatrick & A. L. Vangelisti (Eds.), *Explaining family interactions* (pp. 206–231). Thousand Oaks, CA: Sage.

Garrity, C. B., & Baris, M. A. (1997). *Caught in the middle: Protecting the children of high-conflict divorce.* San Francisco, CA: Jossey-Bass Publishers.

Gibson, H. B. (1969). Early delinquency in relation to broken homes. *Journal of Child Psychology and Psychiatry, 10,* 195–204.

Grych, J. H., & Fincham, F. D. (1993). Children's appraisals of marital conflict: Initial investigations of the cognitive-contextual framework. *Child Development, 63,* 215–230.

Grych, J. H., & Fincham, F. D. (1998). Children of single parents and divorce. In W. K. Silverman & T. H. Ollendick (Eds.), *Developmental issues in the clinical treatment of children and adolescents* (pp. 321–341). Boston, MA: Allyn & Bacon.

Grych, J. H., Seid, M., & Fincham, F. D. (1992). Assessing marital conflict from the child's perspective: The Children's Perception of Interparental Conflict scale. *Child Development, 63,* 558–572.

Hayashi, G. M., & Strickland, B. R. (1998). Long-term effects of parental divorce on love relationships: Divorce as attachment disruption. *Journal of Social and Personal Relationships, 15,* 23–38.

Healy, J. M., Stewart, A. J., & Copeland, A. P. (1993). The role of self-blame in children's adjustment to parental separation. *Personality and Social Psychology Bulletin, 19,* 279–289.

Heider, F. (1958). *The psychology of interpersonal relations.* New York: John Wiley.

Hess, R. D., & Camara, K. A. (1979). Post-divorce family relations as mediating factors in the consequences of divorce for children. *Social Issues, 35,* 79–98.

Hetherington, E. M. (1972). Effects of father absence on personality development in adolescent daughters. *Developmental Psychology, 7,* 313–326.

Hetherington, E. M. (1989). Coping with family transitions: Winners, losers, and survivors. *Child Development, 60,* 1–14.

Hetherington, E. M. (1990). Presidential address: Families, lies, and videotapes. *Journal for Research on Adolescence, 1,* 323–348.

Hetherington, E. M., Cox, M., & Cox, R. (1976). Divorced fathers. *Family Coordinator, 25,* 417–428.

Hetherington, E. M., Cox, M., & Cox, R. (1979). Play and social interaction in children following divorce. *Journal of Social Issues, 35,* 26–48.

Hetherington, E. M., Cox, M., & Cox, R. (1982). Effects of divorce on parents and children. In M. E. Lamb (Ed.), *Nontraditional families* (pp. 233–288). Hillsdale, NJ: Erlbaum.

Johnston, J. R. (1995). Children's adjustment in sole custody compared to joint custody families and principles for custody decision making. *Family and Conciliation Courts Review, 33*, 415–425.

Johnston, J. R., & Campbell, L. E. (1987). Instability in family networks of divorced and disputing parents. In Lawler, E. J. (Ed.), *Advances in Group Processes* (Vol. 4, pp. 243–269). Greenwich, CT: JAI Press.

Johnston, J. R., & Campbell, L. E. (1988). *Impasses of divorce: The dynamics of resolution of family conflict.* New York: The Free Press.

Johnston, J. R., Campbell, L., & Tall, M. (1985). Impasses to the resolution of custody and visitation disputes. *American Journal of Orthopsychiatry, 55*, 112–129.

Johnston, J. R., Gonzalez, R., & Campbell, L. E. (1987). Ongoing post-divorce conflict and child disturbance. *Journal of Abnormal Child Psychology, 15*, 493–509.

Johnston, J. R., Kline, M., & Tschann, J. M. (1989). Ongoing post-divorce conflict in families contesting custody: Effects on children of joint custody and frequent access. *American Journal of Orthopsychiatry, 59*, 576–592.

Kalter, N., & Rembar, J. (1981). The significance of a child's age at the time of parental divorce. *American Journal of Orthopsychiatry, 51*, 85–100.

Kelly, J. B. (1993). Current research on children's postdivorce adjustment: No simple answers. *Family and Conciliation Courts Review, 31(1)*, 29–49.

Kinnaird, K. L., & Gerrard, M. (1986). Premarital sexual behavior and attitudes toward marriage and divorce among young women as a function of their mothers' marital status. *Journal of Marriage and the Family, 48*, 757–765.

Kitzmann, K. M., & Emery, R. E. (1994). Child and family coping one year after mediated and litigated child custody disputes. *Journal of Family Psychology, 8*, 150–159.

Kozuch, P., & Cooney, T. M. (1995). Young adults' marital and family attitudes: The role of recent parental divorce, and family and parental conflict. *Journal of Divorce and Remarriage, 23*, 45–62.

Kurdek, L. A. (1991). Differences in ratings of children's adjustment by married mothers experiencing low marital conflict, married mothers experiencing high marital conflict, and divorced single mothers: A nationwide study. *Journal of Applied Developmental Psychology, 12*, 289–305.

Lampel, A. K. (1996). Children's alignment with parents in highly conflicted custody cases. *Family and Conciliation Courts Review, 34(2)*, 229–239.

Long, N., Forehand, R., Fauber, R., & Brody, G. H. (1987). Self-perceived and independently observed competence of young adolescents as a function of parental marital conflict and recent divorce. *Journal of Abnormal Child Psychology, 15*, 15–27.

Long, N., Slater, E., Forehand, R., & Fauber, R. (1988). Continued high or reduced interparental conflict following divorce: Relation to young adolescent adjustment. *Journal of Consulting and Clinical Psychology, 56*, 467–469.

Luepnitz, D. A. (1986). A comparison of maternal, paternal, and joint custody: Understanding the varieties of post-divorce family life. *Journal of Divorce, 9*, 1–12.

Lutzke, J., Wolchik, S. A., & Braver, S. L. (1996). Does the quality of mother-child relationships moderate the effect of postdivorce interparental conflict on children's adjustment problems? *Journal of Divorce and Remarriage, 25,* 15–37.

Maccoby, E. E., & Mnookin, R. H. (1992). *Dividing the child: Social and legal dilemmas of custody.* Cambridge, MA: Harvard University Press.

Mechanic, D., & Hansell, S. (1989). Divorce, family, conflict, and adolescents' well-being. *Journal of Health and Social Behavior, 30,* 105–116.

Minuchin, S. (1974). *Families and family therapy.* Cambridge, MA: Harvard University Press.

Nelson, R. (1989). Parental hostility, conflict and communication in joint and sole custody families. *Journal of Divorce, 13(2),* 145–157.

Pagani-Kurtz, L., & Deverensky, J. L. (1997). Access by noncustodial parents: Effects upon children's postdivorce coping resources. *Journal of Divorce and Remarriage, 27(1–2),* 43–55.

Parish, T. S., & Taylor, J. C. (1979). The impact of divorce and subsequent father absence on children's and adolescents' self-concepts. *Journal of Youth and Adolescence, 8,* 427–432.

Purcell, D. W., & Kaslow, N. J. (1994). Marital discord in intact families: Sex differences in child adjustment. *American Journal of Family Therapy, 22,* 356–370.

Seltzer, J. A. (1991). Relationships between fathers and children who live apart: The father's role after separation. *Journal of Marriage and the Family, 53,* 79–101.

Shaw, D. S., & Emery, R. E. (1988). Parental conflict and other correlates of the adjustment of school-age children whose parents have separated. *Journal of Abnormal Child Psychology, 15,* 269–281.

Shiller, V. M. (1986). Joint vs. maternal physical custody for families with latency age boys: Parent characteristics and child adjustment. *American Journal of Orthopsychiatry, 56,* 486–489.

Sim, H., & Vuchinich, S. (1996). The declining effects of family stressors on antisocial behavior from childhood to adolescence and early adulthood. *Journal of Family Issues, 17,* 408–427.

Simmons, R. G., Burgeson, R., Carlton-Ford, S., & Blyth, D. A. (1987). The impact of cumulative change in early adolescence. *Child Development, 58,* 1220–1234.

Spanier, G., & Thompson, L. (1984). *Parting: The aftermath of separation and divorce.* Beverly Hills, CA: Sage Publications.

Steinman, S. B. (1981). The experience of children in a joint-custody arrangement: A report of a study. *American Journal of Orthopsychiatry, 51,* 403–414.

Steinman, S. B., Zemmelman, S. E., & Knoblauch, T. M. (1985). A study of parents who sought joint custody following divorce: Who reaches agreement and sustains joint custody and who returns to court. *Journal of the American Academy of Child Psychiatry, 24,* 554–562.

Tschann, J. M., Johnston, J. R., Kline, M., & Wallerstein, J. S. (1990). Conflict, loss, change and parent-child relationships: Predicting children's adjustment during divorce. *Journal of Divorce, 13,* 1–22.

Vandewater, E. A., & Lansford, J. E. (1998). Influences of family structure and parental conflict on children's well-being. *Family Relations, 47,* 323–330.

Wallerstein, J. S., & Kelly, J. B. (1980). *Surviving the breakup: How children and parents cope with divorce.* New York: Basic Books.

Wierson, M., & Forehand, R. (1992). Family stressors and adolescent functioning: A consideration of models for early and middle adolescents. *Behavior Therapy, 23,* 671–688.

Wolchik, S. A., West, S. G., Westover, S., Sandler, I. N., Martin, A., Lustig, J., Tein, J. & Fisher, J. (1993). The children of divorce parenting intervention: Outcome evaluation of an empirically based program. *American Journal of Community Psychology, 21,* 293–331.

Zahn-Waxler, C., Cole, P., & Barrett, K. C. (1991). Guilt and empathy: Sex differences and implications for the development of depression. In K. D. Dodge & J. Garber (Eds.), *Emotion Regulation and Dysregulation* (pp. 243–272). Cambridge: Cambridge University Press.

Zill, N., Morrison, D. R., & Coiro, M. J. (1993). Long-term effects of parental divorce on parent-child relationships, adjustment, and achievement in young adulthood. *Journal of Family Psychology, 7,* 91–103.

14 Marital Conflict in Stepfamilies

Mark A. Fine

A sizeable proportion of children will spend some time living in a stepfamily before they reach the age of 18 years. Glick (1989) has estimated that approximately one-third of children will become stepchildren before they reach the age of 18 and over 40% of marriages involve a remarriage for one or both spouses (Wilson & Clarke, 1992). At any one time, stepfamilies constitute approximately 17% of all two-parent families with children under 18 years of age (Glick, 1989). If one considers cohabiting couples who are not legally married, there are even more children touched by the stepfamily experience, as cohabitation is increasingly becoming a substitute for remarriage (Ganong & Coleman, 1994; Hetherington, Bridges, & Insabella, 1998). There are also gay and lesbian stepfamilies who are not represented in existing statistics, although it is extremely difficult to obtain prevalence data on these families..

In this chapter, I provide an overview of the literature pertaining to how marital, often referred to as interparental, conflict affects children in stepfamilies. I begin with an overview of how stepfamilies are different than first-marriage families, with some attention devoted to how conceptual frameworks help shed light on these differences. Following this overview, our knowledge base related to marital conflict in stepfamilies is reviewed, with attention to the sources, frequency, and resolution of conflict. Next, the limited empirical base regarding how marital conflict affects children in stepfamilies is presented. Finally, methodological limitations of the existing literature and suggestions for future research are presented. Because the manner in which children in stepfamilies react to marital conflict is likely to depend on their developmental level, evidence pertaining to how children of different ages and/or developmental levels respond to marital conflict in stepfamilies will be presented as the literature permits.

Unique Aspects of Stepfamilies Relative to First-Marriage Families

Although stepfamilies look similar to first-marriage families in terms of composition (two adults with children), there are a number of important differences that influence marital conflict and how it is managed. First, stepfamilies are structurally more complex than first-marriage families. Stepfamilies often have more family members than first-marriage families, when one considers that remarriages following divorce can result in a *binuclear* family extended across more than one household, which contains a father, stepmother, mother, stepmother, and (step)children. With the presence of multiple sets of extended kin, such as stepgrandparents and stepaunts, the number of family members can be very large. Not only can the large number of family members increase possibilities for conflict, but the range of types of relationships (e.g., stepkin, biological kin, extended family members of stepkin) also can lead to a greater likelihood of family disputes.

Second, the roles, responsibilities, rights, obligations, and duties of stepparents (as well as other stepfamily members to some extent) are not as clear as are those of biological parents (Fine, Coleman, & Ganong 1998). Stepparents may not know how to behave toward their stepchildren, whether to be an adult friend, a disciplinarian, a supportive adult, a distant adult, or some other possible role. It may not be clear to stepparents and parents whether (and, if so, to what extent) the stepparent should financially support the stepchild. Previous research (see Fine, Ganong, & Coleman, 1999) has suggested that some stepparents, parents, and stepchildren experience a lack of clarity regarding the appropriate role of the stepparent and that this lack of clarity is related to poorer adjustment for stepparents, stepchildren, and the various units within the stepfamily system. In addition, stepparents and stepchildren have an ambiguously defined legal relationship in many important ways (Fine & Fine, 1992). If the stepparent and other stepfamily members are unclear about the nature of the stepparent's role and if family members have different views of this role, marital conflict is more likely to occur.

Third, there are a number of cognitions that are either unique to stepfamily members or that are particularly likely to occur among stepfamily members. For adults, these include unrealistic beliefs or what have been labeled "stepfamily myths" (Visher & Visher, 1988). These unrealistic beliefs include the following (see Ganong, Coleman, & Fine, 1995): (a) Stepkin will immediately love and care for one another; (b) adjustment to life in a stepfamily will and should occur very quickly; and (c) stepfamilies are functionally equivalent to first-marriage families.

These beliefs are considered unrealistic because they are inconsistent with the experiences of most individuals in stepfamilies. For children, these cognitions include (a) self-blame, the belief that they are responsible for current marital conflict, as well as possibly for earlier family conflict that may have precipitated parental divorce; (b) beliefs that the stepparent is attempting to assume the role of parent and the likely negative affect (e.g., resentment) that is likely to accompany those beliefs; and (c) beliefs that the stepparent is causing marital strife by imposing his or her new and different ways of life onto the child's parent and family. These cognitions of adults and children are likely to affect both the amount of conflict in stepfamilies and how children react to it.

Fourth, the lengths of various family relationships are different in stepfamilies than in first-marriage families. In first-marriage families, the relationship between the parents is established before the birth of a child, in most cases allowing the parents some time to become familiar with each other before they begin the task of parenting their child. In stepfamilies, the relationship between the parent and the child predates the relationship between the remarried spouses, as well as the relationship between the stepparent and the stepchild. This may result in the primary affective tie for a remarried parent being to his or her child rather than to the new partner. In addition, newly remarried spouses must work to develop their relationship at the same time that they develop or sustain their relationships with the children in the family. Because the remarried couple relationship has existed for a shorter time period than the parent–child relationship, the likelihood of marital conflict may increase.

The evolutionary perspective can help explain how these differing relationship lengths can exacerbate interparental conflict in stepfamilies. According to this perspective (Daly & Wilson, 1994), because only the parent is biologically related to the child, the two spouses (the parent and stepparent) have different levels of investment in the children. These differing levels of parental investment may lead to conflict stemming from disagreements about a variety of child-related issues, including disciplinary strategies and financial support for children.

The conflict perspective (Klein & White, 1996) also sheds light on how conflict can result from the merging of two groups of individuals, some of whom may not know each other (e.g., stepsiblings). According to this perspective, inequalities in resource allocation contribute to conflict and those with greater resources are more able to negotiate outcomes favorable to them. In stepfamilies, children living with a single parent who remarries have to cope with possible reductions in the amount of attention that they receive from their parent, as the parent directs some of his or her energies to the new partner. In addition, such resources as space may become scarcer as additional people move into a family dwelling.

Finally, family members in stepfamilies have different histories. Adults in first-marriage families develop a mutual family culture with its own rituals, patterns, and characteristics. In the typical scenario, their children adopt that shared family culture, become an integral part of it, and, of course, shape it to a considerable extent. In stepfamilies, by contrast, a parent and one or more children have a shared history, but the newly entering stepparent has not been a part of that previously established family culture. The stepparent brings with him or her a different history, with different interaction patterns, rituals, celebrations, rules, and norms. The merging of these different family histories and cultures can be very confusing, stressful, and difficult, increasing chances for conflict.

The interdependence perspective is helpful in understanding how merging (at least) two sets of family histories and cultures can exacerbate conflict in stepfamilies. According to this perspective (Sabatelli & Shehan, 1993), individuals experience rewards and costs from their relationships with others. To the extent that the rewards exceed the costs, individuals are more likely to be committed to these relationships and to maintain them. However, it is not just the ratio of rewards to costs that influences individuals' relationship thoughts, decisions, and behaviors, it is also how the balance of rewards and costs that they experience compares to what they believe that they can expect to have (i.e., comparison level) or compares to what they believe they could obtain in an alternative relationship (i.e., comparison level for alternatives). The rewards and costs of family life may change dramatically upon entering into a stepfamily. Changes in the ratio of rewards to costs, often involving a reduction in rewards and an increase in costs because of the unique characteristics of stepfamilies described in this section, may affect family relationships in such a way as to increase conflict levels. Further, individuals in stepfamilies, because of their varied family experiences, may have quite different comparison levels. Some may be quite used to and accepting of some of the new resource restrictions in the stepfamily (e.g., lack of personal space in the home), while others may find the new arrangements intolerable.

What Do We Know about Marital Conflict in Stepfamilies?

At the outset, it is important to define marital conflict. Consistent with Fincham, Grych, and Osborne (1994), *marital conflict* is used here to

refer to disagreements that are open enough that the child can potentially observe them; disagreements that the child is not privy to are not
included in this definition. It is also important to draw a distinction
between conflict between the parent and the stepparent (the two adults
in the residential home) and conflict between either the parent or the
stepparent and the nonresidential parent (Bray, 1999; Hanson,
McLanahan, & Thompson, 1996). We know more about conflict
between ex-spouses than we do about conflict involving a stepparent.
In this section, I review the limited evidence pertaining to the sources,
frequency, and resolution of marital conflict.

Sources of Marital Conflict in Stepfamilies

There are a number of potential sources of marital conflict in stepfamilies, including the following:

*Differences between the Parent and Stepparent in Parenting Beliefs
and Styles.* Unlike parents in first-marriage families, parents and stepparents do not have a transition period (e.g., during pregnancy) to foster the development of a shared sense of parenting goals, values, and
practices. Fine and Kurdek (1994), in a survey of members of the
Stepfamily Association of America, found that biological parents, in
contrast to stepparents, generally reported that they engage more frequently in parenting behaviors, that typical parents engage more frequently in parenting behaviors than typical stepparents, and that they
should engage more frequently in parenting behaviors. Therefore, parents and stepparents often have differing parenting styles.

However, whereas these differences between parents and stepparents in their chosen parenting styles may lead to disputes, differences
between spouses in beliefs of how the *stepparent* should function may
be even more likely to generate marital conflict. Fine, Coleman, and
Ganong (1998), in their study of stepparents, parents, and stepchildren
from 40 stepfamilies, found that (a) stepparents and parents similarly
perceived that the stepparent should and does play an active parental
role, (b) stepchildren were more likely to perceive that the stepparent
should assume the less active role of "friend," and (c) consistency in
role perceptions between the parent and stepparent was moderately
strongly related to the interpersonal dimensions of adjustment in stepfamilies. The findings suggest that, although stepchildren have differing perceptions of the stepparent role than do their parents and
stepparents, parents' and stepparents' views are quite similar.

However, there was also evidence from the same study (Fine et al.,
1998) that parents and stepparents had different views of some dimensions of the stepparent role. First, stepparents reported that they were
and should be more active in exhibiting warmth and control parenting

behaviors than parents reported that stepparents were and should be. Second, based on semistructured interviews with a subsample of the stepparents, parents, and stepchildren, stepparents believed that they should play more of a "parental" role than their spouses thought that they should (Fine et al., 1999). In particular, stepparents thought that they had greater obligations to their stepchildren than either their spouses or their stepchildren thought that they had. Thus, stepparents' belief that they should play a more active parenting role than parents think they (the stepparent) should is a source of potential conflict.

Directness of Communication between Remarried Spouses. There is some evidence, both from observations of behavioral interactions and the reports of the individuals themselves, that spouses in stepfamilies tend to be more open and direct in their expression of criticism and anger with each other than are spouses in first marriages (Bray & Berger, 1993; Hetherington, 1993). This greater openness may be related to some general characteristics of remarriages, including that they tend to be more egalitarian with respect to childrearing responsibilities and household maintenance, less romantic, and more practical. In addition, given that at least one spouse has had previous experience in a marriage, it is likely that spouses in remarriages have greater maturity with respect to how to maintain relationships than do spouses in first marriages. These characteristics are likely to lead spouses to feel that it is important that they be open with each other when potential problems emerge. Whereas direct communication can be adaptive and a source of strength, it also can lead to more conflict between the spouses and a greater likelihood that children will be exposed to unresolved marital conflict.

Biological Parent Feeling Divided Loyalties toward the Child or New Spouse. Parents may have competing loyalties in their new stepfamilies. On the one hand, they may feel that their primary allegiance needs to be to their child(ren), who themselves have undergone major transitions as their families have changed from first-marriage to single-parent to remarried. Parents may feel the need to protect their children from further turmoil and stress (Coleman, Fine, Ganong, Downs, & Pauk, 1998) and to maintain the particularly close bond that developed following divorce. On the other hand, however, the parents may feel that they need provide a "united front" to their children by almost unconditionally supporting the stepparent in front of the children (Cissna, Cox, & Bochner, 1990). Some parents may also feel that their new relationship demands careful nurturing and that it should take precedence over the more secure and stable parent–child relationships. Certainly, parents receive both of these disparate messages through the media and the popular literature on stepfamilies. To the extent that the parent takes the former position (i.e., siding with his or her children and protecting them from perceived "danger"), conflict between the spouses is more likely to ensue.

Boundary Issues. In a study by Burrell and Mitchell (1993), spouses from 30 stepfamilies completed questionnaires about partners' perceptions of conflict and how conflict occurred in their families. The spouses were also interviewed about issues and problems that are unique to stepfamilies. Boundary issues, in a variety of forms reflected in the findings described below, were frequently identified as a source of conflict. In many couples, the biological parent felt that he or she needed to support the stepparent in discipline-related situations and to present a united front to the children, perhaps leading to conflict between the spouses and the child. In addition, 75% of the spouses mentioned conflict generated from role-related issues, such as stepchildren challenging and testing the stepparent's authority. Almost one-half of the spouses reported that loyalty issues caused problems in their stepfamilies. Loyalty issues were reflected in a number of ways, including children feeling torn between their stepparent and nonresidential parent, a parent feeling jealous of affection her children showed their stepmother, and children playing one spouse off against the other to get their way.

Coleman et al. (1998) interviewed 57 members from 16 stepfamilies regarding a number of aspects of the role of the stepparent, including a number of specific questions regarding areas of potential contention and conflict. Similar to findings by Burrell and Mitchell (1993), Coleman et al. identified issues related to the negotiation of family boundaries as being at the core of conflict in stepfamilies. More specifically, they identified four general types of conflict discussed by family members: (a) conflicts over resources, ranging from physical space to possessions to finances; (b) loyalty conflicts, particularly children feeling torn between their stepparent and nonresidential parent; (c) individuals holding a "guard and protect" stance, engaging in behaviors that protected the interests of their biological kin (because most of the families in the study were stepfather families, most frequently "guard and protect" behaviors involved mothers protecting their biological children from either the stepfather or the nonresidential father); and (d) conflict with extended family members, most often reported by stepfamily members who were not genetically related to the person initiating the conflict, such as a stepparent reporting friction with new in-laws. Of these four types of conflict, the ones most likely to spur conflict between the spouses in the stepfamily were conflicts over resources and disputes regarding mothers' tendencies to protect their children from either the stepfather or nonresidential father.

Child Playing the Parent off against the Stepparent. Related to the potentially divided loyalties that some parents may experience, children can increase the likelihood of marital conflict by playing one parent off of the other or engaging in triangulating behaviors. For example, a child may have her request to ride her bike to a friend's house turned down by her mother; the child, however, might go to her stepfather, who might agree to her request. If the parents do not have a well thought-out approach to these sorts of situations, they are likely to feel undermined by the other parent, and marital conflict is more likely to occur.

Financial Issues, Particularly Support of the (Step)Child. Although some scholars have speculated that there may be differences in the quality of marital and family life for remarried couples who adopt differing financial management strategies (i.e., pooling resources vs. keeping resources separate), recent evidence suggests that there are no clear adjustment correlates of different approaches to managing resources (Pasley, Sandras, & Edmondson, 1994). However, conflict may be more likely when specific financial issues are discussed, such as the extent to which the spouses have different views regarding how much the stepparent is expected to financially support the stepchild. In the Fine et al. (1999) study, there were two ways that these different views were manifested. First, some parents felt that the stepparent should financially support the stepchild more than the stepparent felt that he or she should. Second, less frequently, some parents did not want the stepparent to financially support the stepchild and the stepparent felt that he or she should do so. These mothers typically had close relationships to their children and felt that their new partner should primarily be a spouse and companion to them, rather than a parent to their child. When these mothers had spouses who felt that they should financially (and in other ways, as well) contribute and who wanted to feel the sense of inclusion that accompanies providing financial support, the potential for conflict was present.

Relationship Issues Involving the Nonresidential Parent(s). There are a variety of ways that relations with the nonresidential parent can become conflictual. The residential and nonresidential parents may continue to carry out the conflicts that characterized their marriage and the immediate postdivorce period (Metts & Cupach, 1995). There is some evidence that the addition of a stepparent can exacerbate some of these conflicts for a number of reasons, including the following: The nonresidential parent may feel displaced by the stepparent; there are three (or four) adults who must work together to some degree to make child-related decisions and rules; financial disagreements can resurface as the stepparent brings more financial resources into the residential household; and children may feel torn between their new stepparent and their nonresidential biological parent. In the Coleman et al. (1998) study described earlier, the semistructured interviews revealed that conflicts with nonresidential parents were very common and had a great deal of influence on stepfamily functioning. For example, as discussed in more detail in Ganong, Coleman, Fine, and Martin (1999), the quality of the stepparent–stepchild relationship was very much dependent on the nature of the child's relationship with the nonresidential parent. When the child's relationship with the nonresidential parent was positive, this seemed to provide a secure base from which the stepchild could attempt to develop a relationship with the stepparent. When the nonresidential parent was disruptive and/or had a negative effect on the child, it was much more difficult for the child and stepparent to develop a mutually satisfying relationship.

Competition among Stepsiblings. If both adults in stepfamilies bring children from previous marriages into the household, the possibility of conflict among stepsiblings is raised (see Ihinger-Tallman, 1987). Stepsiblings, perhaps to a greater extent than biological siblings, may be acutely sensitive to perceived injustices and unfairness in how they are treated by either their parent or stepparent. They may also be protective of their place in the family, such that they become territorial about functions that they served in the family before the stepfamily was formed. In addition, perhaps particularly if they are adolescents, competition among stepsiblings over school performance, appearance, popularity, athletic prowess, and so forth may occur.

Frequency of Conflict

Both parents and children in stepfamilies have reported experiencing more conflict in their families than do their counterparts in first-marriage families. Bray (1999), based on data from a multimethod, multisource, longitudinal study of 200 stepfamilies, found that remarried spouses (both those in 6-month stepfamilies and in 5- to 7-year stepfamilies) were more negative and less positive toward each other in behaviorally observed interactions than were couples in first-marriage families. However, despite the higher levels of conflict, there were few differences between groups in levels of marital satisfaction. Similarly, Hobart (1991), based on interviews of parents in 232 remarried and 102 first-marriage couples, found that remarried participants generally reported higher levels of tension and disagreement than did their counterparts in first marriages. In particular, remarried individuals were more likely to report disagreements over the rearing and disciplining of children than were individuals in first marriages. In addition, both parents reported having more positive relationships with children from the wife's rather than the husband's former marriage, leading Hobart to conclude that children from the husband's former marriage are particularly aversive for the spousal relationship.

Kurdek and Fine (1993), in a sample of 1,017 young adolescents from a number of different family structures, found that adolescents living with stepfathers or stepmothers reported experiencing more conflict in their families than did adolescents from first-marriage or divorced-mother families. Similarly, Barber and Lyons (1994) found that adolescents in remarried families reported more conflict in their families than did those in first-marriage families.

Resolution of Parental Conflict in Stepfamilies

Evidence has consistently suggested that the negative effects of marital conflict on children are reduced to the extent that the conflict is resolved (Cummings & Davies, 1994; Grych & Fincham, 1990). The salutary effects of conflict resolution are robust and appear to extend even to resolutions that the children do not witness (Cummings & Davies, 1994). Given this, what do we know about how conflict is resolved in stepfamilies? Unfortunately, very little.

Coleman et al. (1998), in their interview study described earlier, examined how conflicts were resolved in stepfamilies, although their analyses did not focus only on marital conflict. With respect to the resolution of family conflict, family members reported using a wide array of strategies, some more successfully than others. Consistent with tenets from conflict theory, conflict was not always detrimental and often contributed to positive family changes, particularly when it led to thoughtful discussions and compromise. However, conflict was not always a positive force. In some cases, particularly when it was allowed to persist without being addressed and/or when family members were not able to empathize with each other's views and compromise, conflict lingered and led to more detached family relationships.

Strategies used to resolve conflicts in stepfamilies included compromising and brokering resolutions; sharing feelings and thoughts; arguing; trying to ignore disagreements; forming coalitions against other family members; emotionally and physically distancing specific family members from the rest of the stepfamily; withdrawing from disputes; seeking assistance from professionals, especially attorneys and counselors; and trying to prevent problems (e.g., having family meetings).

As one might expect, some of these strategies (e.g., compromising) were more successful than others.

When conflict was successfully resolved, the resolution often led to more closeness between stepparents and stepchildren and better overall family functioning. As a consequence of conflicts over issues such as childrearing, finances, and privacy, some stepfamilies established new internal and external family boundaries that were effective and workable for them. Another positive outcome of conflict resolution was that better communication and mutual understanding often occurred.

Several families successfully used family meetings to negotiate these conflicts. When preventive strategies such as family meetings were discontinued, conflicts tended to resurface. Particularly painful conflicts were often the stimulus for seeking psychotherapy. In more than half of the stepfamilies that sought some form of counseling or psychotherapy, the intervention was at least partially successful in resolving the conflicts.

Not all families successfully dealt with disagreements. For them, conflict did not contribute to closer, more satisfying relationships. Rather than communicating about differences, some stepfamily members withdrew from each other, both physically and emotionally. Assistance from professionals, such as attorneys (e.g., when the dispute was with former spouses) and counselors (e.g., when household decision making and dynamics were the foci), did not result in positive consequences for every stepfamily. In some of them, family members no longer tried to resolve the disagreements, settling uncomfortably into emotional distance between members and accepting unpleasant feelings toward others as inevitable. For example, in a few stepfamilies, disputes over resources like possessions and space festered, leading to ongoing tension and even open animosity; these families were not characterized by close relationships, but by emotional distance and occasional expressions of anger.

Many of the conflicts with negative outcomes involved former spouses, and occasionally, extended kin. In most of these situations, stepfamily members appeared to have given up in their efforts to find an acceptable solution, expressing sadness and anger about this. In some families, fighting over discipline or external family boundaries was ongoing. Relationships were not close, members expressed considerable anger at each other, and parents and children frequently joined forces against the stepparent. In other families, a child was the outsider; in half of the stepfamilies in which a stepchild left the household (often in response to persistent family conflict), family bonds with the stepchild were severed or damaged.

Effects of Parental Conflict on Children in Stepfamilies

As shown elsewhere in this volume, a consistent body of research has substantiated that frequent marital conflict that is extreme, inadequately resolved, and child-related has negative effects on children. By contrast, conflicts that do not involve children and that are resolved cooperatively and nonaggresively do not (Fincham et al., 1994). To what extent do these general findings pertaining to the effects of marital conflict on children apply to the stepfamily context? Unfortunately, there is limited research that has shed light on this issue. In an extensive review of the literature on the relation between marital conflict and children's adjustment by Grych and Fincham (1990), no studies reviewed specifically focused on children in stepfamilies. However, there have been a few studies since this review was published that have examined this issue. The limited evidence suggests that marital conflict has similarly negative effects on children in a variety of family structures, including stepfamilies. For example, Barber and Lyons (1994) found not only that remarried families were perceived as more conflictual than were first-marriage families but also that perceived conflict had similar and negative effects on adolescents in both types of families. Similarly, Fine and Kurdek (1992), based on self-report data from 118 adolescents in stepfather families and 32 in stepmother families, found that adolescents' reports of conflict in their families were negatively related to their self-reported levels of adjustment. However, Fine and Kurdek (1992) assessed family conflict in general and did not restrict their analysis to marital conflict.

Anderson, Greene, Hetherington, and Clingempeel (1999), based on data from the Virginia Longitudinal Study of Divorce and Remarriage, found that a multirater and multimeasure index of marital negativity (between parent and stepparent) was significantly positively related to adolescents' externalizing behavior problems, but was not related to increases over time in externalizing behaviors, nor did it account for why adolescents in stepfamilies exhibited more externalizing behaviors than did those in first-marriage families. Further, Anderson et al. reported that the number of separations before the divorce (an admittedly crude index of the amount of conflict between the spouses before their divorce) and mothers' perceptions of the amount of current conflict between divorced spouses (based on the extent to which they had arguments over the adolescent) were both positively related to externalizing behavior problems among adolescents in stepfamilies. Levels of current conflict between the ex-spouses were marginally related to increases over time in externalizing behaviors.

Some have suggested that family conflict has a greater impact on stepchildren than children living in first-marriage families (Borrine, Handal, Brown, & Searight, 1991). Bray (1999), for example, reported that overall conflict (including conflict between parent and stepparent, between ex-spouses, and between stepparents and stepchildren) was more predictive of children's adjustment in stepfamilies than in first-marriage families. Further, he found that conflict was more predictive of children's externalizing behaviors than other dimensions of adjustment.

There is also evidence that there are individual differences among children in how they respond to marital conflict. Two examples are provided here, with specific reference to how they may be relevant in the stepfamily context. First, Davies and Cummings (1998) posed an "emotional security" hypothesis, which states that children are motivated to preserve and promote their own sense of emotional security. In a study of 6–9-year-olds, Davies and Cummings found support for the hypothesis that emotional security served to mediate the relations between marital discord and both internalizing and externalizing problems in children. Given the multiple transitions that children in stepfamilies experience and the complexity of stepfamily life, it seems quite possible that stepchildren would be less likely than children in first-marriage families to have a sense of emotional security. For similar reasons, it is also possible that emotional security is more salient to children's well-being when they live in stepfamilies as opposed to first-marriage families.

As a second example, there is some evidence that the children's age is related to the extent to which marital conflict negatively affects them. In a sample of first-marriage families from the National Survey of Families and Households data set (NSFH; see Sweet, Bumpass, & Call, 1988), which was gathered in 1987–88 from a nationally representative sample of 13,017 respondents, Acock and Demo (in press) found that marital conflict had negative relations to the adjustment of children aged 5–11 years old. However, the negative effects were much smaller in magnitude than were the negative effects linked to parent–child conflict. In addition, marital conflict had very weak relations to adolescents' (aged 11–16) adjustment. The authors concluded that marital conflict becomes less important to children's adjustment over time, in contrast to the increasing salience of conflict between the adolescent and parent. In stepfamilies, adolescence seems to be a particularly difficult stage, in which there is an increase in stepparent–stepchild conflict and potentially more conflict between the spouses (Hetherington et al., 1998). However, it is unclear if increased stepparent–stepchild conflict and possibly marital conflict would lead to marital conflict having stronger relations to adolescents' adjustment in stepfamilies than is the case among adolescents in first-marriage families. On one hand, if adolescent stepchildren are brought into their parents or step-parents' disputes and the process of individuation is delayed, marital conflict may become even more salient for them. On the other hand, if adolescent stepchildren respond to the potentially increased conflict by withdrawing and the process of individuation is accelerated, marital conflict may have relatively weak effects on them.

Does marital conflict in stepfamilies explain differences in adjustment levels between children or adolescents in first-marriage and remarried families? Hanson et al. (1996), using the NSFH data set, assessed whether conflict between parents could account for why children in stepfather families were more poorly adjusted than children in first-marriage families. Consistent with the distinction drawn in this chapter, two types of conflict were examined: conflict between the parent and the stepparent (residing in the same household) and conflict between the ex-spouses (residing in different households). Consistent with results reviewed earlier (Hobart, 1991; Kurdek & Fine, 1993), Hanson et al. found that children in stepfather families experienced higher levels of total parental conflict (combined across both types) than were children in first-marriage or single-mother households. Nearly 40% of the children in stepfather families experienced high levels of parental conflict, compared to 28% of those in first-marriage families and 25% of those in single-mother families. Most of the increased risk of experiencing parental conflict came from interhousehold conflict between the exspouses. Further, although they found (consistent with previous research) that the experience of parental conflict detrimentally affects child well-being, lower levels of child well-being in stepfather families relative to first-marriage families (and similar levels of well-being compared to those in single-mother families) could not be accounted for by the higher levels of parental conflict experienced. In other words, parental conflict and family structure generally accounted for independent sources of variation in child well-being. Anderson et al. (1999) reached a similar conclusion based on results reported earlier in this chapter.

Given these considerations, what conclusions can be drawn regarding how marital conflict affects stepchildren? As noted by Hetherington and Stanley-Hagan (in press), the course of adaptation to a family transition like remarriage is likely to be complex, impacted by multiple interacting factors such as characteristics of the children and their parents, the quality of family relationships before the transition, the quality of available support, the nature of the nonresidential parent's involvement, changes in financial status, residential moves, and a host of others. In like manner, children's reactions to marital conflict in stepfamilies are also likely to be multiply determined by a range of interacting factors.

There is sufficient evidence to justify making a perhaps overly simplistic inference: Marital conflict in stepfamilies negatively affects children as it does in other family structures. This inference is supported by the limited empirical evidence available regarding children in stepfamilies, previous findings that marital conflict negatively affects children in various family structures (Vandewater & Lansford, 1998), and the observation that no previous studies have found that children in any family structure were *not* detrimentally affected by marital conflict. Thus, although more definitive conclusions must await the results of future research, children in stepfamilies are, like their counterparts in other types of families, negatively affected by conflict in their families, although, as shown elsewhere in this chapter, the particular types of conflict in stepfamilies are likely to be somewhat different than they are in other types of families. However, it should also be pointed out that there is, as yet, no clear evidence that marital conflict in stepfamilies either partly or completely accounts for the poorer well-being of children in stepfamilies relative to those in other family types.

Methodological Issues and Recommendations for Future Research

There are a variety of issues that need to be addressed in any consideration of the effects of marital conflict on children, including those living in stepfamilies. Below, a number of these are considered, with particular emphasis on how they play out in the stepfamily context. For each issue, some recommendations for future research are made.

First, a distinction needs to be drawn between overt conflict (i.e., the child observes the conflict) and covert conflict (i.e., conflict the child does not observe). With the complexity involved in stepfamily life, not only is there the possibility of a greater amount of conflict, but there is also the possibility of a wider variety of both overt and covert conflicts. For example, even if the nonresidential parent does not overtly criticize the stepparent in front of the parent and/or the child, he or she may implicitly convey his or her negative impressions to other family members, which may lead to children being exposed to more conflict. Thus, even though most of the negative effects of marital conflict on children appear to stem from overt conflict, it is also the case that there is a fine line between covert and overt conflict and, further, that covert conflicts often, over time and aggregated across situations, become overt conflicts that children directly experience. Thus, future researchers need to examine not only overt conflicts, but also attempt to examine the direct and indirect effects of covert conflicts in stepfamilies. Because covert conflicts, and their effects on children, are especially difficult to examine, intensive interviewing and/or observation may be necessary.

Second, the mechanisms underlying the observed relations between marital conflict and child adjustment need to be examined. Not only do we need more studies assessing both the direct and indirect effects of conflict on children in a variety of family structures, but we also need more focused inquiry into these mechanisms in stepfamilies. For example, how does ambiguity regarding the role of the stepparent and the extent to which the spouses have different views of the stepparent role affect the frequency and nature of marital conflict? Does conflict between the residential and nonresidential parent affect children indirectly, through its effects on parenting behaviors, or directly? With the complexities in stepfamily life, there seem to be a greater number of potential mediating mechanisms involved between family conflict and child outcomes than in first-marriage families. Thus, are there greater indirect effects on children in stepfamilies than there are among children in other family structures? These, and other similar questions, should provide helpful guidance to future researchers.

Third, we have to consider whether those providing their views of conflict and/or children's adjustment are "insiders" or "outsiders." This is perhaps particularly salient in the stepfamily context given evidence that stepparents, parents, and (step)children often have quite different views of a number of aspects of their family lives (see Fine, Coleman, & Ganong, 1998; Hetherington & Clingempeel, 1992). On the one hand, an "insider's" view is critically important, because it is this view that forms the basis for an individual's behavioral response to a given situation. On the other hand, the "outsider's" view is also important to consider, as it is less likely to be biased by the immediacy and intensity of the emotions involved in family situations. Thus, it is particularly important that future researchers obtain multiple views, including from other adults who have extensive exposure to the child, such as teachers.

Fourth, it is essential to carefully choose which adjustment dimensions to consider (e.g., social, emotional, academic, economic) when examining how children respond to conflict in stepfamilies. For example, in newly formed stepfamilies, the child's socioeconomic standing often increases dramatically with the addition of the stepparent's income to the household. However, the increase in financial resources does not necessarily result in improved psychosocial and academic functioning for stepchildren. Future researchers need to be guided by their theoretical perspective(s) as they make the important choices of which adjustment dimensions to study.

Fifth, it is important to draw only tentative conclusions about similarities and differences between children in stepfamilies and those in first-marriage families. There is some evidence that the same constructs, when measured with commonly used measures, may have differing meanings for stepfamily members than they do for individuals in first-marriage families. For example, Waldren, Bell, Peek, and Sorell (1990) found that members of stepfamilies reported lower levels of family cohesiveness and adaptability in their families than did individuals in first-marriage families – a consistent finding that has raised the issue among some stepfamily scholars of whether cohesion and adaptability are as important to adjustment in stepfamilies as they are in first-marriage families. Visher and Visher (1988) have suggested that lower levels of cohesion may be adaptive in stepfamilies because of the need for stepfamily members to maintain close ties with others (e.g., the nonresidential parent) outside of the family system. However, inconsistent with this notion, Waldren et al. found that high levels of cohesiveness and adaptability were related to low levels of stress in stepfamilies, and that there were stronger links between stress and cohesiveness/adaptability among stepfamilies than among first-marriage families, although the general nature of the relations was similar between the two groups. Although these findings suggest that cohesiveness and adaptability are as important in stepfamilies as they are in first-marriage families, the general issue of whether measures of commonly assessed family constructs have similar meanings in stepfamilies as they do among other types of families remains important. Future researchers should not blindly assume that a measure validated on individuals from first-marriage families is equally valid or even measures the same construct among members of stepfamilies.

Sixth, although it is extremely difficult to tease apart the relative influences of family structure (e.g., stepfamily vs. first-marriage family) and other factors (e.g., family processes such as conflict), it is essential that researchers continue to attempt to do so. As is true in first-marriage and single-parent families, there is research evidence that suggests that parenting practices and family climate affect children's adjustment in stepfamilies. In general, as in other family structures, certain kinds of parenting practices (i.e., authoritative parenting, involving high levels of parental warmth and supervision) and family climates (high levels of interest, order, supervision, warmth, and low levels of conflict) are related to positive child adjustment in stepfamilies (Fine & Kurdek, 1992; Hetherington & Stanley-Hagan, in press). In addition, perhaps unique to stepfamilies, a number of studies have found that stepparents develop more positive relationships with their stepchildren when they do not initially assume an active role in disciplining their stepchildren (Hetherington & Stanley-Hagan, in press). Stepparents who actively discipline their stepchildren (perhaps as they would if they were the child's biological parent) before they have developed some degree of trust and comfort in their stepparent–stepchild relationship tend to find their efforts resisted and thwarted by their stepchildren. In addition, given that several studies have found that family structure and family process are independently related to children's adjustment (Fine, in press), future researchers need to continue to work to tease apart the relative contribution of each set of variables, possibly by assessing how their interactive effects relate to children's adjustment.

Finally, it is important to consider children's level of cognitive development when trying to understand their responses to marital conflict. Because of the complexities involved in stepfamily life, the cognitive challenges involved in understanding conflict in stepfamilies may be greater than in first-marriage families. For example, because of potential problems with children relating to both a stepparent and nonresidential parent, stepchildren have the difficult challenge of trying to understand that one can be loyal to both a stepparent and a nonresidential parent – a task that children in first-marriage families do not experience. Although our understanding of how children's developmental level affects the nature of their reactions to marital conflict in stepfamilies is still in its infancy, future researchers need to try to take this important developmental variable into account.

Conclusions

In this chapter, I have suggested that a number of qualitative differences between stepfamilies and first-marriage families can lead not only to larger *amounts* of conflict in stepfamilies, but also can produce different *types* of conflicts in the two types of families. Nevertheless, despite the potential differences in the frequency and types of conflict, the available evidence, although limited, suggests that interparental conflict affects children in stepfamilies in the same negative manner that it does children in other family structures. In the interests of acquiring a more complete understanding of how interparental conflict in stepfamilies affects children, a number of recommendations for future research were made. Among the most important of these was a call for future researchers to devote more of their efforts toward furthering our understanding of the *mechanisms* underlying the relation between marital conflict and child adjustment. To the extent that future research is able to shed light on the nature of the relation between interparental conflict and child adjustment in stepfamilies, and enhance our knowledge of the mechanisms underlying this relation, more targeted and effective intervention strategies can be developed.

REFERENCES

Acock, A. C., & Demo, D. H. (in press). Dimensions of family conflict and their influence on child and adolescent adjustment. *Sociological Inquiry.*

Anderson, E. R., Greene, S. M., Hetherington, E. M., & Clingempeel, W. G. (1999). The dynamics of parental remarriage: Adolescent, parent, and sibling influences. In E. M. Hetherington (Ed.), *Coping with divorce, single-parenthood and remarriage: A risk and resiliency perspective* (pp. 295–319). Mahwah, NJ: Erlbaum.

Barber, B. L., & Lyons, J. M. (1994). Family processes and adolescent adjustment in intact and remarried families. *Journal of Youth and Adolescence, 23,* 421–436.

Borrine, M. L., Handal, P. J., Brown, N. Y., & Searight, H. R. (1991). Family conflict and adolescent adjustment in intact, divorced, and blended families. *Journal of Consulting and Clinical Psychology, 59,* 753–755.

Bray, J. H. (1999). From marriage to remarriage and beyond: Findings from the Developmental Issues in StepFamilies research project. In E. M. Hetherington (Ed.), *Coping with divorce, single-parenthood and remarriage: A risk and resiliency perspective* (pp. 253–271). Mahwah, NJ: Erlbaum.

Bray, J. H., & Berger, S. H. (1993). Developmental Issues in Stepfamilies Research Project: Family relationships and parent-child interactions. *Journal of Family Psychology, 7,* 76–80.

Burrell, N. A., & Mitchell, A. K. (1993, May). *The definitional impact on conflict styles as stepfamilies reorganize.* Paper presented at the 43rd annual conference of the International Communication Association, Washington, DC.

Cissna, K. N., Cox, D., & Bochner, A. P. (1990). The dialectic of marital and parental relationships within the stepfamily. *Communication Monographs, 57,* 44–61.

Coleman, M. A., Fine, M. A., Ganong, L. G., Downs, K. M., & Pauk, N. (1998). *Conflict in stepfamilies.* Manuscript submitted for publication.

Cummings, E. M., & Davies, P. (1994). *Children and marital conflict: The impact of family dispute and resolution.* New York: Guilford.

Daly, M., & Wilson, M. I. (1994). Some differential attributes of lethal assaults on small children by stepfathers versus genetic fathers. *Ethology and Sociobiology, 15,* 207–217.

Davies, P. T., & Cummings, E. M. (1998). Exploring children's emotional security as a mediator of the link between marital relations and child adjustment. *Child Development, 69,* 124–139.

Fincham, F. D., Grych, J. H., & Osborne, L. N. (1994). Does marital conflict cause child maladjustment? Directions and challenges for longitudinal research. *Journal of Family Psychology, 8,* 128–140.

Fine, M. A. (in press). Divorce and single parenting. In C. Hendrick & S. S. Hendrick (Eds.), *Sourcebook of close relationships.* Newbury Park, CA: Sage.

Fine, M. A., Coleman, M., & Ganong, L. H. (1998). Consistency in perceptions of the step-parent role among stepparents, parents and stepchildren. *Journal of Social and Personal Relationships, 15,* 811–829.

Fine, M. A., & Fine, D. R. (1992). Recent changes in laws affecting stepfamilies: Suggestions for legal reform. *Family Relations, 41,* 334–340.

Fine, M. A., Ganong, L. H., & Coleman, M. (1999). A social constructionist approach to understanding the stepparent role. In E. M. Hetherington (Ed.), *Coping with divorce, single-parenthood and remarriage: A risk and resiliency perspective* (pp. 273–294). Hillsdale, NJ: Erlbaum.

Fine, M. A., & Kurdek, L. A. (1992). The adjustment of adolescents in stepfather and stepmother families. *Journal of Marriage and the Family, 54,* 725–736.

Fine, M. A., & Kurdek, L. A. (1994). Parenting cognitions in stepfamilies: Differences between parents and stepparents and relations to parenting satisfaction. *Journal of Social and Personal Relationships, 11,* 95–112.

Ganong, L. H., & Coleman, M. (1994). *Remarried family relationships.* Beverly Hills, CA: Sage.

Ganong, L. H., Coleman, M., & Fine, M. A. (1995). Remarriage and stepfamilies. In R. D. Day, K. R. Gilbert, B. H. Settles, & W. R. Burr (Eds.), *Research and theory in family science* (pp. 287–303). Pacific Grove, CA: Brooks-Cole.

Ganong, L. H., Coleman, M., Fine, M. A., & Martin, P. (1999). Stepparents' affinity-seeking and affinity-maintaining strategies in stepfamilies. *Journal of Family Issues, 20,* 299–327.

Glick, P. C. (1989). Remarried families, stepfamilies, and stepchildren: A brief demographic profile. *Family Relations, 38,* 24–27.

Grych, J. H., & Fincham, F. D. (1990). Marital conflict and children's adjustment: A cognitive-contextual framework. *Psychological Bulletin, 108,* 267–290.

Hanson, T. L., McLanahan, S. S., & Thompson, E. (1996). Double jeopardy: Parental conflict and stepfamily outcomes for children. *Journal of Marriage and the Family, 58,* 141–154.

Hetherington, E. M. (1993). An overview of the Virginia Longitudinal Study of Divorce and Remarriage with a focus on early adolescence. *Journal of Family Psychology, 7,* 1–18.

Hetherington, E. M., Bridges, M., & Insabella, G. M. (1998). What matters? What does not? Five perspectives on the association between marital transitions and children's adjustment. *American Psychologist, 53,* 167–184.

Hetherington, E. M., & Clingemepeel, W. G. (1992). Coping with marital transitions. *Monographs of the Society for Research in Child Development, 57*(2–3, Serial No. 227).

Hetherington, E. M., & Stanley-Hagan, M. (in press). Diversity among stepfamilies. In D. H. Demo, K. R. Allen, & M. A. Fine (Eds.), *Handbook of family diversity.* New York: Oxford University Press.

Hobart, C. (1991). Conflict in remarriages. *Journal of Divorce and Remarriage, 15,* 69–86.

Ihinger-Tallman, M. (1987). Sibling and stepsibling bonding in stepfamilies. In K. Pasley & M. Ihinger-Tallman (Eds.), *Remarriage and stepparenting: Current research and theory* (pp. 164–182). New York: Guilford.

Klein, D. M., & White, J. M. (1996). *Family theories: An introduction.* Thousand Oaks, CA: Sage.

Kurdek, L. A., & Fine, M. A. (1993). The relation between family structure and young adolescents' appraisals of family climate and parent behaviors. *Journal of Family Issues, 14,* 279–290.

Metts, S., & Cupach, W. R. (1995). Postdivorce relations. In M. A. Fitzpatrick & A. L. Vangelisti (Eds.), *Explaining family interactions* (pp. 232–251). Thousand Oaks, CA: Sage.

Pasley, K., Sandras, E., & Edmondson, M. E. (1994). The effects of financial management strategies on quality of family life in remarriage. *Journal of Family and Economic Issues, 15,* 53–70.

Sabatelli, R. M., & Shehan, C. L. (1993). Exchange and resource theories. In P. G. Boss, W. J. Doherty, R. LaRossa, W. R. Schumm, & S. K. Steinmetz (Eds.), *Sourcebook of family theories and methods: A contextual approach* (pp. 385–417). New York: Plenum.

Sweet, J. A., Bumpass, L. L., & Call, V. R. (1988). *The design and content of the National Survey of Families and Households* (Working Paper NSFH-1). Madison, WI: University of Wisconsin, Center for Demography and Ecology.

Vandewater, E. A., & Lansford, J. E. (1998). Influences of family structure and parental conflict on children's well-being. *Family Relations, 47,* 323–330.

Visher, E., & Visher, J. (1988). *Old loyalties, new ties. Therapeutic interventions with stepfamilies.* New York: Brunner/Mazel.

Waldren, T., Bell, N. J., Peek, C. W., & Sorell, G. (1990). Cohesion and adaptability in post-divorce remarried and first married families: Relationships with family stress and coping styles. *Journal of Divorce and Remarriage, 14,* 13–28.

Wilson, B. F., & Clarke, S. C. (1992). Remarriages: A demographic profile. *Journal of Family Issues, 13,* 123–141.

PART FOUR. APPLICATIONS

15 Clinical Prevention and Remediation of Child Adjustment Problems

Cynthia M. Turner and Mark R. Dadds

The collection of chapters in this book indicates that we have come a long way in explicating the complex relationship between inter-parental conflict and child adjustment. We now have several frameworks and data bases for delineating the particular aspects of parental conflict that are most detrimental, understanding how children's thinking and processing of the conflict can contribute to their adjustment, and understanding how parenting practices and parent–child relationships can serve as either protective or risk factors for children's adjustment. The challenge for researchers and clinicians alike is to use these bodies of evidence, and the known risk and protective factors, to develop effective prevention and treatment strategies that aim to prevent or minimize the suffering of children exposed to their parents' conflict. Thus, this chapter aims to (1) provide an overview of current intervention technologies that are or could be employed in this area, (2) briefly review examples of specific prevention and intervention programs that have been evaluated and described in the literature, (3) discuss important methodological issues for conducting intervention research, and (4) provide a model for future development of and research into treatment and preventative interventions. Accordingly, we intend to provide a "blueprint" for future investigations, both in terms of program development and evaluation research. It is hoped that our suggestions and guidelines will assist in building upon the foundation research that has already been done in this important area.

The literature describing intervention efforts to enhance the adjustment of children exposed to marital conflict is reviewed in this chapter in accordance with two guiding frameworks. First, the interventions are presented according to current models of categorizing intervention/prevention strategies, and second, they are presented with a developmental perspective, from infancy through to late adolescence and adulthood. Examples of both child-focused and parent-focused interventions are included. These interventions attempt to enhance children's adjustment either by reducing factors associated with adverse outcomes or by increasing factors associated with positive outcomes, or both. We have attempted to be comprehensive; however, space constraints require selectivity. Consequently, where multiple studies were found describing similar types of intervention, a subset were selected as illustrative of the type of work in that area. Table 15.1 summarizes the studies reviewed.

Approaches to Prevention and Intervention

Before proceeding, it is important to discuss the current approaches to prevention and the terminology used to describe these methods. Traditionally, three levels of intervention have been described: primary, secondary, and tertiary (Caplan, 1964). Primary prevention referred to interventions that sought to reduce the incidence of psychopathology by intervening prior to the onset of a disorder. Secondary prevention sought to reduce the prevalence of pathology by intervening once problems had been identified, but before the problems became severe. Tertiary prevention involved treatment of existing disorders and prevention of relapse. The disadvantage of this classification system was that the secondary and tertiary levels related more to treatment than to prevention. Prevention of psychological problems is now recognized as the target of mental health policies across the world, and funding is allocated accordingly (Spence, 1996). The prevention literature has therefore adopted an alternative approach to classifying interventions, based upon the presence and extent of risk factors related to the development of a disorder (Gordon, 1987). These approaches are labeled universal, selective, and indicated.

Universal interventions are those applied to whole populations, regardless of their risk status. In some instances, universal preventive interventions are designed to enhance general mental health or to build resiliency, whereas others are targeted at one specific disorder. Selective prevention efforts are applied to those individuals who are members of a group, the membership of which places them at increased risk for the development of a mental health disorder. Clearly the majority of preventive interventions for children exposed to family conflict, violence, or marital dissolution fall within this category. Indicated prevention approaches are those applied to individuals or groups who are found to manifest mild symptomatology, identifying

Table 15.1. Reviewed Preventive Intervention Programs

Program Title	Targeted Population Group/ Sample Size	Risk Factors Addressed	Outcomes (for total intervention group and/or subgroup)	Principal Investigator(s)/Year(s)
Universal Interventions				
I CAN DO Program	School-age children N = 88	General coping and problem-solving skills	Enhanced self-efficacy, increased repertoire of coping skills and problem-solving ability	Dubow & colleagues, 1993
Resourceful Adolescent Program (RAP Program)	Adolescents N = 261	Depressed mood	Reduced depressive symptomatology & hopelessness, enhanced coping and problem-solving resources	Shochet, Dadds & colleagues, 1998
Prevention and Relationship Enhancement Program (PREP)	Couples N = 135	Couple relationship problems	Better marital adjustment, less divorce, less physical conflict	Markman, 1992
Selected Interventions				
Children of Divorce Intervention Program (CODIP)	School-age children of divorce N = 75	Marital conflict and separation, early conduct problems	Lower anxiety, fewer learning problems, better adjustment	Pedro-Carrol & Cowan, 1985, 1986, 1989
Divorce Education for Parents (resource materials only)	Separated/divorced parents	Parental conflict, children's adjustment to divorce	Greater parent–child involvement with noncustodial parent	Arbuthnot, Poole, & Gordon, 1996

(continued)

Table 15.1 *(continued)*

Program Title	Targeted Population Group/ Sample Size	Risk Factors Addressed	Outcomes (for total intervention group and/or subgroup)	Principal Investigator(s)/Year(s)
Selected Interventions				
Children in the Middle (court-mandated seminar)	Separated/divorced parents N = 131	Parental conflict, children's adjustment to divorce	Reduced exposure of children to parental conflict; increased parental skills & cooperation	Arbuthnot & Gordon, 1996
Indicated Interventions				
Penn Prevention Program	School-age children N = 69	Mild depressive symptoms, adjustment to parental conflict	Relief of depressive symptoms, reduced externalizing behavior, enhanced ability to cope with conflict	Jaycox, Reivich, Gillham, & Seligman, 1994
Positive Adolescent Choices Training (PACT)	African-American Adolescents	Personal history of aggression, victim or witnesses of family violence, social skills deficits	Improved social skills, reduced physical aggression, less involvement in juvenile court	Yung & Hammond, 1998

them as being at extremely high risk for the future development of full-blown mental health disorders.

This current classification is not without its disadvantages. Such an approach assumes that psychopathology can be categorized as present or absent. In reality, most forms of psychopathology lie on a continuum from mild or few symptoms to more severe and/or numerous symptoms. Despite these criticisms, this review will discuss programs in terms of universal, selective, and indicated interventions, as this is currently the most widely accepted model.

Universal Preventive Intervention Programs

School-Age Children. Within the literature on stress and coping research, investigators have identified a number of resources (e.g., social supports, problem-solving skills) that appear to protect children from the potentially negative effects of stressful life events (Compas, 1987; Rutter, 1987). Such findings have led several groups of researchers to advocate for school-based preventive interventions that provide children with the skills and abilities needed to enhance their coping (e.g., Dubow, Schmidt, McBride, Edwards, & Merk, 1993).

The *I CAN DO* program (Dubow et al., 1993) is a 13-session curriculum that teaches children general coping and problem-solving skills, encourages children to seek social support, and shows children how they might be helpful to peers currently experiencing a stressful life event. Pretesting revealed no significant group differences on demographic or life-stress variables. As predicted, the intervention resulted in an improved ability within participants to generate a repertoire of effective solutions to stressful problems, and an improvement in children's self-efficacy for implementing solutions. However, there were no pre- or post-intervention differences found in the size of children's social support networks. These findings suggest that building resiliency in children can assist them to deal with stressful life events. Unfortunately, Dubow et al. (1993) did not collect follow-up data that would allow them to evaluate whether children's behavior in stressful situations would actually change as a result of undergoing such an intervention.

Adolescents. Shochet et al. (1998) reported on a universal preventive program designed to enhance resilience in adolescents and to prevent the onset of clinically significant depression. The *Resourceful Adolescent Program* (RAP) consisted of 11 weekly group sessions of approximately 45 minutes each. Sessions focused on seven major areas: (a) recognition and affirmation of existing strengths, (b) stress management, (c) cognitive restructuring, (d) problem solving, (e) building/accessing support networks, (f) considering the other's perspective, and (g) keeping and making the peace. Adolescents reported lower levels of depressive symptomatology and hopelessness, and greater coping and problem-solving resources at postintervention, compared to controls. Major benefits of the program were evident for those adolescents who began with high or moderate elevations of depressive symptoms. It would be gratifying to see such a program evaluate its long-term efficacy with respect to a variety of life stressors and not just with respect to an absence of depressive symptomatology.

Adults. A number of universal preventive programs have been developed to target relationship satisfaction in couples. These programs are based upon the rationale that negative reciprocity, poor communication, and conflict are the best predictors of poor relationship satisfaction and ultimately divorce. Although not specifically addressing couples' awareness of the effects of conflict on children, such programs are based on the identification of, and intervention with variables that are most predictive of relationship distress. The *Premarital Relationship Enhancement Program* (*PREP*: Markman, 1981; 1984; Markman, Floyd, Stanley, & Storaasli, 1988; Markman, Renick, Floyd, Stanley, & Clements, 1993) is an example of a universal couple intervention which seeks to reduce conflict.

Markman and colleagues developed *PREP* to prevent distress, divorce, and psychological dysfunction in couples who are already married or planning marriage. Couples are taught effective communication skills, and how to thwart behaviors that predict later marital distress (e.g., escalation of disagreements). The central principle underlying the program is that effective communication and problem solving can prevent later marital distress. Clearly such a program has obvious benefits for the mental well-being of children as well as couples.

The *PREP* intervention takes one of two formats. In the original version, groups of four to eight couples attend two-and-a-half hour weekly sessions. They hear lectures on communication skills and then practice their new skills to discuss issues in their relationship. The program facilitator provides feedback. In the second format, groups of 20–40 couples hear the same lectures at a weekend retreat and then use their private rooms to practice skills on their own.

Most of the evaluation findings for the PREP program have focused on the reduction of risk factors for relationship distress rather than on specific mental health outcomes. One of the strongest demonstrations that marital problems predict childhood behavioral and emotional problems came from a longitudinal study by Howes and Markman

(1989). They demonstrated that marital conflict and lack of communication measured at the time of childbirth predicted childhood disturbance 3–5 years later. Therefore, clinical intervention studies that evaluate the long-term impact of marital interventions on child development would be very useful.

Cowan and Cowan (1988) developed a more comprehensive approach directly addressing parenting stress. They devised a group intervention for couples going through the transition to parenthood that was designed to provide support and guidance about marital strains associated with this period and to improve marital communication and conflict resolution concerning parenting issues. The couples who completed the intervention showed lesser declines in marital satisfaction following childbirth and were less likely to divorce 2 and 3 years later than couples in a no-treatment group. Preventive marital interventions are increasingly appearing, but little parallel energy is being invested in evaluating the effects of improving marital relations on child development. Given the high rates of divorce and marital discord currently being observed in the Western world, it is very important that this be addressed.

Selected Preventive Intervention Programs

School-Age Children. Most intervention programs for children of divorce have been school-based to maximize recruitment of children and to produce educational gains as well as gains in emotional adjustment. However, the extent to which such programs are evaluated is quite limited (Grych & Fincham, 1992). Two notable exceptions to this evaluation gap are Stolberg and colleagues' *Divorce Adjustment Program (DAP)* (Stolberg & Garrison, 1985; Stolberg & Mahler, 1994) and Pedro-Carrol and Cowen's (1985) *Children of Divorce Intervention Project (CODIP).* Both these programs are based upon assumptions that divorce is a stressful event in children's lives, and that postdivorce adjustment can be facilitated by teaching cognitive-behavioral skills and providing emotional support (Barber, 1995). Given the similarity between these programs, only one will be reviewed here; however, interested readers are encouraged to consult the references provided.

Pedro-Carrol and Cowen (1985), in the *Children of Divorce Intervention Program (CODIP),* sought to reduce risk and enhance adaptation in children of divorce. Two trained facilitators met with children in grades 4–6 for 10 one-hour weekly sessions. The program included a component for helping children to understand feelings about divorce and divorce-related anxieties, a cognitive skills-building component for resolving interpersonal conflicts, and an anger-management skills component. Parents of participants had been separated for an average of 23.6 months. Participants were matched for gender, grade, length of time since parental separation, and other preadjustment measures before being randomly assigned to the experimental or delayed-treatment intervention.

At posttest, 2 weeks following program completion, teachers rated experimental participants as being significantly better adjusted than control subjects on shy–anxious behaviors and learning problems, and experimental children rated themselves as significantly less anxious than controls. Teachers also rated participants as significantly more socially competent at posttest than controls. Similarly, parents of intervention children rated them as significantly better adjusted than controls on measures of peer relationships, school performance, and feelings about divorce. These findings were replicated 1 year later (Pedro-Carrol, Cowen, Hightower, & Guare, 1986).

Alpert-Gillis, Pedro-Carrol, and Cowen (1989) subsequently modified the program in an effort to make the intervention more accessible to ethnic and urban children. The modified program comprised sixteen 45-minute sessions and was evaluated with children in grades 2–3, whose parents had separated an average of 3.75 years before the intervention.

Pretest comparisons with a group of children from intact families showed children of divorce were significantly less well adjusted. At posttest, experimental children evidenced significant improvements, compared with controls, on (a) self-ratings of coping skills, (b) parent ratings of children's behaviors and problem-solving skills, and (c) teacher ratings of children's competence and peer social skills.

The results of both the *CODIP* and *DAP* evaluations support the effectiveness of selective group-based preventive interventions for school-aged children who have recently experienced parental separation. The findings suggest that a relatively brief intervention can produce immediate reductions in anxiety, adjustment problems, and behavior problems among these children.

However, many families who expose children to marital conflict and separation also expose their children to marital violence. Marital violence is the most severe form of interparental conflict. The most widely suggested treatment intervention for children who have witnessed marital violence is a group-counseling program (Jaffe, Wilson, & Wolfe, 1986). Most of the group programs described in the literature are housed in shelters for battered women, but they may also involve collaboration with other professionals in child protection or mental health centers (Jaffe et al., 1986).

Jaffe, Wolfe, and Wilson (1990) describe a group treatment program for children who have witnessed parental violence. Children are divided into two groups based upon their developmental stage (8–10-year-olds and 11–13-year-olds). The groups aim to deal with the emotional, behavioral, and cognitive problems arising from witnessing wife assault, in addition to addressing more subtle symptoms related to attitudes about violence and responsibility for adult behavior. For example, children are encouraged to understand the impact of violence on their mother and to separate their feelings of love for their father without accepting his violent behavior. The program runs for 10 consecutive weeks, with sessions approximately 90 minutes in duration. Topics covered include labeling feelings, dealing with anger, safety skills, social supports, social competence and self-concept, responsibility for violence, understanding family violence, and wishes about family. Group facilitators try to work in close collaboration with the child's mother in order to maintain open lines of communication and feedback, and to assist mothers to be prepared for any difficult issues that their child may raise.

Jaffe et al. (1990) present group evaluation data for 64 children (aged 7–13 years) and their mothers. Children completed structured interviews pre- and postintervention, while mothers completed the Parent Perception Inventory and the Child Behavior Checklist (CBCL). Although 88% of mothers perceived positive changes in their child's behavioral adjustment, these results were not supported by changes in pre- and postintervention CBCL scores. However, both mothers and children reported children's enjoyment of the group, and participating children demonstrated significant changes in their safety skills and protective strategies.

Jouriles et al. (1998) provide preliminary results of an intervention for families (mothers and children) who have recently sought shelter at a battered women's refuge. To be eligible for inclusion in the program, women were required to be setting up a residence independent of their violent partner, and to have a child (aged 4–9 years) with aggressive and oppositional behavior. There were two primary components to the intervention: (a) providing families with social and instrumental support and problem-solving skills, and (b) teaching child management and nurturing skills to mothers. Weekly in-home sessions were conducted for up to 8 months after departure from the refuge. Families were randomly assigned to either an intervention or comparison condition.

Preliminary results indicated that (a) there were significant reductions in the antisocial behavior of children in the families receiving the intervention; (b) mothers in the intervention group were observed to parent more effectively and become more warm and involved with their children; and (c) mothers in the intervention group reported substantial reduction in psychological distress compared to mothers in the comparison condition. Hughes (1988) and Holden, Geffner, and Jouriles (1998) provide reviews of many other preventive interventions for both children and women exposed to family violence, and interested readers are encouraged to consult these sources as the reviews consider a developmental perspective and take into account the history of violence that children have been witness to.

Adults. There are several examples of programs within the literature that aim to prevent adult mental health problems associated with marital separation. Although such programs are not evaluated by consideration of the mental health status of children, it would seem that children would have secondary benefit from having well-adjusted parents.

Arbuthnot, Poole, and Gordon (1996) sought to evaluate the efficacy of an educational intervention for divorcing parents. The intervention consisted of the dissemination of a 32-page booklet to parents who had recently filed for divorce, with comparisons made against a wait-list control group. The booklet primarily sought to explain the effects of divorce and remarriage on children, and to provide concrete and practical suggestions for eliminating or minimizing parental conflict. The rationale behind the intervention was that parents provided with divorce-specific educational information would be less likely to exhibit behaviors which have been linked to poor postdivorce adjustment in children. Unfortunately, the educational intervention did not reduce reported levels of interparental conflict; however the intervention did result in greater parent–child involvement with the nonresidential parent. Arbuthnot et al. (1996) concluded that while the provision of educational materials is promising, it is likely that intervention effects will be strengthened by the incorporation of such materials into mandated, structured educational programs for parents involved in the separation/divorce process.

Arbuthnot and Gordon (1996) therefore evaluated a court-mandated, child-focused seminar for divorcing parents. They sought to assess (a) parental reactions to mandatory parent education programs, (b) whether divorcing parents could learn communication skills and parenting behaviors that would minimize the problems associated with children being exposed to postdivorce parental conflict, (c) whether the skills that parents learned were maintained over time, and (d) whether completion of the program would serve to reduce parental conflict and increase postdivorce parenting quality. The 2-hour seminar was built around a video, *Children in the Middle,* which illustrates the most common ways in which children are put in the middle of parental conflicts. A male–female team, both of whom had extensive experience in working with families, facilitated discussion groups following the video, and parents were given two resource booklets: a guide to help divorcing parents to work cooperatively together and a booklet to accompany the video.

Parental mastery of the skills taught were evaluated both immediately after the seminar and again 6 months later. Parents perceived the classes to be realistic and useful. Skills were effectively learned and maintained over the evaluation period. Parents reported that they were successful in dramatically lowering exposure of their children to parental conflict. Relative to a comparison group of parents divorcing the year before the classes were initiated, parents completing the class were better able to work through how they would handle difficult child-related situations with their ex-spouses and were willing to let their children spend more time with the other parent.

It seems that researchers have come to acknowledge the importance of influencing parent behavior in order to prevent lasting negative outcomes for their children. While this is a very positive step, these parenting programs need to evaluate their efficacy with respect to child adjustment as well as that of parents.

Indicated Preventive Intervention Programs

As discussed in the previous section, one of the limitations of the current classification system is that it does not recognize the continuum of pathology. Indicated programs aim to focus their efforts on individuals who are found to manifest a risk factor that identifies them as being at high risk for the future development of psychopathology. However, early and/or mild symptomatology is a risk factor for the later development of many forms of psychopathology. For example, conduct disorder in young people tends to develop along a trajectory in which early symptoms are predictive of later development of more severe symptomatology (Farrington, 1995). Once on this trajectory, many children show increasing levels of symptomatology with increasing age. Thus, indicated preventions must target those individuals with early and/or mild symptomatology. With this in mind, the distinction between prevention and remediation becomes blurred. Consequently, this section of the review will also consider programs that remediate existing adjustment problems.

School-Age Children. Jaycox, Reivich, Gillham, and Seligman (1994) report on the development and preliminary efficacy of the

Penn Prevention Program (PPP), a cognitive-behavioral group intervention designed to prevent depressive symptoms and comorbid
conditions such as low self-esteem and conduct problems in children
aged 10–13 years. This study is included in the current review
because of the screening measures that were utilized. PPP is among
the first programs described in the child and youth literature to recognize marital conflict as a risk factor for psychopathology.
Participating children were selected on the degree of parental conflict
they were exposed to and on self-report assessments screening for the
presence of mild depressive symptomatology. Parental conflict was
included because of the weight of previous research showing that
marital conflict and low family cohesion are associated with
increased depressive symptoms in children (Jaycox et al., 1994).
Results on these measures were combined to select a group of children with high base-rate risk for future depression. The sample consisted of 69 children (aged 10–13 years) in the treatment conditions
and 74 children in the control condition.

In this 5-year prospective study, the effectiveness of three versions of
the program were compared to a control group: (a) a cognitive training
component, (b) a social problem-solving component, and (c) a combined treatment including both components. The group intervention
was conducted in 12 weekly sessions of approximately 90 minutes.
Each treatment intervention used cognitive-behavioral techniques
proactively to teach children coping strategies to use in the face of negative life events and to enhance their sense of mastery and competence
across a variety of situations. However, the cognitive training intervention focused on children's interpretations about problems, while the
social problem-solving and coping component focused on children's
actions to solve problems, rather than interpretations.

Due to the relatively small sample sizes within each treatment condition, Jaycox et al. (1994) collapsed all treatment groups to allow
meaningful comparisons between treatment and control conditions.
Results revealed that, compared to the control group, the intervention
was immediately effective in relieving depressive symptoms, and in
preventing depressive symptoms and externalizing behavior at follow-up. Importantly, children who participated in the treatment
groups gained a better sense of how to handle interpersonal problems
and appeared to be more confident in their ability to deal with conflict. Although plagued by self-selection bias and a high attrition rate,
these results are extremely encouraging for researchers attempting to
assist children to overcome the effects of exposure to parental conflict,
and provide considerable support for the efficacy of indicated preventive interventions.

Adolescents. Many of the childhood adjustment problems that are associated with witnessing parental conflict and violence become magnified through the demands and stressors of adolescence. Exposure to such maladaptive family dynamics increases the likelihood that adolescents themselves will repeat the relationship patterns they observe (Jaffe et al., 1990). As adolescents are beginning to become involved in their first intimate relationships outside the family, this is typically the time that learned violent behavior and deviant conflict resolution styles become evident (Jaffe et al., 1990). For this reason, educating youths about relationships and nonviolent problem resolution methods holds great promise as a viable prevention strategy. This is the focus of the *Positive Adolescent Choices Training (PACT)* program (Yung & Hammond, 1998), an excellent example of an indicated prevention program for African-American youth (12–16 years). Targeted adolescents are those identified by teachers as having mild to moderate histories of aggression, to have been victims or witnesses of violence, and/or to have social skills deficits. *PACT* offers adolescents social skills training, anger management training, and education about violence. The skills training components help participants learn to express anger, frustration, or disappointment constructively; listen and react appropriately to criticism or anger from others; problem-solve and compromise in order to overcome disagreements; think through consequences of their angry responses; and control their anger. In the educative component, myths about violence are dispelled and an awareness of the dynamics of violence is raised.

Diverse outcome measures, including observer and self-ratings, school disciplinary records, juvenile court records, and teacher reports, are used in order to evaluate the impact of *PACT*. Results indicate that youths who completed the program demonstrated (a) improvement in the target social skills, (b) a significant reduction in physical aggression at school, and (c) less involvement than untrained youths in violence-related juvenile-court charges. Although only one measure (juvenile court records) is used as a long-term follow-up, Yung and Hammond (1998) have demonstrated that an indicated prevention program can be successful in reducing violent and other criminal behavior in at-risk youth. As former PACT participants enter adulthood, it would be useful to examine the impact of the program on relationships with domestic partners and children.

Treatment Programs for Marital Conflict and Child Behavior Problems

Considerable research has indicated that marital conflict and child behavior problems, particularly conduct disorders in boys, covary in clinical samples and to a lesser extent in the general population (Emery, 1982). However, the role of marital variables in the treatment of children with behavioral disorders has received far less attention .

Dadds, Sanders, Behrens, and James (1987) sought to examine the role of marital conflict on treatment outcome in the behavioral treatment of child conduct disorders. The efficacy of training in Child Management Training (CMT) was evaluated against CMT with an adjunctive treatment for marital conflict called partner support training (PST). Four families presented with an oppositional defiant child and concurrent marital conflict. The marital intervention, occurring as an adjunctive four hour-and-a-half hour sessions to the CMT, involved both communication and problem-solving skills training and was based on the rationale that couples who display the frequent and positive use of such skills are more likely to report satisfying (and less conflictual) relationships. PST initially prevents the escalation of conflict and aims to have both parents working as a team (i.e., not attacking or blaming each other, being supportive of each spouse attempting to resolve the problem, and not giving contrary instructions to the child). Step two involves facilitating daily communication between parents about topics other than the child's behavior and increasing the frequency and enjoyment of this task. Basic skills here are asking and listening. Finally, parents are taught to engage in appropriately timed problem-solving discussions.

The study found that while child behavior problems decreased for those families who could successfully implement the CMT techniques, hostile interactions between spouses continued to occur. However, when PST was added to the CMT intervention, behavior problems were further reduced, significant decreases were noted in hostile spouse interactions, and there was an increase in parental problem-solving behavior. These findings suggest that combined (or adjunctive) parenting and marital interventions are appropriate, and indeed, important. Marital conflict can powerfully influence children's problem behavior via its effects on parenting, and marital conflict can represent a significant impediment for intervention programs that aim to help children by providing parent training.

Dadds, Schwartz, and Sanders (1987) similarly sought to evaluate the role of marital conflict in the overall outcome of child behavior management for parents (CMT). Families with a child diagnosed as oppositional or conduct disordered were assigned to either a marital discord group or a no marital discord group. Families within each group were then randomly assigned to either CMT alone or CMT plus PST. Measures of child behavior, parenting behavior, and marital satisfaction were collected at pre- and posttraining and again at a 6-month follow-up. Results indicated a significant interaction between marital discord and treatment type on most measures at follow-up, but not at posttraining. Significantly, at 6-month follow-up, the group of discordant parents who had received CMT alone evidenced significant relapse. By contrast, the maritally discordant group who received CMT plus PST, and the two nondiscordant groups had maintained treatment effects. Although PST added little to the maintenance of change for the nondiscordant group, it produced significant gains over those who received CMT for the maritally discordant group.

This adjunctive CMT plus PST approach has been extended to encompass child behavior problems and couples' relationship problems in stepfamilies. In a randomized controlled trial, Lawton and Sanders (1994) examined the efficacy of a behavioral intervention combining parent training, partner support techniques, and strategies for enhancing family communication and family relationships. Compared to a wait-list group, the intervention was successful at producing reductions in child behavior problems, with concomitant improvements in the couple's relationship for some families.

For those readers interested in furthering this area, Dadds (1992) and Sanders, Markie-Dadds, and Nicholson (1997) provide therapeutic guidelines for the concurrent treatment of marital and child adjustment problems. Dadds' (1992) model focuses on the therapeutic processes whereby parents can temporarily "moratorium" their relationship conflict in order to work as a team in producing improvements in the child's emotional and behavioral adjustment. As the child's behavior improves, the focus increasingly moves over to the parent's relationship. In contrast, Sanders, Markie-Dadds, et al. (1997) suggest that a relationship between marital problems and child behavior difficulties be established at the outset. In order to do this, they recommend completing a thorough family assessment (incorporating both marital functioning and child functioning) and then using the assessment results to educate parents about the interrelationship between marital and child problems. Once this process is completed, the therapist and parents can work together to determine the best means of pursuing the issues (concurrently, sequentially, by referral, or by using Dadds' moratorium method). Where the initial referral was for marital issues, an initial focus on the couples' relationship is taken. However, when the initial referral was for child problems, this then becomes the focus of attention.

The Sanders, Markie-Dadds, et al. (1997) model approaches marital conflict and child adjustment from a broad community intervention perspective. Their intervention program, known as Triple P (Positive

Parenting Program), outlines five levels of family intervention. On the first level, and in the context of a marital referral, brief child-focused interventions can be successfully integrated with couple issues. For example, the provision of brief, reliable, and effective information (via parenting tip-sheets) about children's development and how to tackle specific problems may be effective for families experiencing mild child behavior problems.

On the second level, parents are given more detailed written parenting information in the form of a parenting educational book and an accompanying workbook. Together, these resources make up a 10-week self-help program for parents with no therapist contact required. This intervention is made more effective when the third level of intervention is added, that is, brief but regular therapist contact. These brief consultations provide minimal support to parents as a means of keeping them focused and motivated while they work through the program.

The fourth level of intervention involves the provision of information in combination with active skills training to teach parents how to manage specific problems, or problem behaviors in specific settings (e.g., bedtime and sleep problems). With narrowly focused interventions, the emphasis is on the management of a specific child behavior rather than developing a broad range of child management skills. Training is continued until parents reach an acceptable criterion level of performance on the skills being taught.

The fifth level of intervention is recommended for moderate to severe child adjustment problems. Similar to level four, information provision is combined with active skills training and support; however, on this level, the skills are applied to a broad range of target behaviors in both the home and community settings, with both the target child and his/her siblings. Generalization enhancement strategies are also included. Sanders and Markie-Dadds (1996) have evaluated each of these five levels of intervention with very positive results.

Commonalities to Successful Interventions

It is worth pausing at this point to consider what common factors underlie the success of the interventions reviewed above. Designing effective interventions primarily stems from clearly understanding the risk and protective factors that contribute to child adjustment. The development of effective interventions then depends upon the accumulation of controlled trials in which well-defined and described interventions are contrasted against each other and various control conditions.

One way of enhancing children's adjustment to interparental conflict is by increasing the factors associated with positive outcomes (protective factors). Universal interventions seemed to do just that. Each of the universal interventions reviewed provided participants with a repertoire of skills, regardless of their age or developmental stage. For example, children and adolescents participating in the *I CAN DO* and *RAP* programs were taught general coping and problem-solving skills, while adolescents and adults participating in the *violence-free* relationships and the *PREP* programs were taught communication and problem-solving skills. All universal interventions emphasized the resolution of interpersonal difficulties. These relatively brief interventions have been demonstrated to increase an individual's repertoire of skills in addition to preventing long-term negative outcomes such as divorce (e.g., Markman, 1981, 1984).

Successful selective and indicated interventions appeared to be similarly skills-focused; however, there was an emphasis on the development of intrapersonal skills in addition to interpersonal skills. For example, children in both the *CODIP* and *DAP* programs were taught skills in cognitive restructuring in order to assist them in processing feelings about parental divorce and in correctly attributing responsibility and blame. Kerig (Chapter 8) also discusses how skill building in children can help them to cope with interparental conflict.

Skills-based interventions focusing on parental skill acquisition were similarly effective. Treatment efficacy was demonstrated for families where separation had occurred as a result of marital conflict (e.g., Arbuthnot & Gordon, 1996), in addition to families whose marital conflict was treated adjunctively with the child's behavior (e.g., Dadds, Schwartz, & Sanders, 1987). The utility of skills-based interventions is further enhanced when considering that some programs compared skills training with a support-only condition. For example, the *DAP* program found that children who received the skills-building component evidenced greater improvements in their emotional and behavioral adjustment than children in the support alone condition. In addition to skills building, education is an important intervention component. Helping parents to understand and identify which aspects of their behavior are detrimental to child adjustment can be a powerful intervention in itself.

Effective interventions appear to draw on our understanding of the causes and risk factors contributing to poor child adjustment and use intervention methods or techniques that are known to change behavior. Most of the interventions described here employ a cognitive-behavioral paradigm. Traditionally, the psychodynamic school has dominated and has emphasized the importance of a cathartic experience, whereby children can reenact the distressing family conflict within the safe confines of the therapeutic relationship, thereby gaining control over their emotions. However, while the literature contains a number of case studies detailing dynamic interventions, there are few that have employed any form of treatment evaluation. Such evaluation is essential in an era where cost-effectiveness is paramount. In addition, it would seem that group-based interventions are an extremely cost-effective form of service delivery. Cognitive-behavioral treatments, which are amenable to group-based delivery and are focused upon outcome evaluation, consequently seem to predominate.

Unfortunately, studies tend to assess only those outcomes that are specifically related to the goals of the program. For example, if children are taught problem-solving skills, the program is evaluated with respect to whether children acquired these new skills. While it is important for researchers to match their treatment evaluation to the treatment goals, it is also important to take a broader life perspective. For example, are interventions that are designed to provide children with general coping skills (e.g., *I CAN DO*) effective in enhancing their adjustment to stressful life situations such as interparental conflict? Similarly, an evaluation of the long-term effects of treatment is required. The effects of treatment and the relative effectiveness of different treatments often vary at posttreatment and follow-up (Kazdin, 1988). A longitudinal perspective of therapy is especially important in relation to children. Without such specific and longitudinal information, we cannot determine which type of intervention (universal, selected, or indicated) receives the strongest empirical support with respect to preventing adjustment problems in children. In a research and clinical environment where cost-effectiveness and outcome evaluation are emphasized, and funding is increasingly difficult to obtain, determining which type of intervention strategy receives the strongest empirical support is increasingly important.

Methodological Issues

Much of the published research relating to the effectiveness of preventive and treatment interventions are limited by methodological problems. These include the use of small, nonrepresentative samples, the lack of appropriate comparison groups, inadequate measures of central constructs, reliance on self-report measures to provide data on multiple variables, low recruitment rates, high attrition rates, and relatively short follow-up periods. Some notable exceptions are Markman et al.'s

(1988, 1993) *PREP* program for relationship enhancement, and Pedro-Carrol and Cowen's (1985) *CODIP* program for children from divorcing families. Such programs provide evidence that preventive interventions can be based upon sound conceptual and empirical foundations, with rigorous design and evaluation strategies.

Rather than dwell on the limitations of the published research, we will review the Institute of Medicine's Committee on Prevention of Mental Disorders criteria for designing and reporting methodologically sound interventions (Marzek & Haggerty, 1994, pp. 217–222). The first criterion pertains to the risk and protective factors that are purported to be addressed by the research. These factors are required to be well-documented and specifically related to the developmental tasks of the target population. The second criterion is a clear description of the targeted or experimental group, the control group, the recruitment and consent process, and the prevention technology that is employed. The third criterion is a description of the intervention itself. All too often, treatment and preventive interventions lack adequate description, sometimes due to restrictions imposed by journal publication formats, but in other cases, it is simply missing information that impedes appropriate evaluation and replication. See Marzek and Haggerty (1994) for the elements that each program description should include.

The fourth criterion addressed is a description of the research methodology. Marzek and Haggerty (1994) suggest that the ideal research design in a prevention trial is a randomized controlled trial of adequate sample size imbedded in a longitudinal study. However, they concede that a variety of other designs, such as pre- and posttest comparisons, are often employed and may be necessary for large-scale community interventions. Details of the research design should include an appropriate description and use of statistical methods. They caution that it is frequently necessary to confirm that randomized assignment has had its intended effects by comparing experimental and control groups on sociodemographic characteristics and on other relevant characteristics in addition to outcome. Furthermore, they add that designs that employ baseline measures are highly desirable because variables that frequently appear extraneous have the potential to be significant.

The fifth criterion comprises details concerning the implementation of the project. For example, how well were the intended objectives and processes of the intervention actually implemented? Finally, there ought to be a description of the outcomes. Most fundamentally, evidence should be provided that risk and protective factors have been changed and that the intervention was successful. Other obvious sources of evidence for a preventive intervention would be an actual reduction in the observed rate of new cases of a disorder or the delayed onset of a disorder in the experimental group.

Methodological issues in clinical research are so important that the American Psychological Society established a task force, led by Richard Price, to develop a set of criteria to guide the development and evaluation of effective prevention programs (Price, Cowen, Lorion, & Ramos-McKay, 1989, p. 50). Many of the criteria correspond to those listed here; however, additional inclusions are (a) a statement of the rationale for the intervention, (b) a description of how the program relates to community groups, (c) the transferability of the intervention to other settings, and (d) the roles of professionals and nonprofessionals in providing caregiver resources.

The final comment we make concerning methodology is that the quality of the measures is of upmost importance in evaluating programs and being able to compare evaluations with existing data. It is beneficial when researchers use similar, well-established measures to facilitate the comparison of findings.

The Potential for Prevention: A Developmentally Informed Prevention Trajectory

One of the aims of this chapter is to provide suggestions and guidelines that will motivate the further development of preventive interventions in the area of children's adjustment to marital conflict. The number of children living in one-parent families is growing at a consistent and dramatic rate. The United States has the highest divorce rate, with recent studies finding that as many as 55% of American couples, 42% of English couples, and 35% of Australian couples divorce (Baris & Garrity, 1997). However, little research has been done on the length of time that couples continue to engage in negative interaction patterns and conflict before reaching a decision to divorce. Certainly, most children of divorce have long histories of exposure to high levels of parental conflict before the divorce occurs. Some researchers (e.g., Block, Block, & Gjerde, 1988) have found evidence of children's distress as long as 11 years prior to the divorce! Clearly, there are substantial numbers of children who remain exposed to the detrimental impact of chronic and destructive marital conflict. Thus, relying on clinical referrals and traditional tertiary interventions for these children is not a useful mental health strategy. Preventive interventions are desperately needed.

Existing research data suggest that no one age group is more vulnerable than another to the effects of marital conflict. We know that children from at least 6 months of age through to late adolescence respond to anger and conflict between adults with visible upset, and with reports of distress and anger (for reviews see Cummings & Davies, 1994; Davies & Cummings, 1994). However, we also know that children's responses to interparental conflict change with age. For example, infants and toddlers rarely mediate their parents' disputes. The disposition to mediate increases sharply at approximately preschool age, and may continue to increase until middle adolescence, thereafter dropping off (Cummings & Davies, 1994). Furthermore, although young children may be less able to cope with the conflict, they are also less likely to be fully aware of the conflict and its implications. Alternatively, older children have a larger repertoire of coping responses but they are likely to be more aware of the causes and consequences of conflict (Cummings & Davies, 1994).

Another developmental consideration is the vulnerability of children at different ages to exhibit different types of mental health problems. For example, infants and young children are more likely to exhibit aggression, noncompliance, and temper tantrums, while dysphoria, passivity, and depression become more prevalent between late childhood and adolescence (Davies & Cummings, 1994; Grych & Fincham, 1990). It is important that clinicians be mindful of these developmental differences and develop intervention strategies that target the vulnerability to specific problems and outcomes at each age.

There are a number of life-cycle stages, for both individuals and relationships, that may be seen as windows of opportunity for establishing comprehensive prevention and treatment programs. Table 15.2 summarizes some of the potential interventions at each point throughout the life cycle.

The Transition from Dating to Marriage. The work of Howard Markman and colleagues (1988, 1993) suggests that couples who are provided with communication and problem-solving skills prior to their marriage report greater relationship satisfaction and less marital distress and conflict than couples who do not receive such training. Clearly this has important preventive implications.

The Transition to Parenthood. Traditionally, marital researchers and therapists have focused on the presence of children as a source of stress that negatively impacts upon the marital relationship (Sanders, Nicholson, & Floyd, 1997). However, the arrival of a new infant into the home can be an opportune time to apply a universal preventive intervention. During this period of transition, family members are often

Table 15.2. Windows of Opportunity: The Potential for Preventive Interventions

Developmental Phase	Potential Interventions
Prenuptial	Marital preparation/skills training (e.g., communication and problem-solving skills)
The transition to parenthood	Lamaze classes Parenthood seminars (perceptions and expectations, stress reduction)
Infancy	Information provided to parents through child-health centers/nurses/pediatricians/daycare centers/playgroups
Childhood	Parent education seminars Education through newsletters School-based interventions (universal or selected) e.g., coping skills, conflict resolution, anger management Indicated interventions concurrently addressing marital issues and children's emotional/behavioral problems Enhancing parent–child relationships
Adolescence	School-based interventions (universal or selected – see childhood) e.g., coping skills, prevention of relationship violence, personal safety Parent–adolescent mediation Pregraduation skills training, e.g., communication, problem-solving, coping, relationship skills Teenage pregnancy and parenting workshops
Marital/couples	Couples therapy, including education Skills training (e.g., anger management, conflict resolution, positive parenting) Parenting groups (e.g., discipline, relationship enhancement) Educative media campaigns
Divorce	Mediation of disputes Neutral third-party involvement Court-mandated parent education programs

open to information that will assist them in caring for their new child, and it is also a time when parents are more likely to accept and appreciate support from others (Larroque & Hendren, 1997). Therefore, adopting a group approach and targeting new parents with education can provide valuable prevention opportunities. The program by

Markman and Kadushin (1986) provides evidence of the potential for such interventions.

A little creative thinking suggests numerous avenues for dissemination of information, for example, in the form of newsletters, community talks or lectures by mental health professionals, and guidance from pediatricians and daycare teachers. Neighborhood get-togethers with parents and their new infants, as well as toddler and preschool playgroups, can provide a wonderful source of information and support. It is, however, increasingly difficult for young families to take advantage of such prevention opportunities. In many families, both parents are working and their infant spends most of the day in a child-care facility. Mental health professionals therefore must not only provide education and guidance to young families, they must find creative ways to relay this information (Larroque & Hendren, 1997).

Studies examining the transition to parenthood have identified that those couples who experience a decline in marital satisfaction and quality at the transition to parenthood appeared to perceive their relationships more as romances than as partnerships (Lindahl, Malik, & Bradbury, 1997). This seems to indicate unrealistic expectations for the relationship in the face of parenthood. Therefore preventive efforts may also (a) explore with parents the perceptions and expectations that each partner holds about the changing nature of their relationship and (b) prepare them for the realities of parenthood and the need to work as teammates and not just romantic partners.

Childhood. Schools are in an ideal position to facilitate preventive interventions because almost all children attend school at some point in their lives, and young people's ability and motivation to stay in school, learn, and utilize what they learn is affected by their mental health (Larroque & Hendren, 1997). Furthermore, when teachers and/or guidance officers are involved in implementing preventive interventions, the interventions can reach generations of children.

Entry to school represents a developmental point in a child's life signaled by movement from the nuclear family into the wider community. Schools are able to facilitate educational evenings or seminars for parents regarding the behavior of their children and the potentially damaging effects of interparental conflict. Typically, all schools relay information about upcoming events and activities to parents via newsletters that are sent home, and it may be worthwhile including a weekly news article encouraging the promotion of mental health within families. In addition to these universal strategies, schools also offer an opportunity to screen children for selected interventions. For example, selection for program participation could result from screening via self-report questionnaires, or children may be selected for involvement in an intervention group on the basis of their family structure.

Alternatively, childhood is often the time when emotional or behavioral problems are first identified and initial referrals to child psychologists are more common. Such referrals provide ideal opportunities for involving children and families in indicated preventive interventions.

Adolescence. As the child matures, peer relationships become more important, making group therapy an extremely relevant mode of intervention throughout high school. Because young adolescents are at an age when potentially harmful situations are surfacing, they are a particularly important target group for interventions designed to prevent or delay the onset of negative pathways (Barber, 1995). The universal preventive intervention described previously (Shochet et al., 1998) provides compelling evidence for the efficacy of a general coping skills program for adolescents.

Despite being a time of heightened autonomy and increasing susceptibility to peer influence, early adolescence is still a period in which family influences are important, making it ideal for programs that target both the youth and the parent. Parent–child relationships are transformed during adolescence as family members continually renegotiate rules and boundaries. Again, schools would be an ideal place to facilitate parent–adolescent mediation workshops. Alternatively, just prior to graduation from high school (with the emotional and often physical separation from the family pending) is an ideal time for a general coping, problem-solving, and communication skills training intervention. Adolescents are also likely to be particularly enthusiastic about adventure or wilderness-based therapies, which draw upon physical exertion and challenge as the avenue for self-discovery and change.

Marital/Couples Interventions. When distressed couples present for therapy, it would seem pertinent to include an educative component into couples' counseling to help them better predict and understand the behavior of their children. In families where interparental conflict is intense, education about the impact this behavior has on children may facilitate couples' attempts to manage their anger better (Sanders, Nicholson, et al., 1997). Education alone, however, may be insufficient, and active skills training interventions may be required. Conflict management, stress reduction, and positive parenting have been identified as potential intervention strategies for parents experiencing relationship distress or undergoing relationship transitions (Sanders, Nicholson, et al., 1997).

There would also seem the potential for offering parents who present for marital therapy an adjunctive parenting group, focusing on family relationships, discipline strategies, and mood enhancement. For example, components of such a group could include positive family activities, teaching parents to attend to and reinforce positive behavior, developing listening skills, encouraging parents to monitor the discipline strategies they use, and emphasizing the importance of consistent consequences for children's behavior.

Direct provision of therapeutic services is only one level at which intervention can occur. Other possibilities are through mass education via media sources. Attitudes, expectations, and beliefs about family relationships are reflected in and shaped by the media, including films, television, newspapers, magazines, and radio. The media can also be used to promote healthy and realistic beliefs about relationships, as well as to model healthy ways to deal with relationship stressors. This strategy has been used successfully in health education, for example, in quit smoking campaigns. There seems little reason why family relationships cannot be targeted in a similar fashion.

Divorce. Parents moving into postdivorce single-parent families may need skills for cooperative parenting and for mobilizing social supports and resources. Divorce mediation is another potentially effective intervention. Mediation focuses on maintaining joint parenting so that the needs of the children are foremost and so that children are protected from the conflict commonly generated between the ex-spouses during and following divorce. Where co-parenting without conflict is impossible, a number of strategies may be introduced to reduce children's exposure to the conflict between divorced parents. These include the development of clear rules regarding pick-up and drop-off of children for access visits and/or negotiating for the handover of children to occur at the home of a neutral third party. Finally, given that parental conflict appears to be such a powerful mediator of children's adjustment to divorce, further attention should be paid to mandated educational programs for divorcing parents. Initial evaluations of such programs are promising (e.g., Arbuthnot & Gordon, 1996).

Summary and Conclusions

This chapter has briefly reviewed the literature relating to prevention and treatment programs for children who have been exposed to interparental conflict, and some suggestions and guidelines for future research and program development were provided. A major limitation of many of the studies reviewed is that the evaluation does not assess the process by which change occurs. To understand how the interventions help (or fail to help) conflictual families, it is important to assess whether the goals of the group are met in addition to assessing the process of change and whether the group improved the child's functioning. Failure to tailor outcome measures to the child's well-being is unfortunate because such research could provide useful information at both theoretical levels (e.g., increasing knowledge about mediators) and applied levels (e.g., identifying which aspects of the program are most useful).

For those studies that did adequately examine the efficacy of their intervention, a number of common factors were identified as contributing to the program success. Effective interventions typically employed a cognitive-behavioral paradigm. For universal preventive interventions, proactive skills training was the common denominator. Where a risk factor was clearly identified, as in selected and indicated interventions, proactive skills training was employed in conjunction with cognitive restructuring. This cognitive component appeared to be necessary for adequately addressing the identified risk factor. Finally, programs that provided skills and education to parents were found to be important in maintaining improvements in children's adjustment.

The development of effective prevention and treatment interventions continues to require the interplay of basic and applied research. In this context, basic research refers to investigations that are designed to understand the risk and protective factors associated with child adjustment. The findings from this basic research provide the underpinnings for informed, well-timed, and targeted interventions. Applied research therefore represents efforts to achieve a therapeutic goal for the participants who are involved in the program. Evaluation of these research goals should be broad and longitudinal.

Intervention strategies that are well articulated but not evaluated are abundant in the literature for both children of divorce and children who are witnesses to family violence. Clearly there is also a need for the rigorous scientific evaluation of these interventions. The literature on prevention is rapidly expanding and with it the amount of funding that such research attracts. However, there is a need to determine which type of preventive intervention is the most efficacious with respect to promoting child adjustment at various points in the life cycles of families. Such information can only be obtained with the inclusion of specific outcome measures imbedded into longitudinal research designs. Child adjustment to interparental conflict is an exciting area of study because of the great potential it has to profoundly affect the lives of many children. We hope that this chapter will serve to motivate further research interest.

REFERENCES

Alpert-Gillis, L. J., Pedro-Carrol, J. L., & Cowen, E. L. (1989). The children of divorce intervention program: Development, implementation, and evaluation of a program for young urban children. *Journal of Counseling and Clinical Psychology, 57*, 583–589.

Arbuthnot, J., & Gordon, D. A. (1996). Does mandatory divorce education for parents work? A six-month outcome evaluation. *Family and Conciliation Courts Review, 34*, 60–81.

Arbuthnot, J., Poole, C., and Gordon, G. (1996). Use of educational materials to modify stressful behaviors in post-divorce parenting. *Journal of Divorce and Remarriage, 25*, 117–137.

Barber, B. L. (1995). Preventive intervention with adolescents and divorced mothers: A conceptual framework for program design and evaluation. *Journal of Applied Developmental Psychology, 16*, 481–503.

Baris, M. A., & Garrity, C. B. (1997). Co-parenting post-divorce: Helping parents negotiate and maintain low-conflict separations. In W. Kim Halford and H. J. Markman (Eds.), *Clinical handbook of marriage and couples intervention* (pp. 619–649). New York: Wiley & Sons.

Block, J., Block, H. J., & Gjerde, P. J. (1988). Parental functioning and the home environment in families of divorce: prospective and concurrent analyses. *Journal of the American Academy of Child and Adolescent Psychiatry, 27*, 207–213.

Caplan, G. (1964). *Principles of preventive psychiatry.* New York: Basic Books.

Compas, B. E. (1987). Coping with stress during childhood and adolescence. *Psychological Bulletin, 101*, 393–403.

Cowan, P. A., & Cowan, C. P. (1988). Changes in marriage during the transition to parenthood: must we blame the baby? In G. Y. Michaels & W. A. Goldberg (Eds.), *The transition to parenthood: Current theory and research* (pp. 114–154). Cambridge: Cambridge University Press.

Cummings, E. M., & Davies, P. (1994). *Children and marital conflict: The impact of family dispute and resolution.* New York: Guilford Press.

Dadds, M. R. (1992). Concurrent treatment of marital and child behavior problems in behavioral family therapy. *Behavior Change, 9*, 139–148.

Dadds, M. R., Sanders, M. R., Behrens, B. C., & James, J. E. (1987). Marital discord and child behavior problems: A description of family interactions during treatment. *Journal of Clinical Child Psychology, 16*, 192–203.

Dadds, M. R., Schwartz, S., & Sanders, M. R. (1987). Marital discord and treatment outcome in behavioral treatment of child conduct problems. *Journal of Consulting and Clinical Psychology, 55*, 396–403.

Davies, P. T., & Cummings, E. M. (1994). Marital conflict and child adjustment: An emotional security hypothesis. *Psychological Bulletin, 116*, 387–411.

Dubow, E. F., Schmidt, D., McBride, J., Edwards, S., & Merk, F. L. (1993). Teaching children to cope with stressful experiences: Initial implementation and evaluation of a primary prevention program. *Journal of Clinical Child Psychology, 22*, 428–440.

Emery, R. E. (1982). Interparental conflict and the children of discord and divorce. *Psychological Bulletin, 92*, 310–330.

Farrington, D. P. (1995). The challenge of teenage antisocial behavior. In M. Rutter (Ed.), *Psychosocial disturbances in young people: challenges for prevention* (pp. 83–130). New York: Cambridge University Press.

Gordon, R. (1987). An operational classification of disease prevention. In J. A. Steinberg & M. M. Silverman (Eds.), *Preventing mental disorders* (pp. 20–26). Rockville, MD: Department of Health and Human Services.

Grych, J. H., & Fincham, F. D. (1990). Marital conflict and children's adjustment: A cognitive-contextual framework. *Psychological Bulletin, 108,* 267–290.

Grych, J. H., & Fincham, F. D. (1992). Interventions for children of divorce: Toward greater integration of research and action. *Psychological Bulletin, 111,* 434–454.

Howes, P., & Markman, H. J. (1989). Marital quality and child functioning: A longitudinal investigation. *Child Development, 60,* 1044–1051.

Holden, G. W., Geffner, R., & Jouriles, E. N. (Eds.). (1998) *Children exposed to marital violence: Theory, research, and applied issues.* Washington, D.C.: American Psychological Association.

Hughes, H. M. (1988). Psychological and behavioral correlates of family violence in child witnesses and victims. *American Journal of Orthopsychiatry, 18,* 77–90.

Jaffe, P., Wilson, S. K., & Wolfe, D. (1986). Promoting changes in attitudes and understanding of conflict resolution among child witnesses of family violence. *Canadian Journal of Behavioral Science, 18,* 356–366.

Jaffe, P., Wolfe, D., & Wilson, S. K. (1990). *Children of battered women.* Developmental Clinical Psychology and Psychiatry, Vol. 21. London: Sage Publications.

Jaycox, L. H., Reivich, K. J., Gillham, J., & Seligman, M. P. (1994). Prevention of depressive symptoms in school children. *Behavior Research and Therapy, 32,* 801–816.

Jouriles, E. N., McDonald, R., Stephens, N., Norwood, W., Spiller, L. C., & Ware, H. S. (1998). Breaking the cycle of violence: Helping families departing from battered womens shelters. In G. W. Holden, R. Geffner, & E. N. Jouriles (Eds.), *Children exposed to marital violence: Theory, research, and applied issues* (pp. 337–369). Washington, D.C.: American Psychological Association.

Kazdin, A. E. (1988). *Child psychotherapy: Developing and identifying effective treatments.* Elmsford, NY: Pergamon Press.

Larroque, C., & Hendren, R. L. (1997). Individual and group interventions. In R. T. Ammerman & M. Hersen (Eds.), *Handbook of prevention and treatment with children and adolescents* (pp. 91–105). New York: John Wiley & Sons.

Lawton, J. M., & Sanders, M. R. (1994). Designing effective behavioral family interventions for step-families. *Clinical Psychology Review, 5,* 463–496.

Lindahl, K. M., Malik, N. M., & Bradbury, T. M. (1997). The developmental course of couples' relationships. In W. K. Halford and H. J. Markman (Eds.), *Clinical handbook of marriage and couples intervention* (pp. 203–223). New York: Wiley & Sons.

Markman, H. J. (1981). Predicting marital distress: A 5-year follow-up. *Journal of Consulting and Clinical Psychology, 49,* 760–762.

Markman, H. J. (1984). The longitudinal study of couples' interactions: Implications for understanding and predicting the development of marital distress. In K. Halweg & N. S. Jacobson (Eds.), *Marital interaction. An analysis and modification* (pp. 253–281).

Markman, H. J., Floyd, F., Stanley, S. M., & Storaasli, R. (1988). The prevention of marital distress: A longitudinal investigation. *Journal of Consulting and Clinical Psychology, 56,* 210–217.

Markman, H. J., & Kadushin, F. S. (1986). Preventive effects of Lamaze training for first-time parents: a short-term longitudinal study. *Journal of Consulting and Clinical Psychology, 54,* 872–874.

Markman, H. J., Renick, M. J., Floyd, F. J., Stanley, S. M., & Clements, M. (1993). Preventing marital distress through communication and conflict management trainings: A 4- and 5-year follow-up. *Journal of Consulting and Clinical Psychology, 61,* 70–77.

Mrazek, P. J., & Haggerty, R. J. (1994). *Reducing risks for mental disorders: Frontiers for preventive intervention research.* Committee on Prevention of Mental Disorders: Institute of Medicine. Washington, D.C.: National Academy Press.

Pedro-Carrol, J. L., & Cowen, E. L. (1985). The children of divorce intervention program: An investigation of the efficacy of a school-based prevention program. *Journal of Counseling and Clinical Psychology, 53,* 603–611.

Pedro-Carrol, J. L., Cowen, E. L., Hightower, A. D., & Guare, J. C. (1986). Preventive intervention with latency-aged children of divorce: A replication study. *American Journal of Community Psychology, 14,* 277–289.

Price, R. H., Cowen, H. L., Lorion, R. P., & Ramios-McKay, J. (1989). The search for effective prevention programs: What we learned along the way. *American Journal of Orthopsychiatry, 59,* 49–58.

Rutter, M. (1987). Psychosocial resilience and protective mechanisms. *American Journal of Orthopsychiatry, 57,* 316–331.

Sanders, M. R. & Markie-Dadds, C. (1996). Triple P: a multilevel family intervention program for children with disruptive behavior disorders. In P. Cotton & H. Jackson (Eds.), *Early Intervention and Prevention Mental Health Applications of Clinical Psychology* (pp. 59–85). Melbourne, Australia: Australian Psychological Society.

Sanders, M. R., Markie-Dadds, C., & Nicholson, J. M. (1997). Concurrent interventions for marital and children's problems. In W. Kim Halford & H. J. Markman (Eds.), *Clinical handbook of marriage and couples intervention.* (pp. 509–535). New York: Wiley & Sons.

Sanders, M. R., Nicholson, J. M., & Floyd, F. J. (1997). Couples' relationships and children. In W. Kim Halford and H. J. Markman (Eds.), *Clinical handbook of marriage and couples intervention* (pp. 225–253). New York: Wiley & Sons.

Shochet, I. M., Dadds, M. R., Holland, D., Whitefield, K., Harnett, P., & Osgarby, S. (1998). *Short-term effects of a universal school-based program to prevent adolescent depression: A controlled trial.* Manuscript submitted for publication.

Spence, S. H. (1996). A case for prevention. In P. Cotton & H. Jackson (Eds.), *Early intervention and prevention in mental health* (pp. 87–107). Melbourne, Australia: The Australian Psychological Society.

Stolberg, A. L., & Garrison, K. M. (1985). Evaluating a primary prevention program for children of divorce. *American Journal of Community Psychology, 13,* 111–124.

Stolberg, A. L., & Mahler, J. (1994). Enhancing treatment gains in a school-based intervention for children of divorce through skill training, parental involvement, and transfer procedures. *Journal of Consulting and Clinical Psychology, 62(1),* 147–156.

Yung, B. R., & Hammond, W. R. (1998). Breaking the cycle: A culturally sensitive violence prevention program for African-American children and adolescents. In J. R. Lutzker (Ed.), *Handbook of child abuse research and treatment* (pp. 319–340). London: Plenum Press.

16 Interparental Conflict and Social Policy

Robert E. Emery

What can social policy do to ease interparental conflict? The enormity of the task begins to come into focus when we consider the potential complexity of interparental conflict. Co-parents are not just parents, but they play multiple roles in their relationship with each other. In addition, there are many possible topics of conflict between parents including but not limited to various issues related to children and parenting. Further, disagreement or anger can be discussed or otherwise communicated in many different ways. Given the diversity of American families, moreover, the interparental relationship may be based on several different legal grounds other than marriage. Finally, the implementation of potential policies is complicated greatly by the historical respect for family privacy and family autonomy found in American family law.

The Multifaceted Co-Parenting Relationship

Consider these complications in a bit more detail. The co-parenting relationship is a multifaceted one. Co-parents are not just parents, but they may be each other's friend (or enemy), lover (or estranged mate), protector (or abuser), economic partner (or competitor), family member (or cast-off). These roles typically are interdependent, thus, for example, inter*parental* conflict may be a result of, or an expression of, an ongoing dispute about altogether different aspects of the co-parents' relationship. It has been suggested, for example, that many child custody disputes may really be attempts to block divorce or to maintain contact with a former spouse rather than (or in addition to) being disagreements about contact and control of the children (Emery, 1994).

The multiple roles co-parents play with each other give them many different topics for potential dispute. Communication, money, extended family, household routines, and sex are just a few of the pos-

sible topics for conflict in addition to disagreements about the children
– and there are many opportunities for disagreement about children.
Moreover, interparental disputes and the anger accompanying them
may be expressed as the silent treatment, through indirect sarcasm, in
direct problem solving, in ongoing battles, in sudden hostile outbursts,
in acts of physical violence, in formal legal battles, or in many other
ways. In short, the manner in which interparental conflict can be
expressed is limited only by the creativity of the disputants.

The Law and the Co-Parenting Relationship

As noted, parents also maintain a variety of different legal relationships with one another, a circumstance that complicates not only the
relationship between the co-parents but also the task of social policy. In
1996, about one out of four children in the United States was born outside of marriage (National Center for Health Statistics, 1997). The parents of only about one quarter of children born outside of marriage are
cohabiting at the time of the birth, which means that the parents are living in different households for about three out of four American children born to unmarried parents (Bumpass & Raley, 1995; Burns &
Scott, 1994). (In most other Western countries, a much higher proportion of unmarried parents, nearly 100%, are cohabiting at the time of
their children's birth.) Three-fourths of American children are born
inside of marriage, but by the time they reach the age of 16, it is estimated that about 40% of children born to married parents will experience their parents divorce (U.S. Census Bureau, 1992). Finally, a
substantial proportion of American children will experience the remarriage of one or both of their parents, since three out of four divorced
men and two out of three divorced women eventually remarry (Sweet
& Bumpass, 1987). Remarriage creates new opportunities for conflict
between the biological parents, as the remarriage and the role of the
stepparent often are topics of dispute. In addition, remarriage potentially exposes children to conflict between the new couple, the child's
parent and stepparent – and between the new stepparent and the former spouse (both of whom also are the child's parents).

In addition to these complexities, social policy makers face another
huge challenge in attempting to promote cooperation and reduce interparental conflict: The relationship between parents largely is a private
one. The privacy is due, in part, to the structure of the nuclear family
household and to social norms about "minding your own business,"
but a respect for family privacy also is embodied in the law. In family
law, there is an ongoing tension between the respective rights and
responsibilities of the child, the family, and the state, but there is a long-

standing tradition of respect for family autonomy in American jurisprudence (Mnookin, 1985).

One example of the deference to family privacy is that, until recent decades, many acts of physical violence between spouses were not illegal; in fact, some states continue to have no statutes against marital rape (Dietz, 1996). A more mundane but equally revealing example is that American courts have refused to hear disputes about parenting between married couples. When a couple is married, courts have consistently denied trial access to disputes about parenting, even disputes about important and serious issues such as the choice of public versus private schooling or different forms of religious upbringing. At the same time, American courts routinely deal with the same controversies between divorced parents, although the legal system increasingly is encouraging the private settlement of such disagreements between divorced parents (Emery, 1999).

The reluctance of the state to intervene in the co-parenting relationship is apparent in the very short list of policies that have been explicitly designed to reduce interparental conflict and to promote interparental cooperation. Given the historical respect for family privacy, it is not surprising, moreover, that these policies come into play primarily when the family is in contact with the legal system for some other reason. Specifically, the social policies explicitly designed to reduce interparental conflict are limited to (1) divorce (especially child custody) mediation, (2) legal interventions in spousal violence, and (3) various educational programs, particularly premarital counseling and education programs for divorcing parents.

Research on each of these topics is selectively reviewed in the following pages. One overriding theme of this review is that policies have only a very limited effect on reducing interparental conflict and increasing interparental cooperation. A second theme, however, is that policies should be judged by their indirect effects as well as their direct consequences. Although a given intervention may not produce substantial, immediate effects on reducing interparental conflict, the policy may produce incremental benefits over time as one of many contributors to shaping cultural views of conflict and the co-parenting relationship.

Divorce Mediation

Divorce mediation is perhaps the clearest example of a social and legal policy that has been explicitly developed to reduce parental conflict and increase parental cooperation. Divorce mediation first emerged as a distinct practice only in the 1970s (Folberg & Taylor, 1984). The first law about divorce mediation in the United States was implemented in 1981 when California legislation mandated that all parents with contested child custody or visitation disputes must attempt mediation before a custody hearing would be held. Since the enactment of the California law, the states of Arizona, Delaware, Florida, Kentucky, Maine, Nevada, North Carolina, Oregon, Utah, and Wisconsin all have adopted legislation mandating the mediation of custody disputes in at least some of their jurisdictions (Hendricks, 1993–94). Indeed, all states (and many other countries) have mounted some form of mediation program, commonly through administrative rather than legislative procedures. It is unusual to find a jurisdiction in the United States where some form of divorce mediation is unavailable.

In divorce mediation, parents meet together with an impartial third party who helps them to identify, discuss, and hopefully resolve disputes that result from divorce. The most frequently practiced form of divorce mediation focuses only on childrearing disputes. The two central childrearing disputes in divorce are: (a) where the children will reside (according to what schedule), or *physical custody*, and (b) how parents will share and/or divide both day-to-day decisions and broader authority over child rearing, or *legal custody*. Mediators commonly also address other areas of conflict (e.g., hurt and anger over the end of the relationship) and encourage cooperative co-parenting, both because these disputes can undermine the legal agreement and because they are important to successful parenting after divorce (Emery, 1994).

Divorce mediation has spread rapidly and widely for a number of reasons. One reason is the rapid increase and continued high incidence of divorce. A second reason is the deregulation of divorce, as evidenced by "no fault" divorce now available in every state, and the related trend toward encouraging the private settlement of divorce disputes. A third reason, specific to the area of child custody, is the indeterminate "best interests of the child" standard, which is the principle guiding the legal settlement of child custody disputes. The best interests rule is a vague directive that particularly encourages private settlement because it presents impossible questions in theory and prolonged, personal, and painful custody hearings (if necessary) in practice (Mnookin, 1975). A fourth impetus for the rapid development of divorce mediation comes from research on divorce and its consequences for children, especially findings that family processes occurring after divorce are strongly related to children's postdivorce adjustment (Emery, 1999). For example, research demonstrates a consistent relation between children's psychological problems and interparental conflict before, during, and after divorce (Cummings & Davies, 1994; Emery, 1982, 1999; Grych & Fincham, 1990), and these findings have provided a strong and explicit motivation for the development of mediation. A special concern has been that, contrary to children's best interests, adversary legal settlements may increase divisiveness and acrimony between divorcing spouses who remain parents (Emery & Wyer, 1987b).

These are compelling rationales for attempting divorce mediation, but does mediation fulfill its ambitious goals of facilitating dispute resolution, improving satisfaction with the process and promoting cooperative co-parenting? Only limited research addresses these important questions, but some clear benefits and apparent limitations of mediation already have been documented empirically (Emery, 1994). Major findings on facilitating dispute resolution, parent satisfaction, and coparenting/psychological health are summarized in the following sections with an emphasis on the author's own research. The research is based on 71 low-income families who petitioned a court for a child custody hearing, and who were randomly assigned either to mediation or allowed to continue with litigation. Families were assessed immediately after dispute settlement, one-and-a-half years later, and recently, in a 12 year follow-up study.

Divorce Dispute Settlement

In the author's own work where families were randomly assigned to mediate or litigate their custody disputes, mediation clearly produced a dramatic reduction in court hearings in both an initial study and in a replication, (Emery & Wyer, 1987b; Emery, Matthews, & Wyer, 1991). Other evidence indicated that disputes also were resolved more quickly in mediation than in adversary settlement (Emery et al., 1991). At least two other studies that used random assignment also found that mediation reduces court hearings (Irving, Benjamin, Bohm, & MacDonald, 1981; Pearson & Thoennes, 1984).

The efficacy of mediation in reducing court hearings seems clear from experimental research, and evaluation research demonstrates the effectiveness of mediation research in settling custody disputes in the real world. A statewide evaluation of California's mandatory custody mediation programs, for example, found that upward of half of all contested custody cases were being resolved in mediation (Depner, Cannata, & Simon, 1992). Since court mediation programs deal with the most acrimonious separated and divorced parents, programs where parents seek mediation voluntarily should and apparently do have much higher rates of reaching a settlement (e.g., Kelly & Duryee, 1992). Finally, it also appears that compliance with agreements may be somewhat higher and relitigaton may be somewhat lower following mediation than adversary settlement (Emery et al., 1991; Kelly, 1990; Margolin, 1973; Pearson & Thoennes, 1989).

Parents' Satisfaction with Mediation

In the author's research, parental satisfaction following mediation and litigation can be summarized in terms of four patterns. First, fathers were significantly and substantially more satisfied with mediation than with litigation. Second, few differences were found between mothers in terms of their satisfaction with mediation or litigation. Third, whether they mediated or litigated, mothers were more satisfied than fathers with the process, outcome, and consequences of dispute settlement. Fourth, these findings were consistent across an initial study, a replication study, and a 1-year longitudinal follow-up study (Emery & Wyer, 1987b; Emery et al., 1991; Emery, Matthews, & Kitzmann, 1994).

This pattern of findings has been interpreted to mean that mediation is bad for mothers and good for fathers (e.g., Grillo, 1991), but this is a misinterpretation. Rather, the findings point more clearly to the disadvantage of men (versus women) in litigation than to a disadvantage of women (versus men) in mediation (see Emery, 1994). In the author's samples, fathers gained more satisfaction from mediation than litigation because fathers were consistent losers in litigation. In contrast, women who mediated had relatively little to gain, because they almost always won in court. Of course, this also means that women potentially had much to lose in mediation, but the evidence indicated that mothers who mediated did not lose. The settlements for the mediation and litigation groups did not differ (except for slightly more joint legal custody in the mediation group), but fathers who mediated nevertheless were much more satisfied than fathers who litigated. Thus, mediation apparently produced win–win outcomes, apparently by giving fathers "voice" in the dispute resolution process (Emery, 1994).

Gender differences have not been carefully examined in much other research, except in Kelly's California studies where she found few gender differences (1989, 1990; Kelly & Gigy, 1989; Kelly, Gigy, & Hausman, 1988). It is important to note that the difference between the Virginia and California studies probably reflects the different experience in *litigation* in the two states. The legal background for determining custody arrangements has been more gender-equal in California than in Virginia (for example, as reflected in the states' joint custody laws). Possible gender differences notwithstanding, research is consistent in finding more satisfaction with mediation than with adversary settlement in studies using random assignment or comparison group designs (Irving et al., 1981; Kelly, 1990; Pearson & Thoennes, 1984). A high level of satisfaction with mediation also has been documented in evaluation research on large samples of mediation cases (e.g., Depner et al., 1992; Keilitz, Daley, & Hanson, 1992).

Co-Parenting Conflict and Psychological Adjustment of Family Members

Divorce mediation produces many settlements at the time of the dispute, parents are very satisfied with their experiences in mediation (more so than in adversary settlement), and mediation may encourage greatly compliance with the terms of the agreement. Does this translate into reduced co-parenting conflict and increased cooperation over time? As with most other policy-relevant research on interparental conflict, the best answer to this question is that not enough research has been conducted to given a definitive answer. However, in the author's research and the work of others, few long-term differences in co-parenting have been found, and no clear differences in children's or parents' psychological adjustment have been demonstrated.

In the author's research, one of the more positive findings was that fathers who mediated reported less co-parenting conflict a year after dispute settlement, although the difference fell just short of statistical significance (Emery et al., 1994). No differences were found between groups on measures of children's mental health or warmth in parent–child relationships, although a decline in parental conflict over time was associated with improved child mental health across both groups (Kitzmann & Emery, 1994). Finally, perhaps the most exciting result comes from data from the author's 12-year follow-up study, which are unpublished as of this writing. Initial data analysis indicates that fathers who mediated maintained significantly (and notably more) contact with their children than did fathers who litigated even many years after dispute settlement. This finding is potentially very important, especially given contemporary concerns about encouraging "deadbeat dads" to be responsible fathers outside of marriage.

As in the author's research, evidence from other studies also fails to indicate differences in mental health between family members using mediation and adversary settlement. No differences in child outcomes were found in a brief assessment in one study (Pearson & Thoennes, 1984), and detailed assessments of the former partners in another study similarly found no differences in adults' psychological adjustment

(Kelly et al., 1988; Kelly, 1990). There could be many explanations for this failure to demonstrate differences, but the most parsimonious conclusion at this point in time is that mediation does not directly produce improved mental health. In reaching this conclusion, however, it is important to note that many possible psychological outcomes have not been measured in the small number of studies conducted to date. Moreover, it *does* appear that mediation improves the co-parenting involvement and cooperation of fathers.

Summary and Implications for Policies on Co-Parenting Conflict

Overall, it is clear that divorce mediation leads to the settlement of a significant number of child custody disputes, many of which would otherwise end in litigation. Parents are generally more satisfied with the process and outcome of mediation as opposed to adversary settlement, and as a result, parents may be more likely to comply with mediated settlements. From the perspective of the efficient and effective administration of justice, these are important and very positive results. Brief mediation (often lasting only 4 to 6 hours) often conducted by mediators with limited training leads to the settlement of many cases that might have ended in expensive, time-consuming, and acrimonious custody hearings.

At the same time, the limited or null effect of mediation on co-parenting and the psychological adjustment of parents and children is inconsistent with the predictions of some of the more optimistic proponents of the process. Mediation reduces co-parenting conflict in the case of the targeted custody dispute, but much less so in terms of the ongoing co-parenting relationship. The positive effects reported by fathers are important, particularly their increased contact with their children even 12 years after dispute settlement. The absence of differences when reported from the mothers' perspective is troubling, however, especially when coupled with the author's finding of gender differences in reported satisfaction.

Both the positive and limited benefits of mediation must be acknowledged squarely, albeit with recognition that the body of sound empirical research on the topic is quite small and conclusions therefore must be reached cautiously. At the same time, the possibility should be considered that many of the most important benefits of mediation are found *outside* of mediation. More specifically, the availability and growth of mandatory or voluntary mediation may have at least two indirect effects in discouraging parental conflict and encouraging parental cooperation. First, mediation may affect the adversarial behavior of lawyers. When courts encourage or perhaps mandate mediation, attorneys have a strong incentive to settle their cases through negotiation rather than litigation, and as a result, this should reduce or at least not escalate conflict between parents. Second, mediation may affect the expression of anger between former partners who remain parents. Former spouses have many legitimate reasons to be angry, and they may have limited abilities to exercise control over their rage. However, the expectations created and the cooperation urged by the philosophy of mediation may influence divorced parents to contain their conflicts in a manner so as to minimize children's exposure to and involvement in the dispute. In short, mediation may have indirect effects on reducing interparental conflict by changing the culture of divorce and divorce settlement, a possibility that is explored together with other policy initiatives at the end of this chapter.

Legal Interventions in Spousal Violence

A number of legal policies have also been developed to alter the most extreme form of interparental conflict, spousal violence. (The terms *spousal violence, spouse abuse, domestic violence,* and *intimate violence* will be used here to refer to violence between unmarried partners or divorced partners, not just to married couples.) The topic of domestic violence is valuable to consider, because more and more stringent policies have been targeted toward the reduction of spouse abuse than in other areas of parental conflict. Like other initiatives, however, even these policies represent only very recent efforts. A review of policies designed to reduce family violence also is helpful in pointing to a number of problems with research evidence on interparental conflict policies in general. The existing body of research is sharply limited, sound intervention research on policy is difficult and expensive to conduct, and, in research that has been completed to date, the effects of intervention typically are rather small and controversial.

Intimate Violence as a Social Problem

Violence between spouses (and others in intimate relationships) has been recognized to have a startling prevalence when viewed either as a proportion of all intimate relationships that are characterized by violence or when viewed as the percentage of violent crimes that involve spouses or partners in intimate relationships. For example, data indicate that 16% of cohabiting partners report at least one incident of violence occurring in the past year, and 3% of women have been designated as victims of "serious" violence in the same survey (Stets & Straus, 1990). As another example, 36% of all the murders of women in the United States in 1992 were committed at the hands of a spouse or boyfriend (Garner & Fagan, 1997). (In calculating this percentage, murders by spouses or boyfriends [N = 1,256] were computed as a percentage of all murders where the relationship between the victim and offender was known [N = 3,454]. The relationship between victim and perpetrator was unknown for another 1,547 murders of women in 1992.)

In part due to increased awareness of the prevalence of the problems since the 1960s and 1970s, spousal violence and child abuse have increasingly been recognized as public health and social policy problems rather than merely as unfortunate events occurring behind closed doors (Fagan, 1990). In conceptualizing and intervening with abusive spouses, an overriding goal for advocates has been to treat episodes of violence against women as criminal problems, not just as family issues. (As an aside, it is interesting to note that, even in serious cases, child abuse has continued to be viewed largely as a family problem with the overriding goal of family reunification [Emery & Laumann-Billings, 1998]). After advocacy efforts resulted in the enactment of laws making most forms of spousal violence illegal, the most important policy initiatives in addressing spouse abuse have taken place in the criminal justice system. The major foci have been (a) the responses of police officers to emergency calls, (b) the prosecution of family violence in the criminal justice system, and (c) the treatment of abusers. We consider these three issues in the following sections. The effects of education about spouse abuse are considered together with other education-based interventions later in this chapter.

Police Intervention: Arrest or Diversion

Even after laws outlawing spouse abuse were enacted, advocates for battered women claimed that police nevertheless failed to make many arrests of abusive men. Research conducted during the 1970s demonstrated that this was, in fact, true. Many police department policies explicitly indicated that, rather than arresting abusive partners, crisis intervention and family counseling were more appropriate responses to domestic violence calls (Garner & Fagan, 1997). The failure to arrest was due, in part, to legal prohibitions against arrest in misdemeanor assaults not witnessed by the police, and, during the 1980s, advocates succeeded in changing state legislation in various ways to allow or encourage arrest in cases of misdemeanor domestic violence. Other policy changes also were enacted to protect battered spouses; for example, laws made it much easier to obtain orders of protection, legal orders that prohibit a perpetrator from contacting or coming into the proximity of a victim.

The push for arrest of abusive spouses was given great impetus by the results of an empirical study of arrest versus diversion in police intervention with domestic violence, the Minneapolis Domestic Violence Experiment (Sherman & Berk, 1984). In this study, police officers responded to domestic violence calls at random by either (1) arresting the suspect, (2) ordering one of the parties out of the residence, or (3) advising the parties. Based on subsequent victim interviews and official police reporters, this investigation indicated that arrest reduced further assault, attempted assault, and property damage by 50% in comparison to the diversion efforts.

The popular media and a U.S. Attorney General's Task Force on Family Violence (Attorney General, 1984) were quick to embrace the apparent substantial effect of arrest, and state laws and local police agency policies were rapidly changed to make arrest the preferred, often the mandatory, response to domestic violence calls (Sherman & Cohn, 1989). Unfortunately, methodological questions raised doubts about the findings of the original study, and the investigators generally failed to replicate the results in studies conducted in five other cities (Garner & Fagan, 1997). The replications did point to one possible explanation for the inconsistency. Arrest may have a deterrent effect in cases where the offender has a stronger attachment to the community (i.e., he was married to the victim or he was employed at the time of the arrest), but arrest may actually *increase* subsequent offending when the perpetrator has a less clear stake in conformity (Berk, Campbell, Klap, & Western, 1992). In any case, it is now clear that the positive effects of arrest in reducing subsequent offending are not uniform and not large (see Buzawa & Buzawa, 1996).

Prosecution of Offenders

Following arrest, prosecution is the next level where policy might be altered in dealing with cases of domestic violence. Historically, as noted, few incidents of domestic violence have resulted in arrest, and it is also true that few arrests lead to the prosecution of offenders. In fact, it has been estimated that as few as 10% of arrests in spouse abuse cases end in prosecution (Ford, 1991). The low rate of prosecution has been attributed to various causes, including victims' refusal to testify, frequent reconciliations between couples, and insensitivity or lack of support for victims in prosecutors' offices. As a way to address the last problem, a number of prosecutors' offices have created a special division either to aid victims as witnesses or to coordinate and strengthen efforts to prosecute spouse abusers (Garner & Fagan, 1997).

Does prosecution lead to lower rates of subsequent offending? Only a few systematic studies have addressed this question, and the answer appears to be that the effects are small or nonexistent. There is some evidence that, as with arrest, prosecution reduces subsequent violence when the offender has a stake in conformity but may actually increase offending in other cases (Garner & Fagan, 1997). Other nonexperimental evidence indicates that prosecution may reduce subsequent *severe* violence when the prosecution is *initiated by the victim* (Ford, 1991). While perhaps important to prosecutory strategies, the limited evidence on prosecution once again suggests that even this very aggressive policy option has only small, null, or mixed effects on subsequent offending.

Treatment of Offenders

A number of treatment programs for abusive spouses have been developed as an alternative either to arrest or to prosecution and/or incarceration following arrest. Programs vary not only in terms of substantive focus (e.g., cognitive behavior therapy, affect awareness training) but also in their basic format, such as individual versus group treatment or self-help versus professionally led groups. There is, however, one thing that unites treatment programs for battering spouses: an absence of research on their effectiveness. Most attempts to study the effectiveness of treatment are flawed in basic ways (e.g., there is no control group), and most of these studies indicate that the positive effects of the program are either small or absent in terms of reducing subsequent episodes of violent behavior (Garner & Fagan, 1997; Hamberger & Hastings, 1989).

Summary and Implications for Policies on Co-Parenting Conflict

Obviously, attempts to end violence between spouses through arrest and prosecution are far different from the usual focus of efforts to alter interparental conflict through the day-to-day management of parenting disputes or perhaps in marital or family therapy. It is useful to consider this extreme, however, both in regard to the unfortunately large number of children who are exposed to interparental violence (Jaffe, Wolfe, & Wilson, 1990) and in regard to the more general implications for policy.

The high prevalence of spouse abuse means that a significant number of children are exposed not only to conflict between their parents but also witness episodes of violence between them. Field research indicates that children of battered women are characterized by a number of psychological problems (Jaffe et al., 1990), and experimental evidence indicates that simulated conflicts involving violence are more distressing to children than other disputes (Cummings & Davies, 1994). In fact, exposure to interparental violence is considered to be a form of child abuse in many states; thus, abused women sometimes face the untenable choice between leaving their husband or losing their children to foster care. The failure of even dramatic interventions like arrest and prosecution to produce notable reductions in spouse abuse thus is sobering not only from the perspective of battered women but also from that of children exposed to parental conflict and violence.

The weak effect of such strong sanctions as arrest and prosecution also holds implications for other policy attempts to reduce interparental conflict and increase interparental cooperation. If arrest and prosecution have little effect on subsequent offending, how can we expect education, therapy, or mediation to help parents to work together better as parents? Part of the answer to the question is that arrest and prosecution do appear to have positive effects for some people in some circumstances; part of the answer is that our expectations must be limited as to how much any social policy can affect this largely private behavior; part of the answer is that acts of misdemeanor violence between spouses often are relationship problems in addition to legal problems (Brown & O'Leary, 1997); and part of the answer is that other forms of conflict may be more tractable than violent actions.

Moreover, it must be acknowledged that social policies, especially legal interventions like arrest and prosecution, can be based on and justified by moral questions, not just empirical ones. It would not be difficult to support an argument, for example, that arrest is the *morally right* response to assault between spouses whether or not it is the *most effective* response. As is discussed at the end of the chapter, strong moral arguments can be made about most policies designed to discourage interparental conflict. In fact, moral codes ultimately may have a strong practical effect in reducing violence and other forms of conflict by changing cultural expectations of and tolerance for conflict between parents.

Education Programs for Marriage and Divorce

Probably the most visible policy initiatives designed to reduce interparental conflict are various education programs, especially premarital education and divorce education. Premarital education programs typically are not targeted at parenting per se, but they may include the topic of parenting as one of several issues that are raised in relation to promoting happy and lasting marriages. In contrast, divorce education programs often are focused directly on parenting, although other issues may be raised in the process. The focus on parenting is most notable in the fact that couples are not expected to attend divorce education classes if they are seeking a divorce but have no minor children.

The logic and success of efforts at educating people about marriage and divorce are similar to other educational policies designed to influence interparental conflict, such as secondary prevention programs designed to reduce spousal violence (Holtzworth-Munroe et al., 1995) and parenting training programs for remarried families (Sanders, Markie-Dadds, & Nicholson, 1997). Thus, the seemingly incompatible topics of marriage and divorce education are reviewed in this section as illustrations of the more general issue of education as a policy intervention. The review begins by considering marriage education.

Marriage Education and Preparation Programs

The idea of offering couples education about and preparation for marriage is hardly a new one. Many premarital education programs have been offered for decades, if not longer, and such programs are widely available throughout the United States. For historical and cultural reasons, most premarital education programs have been run by private groups, particularly religious organizations.

In recent years, however, social policy makers have shown an increasing interest in using public resources to promote marriage education and preparation (and marriage generally). The most notable example of this public involvement is *covenant marriage,* a concept first introduced in 1997 by new legislation passed rapidly in the state of Louisiana. (In the two short years since covenant marriage was first implemented, statutes have been passed in at least one other state, Arizona, and new laws have been proposed if not adopted in many more states.) Covenant marriage gives couples who are to-be-married the option of selecting covenant marriage instead of marriage under the default state legal standards. The two most notable features of covenant marriage, other than the philosophy it embodies, are mandatory premarital education (which presumably will continue to be offered by religious organizations in most cases) and more stringent grounds for divorce (i.e., a longer waiting period for obtaining a nofault divorce, for example, 2 years instead of 1 year in Louisiana). As such, covenant marriage exemplifies the increasing concern of social policy with promoting marriage and marital education. In the review that follows, however, most of the research focuses on privately operated premarital education programs, specifically those operated or developed by professionals as opposed to religious groups. One question about these studies is the extent to which findings generalize to the broader group of premarital education programs run in different settings under different philosophies.

Enough empirical research has been conducted on the effectiveness of premarital education to lead to the publication of two meta-analyses of the literature. Moreover, both empirical reviews concluded that the effect sizes of intervention are moderate to large (Giblin, Sprenkle, & Sheehan, 1985; Hahlweg & Markman, 1988). However, others have raised questions about the quality of research upon which the meta-analyses were based, noting, for example, that effect sizes are much larger for behavioral than for self-report measures (Bradbury & Fincham, 1990). In addition, some evidence indicates that couples who choose to participate in marital education programs are at a lower risk for future marital difficulties than those who do not (Sullivan & Bradbury, 1997). Furthermore, only a few studies have used random assignment and control groups, and evidence of the long-term effectiveness of premarital education in improving marital satisfaction and marital stability is limited to the work of a single research group, Markman's Premarital Education Program (PREP) (van Widenfelt, Markman, Guerney, Behrens, & Hosman, 1997).

The content of the education or preparation is another basic issue that must be considered in relation to premarital education programs and their effectiveness. Programs developed by professionals typically are skills-based, focusing primarily on training couples in using skills such as communication. Substantive issues like sexuality, money, and children typically are secondary foci, if they are addressed at all (van Widenfelt et al., 1997). The content of other premarital education programs varies, but religious programs in particular can be expected to be more substantively based. In fact, issues such as commitment to the marriage necessarily must be treated as "process" issues in secular premarital education programs, but religious groups often offer substantive answers in relation to the question of commitment in marriage. In fact, particular religions often offer clear substantive answers to other controversial issues that may be treated as "process" concerns in secular training, for example, appropriate gender-based marital roles. The effectiveness or relative effectiveness of the more substantive, religious approach to premarital education simply is not known.

Overall, evidence indicates some reason for optimism about the effectiveness of marriage education program at least in the short term. However, whether these education programs produce happier, more stable marriages remains an open question. Obviously, the long-term effectiveness of the programs is the most important concern in relation to the present topic of reducing interparental conflict, since most cohabiting couples bear children after, not before, marriage. The lack of long-term studies is more surprising and disappointing in the marital education literature than the similarly underdeveloped literature on other parenting interventions, since premarital education efforts are much older and more established than divorce mediation or legal initiatives in the area of spouse abuse.

Parenting Education for Divorcing Parents

A much more recent but rapidly growing policy designed to alter interparental conflict is parenting education for divorcing parents. The content of these divorce education programs focuses specifically on children, and it typically includes issues such as the effects of divorce on children and postdivorce parenting, including the detrimental effects of conflict and the benefits of continued, cooperative co-parenting (Braver, Salem, Pearson, & DeLuse, 1996). In this vein, many such programs encourage mediation in cases of disputed custody, and some education programs are linked to mediation services.

Comprehensive divorce education programs are less than a decade old. However, the concept has been embraced rapidly as evidenced by the fact that, as of 1995, 11 state legislatures had enacted laws either mandating divorce education statewide or allowing it to be mandated by various jurisdictions. Many more programs have been developed through local court rules or voluntary participation (Biondi, 1996).

The local implementation and legislative support for divorce education programs have come well in advance of research supporting the effectiveness of these efforts. Several reports indicate that parents report satisfaction with divorce education, but most programs have not been evaluated, and evaluation studies typically include no comparison group, let alone random assignment with control groups. The only known exceptions are a series of studies in which a no-treatment comparison group has been employed without random assignment. The findings of this research are encouraging, as the results suggest that divorce education may produce lower levels of parental conflict, raise levels of parental cooperation, and lower relitigation rates (Arbuthnot & Gordon, 1996; Arbuthnot, Kramer, & Gordon, 1997; Kramer, Arbuthnot, Gordon, Rousis, & Hoza, 1998). The lack of random assignment and high rates of participant attrition raise a number of important uncertainties about the findings of these early studies of a new concept, but the efforts represent a needed step in the right direction. (The only study using random assignment to alternative treatments [Kramer et al. 1998] produced no consistent pattern of results and suffered from high attrition rates.)

The development and evaluation of divorce education programs are too recent to draw firm conclusions about the effectiveness of this form of intervention, but the intent of the programs is laudable and initial outcome data are encouraging. However, when all the results are in, it can be safely predicted that the effects of parenting education programs for divorcing parents will surely disappoint ardent advocates. Given the complexities of divorce, the strong emotions flowing from it, and large individual differences in the divorce experience, brief, generic educational interventions, even skills-based programs, should not be expected to make a substantial difference in postdivorce family life for children. As with other programs that have been reviewed here, perhaps the major effect of parenting education classes will not be the direct impact on participants. Rather, the programs may have indirect, and hopefully cumulative, influences on expectations and attitudes regarding the appropriate control of parental conflict for the sake of children.

Changing the Culture

Several times throughout this chapter, I have suggested that many of the important effects of policies, or interventions driven by policy, may be indirect rather than direct. I have further suggested that these indirect effects sometimes are specific (e.g., mandatory mediation may alter the behavior of attorneys which, in turn, influences parents), but many of the indirect effects alluded to in this chapter are general, not specific. The assertion that policies designed to produce behavioral reductions in interparental conflict may actually have their ultimate effects by changing the "culture" may seem unusual, particularly when offered by a psychologist who has been trained in the behavioral tradition and who remains strongly committed to empirical research. Just what is "culture," and how does one operationalize this construct?

Culture is a difficult, perhaps impossible, construct to operationalize, but like other such constructs, the empirical challenge does not mean that the construct should be banished. According to the *American Heritage Dictionary*, culture is "the totality of socially transmitted behavior patterns, arts, beliefs, institutions, and all other products of

human work and thought characteristic of a community or population." No wonder the construct is difficult to operationalize.

Despite its broad and vague nature, I have been convinced of the
importance of culture as a result of 20 years of research, writing, and
clinical work related to children, families, and the law. I could argue for
the importance of culture, as I have elsewhere (Emery, 1999), from the
perspective of the societal problems that have emerged from the
decline of moral codes of behavior – in society and in law – in favor of
pluralistic policies based on empirical evidence regarding their effectiveness (an approach that sometimes is termed "legal realism"). As a
thought experiment, one might consider what effects the various policies reviewed in this chapter would have had in the United States 100
years ago. On the one hand, some of the policies would be unnecessary,
because divorce, for example, was virtually nonexistent. On the other
hand, other policies would seem ridiculously intrusive, because misdemeanor spouse abuse, for example, was not illegal, and, to a degree, it
was socially accepted. In short, these policies only make sense within
the cultural and historical context. I am suggesting, furthermore, that
such policies not only reflect our culture, but they also help to shape it.

Let me offer one more argument in a very different and perhaps
more concrete vein. Consider the likely effects of any given antismoking education program before American culture had shifted from a
prosmoking to an antismoking stance, for example, a program conducted in a high school in 1964. There surely are data from studies conducted during these times, and my prediction (in the absence of
reviewing past research) is that the effects of intervention were small,
inconsistent, and short-lived. This does not mean, however, that such
programs were unimportant. In fact, I would argue that, together with
repeated advertising in the popular media and related campaigns, antismoking education programs ultimately had a very large if indirect
effect over time. That is, such programs helped to change the culture,
and this cultural change influenced smoking behavior (and was influenced by it as well).

I suggest that a similar, cumulative outcome may eventually be produced by the laws, policies, and educational interventions reviewed in
this chapter. I believe that the culture will be changed if policies continue to discourage interparental conflict and encourage interparental
cooperation, even in the face of legitimate anger between parents. For
example, it seems to me that I have witnessed a partial cultural evolution in regard to the expectations, legal processes, and actual behavior
concerning the co-parenting of children after divorce. The literature I
reviewed almost two decades ago (Emery, 1982) raised concerns about

interparental conflict in divorce, but family structure (e.g., father absence) was the focus of psychological concerns, not family process (e.g., conflict – or contact with nonresidential fathers in father-absent families). The importance of family processes, including interparental conflict, to children's mental health after divorce was convincingly demonstrated in the 1980s and 1990s. The research, in turn, served as a partial impetus for policy change (e.g., mediation, divorce education). Finally, the expectations and actions of divorcing parents, and the professionals who work with them, seem to be changing in manner that is more consistent with the prescriptions of the law and of the empirical evidence (although I know of no data documenting changes in interparental conflict over time).

The coming decades may witness similar cultural change. One change that I anticipate is a rediscovery of the value of commitment to marriage, perhaps commitment based less on personal fulfillment and more on marriage as an institution. Such a change should help to reduce interparental conflict further, especially if marriage comes to be valued more as an institution for raising children and less as a relationship offering (or failing to provide) personal fulfillment.

In summary, research to date indicates that divorce mediation, more stringent policing of spouse abuse, and marriage/divorce education all have modest and limited effects on interparental conflict. To be sure, evidence is limited, but I would be surprised if future research demonstrates that the policies produce substantial changes that have gone undetected in completed research. On the pessimistic side, part of the reason why many policies have produced limited benefits is that the interventions are weak relative to the magnitude of the problems they attempt to address. On the optimistic side, part of the reason why many policies have produced limited benefits is that culture changes slowly. Investigators need to conduct more, and more rigorous, research on policies designed to alter family life. In judging the effectiveness of any given policy, however, it must be recognized that more change may be occurring than can be demonstrated in relatively short-term empirical research.

REFERENCES

Arbuthnot, J., & Gordon, D. A. (1996). Does mandatory divorce education for parents work? A six-month outcome evaluation. *Family and Conciliation Courts Review, 34*, 60–81.

Arbuthnot, J., Kramer, K. M., & Gordon, D. A. (1997). Patterns of relitigation following divorce education. *Family and Conciliation Courts Review, 35*, 269–279.

Attorney General's Task Force on Family Violence (1984). Washington, DC: U.S. Government Printing Office.

Berk, R. A., Campbell, A., Klap, R., & Western, B. (1984). The deterrent effect of arrest: A Bayesian analysis of four field experiments. *American Sociological Review, 49*, 261–271.

Biondi, E. D. (1996). Legal implementaion of parent education programs for divorcing and separating parents. *Family and Conciliation Courts Review, 34*, 82–92.

Bradbury, T. N., & Fincham, F. D. (1990). Preventing marital dysfunction: Review and analysis. In F. D. Fincham & T. N. Bradbury (Eds.), *The psychology of marriage* (pp. 373–401). New York: Guilford.

Braver, S. L., Salem, P., Pearson, J., & DeLuse, S. R. (1996). The content of divorce education programs: Results of a survey. *Family and Conciliation Courts Review, 34*, 41–59.

Brown, P. D., & O'Leary, K. D. (1997). Wife abuse in intact couples: A review of couples treatment programs. In G. K. Kantor & J. L. Jasinski (Eds.), *Out of darkness: Contemporary perspectives on family violence* (pp. 194–207). Thousand Oaks, CA: Sage Publications.

Bumpass, L. L., & Raley, R. K. (1995). Redefining single-parent families: Cohabitation and the changing family reality. *Demography, 32*, 97–109.

Burns, A., & Scott, C. (1994). *Mother-headed families and why they have increased.* Hillsdale, NJ: Erlbaum.

Buzawa, E. S., & Buzawa, C. G. (Eds.). (1996). *Do arrests and restraining orders work?* Thousand Oaks, CA: Sage.

Cummings, E. M., & Davies, P. (1994). *Children and marital conflict.* New York: Guilford.

Depner, C. E., Cannata, K. V., & Simon, M. B. (1992). Building a uniform statistical reporting system: A snapshot of California Family Court services. *Family and Conciliation Courts Review, 30*, 185–206.

Dietz, E. (1996). Violence against women in the United States. *Arizona Journal of International Comparative Law, 13*, 551–595.

Emery, R. E. (1982). Interparental conflict and the children of discord and divorce. *Psychological Bulletin, 92*, 310–330.

Emery, R. E. (1994). *Renegotiating family relationships: Divorce, child custody, and mediation.* New York: Guilford.

Emery, R. E. (1999). *Marriage, divorce, and children's adjustment* (2nd ed.). Thousand Oaks, CA: Sage.

Emery, R. E., & Laumann-Billings, L. (1998). An overview of the nature, causes, and consequences of abusive family relationships: Toward differentiating maltreatment and violence. *American Psychologist, 53*, 121–135.

Emery, R. E., Matthews, S., & Kitzmann, K. (1994). Child custody mediation and litigation: Parents' satisfaction and functioning a year after settlement. *Journal of Consulting and Clinical Psychology, 62*, 124–129.

Emery, R. E., Matthews, S., & Wyer, M. M. (1991). Child custody mediation and litigation: Further evidence on the differing views of mothers and fathers. *Journal of Consulting and Clinical Psychology, 59*, 410–418.

Emery, R. E., & Wyer, M. M. (1987b). Child custody mediation and litigation: An experimental evaluation of the experience of parents. *Journal of Consulting and Clinical Psychology, 55,* 179–186.

Fagan, J. (1990). Contributions of research to criminal justice policy on wife assault. In D. J. Besharov (Ed.), *Family violence: Research and public policy issues* (pp. 53–81). Washington: AEI Press.

Folberg, J., & Taylor, A. (1984). *Mediation: A comprehensive guide to resolving conflicts without litigation.* San Francisco: Jossey-Bass.

Ford, D. A. (1991). Prosecution as a victim power resource: A note on empowering women in violent conjugal relationships. *Law and Society Review, 25,* 313–334.

Garner, J., & Fagan, J. (1997). Victims of domestic violence. In R. C. Davis, A. J. Lurigio, & W. G. Skogan (Eds.), *Victims of crime* (2nd ed., pp. 53–85). Thousand Oaks, CA: Sage.

Giblin, P., Sprenkle, D. H., & Sheehan, R. (1985). Enrichment outcome research: A meta-analysis of premarital, marital and family interventions. *Journal of Marital and Family Therapy, 11,* 257–271.

Grillo, T. (1991). The mediation alternative: Process dangers for women. *Yale Law Journal, 100,* 1545–1610.

Grych, J. H., & Fincham, F. D. (1990). Marital conflict and children's adjustment: A cognitive-contextual framework. *Psychological Bulletin, 108,* 267–290.

Hahlweg, K., & Markman, H. (1988). The effectiveness of behavioral marital therapy: Empirical status of behavioral techniques in preventing and alleviating marital distress. *Journal of Consulting and Clinical Psychology, 56,* 440–447.

Hamberger, K. L., & Hastings, J. E. (1989). Counseling male spouse abusers: Characteristics of treatment completers and dropouts. *Violence and Victims, 4,* 275–286.

Hendricks, C. L. (1993–94). The trend toward mandatory mediation in custody and visitation disputes of minor children: An overview. *Journal of Family Law, 32,* 491–510.

Holtzworth-Munroe, A., Markman, H., O'Leary, K. D., Neidig, P., Leber, D., Heyman, R. E., Hulbert, D., & Smutzler, N. (1995). The need for marital violence prevention efforts: A behavioral-cognitive secondary prevention program for engaged and newly married couples. *Applied and Preventive Psychology, 4,* 77–88.

Irving, H. H., Benjamin, M., Bohm, P., & MacDonald, G. (1981). *Final research report.* Toronto, Canada: Provincial Court (Family Division).

Jaffe, P., Wolfe, D., & Wilson, S. (1990). *Children of battered women.* Newbury Park, CA: Sage.

Keilitz, S. L., Daley, H. W. K., & Hanson, R. A. (1992). *Multi-state assessment of divorce mediation and traditional court processing.* (Project report). Williamsburg, VA: State Justice Institute.

Kelly, J. B. (1989). Mediated and adversarial divorce: Respondents' perceptions of their processes and outcomes. *Mediation Quarterly, 24,* 71–88.

Kelly, J. B. (1990). *Final report. Mediated and adversarial divorce resolution processes: An analysis of post-divorce outcomes.* (Available from the author, Northern

California Mediation Center, 100 Tamal Plaza, Suite 175, Corte Madera, CA 94925).

Kelly, J. B., & Duryee, M. A. (1992). Women's and men's views of mediation in voluntary and mandatory mediation settings. *Family and Conciliation Courts Review, 30,* 34–49.

Kelly, J. B., & Gigy, L. (1989). Divorce mediation: Characteristics of clients and outcomes. In K. Kressel & D. G. Pruitt (Eds.), *Mediation research* (pp. 263–283). San Francisco: Jossey-Bass.

Kelly, J. B., Gigy, L., & Hausman, S. (1988). Mediated and adversarial divorce: Initial findings from a longitudinal study. In J. Folberg & A. Milne (Eds.), *Divorce mediation: Theory and practices* (pp. 453–474). New York: Guilford.

Kitzmann, K. M., & Emery, R. E. (1994). Child and family coping one year after mediated and litigated child custody disputes. *Journal of Family Psychology, 8,* 150–157.

Kramer, K. M., Arbuthnot, J., Gordon, D. A., Rousis, N. J., & Hoza, J. (1998). Effects of skill-based versus information-based divorce education programs on domestic violence and parental communication. *Family and Conciliation Courts Review, 36,* 9–31

Margolin, F. M. (1973). *An approach to the resolution of visitation disputes post-divorce: Short-term counseling.* Unpublished doctoral dissertation, United States International University, San Diego, CA.

Mnookin, R. H., (1975). Child-custody adjudication: Judicial functions in the face of indeterminacy. *Law and Contemporary Problems, 39,* 226–292.

Mnookin, R. H. (1985). *In the interest of children.* New York: Freeman.

National Center for Health Statistics (1997). Births and deaths: United States, July 1995-June 1996. *Monthly Vital Statistics Report, 45* (10), Supplement 2. Hyattsville, MD: National Center for Health Statistics.

Pearson, J., & Thoennes, N. (1984). *Final report of the divorce mediation research project.* (Available from authors, 1720 Emerson St., Denver, CO 80218).

Pearson, J., & Thoennes, N. (1989). Divorce mediation: Reflections on a decade of research. In K. Kressel & D. Pruitt (Eds.), *Mediation research* (pp. 9–30). San Francisco: Jossey-Bass.

Sanders, M. R., Markie-Dadds, C., & Nicholson, J. M. (1997). Current interventions for marital and children's problems. In W. K. Halford & H. J. Markman (Eds.), *Clinical handbook of marriage and couples interventions* (pp. 509–535). New York: Wiley.

Sherman, L. W., & Berk, R. A. (1984). The specific deterrent effects of arrest for domestic assault. *American Sociological Review, 49,* 261–271.

Sherman, L. W., & Cohn, E. G. (1989). The impact of research on legal policy: The Minneapolis Domestic Violence Experiment. *Law and Society Review, 23,* 117–144.

Stets, J. E., & Straus, M. A. (1990). Gender differences in reporting marital violence and its medical and psychological consequences. In M. A. Straus & R. J. Gelles (Eds.), *Physical violence in American families: Risk factors and adaptation to violence in 8,145 families.* (pp. 332–351). New Brunswick, NJ: Transaction.

Sullivan, K. T., & Bradbury, T. N. (1997). Are premarital prevention programs reaching couples at risk for marital dysfunction? *Journal of Consulting and Clinical Psychology, 65,* 24–30.

Sweet, J. A., & Bumpass, L. L. (1987). *American families and households.* New York: Russell Sage Foundation.

U.S. Census Bureau (1992). Marriage, divorce, and remarriage in the 1990s. *Current Population Reports* (P23–180). Washington, DC: U.S. Government Printing Office.

van Widenfelt, B., Markman, H. J., Guerney, B., Beharens, B. C., & Hosman, C. (1997). Prevention of relationship problems. In W. K. Halford & H. J. Markman (Eds.), *Clinical handbook of marriage and couples interventions* (pp. 651–671). New York: Wiley.

PART FIVE. FUTURE DIRECTIONS

Advancing Understanding of the Association between Interparental Conflict and Child Development

Frank D. Fincham and John H. Grych

"Would you tell me, please, which way I ought to go from here?"
"That depends a good deal on where you want to get to," said the Cat.

Lewis Carroll, *Alice in Wonderland*

How do we advance understanding of the association between interparental conflict and child development? Although this question is quite reasonable, it cannot easily be answered. This is because, as hinted by the Cat's answer to Alice, it depends on the context in which it is asked. Understanding for what purpose, making what epistemological assumptions, referring to what aspect of the association, and with what referents for conflict and child development? For the scientist–practitioner, advanced understanding may lie in the identification of processes (e.g., parenting) that can be changed to alleviate child problems that arise in the context of interparental conflict. In contrast, researchers informed by a systemic perspective may find such a definition of causality unduly restrictive for understanding this phenomenon.

Clearly, there is no single answer to the question we posed. Rather than attempt to document the numerous answers that can be given, we believe it is more productive to highlight some issues relevant to addressing the question. This belief rests on the view that advances in any field depend on the questions asked. We therefore address this issue first.

Of Questions

Our field of inquiry has coalesced around a simple question: What is the association between marital satisfaction/discord (more recently, interparental conflict) and child disorder/adjustment (more recently, child development)? Asking this question has brought us a long way but it may have outlived its usefulness. To the extent that it still makes sense to focus energy on a single question, it behooves us to ask: "What aspects of interparental conflict influence what aspects of child development under what conditions?" But, as illustrated by the diversity of questions raised in this volume, it is doubtful if this more sophisticated inquiry captures the interests of those investigating interparental conflict and child development. Even if it does, it provides only a generic question that, upon closer inspection of the literature contained under its rubric, is instantiated in a variety of different ways.

Recognizing that we are really asking a number of questions, and that the questions can be quite diverse, is fundamental to advancing the field. Once we accept that the field is characterized by multiple questions, it is easier to recognize the evolving nature of the questions we ask. As indicated by the alternative terms used in the question that begins this section, there has clearly been an evolution in our inquiry from study of general marital satisfaction/discord to a clear focus on interparental conflict. But we have been slow to integrate the inevitable change that is part of the research enterprise and to recognize its implications. It is axiomatic that as the light we throw on interparental conflict and child development expands, so too does the interface with the darkness, leading us to refine our questions and to ask new ones.

One implication of the evolving nature of our questions bears on the distinction drawn between first- and second-generation research in our domain (see Fincham, 1994). Specifically, first generation research, documenting the conflict–child-outcome association, is never complete; as we refine the constructs involved, we continually (re-)establish and refine the association. This observation bears mention in light of the current emphasis on second-generation research, which focuses on understanding why there is an association between interparental conflict and child outcomes. Although important, the research on mechanism stands in dialectical relation to that on establishing associations and inevitably leads to new questions that require first generation research. Thus, our research process reflects some of the very systemic properties displayed by the families we study, yet our differential valuing of second- over first-generation research points to a need to see both as potential advances over the other. Only then will we accomplish the vast amount of work that is still needed to document phenomena (associations) and rule out artifactual explanations for them. The necessity of this work will become apparent as we turn to highlight some issues relevant to advancing research in this area.

The Journey Ahead: New Terrain, Old Terrain

In this section we highlight seven broad issues. Where we cover familiar ground, we do so to emphasize its importance and to provide a new perspective that might facilitate progress.

What is This Thing Called Conflict?

The move from studying a broad, heterogeneous construct like marital dissatisfaction to a specific aspect of marital dissatisfaction, how couples express and resolve conflict, certainly represents progress in describing what it is about marital problems that may give rise to child problems. However, we are still left with a fairly broad and heterogeneous independent variable that encompasses everything from constructive, respectful disagreements to violence. It is possible that studies on conflict at times may be comparing the proverbial apples and oranges. For example, research on witnessing garden-variety conflict may not be comparable to that examining physical aggression even though both may be conceptualized in terms of conflict intensity and differentiated from other aspects of conflict. In the case of violence, the potential for trauma and for being the victim of aggression can change (implicitly) the question being investigated. Advances are being made in identifying aspects of conflict that are most salient or aversive to children, particularly through experimental analog studies in which specific dimensions of conflict are manipulated (see Cummings, Goeke-Morey, & Papp, in press), but fundamental questions about the nature of conflict remain: Should it be treated as a continuum or are there qualitatively different types of conflict (e.g., constructive vs. destructive, violent vs. nonviolent)? Is the course of a conflict important or simply the occurrence of particular behaviors? What is the relative impact of the emotions expressed during conflict versus the behaviors exhibited? These questions are phrased simplistically but point to the need for continued refinement of what we mean when we talk about conflict.

The Times, They Are A Changing

One third of births in the United States occur outside of marriage, and as more children grow up in households that include single parents or unmarried parents, we need to adapt our language (much of the literature is framed in terms of "marital" conflict) and expand the target of our research efforts. Although the impact of interparental conflict between cohabiting, unwed parents might be similar or identical to that for married parents, matters may be quite different for parents who do not cohabit but where regular contact occurs between the nonresidential parent and the child, what McLanahan et al. (1998) have called "fragile families." We have studied conflict between noncohabiting parents that occurs following a divorce (see Buchanan & Heiges, Chapter 13), but we cannot assume that these findings apply to parents who have never cohabited or experienced the disruption of divorce. Consequently, we know little about interparental conflict and its impact in fragile families. Similarly, we know little about single-parent households where conflict might occur with other adults (e.g., extended family, a series of partners) who take on parenting tasks. The need to expand our study to incorporate different family forms is apparent (see Fine, Chapter 14).

Along with change in family form, we are also witnessing important changes in the ethnic composition of the population which serves to underscore how little we know about interparental conflict in different ethnic groups (see McLoyd, Harper, & Copeland, Chapter 4). This lacuna is further emphasized by the fact that interparental conflict and parenting are more strongly related in European-American samples compared to samples containing different ethnic groups (the effect size is about two-thirds of a standard deviation larger; Krishnakumar & Buehler, 2000). Thus, a strongly favored mechanism whereby conflict influences children (parenting) may not operate, or operate as strongly, in ethnic groups other than European Americans. In short, we need to study samples representative of the broader U.S. population to advance understanding.

Where You Look Is What You Find

Just as we tend to restrict the samples studied, so too have we restricted the child outcomes we study. We offer three observations to facilitate a broader focus of inquiry that might advance our understanding.

First, our preoccupation with negative child outcomes has led us to focus heavily on broad-band internalizing and externalizing childhood problems. Although there is periodic recognition that children might benefit from exposure to some level of parental conflict, the inference is implicit that positive outcomes can be inferred from the absence of negative outcomes. But it is a logical error to assume that healthy functioning is the absence of unhealthy functioning or even its mirror image. For example, the positive relation found between exposure to parental conflict and creativity in adulthood could not emerge from research that focused only on the negative (Koestner, Walker, & Fichman, 1999).

A second, related observation concerns the sensitivity of the measures we use to detect variations that fall within the nonclinical range of functioning. Interparental conflict could be found to have a pro-found effect in some domains (e.g., children's conflict resolution skills) once we allow our attention to focus not only on problematic levels of functioning but also the "normal" range of functioning. Children may display outcomes that are less than optimal as a function of inter-parental conflict but that do not constitute problems.

Third, we have tended to look at general child adjustment without sufficient attention to what aspect of child functioning might be most reactive to exposure to interparental conflict. However, this is clearly changing with the increasing attention that is being paid to how inter-parental conflict may impact children's interpersonal functioning. The emerging study of relationships with siblings (see Dunn & Davies, Chapter 10) and with peer relationships (see Parke et al., Chapter 11) as a function of interparental conflict augers well. But possibly the most obvious need for intensive study in this regard is how interparental conflict may influence the adolescent's functioning in romantic rela-tionships.

Gender (of Child *and* Parent) Matters

Despite the considerable attention we have given to gender, our understanding of the impact of interparental conflict on boys versus girls remains limited (see Davies & Lindsay, Chapter 3). One reason for this is the assumption that children react to their parents as a unit. But the same conflictual behavior performed by a father versus a mother may be experienced quite differently. Not only might responses differ because boys and girls develop different relationships with fathers and mothers, but factors such as size and strength differences can make a slap delivered with the same force more or less threatening depending on whether the mother slaps the father or vice versa. In short, parent as well as child gender matters.

It is insufficient, however, merely to introduce gender into our exam-ination of parental conflict. We also need to consider gender in relation to the mechanisms whereby interparental conflict might influence chil-dren, particularly the parent–child relationship. It is only by examining our questions in relation to mothers, fathers, sons, and daughters that we have been able to document that interparental conflict is especially deleterious for cross-gender parent–child relations (e.g., Kerig, Cowan, & Cowan, 1993), which, unlike same-sex relationships, predict child outcome even though boys and girls reported the same levels of expo-sure to interparental conflict (Osborne & Fincham, 1996). By incorpo-rating gender at the adult *and* child levels in both our conceptual analyses (see Snyder, 1998) *and* empirical investigations we are likely to understand more fully the role that gender plays in the interparental-conflict–child-outcome association.

Snapshots, Time-Lapse Photography, and Video

Virtually all the research in our field involves data gathered at a single point in time and thus provides us a snapshot of the phenomena we study. We previously outlined the critical role of longitudinal research in this area and provided an analysis of how such research can be more informative (Fincham, Grych, & Osborne, 1994). This is not the context in which to repeat our observations, though given the present state of the field, they remain timely. Although the publication of longitudinal studies represents an encouraging first step in responding to this need, it behooves us to note that the few studies conducted to date are, at best, analogous to time-lapse photography and seldom comprise more than two waves of data (e.g., Harold, Fincham, Osborne, & Conger, 1997; Katz & Gottman, 1993). Among other things, this does not even allow us to untangle instability in the constructs investigated from unreliability of measurement (for which at least three waves are necessary; see Kenny & Campbell, 1989).

More importantly, by limiting the number of data collection points, we have forgone the opportunity to examine the trajectory of children's responses to interparental conflict. Such trajectories can be examined in terms of a variety of functions and, importantly, can be examined at the level of the individual. Diversity in developmental pathways among children experiencing similar circumstances (e.g., high levels of destructive conflict) is commonplace but poorly understood. By determining predictors of these individual trajectory parameters we have the potential to advance understanding of the individual differences that are so salient in our field. Among the predictors that can be examined is the initial level (intercept) of child functioning. This serves as an important reminder of the need for prospective studies that will allow us to determine the extent to which child outcomes reflect the onset of significant interparental conflict versus preexisting levels of functioning. The fact that significant amounts of the variance in child functioning, originally attributed to parental divorce, have now been shown to reflect preexisting functioning emphasizes the importance of such research (e.g., Cherlin et al., 1991). In any event, the examination of trajectories or growth curves points to the need for more data points in our longitudinal research and moves us in the direction of approximating the more complete perspective of phenomena offered by video recordings (see Cummings, Goeke-Morey, & Dukewich, Chapter 2).

Conflict in Context

Continued progress also requires us to take more seriously the familiar refrain that conflict occurs in a context. As a field, we are well aware that interparental conflict may have different consequences as a function of familial and nonfamilial contextual factors. For example, conflict in the context of parental substance abuse problems and overcrowding in the home is likely to have a different impact from conflict that occurs alone. It is well documented that marital conflict does not occur in isolation from other stressors (e.g., parental depressive symptoms), yet the range of contextual factors studied remains somewhat limited. The resulting tendency to focus on unitary causation is necessarily limiting because more complex, multifactorial models are necessary to advance our understanding.

In this regard, a recent development in the marital literature is instructive. Until recently, marital researchers tended to focus on conflict in their attempt to understand marital distress without paying attention to the relative importance of conflict behavior compared to other types of behaviors, such as those expressing social support. Attention to a broader range of behavior has led to important advances. For example, Pasch and Bradbury (1998) reported that negative behaviors occurring during a social support interaction had a potentiating effect on poor conflict resolution skills in predicting deterioration in marital quality 2 years later. Similarly, we need to consider interparental conflict in relation to other interparental behaviors to which children are exposed in seeking to understand its impact.

Finally, extrafamilial factors also constitute an important part of the context within which we need to study interparental conflict (see Emery, Chapter 16). We already know, for example, that a good relationship with an adult outside of the family moderates the relation between marital discord and child adjustment, especially in the absence of a good mother–child relationship (Jenkins & Smith, 1990). But we have not ventured much beyond such dyadic relationships to consider the role of social networks, neighborhoods, subcultures, and society itself in understanding how interparental conflict and child development are related. Yet, as Berscheid (1999) reminds us, all relationships are influenced by the broader society in which they exist, and psychologists as a group tend to have overlooked the impact of such factors in their study of relationships.

Integration within an Emergent Relationship Science

As we turn our attention in the direction of examining interparental conflict in the context of couple interaction more generally, we can profit from the broader theoretical frameworks that have emerged in the marital domain (see Fincham, 1998). Indeed, there is much that can be gained by linking our study to the "greening of relationship science" (Berscheid, 1999). There is no doubt that a science of relationships has taken root in psychology with the recognition, long acknowledged by atomic physicists, that understanding comes through study of interactions and interconnections. Over a decade ago, Sroufe (1989) noted that "any understanding of individual behavior divorced from relationships will be seriously incomplete" (p. 104). Although developmental psychology has increasingly embraced this perspective in recent years and placed greater emphasis on the importance of relationships for development, in our area of inquiry we have not looked much at relationship literatures in other subdisciplines, such as social psychology (see Berscheid & Reis, 1998), or at the broader interdisciplinary literature that exists on relationships (see Hinde, 1997). It is important to situate our inquiry within the broader field of relationship science; doing so is bound to further our understanding of the links between conflict and child functioning.

Conclusion

There are more issues relevant to promoting the continued development of research on interparental conflict and child development than those raised in this brief commentary. Many are discussed in the preceding chapters which, together with the reviews they offer, document the state of the art in this vibrant field of inquiry. We have tried to map some new terrain as well as map overlooked features of familiar terrain. Together with the preceding chapters, we hope to have provided a cartography that provides useful sign posts for advancing understanding of the association between interparental conflict and children's development.

REFERENCES

Berscheid, E. (1999). The greening of relationship science. *American Psychologist, 54*, 260–266.

Berscheid, E., & Reis, H. T. (1998). Attraction and close relationships. In D. T. Gilbert, S. T. Fiske, & G. Lindsey (Eds.), *The handbook of social psychology* (Vol. 2, 4th ed., pp. 193–281).

Cherlin, A. J., Furstenburg, F. F., Chase-Lansdale, P. L., Kiernan, K. E., Robins, P. K., Morrison, D. R., & Teitler, J. O. (1991). Longitudinal studies of the effects of divorce on children in Great Britain and the United States. *Science, 252*, 1386–1389.

Cummings, E. M., Goeke-Morey, M., & Papp, L. M. (in press). Couple conflict, children, and families: It's not just you and me, babe. In A. Booth, A. Crouter, & M. Clements (Eds.), *Couples in conflict.* Mahwah, NJ: Erlbaum.

Fincham, F. D. (1994). Understanding the association between marital conflict and child adjustment: Overview. *Journal of Family Psychology, 8,* 123–127.

Fincham, F. D. (1998). Child development and marital relations. *Child Development, 69,* 543–574.

Fincham, F. D., Grych, J. H., & Osborne, L. N. (1994). Does marital conflict cause child maladjustment? Directions and challenges for longitudinal research. *Journal of Family Psychology, 8,* 128–140.

Harold, G. T., Fincham, F. D., Osborne, L. N., & Conger, R. D. (1997). Mom and dad are at it again: Adolescent perceptions of marital conflict and adolescent psychological distress. *Developmental Psychology, 33,* 333–350.

Hinde, R. A. (1997). *Relationships: A dialectical perspective.* Hove: Psychology Press.

Jenkins, J. M., & Smith, M. A. (1990). Factors protecting children living in disharmonious homes. *Journal of The American Academy of Child and Adolescent Psychiatry,* May 29, 60–69.

Katz, L. F., & Gottman, J. M. (1993). Patterns of marital conflict predict children's internalizing and externalizing behavior. *Developmental Psychology, 29,* 940–950.

Kenny, D. A., & Campbell, D. T. (1989). On the measurement of stability in over-time data. *Journal of Personality, 57,* 445–481.

Kerig, P. K., Cowan, P. A., & Cowan, C. P. (1993). Marital quality and gender differences in parent-child interaction. *Developmental Psychology, 29,* 931–939.

Koestner, R., Walker, M., & Fichman, L. (1999). Childhood parenting experiences and adult creativity. *Journal of Research in Personality, 33,* 92–107.

Krishnakumar, A., & Buehler, C. (2000). Interparental conflict and parenting behaviors: A meta-analytic review. *Family Relations, 49,* 25–44.

McLanahan, S., Garfinkel, I., Brooks-Gun, J., & Hongxin, Z. (1998). *Unwed fathers and fragile families.* Paper presented at the Population Association Annual Meeting, Chicago, IL.

Osborne, L. N., & Fincham, F. D. (1996). Marital conflict, parent-child relations, and child adjustment: Does gender matter? *Merrill Palmer Quarterly, 42,* 48–75.

Pasch, L. A., & Bradbury, T. N. (1998). Social support, conflict, and the development of marital dysfunction. *Journal of Consulting and Clinical Psychology, 66,* 219–230.

Snyder, J. R. (1998). Marital conflict and child adjustment: What about gender? *Developmental Review, 18,* 390–420.

Sroufe, L. A. (1989). Relationships and relationship disturbance. In A. J. Sameroff & R. N. Emde (Eds.), *Relationship disturbances in early childhood* (pp. 97–124). New York: Basic Books.

Author Index

Subject Index